Food Security Issues in Asia

Other Titles by the Editor

Bioscience Entrepreneurship in Asia: Creating Value with Biology

Food Matters: Food Security and the Future of Food

Food Reserves: A Comparative Study on Food Reserve Management and Policies in Southeast Asia

STEM Education From Asia: Trends and Perspectives

Food Security Issues in Asia

Editor

Paul Teng

Nanyang Technological University, Singapore

Foreword by

Ambassador Ong Keng Yong

World Scientific

NEW JERSEY • LONDON • SINGAPORE • BEIJING • SHANGHAI • HONG KONG • TAIPEI • CHENNAI • TOKYO

Published by

World Scientific Publishing Co. Pte. Ltd.
5 Toh Tuck Link, Singapore 596224
USA office: 27 Warren Street, Suite 401-402, Hackensack, NJ 07601
UK office: 57 Shelton Street, Covent Garden, London WC2H 9HE

Library of Congress Cataloging-in-Publication Data
Names: Teng, Paul, editor. | Ong, Keng Yong, author of foreword.
Title: Food security issues in Asia / editor, Paul Teng ; foreword, Ong Keng Yong.
Description: Hackensack, New Jersey : World Scientific, [2024] |
Includes bibliographical references and index.
Identifiers: LCCN 2023044873 | ISBN 9789811278280 (hardcover) |
ISBN 9789811278297 (ebook) | ISBN 9789811278303 (ebook other)
Subjects: LCSH: Food security--Asia. | Food supply--Asia. | Agriculture and state--Asia.
Classification: LCC HD9016.A2 F6575 2024 | DDC 338.1/95--dc23/eng/20231220
LC record available at https://lccn.loc.gov/2023044873

British Library Cataloguing-in-Publication Data
A catalogue record for this book is available from the British Library.

For any available supplementary material, please visit
https://www.worldscientific.com/worldscibooks/10.1142/13469#t=suppl

Desk Editor: Shaun Tan Yi Jie

Typeset by Stallion Press
Email: enquiries@stallionpress.com

https://doi.org/10.1142/9789811278297_fmater

Foreword

Food security is not something that the global community can take for granted.

Events in the past few years — when reduced food production, disrupted supply chains, sudden price hikes and increased food waste have all been observed in both developing and developed countries — clearly highlight the importance of preparedness in dealing with the outcomes of climate change, pandemics, and conflicts. Indeed, food insecurity is today a "hot button" issue which requires international collaboration to address.

Global progress against hunger, measured by the Global Hunger Index (GHI), has stagnated in recent years. The prevalence of undernourishment, in the GHI, highlights that the share of people who lack regular access to sufficient calories is increasing. In 2021, nearly 828 million people were undernourished.[1] It is estimated that the number of people who could not afford a healthy diet in 2020 increased globally, across regions. A paradigm shift is necessary now to achieve even low hunger, by 2030.

Asia, which has about 60% of the world's population, many concentrated in cities, has faced its share of challenges to its food

---

[1] FAO, IFAD, UNICEF, WFP and WHO (2022). *The State of Food Security and Nutrition in the World 2022: Repurposing Food and Agricultural Policies to Make Healthy Diets More Affordable.* Food and Agriculture Organization of the United Nations.

security. South Asia has the highest hunger levels and is also most vulnerable to future shocks and crises. South Asia also has one of the highest child-stunting rates and child-wasting rates compared to other regions in the world. In 2021, approximately 425 million people in the world affected by hunger were in Asia, a figure that is more than half of the total.[1] Poverty, income inequality, and the high cost of a healthy diet have all contributed to making healthy diets out of reach of a significant fraction of the population in the region. Additionally, the high incidence of climate shocks, food price inflation, decline in foreign currency reserves, and depreciation of local currencies have also contributed to the affordability challenge.

Some Asian countries like Bangladesh and Pakistan face severe localised food insecurity. At the same time, Sri Lanka has experienced food price inflation combined with a debt crisis, with the possibility of prolonged periods of hunger and poverty for its people. Countries with heavy import needs, like Cambodia, Lao People's Democratic Republic, Nepal, Philippines, and Thailand, were severely affected due to depreciation of currency and rising interest rates. Currently, food prices remain high, and the food security outlook for the region remains uncertain.

Food security challenges are a result of multiple factors. At the global level, the Ukraine crisis and the COVID-19 pandemic have disrupted the food supply chain and resulted in macro-economic challenges, including trade restrictions which have adversely affected food availability across the globe. Climate change has negatively impacted agricultural production and productivity. Extreme flooding in many parts of the world, including East Asia and South Asia, highlights the rapid and rising climate problem.

With such a plethora of issues, what then can individual countries, and Asia as a region, do to be better prepared? An obvious answer is first to appreciate the scope of the problem, followed by a detailed understanding of each problem and its potential solutions. For Asia, there are essential food items to be safeguarded if there is any hope of achieving food security — for example, rice and fish. Additionally, the demand for animal protein is highest in Asia because of a fast-growing urban middle class with rising living standards.

Concomitant with the increase in demand of quantity, quality, and diversity of food in Asia is also increasing awareness of the environment, especially of the importance for sustainable food systems. Asia exemplifies the conundrum of balancing food production with environmental protection. But Asia is also a technology powerhouse and recognisably leads in the development and application of technology-enabled food production such as indoor vertical vegetable farming and the production of alternative, ovel proteins.

This book is therefore a timely contribution to the discourse facing government planners, leaders in the agrifood industry, civil society and, in fact, any consumer with a vested interest in the future of food. The chapter authors are authorities in their respective domains and, collectively, they bring together their rich experiences to discuss, gaze into the crystal ball, and propose solutions to specific issues.

The first section of the book addresses the high-level issues impacting Asia and explicates the situation with key food items such as rice, vegetables, livestock, and fish. The authors in this part further share on how transformation of economies, and policies, plays important roles to shape a country's food security, with the example of how the world's most populous country (until recently), China, has balanced poverty eradication with ensuring enough food for all. Next, the book contains chapters which address the benefits and potential challenges from the plethora of technologies which have surfaced in the 21st century, such as digital technologies, biotechnology, and novel food production systems.

However, food security is premised on production systems which are sustainable, complemented by trade from food-surplus countries. So, the third section of the book digs into issues such as urban agriculture, aquaculture, novel proteins, and the conversion of waste into food. The last section of the book espouses on externality issues in food production, including food regulations and nutrition.

This book seeks to give a comprehensive yet substantive look into the issues confronting food security in Asia. I recommend this timely publication to all with an interest in food security at the nexus of sustainability, environmental preservation, and the future of humanity.

Ambassador Ong Keng Yong
Executive Deputy Chairman
S. Rajaratnam School of International Studies (RSIS)
Nanyang Technological University, Singapore

https://doi.org/10.1142/9789811278297_fmater

Preface

The 21st century was touted as the "Asian century" by many and although much progress has been made in this region in economic growth, reduction of poverty, increase in living standards and urbanisation, the Asian Development Bank (ADB), for example, warned that Asia still has "two faces".[2] On one side, there is growing wealth with improvements in nutrition and well-being BUT, on the other, there remains millions of disadvantaged, hungry and malnourished people without access to basic amenities.

Asia adopted the "globalisation" mantra early on with its accompanying benefits, but its countries were among the first to suffer from disruptions in global food supply chains resulting from conflict, climate change and, recently, the COVID-19 pandemic. And the Asian region is known to be among the most susceptible to unexpected severe weather events each year.

The recent past has certainly shown how vulnerable Asia is to events outside the region and, in particular, in the existential matter of food security. Many countries have come to recognise food security as a "hot button" issue, prompting them to re-evaluate their own situations and at the Asian sub-regional level to formulate plans to address it. An example is the Association of Southeast Asia (ASEAN)'s Vision and Strategic Plan for ASEAN Cooperation in Food,

---

[2] Asian Development Bank (2013, September 5). Food security — Asia's two faces. https://www.adb.org/news/infographics/food-security-asias-two-faces

Agriculture and Forestry, 2016–2025.[3] This plan is endorsed by the agricultural ministries of all ten ASEAN countries and includes collaborative implementation action which additionally makes use of the many mechanisms that exist within the ASEAN framework. The region further lends weight to the observation of the ADB, above, in that within the ASEAN group are countries that are economically strong with low levels of food (nutrition) insecurity co-existing with countries that are economically weak and have high levels of malnutrition. Affirmation of the importance of food security to ASEAN leaders is adoption at the 43rd ASEAN Summit on 5 September 2023 of the "Declaration on Strengthening Food Security and Nutrition in Response to Crises".[4]

In my work in this region as a consultant and adviser to many government entities, private companies and non-profit organisations, it became obvious that there was wide concern about the sustainability of food security, especially with respect to remaining and new issues that would result in insecurity. The broad concern and interest from publishers encouraged me to conceptualise this book and to title it as *Food Security Issues in Asia* to indicate that it is not meant to be like other content textbooks but rather a review and exploration of important issues that currently plague Asia and, additionally, issues that are emerging as key influences on the sustainability of food security and food systems in the region.

The book is organised into four sections, namely a beginning section on macro-level issues, followed by issues in technology, issues in increasing food availability and, finally, externalities that are

---

[3] https://asean-crn.org/vision-and-strategic-plan-for-asean-cooperation-in-food-agriculture-and-forestry-2016-2025/

[4] https://asean.org/wp-content/uploads/2023/09/ASEAN-Declaration-on-Strengthening-Food-Security.pdf

important to be considered in food security. The last chapter deals with futuring and addressing the issues linked to possible scenarios of food for the future. Each of these sections will be elaborated on.

At the outset, Asia faces many of the same issues as other world regions with respect to assuring enough food. The first chapter in the first section explicates this in the context of food security being a multi-dimensional (i.e., multi-component) phenomenon that sits at the nexus of water, energy, climate, labour and human health. This is followed by two chapters which address food insecurity as affected by economic transformation, income inequality and policies. As Asia will not be food secure unless there is sufficient availability of rice, vegetables, livestock and fish, four chapters are devoted to these, with projections and outlook by authors with deep global expertise and experiences in representing the international public sector. Climate change as a macro-level issue is also explained in this section, which lastly presents how two of the largest countries in Asia, China and India, have tackled their food security.

The contribution of technology to food security is the theme of the second section in the book. Three sets of "disruptive technologies" are highlighted, viz. digital technology, biotechnology and novel food. This section also has chapters which address the importance of communicating on new technologies to gain broad acceptance by consumers and, more specifically, of ways to transfer new technologies to farmers. As most new technologies are being commercialised in the growing private sector and fuelled by investments of private equity, the last chapter in this section shares the latest on this trend of increasing private investment in the agrifood space.

A central concern in food security in Asia is about increasing the amount of available food. The next section of the book contains seven chapters that examine different aspects of increasing available food, starting with the role of trade in relation to surplus food production. Four sets of technological innovations with potential to increase food supply in Asia are then highlighted — urban agriculture, aquaculture, novel food, and yellow biotechnology (insect-derived food and feed). The issue of reducing food loss and waste to increase food availability is explained, as is the improvement of plant health by reducing losses caused by pests and diseases as a means to have increased production.

The final section of the book deals with externalities. Asia is highly prone to crises arising from natural and anthropogenic causes which result in food insecurity, particularly felt in poor, developing countries. A social-anthropogenic approach is needed to understand the impact of such crises on society; this is demonstrated by a chapter which uses a West Timor narrative to illustrate the impact. With technology being considered by many as providing potential solutions for food security, another chapter examines the policy and regulatory frameworks required to enable innovations to be fully commercialised and reach the end user, be it the farmer or the urban consumer. Furthermore, with the growing input of novel foods into food systems in Asia, research presented will show that public perceptions and attitudes are important for acceptance of these novel foods.

The last chapter in the book provides a look into uncertainties (such as climate, geopolitics, technological advances) that have potential to impact on future food systems in Asia, and how these can result in different scenarios for future food security. Very aptly, this last chapter raises the question of which scenario Asian countries choose to be in 2033 based on what they know today.

In identifying the sections and chapter topics for this book, I have drawn on conversations with many colleagues across a broad spectrum of professions, sectors and disciplines. Admittedly, not all readers may agree with my selection of issues affecting food security in Asia and I make no apologies for omitting a few which have been much discoursed. My hope in this selection is that they will provide much "food for thought" in the continuing discourse on how best to assure food security in Asia.

This book would not have been possible without the commitment and strong support of all the authors. I wish also to thank and acknowledge the support of the institutions, consciously or unconsciously, which have allowed me to spend time on the book, namely the National Institute of Education (NIE) and NIE International, and the S. Rajaratnam School of International Studies (RSIS), Centre for Non-Traditional Security Studies, both of Nanyang Technological University. I am also grateful to the Agency for Science, Technology and Research (A*STAR) which, in my role there as Senior Adviser in the Biomedical Research Council, exposed me to some exciting frontiers in science and technology and shaped some of the topics covered in this book.

Paul Teng
15 September 2023

https://doi.org/10.1142/9789811278297_fmater

About the Editor

Professor Paul Teng is Managing Director and Dean, National Institute of Education International (NIEI), Nanyang Technological University (NTU), Singapore, and Adjunct Senior Fellow, S. Rajaratnam School for International Studies (RSIS), NTU, Singapore. He is an elected Fellow of the International Society of Plant Pathology (first Singaporean to achieve this), the American Phytopathological Society, the Third World Academy of Sciences, and the ASEAN Academy of Engineering and Technology. He also holds *pro bono* positions as Chair, International Service for the Acquisition of Agribiotechnology Applications (ISAAA); Adjunct Professor, Murdoch University, Australia; Senior Fellow, Southeast Asian Regional Center for Graduate Study and Research in Agriculture (SEARCA), Philippines; Fellow, The Head Foundation; and Affiliate Senior Fellow, Institute of Southeast Asian Studies (ISEAS), Singapore. He has co-authored over 250 journal papers and 8 books. He was the first Asian to obtain a Ph.D. in agricultural microbiology/systems research from University of Canterbury, New Zealand.

Professor Paul Teng is internationally recognised for his expertise in education, research, entrepreneurship and outreach in the areas of agriculture, food security and sustainable development. Between

1984 and the present, he has made visits to more than 44 countries in support of food security and sustainable development projects through consultancies with the World Bank, the Asian Development Bank, the UN Food & Agriculture Organization, etc. He has won numerous awards and recognition for his work such as the Eriksson Prize in Plant Pathology from the Royal Swedish Academy of Sciences, an Honorary Doctor of Science from Murdoch University, Honorary Member of the Philippines Society of Agricultural Economics, and Honorary Fellow of the Indian Society for Cotton Improvement.

https://doi.org/10.1142/9789811278297_fmater

Contents

Macro-Level Issues

https://doi.org/10.1142/9789811278297_0001

Chapter 1

Asian Food Security — Issues and Opportunities

Paul Teng

Centre for Non-Traditional Security Studies, S. Rajaratnam School of International Studies, Nanyang Technological University, Singapore

1.1 Introduction

Asia remains, in the 21st century, one of the most dynamic regions of the world with many fast-growing economies spearheading technological innovations in different sectors. The Asian region has about 60% of the world's population, the greatest number of poor and undernourished people, but only 34% of the world's arable land and 36% of the world's water resources [Teng and Escaler, 2012]. The world's population reached eight billion in mid-November 2022, with the two most populous countries being in Asia — China and India.[1] Population pressure together with limited land and water resources mean that Asia will face increasing pressures to feed itself. Paradoxically some

[1] https://www.un.org/en/global-issues/population#:~:text=Our%20growing%20population,and%202%20billion%20since%201998.

of the largest producers of food and feed are in this region, as are some of the largest importers. The complex social, political, and economic dynamics in Asia have led to large differences in the level of food security amongst its 48 countries. And underpinning this complexity are the eco-geographic differences in agricultural production as Asia has large intra-regional variations in climate and soils.

This complexity underscores the issues and dilemmas facing food security in the region, some of which are unique to the region and others which are common to other geographic regions. This chapter provides an overview of the trends in Asian food security, and discourses on how the context, scope and meaning of food security have changed from the previous to the current century. This is followed by discussion on the unresolved issues facing Asian food security from two perspectives — food demand (consumption) issues and food supply (production) issues. Opportunities are then highlighted to tackle some of these unresolved issues.

1.2 Trends in Asian Food Security

1.2.1 *Global Influences on Asia*

Asia's food security has been and remains under pressure from a variety of factors that include population growth and urbanisation, the declining performance of agriculture, natural resource constraints, climate change, high and volatile food and fuel prices, and the rapid transformation of supply chains.

The world's population is expected to increase from 8.0 billion in 2022 to 9.3 billion in 2050, with Asia capturing the lion's share. At the same time, the population living in urban areas is projected to gain 2.9 billion, passing from 3.4 billion in 2009 to 6.3 billion in

2050 with most growth concentrated in the cities and towns of the less developed regions [Our World in Data, 2022]. Urbanisation, in combination with rising incomes, will increase food demand and accelerate the diversification of diets [Escaler and Teng, 2014]. As incomes rise, diets will come to include more resource-intensive food products, such as meat, dairy, eggs, fruits and vegetables, thus unleashing a rapid increase in demand for raw agriculture commodities. It is unlikely that the Asian region can produce enough to meet these increases [Dy, 2021].

Agricultural performance in the Asian region has declined over the last few decades. Annual growth in crop productivity, measured in terms of average aggregate yield, has been slowing over the years. Global aggregate yield growth of grains and oilseeds averaged 2.0% per year between 1970 and 1990, but declined to 1.1% between 1990 and 2007. Crop yield growth is projected to continue declining over the next ten years to less than 1.0% per year, including in Asia [Montesclaros and Teng, 2021]. As an economic activity, the share of agriculture to gross domestic product has fallen across the region, for example, from 43% to 15% between 1961 and 2019 in South Asia. The number of people working in agriculture has also steadily declined from 70% to 55% between 1980 and 2010, and is projected to further fall to 29% in 2019 [Asian Development Bank, 2020a]. This is largely due to the structural transformation occurring in the rural sector, and attributed to the fact that farmers are getting older across Asia, rural to urban migration has increased, and the replacement rate by young farmers is not happening fast enough.

Many of the agroecosystems being used as food production systems in Asia are already showing worrying signs of stress. Climate change will put additional pressure on natural resources and food security through higher and more variable temperatures, changes in precipitation patterns, and increased occurrences of extreme weather events. According to projections compiled from various sources by Montesclaros and Teng [2021], Asia's production of irrigated wheat and rice will be 14% and 11% lower, respectively, in 2050 than in 2000 due to climate change.

International prices of major food commodities have risen sharply in the recent past, only a few years after the 2007–2008 food crisis. Since June 2010, international maize prices have more than doubled, and wheat prices have almost doubled. Domestic food prices in many countries in Asia have also increased rapidly (Teng, 2021a).

The rising costs of fuel, fertiliser and transport further contribute to fluctuations in the price of food, and also result in the expansion of biofuel production and its competition with food crops for available land. Recently, the impact of the Russia-Ukraine crisis has intensified supply shortages of some food items and fertilisers, and exacerbated the price spirals [Donnellon-May and Teng, 2022c].

The last decade of the 20th century has also shown a rapid transformation of Asia's supply chains, changing the way food is being produced, processed, packaged, transported and distributed. The fast diversification of diets towards high-value agricultural products associated with urbanisation and increasing incomes, and the rapid rise of organised retail in food, have resulted in a "supermarket revolution" [Reardon *et al.*, 2004]. Over the past two decades, countries like China, India and Vietnam have seen their share of supermarkets in food retail reach 5–20% of the market, thereby experiencing the fastest supermarket spread in history. This rapid transformation has obvious implications for food security. While supermarkets may provide higher quality and cheaper produce for urban consumers, market participation by poorer farmers is lower [Teng and Escaler, 2014].

1.2.2 *Unpacking Food Security in the Asian Context*

Food security is broadly defined by the Food and Agriculture Organization (FAO) of the United Nations as "(a) situation that exists when all people, at all times, have physical, social and economic access to sufficient, safe, and nutritious food that meets their dietary needs and food preferences for an active and healthy life" [FAO *et al.*, 2013]. This may be unpacked into four representative dimensions, namely food availability, physical access, economic access and food utilisation. Using this definition and its unpacked components, it is possible to benchmark how viewpoints on Asia's food security have changed, from the Green Revolution in the 1960s where emphasis was on making more food available (production) to stave off famine, to the present where there is more concern about distribution, affordability and nutrition accompanied by food safety (utilisation).

1.2.2.1 *Food Availability*

This is about having sufficient food available to meet growing demand, and is commonly based on the amount of food produced [Montesclaros and Teng, 2021]. Most countries have two major sources of food — domestic production and imports. There are a few economies that, even without significant agriculture, are still able to secure food through imports (trade). Singapore, for instance, only produces about 10% of its food needs and yet is considered one of the most food-secure countries in Asia [Teng, 2020]. It does so by having the financial and logistical capacity to import food from over 170 countries worldwide. However, because all imports draw from the global pool of commodities for export, it is important that production as a whole keeps up with the demand of a global population of ten billion by 2050. For the majority of countries in Asia, domestic production still makes up a large proportion of total consumption, making the performance of the agricultural sector critical. Production is driven by the land available and the yield or amount of harvest for every unit of space planted/allocated for production. The production base for agriculture, traditionally done in rural areas, has been shrinking over the past decades due to multiple factors like soil degradation, industrialisation and urbanisation [Asian Development Bank, 2021] and has led to the search for new spaces to farm, such as in urban areas and in oceans. Having food available by whatever means is a top priority in every Asian country. As a region, Asia is a net food importer for many food items.

1.2.2.2 *Physical Food Access*

Even if food is available, the countries that need it may not always have physical access to it, especially if it needs to be transported from long distances through complex supply chains. During the 2007–2008 crisis, countries like Thailand and India banned the export of rice in order to meet domestic demand [Timmer, 2009] and this precipitated supply shortages and price hikes which affected millions of rice consumers in Asia. More recently, the Russia-Ukraine crisis, preceded by the COVID-19 pandemic, prevented or slowed physical access to food in countries which were net importers [Donnellion-May and Teng, 2022c] by disrupting activities along supply chains such as the loading of grain shipments and the movement of ships along trade routes. At the domestic level, measures to control the spread of the COVID-19 pandemic caused much raw produce to rot in farms and storage facilities as there was no labour to move the goods.

1.2.2.3 *Economic Food Access*

Economic access is a key factor in food security, in which employment and the support given by governments need to provide people with sufficient purchasing power to obtain needed quantities of food. Regardless of the amount of food available through either imports or production, people may still not have the means to purchase the required amounts of food for a healthy life. Economic access becomes particularly apparent during times of crisis when people such as daily wage workers lose their jobs [Donnellion-May and Teng, 2022c]. Any increase in food prices affects mainly those in the lower echelons of the socio-economic ladder. So when international crises affect trade and international prices of traded food increase, a "pass through" effect occurs to cause domestic price increases [Durevall and van der Weide, 2014].

1.2.2.4 *Food Utilisation*

This generally involves the way in which food addresses hunger and brings about desirable nutritional and health outcomes among the populace [Montesclaros and Teng, 2021]. Concerns about food utilisation have led to work on "nutrition security", focussing on not just the adequacy of food to meet the calories per day, but also to supply essential minerals and vitamins needed for health. The "triple burden" of malnutrition as expressed by the International Food Policy Research Institute is of particular interest when manifested through under-nutrition (stunting, slow cognitive development), over-nutrition (obesity, non-communicable diseases) and mineral deficiencies [Fan, 2014]. Even before the COVID-19 pandemic in 2020, the Asia-Pacific region had been confronting high burdens of food insecurity and all forms of malnutrition as highlighted repeatedly by the FAO reports on State of Food Security and Nutrition [FAO, 2022]. 375 million people in the region were malnourished in 2020, an increase of 53.9 million people over 2019 — most of them in South Asia. 40% of the population in this region cannot afford a healthy diet. Overweight and obesity are also rising in the region. This is paradoxical in a region that is the engine of the world's economic growth and is a large producer of major food commodities such as rice, fish, pork, milk, eggs, fruits and vegetables, among many others.

However, on the bright side, given per capita income growth, hunger across all regions has fallen since 1990. Based on data from the Asian Development Bank (ADB), over 707 million people in the Asia-Pacific have been brought out of poverty since the start of the millennium [ADB, 2021].

Another aspect of food utilisation is food safety, which may be affected by improper feeding practices, excessive use of plant chemicals or microbial contamination, all of which can worsen malnutrition, especially among the poor. The food safety aspect of food security has further taken on new consideration due to the introduction of novel foods like "cultivated meat" and food from novel technologies like precision fermentation and indoor farms [Teng, 2021b].

1.3 Remaining Issues in Asian Food Security

While Asia generally shows dynamic economic growth, many challenges remain to assure food security for all its people, and the ADB has aptly described the situation using a "two-face" analogy — one face showing the bright side of plentiful food with strong economies and the other showing much malnutrition and hunger in poorly performing economies [ADB, 2013]. However, the unresolved issues in Asian food security may also be viewed positively — that they present opportunities for innovation.

Agricultural productivity proved vital in the last few decades for the region's economic transformation. Agriculture is vulnerable to climate change and extreme weather conditions. Extreme temperatures, land degradation, water stress and scarcity are limiting crop production and causing livestock and fishery losses. Transboundary plant and animal pests and diseases are further worsening the situation. In developing economies, agriculture absorbs 63% of the damage and loss caused by climate-related disasters across all economic sectors, and crops absorb 49% of all damage and loss from disasters triggered by natural hazards [FAO, 2021a]. Concurrently, the demand for the primary staple, rice, is expected to increase by 18% by 2050 while its yield is stagnating in major rice-producing and -exporting countries with arable land and water becoming scarce [ADB, 2021; Yuan *et al.*, 2022]. Major trends in the region — urbanisation and changes in consumer demand, migration from rural to urban areas, ageing populations in some countries, among others — are rendering the task of transforming agriculture more complex.

1.3.1 *Food Demand (Consumption) Issues*

A 34% increase in global population is expected by 2050 and, combined with income growth, leads to an estimated 70% growth in global food demand [FAO, 2015]. The current population of Asia is 4.7 billion as of November 11, 2022, based on the latest United Nations estimates, equivalent to 59% of the total world population. It is generally predicted that the Asian population will increase to 5.3 billion by 2050, equivalent to 54% of the global population of

9.7 billion [East-West Center, 2002]. So arithmetically, there can be an expected increase in demand for food.

The demographic phenomena of increasing population, ageing farmers, increasingly urban population accompanied by diet changes, a rising middle class, all together cause changes in the demand for food in Asia, three of which are discussed in this section.

1.3.1.1 *Impact of Urbanisation on Food Demand*

With more and more Asians living in cities, urban food security will be an increasingly important consideration in maintaining peace and stability. The food crisis in 2007–2008 and the resulting food riots that occurred in cities all over the world not only exposed the vulnerability of the global food system but, more importantly, highlighted the increasing problem of urban food security [Teng and Escaler, 2012]. Food supply, food consumption, and food stability in cities are very different from traditional rural patterns, as some governments (e.g., Egypt and Tunisia) learnt to their cost. The urban environment presents unique challenges which potentially render its residents more vulnerable to disruptions in the global food supply chain and to price fluctuations.

Urban residents have to purchase almost all of their food as well as other goods and services. For the millions of urban poor who spend 50% to 70% of their income on food, soaring prices may mean going from two meals a day to one or, at worst, to no food at all. Urban residents face more threats to their economic access to food compared to their rural brothers.

Due to increased incomes in towns and cities, the basket of food which households depend on for their existence has further become more varied and more diverse in origin. Thus, the urban poor may be more vulnerable than their rural counterparts to variations in the international market since many of their food items tend to be internationally traded. Many urban residents are also more vulnerable to global economic events since they depend on overseas remittances, exports, employment, and foreign direct investment. As recent food crises have demonstrated, urban households can be among the hardest hit as they see their purchasing power decline drastically with limited capacity to produce their own food. Because urban areas are centres of economic opportunity, there are more women working outside the home which may mean they have less time for traditional food preparation. In addition, because of greater exposure to advertising and easier access to supermarkets, urban dwellers often consume more processed and fast food, which mean higher intakes of saturated and total fat as well as sugar and lower intake of fibre. This diet, together with a more sedentary lifestyle in cities, increases the risk of chronic diseases including diabetes and obesity, diseases associated with wealth and industrialisation.

Foremost among the changes in urban diets is the increased consumption of animal protein, which has resulted in Asia being now the main importer of the world's supply of soybean and corn for animal feed. China alone imports 70–80 million tons of soybean each year to meet the needs of its animal industry, projected to increase up to 112 million tons by 2023 [Gale *et al.*, 2015].

The determinants of nutritional status go beyond income alone. Food availability is not enough for good nutrition, a reality which tends to impact city dwellers more than their rural counterparts. The urban poor live in crowded living conditions with poor quality housing, poor to non-existent garbage disposal systems, unsafe drinking water, and non-functional or non-existent sewage systems — thus affecting their nutritional status. For the urban poor living in slums, their living conditions could affect their nutritional status in the form of malnutrition and poor health. Lastly, jobs of the urban poor are casual, insecure, uncertain, low-paying and vulnerable to outside forces such as macroeconomic policies, social security programmes and, of course, the availability of food through its impact on supplies in the market, and therefore on market prices.

1.3.1.2 *The Demand for Animal Meat*

In recent decades, meat production and consumption have increased in Asia, for example, in China where, following market reforms in 1978, per capita meat consumption jumped almost six-fold in four decades alongside the rise of domestic production. The three biggest beef-eating countries in Asia — China, India and Japan — are expected to further increase consumption to an estimated 10.2 million metric tonnes (mmt), 2.9 mmt and 1.3 mmt respectively in 2022 [USDA FAS, 2022]. Other Asian countries such as Japan and South Korea as well as the ASEAN economies of Indonesia, Malaysia, the Philippines, Vietnam and Thailand are also part of the 'meatification' process of Asia [Jakobsen and Hansen, 2020].

Pork production in Asia is also expected to rise in response to increased consumption demand. China leads in pork production with a forecast of 51.0 mmt in 2022, 7% higher than in 2021 [USDA FAS, 2022]. Currently, Asia's top poultry producers include China and Thailand which are projected to reach 14.3 mmt and 3.3 mmt respectively this year.

Meat production requires feed, of which the main components are corn and soybean. Asian countries generally do not produce enough corn or soybean, despite countries like China, the Philippines and

Thailand having substantial areas of corn. Any reduction in feed availability will affect Asia's meat production. Supply chain delays arising from the Russia-Ukraine area caused temporary shortages which drove up commodity prices, especially in the more feed-intensive poultry and pork sectors. The deficit in feed production is an unresolved issue in Asian food security that requires concerted and integrated action between policy, research and investment [Donnelon-May and Teng, 2022a].

1.3.1.3 *The Demand for Fish Protein*

The global demand for fish follows the unprecedented growth in demand for protein worldwide since the beginning of the 21st century [Donnellon-May and Teng, 2022b]. In Asia, fish is both a vital source of protein as well as a legacy food for many of its countries.

The latest report by the FAO on world fisheries and aquaculture estimated that 156 million tonnes of fish were eaten as food in 2018 [FAO, 2020]. Of these, 82 million tonnes or 52% were produced from aquaculture. Today, each person eats about twice as much fish as 50 years ago on average. Nevertheless, by 2030 fish consumption is expected to jump by another 30 million tonnes due to the expansion of the middle class.

Increasing the availability of fish by harvesting from the wild is no longer a viable option. Some of the world's richest fisheries have already fallen into a perilous state. An estimated 70% of fish populations are overused or entirely used, while one-third of commercial fish stocks are being harvested at unsustainable levels. By 2050, all fisheries are expected to have collapsed. This crisis has been caused by a combination of factors, including large, destructive industrial fishing fleets with sophisticated technologies supplanting local fishermen and destroying habitats, and overfishing. At the same time, climate change is causing warmer temperatures in the oceans, much to the detriment of many fish species [Teng *et al.*, 2017].

One approach to meeting Asia's enormous appetite for fish is through aquaculture or 'fish farming', generally considered a more sustainable alternative to commercial fishing. Asia accounted for 92% of all aquaculture production worldwide and is the region's biggest source of fish for human consumption, accounting for 23% of animal protein in Asian diets [Donnellon-May and Teng, 2022b].

In Asia, China is the biggest farmed fish producer, but strong production growth is seen in India, Indonesia, Vietnam and Thailand. Various countries in Asia such as Singapore and China have implemented frameworks and policies to harness the benefits of new forms of aquaculture. Apart from its role in food security, aquaculture and related industries are also a major source of employment, with 20.5 million people working in aquaculture in 2018, of which Asia accounted for 85% [FAO, 2020]. With the continuing importance and preference for fish as healthy protein, Asia will need to invest more in aquaculture research and development (R&D) to increase productivity, i.e., more fish per unit volume of water.

1.3.2 *Food Supply (Production) Issues*

Agriculture has been the engine of growth to meet Asian's food demands since the Green Revolution of the 1960s [Montesclaros and Teng, 2021]. However, food supply from agriculture, which traditionally has been labour demanding, is also facing demographic changes. The inadequate level of generational turnover in farming, and the lack of opportunities for on- and off-farm employment of youth in rural areas, seriously affect the composition of the rural labour force, patterns of agricultural production, land tenure, social organisation within rural communities, and socio-economic development in general. This constitutes a major risk to increasing and sustaining agriculture productivity [FAO, 2017].

1.3.2.1 *Eco-Geography and Climate (Change)*

The ecology and geography (influenced by climate) of a locale determines its potential for agriculture and hence food production. As noted earlier in this chapter, Asia has 34% of the world's arable land while hosting about 60% of its population. A major issue confronting Asia is therefore how to grow more food with declining land resources which in turn are limited by the climate in a locale, i.e., the eco-geography.

The changing dynamics of temperature and precipitation, among others, has the potential to shape the landscape of areas suitable for crop production. Changes in climate will have particular impacts on crop yields in the region. Estimates from various sources show the potential for 8–14% declines in rice yields in South Asia, as well as East Asia and the Pacific [IPCC, 2022]. The implications of these, combined with global demand growth and changes in dietary patterns, are that prices of agricultural commodities could increase further by 2050, in rice (by 113–121%), wheat (by 171–194%), and maize (by 148–153%).

Looking forward, climate change presents a pessimistic picture of suitable temperatures and precipitation, which are needed for agricultural production. The United Nations Climate Change Conferences — e.g., COP26 — have so far provided little evidence that countries, whether acting individually or together, have the will to formulate concrete and meaningful action to provide financial support for the millions of small-scale farmers in developing countries.

Climate action has to take into account economic aspects of small-scale farming. But there is a gap between actual livelihoods and practices at the farming community level and high-level pronouncements of policies and aspirations in international forums. How do we also ensure that the livelihoods of small-scale farmers in sustainable agriculture are not jeopardised by climate change action? These are but a sample of the questions that will continue to be associated with attempts to balance out the carbon equation in farming — the "net-zero" solution.

1.3.2.2 *The Water Crisis*

Water is indispensable for agriculture. The Sixth Assessment Report of the Inter-Government Panel on Climate Change (IPCC) warned that further water insecurity — too little (droughts) or too much (floods) — along with the timing and duration of occurrences of excess or deficit will be expected to affect food production [IPCC, 2022].

In Asia, water insecurity has become almost a recurrent phenomenon. The two largest countries, China and India, and the Southeast Asian region suffer from extremes of water availability. Southeast Asia has the world's most vulnerable coastal area and is a significant producer of staples like rice [Teng and Donnellon-May, 2022].

In Asia, the growing water insecurity has caused unpredictable food production, requiring enormous imports from other regions [Donellion-May and Teng, 2022a]. Growing population and income will also lead to competing uses of water, across agricultural products and between agricultural and non-agricultural uses, i.e., energy/industry purposes. Today, 80% of the region's water is utilised for agricultural purposes, with the remaining 20% being used for non-agricultural purposes, including industry and energy production [ADB, 2020b]. Agricultural demand for water is expected to increase by 55%, from 3,500 km^3 in 2000 to 5,500 km^3 in 2050, to be accompanied by a 400% increase in water demand for manufacturing purposes, a 140% increase for electricity generation purposes, and a 130% increase for domestic water use [OECD, 2012].

The impact of water insecurity on food production will most affect marginal farmers, fishers and poor urban consumers due to their limited capacities to adapt to and recover from extreme weather events.

1.3.2.3 *Biological Environment and Declining Crop Yield Growth*

Declines in crop yield growth across Asia's sub-regions, notably in rice and wheat, have been documented as yield declines in long-term experiments [Dawe *et al.*, 2000] and also in terms of reduced growth in average yields in farmers' fields [Savary *et al.*, 2022]. While gross crop yields continue to grow in Asia, they have not grown as fast as they did in previous periods, i.e., decline in yield growth. They have been variously interpreted as indications of declining soil health, pests and diseases, negative externalities of agricultural practices, climate change effects, etc. [Montesclaros and Teng, 2021].

In particular, the growth rate in yields in 1990–2010 when compared with the previous 20-year period, 1970–1990, shows that yield growth in cereals was slower in the 1990–2010 period. The same applies to coarse grain, fibre crops, jute, oilcakes, oils, and pulses [Montesclaros and Teng, 2021].

Disaggregating yield growth trends by region, the data shows changes in yields across East, Southeast, South, and Western Asia. In East Asia, there are consistent trends of declines in the growth rate in yields of cereals, coarse grains, and roots, among others. In contrast, perennial plants, such as fruits, seem to show trends of increasing yields. In addition, vegetable production yields grew faster in this sub-region.

In the first decade of the Green Revolution, crop yield growth in rice and wheat exceeded the growth in demand per capita attributable to population growth. That yield growth is now less than the growth in demand remains an important issue for Asia to maintain its food security, especially for a staple like rice [Yuan *et al.*, 2022].

1.3.2.4 *Negative Externalities in Food Production*

Agricultural practices are known to have negative effects on the environment [Shortle and Uetake, 2015], with two well-known examples being eutrophication and pesticide poisoning of humans and ecosystem fauna. Use of chemical inputs such as pesticides has increased agricultural production and productivity. However, negative externalities from such use have resulted in damage to agricultural land, fisheries, fauna and flora, and the unintentional destruction of beneficial predators of pests thereby increasing the virulence of many species of agricultural pests. Furthermore, increased mortality and morbidity of humans due to exposure to pesticides are recorded especially in developing countries [Rahman *et al.*, 2021]. The costs from these externalities are large and affect farmers' returns. However, despite these high costs, farmers continue to use pesticides in most countries in increasing quantities [Wilson and Tisdell, 2001].

A more recent externality of concern is in the context of climate change. Agriculture is generally acknowledged as a significant source of greenhouse gas (GHG) emissions (a negative externality), contributing around 18.4% of the global total, mainly through cattle farming and rice cultivation. The FAO has warned that rice production must increase by 5 million tonnes per year to keep up with demand from increasing populations. But areas of high rice production are simultaneously areas of high GHG emissions. Growing more rice will inevitably lead to more methane and nitrous oxide emissions. The importance of this is reinforced by the fact that Asia grows about 90% of the world's rice [Teng, 2022a].

There are also growing concerns over aquacultural practices and their damage to the environment [FAO, 2020]. Aquaculture has been linked to habitat destruction (e.g., mangrove destruction), environmental degradation, biodiversity loss, and ecosystem loss due to factors like the introduction of exotic species that can displace native fish species and the excess of nutrients such as nitrogen and phosphorous from non-consumed feed (mainly due to overfeeding) flowing into natural ecosystems.

The need to produce more food and feed per unit area of arable land suggests that so-called modern agricultural inputs like pesticides will continue to be used by farmers. The unresolved issue in Asian food security is therefore to ensure that there is increased crop productivity without any accompanying negative effect, and for this, R&D into sustainable practices backed by working extension systems are needed.

1.3.2.5 *Sustainability Issues*

Sustainable agriculture does not have a generally accepted definition, although Crosson's (1992) captures succinctly the aspirations for sustainable agriculture: "*A sustainable agricultural system is one that can indefinitely meet the requirements for food and fibre at socially acceptable, economical and environmental costs.*" This suggests that sustainable agriculture may be described using three rubrics, Environment, Economics and Social (EES), expanded as follows: environmentally friendly (conserves natural resource base, minimises negative externalities like pesticides, etc.), economically viable (enables farmer livelihood) and socially just (benefits small and large farms, benefits producers and consumers).

However, sustainable agriculture also needs to be contextualised as an integral part of sustainable development which aims at "meeting the needs of the present without compromising the ability of future generations to meet their own needs", as proposed by the seminal "Brundtland Report" [World Commission on Environment and Development, 1987].

The call for sustainable farming has gotten louder, especially as we approach the 2030 deadline to achieve the United Nations' Sustainable Development Goals (SDGs). Increased sustainability, however, can only be achieved by intensifying research, adopting new farming approaches, technologies that contribute to a circular economy, and game-changing policies — all backed by political will and support to implement practices.

Ultimately, there can be no sustainable development without addressing the interlinked issues of climate change, livelihoods and food production.

Currently, much of the discourse on sustainability appears focused on the environmental, social and governance (ESG) aspects [Teng, 2017]. The distinction between "EES" and "ESG" is particularly important for the world's small-scale farmers and animal herders in the Asian-African regions who are responsible for most of the world's food production. The economic (E) rubric recognises that small-scale farmers need to have decent livelihoods, without which they cannot sustain their farming and their families.

1.4 Opportunities to Ensure Future Food Security

When the issues of climate change, sustainable agriculture, food security and farmer livelihoods are considered together, they represent a "wicked problem". Can a wicked problem be unpacked into parts which can be addressed separately and, in their solutions, contribute to the overall solution? Pragmatically, this may be the only approach. Agriculture contributes to climate change and climate change affects agriculture. The "whole is more than the sum of its parts", and food production is only one component of food systems. The FAO views food systems as comprising "the entire range of actors and their interlinked value-adding activities" [FAO, 2018]. This involves "the production, aggregation, processing, distribution, consumption and disposal of food products that originate from agriculture, forestry or fisheries, <u>and</u> parts of the broader economic, societal and natural environments in which they are embedded". So the hope for humankind may be to unpack a big wicked problem into its components. Then follow this by solving the component issues through cooperative efforts. This in the hope that they may lead at least to a partial solution of the bigger wicked problem.

In response to the many challenges posed by a complex situation, governments in Asia have put forward measures to safeguard food security amidst fear of food shortages and social and political instability. The "New Normal" [Donellon-May and Teng, 2022c] has prompted countries to look for opportunities to buffer themselves against potential food insecurity. Several of these opportunities include the exploitation of disruptive technologies, urban-periurban agriculture, and rebalancing self-production levels with imports via trade.

1.4.1 *Disruptive Technologies*

Asian agriculture faces many challenges that lend themselves to technological solutions. While political and social solutions meet some of these challenges, experts generally agree that technological innovations offer much potential. A perfect example of this is the "Green Revolution" which in the 1960s saw many large Asian countries increase yields with new rice and wheat varieties and agricultural inputs. China and India staved off mass starvation. If not for the positive impact of these disruptive innovations, Asia would not have had the food security necessary for economic development [Teng, 2021b]. Clayton Christensen, a professor at the Harvard Business School, coined the term "disruptive technology" — one that displaces an established technology and shakes up the industry or a ground-breaking product that creates a completely new industry [Christensen *et al.*, 1997].

Agriculture is now strongly influenced by agricultural technology or "agtech", which is the milieu of exciting new technologies that have already started to make a difference to small farmers in Asia. These include the following [Teng, 2021b]:

- Agronomy and agricultural biotechnology to innovate inputs for crop and animal agriculture such as seeds, pest control, seeds with new genetics, microbiome and animal health;
- Mechanisation, robotics and equipment such as on-farm machinery, automation, drones guided by Global Positioning

Systems or Geographic Information Systems, environmental sensors, and growing equipment;
- Farm management software, Internet of Things (IoT) systems with sensing and intervening — these include environmental, farming data capture devices, decision support software, big data analytics and miniaturised portable applications; most from the so-called fourth Industrial Revolution;
- Novel farming systems such as indoor farms, plant factories with controlled environment, aquaculture systems, and grow-out facilities for insects, algae and microbes; and
- Novel, future foods made using precision fermentation and biotechnology processes, as exemplified by plant-based protein and cultivated meat.

In countries like China, India and the Philippines, many digital agtech applications are offered through young entrepreneurs to farmers as part of a consulting service to make profits and represent a form of "Smart Farming" in which up-to-date data on crop and environment are linked through IoT systems to provide timely action.

Biotechnology is an important disruptive technology, in the form of crop varieties developed using biotechnology, including genetic modification. Asia in 2019 grew 11% of the world's bio-tech (genetically modified) crops, about 19.5 million hectares in nine countries [ISAAA, 2020]. The crops are cotton, papaya, canola, maize, eggplant and sugarcane, benefiting millions of smallholders and, in some cases, allowing crops to be grown in areas which hitherto had to be abandoned due to insect-pest pressure and the ineffectiveness of insecticides. Going forward, a new biotechnology called gene editing is likely to have even greater impact.

A disruptive technology that has risen in response to urbanisation, climate change and increased demand by consumers to have vegetables grown close by is the "Plant Factory with Artificial Light" — which is essentially an enclosed, environment-controlled greenhouse in which vegetables are grown in tiered trays. These plants grown indoors generally have no need to use insecticides and can produce many times more per unit area using artificial lights.

Two other technologies that have potential to become disruptive technologies are alternative proteins (such as plant-based protein, cultivated meat and insect protein) and blockchain. Although the alternative protein space is currently dominated by plant proteins, fungal proteins are gaining popularity due to their nutritional values and other health benefits. Blockchain technology safeguards the integrity of food supply from farm to consumer and are also spawning the development of techniques to quickly detect food fraud or guarantee food identity.

Many developing countries are already benefitting from disruptive technologies. However, many more are not even starting to use them, leaving much untapped potential to increase food production and promote entrepreneurship in Asia. Care has to be taken to see that no "technology divide" is created between farmers because of affordability, as had happened in the early days of the Green Revolution when poor farmers in unfavourable lands could not afford the price of inputs like new seeds and fertilisers.

1.4.2 *Urban-Periurban Agriculture*

An emerging trend in Asia is that of farming in and around cities (urban and periurban agriculture), contributing complementary food sources as well as greenery for urban environments. Agriculture also provides green spaces within the core of urban centres, as a means toward sustainable landscape planning with not only environmental but also cultural and socio-economic benefits [Carlet *et al.*, 2017]. In Seoul, such a movement started to take shape in the mid-2000s, with the cultivation of edible vegetables by urban dwellers in unused land, after a key policy was introduced in 2005 that offered tax benefits to farmers [Suk, 2014]. These offer cities some remedy from the heat-island effect, wherein densely populated areas are a few degrees warmer than their surroundings [Teng and Escaler, 2014]. Having agriculture enhances the ability of cities to cope with this, thereby also reducing energy costs for cooling.

In Asia, there were reportedly over 450 'Plant Factories with Artificial Light' as of 2016 and the number is growing in countries like China, Japan, Singapore, South Korea and Taiwan. Collectively, these will increase the FAO estimate of 20% of food produced in urban areas [Teng, 2021b]. However, Plant Factories with Artificial Light require large financial resources to set up and their produce is costlier than outdoor vegetables. The expectation, though, is that efficiency will improve and produce will become cheaper as the technology is improved and scaled up.

1.4.3 *Rebalancing Food Self-Production with Imports Via Trade*

The food insecurity caused by the three Cs — COVID-19 pandemic, climate change and conflicts — has highlighted the reliance of many Asian states on imported staple food and feed. The ASEAN sub-region within Asia exemplifies the vulnerability to imports of foodstuffs, and several ASEAN states are now rethinking their agrifood policies in favour of more localised production and shorter (and more reliable) supply chains [Donnellon-May and Teng, 2022c].

The ASEAN region is an illustration of the importance to rebalance food flows [Teng, 2022c]. The ASEAN Secretariat estimated that in

2020, ASEAN imported US$61 billion of agricultural commodities from outside ASEAN. This reflects insufficient production within ASEAN of the region's main foodstuffs (and feedstuffs). However, even though ASEAN member states differ widely in their food production capacities [Teng, 2022c], the region still produced 46 mmt of maize, 735,000 mt of soybean and 113,400 mt of wheat.

For maize, ASEAN production meets about 75% of the region's needs. ASEAN produces less than one-tenth of its soybean needs, mainly from Indonesia (395,000 mt), Myanmar (195,000 mt), Vietnam (81,000 mt), Cambodia (31,000 mt) and Thailand (27,000 mt) in 2020. ASEAN also produced less than half a percent of its wheat needs, some 113,400 mt, almost all from Myanmar, with a small amount from Thailand. ASEAN states are among the world's largest importers of wheat, together with significant amounts of soybean and maize. In fact, ASEAN took up 15% of global wheat imports in 2021 [Teng, 2022c]. Wheat imports exceed production in ASEAN by a whopping ratio of 244:1. Soybean imports exceed local production by a ratio of 10:1. The deficit has to be made up with imports through trade from countries with surplus to export. Reducing these trade deficits will require extra effort by this Asian sub-region alone in the coming years.

1.5 Concluding Remarks

The recent past has shown how interconnected the world is with respect to food. Indeed, the world seems to be entering an era of "Volatile Deficits", in which the stability of food security is not assured, and countries will have to be better prepared to deal with uncertainty [Teng, 2022b]. The impact of disruptions on food security can be very dire if food production, access and distribution are severely affected, as has been seen in the first half of 2020 because of COVID-19 [Caballero-Anthony *et al.*, 2020]. Absent well-thought preparedness planning and policy responses, this disruptive impact can rapidly escalate into a food crisis of huge proportions, aggravating problems of malnutrition and hunger, and triggering conflicts. Thus, having 'disruption-proof' food security strategies at national and regional levels becomes more urgent than ever if states are to adequately respond to multi-faceted disruptions.

The year 2022 saw many countries aiming to transform or reform their food systems to deal with periods of deficits, whether in imports or in their self-production. What 2022 has shown is that countries need to have some level of resilience in their food supplies, conferred through self-production or assured supply chains; the latter through contractual agreements which are binding and prevent exporting countries from reneging on their contracts.

However, 2022 has also shown that when countries limit exports to protect their domestic constituencies, the action may have unintended effects on that country's food production sector, a phenomenon tantamount to "shooting oneself in the foot". Exporters in exporting countries which limited their exports found themselves deprived of their former markets when the limitations were lifted as importing countries secured new sources of food. A key lesson from the crisis caused by the 3Cs is also that countries which export the majority of their production are more unlikely to ban or reduce their exports. So this translates into a key learning point for investment and cooperation, which is to choose those exporting countries whose domestic consumption are a small fraction of their total production, such as Australia and New Zealand in the Asia-Pacific region.

The past years of 2020–2022 have also highlighted the weakness in regional cooperation because countries have relied for decades on global supply chains. A reaction to this weakness is the increase in national food protectionism, as witnessed by disengagement from global supply chains and increasing self-production of staples. However, as shown by the Sri Lanka disaster, disengagement without proper planning and supportive policy and science also has disastrous outcomes on people's lives [Teng and Montesclaros, 2022]. So while food system transformation towards more sustainability and reliability at the national level is a laudable aspiration, 2022 has shown that this has to be handled delicately.

A bright spark in 2022, though, has been the rise in local support groups to provide food security to the disadvantaged groups within a country [Teng, 2022b]. Food banks, safety nets of different types, volunteerism by individuals and organisations increased in many countries — all signs of social cohesion in the face of calamity. Perhaps in Asia, the cultural history has positioned the continent to be more caring despite limited capabilities.

There are many potential solutions available — policy-based, evidence-based, regenerative, innovative, technological — and many of these will be needed to overcome key challenges. These measures also include strengthening actions to sustainably manage natural resources and enhance forest and landscape restoration. The Asia-Pacific region has thousands of years with agriculture-based systems and hundreds of generations of traditional knowledge which are coupled with a fast-growing entrepreneurial ecosystem.

Feeding and nourishing a larger, more urban and increasingly affluent Asian population sustainably and equitably will remain an unprecedented challenge that will require a more holistic approach to address food security more effectively [Teng and Escaler, 2014]. The more obvious solution of increasing food production is only one among many strategies needed to meet this challenge. While rural areas currently hold most of the world's poor and hungry and will continue to do so for many years to come, the urban dimensions of food security merit distinct attention and focus from national governments. As it is, the world is already witnessing the shifting of poverty and the food insecure to cities, with most of the poor being absorbed into life-threatening slums. Factors of production, technologies, employment and indeed policies which were predominantly aimed at rural populations must now adapt to address urban situations. Specific attention needs to be given to the links that connect urban and rural communities, shape the economic relationships between them and determine how resources can be shared and used sustainably. Cities, with their unique features, must be included on the agenda of food and agriculture policymakers, planners and institutions and, conversely, food security and agriculture must be integrated into the agenda of city planners and local urban authorities. By addressing urban-rural linkages from social, economic and environmental perspectives, a more coherent and holistic approach can be developed.

'Disruptive technologies' are anticipated to play a key role in safeguarding food production. Biotechnology using genetic modification and gene editing is anticipated to provide farmers with better crop varieties and animal breeds to tolerate climate change and pests and inherently yield more. Digital technologies have been used to improve smallholder rice farming in countries including China, India and the Philippines with the use of drones, sensors and the IoT: a network of software and other technologies connecting physical objects and exchanging data online.

But these will have to be accompanied by supportive public sector policies, sufficient private investment and an environment which incentivises farmers to produce more.

The 2030 SDG Agenda is intended to guide countries of the world towards the attainment of the 17 SDGs, leaving no one behind. Yet, years after its adoption, the Asia-Pacific region is significantly off track and is now expected to achieve them only by 2065 — three-and-a-half decades behind schedule [ESCAP, 2022]. The United Nations was already cognisant of the inequalities across the globe in terms of access to safe and nutritious food. Besides ensuring food security and nutrition for all, the urgent need to reshape and re-imagine agrifood systems is now recognised as also necessary to contribute to combating climate change by keeping the temperature rise of the planet to no more than 1.5°C [IPCC, 2021].

In order to maximise the potential of Asia's agricultural sector to improve food security in the region and beyond, governments must embark on a multi-faceted and integrated strategy, one that is broader in scope and adapted to these dynamic challenges.

References

Asian Development Bank. (2013). Food security — Asia's two faces. https://www.adb.org/news/infographics/food-security-asias-two-faces

Asian Development Bank. (2020a). Key Indicators for Asia and the Pacific 2020. https://www.adb.org/publications/key-indicators-asia-and-pacific-2020

Asian Development Bank. (2020b). Asian Water Development Outlook 2020: Advancing Water Security across Asia and the Pacific. https://www.adb.org/publications/asian-water-development-outlook-2020

Asian Development Bank. (2021). Asian Development Outlook 2021 Update: Transforming Agriculture in Asia. https://www.adb.org/publications/asian-development-outlook-2021-update

Caballero-Anthony, M., Teng, P. and Montesclaros, J. M. L. (2020). COVID-19 and food security in Asia: How prepared are we?. *NTS Insight*, No. IN20-03, RSIS Centre for Non-Traditional Security Studies (NTS Centre), Nanyang Technological University, Singapore. https://www.rsis.edu.sg/wp-content/uploads/2020/06/NTS-Insight_Food-Security-Preparedness_June-9-2020.pdf

Carlet, F., Schilling, J. and Heckert, M. (2017). Greening U.S. legacy cities: Urban agriculture as a strategy for reclaiming vacant land. *Agroecology and Sustainable Food Systems*, 41(8), pp. 887–906.

Christensen, C. M., Raynor, M. E. and Mcdonald, R. (2015). What is disruptive innovation?. *Harvard Business Review*, December, pp. 44–53.

Crosson, P. (1992). Sustainable agriculture. *Resources*, 106, pp. 14–17.

Dawe, D., Dobermann, A., Moya, P., Abdulrachman, S., Singh, B., Lal, P., Li, S. Y., Lin, B., Panaullah, G., Sariam, O., Singh, Y., Swarup, A., Ta, P. S. and Zhen, Q. X. (2000). How widespread are yield declines in long-term rice experiments in Asia?. *Field Crops Research*, 66, pp. 175–193.

Donnellon-May, G. and Teng, P. (2022a). Animal feed & meat: Asia's looming food crisis. RSIS Commentary no. 061. https://www.rsis.edu.sg/rsis-publication/nts/global-food-insecurity-animal-feed-and-meat-asias-looming-food-crisis/#.Yp7mYVN_WdM

Donnellon-May, G. and Teng, P. (2022b). Asia's huge appetite for fish: can it be met?. RSIS Commentary no. 062. https://www.rsis.edu.sg/wp-content/uploads/2022/06/CO22062.pdf

Donnellon-May, G. and Teng, P. (2022c). Ukraine crisis — Asia's food security in trouble?. RSIS Commentary No. 035. https://www.rsis.edu.sg/rsis-publication/nts/invasion-of-ukraine-asias-food-security-in-trouble/

Durevall, D. and van der Weide, R. (2014). Importing high food prices by exporting: Rice prices in Lao PDR. Policy Research Working

Paper 7119, Poverty and Inequality Team, Development Research Group, World Bank Group. http://documents.worldbank.org/curated/en/894041468278696193/pdf/WPS7119.pdf

Dy, R. T. (2021). Measuring food security across countries. *Food and Agri Business Monitor*, pp. 2–3.

East-West Center. (2002). The Future of Population in Asia. https://www.eastwestcenter.org/publications/the-future-population-in-asia

Economic and Social Commission for Asia and the Pacific (ESCAP). (2022). Asia and the Pacific SDG Progress Report 2022: Widening Disparities amid COVID-19. https://www.unescap.org/kp/2022/asia-and-pacific-sdg-progress-report-2022

Escaler, M. and Teng, P. (2014). Urban Food Security and Urban Agriculture in Asia: Cities as Part of the Solution. In S. Bazoobandi (Ed.), *The Politics of Food Security: Asian and Middle Eastern Strategies*, pp. 159–178. Gerlach Press.

Fan, S. (2014). Overcoming the triple burden of malnutrition in the MENA region. International Food Policy Research Institute. https://www.ifpri.org/blog/overcoming-triple-burden-malnutrition-mena-region%E2%80%A8

Food and Agriculture Organization (FAO). (2015). The Future of Food and Agriculture — Trends and Challenges. https://www.fao.org/3/i6583e/i6583e.pdf

Food and Agriculture Organization (FAO). (2017). The Future of Food and Agriculture — Trends and Challenges. https://www.fao.org/3/i6583e/i6583e.pdf

Food and Agriculture Organization (FAO). (2018). Sustainable Food Systems — Concept and Framework. https://www.fao.org/3/ca2079en/CA2079EN.pdf

Food and Agriculture Organization (FAO). (2020). The State of World Fisheries and Aquaculture 2020: Sustainability in Action. https://doi.org/10.4060/ca9229en

Food and Agriculture Organization (FAO). (2021a). The Impact of Disasters and Crises on Agriculture and Food Security: 2021. https://www.fao.org/3/cb3673en/cb3673en.pdf

Food and Agriculture Organization (FAO). (2021b). State of Food Security and Nutrition — Regional Overview of the Asia and Pacific. https://www.fao.org/3/cb7494en/cb7494en.pdf

Food and Agriculture Organization (FAO). (2022). The State of Food Security and Nutrition in the World. https://www.fao.org/3/cc0639en/cc0639en.pdf

Food and Agriculture Organization (FAO), International Fund for Agricultural Development (IFAD) and World Food Programme (WFP). (2013). The State of Food Insecurity in the World 2013: The Multiple Dimensions of Food Security. https://www.fao.org/3/i3434e/i3434e.pdf

Gale, F., Hansen, J. A. and Jewison, M. (2015). China's growing demand for agricultural imports. Economic Information Bulletin 136, Economic Research Service., U.S. Department of Agriculture. https://www.ers.usda.gov/webdocs/publications/43939/eib-136.pdf?v=42058.

Inter-Government Panel on Climate Change (IPCC). (2021). Climate Change 2021: The Physical Science Basis. Contribution of Working Group I to the Sixth Assessment Report of the Intergovernmental Panel on Climate Change. https://www.ipcc.ch/report/ar6/wg1/

Inter-Government Panel on Climate Change (IPCC). (2022). Climate Change 2022 — Impacts, Adaptation and Vulnerability. https://www.ipcc.ch/report/sixth-assessment-report-working-group-ii/

International Service for Acquisition of Agribiotechnology Applications (ISAAA). (2020). Global Status of Commercialized Biotech/GM Crops: 2019. *ISAAA Brief no. 55.*

Jakobsen, J. and Hansen, A. (2020). Geographies of meatification: an emerging Asian meat complex. *Globalizations*, 17(1), pp. 93–109._

Montesclaros, J. M. L. and Teng, P. (2021). Agriculture and Food Security in Asia. In J. Pulhin, M. Inoue and R. Shaw (Eds.), *Climate Change, Disaster Risks, and Human Security: Asian Experience and Perspectives*, pp. 137–168. Springer.

OECD. (2012). OECD Environmental Outlook to 2050: The Consequences of Inaction. http://dx.doi.org/10.1787/9789264122246-en

Our World in Data. (2022). Urbanisation across the world today. https://ourworldindata.org/urbanization#:~:text=By%202050%2C%20global%20population%20is,rural%20settings%20(3.1%20billion). Accessed 07 January 2023.

Rahman, M. M., Chowdhury, S. R., Bohara, A. K. and Karmacharya, B. (2021). A case of negative externality: use of pesticide and its impact on health among farmers in Salumbhu Village, Nepal. *Journal of Health Management*, 23(2), pp. 302–314.

Reardon, T., Timmer, P. and Berdegue, J. (2004). The rapid rise of supermarkets in developing countries: induced organizational, institutional, and technological change in agrifood systems. *Electronic Journal of Agricultural and Development Economics*, 1(2), pp. 168–183.

Savary, S., Willocquet, L., Castilla, N., Nelson, A., Singh, U. S., Kumar, J. and Teng, P. (2022). Whither rice health in the lowlands of Asia: Shifts in production situations, injury profiles, and yields. *Plant Pathology*, 71, pp. 55–85.

Shortle, J. and Uetake, T. (2015). Public goods and externalities: agri-environmental policy measures in the United States. *OECD Food, Agriculture and Fisheries Papers*, No. 84. http://dx.doi.org/10.1787/5js08hwhg8mw-en

Suk, G.-h. (2014). City agriculture sprouts in Korea. *The Korea Herald*, March 28. http://www.koreaherald.com/view.php?ud=20140328001435

Teng, P. (2017). Sustainability — beware of greenwashing. RSIS Commentary No. 072. https://www.rsis.edu.sg/wp-content/uploads/2017/04/CO17072.pdf

Teng, P. (2020). Assuring food security in Singapore, a small island state facing COVID-19. *Food Security*, 12, pp. 801–804.

Teng, P. (2021a). Southeast Asia and food price inflation: double whammy. *ISEAS Fulcrum*. https://fulcrum.sg/southeast-asia-and-food-price-inflation-double-whammy/

Teng, P. (2021b). INDUSTRY NOTE: New disruptive technologies and mindsets for Asian agriculture in the 21st century. *International Journal of Agriculture Innovation, Technology and Globalisation*, 2(2), pp. 186–191.

Teng, P. (2022a). Sustainability and security concerns feed Southeast Asia's rice conundrum. *GLOBEMEDIA ASIA* 10MAY2022. https://southeastasiaglobe.com/southeast-asia-rice-conundrum/

Teng, P. (2022b). 2022 — a year of reckoning on food security. In L. Gong and J. C. Trajano (Eds.), *Centre for Non-Traditional Security Studies Year in Review 2022*, pp. 14–15. S. Rajaratnam School of International Studies, Nanyang Technological University.

Teng, P. (2022c). Food import: reducing ASEAN's dependency. RSIS Commentary No. 073. https://www.rsis.edu.sg/rsis-publication/nts/global-food-insecurity-food-import-reducing-aseans-dependency/

Teng, P. and Donnellon-May, G. (2022). Growing food insecurity — global water crisis: options for food security. RSIS Commentary No. 068. https://www.rsis.edu.sg/rsis-publication/nts/growing-food-insecurity-global-water-crisis-options-for-food-security/

Teng, P. and Escaler, M. (2012). Food Security in Asia: The Changing Landscape. In B. L. Job (Ed.), *CSCAP Regional Security Outlook 2012*, pp. 40–45. Council for Security Cooperation in the Asia Pacific.

Teng, P. and Escaler, M. (2014). Food Security in Asia. In W. Hofmeister, P. Rueppel and J. Wong (Eds.), *Food Security: The Role of Asia and Europe in Production, Trade and Regionalism*, pp. 11–36. European Policy Centre.

Teng, P. and Montesclaros, J. M. L. (2022). The danger of misguided food production policies: the case of Sri Lanka. RSIS Commentary No.106. https://www.rsis.edu.sg/wp-content/uploads/2022/10/CO22106.pdf

Teng, P., Lassa, J. and Caballero-Anthony, M. (2017). Climate change and fish availability. *COSMOS*, 12(1), pp. 1–14.

Timmer, P. (2009). Rice price formation in the short run and the long run: The role of market structure in explaining volatility. Working Paper Number 172, Center for Global Development. https://www.cgdev.org/sites/default/files/1422136_file_Timmer_Rice_Price_FINAL.pdf

USDA, FAS. (2022). Livestock and Poultry: World Markets and Trade, October 2022. https://apps.fas.usda.gov/psdonline/circulars/livestock_poultry.pdf

World Commission on Environment and Development. (1987). Our Common Future, From One Earth to One World. https://sustainabledevelopment.un.org/content/documents/5987our-common-future.pdf

Wilson, C. and Tisdell, C. (2001). Why farmers continue to use pesticides despite environmental, health and sustainability costs. *Ecological Economics*, 39(3), pp. 449–462.

Yuan, S., Stuart, A. M., Laborte, A. G., Edreira, J. I. R., Dobermann, A., Kien, L. V. N., Thúy, L. T., Paothong, K., Traesang, P., Tint, K. M., San, S. S., Villafuerte, M. Q., Quicho, E. D., Pame, A. R. P., Then, R., Flor, R. J., Thon, N., Agus, F., Agustiani, N., Deng, N., Li, T. and Grassini, P. (2022). Southeast Asia must narrow down the yield gap to continue to be a major rice bowl. *Nature Food*, 3, pp. 217–226.

https://doi.org/10.1142/9789811278297_0002

Chapter 2

Reducing Poverty and Malnutrition in Asia: The Role of Structural Change and Income Inequality

Roehlano M. Briones

Philippine Institute for Development Studies, Quezon City, The Philippines

2.1 Introduction — Statement of the Problem

Nutrition is an important aspect of food security which, in turn, is strongly linked to poverty. In Asia, income inequality is responsible for high poverty levels in developing countries, which further explains the presence of high malnutrition among poor households. In a seminal report, the Asian Development Bank [Asian Development Bank, 2013] described Asia as having two "faces" — one face with strong economic growth and wealth, and another face in which poverty and malnutrition are prevalent, and warned that this was an important issue that the region had to address to ensure sustained economic growth. Additionally, data from the Global Food Security Index [Economist Intelligence Unit, 2022] show that there are strong correlations between increased household income and decreased malnutrition.

The structural transformation of economies plays a key role to reduce income inequalities and, consequently, poverty levels and malnutrition in populations.

Postwar Asian economies have undergone considerable structural change. Whereas economic activity was previously dominated by agriculture, there is now a heavy dependence on industry and services. Over the course of economic transformation, poverty and malnutrition rates have fallen dramatically. This is no coincidence — structural change is a key driver of growth of household income, and therefore living standards and nutrient intake.

Nonetheless, there remain severe disparities in poverty and nutrition outcomes across Asia. These variations are partly explained by differences in the pace and extent of structural change. However, I propose here an additional determinant, which is income inequality. While income inequality is partly influenced by structural change, it is more importantly driven by historical and institutional processes. Furthermore, there are policy levers that can improve a society's income inequality, beyond simply promotion of economic growth and transformation, that can achieve faster reductions in poverty and malnutrition.

The rest of the chapter is organised as follows: Section 2.2 presents the conceptual framework of structural change in relation to income inequality. Section 2.3 presents empirical data to support the conceptual framework. Section 2.4 discusses trends in structural change, poverty, malnutrition, and income inequality for Asian countries.

2.2 Conceptual Framework on Poverty and Malnutrition

2.2.1 *Poverty and Malnutrition at the Micro-Level*

Food security is closely associated with **nutrition**, which involves translating food intake into nutrient intake. Intake of nutrients is of course a major contributor to nutritional status (the additional contributors are other aspects of human health, such as presence of parasites, disease, physical fitness, etc.).

In the modern economy, most households obtain their daily needs largely from the market. The standard of living therefore greatly depends on a household's ability to exchange money for goods and services, i.e., its "purchasing power".

Poverty involves comparing household income to an income threshold, which is just sufficient to purchase a basket of goods and services corresponding to a minimum standard of living. For example, the World Bank sets the poverty threshold at USD 2.15 a day based on 2017 purchasing power parity-adjusted dollars; households whose average per income fall below this line are deemed "poor". Household income and poverty are the long-run drivers of nutritional outcomes [Bouis *et al.*, 2011].

Development economics has shown that changes in household income can be described by macro-level determinants associated with changes in average per capita incomes, or *economic growth*, and the distribution of income across the population, or income inequality. Macro-level factors are discussed in the next sub-section.

2.2.2 *Economic Growth and Structural Change at the Macro-Level*

A common indicator of economic development is output per capita. Standard economic theory as represented by growth models can explain increasing output per capita in terms of population growth, capital formation, and technological change. Economic growth is not only characterised by factor accumulation and rising productivity; it is also strongly correlated with the changing composition of economic activity, or **structural change**. This can also be explained by standard economics by incorporating an Engel effect on the demand side, in which the share of food in household expenditure declines as household income and expenditure increase [Kongsamut *et al.*, 2001]. On the supply side, capital accumulation causes Rybczynski-type effects leading to the increasing share of capital-intensive activities, which tend to be outside agriculture [Acemoglu and Guerriri, 2008].

These "new classical" or "neoclassical" explanations derive structural change as incidental to the development process. Lewis [1954] proposed a "dual development" model based on the older, classical approach, where structural change is a key feature of the development process. He posits two types of economies, a traditional and a modern economy, with the distinguishing characteristic of the latter being a) capital accumulation; and b) scarcity of labour. In contrast, in the traditional economy, labour is in surplus, and there are essentially no savings as income is set to subsistence. Meanwhile, savings and investment in the modern economy draws in surplus labour and drives economic growth.

The model predicts that wages tend to remain depressed over a prolonged period of economic development and migration out of the traditional sector, until a "turning point" is reached when surplus labour is exhausted and wages equal marginal product in the modern economy.

Subsequent authors such as Ranis and Fei [1961] associate the traditional and modern economies with, respectively, agriculture and industry. In particular, in the face of rapid population growth, agriculture cannot remain "traditional" in terms of zero change in technology; rather, growth in productivity may be necessary for food production to remain sufficient even as workers move from agriculture to industry, else the process of modernisation may "grind to a halt". It may be argued, however, that imports are an alternative source of food — the products of modern industry may be traded internationally for food without the need for domestic productivity growth. This indeed may be the case for a small open economy such as Singapore. However, for large open economies, Gollin *et al.* [2003] point out that food requirements cannot all be imported, and that most consumption will have to be sourced domestically, requiring agricultural productivity to increase to remain cost competitive. For instance, the Philippines consumes about 15 million tons of milled rice [PSA, 2023]; this is already over 30% of total annual trade in rice [FAO, 2023], comprising an unrealistically high market share for a single country. In fact, the Philippines normally imports about 15–20% of its annual requirement.

2.2.3 *Income Inequality*

Household income is simply the return on assets held by the household under a regime of property rights. These include physical assets such as land, buildings, and equipment; labour endowments, which embodies human capital; and intangible assets such as intellectual property. Typically these assets, or claims to these assets, except for human capital, can be passed on via inheritance laws to the next generation; even human capital can be to a large extent passed on by making expensive schooling investments. Initial levels of inequality may end up perpetuating or even intensifying over time [Piketty, 2014].

The link to poverty is obvious: for a given mean income, and some regularity features of the size distribution of income, a greater income inequality will imply higher poverty and lower incomes among the poorer segment; this in turn links to greater extent and depth of malnutrition. Over time, what matters for poverty reduction and eventually, better nutrition, is not just the increase in mean income, but also the distribution of those incomes. The response of poverty to economic growth may be weakened by a highly concentrated distribution of income.

The property rights explanation suggests that inequality is independent of per capita output and its change over time. There are of course hypothesised links between inequality and growth; even the Lewis model already suggests that some income inequality is essential to endowing the modern sector households with enough wealth to generate savings for investment. Moreover, the model predicts a prolonged phase of income inequality despite economic growth.

2.3 Empirical Basis of the Links

2.3.1 *Growth and Structural Change*

Back in the 1930s and 1940s, Fisher [1939] and Clarke [1940] had already pointed out the stylised fact of structural change, in which a developing economy transitions from one that is agriculture-based, to one dominated by industry. The data on economic growth and structural shifts was compiled and assessed systematically in Kuznets [1965]. Other aspects of the Lewis model have also been studied empirically; Fei and Ranis [1975] point to the experience of South Korea and Taiwan as confirming a prolonged period of stagnant agricultural wages, after which a turning point was reached in the late 1970s. The "turning point" was also found for China, although the exhaustion of surplus labour occurred much later, at around 2003 [Zhang *et al.*, 2011].

Accordingly, over the initial phase of development, poverty reduction may occur relatively slowly, later accelerating as the turning point is reached. This closely ties in with trends in malnutrition. For instance, Bangladesh has seen a remarkable decline in stunting over the period 1997 to 2011, largely due to economic growth and demographic change, with minimal reliance on high-quality, nutrition-specific public programs [Headey *et al.*, 2015].

2.3.2 *The Role of Inequality*

As mentioned earlier, while inequality may legitimately be deemed independent of economic growth, there are hypothesised linkages between the two. The empirical link was already suggested by Kuznets [1955], who found that, for the United States, England, and Germany, rising per capita incomes were associated with a more equal income distribution. In the same paper, he conjectured that, at the initial development phase, income inequality might actually increase together with average incomes. One reason is the concentration of savings, and therefore wealth formation, among the upper classes. Another reason is the wider dispersion of incomes among urban households, together with migration outside rural areas, where income dispersion tends to be narrower.

Subsequently, this conjecture was stylised as the "inverted-U" hypothesis [Paul, 2018]. Analysis of 217 countries over the period 1991–2014 shows the positive impact of structural change on income inequality [Roy and Roy, 2018]. The same study shows other determinants of income inequality, such as trade liberalisation (negative impact), and foreign direct investment (negative impact, though weak).

Mdingi and Ho [2021] undertook a comprehensive review of the theoretical and empirical links between inequality and growth. Hypothesised transmission mechanisms include the level of technological development; socio-political unrest; political economy factors; credit market imperfections; the savings rate; institutions; and the fertility rate. Theoretically, depending on the transmission mechanism and the stage of development process, inequality may be linked to growth in a positive or negative way, or else the link is inconclusive. The voluminous empirical literature bears this out, with some studies finding a positive relationship, some a negative link, and others being inconclusive. The authors argue that varying results obtained are due to issues of data comparability and methodology adopted.

2.4 Trends for Asian Economies

2.4.1 *Structural Change*

Asia has undergone structural change unprecedented in extent and pace [Aizenman *et al.*, 2012]. In terms of agriculture share in gross domestic product (GDP), East Asia and the Pacific (EAP) has undergone an average of 0.31 percentage point decline from 1960 to 2021, while South Asia has undergone a 0.41 percentage point decline over the same period (Figure 2.1). In contrast, Sub-Saharan Africa has undergone only 0.08 percentage point decline (1990–2021); Latin America and the Caribbean (LAC) only 0.1 percentage point decline (1970–2021): and Middle East and North Africa (MENA) a 0.20 percentage point decline (2000–2021).

The record of structural change for Asia is even more impressive in terms of the employment share of agriculture (Figure 2.2). In 1991, the majority of workers in EAP, SSA, and South Asia were in

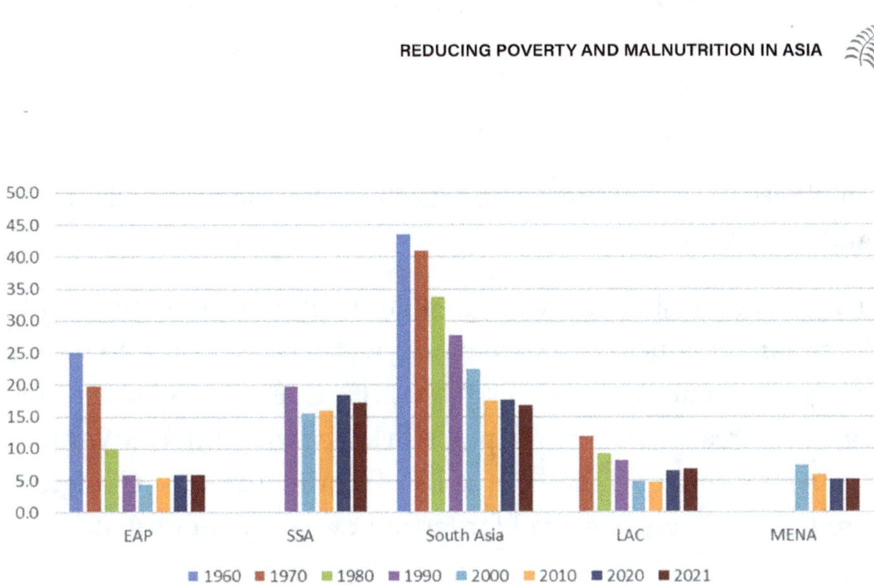

Figure 2.1 Share of agriculture in GDP, by region, 1960–2021 (%). Source: World Bank [2022a].

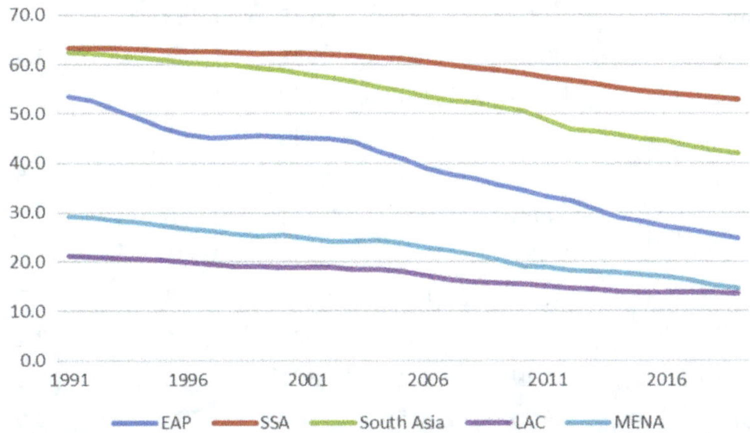

Figure 2.2 Share of agriculture in employment, by region, 1991–2016 (%). Source: World Bank [2022a].

agriculture, with the latter two reaching 63.5% and 62.5% shares, respectively. By 2021 the employment share of agriculture fell to just a quarter of workers in EAP, while that of South Asia fell to just two-fifths. In SSA, however, the majority of workers are still employed in agriculture. Smaller declines are also observed for LAC and MENA regions.

The declining share of workers in agriculture is accompanied by increasing productivity of remaining workers, as measured by output per agricultural worker (Table 2.1). Countries with the most rapid increases in output per worker were China, Myanmar, Vietnam, Cambodia, and Republic of Korea. The least changes in productivity were observed for Japan (a wealthy country in 1991),

Table 2.1 Agricultural Gross Value Added per worker, in constant 2015 USD. Source: World Bank [2022a].

	1991	2000	2010	2019	Growth rate (%)
Afghanistan	..	..	1,145	1,285	1.3
Bangladesh	506	552	929	1,284	3.4
Bhutan	1,153	1,257	1,362	1,569	1.1
Cambodia	..	654	945	1,547	4.9
China	955	1,437	2,795	5,609	6.5
India	865	1,006	1,321	2,076	3.2
Indonesia	1,322	1,609	2,219	3,601	3.6
Japan	..	20,179	20,020	17,763	-0.7
Laos	..	803	1,004	1,184	2.2
Malaysia	9,629	9,671	13,891	16,576	2.0
Mongolia	2,666	1,875	2,362	5,705	2.8
Myanmar	..	524	1,152	1,390	5.6
Nepal	409	444	557	705	2.0
Pakistan	2,138	2,475	2,284	2,634	0.7
Philippines	1,732	1,981	2,445	3,531	2.6
Republic of Korea	7,227	10,349	16,999	20,572	3.8
Sri Lanka	1,318	1,357	2,145	3,248	3.3
Thailand	1,997	1,685	2,346	3,217	1.7
Vietnam	573	750	1,140	1,735	4.0

Pakistan, Bhutan, and Afghanistan. Given consistent expansion of agriculture in these countries over the decades, the declining share of workers must have been accompanied by increasing deployment of capital. According to the FAO [2023], net capital stocks in Asian agriculture in USD increased four-fold between 1995 and 2021.

Similarly, productivity of land had been increasing in the course of structural change, further buttressing the argument that transformation of the economy as a whole coincided with transformation of agriculture in particular. For rice in particular, the 1960s to 1970s were the period of transformation as "Green Revolution" technologies were developed and adopted widely throughout Asia (Table 2.2).

Table 2.2 Yield of paddy rice in tons per ha, 1961–2021. Source: FAO [2023].

	1961	1970	1980	1990	2000	2010	2020	2021
Afghanistan	1.5	1.8	2.2	1.9	2.0	3.2	3.0	3.0
Bangladesh	1.7	1.7	2.0	2.6	3.5	4.3	4.8	4.9
Cambodia	1.1	1.6	1.2	1.3	2.1	3.0	3.4	3.5
China	2.0	3.4	4.1	5.7	6.3	6.6	7.0	7.1
India	1.5	1.7	2.0	2.6	2.9	3.4	4.1	4.2
Indonesia	1.8	2.4	3.3	4.3	4.4	5.0	5.1	5.2
Japan	4.9	5.6	5.1	6.3	6.7	6.5	7.2	7.5
Laos	0.9	1.4	1.4	2.3	3.1	3.6	3.8	4.1
Malaysia	2.1	2.4	2.9	2.8	3.1	3.6	3.7	3.7
Myanmar	1.6	1.7	2.8	2.9	3.3	4.0	3.8	3.8
Nepal	1.9	1.9	1.9	2.4	2.7	2.7	3.8	3.8
Pakistan	1.4	2.2	2.4	2.3	3.0	3.1	3.8	4.0
Philippines	1.2	1.7	2.2	3.0	3.1	3.6	4.1	4.2
Republic of Korea	4.1	4.6	4.3	6.2	6.7	6.5	6.5	7.1
Sri Lanka	1.9	2.2	2.6	3.1	3.4	4.1	4.8	4.6
Thailand	1.7	2.0	1.9	2.0	2.6	3.0	2.9	3.0
Vietnam	1.9	2.2	2.1	3.2	4.2	5.3	5.9	6.1

Green Revolution technologies included modern varieties of rice, fertiliser application, application of other chemicals, and water management through irrigation. Over a 60-year period (1961–2021), countries in East Asia reached a frontier yield of seven or more tons per hectare (China, Japan, Republic of Korea), while yields in various countries more than tripled (Cambodia, Philippines, Vietnam) or nearly quintupled (Laos).

2.4.2 *Poverty and Malnutrition*

Alongside structural change was a rapid decline in poverty in Asia (Table 2.3). The steepest fall was observed in China, where poverty

Table 2.3 Poverty incidence of selected Asian countries, 1983–2018 (%). Source: World Bank [2022a].

	Starting value	Year	Ending value	Year	Annual decline
Bangladesh	82.7	1983	51.6	2016	–0.9
Bhutan	41.6	2003	9.4	2017	–2.3
China	92.7	1990	3.0	2019	–3.1
India	88.9	1977	44.8	2019	–1.1
Indonesia	92.4	1984	22.4	2021	–1.9
Japan	1.0	2008	0.9	2013	0.0
Laos	62.5	1992	32.5	2018	–1.2
Malaysia	14.9	1984	0.4	2015	–0.5
Mongolia	41.1	1995	6.9	2018	–1.5
Myanmar	30.0	2015	19.6	2017	–5.2
Nepal	83.8	1995	40.0	2010	–2.9
Pakistan	70.0	1996	39.8	2018	–1.4
Philippines	39.2	2000	18.3	2018	–1.2
Republic of Korea	0.7	2008	0.5	2016	0.0
Sri Lanka	51.8	1985	13.8	2016	–1.2
Thailand	48.0	1981	0.7	2020	–1.2
Vietnam	76.1	1992	5.3	2018	–2.7

shrank from 93% in 1990 to just 3% in 2019. Also seeing a rapid decline is Nepal, at rates similar to that of China (though the interval with data is shorter). Similarly on the upper echelon of the poverty reducers were Vietnam and Bhutan; Myanmar made very rapid progress but only over a very short interval. The weakest reduction in poverty is observed for Japan, Republic of Korea, and Malaysia (with low initial values), but on the lower end as well are Bangladesh, India, Laos, Philippines, Sri Lanka, and Thailand, countries with relatively high initial values of poverty.

A common indicator of malnutrition is prevalence of stunting among children under five (Table 2.4). Over the period 2000–2020, the

Table 2.4 Stunting rate in selected Asian countries, 2000–2020 (%). Source: FAO [2022].

	2000	2005	2010	2015	2020	Annual decline
Afghanistan	54.6	52.2	47.2	41.1	35.1	-0.98
Bangladesh	56.0	47.1	40.2	35.0	30.2	-1.29
Bhutan	46.5	40.3	33.0	26.4	22.4	-1.21
Cambodia	51.1	44.8	37.5	31.3	29.9	-1.06
China	17.8	9.1	..	8.1	4.8	-0.65
India	49.8	48.2	44.5	37.5	30.9	-0.95
Indonesia	41.5	38.3	35.7	32.9	31.8	-0.49
Japan	8.4	7.6	6.9	6.1	5.5	-0.15
Laos	49.7	47.6	43.2	36.5	30.2	-0.98
Malaysia	20.0	18.3	17.9	19.1	20.9	0.04
Mongolia	29.4	23.3	15.2	10.1	7.1	-1.12
Myanmar	47.0	39.1	33.2	29.5	25.2	-1.09
Nepal	57.9	49.5	42.8	36.4	30.4	-1.38
Pakistan	42.1	43.8	44.2	41.3	36.7	-0.27
Philippines	35.7	34.0	32.7	31.1	28.7	-0.35
Republic of Korea	2.9	2.6	2.3	2.2	2.2	-0.04
Sri Lanka	20.6	18.3	17.2	16.3	16.0	-0.23
Thailand	16.9	16.4	14.9	12.9	12.3	-0.23
Vietnam	41.8	32.9	27.6	24.4	22.3	-0.98

fastest progress against malnutrition was made by Bangladesh, Bhutan, Cambodia, Mongolia, and Nepal. China's pace was not as rapid, though it had started at a low initial value of 17.8% by 2000. Likewise showing slow declines are Sri Lanka (initial value of 20.6%) and Thailand (initial value of 16.9%). However, in spite of a high initial value, relatively slow progress was observed in Pakistan (initial value 42.1%) and Philippines (35.7%).

2.4.3 *Income Inequality*

The Gini ratio is a common indicator of income inequality (Table 2.5). Unlike the foregoing indicators of economic development, not all countries have experienced an improvement over time

Table 2.5 Gini ratio for selected Asian countries, 1977–2021 (%). Source: World Bank [2022].

	Starting value	Year	Ending value	Year	Annual change
Bangladesh	25.9	1983	32.4	2016	0.20
Bhutan	40.9	2003	37.4	2017	-0.25
China	32.2	1990	38.2	2019	0.21
India	33.3	1977	35.7	2019	0.06
Indonesia	33.5	1984	37.9	2021	0.12
Laos	34.3	1992	38.8	2018	0.17
Malaysia	48.6	1984	41.1	2015	-0.24
Mongolia	33.2	1995	32.7	2018	-0.02
Myanmar	38.1	2015	30.7	2017	-3.70
Nepal	35.2	1995	32.8	2010	-0.16
Pakistan	33.3	1987	29.6	2018	-0.12
Philippines	47.7	2000	42.3	2018	-0.30
Republic of Korea	31.7	2006	31.4	2016	-0.03
Sri Lanka	32.5	1985	39.3	2016	0.22
Thailand	45.2	1981	35.0	2020	-0.26
Vietnam	35.7	1992	35.7	2018	0.00

for the inequality measure; several countries have actually experienced worsening inequality as seen by the increasing Gini ratio, i.e., Bangladesh, China, India, Indonesia, and Sri Lanka. For countries with decreasing inequality, the changes in Gini ratio are quite slow, ten percentage points over three decades in Thailand, and five percentage points over two decades in the Philippines.

Another indicator of income inequality is the relative income share, measured as the ratio of the income share of the top 10% of households by income, to the income share of the bottom 20% of households (Table 2.6). For instance, in Bangladesh, the top 10% earned more than double the income of the bottom fifth in 1983; by 2016

Table 2.6 Relative income share, top 10% to bottom 20% ratio, 1983–2020. Source: World Bank [2022a].

	Starting value	Year	Ending value	Year	Annual change
Bangladesh	2.3	1983	3.1	2016	0.03
Bhutan	5.0	2003	4.2	2017	-0.06
China	3.1	1990	4.4	2019	0.04
India	3.4	1977	3.8	2019	0.01
Indonesia	3.3	1984	4.3	2021	0.03
Laos	3.4	1992	4.5	2018	0.04
Malaysia	8.4	1984	5.4	2015	-0.10
Mongolia	3.4	1995	3.3	2018	-0.01
Myanmar	4.3	2015	2.9	2017	-0.74
Nepal	3.7	1995	3.2	2010	-0.04
Pakistan	3.3	1987	2.7	2018	-0.02
Philippines	7.4	2000	5.4	2018	-0.11
Republic of Korea	3.3	2006	3.2	2016	-0.01
Sri Lanka	3.2	1985	4.6	2016	0.05
Thailand	5.8	1988	3.6	2020	-0.07
Vietnam	3.7	1992	4.1	2018	0.02

the ratio had become triple. Also seeing increases in the relative income share are China, India, Indonesia, Laos, Sri Lanka, and Vietnam. The trend for Vietnam is striking, as the relative share increased by 10% over three decades, even though the Gini ratio did not change over the same period.

Table 2.7 categorises Asian countries based on changes over time and relative income share (latest year available). Countries with the

Table 2.7 Country groupings based on changes over time, and relative income share (most recent period).

	Change over time			Relative income share, 2015–2020	
	Poverty	**Stunting prevalence**	**Agriculture employment share**		
Fastest Group	Myanmar	Nepal	Cambodia	Most equal group	Pakistan
	China	Bangladesh	China		Myanmar
	Nepal	Bhutan	Vietnam		Bangladesh
	Vietnam	Mongolia	Bangladesh		Nepal
	Bhutan	Myanmar	Thailand		Republic of Korea
	Indonesia	Cambodia	Indonesia		Mongolia
Middle Group	Mongolia	Laos	Laos	Moderately equal group	Thailand
	Pakistan	Afghanistan	Philippines		India
	Sri Lanka	Vietnam	Myanmar		Vietnam
	Thailand	India	Afghanistan		Bhutan
	Philippines	China	India		Indonesia
Slowest Group	Laos	Indonesia	Mongolia	Most unequal group	China
	India	Philippines	Nepal		Laos
	Bangladesh	Pakistan	Sri Lanka		Sri Lanka
	Malaysia	Sri Lanka	Bhutan		Malaysia
		Thailand	Malaysia		Philippines
		Japan	Pakistan		
		Republic of Korea			
		Malaysia			

least income inequality currently are Pakistan, Myanmar, Bangladesh, Nepal, Republic of Korea, and Mongolia; meanwhile the countries with the most unequal incomes are China, Laos, Sri Lanka, Malaysia, and the Philippines. A few patterns emerge:

- Philippines belongs to the slowest group in terms of malnutrition improvement, and the middle group in terms of poverty reduction; China is now in the most unequal income group, but started out among the more equal group of countries in 1990.
- Bangladesh, which is among the most equal group of countries, also belongs to the fastest group in terms of malnutrition improvement, and structural change.
- Middle group countries in terms of income inequality such as India, Vietnam, Indonesia, and Bhutan are countries with the most rapid decline in poverty and structural change, as well as decline in stunting prevalence (in case of Bhutan).

2.4.4 *Historical Roots of Income Inequality*

Philippines stands out in Asia as having one of the worst levels of income inequality, next only to Malaysia. Explaining income inequality requires a review of the historical roots of wealth patterns in a society. Both Malaysia and Philippines underwent a colonial period where an elite class came to acquire an extremely lopsided share of agricultural land; as agriculture was the dominant economic activity at the time, this implied a highly skewed distribution of wealth. For Philippines, under Spanish rule, the Spanish King laid claim to all lands in the Philippines. Corpuz [1992] traces inequality to the formation of friar estates (*haciendas*) starting from the 18th century, and takeover by private capital over-unsettled frontier lands. Similarly in Malaysia, the British introduced a system of land rights which allowed investors to occupy frontier lands for plantation crops. Upon independence, Malaysia had a land Gini ratio of 68.0, the highest in Asia where data is present [Frankema, 2010]. On the other hand, a similar colonial heritage was much less prominent in Indonesia, where settlement of frontier lands occurred after independence and was able to favour smallholders as well [Dib *et al.*, 2018].

2.5 Conclusion

This brief analysis has shown that structural change has been accompanied by declining poverty and malnutrition. However, a confounding factor in the progress against poverty and malnutrition is income inequality. Where income distribution was more even, more progress has been observed, whereas in countries such as the Philippines and Sri Lanka, high income inequality seems associated with slower declines in poverty and malnutrition.

Philippines is quite a unique case, given its relatively high and persistent level of income inequality, even compared with other countries in the same group, i.e., China (a newcomer to high levels of income inequality) and Malaysia (which managed rapid economic growth notwithstanding a highly unequal income distribution).

World Bank [2022b] has recently prepared an extensive poverty and inequality assessment of the Philippines. Inequality in the Philippines has evolved far from its historic, agrarian roots; structural determinants now cover unequal access to tertiary education, scarcity of skills, spatial gaps, and gendered social norms. Nonetheless, expansion of secondary education and employment shifts, broader access to basic services, and expanded governmental social assistance, have helped reduce inequality since the mid-2000s.

Policies can be designed to accelerate the decline in inequality by improving education access, promoting inclusive rural development, and strengthening social protection. Especially urgent is to address the unprecedented human capital scarring brought about by a mismanaged response to the COVID-19 pandemic. Prolonged school closures have inflicted a massive learning loss, combined with de-skilling due to prolonged unemployment. Reversing these learning losses should be a top priority to bringing the country back on track to reducing poverty, boosting food security, and achieving greater social equity.

References

Acemoglu, D. and Guerrieri, V. (2008). Capital deepening and nonbalanced economic growth. *Journal of Political Economy,* 116(3), pp. 467–498.

Aizenman, J., Lee, M. and Park, D. (2012). *The Relationship Between Structural Change and Inequality: A Conceptual overview with Special Reference to Developing Asia.* ADBI Working Paper 396. Asian Development Bank Institute.

Asian Development Bank. (2013). *Food Security in Asia and the Pacific.* Asian Development Bank.

Bouis, H., Eozenou, P. and Rahman, A. (2011). Food prices, household income, and resource allocation: Socioeconomic perspectives on their effects on dietary quality and nutritional status. *Food and Nutrition Bulletin,* 32(1 — Supplement), pp. S14–S23.

Clark, C. (1940). *The Conditions of Economic Progress.* Macmillan.

Corpuz, O. (1992). Land and agriculture in the Philippines: an economic history perspective. *Philippine Review of Economics and Business,* 29(2), pp. 137–160.

Dib, J. B., Alamsyah, Z. and Qaim, Z. M. (2018). Land-use change and income inequality in rural Indonesia. *Forest Policy and Economics,* 94(1), pp. 55–66.

Economist Intelligence Unit (EIU). (2022). *Global Food Security Index.*

Fei, J. and Ranis, G. (1975). A model of growth and employment in the open dualistic economy: The cases of Korea and Taiwan. *Journal of Development Studies,* 11(2), pp. 32–63.

Fisher, A. (1939). Production, primary, secondary and tertiary. *Economic Record*, 15(1), pp. 24–38.

Frankema, E. (2010). The colonial roots of land inequality: Geography, factor endowments, or institutions?. *Economic History Review*, 63(2), pp. 418–451.

Gollin, D., Parente, S. and Rogerson, R. (2002). The role of agriculture in development. *American Economic Review*, 92(2), pp. 160–64.

Kongsamut, P., Rebelo, S. and Xie, D. (2001). Beyond balanced growth. *Review of Economic Studies*, 68(4), pp. 869–882.

Kuznets, S. (1955). Economic growth and income inequality. *American Economic Review*, 45(1), pp. 1–28.

Kuznets, S. (1966). *Modern Economic Growth*. Yale University Press.

Lewis, A. (1954). Economic development with unlimited supplies of labor. *Manchester School of Economic and Social Studies*, 22(2), pp. 139–91.

Mdingi, K. and Ho, S.-Y. (2021). Literature review on income inequality and economic growth. *MethodsX*, 8, 101402.

Paul, S. (2018). Structural transformation, growth, and inequality in Asia since the 1990s. In S. Paul (Ed.), *Kuznets Beyond Kuznets: Structural Transformation and Income Inequality in the Era of Globalization in Asia*. Asian Development Bank Institute.

Piketty, T. (2014). *Capital in the Twenty-first Century*. Harvard University Press.

Roy, R. and Roy, S. (2018). Structural change, trade, and inequality: cross-country evidence. In S. Paul (Ed.), *Kuznets Beyond Kuznets: Structural Transformation and Income Inequality in the Era of Globalization in Asia*. Asian Development Bank Institute.

World Bank. (2022a). *World Development Indicators*. https://databank.worldbank.org/source/world-development-indicators. Accessed 11 January 2022.

World Bank. (2022b). *Overcoming Poverty and Inequality in the Philippines: Past, Present, and Prospects for the Future*. World Bank.

Zhang, X., Yang, J. and Wang, S. (2011). China has reached the Lewis turning point. *China Economic Review*, 22(4), pp. 542–554.

https://doi.org/10.1142/9789811278297_0003

Chapter 3

Policies and Policy Instruments to Address Food Security in Asian Developing and Developed Economies

Suresh Chandra Babu and Nandita Srivastava

International Food Policy Research Institute (IFPRI), Washington, DC, USA

3.1 Introduction

In 2021, approximately 425 million people in the world affected by hunger were in Asia. This figure constitutes more than half of the people in the world affected by hunger that year. It is estimated that the number of people who could not afford a healthy diet in 2020 increased globally, across regions, although the increase was mainly driven by Asia. There are also differences in the proportion of the population facing hunger in different regions of Asia. In Central Asia and Eastern Asia, it was low in comparison to Southern Asia and Western Asia [Food and Agriculture Organization (FAO) *et al.*, 2022]. Poverty, income inequality, and the high cost of a healthy diet have all contributed to making healthy diets out of reach for a significant proportion of the population in the region [FAO and UNICEF, 2021]. Additionally, the high incidence of climate shocks, food price inflation, the decline in foreign currency reserves, and the depreciation of local currencies have also affected the affordability of a healthy diet [World Bank, 2022].

In Asia, some countries like Bangladesh and Pakistan face severe localised food insecurity. At the same time, Sri Lanka has experienced food price inflation combined with a debt crisis, with the possibility of prolonged periods of hunger and poverty. Countries with heavy import needs, like Cambodia, Laos, Nepal, Philippines, and Thailand were severely affected due to depreciation and rising interest rates. Currently, food prices remain high, and the food security outlook for the region remains uncertain [Asian Development Bank (ADB), 2022a].

Food security challenges are a result of multiple factors. At the global level, the Ukraine crisis and the COVID-19 pandemic have disrupted the food supply chain and resulted in macro-economic challenges, including trade restrictions which have adversely affected food availability across the globe. Climate change has negatively impacted agricultural production and productivity. Extreme flooding in many parts of the world, including East and South Asia, highlights the rapid and rising climate problem [ADB, 2022a]. This chapter provides a conceptual framework that looks at different integration aspects for food systems transformation with the aim to achieve food and nutrition security. It discusses the food security challenges in the Asian region. Providing a brief background analysis of the evolution of food systems in the region, the chapter analyses the policy actions undertaken, existing constraints, and the way forward.

3.2 Conceptual Framework for Food Systems Transformation

Across the globe, governments face interconnected challenges such as food insecurity, climate change, and biodiversity loss, which are often dealt with disjointedly [Organization for Economic Co-operation and Development (OECD), 2019]. To accomplish food security, using the Agriculture Innovation Systems (AIS) approach helps — it integrates a subset of innovation entities in agriculture with the policy and institutional environments and then connects them to the larger investment strategies and frameworks at the national levels [World Bank, 2012].

The International Food Policy Research Institute (IFPRI), in collaboration with FAO, has developed an analytical framework that identifies critical aspects of integration within AIS to accomplish food systems transformation [FAO and IFPRI, 2019]. This has been done after a careful review of available guidelines, frameworks, and country experiences for strengthening integrated policies and investments across sectors within AIS. These include policy integration, political economy integration, institutional integration, monitoring and evaluation framework integration, market system integration, and global integration.

Policy integration is a key aspect — it is essential that the policy is preceded by an *ex ante* analysis, tied closely to the overall agriculture strategy/policy/innovation framework of the country, backed by investment, and has the adequate infrastructure, capacity, and technology-related support to be effective. Policy integration can help establish common objectives, achieve coherence, and minimise overlaps and trade-offs across sectors. This is especially valuable in the case of food systems transformation due to the high degree of interconnectedness between sectors. Integration at the policy level entails multi-stakeholder engagement at different policy stages — agenda setting, policy design, policy implementation, policy adoption, and policy evaluation and reform. Policies need to be backed by sustainable investment for effective implementation. To ensure that policy integration achieves its desired objectives, certain supporting mechanisms are required. For ensuring transparency and accountability at the institutional and program policy level, political will is key. Good governance encompasses transparency and accountability to increase policy effectiveness, efficiency, and trust. This includes periodic reporting, disclosure of accurate information, information access, and a grievance redressal mechanism to settle any disputes. State capacity, including budget and technical capacity, is crucial to implement the policy/initiative [Resnick *et al.*, 2018]. For farmers to improve productivity and achieve sustainable growth from any innovation, they need adequate training and advisory support. This support can be provided through local-level extension services and program-based extension [OECD, 2019].

The sustainability of food systems can be constrained by climate change-related phenomena — rising temperatures and extreme climate events have contributed to reductions in land and soil quality, availability of water resources for irrigation and human use, and crop yields. To address these concerns, measures such as climate-smart agriculture and resilience building are essential. Natural Resource Management such as sustainable land use management can help reverse declining biodiversity, mitigating the effects of climate change while still achieving food security goals. Monitoring and evaluation is another crucial integration aspect. To ensure that the policies and programs within are achieving desired objectives and accommodating changing needs, there is a need for a strong monitoring and evaluation framework. A monitoring and evaluation framework will help track progress, conduct impact assessments, identify gaps, and avoid duplication of support [Intergovernmental Panel on Climate Change (IPCC), 2022].

While progress has been made in improving nutrition levels of the population in recent years, significant challenges remain. The government should focus on providing an enabling environment for investment in food and nutrition security. A coherent national plan should be developed on strategies to achieve food security, food safety and better nutrition [FAO *et al.*, 2022]. Global markets present opportunities to sell domestically produced products and create products which meet international quality standards. Being integrated with global markets can help in getting access to high-quality research, inputs, technology, and finance. At the national and local levels, AIS should ensure that markets are competitive and inclusive. They should create strong market linkages for farmers with potential local buyers and ensure that farmers receive a fair price [OECD, 2019].

At the institutional level, capacity development should create transparency, accountability, clarity in roles and responsibilities amongst collaborators, and the ability to undertake cross-disciplinary research to improve integration in AIS. Within institutions, delegated actors should have the technical, managerial, and financial skills to create and implement policies and programs [Garrett, 2011; Babu, 2019]. To ensure that the network of actors across the value chain in the AIS collaborate in a sustainable manner, it is imperative that investments are integrated from the stage of research and development to the stage of commercialisation [FAO, 2016]. Additionally, to ensure conservation of biodiversity, integrated production systems which include aquaculture and forestry are being promoted [OECD, 2020].

Tables 3.1 and 3.2 highlight the overall and specific integration of AIS aspects from the food systems transformation perspective.

Table 3.1 AIS conceptual framework: Broader integration aspects. Source: FAO and IFPRI [2019].

Policy Integration
Policy domain
Overview of the policy
Geographic classification (global/regional/national)
Thematic area (examples: overall innovation policy, digital, extension, information and communication technology, and natural resource management)
Development status of the nation (developed/developing)
Sector initiating the innovation (public, private, public-private partnership, intergovernmental organisation, non-governmental organisation)
Is the policy integrated with the general innovation framework of the country?
Is the policy backed by investment?
Was any *ex ante* assessment done to understand the level of need for the innovation?
Were any pre-sensitisation activities conducted before the launch of the policy/initiative?
Supporting Mechanisms Integration
Are there any initiatives for filling infrastructural gaps/improving infrastructure?
Are there any initiatives to access information and skills training/education?
Are there any initiatives to improve technologies and technology access?
Are there any initiatives to improve natural resource management?
Are there any initiatives to improve access to key inputs?
Are there any initiatives to address regulatory barriers/improve regulation enforcement?
Political Economy Integration
Is there political will to implement the policy/initiative?
Are there any transparency and accountability mechanisms?
Is there state capacity, including budget and technical capacity, to implement the policy/initiative?

Table 3.2 Conceptual framework: Specific integration aspects. Source: FAO and IFPRI [2019].

Risk Management Integration
Are there any initiatives for climate-smart agriculture?
Are there any initiatives for resilience building (including disaster management)?
Is agroecology integrated?
Are there any initiatives for risk management (production, sale, and price risk)?
Monitoring and Evaluation Framework Integration
Is the policy/initiative inclusive?
Are targets/indicators for policy/initiative performance clearly defined and measurable?
Institutional Integration
Are there initiatives to improve human and technical capacity at the institutional level to implement the policy?
Are the roles and responsibilities of all involved institutions clearly defined?
Are there initiatives to integrate agriculture research and innovation to the AIS?
Are there initiatives to improve/ensure coordination across institutions integrated in the policy?
Are there initiatives to improve access to credit and insurance?
Market System Integration
Are there initiatives to improve access to farmers/sellers to potential local buyers?
Does the policy provide any price-setting mechanism?
Value Chain Integration
Is investment integrated across the value chain?
Global Integration
Is there investment integration to ensure that domestic products are recognised and competitive in global markets?
Nutrition Integration
Are there initiatives to ensure the integration of nutrition/health priorities in the policy?
Aquaculture and Forestry Integration
Are there initiatives to ensure the integration of aquaculture and forestry?

3.3 Review of the Current Situation with Retrospective Analysis and Literature Review

Strengthening food systems requires a holistic approach. Given the multi-sectoral and multi-stakeholder nature of food systems, integration across sectors and related coordination between stakeholders is crucial. The framework discussed in the previous section identifies different integration aspects which should be considered to ensure that strategies focused on food systems transformation are effective. The review of literature in this section analyses the evolution of the food system in the Asian region and highlights existing challenges. The key takeaways from the analysis further strengthen the rationale for referencing the conceptual framework as a starting point for policymakers, regulators, investors, non-governmental organisations, and development partners who aim to create a sustainable and inclusive food system.

In the late 1960s, the Green Revolution reduced food insecurity by focusing on high-yielding varieties for wheat, rice, and maize, increased input intensity, irrigation investments, and new farm management practices [Abraham and Pingali, 2020a]. In the Asian context, the Green Revolution was instrumental in eradicating famine. Following the Green Revolution, the high mortality from food unavailability declined significantly in the region [Devereux, 2000].

The opening up of the Asian economies in the 1980s and 1990s, with liberalisation, privatisation, and globalisation measures, led to a rise in urbanisation and the proportion of the middle class in many countries. This impacted consumer tastes and preferences, with the focus shifting from quantity to quality and food diversity. The signing of the Agreement on Agriculture under the General Agreement on Tariffs and Trade led to foreign direct investment flow in food retail. In the last decade, the sales of processed foods increased in all major Asian economies. However, the growth rates in processed foods sales were higher in lower-middle-income countries like India, Bangladesh, Indonesia, and Vietnam compared to middle-income countries like Thailand and China. Demand side factors such as urbanisation, higher women's participation in the workforce, and rising incomes resulted in the increase in demand for processed food, thus fast-tracking the diffusion of supermarkets [Reardon and Zilberman, 2022]. Dietary changes have also led to rising levels of obesity. It may be noted that the problems of hunger and micronutrient malnutrition persist, and the burden of non-communicable diseases is on the rise in the region [Pingali and Abraham, 2022].

The agricultural sector is a major contributor to greenhouse gas (GHG) emissions in Asia and the Pacific region. To achieve food security for growing populations, there has been a massive increase in the use of synthetic fertilisers and energy in agricultural production. The increase in livestock production has increased methane emissions [ADB, 2022b; Aryal *et al.*, 2021a; Aryal *et al.*, 2021b]. Climate change-related events are adversely affecting food systems in Asia. In Central Asia, rising temperatures and extreme climate events have contributed to reductions in land and soil quality, availability of water resources for irrigation and human use, and crop yields. Land degradation is a major challenge. There is a lack of reliable data on climate change and food systems and weak analytical capacity in the region. Yield decline, production losses, and depleted natural resources are some key negative impacts of climate change on South Asia's food system. The impacts of climate change in South Asia, alongside the challenges due to COVID-19, will make it challenging to achieve the goal of zero hunger by 2030. In East and Southeast Asia, the intensity and frequency of extreme weather events, including droughts, floods, typhoons, and heat waves threaten the region's role as a major producer of grain and industrial crops. Also, rising household income and urbanisation have changed food preferences from cereals towards animal products, which have more resource-intensive production and produce more GHG emissions than plant-based products [IFPRI, 2022; IPCC, 2022; FAO *et al.*, 2022].

Many countries in the region have policies which give fertiliser subsidies that encourage overuse, causing environmental pollution. A recent OECD study found that several countries provided agricultural sector support through policies that artificially maintain domestic farm prices in instances where there are payments linked to output or the use of variable inputs such as groundwater, fertilisers, and pesticides. But such policies oftentimes lead to overuse of inputs and unsustainable production. Water scarcity has also worsened in Asia with weak collective management of irrigation systems [ADB, 2021a; ADB, 2021b; OECD, 2020].

While significant progress has been made in reducing hunger and malnutrition in the region, nutrition challenges persist. The number of children in the region under age five who suffer from stunting remains high. There is still a prevalence of child wasting and anaemia, while obesity has become a growing problem in the region [ADB, 2021a; ADB, 2021b].

In many developing countries, land scarcity, along with continued population pressure, has led to further fragmentation of landholdings and added pressure on already degraded land and scarce water resources. The Asia-Pacific region is characterised by smallholder farming — 450 million smallholder farmers produce more than 80% of the food consumed in the region [Macfarlane, 2022]. They work on small land plots and have limited access to markets and services. These challenges, combined with a lack of access to knowledge and resources, keep the production levels below potential and generate low incomes for the farmers. In recent times, with the rising outmigration of male workers to urban areas, the region's agricultural sector is becoming increasingly reliant on women and the elderly to provide labour. This is especially the case in countries like Bangladesh, Cambodia, and Nepal, with high labour migration. Despite the contribution of women to the agricultural sector, they still have limited access to resources, especially land [ADB, 2021a; ADB, 2021b; Syngenta, 2022].

Public extension systems in many countries remain largely supply-side driven, with limited reach. There are also several knowledge- and skills-based capacity constraints — the capacity of agricultural extension agents continues to be inadequate to address the rapidly changing demands for extension services [Joshi and Babu, 2019].

As a result of COVID-19 restrictions, food supply chains in many urban areas were disrupted for prolonged periods due to transport and movement restrictions. Several food sector businesses had significant income losses. Many small and medium enterprises were unable to access the financial support and technical assistance they needed during the pandemic. A study showed that food systems in selected cities did not have the transformative capacity to respond effectively to the pandemic [World Food Programme (WFP), 2022].

3.4 Policy Actions and Gaps

Several countries in the region experienced a rise in natural disasters between 1970 and 2020. Some of the countries are also reliant on international humanitarian assistance, including food assistance, during a conflict situation. Despite the growing need, early warning systems are not yet well integrated with the overall social protection mechanisms in the countries. While efforts have been made at the local level by non-governmental institutions, there is a need for consistent and large-scale efforts at the national level using flagship programs [World Bank, 2022]. Policies should also focus on improving the adaptive capacity of key institutions and actors by providing training. To ensure access to the most updated need-based knowledge and technology, policies should focus on knowledge sharing, technology transfer for adaptation and mitigation, and integrating climate change into national and sectoral policies and plans. From the investment perspective, facilitating access to finance is essential [United Nations Environment Programme (UNEP), 2022].

The current and anticipated climate change challenges in the region build a strong case for making food supply chain infrastructure climate resilient. This includes storage facilities, rural connectivity, and digital services that are accessible and affordable for farmers. Countries must invest in weather advisory and forecasting services. Governments should promote remote sensing to improve land-use planning and management. Climate-smart approaches should be integrated across the entire value chain, from the production to the consumer stage. Policies focused on the conservation or rehabilitation of natural ecosystems should be advanced. GHG emissions reduction through investments in sustainable livestock, and CO_2 sequestration by forests and biomass, is another important strategy. The goal should be to develop climate policies that not only result in reduction in GHG emissions but also enhance productivity and improve food availability [Lin *et al.*, 2022; Bruno and Qingfeng, 2022].

Fertiliser subsidies have helped to improve agricultural production. However, the burden associated with these subsidies outweighs the costs. These subsidies have placed a significant financial burden on governments in the region. Recent data show the share of fertiliser subsidies in the national budget of countries like Bangladesh and Indonesia to be significant [Suryana, 2019]. Besides, overuse has led to environmental pollution and GHG emissions in countries like India. China is an important example to learn how to effectively phase out fertiliser subsidies. The Chinese government has undertaken interventions to enhance production efficiency through improved nitrogen use and the increased use of natural fertilisers [Searchinger, 2020].

The region faces significant nutrition challenges. Thus, the urgent focus must be on making nutritious food more accessible and affordable. According to FAO *et al.* [2022], this would require complementary policies that promote shifting in food environments and consumer behaviour toward healthy eating patterns. Mandatory limits or voluntary targets to improve the nutritional quality of food and drinks, food marketing legislation, and behavioural interventions are some such policy interventions that can be promoted.

Regarding land size, some countries in the region have witnessed a change in the declining trend of average farm size, which can be attributed to active land rental markets and emerging labour shortages. However, there continues to be the dominance of smallholder farmers in the region [Yamauchi, 2021]. Thus, policies to support smallholder farmers should focus on promoting land rights and efficient land markets, inclusive food value chains, empowering women and youth, and providing social safety nets. Policy interventions such as access to cheap and low-cost credit, research and development to promote diversification, market access, and access to local extension support, technology, and inputs should also be emphasised [Fan and Rue, 2020; Abraham and Pingali, 2020b].

Extension and advisory services must be demand-driven, focusing on the farmer's needs. Since food systems have become more knowledge- and technology-intensive, the role and value of information have become more profound. The policy system should understand how farmers access and use available information, their information needs, and information search behaviour to create more targeted programs. There should also be capacity enhancement of the extension workers alongside building an organisational structure to suit the needs, including building resilience to cope with climate change and ensure food and nutritional security. Since public extension systems have their constraints both in terms of nature and coverage, the focus should be on developing a pluralistic system with an enhanced role of private extension [Joshi and Babu, 2019; FAO, 2020].

Governance plays a critical role by creating an enabling environment for food systems transformation. Good governance can enable regional and local perspectives to be aligned with commitments at the national and global levels. Given the food and nutritional security challenges currently facing the region, there is a clear need to understand governance processes as well as implementation and action on the ground. Governance encompasses commitment, power, accountability, coherence, data, leadership, and capacity [Gillespie, 2019]. Agricultural and food system governance should determine which dietary changes can improve public health and the environment and which policy instruments may promote adoption by the different food systems' relevant actors. According to Mbow *et al.* [2019], effective governance of food systems and climate change requires setting up institutions that coordinate across multiple sectors, levels, and actors. Positive outcomes can be accomplished with participation, mutual learning, adaptability, and cooperation.

3.5 Concluding Remarks

While significant progress has been made through policy actions to achieve food and nutrition security in Asia, challenges remain. The region faces problems related to poverty reduction, climate change and environmental constraints, and adequate and affordable supply of diverse foods required for a sustainable healthy diet. The region has social, economic, and geographic inequalities which create significant barriers to food systems transformation. The COVID-19 pandemic and Ukraine crisis have shown the fragility of agrifood systems, contributing to a rise in world hunger and severe food insecurity.

This chapter provided an overview of how food systems evolved in the region and highlighted existing challenges, analysing policy actions and recommendations to fill the existing gaps. It presented a conceptual framework identifying different integration aspects which must be considered while designing and implementing policies.

Based on the analysis, it is evident that current and future emphasis should be to meet food security needs while addressing associated challenges. Governments must incentivise sustainable production, supply, and consumption of nutritious foods. Support in the domain of health, climate change-related adaptation and mitigation, and the environment needs to be strengthened. Smallholder farmers should remain a pivotal support area given that a significant proportion of agriculture in the region is still dominated by them.

Policy actions undertaken in the region will be largely driven by political and social backgrounds, governance structures, and the degree of influence of stakeholders. Food systems require different actors to be engaged to better align actions across sectors.

Thus, coordination of multiple actors and decision-making processes is fundamental. By focusing on a participatory approach, inclusiveness, adaptive capacity, leadership, and clarity on roles and responsibilities, holistic food systems transformation is more likely to be achieved.

References

Abraham, M. and Pingali, P. (2020a). Climate Change and Food Security. In J. P. Gustafson, P. Raven and P. Ehrlich (Eds.), *Population, Agriculture, and Biodiversity: Problems and Prospects*, pp. 97–122. University of Missouri Press.

Abraham, M. and Pingali, P. (2020b). Transforming Smallholder Agriculture to Achieve the SDGs. In S. Gomez y Paloma, L. Riesgo and K. Louhichi (Eds.), *The Role of Smallholder Farms in Food and Nutrition Security*. Springer.

ADB. (2021a). *Asian Development Outlook 2021 Update: Transforming Agriculture in Asia*. https://dx.doi.org/10.22617/FLS210352-3

ADB. (2021b). *Financing Sustainable and Resilient Food Systems in Asia and the Pacific*. https://dx.doi.org/10.22617/SPR210428-2

ADB. (2022a). *Short and Long-Term Actions Needed to Help Asia and the Pacific Beat the Global Food Crisis*. https://www.adb.org/news/features/short-and-long-term-actions-needed-help-asia-and-pacific-beat-global-food-crisis

ADB. (2022b). Contribution of agriculture to climate change and low-emission agricultural development in Asia and the Pacific. https://doi.org/10.56506/WDBC4659

Aryal, J. P., Sapkota, T. B., Krupnik, T., Rahut, D. B., Jat, M. L. and Stirling, C. (2021a). Factors affecting farmers' use of inorganic fertilizers and manure in South Asia. *Environmental Science and Pollution Research*, 28, pp. 51480–51496.

Aryal, J. P., Sapkota, T. B, Rahut, D. B, Marenya, P. and Stirling, C. (2021b). Climate risks and adaptation strategies of farmers in East Africa and South Asia. *Scientific Reports*, 11, 10489.

Babu, S. C. and Joshi, P. K. (Eds.) (2019). *Agricultural Extension Reforms in South Asia: Status, Challenges, and Policy Options*. Academic Press.

Babu, S. C. (2019). Nutrition sensitive food system: Policy analysis and investment framework for Myanmar. *IFPRI Discussion Paper 1840*. https://doi.org/10.2499/p15738coll2.133269

Bruno, C. and Qingfeng, Z. (2022). Confronting Asia's triple threat: climate change, biodiversity loss, food insecurity. https://blogs.adb.org/blog/confronting-asia-s-triple-threat-climate-change-biodiversity-loss-and-food-insecurity

Devereux, S. (2000). Famine in the twentieth century. *IDS Working Paper No. 105*. https://www.ids.ac.uk/publications/famine-in-the-twentieth-century/

Fan, S. and Rue, C. (2020). The Role of Smallholder Farms in a Changing World. In S. Gomez y Paloma, L. Riesgo and K. Louhichi (Eds.), *The Role of Smallholder Farms in Food and Nutrition Security*. Springer.

FAO. (2016). *Sustainable Value Chains for Sustainable Food Systems: A Workshop of the FAO/UNEP Programme on Sustainable Food Systems*. https://www.fao.org/publications/card/en/c/bc620ddb-dfed-42a8-8742-1dfa69989ba2

FAO. (2020). *Strengthening the Capacity of Agricultural Extension Services in Central Asia on Sustainable Intensification of Crop Production*. https://www.fao.org/3/ca9081en/ca9081en.pdf

FAO. (2021). *Agricultural Transformation in Asia — Policy and Institutional Experiences*. https://doi.org/10.4060/cb4946en

FAO and IFPRI. (2019). Integrating innovation policies and investments for food systems transformation: Global lessons.

FAO and UNICEF. (2021). *Asia and the Pacific — Regional Overview of Food Security and Nutrition 2021: Statistics and Trends*. https://doi.org/10.4060/cb7494en

FAO, IFAD, UNICEF, WFP and WHO. (2022). *The State of Food Security and Nutrition in the World 2022: Repurposing Food and Agricultural Policies to Make Healthy Diets More Affordable*. https://data.unicef.org/resources/sofi-2022/

Garrett, J. and Natalicchio, M. (Eds.) (2011). *Working Multisectorally in Nutrition: Principles, Practices, and Case Studies*. International Food Policy Research Institute.

Gentilini, U. (Ed.) (2022). *Social Protection, Food Security and Nutrition: An Update of Concepts, Evidence and Select Practices in South Asia and Beyond*. World Bank.

Gillespie, S., Bold, M., and Hodge, J. (2019). Nutrition and the governance of agri-food systems in South Asia: A systematic review. *Food Policy*, 82, pp. 13–27.

IFPRI. (2022). *Global Food Policy Report: Climate Change and Food Systems*. https://doi.org/10.2499/9780896294257

IPCC. (2019). *Climate Change and Land: an IPCC special report on climate change, desertification, land degradation, sustainable land management, food security, and greenhouse gas fluxes in terrestrial ecosystems*. www.ipcc.ch/site/assets/uploads/2019/11/SRCCL-Full-Report-Compiled-191128.pdf

IPCC. (2022). *Climate Change 2022: Impacts, Adaptation, and Vulnerability*. https://www.ipcc.ch/report/ar6/wg2/

Lin, H. I., Yu, Y. Y., Wen, F. I. and Liu, P. T. (2022). Status of food security in East and Southeast Asia and challenges of climate change. *Climate*, 10(3), p. 40.

Macfarlane, A. (2022). *Building Resilient, Equitable and Sustainable Food Systems in Asia*. International Finance Cooperation.

OECD. (2019). *Innovation, Productivity and Sustainability in Food and Agriculture: Main Findings from Country Reviews and Policy Lessons*. https://www.oecd.org/publications/innovation-productivity-and-sustainability-in-food-and-agriculture-c9c4ec1d-en.htm

OECD. (2020). *Towards Sustainable Land Use: Aligning Biodiversity, Climate and Food Policies*. https://www.oecd.org/environment/towards-sustainable-land-use-3809b6a1-en.htm

OECD. (2022). *Agricultural Policy Monitoring and Evaluation 2022: Reforming Agricultural Policies for Climate Change Mitigation*. https://doi.org/10.1787/7f4542bf-en

Pingali, P. and Abraham, M. (2022). Food systems transformation in Asia — A brief economic history. *Agricultural Economics*, *53*, pp. 895–910.

Reardon, T. and Zilberman, D. (2022). Symbiotic, Resilient, and Rapidly Transforming Food Supply Chains in LMICs: Supermarket and E-commerce Revolutions Helped by Wholesale and Logistics Co-pivoting. In P. Antras and D. Zilberman (Eds.), *Risks in Agricultural Supply Chains*. University of Chicago Press.

Resnick, D., Haggblade, S., Babu, S., Hendriks, S. L. and Mather, D. (2018). The kaleidoscope model of policy change: Applications to food security policy in Zambia. *World Development*, 109, 101–120.

Searchinger, T., *et al.* (2020). *Revising Public Agricultural Support to Mitigate Climate Change*. World Bank.

Suryana, A. (2019). *Fertilizer Subsidy and Retail Price Policies to Support Food and Nutrition Security in Indonesia.* Food and Fertilizer Technology Center for the Asian and Pacific Region.

Syngenta. (2022). Seeding the future of agriculture in Asia. https://www.syngenta.com.sg/seeding-future-agriculture-asia

UNEP. (2022). Helping countries tackle climate change. https://www.unep.org/regions/asia-and-pacific/regional-initiatives/helping-countries-tackle-climate-change

WFP. (2022). *Food Security and Diets in Urban Asia: How Resilient are Food Systems in Times of COVID-19?*. https://www.wfp.org/publications/food-security-and-diets-urban-asia-how-resilient-are-food-systems-times-covid-19

World Bank. (2012). *Agricultural Innovation Systems: An Investment Sourcebook. Agricultural and Rural Development.* https://doi.org/10.1596/978-0-8213-8684-2

World Bank. (2022). *Food Security Update: December 15, 2022*. https://reliefweb.int/report/world/food-security-update-december-15-2022

Yamauchi, F. (2021). Changing Farm Size and Agricultural Productivity in Asia. *ADB Background Paper.* https://www.adb.org/sites/default/files/institutional-document/731791/adou2021bp-farm-size-agri-productivity-asia.pdf

https://doi.org/10.1142/9789811278297_0004

Chapter 4

Climate Change and Its Implications for Asian Agriculture and Food Security

Rathana Peou Norbert-Munns[1,2], Beau Damen[3] and Imelda Baccudo[4]

[1]*Office of Sustainable Development Goals (OSG), FAO, Italy*
[2]*Copernicus Center, Utrecht University, The Netherlands*
[3]*FAO Regional Office for Asia and the Pacific, Thailand*
[4]*Association of Southeast Asian Nations Climate Resilience Network (ASEAN-CRN), Indonesia*

4.1 Introduction

Climate change is a current and future risk to food security in Asia and globally. The latest report of the Intergovernmental Panel on Climate Change (IPCC) states that there is significant evidence that climate change undermines both agricultural production and food security in Asia [IPCC, 2023]. Increasing evidence from sub-regions and individual countries suggests that climate-related hazards, such as increasing temperature, changing rainfall, sea-level rise, drought, flooding, and the more frequent and intense occurrences of El Niño–Southern Oscillation events, all impact agricultural production with significant effects on food security [ADB, 2017]. All these hazards interact with non-climatic factors, such as competing demand for scarce water resources, rural-urban migration, aging workforce, food prices and poor governance, among other things, which may worsen food insecurity in the region [Montesclaros and Teng, 2021].

Asia accounts for 67% of global agricultural production [Mendelsohn, 2014] and food demand is expected to increase anywhere between 59% and 98% by 2050. The majority of producers in the region are and will continue to be smallholder farmers for the foreseeable future. But rapid urbanisation and economic development have seen shifts in production systems and also diets. The interactions between the elements of the food system and natural and socio-economic systems have become more intricate and complex [Food and Agriculture Organization (FAO), 2018b]. Ongoing and projected future climate change is a risk multiplier of food insecurity [Krishnamurthy *et al.*, 2012].

The risks climate change presents for food security and nutrition have been a concern of the sustainable development agenda since the early 1990s [Alpino *et al.*, 2022] and were highlighted in the objective for the establishment of the United Nations Framework Convention on Climate Change (UNFCCC), [UNFCCC, 1992]. Recent studies and syntheses including the 5th and 6th Assessment reports of the IPCC have offered more insights into these risks. The authors of this chapter aim to provide a concise synthesis of recent assessments of climate change risks to food security in Asia and highlight the potential of coordinated action to promote climate-resilient food systems that deliver food security and improved nutritional outcomes using an example from the Association of Southeast Asian Nations (ASEAN).

This chapter will first present an overview analysis of the observed and potential impacts of climate change on agriculture and food security in Asia. Then a case study is presented outlining coordinated action by ASEAN to address systematic risks from climate change to food security at the sub-regional level. Finally, based on the case study, some suggestions for ways forward to address climate change risk to food security in Asia and beyond will be discussed.

4.2 Climate Change and Food Security in Asia

Food security can be referred to as the condition in which all people have physical, social, and economic access to sufficient, safe, and nutritious food that meets their dietary needs and food preferences for an active and healthy life [FAO, 1996]. It is a multidimensional concept that encompasses availability, access, utilisation, and stability of food. Both agriculture and food security are fundamentally interlinked as per Figure 4.1.

Climate change has significant impacts on agriculture in Asia, affecting various aspects of crop production, livestock, fisheries and overall food security. Climate change is projected to negatively impact the four pillars of food security — availability, access, utilisation and stability — and their interactions [FAO, 2018a].

The IPCC Working Group II AR5 chapter on Food Security and Food Production Systems broke new ground by expanding its focus beyond the effects of climate change primarily on agricultural production (crops, livestock and aquaculture) to include a food systems approach as well as directing attention to undernourished people [Porter *et al.*, 2014].

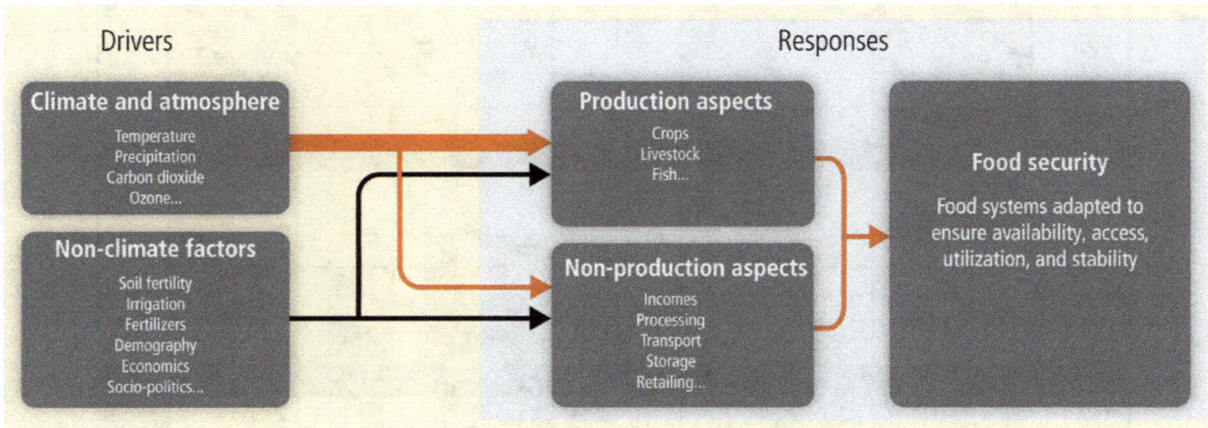

Figure 4.1 Climate change drivers on agriculture and food security [Porter *et al.*, 2014].

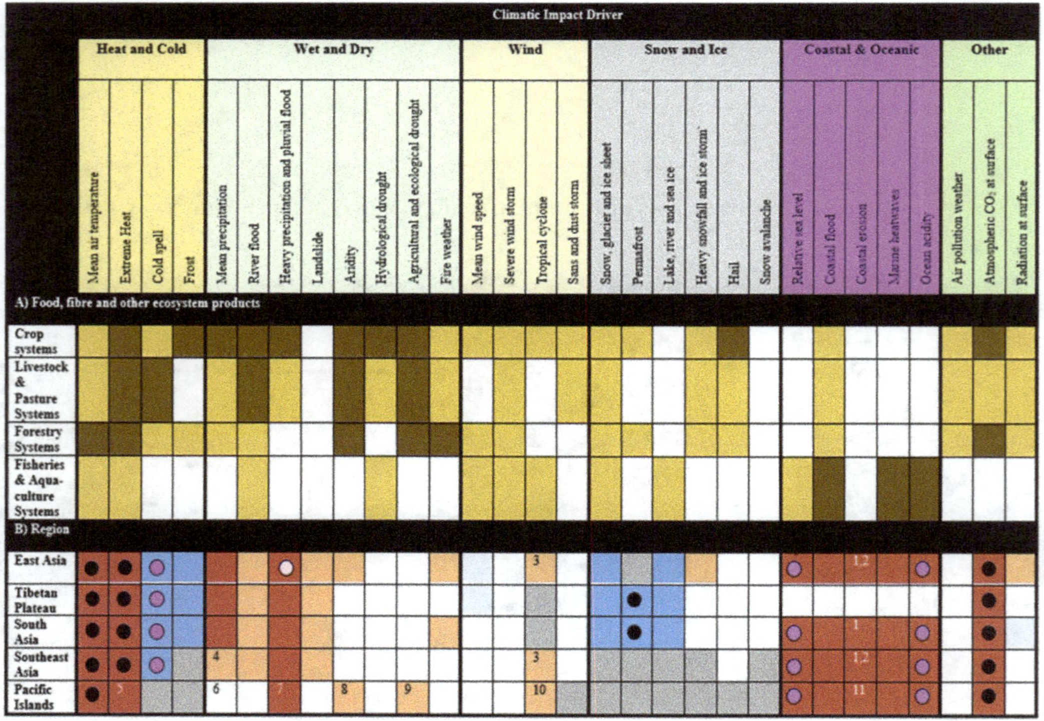

Figure 4.2 A) Relevance of key climate impact drivers (CID) for the food, fibre and other ecosystems sector and sectoral assets. B) Summary of confidence in direction of projected change in CIDs in Asia and the Pacific, representing their aggregate characteristic changes for mid-century for scenarios RCP4.5, SSP3-4.5, SRES A1B, or approximately corresponding (for CIDs that are independent of sea-level rise) to global warming levels between 2°C and 2.4°C. Source: FAO [2022]. Adapted from Ranasinghe, R. A., *et al.* [2021].

Notes:

A)

'High relevance' indicates climatic 14 impact-drivers that are most prominent and widely studied for their direct connection to assets, while lower relevance indicates weaker linkages and less commonly-studied driving behaviours.

B)

● **Already emerged in the historical period (medium to high confidence)**

● **Emerging by 2050 at least in Scenarios RCP8.5/SSP-8.5 (medium to high confidence)**

○ **Emerging after 2050 and by 2100 at least in Scenarios RCP8.5/SSP-8.5 (medium to high confidence)**

1. Along sandy coasts and in the absence of additional sediment sinks/sources or any physical barriers to shoreline retreat.
2. Substantial parts of the EAS and SEA coasts are projected to prograde if present-day ambient shoreline change rates continue
3. Tropical cyclones decrease in number but increase in intensity
4. High confidence of decrease in Indonesia.
5. Very high confidence in the direction of change, but low to medium confidence in the magnitude of change due to model uncertainty.
6. Decrease in eastern Pacific and southern Pacific subtropics, but Increase in parts of western and equatorial Pacific; with seasonal variation in future changes.
7. High confidence in increase in extreme rain frequency and intensity in western tropical Pacific; low confidence in magnitude of change due to model bias.
8. Increase in southern Pacific.
9. Particularly in parts of the Pacific with projected rainfall declines.
10. Increase in intensity; decrease in frequency except over central north Pacific.
11. Along sandy coasts and in the absence of additional sediment sinks/sources or any physical barriers to shoreline retreat.

Key	
	A)
	None/low confidence
	Low/moderate
	High
	B)
	High confidence of decrease
	Medium confidence of decrease
	Low confidence in direction of change
	Medium confidence of increase
	High confidence of increase
	Not broadly relevant

Figure 4.2 *(Continued)*

Over the past century, and across most of Asia, warming trends and increasing temperature extremes have been observed [Shaw *et al.*, 2022]. Working Group I of the IPCC AR6 report identified climate impact drivers (CID) relevant to various elements of food systems including crops, livestock and pasture, forestry, fisheries and aquaculture subsectors. In Asia, some CIDs such as increased mean temperatures and extreme heat were found to already have changed compared to the climate of the recent past, with potential implications for food security (Figure 4.2). Major documented impacts to agricultural production, such as those observed by the farmers in the Philippines and Indonesia, include among others delays in crop harvesting, declining crop yields and quality of produce, increasing incidence of pests and diseases, stunted growth, livestock mortality and low farm income [Tolentino and Landicho, 2013].

The IPCC AR6 also indicated with high confidence that overall, at the regional level, the projected negative impacts will far outweigh the expected benefits, with India emerging as the most vulnerable nation in terms of crop production (Figure 4.3). Climate-related risks to agriculture and food security in Asia are expected to progressively escalate as global warming reaches 1.5°C and higher above pre-industrial levels [IPCC, 2018].

The review below highlights the key findings regarding the observed impacts of climate change on each element of food security in Asia.

4.2.1 *Availability*

Reliable estimates of the impacts of climate change on crop production are critical for assessing the sustainability of food systems. Distinguishing observed climate change impacts on food

Figure 4.3 Projected impacts of climate change to agriculture and food systems in sub-regions of Asia based on post-IPCC-AR5 studies.[2]

[2] Figure 10.6 in Shaw, R., *et al.* (2022). 2022: Asia. In H.-O. Pörtner, *et al.* (Eds.), *Climate Change 2022: Impacts, Adaptation and Vulnerability*, pp. 1457–1579. Cambridge University Press.

production is difficult due to inherent problems in defining a unique baseline scenario that accounts for the number and strength of non-climate drivers and accounting for farmer behaviour in response to changes in climate [Porter *et al.*, 2014]. Global, regional, and site-specific crop simulation studies have been conducted for nearly four decades, representing valuable sources of information for climate change impact assessments [Hasegawa *et al.*, 2022]. The IPCC AR5 singled out food production as one clear example where the impacts of climate change were already having an impact [Cramer *et al.*, 2014].

Rising temperatures affect crop growth and development. Higher temperatures can lead to reduced crop yields, especially for heat-sensitive crops like rice and wheat. Shifts in temperature patterns also disrupt plant pollination and affect the timing of planting and harvesting seasons. Climate change can also bring changes in rainfall patterns, leading to both increased and decreased precipitation in different regions. More frequent and intense droughts reduce water availability for irrigation, affecting crop productivity and livestock water supply. Conversely, heavy rainfall events and floods can damage crops, cause soil erosion, and increase the risk of waterlogging. The impacts from these changes in climate will not be distributed evenly. The spatio-temporal diversity of projected future impacts on food production is projected to vary across the region. The direction of the cumulative impacts on yield will be negative in most countries [IPCC, 2022b; Shaw *et al.*, 2022].

4.2.2 *Accessibility*

Food access is the availability and affordability of nutritious and suitable foods for people. It depends on physical, economic and social factors. It refers to, for example, how far you must travel to buy food, how much it costs, and what kind of food you prefer. The key assumptions regarding climate change impacts on food accessibility are not only that it can limit access to food through its direct and negative effects on rural incomes and livelihoods but also by higher food prices resulting from climate change [FAO, 2016].

It is noted that climate-related impacts on food access depend to an extent on the distribution of net food buyers and net food sellers, and the process and level of economic development. However, assessing the impacts of climate change on households' ability to access food depends as much on the various income sources available to households as on climate impacts on agricultural productivity [Porter *et al.*, 2014]. The impacts of climate change on food access can vary according to the geographical variations in climate change impacts and income, household resources, agricultural productivity, the connectedness of farm households to markets, and the diversity of income-generating opportunities available to households. There has been linkages drawn between food price fluctuations and spikes and climate extremes in major producing regions, implying a link between climate change and food access [Porter *et al.*, 2014]. Domestic policy responses to these spikes can amplify international price responses with flow-on implications for food access.

Looking to evidence from the region, a recent report from Oxford Economics finds that variability in climate conditions may have had a significant impact on the cost of food production and resulted in increased food price volatility. Across Southeast Asian economies a 1% increase in temperature was found to increase food production costs year on year by 0.5–0.8%. Extreme heat events in Thailand and Vietnam in recent years have driven price spikes of 5–6%. Climate futures in which temperatures rise fastest and weather volatility increases most have the potential to generate ever-faster food price growth and greater price spikes [Oxford Economics, 2022].

4.2.3 *Stability*

Climate change leading to more variability and extreme climate events upsets the stability of food systems [FAO, 2016]. Smallholder farmers are particularly at risk of disruption from climate shocks resulting in reduced consumption and the liquidation of productive assets that can lead to long-term deterioration of capacity to cope with climate shocks [Porter *et al.*, 2014]. Asia experiences an increased frequency and intensity of extreme weather events such as hurricanes, cyclones, and typhoons. It has been estimated that as much as 75% and 73% of the global population exposed to coastal and riverine flooding respectively live in Asia. These events can result in devastating crop and infrastructure damage, loss of livestock, and displacement of rural communities, leading to food shortages and increased vulnerability. It is to be noted that the health impacts and needs of rural populations following disasters such as drought and flood are greater and that access to support in these areas is lower than for the general population [Davis *et al.*, 2010]. Climate change also affects the distribution and behaviour of pests and diseases, impacting agricultural productivity. Higher temperatures and altered rainfall patterns can create more favourable conditions for pests, leading to increased infestations and crop damage. Changes in disease patterns can also affect livestock health and decrease productivity.

4.2.4 *Utilisation*

Climate change can impact food utilisation by altering crop yields and nutritional content, potentially affecting the quality and quantity of food available for consumption. These changes can have profound implications for both food security and public health. Utilisation of food may be affected by negative impacts on factors such as diets, availability of clean water, sanitation, and health care [FAO, 2016]. Shifts in temperature and precipitation patterns can disrupt crop yields and reduce the availability of essential foods, leading to potential shortages of key nutrients like vitamins and minerals. Extreme climate events have been linked to increased prevalence of numerous negative nutritional outcomes such as stunting, wasting and micro-nutrient deficiency. This research has highlighted specific cases in Afghanistan, China, India, North Korea, and Indonesia in Asia [Stanke *et al.*, 2013]. Increased exposure to flood and drought has also been linked to increased exposure to pathogenic bacteria, parasites, mycotoxins, and a host of viruses [Myers *et al.*, 2017]. Extreme climate events can also damage infrastructure, making it difficult for communities to access nutritious foods. Additionally, changes in climate can alter the composition of certain crops, potentially reducing their nutritional value [Shindell, 2016]. All these factors can contribute to malnutrition and deficiencies in essential nutrients, posing serious health risks, particularly for vulnerable populations, and exacerbating the global challenge of achieving adequate nutrition for all in the face of a changing climate.

4.2.5 *Broader Impacts and Linkages of Climate Change to Food Security*

The food system is interconnected with other biophysical and socio-economic systems. Climate change can also affect food security through these interconnections, while acting as a driver of climate change itself. For example, climate change contributes to the loss of biodiversity, including pollinators and natural pest control agents. Pollinators, such as bees, are crucial for crop production, and their decline can negatively impact yields [Habibullah *et al.*, 2022]. Additionally, the loss of ecosystem services, such as soil fertility and water regulation, further affects agricultural productivity. Climate change impacts can also force farmers to adapt or abandon traditional agricultural practices. Adaptation strategies include changing land and cropping practices, and the development of improved crop varieties [Anderson *et al.*, 2020].

Agriculture also contributes a significant share of the greenhouse gas (GHG) emissions that cause climate change — 17% directly through agricultural activities and an additional 7–14% through land use changes. It is therefore both part of the problem — and an important part of the solution [OECD, 2019].

4.3 Potential Drivers of Future Risk to Food Security

Although most studies continue to focus on food availability by looking at climate change impacts on food production, more studies are addressing related issues of access (e.g., impacts on food prices), utilisation (e.g., impacts on nutritional quality), and stability (e.g., impacts of increasing extreme events) as they are affected by a changing climate [Bailey *et al.*, 2015].

Major trends driving agriculture development in the region — rural urbanisation and the development of agro-industry, opportunities in export markets (i.e., China), restrictions in export markets (i.e., the European Union), urbanisation and nutrition transitions (impact on nutrition), changes in food preferences (more consumption of high calorie and fast foods, consumption of foods outside of home) and emissions profiles need to be considered. Dietary shifts in the region towards processed, packaged and convenience foods and increased consumption of oils and fats, caloric sweeteners and meat result in substantial levels of agrifood systems emissions and other externalities. Non-communicable diseases, linked to changes in diet, are now a much greater public health issue than undernourishment in certain regions of Asia. In the Technical Summary to the IPCC Special Report on Climate Change and Land, the consumption of healthy and sustainable diets are presenting major opportunities for reducing GHG emissions from food systems and improving health outcomes [IPCC, 2018; Shukla *et al.*, 2019].

Trade and urbanisation may also play a role in increasing food system emissions. As much as one-third of total agricultural land use at the global level is embodied in interregional trade [Wu *et al.*, 2018]. Deforestation in tropical regions to accommodate expansion in the production of a few key commodities in traded agricultural products has been significant in Asia. The demand driving these land use changes is strongly linked to consumption choices for food and agriculture products in urban areas [Meyfroidt, 2013].

Climate change has already begun to significantly impact agriculture, food security and nutrition in Asia, and these impacts are expected to intensify in the future along with additional drivers of climate change and food system risk. It is crucial to implement adaptation strategies such as developing climate-resilient crop varieties, promoting water-efficient irrigation techniques, improving early warning systems, and supporting smallholder farmers to build resilience and ensure food security in the face of climate change. International cooperation, policy support, and financial assistance are key to addressing these challenges effectively and ASEAN presents a useful case study to illustrate this.

4.4 ASEAN as a Case Study

4.4.1 *ASEAN and Climate Change Risks to Food Security*

The ASEAN region, consisting of 10 member states across Southeast Asia, has in 2022 a combined population of 672 million people. Agriculture[2] plays an important role in the economy of the countries of Southeast Asia. At the regional level, the agricultural sector contributes to more than 10% of the region's gross domestic product (GDP) and provides jobs for over one-third of the working population. In 2021, the average rural population in ASEAN was 47.28%, with the highest value in Cambodia with 75.33% and the lowest value in Singapore with 0% [ASEAN, 2021–2022], and an average of 38.9% of the employed population engaged in the agricultural sector [ASEAN, 2020]. The ASEAN population is projected to reach 717 million people to be fed by 2030 [United Nations, Department of Economic and Social Affairs, 2019], accompanied by diet changes, environmental degradation, and natural resources pressures paired with climate change, all of which are major threats to this region and its food baskets.

Trade is an important element of the food system in ASEAN. Some countries are heavily dependent on food imports, such as Singapore and Brunei Darussalam. Others are significant producers and exporters of many major food items such as Thailand and Vietnam, while Indonesia and Philippines are major producers and importers of food commodities.

The region is at risk of hotter weather, longer monsoon seasons, and increased droughts, as global temperatures are predicted to

---

[2] The FAO definition of agriculture includes crops, livestock, forestry, fisheries and aquaculture.

increase by 1.5°C above pre-industrial levels over the next 20 years [IPCC, 2023]. In 2021, the Global Climate Risk Index, which calculates impacts of extreme weather events, found that changes in rainfall patterns and temperature will cause major consequences for ASEAN's ecosystems and agricultural activities. The index ranked Myanmar 2nd, the Philippines 4th, and Thailand 9th as the top three ASEAN countries at risk from 2000 to 2019. Meanwhile, Brunei Darussalam at 176th and Singapore at 179th, were ranked the least at risk [Eckstein *et al.*, 2021]. Member states are unevenly at risk due to their exposures, vulnerabilities, and readiness of their agricultural sector.

ASEAN is at risk of losing over 35% of its GDP by 2050 to climate change and natural hazards, severely impacting key sectors such as agriculture, tourism, and fishing, along with human health and labour productivity [Renaud *et al.*, 2021]. The workforce in some ASEAN member states dedicated to this sector are above one-third of the total employed with the top of the list being Laos (61%), Vietnam (37%) and Cambodia (34%). When looking at the land uses, agriculture and forestry constitute almost 79% (342,454,000 ha) of Southeast Asia's total land area with 30.08% and 48.82% respectively.

Agriculture is a critical livelihood for smallholder farmers as drivers of economic growth, food security and poverty alleviation. It is a key driver of economic development for most of the ASEAN member states as most of the food consumed in ASEAN is produced in ASEAN. At the same time, the growing impacts of climate change also threaten the agricultural sector affecting productivity, prices, quality, safety, food security and millions upon millions of livelihoods. Changes, shocks, or crises in agriculture that affect the ASEAN food system will be felt across the region and globally.

4.4.2 *Working with Global and National Frameworks*

Countries in Southeast Asia, both individually and as members of ASEAN, have committed to addressing the challenges of food security and climate change in the agricultural and land use sectors. There are several relevant action frameworks that have been developed to address the challenges posed by climate change. These frameworks provide guidance and strategies for governments, organisations, and communities to mitigate GHG emissions, adapt to climate change impacts, and foster sustainable development. Some notable action frameworks are the UNFCCC and the Paris Agreement (adopted in 2015 under the UNFCCC). The agreement emphasises mitigation, adaptation, finance, technology transfer, and capacity building to address climate change at the national and global levels. The Nationally Determined Contributions (NDCs) also specify specific mitigation and adaptation targets and actions that countries commit to under the Paris Agreement. The Sustainable Development Goals (SDGs) provide a comprehensive framework for sustainable development, including addressing climate change. Goal 13 specifically focuses on climate action, aiming to strengthen resilience and adaptive capacity, and promote low-carbon development while Goal 2 is on zero hunger.

The Sendai Framework for Disaster Risk Reduction adopted in 2015 aims to reduce the risk of disasters and enhance resilience to climate-related hazards. It emphasises the integration of disaster risk reduction with climate change adaptation and sustainable development. Along with Regional and National Climate Action Plans, many countries and regions have developed their own climate action plans that align with international frameworks and address specific national or subnational challenges. These plans outline strategies, policies, and measures to reduce emissions, enhance resilience, and promote sustainable development at the local level.

In their first round of NDCs, several Southeast Asian countries identified a variety of measures and priorities for tackling climate change. Many of the countries in the region included agriculture and land use, land-use change and forestry sectors (90%) in their economy-wide mitigation target, but mainly through non-GHG targets and/or policies and measures. All countries in the region have also indicated that adaptation in agriculture is a priority, through the identification of different policies and measures to strengthen resilience of the sector. Most ASEAN member states (90%) have identified specific adaptation measures for all sub-sectors including forestry, fisheries, crops, and others. However, based on the analysis by FAO, most of the policies and measures for both mitigation and adaptation in the agriculture and land use sector are not quantified and, as a result, cannot inform a full assessment of their potential impact or of the technical and financial needs that may be required to support their implementation [Crumpler *et al.*, 2020].

Increasing the resilience of the agricultural sector and furthering progress toward food security and better nutrition have been identified as key priorities for the region, and are prominent not only in the NDCs of all Southeast Asian Countries but as well in their Long-Term Strategy for Carbon Neutrality. Of the ten ASEAN countries, eight have announced national targets to achieve net-zero GHG emissions or to become carbon neutral by 2050, corresponding to the 1.5°C target set by the IPCC, except Indonesia, which committed to net zero by 2060, and the Philippines, which is the only ASEAN country that has not committed to a net-zero target.

Key adaptation and mitigation strategies identified in the sector-specific climate change strategies and NDCs of the countries in the region can be grouped around different practices and approaches. These groupings can include, but are not limited to:

1. Drought-Tolerant Varieties: Planting drought-tolerant crop varieties is a common adaptation strategy. These varieties are bred to withstand water stress and have higher resilience to drought conditions, allowing farmers to maintain productivity even during dry periods.
2. Crop Rotation and Diversification: Changing farming sequences through crop rotation and diversification can enhance climate resilience. Rotating crops helps break pest and disease cycles, improves soil health, and reduces the risk of crop failure. Diversifying crops can spread risks associated with climate variability and provide alternative income sources.
3. Conservation Agriculture: Conservation agriculture practices, such as minimal tillage, cover cropping, and crop residue management help improve soil health, reduce erosion, and enhance water retention. These practices enhance the resilience of agricultural systems to climate change impacts.
4. Agroforestry Systems: Agroforestry involves integrating trees with crops or livestock in the same farming system. Agroforestry provides multiple benefits, including soil conservation, microclimate regulation, biodiversity conservation, and increased farm productivity. It can help buffer against climate extremes and improve long-term resilience.
5. Water Management Techniques: Improved water management practices are essential for climate adaptation. These include water harvesting, drip irrigation, efficient irrigation systems, and the use of mulching to conserve soil moisture. Efficient

water use helps mitigate the impacts of water scarcity and supports crop growth during droughts.

6. Climate Information Services: Providing farmers with timely and accurate climate information helps them make informed decisions. Climate information services offer weather forecasts, early warning systems, and advisory services tailored to agricultural needs. These services enable farmers to adjust planting and harvesting schedules, optimise resource use, and mitigate climate risks.
7. Sustainable Land and Natural Resource Management: Sustainable land and natural resource management practices, such as terracing, contour ploughing, agroecology, and watershed management help protect soil health, conserve water resources, and enhance biodiversity. These practices contribute to long-term resilience and sustainable agriculture.
8. Farmer Field Schools and Capacity Building: Farmer field schools and capacity-building programs educate farmers on climate-smart practices, sustainable farming techniques, and risk management strategies. These initiatives enhance farmers' knowledge and skills, empowering them to adopt climate adaptation measures effectively.

ASEAN has developed a program of regional cooperation to help facilitate countries to collaborate and share knowledge in the adoption and scaling up of measures such as those outlined above to address climate change risks to food security.

4.4.3 *Regional Cooperation to Address Risks from Climate Change to Food Security*

At the regional level, in September 2015, ASEAN included the need to address climate change through the promotion of appropriate agricultural practices in the Vision and Strategic Plan for ASEAN Cooperation in Food, Agriculture and Forestry 2016–2025 (FAF) [ASEAN, 2015]. The FAF 2025 identifies and prioritises the main areas for cooperation in response to socio-economic and demographic changes in the region, including pressures on the natural resource base. Under the FAF 2025 Southeast Asian countries have prioritised approaches and measures including climate-smart agriculture, enhancing regional and international collaboration, and enhancing access to financial resources. Furthermore, the FAF looks to encourage coordination and joint approaches on issues affecting food, agriculture, and forestry, and present its common positions on these matters. A successful past example of such collaboration is the ASEAN Plus Three Emergency Rice Reserve, which was established in 2011 to strengthen food security, poverty alleviation, and malnourishment eradication among its members without distorting normal trade. The Rice Reserve has been mobilised recently to address problems arising from the COVID-19 pandemic. The ASEAN Technical Working Group on Agricultural Research and Development (ATWGARD) under the ASEAN Ministers for Agriculture and Forestry supports the implementation of the FAF. Based on mutual interest in defining climate-smart agriculture practices and policies, ATWGARD focal points worked to form the ASEAN Climate Resilience Network (ASEAN-CRN). ASEAN-CRN is a platform for regional exchange of information, experience and expertise on climate-smart land use. The network facilitates the translation of science into policies to promote resilient agriculture and explore its mitigation potential, through resource matchmaking with various stakeholders. These commitments and initiatives demonstrate a strong commitment to tackling climate change risks to the agricultural sector and broader regional food system in a collaborative and coordinated manner.

In acknowledgement of those challenges and with the opportunities that tackling climate change presents for agriculture and food security, the ASEAN member states have been deploying alongside international bodies such as the UNFCCC resources to build knowledge from the past and towards the future. Moreover, before the Paris Agreement in 2015, the awareness of the critical environmental issues, especially on global warming, has been blooming among Southeast Asian countries [Lee *et al.*, 2013]. At the political level, the ASEAN leaders have expressed a common will to further develop and promote resilience to climate change throughout the ASEAN community, while adopting a joint position and bringing forward the interests and priorities of the ASEAN region in international negotiations [Fasting *et al.*, 2021]. To support implementation of specific measures, ASEAN policy frameworks and regional priorities for climate adaptation in the agricultural sector offer guidance and strategies for member states to adopt and implement climate-smart agricultural practices, sustainable land management, and water resource management to enhance resilience to climate change impacts (Table 4.1).

4.5 Ways Forward

The urgency of tackling climate change on global, regional, national, and subnational scales cannot be overstated. Climate change also intersects with other risk factors, such as pandemics, supply chain disruptions stemming from conflicts or natural disasters, and the degradation of our precious natural resources. Solutions require input from different stakeholders, both public and private, as well as a range of government ministries, including Health, Finance, Education, Environment, Trade and Social Welfare in addition to Agriculture [FAO, 2018b]. These converging threats demand

Table 4.1 Key ASEAN climate-related agriculture policies, strategies and guidance.

Title	Summary
ASEAN Climate Change Initiative (ACCI)	The ACCI is an initiative under the ASEAN Framework on Climate Change that focuses on addressing climate change impacts in the region. It promotes climate adaptation measures, including those specific to the agricultural sector, through regional cooperation and capacity-building activities.
ASEAN Guidelines on Promoting Climate-Smart Agriculture Practices	These guidelines, developed by the ASEAN Working Group on Climate Change, provide a framework for promoting climate-smart agriculture practices across ASEAN member states. The guidelines highlight practices such as crop diversification, conservation agriculture, water management, and sustainable land management.
ASEAN Strategy on Climate Change and Agriculture	This strategy, developed by the ASEAN Climate Resilience Network, outlines the regional priorities and action plans for climate change adaptation in the agricultural sector. It emphasises the importance of promoting climate-resilient agricultural practices, enhancing water and soil management, and integrating climate considerations into policy and planning.
ASEAN Guidelines on Mainstreaming Climate Change Adaptation into Agriculture and Forestry Sectors	These guidelines, developed by the ASEAN Working Group on Climate Change Adaptation, provide a framework for integrating climate change adaptation into agricultural and forestry sectors. The guidelines emphasise the need for sustainable land and water management, diversification of crops and livestock, and capacity building for farmers.
ASEAN Strategic Plan of Action on Food Security	This strategic plan aims to enhance food security in ASEAN member states. It recognises the importance of climate change adaptation in the agricultural sector and highlights the need to promote climate-smart agricultural practices, sustainable land and water management, and technology transfer for improved productivity and resilience.
ASEAN Declaration on Environmental Sustainability	While not specific to agriculture, this declaration acknowledges the importance of environmental sustainability and climate change adaptation in ASEAN member states. It calls for the promotion of sustainable development practices, including those related to agriculture, to address environmental challenges and build resilience.

immediate attention and robust action, as they collectively pose a formidable challenge to the stability of our food systems and achieving food security. There is high confidence that currently implemented climate action in Asia (such as climate-smart agriculture, ecosystem-based disaster risks reduction and investing in urban blue-green infrastructure) can meet adaptation, mitigation and SDGs simultaneously, presenting opportunities for climate-resilient development in food systems [IPCC, 2022b].

However, there also exist significant barriers to climate-resilient food systems such as fragmented, reactive governance, political myopia, inadequate evidence on which actions to prioritise and how to sequence them, and inadequate financing mechanisms.

Climate foresight and scenario analysis have emerged as useful tools, gaining increasing recognition and adoption among governments and key stakeholders within the agrifood sector. These tools support governments and other food system stakeholders to anticipate and experiment with possible responses to multiple potential climate futures and food system configurations with the aim of identifying and considering complex risks to food security through multi-stakeholder processes. These tools enable food system actors to grapple with the uncertainty posed by climate change and proactively plan and strategise for a more resilient and sustainable future. Foresight planning, particularly through participatory scenario planning, offers a dynamic approach that combines quantitative modelling with qualitative narratives. This approach encourages holistic, long-term thinking, shedding light on diverse potential futures and their implications for various facets of the agrifood system, as well as their intricate interplay with other sectors and sources of uncertainty [Eckstein *et al.*, 2021]. Importantly, foresight planning serves as a catalyst for the integration of sustainability-focused policies within the agricultural sphere. It illuminates the intricate web of connections between agricultural sustainability, encompassing environmental health, human well-being, food security, nutrition, safety, animal and crop health, economic viability, digital innovation, and the development of rural communities.

In this context, adopting a food system approach through the lens of the Asian countries' food systems pathways represents a profound evolution, rooted in a systemic perspective, to tackle the multifaceted challenges and risks of today and tomorrow, shaping a promising trajectory towards a more secure, nutritious, sustainable, and resilient future. As part of the 2021 United Nations Food System Summit, all ASEAN member states crafted strategic pathways for the transformation of their national food systems. A range of organisations have since taken on roles to support governments in the implementation of these pathways that are looking at building a resilient, climate-adapted and sustainable future. These efforts provide a clear example for food system actors in Asia and globally looking to strengthen the resilience of food systems and eradicate hunger and malnutrition under climate change.

References

ADB. (2017). *A Region at Risk: The Human Dimensions of Climate Change in Asia and the Pacific*. https://dx.doi.org/10.22617/TCS178839-2

Alpino, T. D. M. A, Mazoto, M. L., de Barros, D. C. and de Frietas, C. M. (2022). The impacts of climate change on Food and Nutritional Security: a literature review. *Ciência & Saúde Coletiva*, 27(1), pp. 273–286.

Anderson, R., Bayer, P. E. and Edwards, D. (2020). Climate change and the need for agricultural adaptation. *Current Opinion in Plant Biology*, 56, pp. 197–202.

ASEAN. (2015). *Vision and Strategic Plan for ASEAN Cooperation in Food, Agriculture and Forestry 2016–2025.* https://asean-crn.org/vision-and-strategic-plan-for-asean-cooperation-in-food-agriculture-and-forestry-2016-2025/

ASEAN. (2020). *ASEAN Key Figures 2020.* https://asean.org/book/asean-key-figures-2020-3/

ASEAN. (2021–2022). *Transforming ASEAN's Rural Landscape.* https://theaseanmagazine.asean.org/edition/transforming-aseans-rural-landscape/

Bailey, R., *et al.* (2015). *Extreme Weather and Resilience of the Global Food System: Final Project Report from the UK-US Taskforce on Extreme Weather and Global Food System Resilience.* The Global Food Security Programme, UK.

Cramer, W., Yohe, G. W., Auffhammer, M., Huggel, C., Molau, U., Da Silva Dias, M. A. F. and Tibig, L. (2014). Detection and Attribution of Observed Impacts. In C. B. Field (Ed.), *Climate Change 2014: Impacts, Adaptation and Vulnerability*, pp. 979–1037. Cambridge University Press.

Crumpler, K., Dasgupta, S., Federici, S., Meybeck, M., Bloise, M., Slivinska, V., Salvatore, M., Damen, B., Von Loeben, S., Wolf, J. and Bernoux, M. (2020). Regional analysis of the nationally determined contributions in Asia — Gaps and opportunities in the agriculture and land use sectors. *Environment and Natural Resources Management Working Paper No. 78.* https://doi.org/10.4060/ca7264en

Davis, S. J., Calderia, K. and Matthews, H. D. (2010). Future CO2 emissions and climate change from existing energy infrastructure. *Science*, 329(5997), pp. 1330–1333.

Deloitte. (2022). *The Turning Point.* https://www.deloitte.com/global/en/issues/climate/global-turning-point.html

Duasa, J. and Adibah Mohd-Radzman, N. (2022). The impact of climate change on ASEAN rice production in the short and long run. *Journal of Tourism Hospitality and Environment Management*, 7, pp. 94–111.

Eckstein, D., Künzel, V. and Schäfer, L. (2021). *Global Climate Risks Index*. Germanwatch e.V.

ESCAP. (2022a). *Asia and the Pacifics SDG Progress Report 2022: Widening Disparities amid COVID-19*. https://www.unescap.org/kp/2022/asia-and-pacific-sdg-progress-report-2022

ESCAP. (2022b). *Asia and the Pacific SDG Progress Report 2023: Championing Sustainability Despite Adversities*. https://www.unescap.org/kp/2023/asia-and-pacific-sdg-progress-report-2023

FAO. (1996). Rome Declaration on World Food Security and World Food Summit Plan of Action. https://www.fao.org/3/w3613e/w3613e00.htm

FAO. (2015). *Statistical Pocketbook*. https://www.fao.org/fsnforum/resources/trainings-tools-and-databases/fao-statistical-pocketbook-2015

FAO. (2016). *The State of Food and Agriculture*. https://www.fao.org/family-farming/detail/en/c/447860/

FAO. (2018a). *The Future of Food and Agriculture: Alternative Pathways to 2050*. https://www.fao.org/global-perspectives-studies/resources/detail/en/c/1157074/

FAO. (2018b). *Dynamic Development, Shifting Demographics, Changing Diets*. https://www.fao.org/documents/card/en/c/I8499EN

FAO. (2022). *Actions to Promote Climate Resilient Agrifood Systems in Asia and the Pacific Region*. https://www.fao.org/documents/card/en/c/NH656en

Fasting, S., Bacudo, I., Damen, B. and Dinesh, D. (2021). Climate governance and agriculture in Southeast Asia: learning from a polycentric approach. *Frontiers in Political Science*, 3, p. 698431.

Habibullah, M. S., Din, B. D., Tan, S. H. and Zahid, H. (2022). Impact of climate change on biodiversity loss: global evidence. *Environmental Science and Pollution Research*, 29(1), pp. 1073–1086.

Hasegawa, T., Wakatsuki, H., Ju, H., Vyas, S., Nelson, G. C., Farrell, A., Deryng, D., Francisco Meza, F. and Makowski, D. (2022). A global dataset for the projected impacts of climate change on four major crops. *Scientific Data*, 9, p. 58.

IPCC. (2018). Global warming of 1.5°C. https://www.ipcc.ch/sr15/

IPCC. (2022a). *AR6 Synthesis Report: Summary for Policymakers*. https://www.ipcc.ch/report/ar6/syr/downloads/report/IPCC_AR6_SYR_SPM.pdf

IPCC. (2022b). *AR6-chapter 10*. IPCC.

IPCC. (2023). *AR6 Synthesis Report*. https://www.ipcc.ch/report/sixth-assessment-report-cycle/

Krishnamurthy, P. K., Lewis, K. and Choularton, R. J. (2012). *Climate Impacts on Food Security and Nutrition — A Review of Existing Knowledge*. Met Office and World Food Programme, UK.

Lee, Z. H., Sumathi, S., Lee, K. T., Bhatia, S. and Mohamed, A. R. (2013). An overview on global warming in Southeast Asia: CO2 emission status, efforts done, and barriers. *Renewable and Sustainable Energy Reviews*, 28(C), pp. 71–81.

Lim, C.-H., Kim, S. H., Chun, J. A., Kafatos, M. A. and Lee, W. K. (2019). Assessment of agricultural drought considering the hydrological cycle and crop phenology in the Korean Peninsula. *Water*, 11(5), p. 1105.

Mendelsohn, R. (2014). The impact of climate change on agriculture in Asia. *Journal of Integrative Agriculture*, 13(4), pp. 660–665.

Meyfroidt, P., Lambini, E. F., Erb, K. H. and Hertel, T. W. (2013). Globalization of land use: Distant drivers of land change and geographic displacement of land use. *Current Opinion in Environmental Sustainability*, 5, pp. 1–7.

Montesclaros, J. L. M. A. and Teng, P. (2021). Agriculture and Food Security in Asia. In J. M. Pulhin, M. Inoue and R. Shaw (Eds.), *Climate Change, Disaster Risks, and Human Security: Asian Experience and Perspectives*, pp. 137–168. Springer.

Myers, S. S., Smith, M. R., Guth, S., Golden, C. D., Vaitla, B., Mueller, N. D., Dangour, A. D. and Huybers, P. (2017). Climate change and global food systems: potential impacts on food security and undernutrition. *Annual Review of Public Health*, 38(1), pp. 259–277.

OECD. (2019). *Enhancing Climate Change Mitigation through Agriculture.* https://www.oecd.org/publications/enhancing-the-mitigation-of-climate-change-though-agriculture-e9a79226-en.htm

Oxford Economics. (2022). Climate change and food prices in Southeast Asia. https://www.oxfordeconomics.com/resource/climate-change-and-food-prices-in-southeast-asia/

Porter, J. R., Xie, L., Challinor, A. J., Cochrane, K., Howden, S. M., Iqbal, M. M., Lobell, D. B. and Travasso, M. I. (2014). Food Security and Food Production Systems. In C. B. Field (Ed.), *Climate Change 2014: Impacts, Adaptation and Vulnerability*, pp. 485–533. Cambridge University Press.

Ranasinghe, R., Ruane, A. C., Vautard, R., Arnell, N., Coppola, E., Cruz, F. A., Dessai, S., Islam, A. S., Rahimi, M., Carrascal, D. R., Sillmann, J., Sylla, M. B., Tebaldi, C., Wang, W. and Zaaboul, R. (2021). Chapter 12: Climate Change Information for Regional Impact and for Risk Assessment. In *Climate Change 2021: The Physical Science Basis*, pp. 1767–1926. Cambridge University Press.

Renaud, F., Chardot, L., Hamel, P., Cremin, E., Ng, D. K. S. Balke, T., Lallemant, D., Friend, R., Shi, X., Lee, J. S. H., Ng, L. Y., Andiappan, V., Le, H., Djalante, R., Tortajada, C., Ebeler, L. and Horton, B. P. (2021). *Adaptation and Resilience in ASEAN: Managing Disaster Risks from Natural Hazards*. United Kingdom — government, University of Glasgow, Earth Observatory of Singapore — Nanyang Technological University, University of York, Centre for Regional Change in the Earth System.

Shaw, R., Luo, Y., Cheong, T. S., Halim S. A., Chaturvedi, S., Hashizume, M., Insarov, G. E., Ishikawa, Y., Jafari, M., Kitoh, A., Pulhin, J., Singh, C., Vasant, K. and Zhang, Z. (2022). Asia. In *Climate Change 2022: Impacts, Adaptation and Vulnerability*, pp. 1457–1579. Cambridge University Press.

Shindell, D. T. (2016). Crop yield changes induced by emissions of individual climate-altering pollutants. *Earth's Future*, 4(8), pp. 373–380.

Shukla, P. R., Skea, J., Slade, R., van Diemen, R., Haughey, E., Malley, J., Pathak, M. and Pereira, J. P. (Eds.) (2019). Technical Summary, 2019. In *Climate Change and Land*. Intergovernmental Panel on Climate Change.

Stanke, C., Kerac, M., Prudhomme, C., Medlock, J. and Murray, V. (2013). Health effects of drought: a systematic review of the evidence. *PLoS Currents*, 5, 10.1371/currents.dis.7a2cee9e980f91ad7697b570bcc4b004.

Tolentino, L. L. and Landicho, L. D. (2013). Climate change adaptation strategies of selected smallholder upland farmers in Southeast Asia: Philippines and Indonesia. *APN Science Bulletin*, 3(1), 61–64.

United Nations, Department of Economic and Social Affairs. (2019). World Population Prospects 2019. Data Booklet. https://population.un.org/wpp/publications/files/wpp2019_databooklet.pdf

UNFCCC. (1992). United Nations Framework Convention Convention on Climate Change. https://unfccc.int/resource/docs/convkp/conveng.pdf

Wu, X. D., Guo, J. L., Han, M. Y. and Chen, G. Q. (2018). An overview of arable land use for the world economy: From source to sink via the global supply chain. *Land Use Policy*, 76(C), pp. 201–214.

https://doi.org/10.1142/9789811278297_0005

Chapter 5

Future of Rice in Asia: Perspectives and Opportunities, 2050

Valerien O. Pede[1], Harold Glenn Valera[1], Ashok K. Mishra[2] and Jean Balié[1]

[1]*International Rice Research Institute, Los Banos, Philippines*
[2]*Morrison School of Agribusiness, W.P. Carey School of Business, Arizona State University, Tempe, AZ, USA*

5.1 Introduction

The South and Southeast Asia regions are the world's leading rice producer, accounting for 58% of global rice production in 2021 [United States Department of Agriculture (USDA), 2022]. Asian agriculture, especially rice farming, has been facing issues such as stagnant yields [Ladha *et al.*, 2003], declining productivity of production factors, nutrient deficiencies, soil degradation [Tripathi and Das, 2017], depleting groundwater, labour scarcity, over-exploitation of natural resources such as water [Humphreys *et al.*, 2010], and higher cost of cultivation. In a nutshell, agricultural and food systems' sustainability is at risk. Rice remains closely tied to national and sub-national food security imperatives. Rice production systems in South and Southeast Asia in recent years have become increasingly threatened by climate change — such as the increased occurrence of severe weather, including heatwaves, droughts, unpredictable precipitation, increased salinity, rising sea levels, flooding and submergence [Yan *et al.*, 2022; Redfern *et al.*, 2012]. Asian countries are more primed and vulnerable at the same time to changes in economic progress. In the past two decades, countries in Asia have witnessed faster rates of urbanisation, rising wages, more diversity of diets, and increased population density leading to a decreased area in production agriculture [Mishra *et al.*, 2022; Mottaleb and Mishra, 2022]. As noted by Furuya and Koyama [2005], Li and Wassmann [2011] and Yan *et al.* [2022], weather variability or climate change can cause a decline in world rice production and yield gaps, and have already proven to have negative effects on agricultural production and the socioeconomic conditions of the farmers.

Meanwhile, most of the world is experiencing rapid income growth and urbanisation that will profoundly affect food production, crop diversity, food quality, diets, and nutrition. With subsequent lifestyle changes, changes in diets, and the proliferation of fast food restaurants, households consequently consume relatively more packaged and processed foods. They tend to consume meat, sugar, fats, and oils [Gaiha *et al.*, 2013; Pingali, 2007; Mottaleb and Mishra, 2022] and not enough fruits, vegetables, and other healthy foods. Consumption and, therefore, demand for feed grains for other livestock feeds increase. Thus, growing and evolving food patterns will pressure food production, specifically sustainable food production. However, growth in sustainable food production faces challenges on several fronts, including climate change — higher temperatures and weather variability, and increased variability in rainfall. Pingali *et al.* [1997] in their book highlighted slowing yield growth and signs of severe environmental degradation due to increased fertilisation and water usage by rice farmers.

Additionally, Pandey *et al.* [2010] noted that the food economy is more integrated with other sectors of the global economy, including both energy and financial markets. Women make significant contributions to rice farming, processing, and marketing and play a dominant role in buying rice for consumption [Medagbe *et al.*, 2020]. Addressing social considerations with a focus on women and youth is expected to lead to policies and technological changes that promote gender and youth equality in terms of access to productive resources and opportunities that will contribute to household food and nutrition security. Finally, government policies, domestic support, and trade policies alter the supply and demand of rice around the globe. Governments,[1] like the Philippines, have had import restriction policies[2] to protect Filipino farmers from foreign competition and secure lower prices for domestic consumers [Balié and Valera, 2020;[3] Balié *et al.*, 2021].

[1] For instance, Tanaka and Hosoe [2011] opposed the Japanese government's rice trade liberalisation because it would threaten national food security. In India's case, Srinivasan and Jha [2001] note that rice trade liberalisation reform would likely increase domestic price variability and increase the costs of price stabilisation.

[2] In March 2019, the government of the Philippines promulgated a bill called the Rice Tariffication Law (Republic Act No. 11203). The policy reform abandoned the quantitative restrictions on imports that have been in place for more than 30 years, replacing them with *ad valorem* tariffs to finally comply with the principles and rules of the World Trade Organization. Another important aspect of the reform was the elimination of the role of the National Food Authority (NFA) in rice imports. The NFA has long been considered a source of huge inefficiencies and inappropriate interventions in markets [Balié *et al.*, 2021].

[3] Replacing import quota with tariffs would decrease domestic production, and lower farm and retail prices. Thus, tariffs could have a beneficial impact on fining inflation in Philippines.

Rice, a staple food for some four billion people globally, provides 21% of global human per capita energy and 15% of per capita protein [United Nations, 2017]. Rice is still the dominant crop in Asia, covering 85% of the arable land. Rice is grown in diverse agroecosystems in South Asia, Southeast Asia, Africa, and Latin America. Asians consume 84% of the world's rice. However, rice production and consumption vary by region [Mishra *et al.*, 2022]. Rice farming is associated with poverty in many areas. About 900 million of the world's poor depend on rice as producers or consumers. Mishra *et al.* [2022] notes that about 400 million poor and undernourished people are engaged in rice-based farming systems, mostly on less than 2 hectares of landholding. Finally, the authors note that about 144 million farm households, usually small farms, are engaged in rice production for subsistence and employment. Therefore, an abundant and stable supply of affordable rice is critical for reducing poverty and hunger in developing and emerging economies. Figure 5.1 shows the area, production, and rice yield growth rate

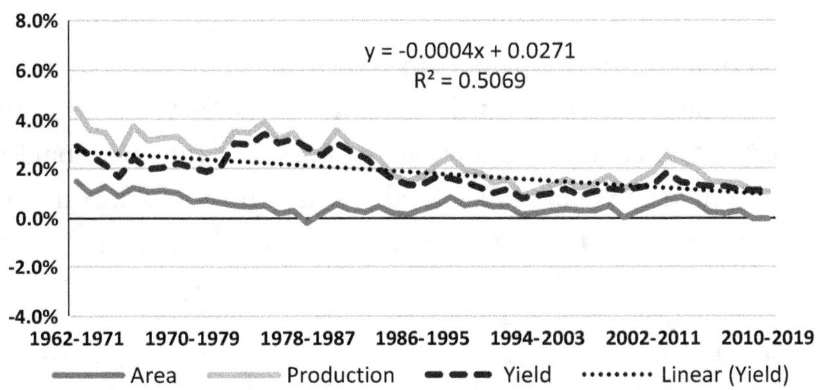

Figure 5.1 Average growth rate (%) of area (hectares), production (tons), and rice yield (t/ha), 1962–2019 for South Asia, Southeast Asia and the Pacific. Source: Mishra *et al.* [2019].

from 1962 to 2019 for South and Southeast Asia and the Pacific region. The figure shows the high growth during the Green Revolution (1966–1985), which increased world rice production and yield by 2.5% per year. However, over the past 20 years, land used for rice farming has been declining.

Food security remains fragile despite the economic progress made in the last four decades. The 2008 world food crisis and the recent COVID-19 pandemic reinstate the need to ensure a stable, affordable, quality, and sustainable food supply for the poor. Thus, there is a need to develop a new vision for future rice farming in the context of Asia. The vision is needed to strategically position rice research and technology investments and induce policymakers to design policies that help accelerate reforms. Rural-urban migration has increased labour scarcity, rural wages, and feminisation[4] and aging of the agricultural labour force. The aging of the rural labour force has many countries worrying about who will grow their food in the coming decades, especially in many countries in Asia.

This chapter presents a perspective and outlines the opportunities for the future of rice farming in Asia. It is forward looking in the context of major developments in the Asian economy. The chapter has two objectives. First, it documents the current situation and projected status of the rice economy in Asia. The International Rice Research Institute Global Rice Model is used to assess the direction of supply and demand among rice economies over the next three

---

[4] Factors affecting feminisation of rice farming include out-migration of rural male workers [Radel *et al.*, 2012], mechanisation and labour-saving technologies [Pandey *et al.*, 2012], rice production systems (subsistence farming where women contribute significant amount of labour [Radel *et al.*, 2012]), and sociocultural norms and values [Paris *et al.*, 2008].

decades. The outlook of countries with a significant role in the global rice economy will also be analysed. Then it briefly discusses the key lessons from the supply and demand outlook. Second, it will identify key challenges that countries must address in the intermediate and long-term periods. It also examines how the design of coherent and coordinated policy actions will meet those challenges.

5.2 Key Drivers of Rice Supply and Demand

To meet the rice demand by 2050, the International Rice Research Institute (IRRI) estimates that an extra 75 million tons of rice will need to be produced worldwide compared to 2020. This represents a substantial leap forward when rice yields are plateauing in most countries. Asia's ongoing demographic transformation is expected to affect future rice production and consumption [Bhandari and Mishra, 2018].[5] Several factors are likely to drive the supply response. On the supply side, major factors include growth in the actual area planted, rice cropping intensity and rice yields through the adoption of high-yielding varieties, aging farmers, out-migration, and off-farm income opportunities [Bhandari and Mishra, 2018]. Rural out-migration affects rice farming by influencing the farming population, labour supply, and geographic shifting of rice demand. The aging of farmers is a matter of concern because it affects the farming population and the available amount of food to feed the growing population. Other effects of the aging farm population on agriculture and rice farming are labour market, land market, land use, production practices, farming intensification and commercialisation, technology adoption, livelihood strategies, food and nutrition security, poverty, and farm consolidation. Rice

[5] The Asian population is projected to reach 4.6 billion in 2050.

production growth can be accomplished by adopting new technologies and sustainable practices, improving access to credit, increasing investment in agriculture research and development (R&D), repurposing the policy support from the national government, and redesigning national and international trade policies.

Meanwhile, the drivers of rice demand include population growth, income, family size, household labour reallocation, urbanisation [Mottaleb *et al.*, 2018], and changing consumer preferences. Bhandari and Mishra [2018] predicted that the urban population will surpass the rural population for the first time in history in 2025. Empirical studies demonstrate that with the increase in income and urbanisation, people diversify their food consumption from cereal to more high-value-added items [Huang and David, 1993; Huang and Bouis, 1996; Pingali, 2007; Timsina *et al.*, 2016]. In addition, in Bangladesh, Mottaleb *et al.* [2017] argue that with rising income and urbanisation, consumers will be demanding more high-quality rice — long grain and fragrant rice. Indeed, one would recognise a similar pattern across East and Southeast Asian countries.

To meet the demand for quality rice and rice with attributes (like smell, taste, texture, grain shape, and other characteristics), rice value chains are rapidly changing in many parts of the world. Since rapid urbanisation is occurring in Asia, rice value chains will attempt to tap into growing market opportunities by tailoring their products to the increasingly demanding taste of urban consumers, who spend more on food per person than rural consumers. However, food represents a lower share of their total expenditures [Mottaleb *et al.*, 2016]. Thus, the above supply and demand drivers will shape the rice sector's transformation. Other factors include mechanisation, feminisation, land consolidation, branding, quality upgrading, healthier, more nutritious products, and globalisation.

5.2.1 *The Global Rice Supply and Demand Outlook Using the International Rice Research Institute Global Rice Model*

In this chapter, a long-term supply and demand outlook is developed using the IRRI Global Rice Model[6] (IGRM) managed by researchers at IRRI. This model has been extensively used for policy analyses in the Philippines and other parts of the world [Hoang and Meyers, 2015; Balié and Valera, 2020]. Figure 5.2 shows a representative country model[7] that includes supply, demand, trade and market equilibrium conditions. The supply comprises production, beginning stocks, and imports. Demand is composed of domestic consumption, ending stock, and exports. The model's representation of the global rice market comprises 25 countries and four regional aggregates. Those countries account for about 90% of worldwide rice consumption and production. The world reference price for the model is the Thai Free-on-Board 5% broken price. The Thai 5% broken price is solved to close the model such that Thailand's net exports equal the sum of the net trade of the remaining countries.

On the supply side, the rice area is specified as a function of the previous year's harvested area and expected gross returns or prices received by producers for rice and competing crops. In general, partial adjustment expectations of the prior year are the most representative, but there are some variations in specific variations by country. The model specified yield as a function of expected output,

[6] IGRM is a dynamic partial equilibrium framework with a structure similar to the well-established Arkansas Global Rice Model of the University of Arkansas [Wailes and Chavez, 2011]. IGRM has been used as an analytical framework for rice trade liberalisation studies in the Southeast Asian rice markets [Hoang and Myers, 2015; Balié and Valera, 2020; Balié *et al.*, 2021].

[7] IGRM representative country model for the Philippines employed in the rice tariffication policy simulation [Balié and Valera, 2020].

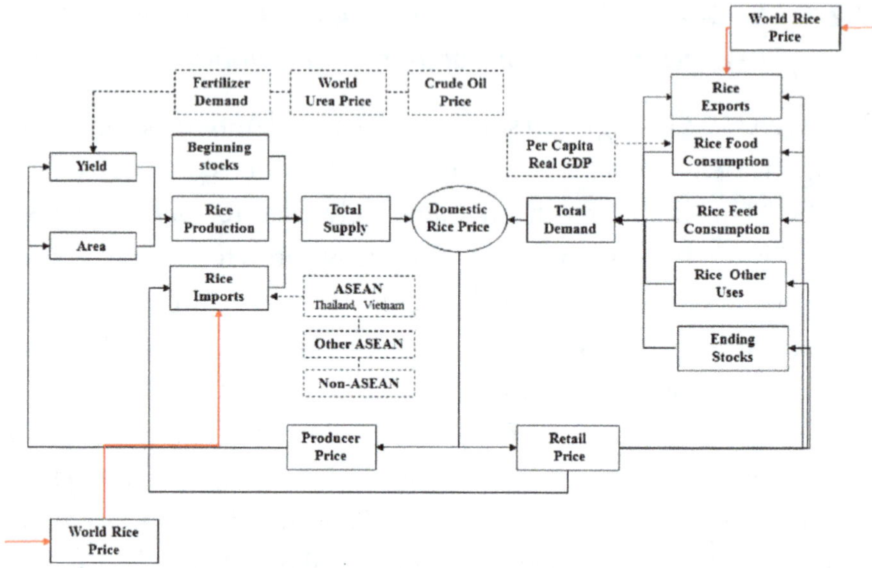

Figure 5.2 IGRM model structure. Source: Balié and Valera [2020].

input prices, and R&D expenditures or trend assumptions to capture technological change. On the demand side, per capita food consumption is estimated based on real per capita income and real retail prices of rice and substitute food.

5.2.2 *Global Rice Outlook*

In this chapter, we develop long-term baseline deterministic estimates of global supply and demand for rice between 2022 and 2050. The estimates are generated under a set of assumptions regarding population, income, exchange rate, and other macroeconomic indicators. In addition, the estimates assume a continuation of existing rice sector policies and average weather conditions.

Before presenting our long-term baseline estimates, it is worthwhile to mention some key developments in the Asian rice market.

In 2020–2021, for example, there was a record production in the rice market fundamentals in Asia along with high levels of global stocks, which were well above the levels observed in 2008 and 2011 when the global rice market experienced a surge in prices. While key rice exporters in the region, such as Vietnam, Cambodia, and Myanmar, abandoned the rice trade restrictions at the initial stage of the COVID-19 pandemic, India imposed a ban on the export of broken rice and a 20% export tax on other rice grades in September 2022. The rice export restrictions were mainly imposed to protect the domestic rice market and food security. The baseline estimates we developed did not account for India's recent rice trade restrictions.

As shown in Table 5.1, the IGRM model estimates that the world rice area will increase by 2% between 2022 and 2050. However, rice yield would increase by 10.6% during the same period. World rice consumption would increase by 11.2% and net trade in rice would increase by about 17% during the 2022–2050 period. For Asia, our analysis reveals that the rice area would only increase by 0.2% between 2022 and 2050. However, rice yield would increase by nearly 8%, perhaps due to technological changes in rice production, during the same period. Asian rice consumption would increase by 4.6%, well below the yield increase, and as a result, net trade in rice would increase by about 51% during the 2022–2050 period.

The rice outlook in Africa is quite different. For instance, our analysis using IGRM shows that Africa's rice area would increase by 18.3% between 2022 and 2050. However, rice yield would increase by three folds compared to rice area — by 55.3% during the same period. Interestingly, African rice consumption would grow at a faster rate. Our analysis reveals that African rice

Table 5.1 Rice supply and use in selected years: World, Asia, Africa, and Americas.

	Unit	2021	2022	2025	2030	2040	2050	Growth rate
World								
Area	1,000 HA	163,304	162,332	163,559	165,315	166,833	165,656	2.05
Yield	MT/HA	4.60	4.61	4.70	4.78	4.94	5.10	10.58
Milled Production	1,000 MT	503,101	501,604	514,924	528,919	550,400	564,098	12.46
Beginning Stocks	1,000 MT	188,087	185,049	179,304	179,516	181,269	184,704	–0.19
Consumption	1,000 MT	515,733	517,687	525,738	539,848	561,654	575,573	11.18
Ending Stocks	1,000 MT	185,049	179,462	179,191	179,608	181,512	185,019	3.10
Total Trade	1,000 MT	40,650	40,312	40,729	40,997	42,523	47,186	17.05
Asia								
Area	1,000 HA	140,613	139,748	140,551	141,518	141,790	139,981	0.17
Yield	MT/HA	4.76	4.79	4.86	4.92	5.04	5.17	7.97
Milled Production	1,000 MT	449,110	448,809	458,237	466,593	478,098	484,082	7.86
Beginning Stocks	1,000 MT	177,057	173,824	168,565	168,729	169,999	172,248	–0.91
Consumption	1,000 MT	434,296	434,890	439,174	447,033	455,524	454,846	4.59
Ending Stocks	1,000 MT	173,824	168,553	168,491	168,789	170,185	172,496	2.34
Net Trade	1,000 MT	18,047	19,190	19,137	19,500	22,388	28,989	51.06
Africa								
Area	1,000 HA	15,562	15,562	15,810	16,454	17,606	18,403	18.26
Yield	MT/HA	2.34	2.32	2.48	2.75	3.20	3.60	55.31

Milled Production	1,000 MT	23,677	23,410	25,485	29,314	36,562	42,902	83.26
Beginning Stocks	1,000 MT	4,280	4,308	3,787	3,631	3,669	3,826	-11.19
Consumption	1,000 MT	41,149	42,110	45,127	50,381	61,316	73,164	73.74
Ending Stocks	1,000 MT	4,308	3,985	3,721	3,623	3,680	3,845	-3.51
Net Trade	1,000 MT	-17,500	-18,377	-19,576	-21,059	-24,765	-30,281	64.78
Americas								
Area	1,000 HA	5,501	5,448	5,531	5,650	5,735	5,571	2.26
Yield	MT/HA	6.44	6.36	6.57	6.77	7.21	7.66	20.51
Milled Production	1,000 MT	24,091	23,546	24,707	26,023	28,070	28,974	23.05
Beginning Stocks	1,000 MT	4,279	4,038	3,908	4,023	4,376	4,790	18.62
Consumption	1,000 MT	24,527	24,585	25,025	25,590	26,688	27,716	12.73
Ending Stocks	1,000 MT	4,038	3,901	3,916	4,048	4,414	4,827	23.73
Net Trade	1,000 MT	-195	-902	-327	409	1,344	1,221	-235.32
European Union-28								
Area	1,000 HA	403	357	409	419	424	424	18.67
Yield	MT/HA	6.53	5.84	6.51	6.83	7.15	7.10	21.44
Milled Production	1,000 MT	1,713	2,087	2,666	2,862	3,031	3,007	44.11
Beginning Stocks	1,000 MT	663	737	603	632	620	1,134	53.83
Consumption	1,000 MT	3,500	3,559	3,655	3,770	4,145	4,684	31.60
Ending Stocks	1,000 MT	737	615	609	635	619	1,134	84.38
Net Trade	1,000 MT	-1,861	-2,101	-1,953	-1,941	-2,203	-2,758	31.29

consumption between 2022 and 2050 would increase by about 83%. Thus, African countries would have to import much of the rice from Asia and the rest of the world (the United States and others) to meet the consumption demand. Import of rice (net trade negative) would have to increase by about 65% during the 2020–2050 period.

Next, Table 5.1 also shows the rice situation in the Americas. The IGRM baseline projections show that America's rice area would increase by only 2.3% between 2022 and 2050. However, rice yield would increase ten folds compared to rice area — by 20.5% during the same period. Interestingly, America's rice consumption would grow at a slower rate. Our analysis reveals that America's rice consumption between 2022 and 2050 would increase by about 12.7%. Finally, the bottom part of Table 5.1 shows the long-term outlook on rice in the European Union. The IGRM baseline projections show that the rice area in this region would increase by 18.7% between 2022 and 2050. Rice yield is expected to increase by 21.4% during the same period. European Union's rice consumption is expected to grow much faster — by 31.6% between 2022 and 2050. Accordingly, rice imports of the European Union would increase by 31.3% during the same period.

5.2.3 *Asian rice Sector Outlook*

USDA (2021) reports that globally 503.17 MT of rice is produced, where China has 29.5% of the total, followed by India (23.8%), Bangladesh (7.0%), Indonesia (6.9%), Vietnam (5.4%), and Thailand (3.7%) [Al Mamun *et al.*, 2021]. Using the IGRM model, we also projected the outlook of the rice industry in selected Asian countries (see Table 5.2). These countries represent high producers,

Table 5.2 Rice supply and use in selected Asian countries, IGRM model, 2022–2050.

	Unit	2021	2022	2025	2030	2040	2050	Growth rate
Bangladesh								
Area	1,000 HA	8,410	8,323	8,461	8,673	8,920	9,004	8.18
Yield	MT/HA	4.51	4.53	4.58	4.65	4.77	4.89	7.91
Milled Production	1,000 MT	25,299	25,154	25,845	26,866	28,393	29,365	16.74
Beginning Stocks	1,000 MT	1,461	2,101	1,552	1,539	1,559	1,621	–22.85
Per capita consumption	KG/Year	219.48	219.20	219.00	216.57	215.05	216.78	–1.10
Consumption	1,000 MT	36,500	36,801	37,756	38,765	40,518	41,745	13.44
Ending Stocks	1,000 MT	2,101	1,542	1,548	1,538	1,563	1,629	5.64
Net Trade	1,000 MT	–1,290	–592	–1,205	–879	–632	–598	0.89
China								
Area	1,000 HA	29,921	30,000	30,004	29,793	29,236	28,576	–4.75
Yield	MT/HA	7.11	7.10	7.19	7.21	7.25	7.28	2.67
Milled Production	1,000 MT	148,990	149,000	151,044	150,341	148,291	145,719	–2.20
Beginning Stocks	1,000 MT	116,500	113,000	108,985	108,854	108,809	109,048	–3.50
Per capita consumption	KG/Year	107.61	107.52	105.49	104.78	103.87	103.36	–3.87
Consumption	1,000 MT	156,290	156,631	154,690	154,353	151,436	145,864	–6.87
Ending Stocks	1,000 MT	113,000	108,993	108,956	108,828	108,823	109,081	0.08
Net Trade	1,000 MT	–3,800	–3,625	–3,618	–3,986	–3,159	–178	–95.09
India								
Area	1,000 HA	47,000	45,999	46,412	46,561	46,734	46,852	1.85

(Continued)

Table 5.2 *(Continued)*

	Unit	2021	2022	2025	2030	2040	2050	Growth rate
Yield	MT/HA	4.14	4.19	4.27	4.36	4.50	4.66	11.28
Milled Production	1,000 MT	129,660	128,500	132,099	135,229	140,295	145,652	13.35
Beginning Stocks	1,000 MT	37,000	36,500	36,201	36,550	37,072	37,723	3.35
Per capita consumption	KG/Year	77.80	76.49	76.38	76.17	75.70	75.08	–1.84
Consumption	1,000 MT	108,410	107,592	110,365	114,526	120,571	123,070	14.38
Ending Stocks	1,000 MT	36,500	36,050	36,271	36,605	37,131	37,793	4.84
Net Trade	1,000 MT	21,750	21,358	21,664	20,647	19,664	22,512	5.40
Indonesia								
Area	1,000 HA	11,600	11,650	11,672	11,674	11,658	11,620	–0.26
Yield	MT/HA	4.67	4.68	4.74	4.83	5.02	5.20	11.21
Milled Production	1,000 MT	34,400	34,600	35,143	35,835	37,136	38,378	10.92
Beginning Stocks	1,000 MT	3,060	2,860	3,142	3,269	3,487	3,707	29.62
Per capita consumption	KG/Year	127.19	125.39	124.80	123.81	121.48	118.29	–5.66
Consumption	1,000 MT	35,150	35,001	35,828	37,044	38,710	39,143	11.83
Ending Stocks	1,000 MT	2,860	3,011	3,172	3,290	3,509	3,729	23.85
Net Trade	1,000 MT	–550	–552	–715	–1,231	–1,595	–788	42.68
Philippines								
Area	1,000 HA	4,800	4,800	4,885	4,997	5,143	5,209	8.53
Yield	MT/HA	4.17	4.10	4.28	4.28	4.29	4.29	4.43
Milled Production	1,000 MT	12,600	12,411	13,172	13,481	13,885	14,067	13.34
Beginning Stocks	1,000 MT	3,763	4,513	4,494	4,491	4,499	4,521	0.18

Per capita consumption	KG/Year	138.68	138.64	137.85	136.70	131.92	128.64	−7.21
Consumption	1,000 MT	15,400	15,598	16,105	16,910	17,890	18,588	19.16
Ending Stocks	1,000 MT	4,513	4,424	4,492	4,490	4,500	4,524	2.25
Net Trade	1,000 MT	−3,550	−3,099	−2,931	−3,427	−4,007	−4,523	45.97
Thailand								
Area	1,000 HA	10,587	10,700	10,619	10,848	10,890	10,421	−2.60
Yield	MT/HA	2.81	2.80	2.85	2.93	3.09	3.24	15.56
Milled Production	1,000 MT	19,650	19,800	19,965	20,991	22,213	22,285	12.55
Beginning Stocks	1,000 MT	4,280	3,930	3,037	3,120	3,530	3,869	−1.55
Per capita consumption	KG/Year	185.84	187.02	186.08	182.91	179.45	179.55	−4.00
Consumption	1,000 MT	13,000	13,106	13,087	12,867	12,383	11,840	−9.66
Ending Stocks	1,000 MT	3,930	3,334	2,995	3,159	3,566	3,896	16.83
Net Trade	1,000 MT	7,000	7,289	6,921	8,084	9,794	10,418	42.93
Vietnam								
Area	1,000 HA	7,285	7,290	7,313	7,385	7,440	7,399	1.49
Yield	MT/HA	5.95	6.01	6.10	6.21	6.45	6.68	11.10
Milled Production	1,000 MT	27,069	27,400	27,868	28,683	29,985	30,896	12.76
Beginning Stocks	1,000 MT	2,639	2,808	2,931	2,812	2,866	3,294	17.33
Per capita consumption	KG/Year	219.01	219.29	218.37	216.13	211.64	207.57	−5.35
Consumption	1,000 MT	21,500	21,700	22,079	22,512	22,813	22,751	4.84
Ending Stocks	1,000 MT	2,808	2,910	2,892	2,797	2,893	3,351	15.17
Net Trade	1,000 MT	5,400	5,598	5,828	6,185	7,144	8,089	44.50

exporters, and rice consumers (about 74% of global trade).[8] We explore in depth the outlook for rice in several of the major rice-growing countries in the sections which follow.

5.2.3.1 *Bangladesh*

The top panel of Table 5.2 shows the area, yield, consumption, per capita consumption, net trade, and farm and retail rice prices in Bangladesh. Bangladesh's rice production heavily depends on rainfall and has three growing seasons (Aman, Aus and Boro). Rice is also the staple food in Bangladesh and accounts for approximately 78% of the country's total net cropped areas in cultivation. The IGRM baseline projections show that Bangladesh's rice area and yield would increase by approximately 8% between 2022 and 2050. Although the total consumption would increase by 13.4%, per capita consumption would decrease by 1.1% during the same period — perhaps due to the high population growth rate. To meet rice demand, Bangladesh would have to increase rice imports by 1% from 2022 to 2050.

5.2.3.2 *China*

China is the world's largest producer of rice, with an average yield of about 6.5 tons per hectare, among the highest in Asia. More than 90% of China's rice is irrigated and, in some parts of China, two harvests per year can be grown. The IGRM baseline projections

[8] India exports about 37.5% of rice to the world market, followed by Thailand, 13%, Pakistan, 8.4%, Vietnam, 7.7%, China, 3.3%, Myanmar, 2.1% and Cambodia, 1.6%.

show that China's rice area would decrease by about 4.8% between 2022 and 2050 (Table 5.2). This may be due to increased urbanisation and higher demand for land for other activities. However, rice yield would increase by about 2.7% during the same period. Interestingly, our baseline projections show that total and per capita rice consumption would decrease by about 6.9% and 3.9%, respectively, during the same period. This may be due to the increased consumption of other types of food and the westernisation of Chinese diets. As a result, China will be able to reduce its rice imports.

5.2.3.3 *India*

Rice is a staple food for most Indians. Rice farming is directly and indirectly linked to poverty, food security, and economic, social, cultural, political, and environmental aspects of India. India accounts for 23% of overall global rice production. India, the world's second biggest rice consumer after China, has a market share of more than 40% of the global rice trade. India exports rice to more than 150 countries. The IGRM baseline projections show that India's rice area would increase by about 1.9% between 2022 and 2050 (Table 5.2). However, rice yield would increase significantly by about 11.3% during the same period. This may be accomplished by increased use of modern rice technologies like hybrid rice and water management techniques. Our results show that total and per capita rice consumption would increase by 14.3% and decrease by 1.8%, respectively, during the same period. This may be due to a slower rate of population growth and the westernisation of Indian diets. Rice export from India would also increase by 5.4% during 2022–2050.

5.2.3.4 *Indonesia*

Indonesia is the third largest producer of rice and one of the top five importers of rice. Indonesia imports rice mainly from Thailand, Vietnam, and India. Indonesia's rice consumption will likely increase because of the growing population. Table 5.2 shows the baseline projection for Indonesia's rice area would decrease by 0.3%. In contrast, rice yield would increase significantly by 11.2% during the same period. This may be accomplished by the increased use of modern rice technologies. Our analysis shows that total and per capita rice consumption would increase by 11.8% and decrease by 5.7%, respectively, during the same period. Rice imports would increase by 43% during 2022–2050.

5.2.3.5 *Philippines*

In the Philippines, rice is the national staple and a political crop. It is a primary source of income for millions of farmers. Rice represents almost 23% of the total consumption of poor households and 10% of non-poor. The contribution of the rice sector to GDP is low, about 0.7%. Our baseline projections show that the Philippines' rice area would increase by about 8.5% between 2022 and 2050 (Table 5.2). However, rice yield would increase by about 4.4% during the same period. The results further show that total and per capita rice consumption would increase by 19.2% and decrease by 7.2% during the same period. Indeed, as Balié and Valera [2020] pointed out, it is unsurprising that this pattern conforms to the literature that indicates an increase in global rice consumption due to population growth. Rice imports would increase by 46% during 2022–2050.

5.2.3.6 *Thailand*

Rice has long been Thailand's traditional food crop and main export product. Thailand remains the world's second-largest rice exporter after India. According to the United Nations Food and Agriculture Organization's Rice Market Monitor, rice occupies about 55% of the total arable land, and over 80% of the Thai population eats rice as their main meal. The annual per capita consumption is about 100.8 kg. Table 5.2 shows that Thailand's rice area would decrease by about 2.6% between 2022 and 2050 (Table 5.2). This is because of climate change and rising sea levels that have made arable land inoperable because of salinity and flooding [Kawasaki, 2010]. The USDA reports that a decline in output is likely due to reduced area of off-season rice as reservoirs are at critically low levels and the government restricts irrigation for rice production. Production costs have risen over the past decade due to rising fertiliser and fuel prices. These issues are only exacerbated by the more recent energy crisis resulting from Russia's invasion of Ukraine. Meanwhile, rice yield would increase considerably by more than 15% during the same period. Our baseline projections show that total and per capita rice consumption would decrease by 9.7% and 4.0%, respectively, during the same period. Rice exports would increase by 42.9% during 2022–2050.

5.2.3.7 *Vietnam*

Rice is Vietnam's leading staple food, and total rice output ranks fifth in global production, behind China, India, Indonesia, and Bangladesh. The Mekong River Delta and the Red River Delta cover approximately 70% of the total rice area in Vietnam. Rice is essentially cultivated year-round. However, seasonal weather drives planting cycles phased into three planting periods, Lua Mua

(Winter), Winter-Spring, and Summer-Autumn. Our analysis using the IGRM baseline projection shows that Vietnam's rice area would increase by about 1.5% between 2022 and 2050 (Table 5.2). However, rice yield would increase significantly, ten times more (about 11.1%) during the same period. This may be accomplished by increasing production area, using modern rice technologies like hybrid rice and improved water management techniques, and the government's decision to make the rice sector low carbon in the next 10 years. Our baseline projections show that total and per capita rice consumption would increase by 4.8% and decrease by 5.4%, respectively, during the same period. When it comes to trade, Vietnam has the upper hand. For instance, in 2022 the European Union-Vietnam Free Trade Agreement (EVFTA) came into effect. According to EVFTA, the European Union provides Vietnam with 80,000 tons of rice for export at a 0% tax rate annually (including 30,000 tons of milled rice, 20,000 tons of unmilled rice, and 30,000 tons of aromatic rice). Table 5.2 shows that rice export from Vietnam would increase by 44.5% during 2022–2050.

Note that the findings reported in the preceding paragraphs are based on a five-year time horizon of the IGRM baseline projection from 2022 to 2026. The performance of the model is validated by comparing projection results of 2022 with the USDA's 2022 actual production, consumption and trade data.

5.3 Trade-offs between Food and Nutrition Security and Opportunities

The above outlook of the rice sector globally and regionally (Asia) assumes that the prevailing paradigm of feeding the world is one with abundant and cheap agricultural produce out of sustained intensification.

5.3.1 *Food Versus Nutrition Security*

However, in the recent decade, the paradigm of agricultural research, including rice research, has been shifting to incorporate food systems thinking about economic, social, and environmental sustainability and food and nutrition security under a climate change imperative. As a result, funding for technological development and other innovations in the food system has shifted to focus on healthy, affordable, nutritious, and sustainably produced food, particularly nutritious rice [Balié, 2020]. In other words, we have enough food to eat, but the population in developing and emerging economies lacks diet diversity leading to micronutrient deficiencies [Palanog *et al.*, 2019]. Iron deficiency anaemia and zinc deficiency are two severe nutritional problems. Thus, future opportunities in the rice sector would have to focus on developing nutritional rice varieties, such as low glycaemic index rice, high-zinc rice, high-iron rice and rice with high protein content. In the Philippines, the government[9] has proactively initiated various programs and policies to address micronutrient deficiencies, particularly fortifying essential food commodities. Thus, developing rice varieties with high micronutrient concentrations within rice grains is a cost-effective and sustainable strategy to address micronutrient needs among populations unable to access a healthy and diverse diet [Stein *et al.*, 2005].

5.3.2 *Opportunities to Address the Rice Complex*

5.3.2.1 *Addressing Production Issues*

Regarding the future of the rice sector, national rice research institutions in countries and/or the IRRI need to strengthen their capacity

[9] Currently, only two biofortified rice varieties, Zn rice, NSIC Rc460, and Fe rice, NSIC Rc172 (MS13), are commercially available for production and multiplication.

to deal with more diverse and complex topics that relate to rice production with complementary, holistic views that deal with significant problems such as climate change, nutrition, and environmental sustainability as well as the prosperity of rice growers and the communities around them. Soil, water and other environmental issues, as well as farming households' resilience to shocks, require that rice research in Asia and globally increasingly focus on sustainable farming practices, soil fertility, regeneration and conservation practices, efficient water management and conservation technologies as well as water pricing policies in rice cultivation. Research on short-duration, high-yielding, and stress-tolerant rice varieties and the benefits of direct seeded rice and mechanised transplanting on zero-tilled/un-puddled fields can improve the input use efficiency in rice cultivation under medium- to heavy-textured soils. By the same token, more research is warranted on developing and replacing varieties to adapt to rapidly evolving stress conditions for rice cultivation.

5.3.2.2 *Improving Market Intelligence*

Other opportunities that have yet to be explored in the Asian rice sector include consumer-based market intelligence-driven varietal development, contract farming, and using futures markets to manage commodity risk. Commodity growers, including rice farmers, in Asian countries[10] could benefit tremendously from creating market intelligence centres. The centres would forecast market conditions (supply and demand) and market prices and anticipate the emergence of new market segments driven by fast-evolving consumer preferences. The centre would also develop a commodity

[10] Developed countries already have government agencies that provide this information, for example, USDA and its several services (Agricultural Marketing Service, Economic Research Service, Foreign Agriculture Service).

market outlook and provide commodity market research and services for traders, investors, and other value chain stakeholders. The centres would also provide information on export procedures, post-harvest technologies, good management practices, and infrastructure development (rail, storage, cold chain, warehousing, ports, etc.). The centres can accelerate information delivery by providing timely and appropriate market intelligence to guide the development of new rice varieties. Examples of such centres have started to emerge. For instance, India has established centres called "Networking of Agricultural Market Intelligence Centres," comprising university researchers, private companies, and the central government. The One-CGIAR has recently launched a new initiative called 'Market Intelligence' which aims to maximise CGIAR and partners' returns on investment in breeding, seed systems, and other initiatives based on reliable and timely market intelligence, enable stronger demand orientation and strengthen co-ownership and co-implementation by CGIAR and partners.[11]

5.3.2.3 *Farming Modalities*

Contract farming has emerged as a popular vertical coordination mechanism for smallholders to diversify risk and receive higher product prices [Otsuka *et al.*, 2016]. Production contracts can shift farming risk and provide smallholders with transportation, storage, and capital needs. Smallholders producing both high-value and low-value crops in many Asian countries have used contract farming arrangements. Empirical evidence [Meemken and Bellemare,

[11] More information about the Market intelligence Initiative is available at https://www.cgiar.org/initiative/05-market-intelligence-for-more-equitable-and-impactful-genetic-innovation/.

2020; Mishra *et al.*, 2016, 2017, 2018a, 2018b, 2018c] from Africa and Asia shows that contract farming positively impacts growers' profit, yield, and technical efficiency. Finally, governments in Asia should start exploring the use and potential benefits of futures markets for rice trading. Both consumers and rice producers can manage price risk by purchasing and selling rice futures.[12] The futures contract would enable rice growers to obtain greater security for the sale of their harvest, locking in prices at acceptable levels. For instance, the Dojima Rice Exchange in Japan started in 1967. It is a commodity futures exchange specialising in rice. In the futures market, buyers (smallholders in our case) could purchase rice at predetermined prices, eliminating the risk of sudden price increases and securing valuable rice supplies ahead of time. The risk management benefits of an active Asian rice futures contract could be significant. Public/state agencies and private market firms could use the futures market to lock in or fix the price they buy/sell rice months in advance — removing the risk associated with price spikes.

5.4 Concluding Remarks

The Asian rice market fundamentals in 2020–2021 indicated record production and high levels of global stocks. These production and stock levels were much higher than in 2008 and 2011. At the onset of the COVID-19 pandemic, many rice-exporting countries such as Vietnam, Cambodia, and Myanmar restricted exports for food security reasons in their own country, thus pushing international rice prices higher. Since then, global reference prices for rice, based on

---

[12] For example, rice producers could employ short hedge to lock in selling price for their rice. Businesses that require rice could use long hedge to secure a purchase price for the rice.

Thai 5% broken rice, have declined significantly. Additionally, the rice-exporting countries rolled back their export restrictions because of the influx of Indian rice in the global market. However, India recently imposed a ban on the export of broken rice and a 20% export tax on other rice grades to lower domestic prices and ensure enough local rice supply for Indians. The global rice economy could see a dramatic shift or tightening quickly if India continues to restrict rice exports and experiences a bad monsoon season. The global rice market will be in peril if rice-exporting countries like Vietnam, Cambodia, Myanmar, and Thailand follow the Indian philosophy of export ban.

Considering the vital role played by Asia in tackling the challenge of eradicating hunger and improving food security, this chapter provides a long-term outlook for the regional and global rice market, assuming average weather and non-imposition of India's recent rice export restrictions and a continuation of current policies in other countries. The baseline projections presented in this book chapter indicate that global rice output, consumption, stocks, and trade can be expected to grow. The growth in rice yield in Asia is expected to be much slower than in Africa, where yield is projected to increase by 55% between 2022 and 2050. Over the long run, total rice consumption in Asia and Africa is projected to rise by 5% and 73%, respectively. To meet the rice consumption demand in Africa, the region would have to import much of the rice from Asia and the rest of the world. The baseline projections further indicate a decline in per capita rice consumption over the long run. The decline in per capita rice consumption in many Asian countries is being offset by a rise in rice consumption in Africa.

Lastly, for yield improvement and food security of billions of Asians, policymakers need to focus on addressing natural and man-made challenges such as climate change, nutrition, environmental sustainability, efficient water management, soil fertility, sustainable farming practices, and prosperity of rice growers. We argue that a significant amount of resources should be devoted to developing varieties that can grow in unfavourable environments. To this end, it is not surprising that scientists and policymakers have been forward looking and joined the cause. They have been working relentlessly to develop stress-tolerant varieties that can withstand submergence, drought, and salinity and climate-smart technologies that can reduce input usage.

Acknowledgement

We would like to thank all funders who support this research through their contributions to the CGIAR Trust Fund. In particular, funding from the CGIAR Initiative on Market Intelligence and Foresight Initiatives is greatly acknowledged. We also gratefully acknowledge the research assistance provided by Ronald Jeremy Antonio.

References

Al Mamn, M. A., Nihad, S. A. I., Sarkar, M. A. R., Aziz, M. A., Qayum, M. A., Ahmed, R., Rahman, N. M. F., Hossain, M. I. and Kabir, M. S. (2021). Growth and trend analysis of area, production and yield of rice: A scenario of rice security in Bangladesh. *PLoS One*, 16(12), p. e0261128.

Balié, J., Minot, N. and Valera, H. A. (2021). Distributional impacts of the rice tariffication policy in the Philippines. *Economic Analysis and Policy*, 69, pp. 289–306.

Balié, J. (2020). The trade-offs of healthy food from sustainable agriculture in the Global South. *Global Food Security*, 26, p. 100384.

Balié, J. and Valera, H. A. (2020). Domestic and international impacts of the rice trade policy reform in the Philippines. *Food Policy*, 92, p. 101876.

Bhandari, H. and Mishra, A. K. (2018). Impact of demographic transformation on future rice farming in Asia. *Outlook on Agriculture*, 47(2), pp. 135–132.

Francisco, S., Mataia, A., Eusebio, A., Sanguyo, E., Constantino, M., Causon, E., Quilloy, K. and Sombillia, M. (2013). Per capita rice consumption in the Philippines: reasons behind increases. *Crop Protection Newsletter*, 38, pp. 33–42.

Furuya, J. and Koyama, O. (2005). Impacts of climatic change on world agricultural product markets: estimation of macro yield functions. *JARQ*, 39, pp. 121–134.

Gaiha, R., Jha, R. and Kulkarni, V. S. (2013). How pervasive is eating out in India? *Journal of Asian and African Studies*, 48, pp. 370–386.

Hoang, H. K. and Meyers, W. H. (2015). Price stabilization and impacts of trade liberalization in the Southeast Asian rice market. *Food Policy*, 57, pp. 26–39.

Huang, J. and David, C. (1993). Demand for cereal grain in Asia: the effect of urbanization. *Economics*, 8, pp. 107–124.

Ladha J. K., Dawe, D., Pathak, H., Padre, A. T., Yadav, R. L., Singh, B., Singh, Y., Singh, Y., Singh, P., Kundu, A. L. *et al.* (2003). How extensive are yield declines in long-term rice–wheat experiments in Asia? *Field Crop Research*, 81, pp. 159–180.

Kinkingninhoun Medagbe, F. M., Komatsu, S., Mujawamariya, G. and Saito, K. (2020). Men and women in rice farming in Africa: a cross-country investigation of labor and its determinants. *Frontiers in Sustainable Food Systems*, 4, p. 117.

Meemken, E. M. and Bellemare, M. F. (2020). Smallholder farmers and contract farming in developing countries. *Proceedings of the National Academy of Sciences*, 117, pp. 259–264.

Mishra, A., Kumar, A., Joshi, P. K. and Dsouza, A. (2016). Impacts of contracts in high yielding varieties seed production on profits and yield: the case of Nepal. *Food Policy,* 62, pp. 110–121.

Mishra, A., Kumar, A., Joshi, P. K. and Dsouza, A. (2018a). Production risks, risk preference, and contract farming: Impact on food security in India. *Applied Economic Perspectives and Policy*, 40, pp. 353–378.

Mishra, A., Kumar, A., Joshi, P. K. and Dsouza, A. (2018b). Cooperatives, contract farming, and farm size: The case of tomato producers in Nepal. *Agribusiness: An International Journal*, 34(4), pp. 865–886.

Mishra, A., Kumar, A., Joshi, P. K. and Dsouza, A. (2018c). How can organic rice be a boon to smallholders? Evidence from contract farming in India. *Food Policy*, 75, pp. 147–157.

Mishra, A., Pede, V. O., Arouna, A., Labarta, R., Andrade, R., Veettil, P. C., Bhandari, H., Laborte, A. G., Balie, J. and Bouman, B. (2022). Helping feed the world with rice innovations: CGIAR research adoption and socioeconomic impact on farmers. *Global Food Security*, 33, p. 100628.

Mishra, A., Shaik, S., Khanal, A. R. and Bairagi, S. (2017). Contract farming and technical efficiency: evidence from low-value and high-value crops in Nepal. *Agribusiness: An International Journal,* 34, pp. 426–440.

Mottaleb, K. A. and Mishra, A. (2022). Income, urbanisation and consumption of processed foods: Implications for nutrition and health policies for India. *Journal of International Development*, 35(5), pp. 688–715.

Mottaleb, K. A., Rahut, D. B., Kruseman, G. and Erenstein, O. (2018). Evolving food consumption patterns of rural and urban households in developing countries. *British Food Journal*, 120, pp. 392–408.

Mottaleb, K. A., Rahut, D. B. and Mishra, A. (2017). Modeling rice grain-type preferences in Bangladesh. *British Food Journal*, 119, pp. 2049–2061.

Mottaleb, K. A. and Mishra, A. (2016). Rice consumption and grain-type preference by household: a Bangladesh case. *Journal of Agricultural and Applied Economics*, 48, pp. 298–319.

Otsuka, K., Nakano, Y. and Kazushi, T. (2016). Contract farming in developed and developing countries. *Annual Review of Resource Economics*, 8, pp. 353–376.

Pandey, S., Suphanchaimat, N. and Velasco, L. (2012). The patterns of spread and economics of a labor-saving innovation in rice production: the case of direct seeding in Northeast Thailand. *Quarterly Journal of International Agriculture*, 51, pp. 333–356.

Pingali, P. L. (2007). Westernization of Asian diets and the transformation of food systems: Implications for research and policy. *Food Policy*, 32, pp. 281–298.

Pingali, P. L., Hossain, M. and Gerpacio, R. V. (1997). *Asian Rice Bowls: The Returning Crisis*. CAB International.

Radel, C., Schmook, B., Mcevoy, J., Mendez, C. and Petrzelka, P. (2012). Labor migration and gendered agricultural relations: the feminization of agriculture in the Ejidal sector of Calakmul, Mexico. *Journal of Agrarian Change*, 12, pp. 98–119.

Redfern, S. K., Azzu, N. J. and Binamira, S. (2012). Rice in Southeast Asia: facing risks and vulnerabilities to respond to climate change. *Building Resilience for Adaptation to Climate Change in the Agriculture Sector, FAO/OECD Workshop Proceedings*, 23–24 April 2012, pp. 295–314. http://www.fao.org/docrep/017/i3084e/i3084e18.pdf

Srinivasan, P. V. and Jha, S. (2001). Liberalized trade and domestic price stability. The case of rice and wheat in India. *Journal of Development Economics*, 65, pp. 417–441.

Tanaka, T. and Hosoe, N. (2011). Does agricultural trade liberalization increase risks of supply-side uncertainty?: Effects of productivity shocks and export restrictions on welfare and food supply in Japan. *Food Policy*, 36, pp. 368–377.

Timsina, J., Wolf, J., Gulipart, N., van Bussel, L. G. J., Grassini, P., van Wart, J., Hossain, A., Rashid, H., Islam, S. and van Ittersum, M. K. (2016). Can Bangladesh produce enough cereals to meet future demand? *Systems*, 163, pp. 36–44.

Tripathi, S. C. and Das, A. (2017). Bed planting for resource conservation, diversification and sustainability of wheat based cropping system. *Journal of Wheat Research*, 9, pp. 1–11.

USDA Foreign Agricultural Service. (2021). Production and supply and distribution database. Accessed: September 15, 2021. https://apps.fas.usda.gov/psdonline/app/index.html#/app/advQuery

Yuan, S., Stuart, A. M., Laborte, A. G., *et al.* (2022). Southeast Asia must narrow down the yield gap to continue to be a major rice bowl. *Nature Food*, 3, pp. 217–226.

https://doi.org/10.1142/9789811278297_0006

Chapter 6

The Role of Vegetables in Asia's Food and Nutrition Security

Marco C. S. Wopereis[1], C. George Kuo[1], Delphine Larrousse[2], Maarten van Zonneveld[1] and Pepijn Schreinemachers[2]

[1]*World Vegetable Center, P.O. Box 42, Shanhua, Tainan 74199, Taiwan*
[2]*World Vegetable Center, P.O. Box 1010, Bangkok 10903, Thailand*

6.1 Introduction

There are an estimated 150 species of vegetables cultivated in Asia [Ma *et al.*, 2010]. Major vegetables (e.g., tomato, chili, pepper, onion, cabbage, and cucumber) and vegetables of sub-regional importance (e.g., pumpkin, bitter gourd, mung bean, vegetable soybean, okra, kangkong, and amaranth) are terrestrial herbaceous plants, whereas other vegetables include aquatic plants (e.g., water bamboo, water-cress, lotus), lower vascular plants (ferns), ocean algae (e.g., kelp, seaweed), and saprophytic fungi (mushrooms). Edible plant parts include sprouts, seedlings, leaves, petioles, heads, fronds, stems, pseudo-stems, non-starchy roots, rhizomes, corms, non-starchy tubers, bulbs, flowers, fruits, seeds, and fungal fruiting bodies that contain diverse types and different concentrations of beneficial compounds. This enormous diversity of vegetables in Asia is a great asset; it provides many opportunities to adapt to local growing conditions, adding colour, flavour, nutrients and health qualities to people's diets [Rubatzky and Yamaguchi, 1999].

Vegetables have tremendous nutritional value. They provide important sources of essential micronutrients (vitamins and minerals), plant-based proteins, edible fibres and antioxidants, all of which are vital to healthy development, disease prevention, and wellbeing. For instance, the antioxidant properties of phytochemicals inherent in various vegetables have protective functions against the oxidation of omega-3 oils, essential for good health [Cheng *et al.*, 2022]. An adequate vegetable intake therefore helps to protect against malnutrition in all its forms, as well as against chronic and non-communicable diseases. The World Health Organization (WHO) and the Food and Agriculture Organization (FAO) recommend a daily minimum fruit and vegetable (F&V) intake of five portions or 400 g per adult per day, including at least three portions of vegetables (~240 g) [WHO/FAO, 2003]. The EAT-Lancet Commission on Healthy Diets from Sustainable Food Systems and the Global Burden of Disease study [Afshin *et al.*, 2019] even recommended daily mean F&V intakes of 300 g and 360 g, respectively.

Globally, dietary risks are among the top five global health risk factors, with over 3.5 million deaths and 99 million Disability-Adjusted Life Years (DALYs). Each DALY represents the loss of the equivalent of one year of full health attributable to poor quality diet [Afshin *et al.*, 2019]. However, the reality is that three billion people on our planet are unable to afford a healthy diet. More than half of them (1.9 billion people) live in Asia — the majority in South Asia (1.3 billion people, 57% of the South Asia population), followed by

Southeast Asia (0.32 billion, 46% of the Southeast Asia population) and East Asia (0.23 billion, 16% of the East Asia population). This is strongly related to the cost of food with dairy, F&V and protein-rich foods accounting for more than 79% of the cost of diets across Asia [FAO *et al.*, 2021].

Asia's population is affected by multiple forms of malnutrition — hunger, hidden hunger (lack of micronutrients), overweight and obesity. Half of the world's undernourished people are living in the Asia and Pacific region (about 351 million people): South Asia accounts for the largest number (257 million), followed by Southeast Asia (65 million), while the numbers in East Asia are very small [FAO *et al.*, 2021]. These numbers have fallen rapidly since the 1990s and the burden of hidden hunger, measured in DALYs, has surpassed that of chronic hunger across Asia. South Asia has the highest burden of hidden hunger of all regions in the world [Lenaerts and Demont, 2021]. For example, 56 million children under five years of age affected by stunting (one dimension of hidden hunger) are living in South Asia [FAO *et al.*, 2021].

Because of the rapidly increasing consumption of highly processed food, salt, sugar and sugar-sweetened drinks, malnutrition has increased in all Asian countries over the last 20 years. Overweight and obesity now affect between 20% and 55% of adult populations in Asia. This has become an enormous public health issue. Diabetes alone is associated with US$321 billion of economic loss in East Asia and the Pacific in 2015 and is projected to reach US$800 billion by 2030. Comparative figures in South Asia are US$26 billion, projected to reach US$84 billion by 2030 [Bommer *et al.*, 2018].

Besides their importance for healthy lives, vegetables are also important to raise the living standards and resilience of smallholder farmers and other actors along the vegetable value chain. Vegetables can be grown on small spaces and profits per hectare are 3–14 times higher in vegetable production than in rice production [Schreinemachers *et al.*, 2018]. However, Asia's agriculture remains strongly rice-based (and based on wheat in parts of South Asia). While rice production is key to national food security, most rice farmers have remained poor and food insecure as productivity growth has been accompanied by price declines benefiting consumers rather than producers [Timmer, 2009]. Given that vegetables can be grown on relatively small areas of land and are labour intensive, opportunities for jobs and income generation are important considerations in particular in low- and middle-income countries.

The objective of this chapter is to: (i) describe the diverse and colourful world of vegetables in terms of varieties, production systems and diets in Asia and the drivers of change; (ii) analyse how to reduce the vegetable dietary gap across Asia, enabling healthier lives, with maximum benefits to people's livelihoods and with minimal environmental footprint; (iii) highlight enablers and constraints related to the policy- and decision-making environment; and (iv) reflect on future prospects related to the role of vegetables to boost food and nutrition security in Asia. While the chapter focuses on vegetables, many of the issues equally apply to fruit.

6.2 Status of Vegetables in Asia

6.2.1 *Production*

The total value of vegetables produced worldwide, measured at farmgate prices, was 568 billion US dollars in 2020 according to FAO estimates [FAOSTAT, 2022]. Asia accounted for 78% of this value (Figure 6.1), or a total of 441 billion US dollars from a harvested

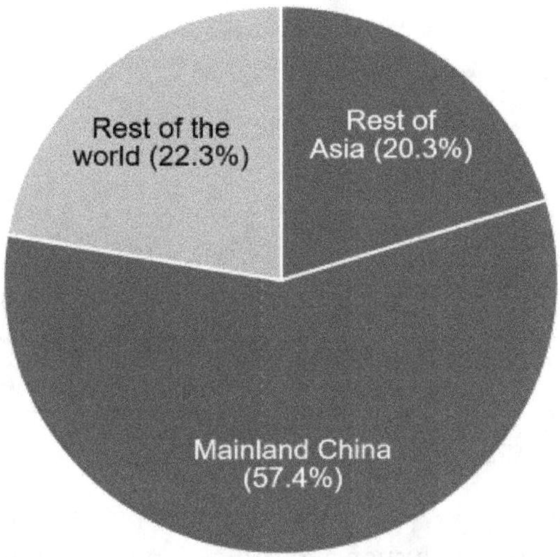

Figure 6.1 Share of Asia in global vegetable production. Note: Based on gross production value (current thousand US$) for 2020. Vegetables in FAOSTAT include melons and mushrooms. Source: FAOSTAT [2022].

area of 19.5 million hectares and a production volume of 332.3 million tons. However, mainland China dominates production in Asia as well as globally. Mainland China accounted for 57.4% of global vegetable production by value, 37.3% by area, and 45.5% by volume, although the country only accounts for 20.0% of global population.

The rise of China's vegetable production, as documented by FAO data, has been phenomenal (Figure 6.2a). China's vegetable production expanded at a mean growth rate of 5.7% per annum over the period 1990–2020, while this was 2.8% for the rest of Asia, and 1.5% for the rest of the world. Factoring in population growth (Figure 6.2b), China's growth in vegetable production remains impressive while there is hardly any increase for the rest of Asia or the world. While China exports vegetables to other countries in Asia, FAO Food Balance data suggest that only about 2% is exported.

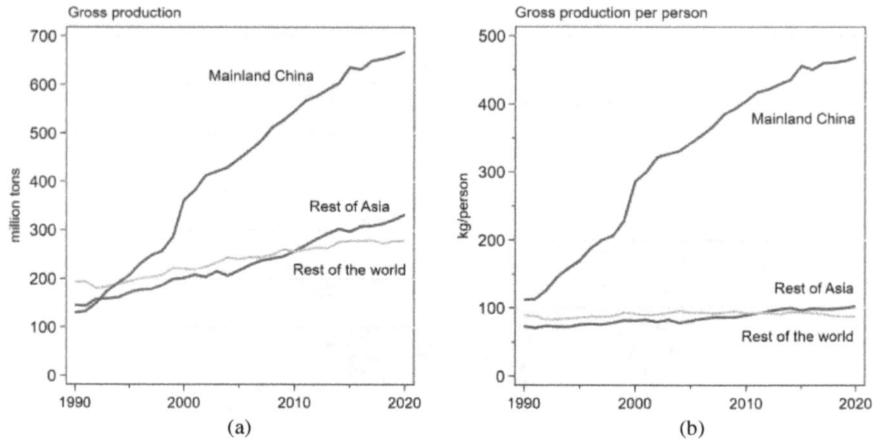

Figure 6.2 The role of Asia in global vegetable production by volume from 1990–2020: (a) gross production and (b) gross production per person. Note: Based on production volume (tons). Vegetables in FAOSTAT include melons and mushrooms. Source: FAOSTAT [2022].

6.2.2 *Diversity in Varieties*

Asia has an incredible range of vegetable species and varieties grown in diverse production systems and climates, resulting in a vast diversity of local dishes. Asia is an extremely rich source of vegetable origin and diversity. Central Asia and West Asia are the centres of origin for carrot, garlic, onion, peas, broad bean, and spinach; East and Southeast Asia for Asian types of amaranth, bamboo shoot, various subspecies of *Brassica rapa* (Chinese cabbage), kangkong, radish and vegetable soybean; and South Asia for bitter gourd, cucumber, eggplant, Malabar spinach, sponge gourd, wax gourd, and yard-long bean [Siemonsma and Piluek, 1993]. However, some of the most widely grown vegetables in Asia find their origin in other regions of the world, such as green bean, pepper, tomato, okra, pumpkin, and various sub-species of cabbages (*B. oleracea*).

Vegetables are an attractive food group for farmers to diversify food production systems at farm and landscape level to make food supply more climate resilient and nutritious because they require little space, have short rotations, and offer high-value products [van Zonneveld *et al.*, 2020]. However, little research has been carried out on climate stress tolerance in vegetable species compared with species from other food groups such as grain legumes, cereals, and fruit trees [van Zonneveld *et al.*, 2020]. A meta-analysis of experimental studies calculated a one-third yield reduction in vegetable crops if water availability dropped by 50% or if temperature increased by 4°C, while the combined effects of heat and water scarcity likely lead to even more severe reductions in vegetable yield [Scheelbeek *et al.*, 2018]. At the same time, preliminary results from environmental niche modelling show that many commercial and traditional vegetables have been grown in a wide range of environments; this diversity provides a wealth of vegetable crop choices for tailored adaptation of local food production to changing climates [van Zonneveld *et al.*, 2023]. This diversity can be further evaluated in different environments to better understand the agronomic and physiological responses of vegetable crops to different climate stresses [van Zonneveld *et al.*, 2020]. These evaluations allow selection of crops that are best-bet options for diversification and to identify germplasm that is promising for development of more climate-resilient varieties [van Zonneveld *et al.*, 2023].

The World Vegetable Center (WorldVeg) holds the largest international and public collection of vegetable germplasm in its gene bank in Taiwan. Of its total collection of close to 65,000 accessions (November 2022), 37,092 accessions come from Asia, covering 280 species, and representing 38 countries. Of these, 9,023 accessions of 226 species representing 16 countries were collected directly by WorldVeg and partners in these countries. Many of these may no longer be found in their places of origin. Vegetable biodiversity in Asia is rapidly declining in farmers' fields and natural ecosystems [Pilling *et al.*, 2020; Schunko *et al.*, 2022] while it is poorly conserved *ex situ* and therefore at risk of being lost [van Zonneveld *et al.*, 2021]. The decline is a result of multiple factors, which include overexploitation of local food plants, natural and diversified farm land being taken out of production because of urbanisation and industrialisation, and a gradual homogenisation of consumer preferences and diets leading to reduced emphasis on a diversity of vegetable crops [Pingali, 2007; Khoury *et al.*, 2022; Schunko *et al.*, 2022], although this is not seen in all Asian countries (see below). In specific countries and in local societal settings, people continue to eat a diverse set of vegetables [e.g., Xu *et al.*, 2004; Sthapit *et al.*, 2008].

This reduction in diversity is narrowing the range of options to select new vegetable crops or breed new varieties providing resilience to climate change (e.g., tolerance to heat, resistance to pests and diseases, enhanced shelf life) or providing better health and nutrition benefits for different segments of the Asian population. This is a major concern that requires concerted action at country and regional levels to rescue, safeguard and use vegetable biodiversity, either directly or in breeding programs.

Many farmers in Asia nowadays buy vegetable seed supplied by seed companies, in particular improved varieties of global vegetables. For instance, it is estimated that in India, F_1 hybrids now occupy about 70% of the vegetable market by value [Schreinemachers *et al.*, 2021]. Asia has a large number of seed companies. The Asia and Pacific Seed Association is the largest association of private seed companies in the world with over 500 members. Vegetable seed is the most important business for most of these companies.

With climate change, heat tolerance and resistance to increasing and newly emerging pest and disease pressure are becoming increasingly important. WorldVeg monitoring data show that its vegetable collection is used as a source for climate resilience by at least 43 seed companies, members of the WorldVeg-Asia & Pacific Seed Association consortium [Schreinemachers and Lin, 2022]. Informal seed systems, such as farmer-to-farmer exchange, are also important in particular for more traditional Asian varieties and their complementarity to formal vegetable seed systems needs further study.

6.2.3 *Diversity in Systems*

Commercial vegetable production systems in Asia range from rainfed open-field cultivation to plant factories, resulting in vastly different performance in terms of productivity, product quality, length of growing season and environmental footprint. Vegetable production in Asia is mostly from open-field production; however, there are enormous differences between countries. Open-field production in tropical Asia is often subject to climate variability and change of temperature, storms, heavy rainfall, flooding, drought, etc., that impact vegetable growth and development and increase biotic stresses such as diseases and pests on the vegetable value chain. To overcome these stresses, protected cultivation such as greenhouses is often used for growing vegetables.

Taking tomato as a proxy, compared to open-field production, high-tech greenhouses resulted in 6.4 times more yield per unit area [Maureira *et al.*, 2022]. Scarcity of water and land and abundant capital drives a country like Singapore towards vertical farming and plant factories. For a country like India, capital is most limiting, therefore expansion of vegetable production will have to come from field-based production, with the exception of production in urban areas — where vertical farming and plant factories are taking off.

Asia has approximately 0.2 million hectares of greenhouses, based on international greenhouse vegetable production figures in 2018 [Hickman, 2019]. Nearly half of the world's greenhouse vegetable areas are located in Asia; most of these can be found in China, Japan, South Korea and Taiwan. Singapore plans to expand vegetable production through indoor farms and rooftop gardening, using hydroponics and aeroponics cultivation techniques [Klein-Hessling and Zimmermann-Loessl, 2021].

Plant factories are also increasingly common, currently focusing mostly on leafy vegetables such as lettuce, spinach and other leafy greens. Efforts are being made to popularise the commercial production of head vegetables with plant factories [Kozai *et al.*, 2022]. These factories may gain in prominence if they could focus on health-promoting vegetable crops, or crops produced for a specific nutrition or health product.

The environmental footprint of vegetable production is a major concern, even for open-field systems. Commercial vegetable production is associated with the intensive use of mineral fertilisers and pesticides. For greenhouse production, the construction itself, the media used to grow vegetables, climate control (cooling or heating) and artificial lighting all contribute to greenhouse gas emissions. Agricultural plastics are widely used in horticulture, often for one-time use (e.g., for mulching), and may lead to the accumulation of microplastics in soil and water resources, creating a food hazard [Conti *et al.*, 2020].

Life cycle analysis comparing environmental footprint for vegetables, from the production of inputs all the way to the consumer in Asia, are rare. Evidence from Australia for tomatoes showed that carbon and water footprint varied considerably depending on the season and the type of production system used. In the case of field-grown tomatoes, transportation to the market contributed most to the carbon footprint, while for greenhouses it was artificial heating [Page *et al.*, 2012]. A study by Li *et al.* [2022] showed that 27% of greenhouse gas emissions from total freight miles are related to food miles. F&V (transported at high tonnage and requiring temperature control) contribute more than a third of global food-mile emissions. For nearly all regions, emissions related to food miles of F&V were greater from domestic than international transport.

In many parts of Asia, poor road conditions, lack of refrigerated transport, poorly designed market infrastructure (often without cold storage facilities) and large distances between farmers, processors and consumers lead to high losses. Postharvest losses in the vegetable sector are typically large, ranging from 30–50% of farm production [FAO, 2011]. Market gluts may also cause farmers to be unable to sell their produce.

Because of rapid urbanisation, consumer behaviour in Asia is shifting towards convenience food. These trends create opportunities for farmers and other actors in the value chain to supply urban markets and add value through processing and target higher-value market segments, e.g., plant-based substitutes for animal-sourced products. This may also lead to reduced losses. Cutting back on losses and waste and reducing the distance between producers and consumers will also bring down the environmental footprint, as is the use of renewable energy for storage and processing. Processing, and more durable packaging and greater usage of coproducts, can reduce food losses and waste. Wastage of processed F&V is 14% lower than that of fresh F&V [Poore and Nemecek, 2019].

A substantial quantity of vegetables comes from home gardens or is collected from the wild. The quantities can be very substantial in some countries but are usually not reflected in official data.

The home garden production of vegetables makes a tremendous yet undervalued contribution to food and nutrition security. Evidence is strong that the promotion of home gardens through training in gardening and nutrition increases household production and consumption of vegetables [Schreinemachers *et al.*, 2020; Baliki *et al.*, 2022; Depenbusch *et al.*, 2022]. The COVID-19 pandemic has raised the interest in this type of cultivation, not just for consumption but also because gardening can contribute to relieving stress in people's busy lives.

Although some efforts are made by Asian governments, more needs to be done to promote greater diversity of production systems, using environmentally safe and sustainable practices. More diversified systems can improve soil health, reduce environmental footprint, while increasing the availability of vegetables. They also contribute to increased economic opportunities and have a great potential to enhance resilience against climate change and different types of shocks.

6.2.4 *Diversity in Diets*

Many Asian dishes traditionally contain a wide variety of vegetables. Preparation methods of vegetables vary depending on the local cuisine. They can enhance or reduce the nutrition quality of vegetables eaten [Fabbri and Crosby, 2016]. While some Asian cultures eat fresh vegetables as salads, the vast majority of vegetables are cooked. Cooking methods include cooking and blending as a puree, blanching in boiling water or steam, stir-frying with oil or water, battering and deep-frying, sautéing, roasting, broiling, boiling as a soup, etc. Many vegetables are also processed — e.g., pickled, fermented or dried — to transform perishable produce into stable foods with long shelf lives.

Unhealthy diets lacking fruits, vegetables and other nutrient-rich foods are among the major drivers of illness and death globally, underpinning 11 million deaths worldwide each year [Afshin *et al.*, 2019]. Low vegetable consumption is a global problem affecting high- and low-income countries: only 5% of people in low-income countries meet WHO F&V recommendations of 400 g per person per day, and only 27% of people in upper-middle-income countries do [Frank *et al.*, 2019].

As incomes rise in Asia, the consumption of meat and ultra-processed food often takes precedence over nutritious foods like vegetables. The expanding market share of large international food companies producing ultra-processed foods and beverages and their aggressive marketing and sales strategies are a key driver of the nutrition transition away from traditional diets. There are also food safety concerns related to pesticide residues that dissuade consumers from buying fresh vegetables [e.g., Ha *et al.*, 2020]. However, with rapid urbanisation in Asia, a growing middle class is also becoming more demanding in terms of quality food, which opens up, in principle, economic opportunities for vegetable value chain actors, from seed companies, farmers, to processors and retailers.

6.3 Boosting Vegetable Supply and Intake

Consumption patterns, climates and socio-economic settings in Asia differ greatly and this has important consequences for pathways to closing dietary gaps. Diets are moving away from vegetables and towards highly processed unhealthy food. In many urban areas in Asia, quality and healthy fresh food items are not easily accessible or affordable to all.

6.3.1 *Boosting Supply*

Asia's population is projected to grow from 4.72 billion in 2022 to 5.29 billion in 2050, with the share of the urban population growing from 52% in 2022 to 66% in 2050.[1] Mason-D'Croz *et al.* [2019] estimated dietary gaps in F&V consumption between 1965 and 2015 for 150 countries by comparing the minimum F&V intake recommended by WHO of 400 g per capita per day and F&V availability based on FAOSTAT commodity balance sheets[2] and the IMPACT simulation model developed by the International Food Policy Research Institute. Only five countries (out of 22) in the East Asia and Pacific region had greater F&V availability than 400 g per person per day in 1965. This increased to 12 (out of 23) by 2015, representing 1.9 billion people (out of 2.2 billion, so 86%), for which F&V are available in their countries, although not necessarily accessible and affordable. The situation was very different for South Asia. None of the South Asian countries in 1965 had sufficient F&V availability with respect to the 400 g target — and although average F&V intake levels increased substantially to an average of 326 g per person per day, the situation was the same in 2015, representing 1.7 billion people with insufficient F&V availability. There are, therefore, huge differences in terms of dietary gaps when it comes to F&V across Asia, with East Asian countries generally best positioned. Because the majority of Asia's population growth towards 2050 will occur in South Asia, this trend will be amplified in the future. These results underline the need for policies and incentives

---

[1] https://ourworldindata.org/ accessed on 13 July 2022.

[2] FAO commodity balance sheets do not include waste from retail to consumer and neglect F&V not commonly traded or grown for home consumption. They also do not account for intra-country variation and production levels of F&V are highly aggregated.

adapted to local contexts that enhance F&V availability, accessibility and affordability, by enhancing year-round production and reducing losses and waste.

In higher-income countries, vegetables are mostly produced in high-input field systems, often protected with insect-proof nets and/or plastic roofing and use of plastic mulch, or produced in polyhouses or greenhouses near cities. Because yield levels are generally high, boosting local production can be achieved through area expansion, either vertically in urban areas or horizontally in peri-urban and rural areas. In high-input field-based systems, the environmental footprint is often of great concern. Agroecological approaches, such as the introduction of biocontrol measures, cover crops, crop rotations and strip cropping (two or more crops grown side by side in narrow strips), increase diversity, enhance soil and plant health, and can lead to reduced reliance on chemical pesticides and fertilisers. Introduction of traditional Asian vegetables that are generally more robust and nutritious than global vegetables may further cut back on the need to use external inputs.

In lower-income countries, vegetable yield levels are often far below what would be possible under optimal management conditions. Here, vegetable production can be enhanced by introducing improved varieties, or sturdy traditional Asian vegetables, which are better adapted to local growing and market conditions, and introducing improved management practices, thereby increasing yields per m^2 surface area per day, and/or lengthening the growing season. A study for Bangladesh showed that training farmers in off-season vegetable production increased their seasonal income by 48% [Schreinemachers *et al.*, 2016]. Ideally, agroecological approaches should be combined with judicious use of external inputs. There are major opportunities for producing vegetables in the off-season or replacing lower-value crops such as cereals with higher-value vegetables. This will often require introducing protected cultivation measures that reduce risk to the farmer and allow them to intensify and/or diversify production in space and time. It will also require improvements in market functioning and postharvest practices. The best approach will be very context specific. Protecting crops with polyethylene film and insect-proof nets reduce incoming radiation by about 20% and increase air temperature by 4% and 10% respectively [Nordey *et al.*, 2017]. This may open up opportunities to cultivate vegetables in colder climates or growing seasons, but may require varieties that are more tolerant to heat stress. Climate change may also require farmers to adopt heat-tolerant and pest- and disease-resistant varieties or different vegetable crops altogether.

Across Asia, reducing losses and waste from field to fork will have a major positive effect on availability. Moreover, having significant losses and waste of food mean that all efforts to produce vegetables are in vain. This represents an unnecessary burden to the environment, and a loss of nutritious food and economic opportunities.

Food safety is a major concern for Asian consumers and is mostly related to fear of pesticide residues [e.g., Ha *et al.*, 2020; Wertheim-Heck *et al.*, 2014 for Vietnam]. Overuse of pesticides in vegetable production is common in Asia [Schreinemachers *et al.*, 2017], leading to health risks for farmers, consumers and the environment. However, microbial contamination is another and often greater threat that becomes more prominent moving from the field to storage, wholesale and retail markets. Vegetables produced in urban contexts may also be contaminated with heavy metals, particularly if fields are close to roads or factories. It is critical that vegetables can be traced along the supply chain back to the producer to instil trust in local consumers for local produce. The shorter the supply chain and the distance between producer and consumer, the easier this will be.

6.3.2 *Stimulating Intake*

Focusing solely on increasing the availability of vegetables would not be a wise strategy, given that current dietary trends show little to no increase in vegetable consumption despite income growth, while the consumption of ultra-processed food is increasing rapidly — associated with a range of health risks such as type 2 diabetes, heart disease, and cancer. In general, much work will need to be done in Asia to stimulate the intake of vegetables as a strategy to fight malnutrition. Overweight and obesity affect both urban and rural populations.

While marketing campaigns can influence consumer behaviour, there is little evidence that large-scale marketing of vegetables is effective to create long-term changes in food behaviour. Besides, investments in the marketing of ultra-processed foods with high profit margins would always dwarf public investments in healthy eating campaigns. While nutrition literacy is important to stimulate healthy eating, it will need to be combined with restrictions on how ultra-processed food is marketed.

Key challenges are to make vegetables more affordable (cheaper without compromising on quality), more widely accessible, and more acceptable and desirable. Food safety concerns (related to microbial contamination and pesticide residues) need to be addressed. Healthy vegetable preferences in children can be developed through taste exposure, sensory learning, food preparation, and nutrition education. WorldVeg and other organisations have shown that home and school gardens are one effective approach to accomplish this. A study in Nepal showed that children's vegetable intake increased after setting up vegetable gardens in schools and training both children and their parents in gardening and nutrition [Schreinemachers *et al.*, 2020]. Training rural, low-income people in gardening has also shown to be effective in various countries such as Bangladesh, Cambodia, and India.

More innovations are needed in food environments so that these enable healthier eating. This may involve stimulating procurement of F&V for schools, canteens, hospitals, and prisons; price subsidies for F&V; or zoning and market regulations, e.g., banning sale of unhealthy food items in a radius of 500 m around schools. Another possibility is to bring vegetables closer to consumers, e.g., by designing new retail options, such as door-to-door delivery, mobile vendors, etc. One can also think of more prominent places for F&V in shops and canteens. It is critical to create and promote more attractive ways to present and prepare vegetables to increase desirability and stimulate demand.

6.3.3 *Enabling Policy*

Food systems policy decisions shape how vegetables are available, accessible, desirable and affordable over time. Policies in Asia related to vegetables are mostly geared towards facilitating export and generating income. Governments need to be encouraged to design national F&V strategies that focus on the health of local consumers and livelihoods of small-scale farmers rather than export earnings. In Thailand, the government is increasingly interested in food systems approaches to healthy diets, evidenced by multiple events and commitments around the 2021 United Nations Food Systems Summit and national dialogues organised by the Ministry of Agriculture and Cooperatives. This included a debate on the need for Thailand to adopt a sustainable vegetable policy.[3]

Thailand is also one of the few Asian countries that introduced a tax on sugar-sweetened beverages in 2019. Yet what is often lacking is evidence through which policy actors can decide on appropriate changes to support vegetable food systems towards healthy diets. It is critical to fill that evidence gap and accompany governments in the development and implementation of concrete action plans. Another priority is to boost investments in vegetable research and development (R&D) to stimulate supply of and demand for safe, locally produced vegetables. For both national and international research, the fraction allocated to vegetables and other nutritious foods like fruits, nuts and pulses is extremely low [Schreinemachers *et al.*, 2018]. There is an urgent need to shift the focus of food policies and research investments from 'calories' to 'diet quality'.

To nourish Asia's growing urban population with safe, locally produced vegetables, there will be a need for innovative policies and incentives to protect peri-urban agricultural land as a vital resource for vegetable production that are free of contaminants from urban waste. The city of Beijing (China), as part of its Urban Master Plan, preserves farmland and green spaces and has designated permanent green areas in city fringes and corridors [Dubbeling *et al.*, 2019]. Singapore actively promotes high-tech indoor farming next to leasing out plots of land across the city to encourage people to grow food [Bettinazzi, 2022].

Investments are also needed in wholesale and retail market infrastructure to ensure vegetables can be cleaned, sorted and

[3] https://summitdialogues.org/dialogue/15703/

stored safely with renewable energy, as well as applications of new technologies to improve traceability of vegetables for food safety. To boost the availability and affordability of vegetables, policies are needed that promote investments in off-season horticulture, aggregation, processing and storage facilities as much as possible using durable and recyclable materials and green energy sources.

Much more attention is also needed for traditional Asian vegetables, getting them on the policy agenda, on the R&D agenda, on the farm, and ultimately on the plate. Breeding efforts also need to expand for controlled environment conditions to enhance the diversity of vegetables produced through indoor farming.

6.4 Conclusions

Vegetable production in Asia will need to increase substantially to close dietary intake gaps and cater for population growth. There is a tremendous need for innovation and targeted action at multiple levels. This requires addressing the huge research funding disparity at national and international levels that still focuses largely on the big staples and not on nutritious food, and to redirect agricultural subsidies towards healthy food systems.

Transforming food systems towards a healthier and more sustainable diet requires partnerships among international development organisations, international agricultural research centres like WorldVeg, governments, the private sector, national agricultural research systems and the civil society to encourage and support innovation, infrastructure development and extension services. These partnerships involve coordination and leveraging private- and public-sector resources towards strengthening the vegetable sector and shortening the time to impact from R&D.

Current production systems carry a heavy environmental footprint and are the cause of food safety issues. Vegetable producers in Asia must be enticed to embrace greener and safer ways of production and investments in market and transport logistics, and infrastructure must be made to cut back on losses and waste, and consciously reduce the carbon footprint of vegetable supply chains. Vegetable waste can be valorised, e.g., by conversion into biofertiliser, animal feed, bioenergy fuels, chemicals and compounds of high value, and for use in soft drinks.

Vegetables are valuable in monetary terms. However, beyond their economic value, these foods are not sufficiently prioritised in people's diets. There is a need to better understand consumers' preferences and behaviours with respect to vegetables and what incentives might increase consumption in different contexts. Governments can make a start to value vegetables more as part of a healthy diet, rather than just focusing on economic value and exports. National horticultural policies and strategies must focus on domestic consumption, and ideally such policies should link with public health policy. Much more attention is also needed for traditional Asian vegetables.

The health and economic burden of unhealthy diets is enormous. The consumption of ultra-processed foods is likely to rise in many countries in Asia and, with it, the burden of many non-communicable diseases. While there is a big need to substantially increase the quantity of vegetables consumed, it will be challenging to even maintain current quantities in some countries. Success in this area will partly depend on governments' ability to restrain the growth in ultra-processed foods.

Last but not least, there is an urgent need to stem the rapid decline in vegetable biodiversity, because much valuable material that current and future generations will need is being lost forever.

This diversity must be rescued, conserved and put to good use to transition to healthier lives and a healthier planet.

Acknowledgements

The authors wish to acknowledge long-term strategic funders to the World Vegetable Center: Taiwan, UK aid from the UK government, United States Agency for International Development (USAID), Australian Centre for International Agricultural Research (ACIAR), Germany, Thailand, Philippines, Korea, and Japan.

References

Afshin, A., Sur, P. J., Fay, K. A., ..., and Murray, C. J. L. (2019). Health effects of dietary risks in 195 countries, 1990–2017: A systematic analysis for the global burden of disease study 2017. *Lancet*, 393, pp. 1958–1972.

Baliki, G., Schreinemachers, P., Brück, T. and Uddin, N. M. (2022). Impacts of a home garden intervention in Bangladesh after one, three and six years. *Agriculture & Food Security,* 11, p. 48.

Bettinazzi, G. (2022). Farming takes Singapore by storm. *Fair Planet.* https://www.fairplanet.org/story/passion-for-urban-farming-takes-singapore-by-storm/

Bommer, C., Sagalova, V., Heesemann , E., Manne-Goehler, J., Atun, R., Bärnighausen , T. Davies , J. and Vollmer, S. (2018). Global economic burden of diabetes in adults: Projections from 2015 to 2030. *Diabetes Care,* 41, pp. 963–970.

Cheng, L. J., Sanguansri, L., Hlaing, M. M., Singh, T., Shreshta, P. and Augustin, M. A. (2022). Use of vegetables for enhancing oxidative stability of omega-3 oils in the powdered state. *Food Chem.*, 370, p. 131340.

Conti, G. O., Ferrantea, M., Bannib, M., Favara, C., Nicolosi, I., Cristaldi, A., Fiore, M. and Zuccarello, P. (2020). Micro- and nano-plastics in edible fruit and vegetables. The first diet risks assessment for the general population. *Environmental Research,* 187, p. 109677.

Depenbusch, L., Schreinemachers, P., Brown, S. and Roothaert, R. (2022). Impact and distributional effects of a home garden and nutrition intervention in Cambodia. *Food Security,* 14, pp. 865–881.

Dubbeling, M., van Veenhuizen, R. and Halliday, J. (2019). Urban agriculture as a climate change and disaster risk reduction strategy. *Field Actions Science Reports*, 20, pp. 32–39.

Fabbri, A. D. T. and Crosby, G. A. (2016). A review of the impact of preparation and cooking on the nutritional quality of vegetables and legumes. *International Journal of Gastronomy and Food Science,* 3, pp. 2–11.

FAO. (2011). *Global Losses and Food Waste — Extent, Causes and Prevention.* https://www.fao.org/3/i2697e/i2697e.pdf

FAO, UNICEF, WFP and WHO. (2021). *Asia and the Pacific Regional Overview of Food Security and Nutrition, 2020: Maternal and Child Diets at the Heart of Improving Nutrition.* https://doi.org/10.4060/cb2895en

FAOSTAT. (2022). Food and agriculture data. http://www.fao.org/faostat/ (accessed 12 December 2022).

Frank, S. M., Webster, J., McKenzie B, ..., and Jaacks, L. M. (2019). Consumption of fruits and vegetables among individuals 15 years and older in 28 low- and middle-income countries. *Journal of Nutrition*, 149, pp. 1252–1259.

Ha, T. M., Shakur, S. and Pham Do, K. H. (2020). Risk perception and its impact on vegetable consumption: A case study from Hanoi, Vietnam. *Journal of Cleaner Production,* 271, p. 122793.

Hickman, G. W. (2019). *International Greenhouse Vegetable Production — Statistics.* Cuesta Roble Greenhouse Vegetable Consulting.

Khoury, C. K., Brush, S., Costich, D. E., ..., and Thormann, I. (2022). Crop genetic erosion: Understanding and responding to loss of crop diversity. *New Phytologist,* 233, pp. 84–118.

Klein-Hessling, H. and Zimmermann-Loessl, C. (2021). A little history on the most recent evolution of vertical, urban farming in Singapore. https://vertical-farming.net/blog/2021/03/11/a-little-history-on-the-most-recent-evolution-of-vertical-urban-farming-in-singapore

Kozai, T., Amagai, Y., Lu, N., ..., and Maruo, T. (2022). Chapter 23-Toward Commercial Production of Head Vegetables in Plant Factories with Artificial Lighting. In T. Kozai, G. Niu and J. Masabni (Eds.), *Plant Factory Basics, Applications, and Advances*, pp. 417–434. Elsevier.

Lenaerts, B. and Demont, M. (2021). The global burden of chronic and hidden hunger revisited: new panel data evidence spanning 1990–2017. *Global Food Security*, 28, p. 100480.

Li, M., Jia, N., Lenzen, M., ..., and Raubenheimer, D. (2022). Global food-miles account for nearly 20% of total food-systems emissions. *Nature Food,* 3, pp. 445–453.

Ma, D., Ma, Y., Ma, C., ..., and Yan, W. (2010). *Cultivation of Vegetables in China* (in Chinese). China Agricultural Press Co., Ltd.

Mason-D'Croz, D., Bogard, J. R., Sulser, T. B., ..., and Wiebe, K. (2019). Gaps between fruit and vegetable production, demand, and recommended consumption at global and national levels: an integrated modelling study. *Lancet Planet Health,* 3, pp. e318–329.

Maureira, F., Rajagopalan, K. and Stöckle, C. O. (2022). Evaluating tomato production in open-field and high-tech greenhouse systems. *Journal of Cleaner Production,* 337, p. 130459.

Nordey, T., Basset-Mens, C., De Bon, H., ..., and Malézieux, E. (2017). Protected cultivation of vegetable crops in sub-Saharan Africa: limits and prospects for smallholders. A review. *Agronomy for Sustainable Development,* 37, p. 53.

Page, G., Ridoutt, B. and Bellotti, B. (2012). Carbon and water footprint tradeoffs in fresh tomato production. *Journal of Cleaner Production,* 32, pp. 219–226.

Pilling, D., Bélanger, J. and Hoffmann, I. (2020). Declining biodiversity for food and agriculture needs urgent global action. *Nature Food,* 1, pp. 144–147.

Pingali, P. (2007). Westernization of Asian diets and the transformation of food systems: Implications for research and policy. *Food Policy,* 32, pp. 281–298.

Poore, J. and Nemecek, T. (2019). Reducing food's environmental impacts through producers and consumers. *Science,* 360, pp. 987–992.

Rubatzky, V. E. and Yamaguchi, M. (1999). *World Vegetables: Principles, Production and Nutritive Values*. Aspen Publishing, Inc.

Scheelbeek, P. F., Bird, F. A., Tuomisto, H. L., …, and Dangour, A. D. (2018). Effect of environmental changes on vegetable and legume yields and nutritional quality. *Proceedings of the National Academy of Sciences,* 115, pp. 6804–6809.

Schreinemachers, P., Wu, M.-H., Uddin, M. N., Ahmad, S. and Hanson, P. (2016). Farmer training in off-season vegetables: Effects on income and pesticide use in Bangladesh. *Food Policy,* 61, pp. 132–40.

Schreinemachers, P., Chen, H.-P., Loc, N. T. T., ..., and Srinivasan, R. (2017). Too much to handle? Pesticide dependence of smallholder vegetable farmers in Southeast Asia. *Science of the Total Environment,* 593–594, pp. 470–477.

Schreinemachers, P., Simmons, E. B. and Wopereis, M. C. S. (2018). Tapping the economic and nutritional power of vegetables. *Global Food Security,* 16, pp. 36–45.

Schreinemachers, P., Baliki, G., Shrestha, R. M., …, and Brück, T. (2020). Nudging children toward healthier food choices: An experiment combining school and home gardens. *Global Food Security,* 26, p. 100454.

Schreinemachers, P., Howard, J., Turner, …, and Wopereis, M. C. S. (2021). Africa's evolving vegetable seed sector: status, policy options and lessons from Asia. *Food Security,* 13, pp. 511–523.

Schreinemachers, P. and Lin, M. (2022). *Use of World Vegetable Center breeding lines among seed companies in Asia in 2021*. WorldVeg Staff Publication Pub. No. 22-1042. World Vegetable Center.

Schunko, C., Li, X., Klappoth, B., …, and Reyes-García, V. (2022). Local communities' perceptions of wild edible plant and mushroom change: A systematic review. *Global Food Security,* 32, p. 100601.

Siemonsma, J. S. and Piluek, K. (Eds.) (1993). *Plant Resources of South-East Asia. No. 8. Vegetables*. Pudoc Scientific Publishers.

Sthapit, B., Rana, R., Eyzaguirre, P. and Jarvis, D. (2008). The value of plant genetic diversity to resource-poor farmers in Nepal and Vietnam. *International Journal of Agricultural Sustainability,* 6, pp. 148–166.

Timmer, C. P. (2009). *Rice price formation in the short run and long run: The role of market structure in explaining volatility*. Working Paper 172. Center for Global Development.

van Zonneveld, M., Turmel, M.-S. and Hellin, J. (2020). Decision-making to diversify farm systems for climate change adaptation. *Frontiers in Sustainable Food Systems,* 4, p. 32.

van Zonneveld, M., Volk, G. M., Dulloo, M. E., …, and Guarino, L. (2021). *Safeguarding and Using Fruit and Vegetable Biodiversity*. Center for Development Research.

van Zonneveld, M., Kindt, R., McMullin, S., …, and Dawson, I. K. (2023). Forgotten food crops in sub-Saharan Africa for healthy diets in a changing climate. *Proceedings of the National Academy of Sciences*, 120(14), e2205794120.

Wertheim-Heck, S. C. O., Spaargaren, G. and Vellema, S. (2014). Food safety in everyday life: Shopping for vegetables in a rural city in Vietnam. *Journal of Rural Studies,* 35, pp. 37–48.

WHO/FAO. (2003). *Diet, Nutrition and the Prevention of Chronic Diseases*. https://www.who.int/publications/i/item/924120916X

Xu, Y.-K., Tao, G.-D., Liu, H.-M., Yan, K.-L. and Dao, X.-S. (2004). Wild vegetable resources and market survey in Xishuangbanna, Southwest China. *Economic Botany,* 58, pp. 647–667.

https://doi.org/10.1142/9789811278297_0007

Chapter 7

The Crisis of Fisheries and Prospects for Fish as Food in Asia

Uttam Deb[1] and Madan Dey[2]

[1]*Department of Aquaculture and Fisheries, University of Arkansas at Pine Bluff, Pine Bluff, AR 71601, USA*
[2]*Department of Agricultural Sciences, Texas State University, San Marcos, Texas 78666, USA*

7.1 Introduction

Fish and fishery products (also called seafood) play an important role in meeting our protein consumption needs, often one of the only animal protein sources available for increasing dietary diversity in populations where starch-based staples predominate, especially because seafood is usually less costly and more accessible than other animal-source foods [Belton and Thilsted, 2014]. Seafood is an important contributor to food and nutritional security [Golden *et al.*, 2016] and a rich source of both macronutrients (e.g., proteins and omega-3 fatty acids) and essential micronutrients (e.g., vitamin A, vitamin B12, iron, zinc, and calcium) [Thilsted *et al.*, 2016]. The term "seafood" typically refers to all aquatic foods, including those from oceans, estuaries, lakes, rivers, and streams, as well as aquatic animals and plants farmed in tanks and other artificial environments. Thus, a large share of aquatic food does not actually come from the "sea" [Cojocaru *et al.*, 2022]. In this chapter, we have used the terms fish, fishery products, and seafood as synonyms, and the term "seafood" is limited to all aquatic animal foods except mammals. We have not included aquatic plants in our study.

Fish and fishery products originate from capture (wild-caught) and aquaculture (farmed fish). Capture fisheries have two sources: inland capture fisheries and marine capture fisheries. Capture fisheries significantly contribute to human well-being, including food security, employment, and poverty alleviation. Inland fish provides nutritional quality to countries with otherwise poor diets due to poverty and limited access to other forms of quality food [Food and Agriculture Organization (FAO), 2021]. At least 43% (4.9 million tons in 2015) of the world's inland capture fisheries harvest comes from 50 low-income, food-deficit countries, including India, Bangladesh, Nepal, and Vietnam [FAO, 2021]. At least 11% of global inland fishery production (1.3 million tons in 2015) comes from landlocked countries, including Laos and Nepal [FAO, 2021].

In addition to direct consumption, fisheries contribute to food and nutrition security through income generation, increasing the household's ability to purchase food and providing a source of employment for women who participate in fishing and post-harvest activities [Kawarazuka and Béné, 2010]. FAO estimated that 30.8 million people were engaged in Asia's primary sector of marine and inland capture fisheries in 2018 [FAO, 2018]. Many more are involved in auxiliary activities, particularly in the post-harvest sector, where women play an essential role. Unfortunately, the fisheries sector in many Asian countries, like other parts of the world, has been facing the challenges of over-exploitation, illegal fishing, and pollution.

Moreover, climate change has already affected or would likely have substantial adverse impacts on Asian fisheries. Poor management and external stressors can undermine these fisheries' environmental, economic, and social sustainability [Kroetz *et al.*, 2022]. Therefore, it is essential to study the trends and status of capture fisheries in Asian countries, the management practices followed by various countries, and their outcome of fish harvest and food and nutrition security. This chapter addresses four critical questions: What are the trends and current state of capture fisheries harvest in Asia? What has happened to the harvest of economically important species from capture fisheries in Asia? What are the consequences of the changes in capture fisheries on food and nutrition security in Asia? What is the future of capture fisheries in Asia?

This chapter is organised as follows. The next section discusses the fish production trends and harvest situation in Asian countries. Then, there is an examination of the dependence on fish for protein consumption and employment in different countries. The chapter subsequently describes the association between protein consumption and capture fisheries harvest and the challenges in capture fisheries. The chapter concludes that the future directions for capture fisheries for food and nutrition security in Asian countries would depend on evidence-based decision and policymaking.

7.2 Fish Production and Harvest

7.2.1 *Total Production of Fish and Fishery Products in Asia*

Total production of aquaculture and fisheries in Asia has increased by 215% over the last three decades (Figure 7.1), from 50.86 million tons in 1990 to 160.26 million tons in 2020. During this period, capture fisheries production increased by 33.5% (from 35.9 million

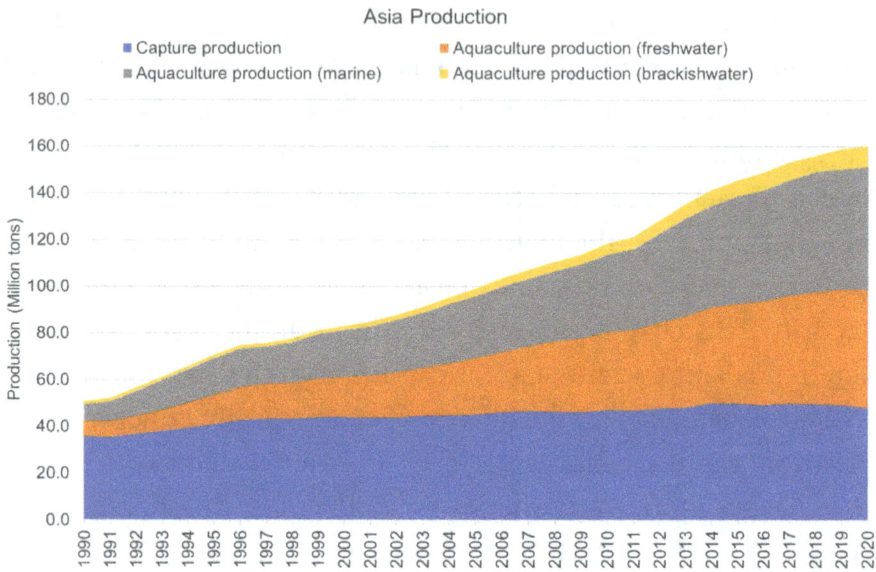

Figure 7.1 Trends in aquaculture and fisheries production (million tons) in Asia, 1990–2020.

tons to 48.0 million tons), and aquaculture production by 652% (from 14.9 million tons to 112.3 million tons). Aquaculture has three components: freshwater aquaculture, marine aquaculture, and brackish water aquaculture. Freshwater aquaculture increased by 672%, marine aquaculture by 621%, and brackish water aquaculture by 735%.

Over the last three decades (1990–2020), annual compound growth rates in total production of aquaculture and fishery products were 3.78% (Table 7.1). During this period, annual growth in aquaculture and capture fisheries production was 6.34% and 1.00%, respectively. Although overall total production has increased in Asia, there was wide variation across countries. Most of the countries experienced an increase in total production. However, total production declined in more than one-fourth of countries/areas (including Japan, Taiwan,

Table 7.1 Annual compound rate of growth in aquaculture and capture fisheries harvest in major fish-producing countries of Asia, 1990–2020.

Sector	Growth experience (%) by countries/areas
Total aquaculture and fisheries production	High growth (≥5.0 to 16.3): Bangladesh, Cambodia, Georgia, Indonesia, Iran, Laos, Myanmar, and Vietnam. Moderate growth (≥3.0 to <5.0): ASIA, China, India, Oman, Saudi Arabia, and Sri Lanka. Slow growth (>0.0 to <3.0): Malaysia, Maldives, Pakistan, Philippines, South Korea, Tajikistan, Turkey, and Yemen. Negative growth (–5.0 to <0.0): Hong Kong, Japan, Kazakhstan, North Korea, Taiwan, Thailand, and UAE.
Total aquaculture production	High growth (≥5.0 to 16.3): ASIA, Bangladesh, Cambodia, China, Georgia, India, Indonesia, Iran, Laos, Malaysia, Myanmar, Pakistan, Saudi Arabia, Sri Lanka, Turkey, and Vietnam. Moderate growth (≥3.0 to <5.0): Philippines, South Korea, and Thailand. Slow growth (>0.0 to <3.0): Taiwan. Negative growth (–5.0 to <0.0): Hong Kong, Japan, Kazakhstan, North Korea, and Tajikistan.
Total capture fisheries production	High growth (≥5.0 to 16.3): Cambodia, Georgia, and Tajikistan. Moderate growth (≥3.0 to <5.0): Bangladesh, Indonesia, Iran, Laos, Myanmar, Oman, Sri Lanka, and Vietnam. Slow growth (>0.0 to <3.0): ASIA, China, India, Malaysia, Maldives, Philippines, Saudi Arabia, and Yemen. Negative growth (–5.0 to <0.0): Hong Kong, Israel, Japan, Kazakhstan, North Korea, Pakistan, South Korea, Taiwan, Thailand, Turkey, and UAE.
Inland capture fisheries production	High growth (≥5.0 to 16.3): Cambodia and Myanmar. Moderate growth (≥3.0 to <5.0): Bangladesh, India, Laos, Malaysia, and Sri Lanka. Slow growth (>0.0 to <3.0): ASIA, China, Indonesia, Iran, Pakistan, Thailand, and Vietnam. Negative growth (–5.0 to <0.0): Georgia, Kazakhstan, Philippines, South Korea, and Turkey. High negative growth (–13.1 to ≤–5.0): Japan, North Korea, and Taiwan.

(Continued)

Table 7.1 (*Continued*)

Sector	Growth experience (%) by countries/areas
Marine capture fisheries production	High growth (≥5.0 to 16.3): Georgia and Tajikistan. Moderate growth (≥3.0 to <5.0): Bangladesh, Indonesia, Iran, and Oman. Slow growth (>0.0 to <3.0): ASIA, China, India, Malaysia, Maldives, Myanmar, Philippines, Saudi Arabia, Sri Lanka, and Yemen. Negative growth (−5.0 to <0.0): Hong Kong, Japan, North Korea, Pakistan, South Korea, Taiwan, Thailand, Turkey, and UAE.

Note: Annual compound rate of growth in aquaculture and fisheries production was estimated using $\ln Y = a + bt$, where $\ln Y$ is the production (in metric tons) expressed in natural log form, t is the time trend denoting years, and b represents the regression coefficient and the growth rate.

Thailand, and the United Arab Emirates (UAE)) in Asia in TE2020[1] (i.e., the average for 2018–2020), compared to TE1990 (i.e., the average for 1988–1990). Asian countries' contribution to the global production of aquaculture and fisheries increased from 48.1% in TE1990 to 74.2% in TE2020.

7.2.2 *The Share of Capture Fisheries Harvest*

There are two sources of capture fisheries in Asia: inland capture fisheries and marine capture fisheries. One-fourth of countries/areas in Asia has only marine capture fisheries. On the other hand, about one-fourth of countries/areas have only inland capture fisheries. All others (half of all Asian countries) have both inland and marine capture fisheries. 13 countries (Bangladesh, Cambodia, China, India, Indonesia, Iran, Japan, Myanmar, Pakistan, the Philippines,

[1] TE2020 indicates triennium ending 2020, i.e., the average for 2018–2020. TE is used to remove the effect of annual fluctuations in the production level.

Sri Lanka, Thailand, and Vietnam) are major fish producers of both inland and marine capture fisheries. Two countries (Kazakhstan and Laos) are major producers of inland capture fisheries only. Another 13 countries/areas (Hong Kong, Georgia, North Korea, South Korea, Malaysia, Maldives, Oman, Saudi Arabia, Taiwan, Tajikistan, Turkey, the UAE, and Yemen) are major producers of marine capture fisheries only. A country/area is considered a major fish producer if its inland/ marine fisheries production was >50,000 tons in TE2020 or TE1990. If a country/area is a major producer of inland or marine capture fisheries production, then we have considered it a major capture fish producer for total capture fisheries analysis.

Total harvest from capture fisheries in Asia has increased by 33.5% over the last three decades (Figure 7.2). Between 1990 and 2020, harvest from inland fisheries more than doubled, from 3.5 million tons to 7.3 million tons. On the other hand, harvests from marine

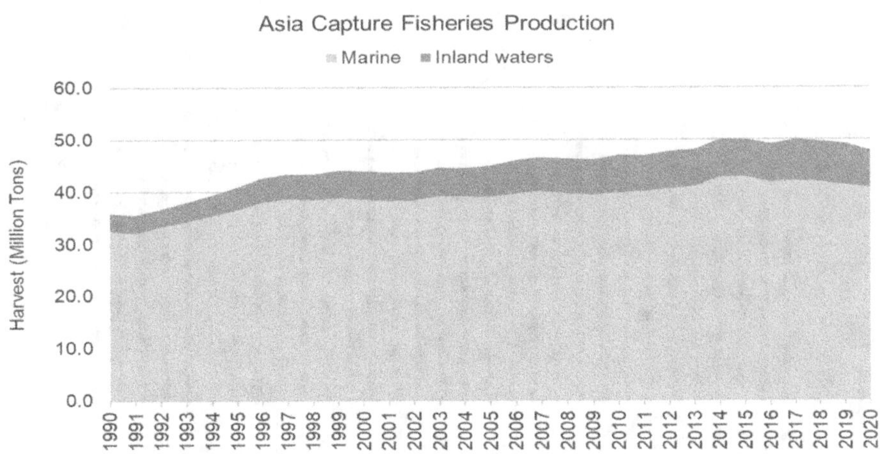

Figure 7.2 Trends in capture fisheries production (million tons) in Asia, 1990–2020.

capture fisheries increased by 25.2%, from 32.5 million tons to 40.7 million tons. Over the last three decades (1990–2020), the annual compound growth rate in capture fisheries harvest was 1.00%. During this period, annual growth in inland and marine capture fisheries harvest was 2.82% and 0.74%, respectively. With the increase in aquaculture in many Asian countries, the share of capture fisheries in total production has declined from 70.6% in 1990 to 29.9% in 2020 (Figure 7.3).

In TE2020, compared to TE1990, absolute harvest from capture fisheries declined in one-fourth of Asian countries, including Japan, South Korea, Taiwan, Thailand, and the UAE (Figure 7.4). All other Asian countries have experienced a significant increase in capture fisheries harvest except the Philippines, which had less than a 5% increase. In TE2020, the share of inland and marine capture fisheries to the total harvest from capture fisheries in Asia was 15.2% and 84.8%, respectively. On the other hand, the contribution of Asia

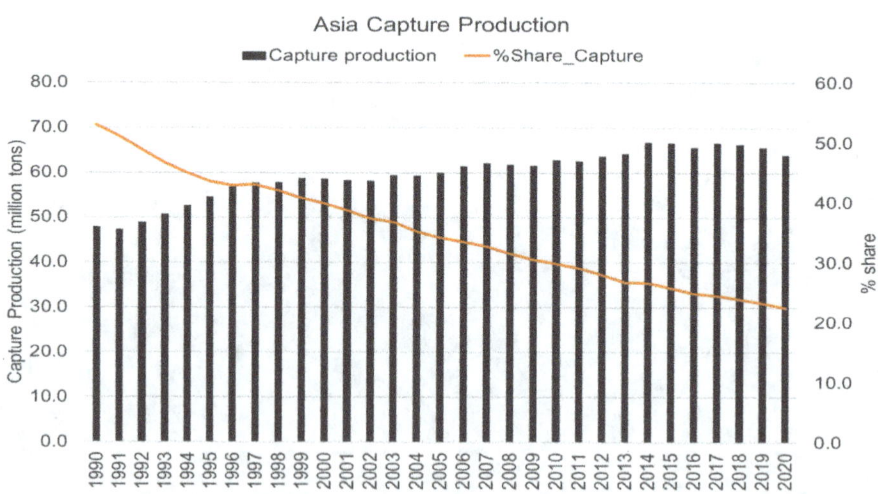

Figure 7.3 Trends in capture fisheries production (million tons) and its share (%) to the total aquaculture and fisheries production in Asia, 1990–2020.

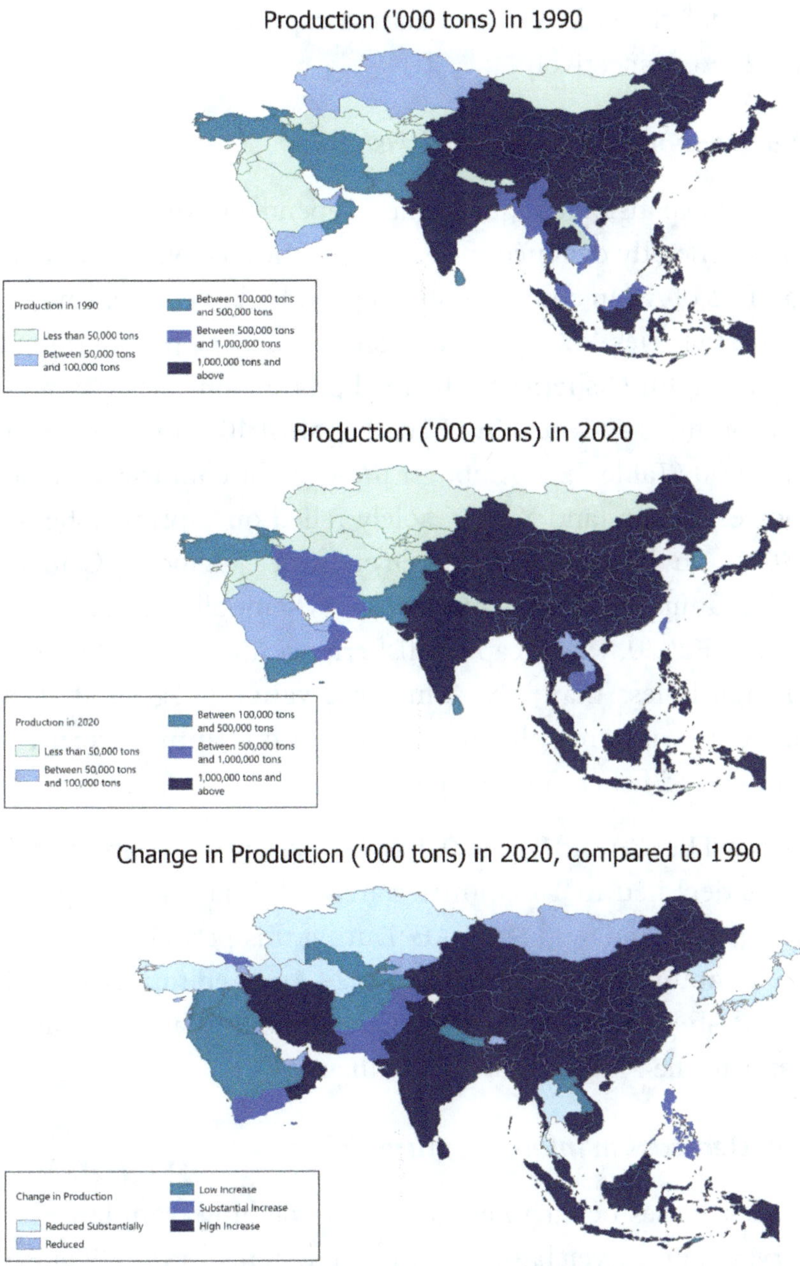

Figure 7.4 Changes in average catch from capture fisheries in Asian countries, TE1990 and TE2020.

to the total global inland and marine capture fisheries was 40.8% and 52.0%, respectively.

7.2.3 *Dependency on Capture Fisheries*

With the expansion of aquaculture, dependence on capture fisheries has generally declined in Asian countries. However, more than two-fifths of Asian countries still depend highly (70% or more) on capture fisheries for their total fish and fishery production. The share of capture fisheries to the total production was 70% or more in 24 countries and areas in TE2020, against 40 countries and areas in TE1990 (Table 7.2). Amongst these, eight countries, including Maldives, Oman, and Yemen, solely relied on capture fisheries in TE2020. On the other hand, seven countries, including Cambodia, Iran, Myanmar, and Thailand, relied substantially on capture fisheries in TE2020, where capture fisheries contributed between 50% and slightly less than 70%. This observation suggests that most Asian countries are still very dependent on capture fisheries for their fish and fishery production.

Between TE1990 and TE2020, harvest from marine capture fisheries has declined in 13 countries/areas of Asia, including Japan, Taiwan, Thailand, and the UAE. During this period, harvest from marine capture fisheries increased in 24 Asian countries, including Bangladesh, Cambodia, China, India, Indonesia, Malaysia, Maldives, Myanmar, the Philippines, and Vietnam.

7.2.4 *Decrease in Inland Capture Fisheries*

Inland fisheries occur in environments ranging from large lakes, reservoirs, and river basin–floodplain systems to the diverse and diffuse fisheries in ponds, canals, rice fields, and upland streams [Gregory *et al.*, 1996; Welcomme *et al.*, 2010]. The most productive

Table 7.2 Total fish production and dependence on (% share of) capture fisheries production to the total aquaculture and fisheries production in Asia, by countries and territories, TE1992 and TE2020.

Total production (p) and dependence on capture fisheries (d)	Countries in TE1990 (average of 1988–1990)	Countries in TE2020 (average of 2018–2020)
P1D1 (Very High Production & Very High Dependence)	Thailand	None
P1D2 (Very High Production & High Dependence)	India, Indonesia, Japan, Philippines, Taiwan, and South Korea	Japan, Malaysia, and Taiwan
P1D3 (Very High Production & Medium Dependence)	None	Iran, Myanmar, and Thailand
P1D4 (Very High Production & Low Dependence)	China	Bangladesh, China, India, Indonesia, Philippines, South Korea, and Vietnam
P2D1 (High Production & Very High Dependence)	Malaysia, Myanmar, and Turkey	Sri Lanka
P2D2 (High Production & High Dependence)	Bangladesh and Vietnam	Pakistan
P2D3 (High Production & Medium Dependence)	None	Cambodia and Turkey
P2D4 (High Production & Low Dependence)	North Korea	None
P3D1 (Medium Production & Very High Dependence)	Hong Kong, Georgia, Iran, Oman, Pakistan, and Sri Lanka	Georgia, Hong Kong, Maldives, Oman, and Yemen
P3D2 (Medium Production & High Dependence)	None	None
P3D3 (Medium Production & Medium Dependence)	None	Iraq
P3D4 (Medium Production & Low Dependence)	None	Laos, North Korea, Saudi Arabia, and Uzbekistan

(*Continued*)

Table 7.2 (*Continued*)

Total production (p) and dependence on capture fisheries (d)	Countries in TE1990 (average of 1988–1990)	Countries in TE2020 (average of 2018–2020)
P4D1 (Low Production & Very High Dependence)	Cambodia, Kazakhstan, Maldives, UAE, and Yemen	UAE
P4D2 (Low Production & High Dependence)	None	None
P4D3 (Low Production & Medium Dependence)	None	None
P4D4 (Low Production & Low Dependence)	None	Nepal
P5D1 (Very Low Production & Very High Dependence)	Azerbaijan, Bahrain, Brunei Darussalam, Cyprus, Kuwait, Lebanon, Macao, Mongolia, Qatar, Saudi Arabia, and Turkmenistan	Bahrain, Macao, Mongolia, Timor-Leste, Turkmenistan, and Qatar
P5D2 (Very Low Production & High Dependence)	Afghanistan, Bhutan, Iraq, Jordan, Laos, and Singapore	Azerbaijan, Brunei Darussalam, Kazakhstan, Kuwait, Lebanon, and Tajikistan
P5D3 (Very Low Production & Medium Dependence)	None	Syria
P5D4 (Very Low Production & Low Dependence)	Armenia, Kyrgyzstan, Nepal, Syria, Israel, Tajikistan, and Uzbekistan	Afghanistan, Armenia, Bhutan, Cyprus, Israel, Jordan, Kyrgyzstan, and Singapore

Note: (a) Total aquaculture and fisheries production level: (1) P1: Very High Production (equals or more than 1,000,000 tons), (2) P2: High Production (between 500,000 tons and 1,000,000 tons), (3) P3: Medium Production (between 100,000 tons and 500,000 tons), (4) P4: Low Production (between 50,000 tons and 100,000 tons), and (5) P5: Very Low Production (less than 50,000 tons). (b) Dependence on capture fisheries (% share of capture fisheries to total fish and fisheries production): (1) D1: Very High Dependence (≥90%), (2) D2: High Dependence (≥70% to <90%), (3) D3: Medium Dependence (≥50 to <70%), and (4) D4: Low Dependence (<50%).

capture fisheries are found in the tropical and subtropical latitudes, with around 46% of global inland fish production coming from Asia (excluding China). Harvest from inland capture fisheries has decreased in one-fourth of Asian countries/areas. Most inland fish production is from small-scale operations, harvesting for household consumption and local trade or barter [Bartley *et al.*, 2015], accounting for almost 90% of total production [Funge-Smith, 2018].

Over the last four and a half decades, Asia's area under floodplain fisheries has substantially shrunk, and river basins have been polluted through industrial waste and plastics. Traditionally, South and Southeast Asian countries used to grow deepwater rice in the monsoon season. The vast rice fields in the rainy season were spawning and production grounds for freshwater fisheries in these countries. These open-access fish habitats provided fish-harvesting opportunities to all segments of society and, most importantly, the poor households for their consumption and earning opportunities. With the development of modern rice varieties and the success of the Green Revolution, rice production technology and the primary rice-growing season shifted from the rainy to the dry season. Many previously rainy-season rice-growing areas are also converted to fishponds for year-round fish cultivation. This transformation has resulted in a decline in fish breeding grounds during the dry season, floodplain fisheries areas, fish harvest, and the availability of diverse fish and seafood species. Thus, vast rice fields in Asia, which used to be open-water rice-fish habitats and production grounds, are lost or have largely declined. Recently, some countries have promoted aquaculture in open-water bodies, fish farming in the rainy season, and rice farming in the dry season.

Most importantly, access to open-water fisheries for poor people declined substantially. In addition, other transboundary and domestic factors adversely affected inland water quality, fish habitat, and production. Deforestation in hills where most of the Asian rivers originated has increased soil erosion and increased siltation in riverbeds and floodplains. Increased siltation has reduced the water-carrying capacity of rivers and damaged water quality and fish habitat in many Asian countries.

Over the last three decades, harvest from inland capture fisheries decreased in one-fourth (13) of Asian countries, including Japan, the Philippines, and Taiwan. On the other hand, harvest from inland capture fisheries increased in more than one-third (19) of Asian countries, including Bangladesh, Cambodia, China, India, Indonesia, Iran, Laos, Malaysia, Myanmar, Pakistan, Sri Lanka, Thailand, and Vietnam. Improvement in statistics and documentation of catch from open-water fisheries and an actual increase in production in these countries resulted in the increased catch level data.

Table 7.3 reports the production trends in catch from inland fisheries and their relative contributions to the Asia-Pacific region catch.

Table 7.3 Production trends (inland fisheries) and the relative contributions to the Asia and Pacific region catch. Source: FAO [2021], Tables 2–3, p. 23.

Catch trend, 2007 to 2016	Aggregate catch (tons)	Percentage of Asia-Pacific region catch	Countries
Increasing catch	5,102,047	70	China, India, Cambodia, Indonesia, Philippines, Pakistan, Sri Lanka, Malaysia
Decreasing catch	323,869	4.4	Thailand, Vietnam, Japan, Australia, Taiwan, Mongolia
Stable catch	21,500	0.3	Nepal
No clear trend	1,082,305	14	Bangladesh, Nepal, South Korea, Fiji, New Zealand, French Polynesia
Excluded from analysis	793,541	11	Major countries: Myanmar, Laos, Papua New Guinea

Table 7.4 Inland fisheries catch per capita population. Source: Raw data from FAO [2022a].

Kg catch per capita of population	TE1990 (Average of 1988–1990)	TE2020 (Average of 2018–2020)
10 to 26	None	Cambodia and Myanmar
5 to 10	Cambodia	Bangladesh and Laos
2 to 5	Bangladesh, Laos, Myanmar, Philippines, Thailand, and Vietnam	Indonesia, Kazakhstan, Sri Lanka, Thailand, and Turkmenistan
1 to 2	ASIA, Indonesia, Iraq, North Korea, and Sri Lanka	ASIA, China, India, Iran, Philippines, Uzbekistan, and Vietnam
0.1 to 1	Afghanistan, Bhutan, Brunei Darussalam, China, India, Iran, Israel, Japan, Jordan, South Korea, Malaysia, Mongolia, Nepal, Pakistan, Singapore, Syria, Taiwan, and Turkey	Afghanistan, Armenia, Azerbaijan, Iraq, Israel, Japan, North Korea, South Korea, Malaysia, Nepal, Pakistan, Syria, Taiwan, Tajikistan, and Turkey

Increasing catch was observed in China, India, Cambodia, Indonesia, the Philippines, Pakistan, Sri Lanka, and Malaysia. On the other hand, there was decreasing catch in Thailand, Vietnam, Japan, and Taiwan. There was no clear trend in South Korea. Table 7.4 shows the inland fisheries catch per capita population. TE2020 per capita inland fisheries catch was at least 10 kg in Cambodia and Myanmar and at least 5 kg in Bangladesh and Laos. The average per capita catch from inland fisheries in Asia was 1.7 kg in TE2020, against 1.1 kg in TE1990.

7.2.5 *Changes in the Composition of Captured Fish Species*

Harvest of many economically important species declined in recent years, but affirmative actions resulted in an increased catch of some species in some countries. Our analyses revealed that many important species have decreased over the last three decades. Harvest of Indian oil sardines in India and the UAE and Pacific sardines in Japan and South Korea declined. Narrow-barred Spanish mackerel harvest declined in Oman, Saudi Arabia, and Sri Lanka. Harvest of many important species (e.g., silver barb (*Barbonymus gonionotus*) in Indonesia, freshwater prawns in Japan, climbing perch and striped snakehead in Thailand) substantially declined over the last three decades (Figures 7.5 and 7.6). Fluctuations in silver barb harvest in Thailand may be linked with the stocking of this species. Kamonrat [1996] reported that in samples of silver barb from stocked waters in Thailand, up to 70% was of hatchery origin. There were also examples of species whose harvest declined rapidly in the nineties but started to increase due to affirmative action by governments and citizens. Hilsa shad harvest in Bangladesh is an example of such a case. Another example is the Skipjack tuna harvest in the Maldives (the western part of the Indian Ocean). Harvest of Japanese

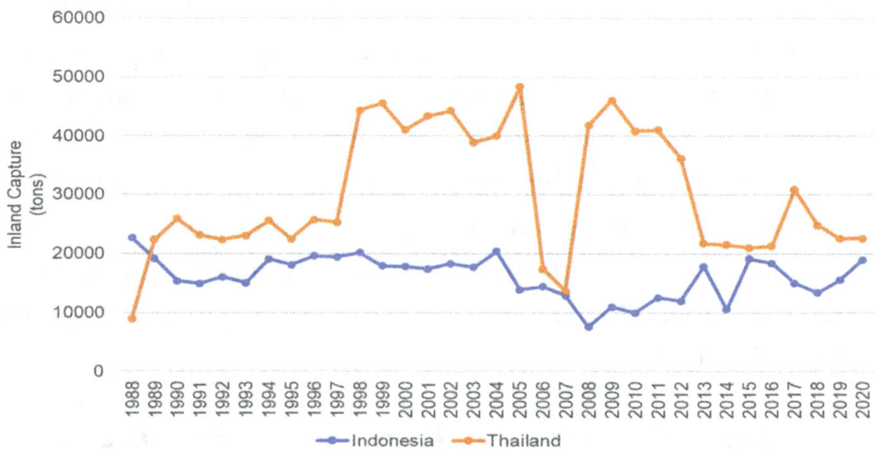

Figure 7.5 Trends in silver barb catch in inland capture fisheries in Indonesia and Thailand: 1988 to 2020. Source: Raw data from FAO FishStatJ.

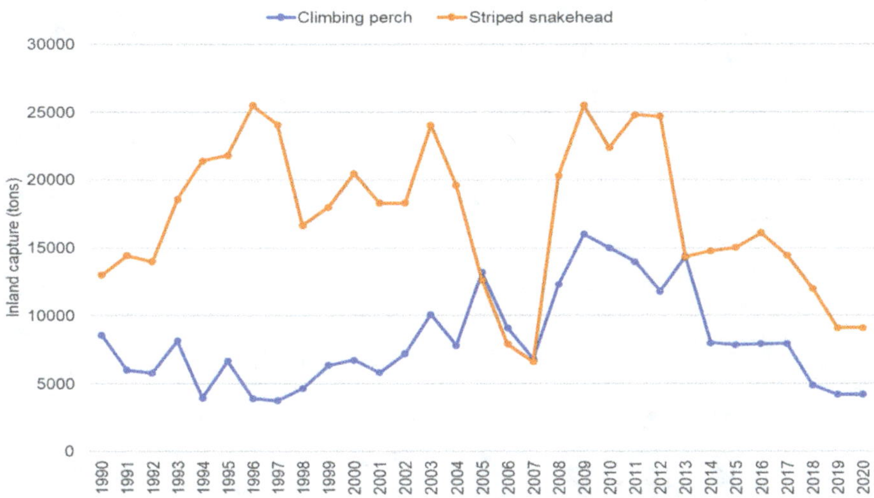

Figure 7.6 Trends in climbing perch and striped snakehead harvest in inland capture fisheries in Thailand: 1990 to 2020. Source: Raw data from FAO FishStatJ.

anchovy in China and South Korea and Skipjack tuna in Indonesia, the Philippines, and Taiwan increased. Harvest of yellowfin tuna increased in the Maldives, Oman, and Yemen.

7.3 Dependence on Fish for Protein Consumption

7.3.1 *Consumption of Fish Protein in Asia*

Per capita fish protein consumption has increased in Asian countries. Figures 7.7 and 7.8 report the per capita availability of fish and seafood (kg/year) in Asian countries and geographical areas in TE1992 and TE2019. Our analysis revealed a general increase in the per capita availability of fish and seafood in most of Asia. Per capita fish consumption increased in about three-fifth of Asian countries, including Bangladesh, Cambodia, China, India, Indonesia,

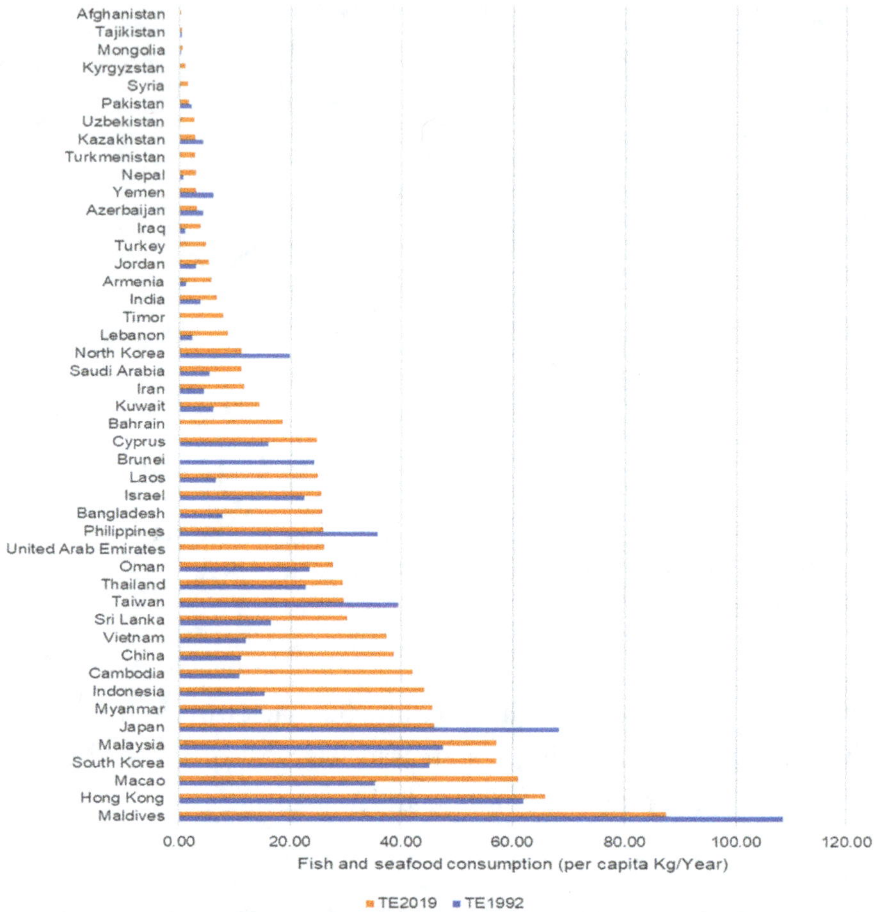

Figure 7.7 Per capita fish (seafood) availability and consumption in Asia by geographical area, TE1992 and TE2019. Source: Raw data from FAO Food Balance Sheet.

Malaysia, Myanmar, Saudi Arabia, Sri Lanka, Thailand, and Vietnam. However, availability declined significantly in one-fifth of Asian countries/areas, including Japan, Maldives, Pakistan, the Philippines, and Taiwan. Relevant data were unavailable for six countries, including Turkey and the UAE.

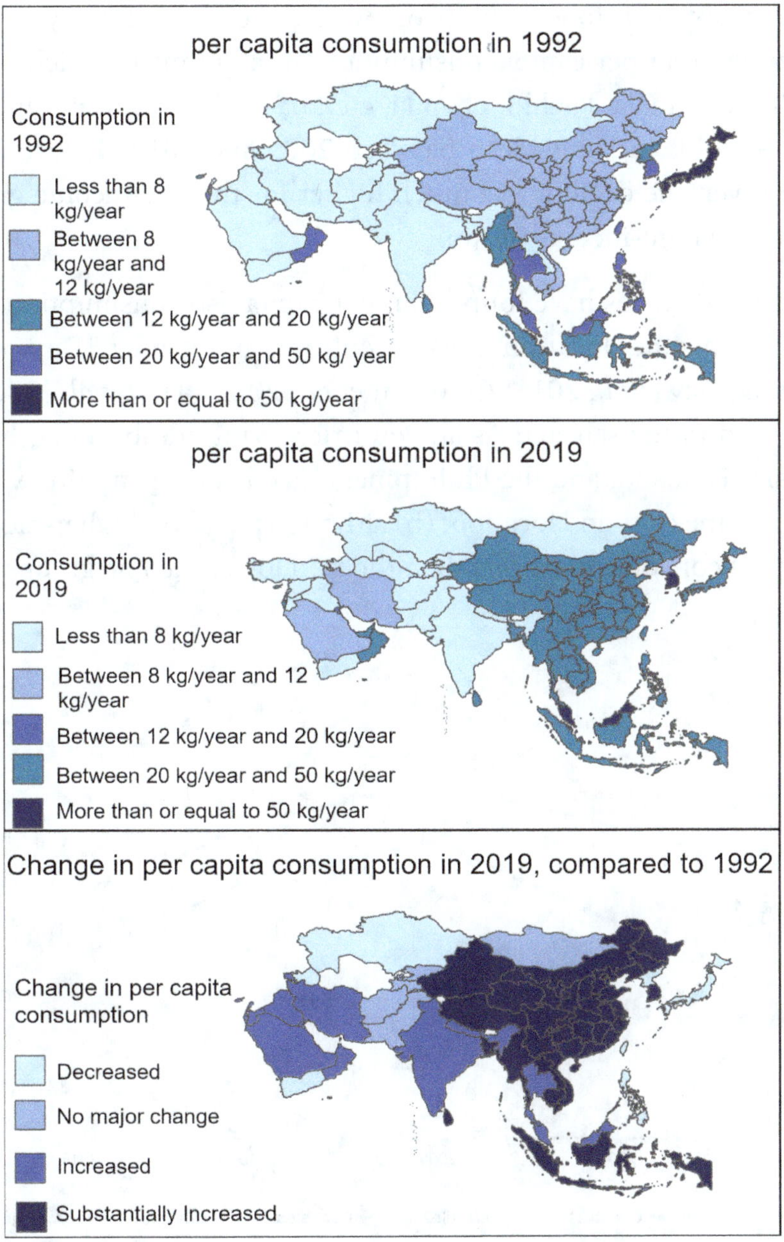

Figure 7.8 Changes in per capita seafood consumption in different countries of Asia in TE2019, compared to TE1992.

Our analysis of Household Income and Expenditure Survey reports revealed that per capita consumption of micronutrient-rich small fishes like mala, kachki, chapila, etc., has reduced for all types of households in Bangladesh between 2005 and 2016 (Figure 7.9). However, the decline was much higher for the low-income group than the high-income group.

Previous studies have found that per capita fish consumption varies by income, location, season, culture, and gender [Dey *et al.*, 2005a; Dey *et al.*, 2011; Cojocaru *et al.*, 2022]. Dey *et al.* [2005a] showed in the selected Asian countries (Bangladesh, India, Indonesia, Thailand, and the Philippines): (a) fish consumption varies by income class and location; (b) although people in higher-income groups consume more fish than those in lower-income groups, the

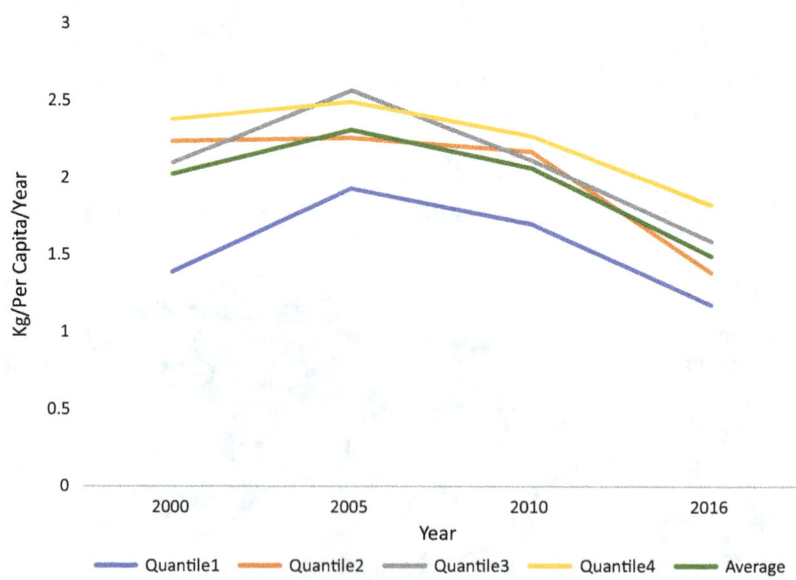

Figure 7.9 Per capita (adult equivalent) consumption trends in micronutrient-rich small fishes (mala, kachki, chala and chapila fish) in Bangladesh by income groups, 2000 to 2016.

proportion of the food budget allocated to fish is higher among the low-income groups; (c) rural people consume more fish than urban dwellers; (d) fish producers, in general, consume more fish than non-producers; and (e) poor people consume low-value fish, many of which are freshwater fish. A study of nine Asian countries reported that the price and income elasticities of seafood are considerably higher for affluent consumers than for poor consumers [Dey *et al.*, 2008]. Empirical studies have argued that small-scale inland fisheries and small-scale marine fisheries contribute substantially to the consumption need of poor people in South and Southeast Asia.

7.3.2 *Dependence on Fish to Meet Dietary Protein Requirements*

Asian countries depend highly on fish and fishery products to meet their animal protein consumption. Fish and fishery products have contributed substantially to the per capita total animal protein consumed in Asia. Figure 7.10 reports the fish dependency of Asian countries. Fish dependence is defined in this study as the percent of animal source protein from fish. Based on the estimated values, there are five categories of fish dependency: (i) below 7%, (ii) between 7% and 25%, (iii) between 25% and 40%, (iv) between 40% and 60%, and (v) 60% and above. In TE2019, fish and seafood contributed more than 40% of animal protein consumed in about one-fifth of Asian countries: Bangladesh, Cambodia, Indonesia, Japan, Laos, Malaysia, Maldives, Myanmar, Sri Lanka, and Thailand. During this period, the contribution of fish and seafood to the per capita animal protein consumption was more than 71% in Cambodia, about 61% in Bangladesh, 57% in Indonesia, 58% in the Maldives, and about 50% in Sri Lanka. In four countries (North Korea, the Philippines, South Korea, and Vietnam), fish and seafood contributed between 25% and 35% of per capita animal protein consumption in TE2019.

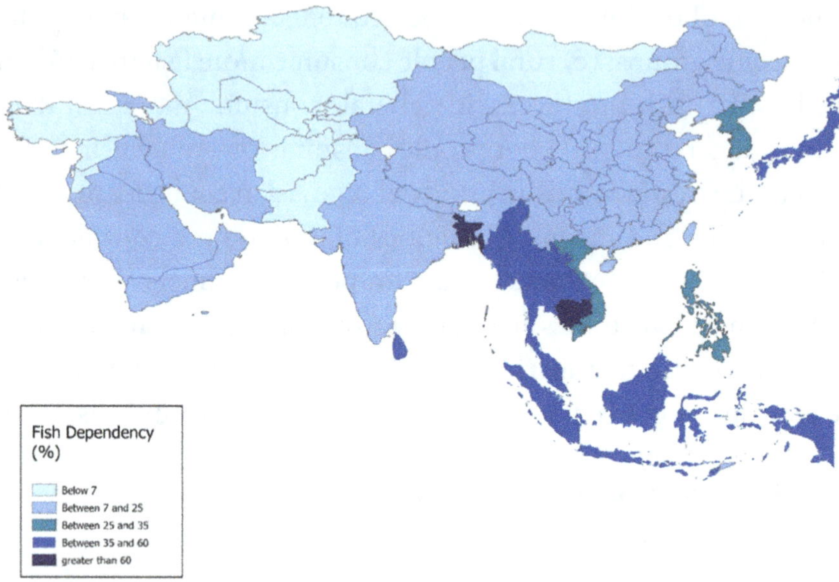

Figure 7.10 Fish dependency of Asian countries (measured in percent of animal source protein derived from fish) in TE2019.

Income and geography do not fully explain heterogeneity in seafood consumption, which suggests that cultural differences also play a role [Cojocaru *et al.*, 2022]. India's average fish dependency is low due to its large share of the vegetarian population. Even though most Indians are not vegetarians, majorities follow at least some restrictions on meat in their diet.

7.4 Association between Protein Consumption and Capture Fisheries Harvest

7.4.1 *Association Between Capture Fisheries Harvest and Protein Intake*

Figure 7.11 shows the associations between the change in per capita protein consumption and capture fisheries harvest in Asia. There are four types:

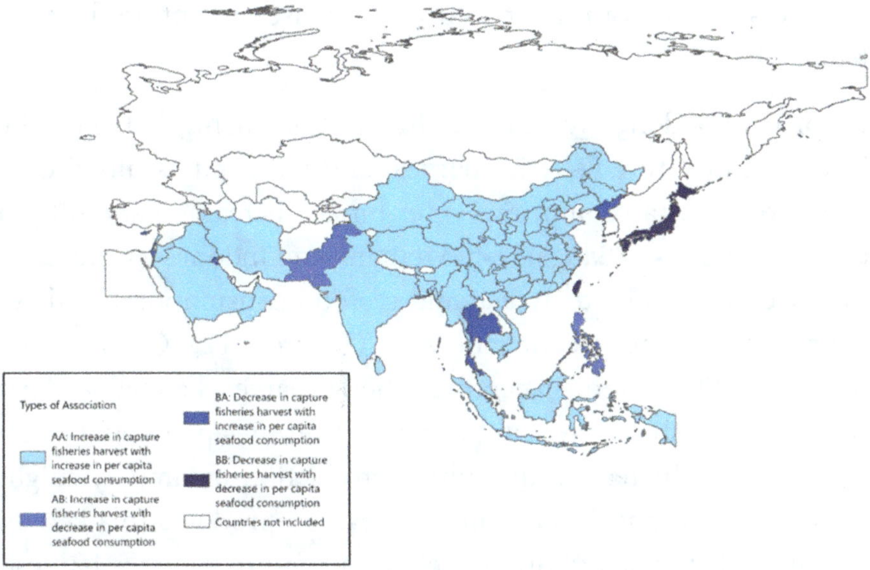

Figure 7.11 Association between changes in per capita protein consumption and decline in capture fisheries harvest in Asia in TE2019, compared to TE1992.

AA: Increase in capture fisheries harvest with an increase in per capita seafood consumption. AB: Increase in capture fisheries harvest with a decrease in per capita seafood consumption. BA: Decrease in capture fisheries harvest with an increase in per capita seafood consumption. BB: Decrease in capture fisheries harvest with a decrease in per capita seafood consumption.

There was an increase in capture fisheries harvest with an increase in per capita seafood consumption in half of the major fish-producing countries, including Bangladesh, Cambodia, China, India, Indonesia, Malaysia, Myanmar, Sri Lanka, and Vietnam. Japan is one of the world's top fish and fishery product importers. Japan imported fish and fishery products worth USD 11.88 billion in 2018 and USD 11.54 billion in 2019 from the world [UN Comtrade, 2022]. Despite massive imports, per capita consumption of seafood products declined in Japan, with a decrease in capture fisheries harvest in TE2020.

Empirical evidence revealed a direct relationship between the changes in capture fisheries harvest and per capita seafood consumption in Asian countries. For example, increased harvest from capture fisheries in Bangladesh, Vietnam, and Indonesia resulted in increased per capita daily fish and seafood consumption in these countries over the last three decades (Figure 7.12). On the other hand, a declining trend in capture fisheries harvest had reduced per capita daily fish and seafood consumption in Japan and Taiwan (Figure 7.13). Increased aquaculture production and imports might increase the physical availability of seafood products to a certain extent. Unfortunately, with a decline in capture fisheries harvest, the poor and marginalised people do not have economic access to seafood products available in the market. Both developed and developing countries faced similar situations.

7.4.2 *Impact of COVID-19 Pandemic on Fish Harvests and Consumption*

The COVID-19 pandemic has decreased harvest from capture fisheries, reduced per capita fish availability, and increased undernourishment in Asian countries. Stay-at-home orders, curfews, bans, and travel restrictions for national and international air and land travel have led to complete or partial closures of hotels, restaurants, catering services, and local markets and disruption of transportation and cold-chain systems [FAO, 2020b]. Our analysis of the inland capture fisheries production data revealed a general decline in inland fisheries harvest in 2020 than in 2019 in most Asian countries (Table 7.5). The decline in catch was mainly due to the pandemic-induced lockdown, restrictions on movement, and other embargoes. In 2020,

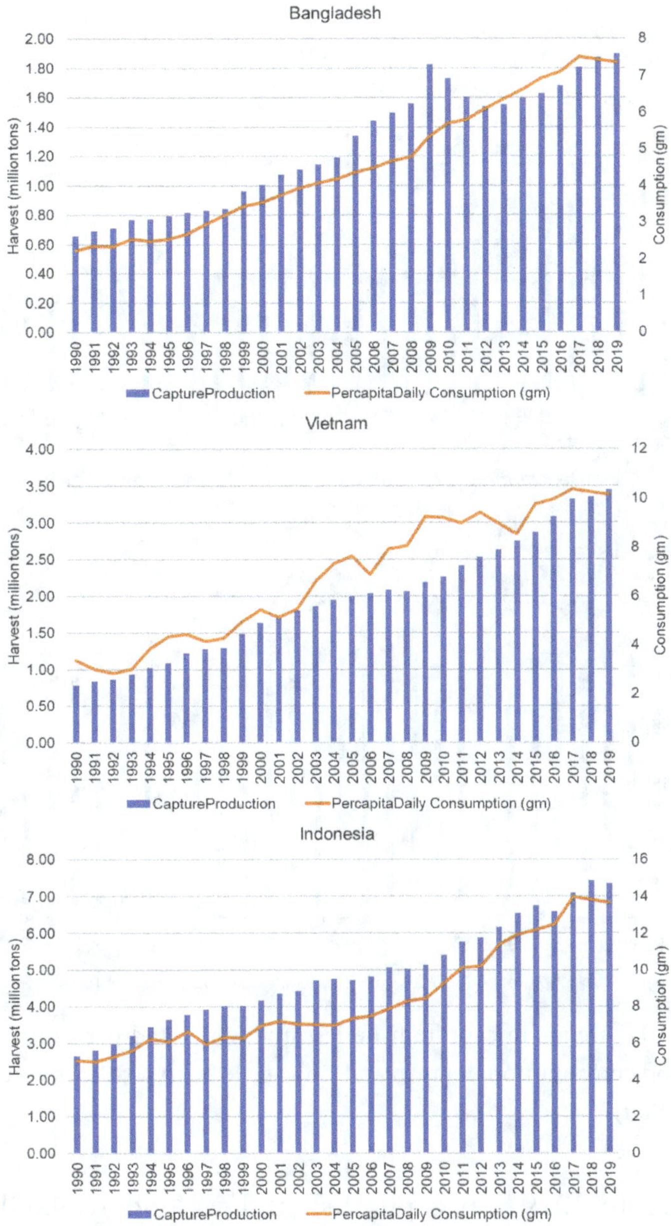

Figure 7.12 Trends in capture fisheries production and per capita daily fish and seafood consumption in Bangladesh, Vietnam, and Indonesia, 1990 to 2019. Source: Raw data from FishStatJ.

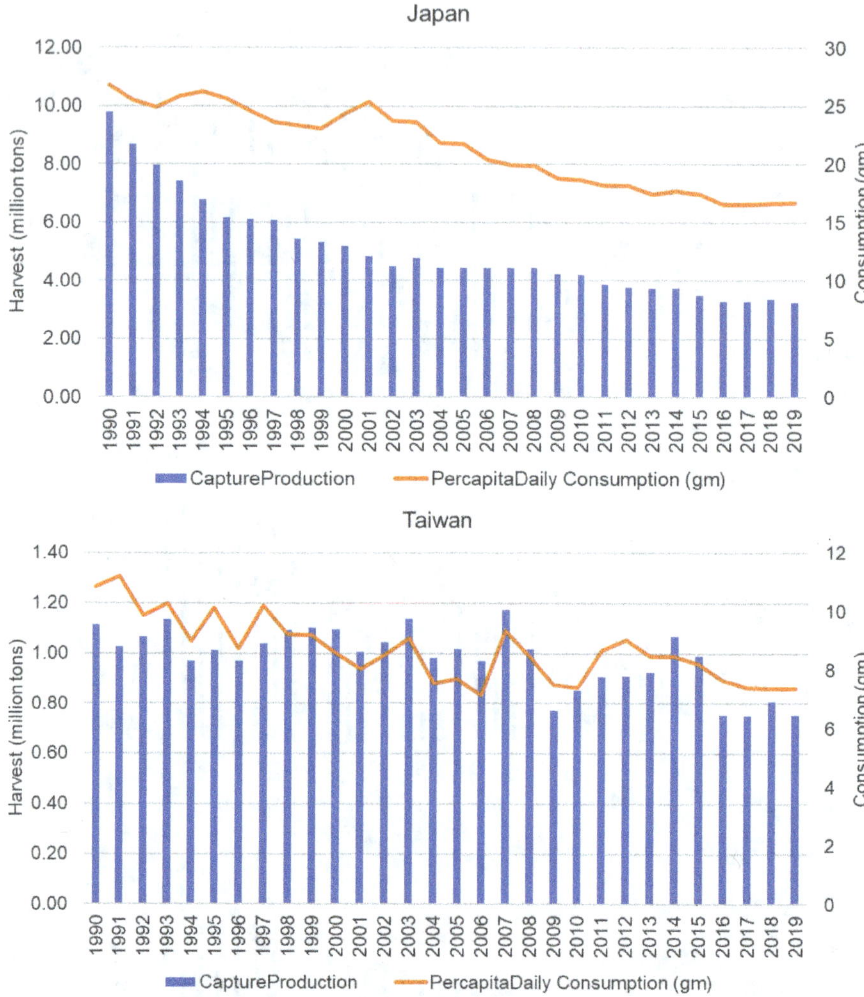

Figure 7.13 Trends in capture fisheries production and per capita daily fish and seafood consumption in Japan and Taiwan, 1990 to 2019. Source: Raw data from FishStatJ.

compared to 2019, per capita fish and seafood availability also decreased, ranging between –0.09% and –2.7% decline for all Asian countries except Japan, where no notable change (less than 0.5% increase) in per capita fish availability was observed. Our analysis

Table 7.5 Impact of the COVID-19 pandemic on inland capture fisheries harvests, per capita fish and seafood consumption, and undernourishment in major fish-producing Asian countries.

Type of change	Inland capture fisheries harvest in 2020, compared to 2019	Per capita fish and seafood availability (kg/yr) in 2020, compared to 2019	Prevalence of undernourishment (% of the population) in 2020, compared to 2019
Increased	Bangladesh, Cambodia, India, Kazakhstan, Laos, Pakistan, Sri Lanka, and Vietnam	Japan	Bangladesh, Cambodia, India, Indonesia, Japan, Myanmar, Oman, Pakistan, and Thailand
No change	None	None	China, Cyprus, Hong Kong, Kazakhstan, South Korea, and Turkey
Decreased	China, Indonesia, Iran, Japan, Malaysia, Myanmar, Philippines, Taiwan, Thailand, and Vietnam	Bangladesh, Cambodia, China, Hong Kong, India, Indonesia, Iran, Kazakhstan, North Korea, South Korea, Laos, Malaysia, Maldives, Myanmar, Oman, Pakistan, Philippines, Saudi Arabia, Sri Lanka, Taiwan, Tajikistan, Thailand, Turkey, UAE, Vietnam, and Yemen	Iran, North Korea, Laos, Malaysia, Philippines, Saudi Arabia, Sri Lanka, Vietnam, and Yemen

also revealed that undernourishment increased in many Asian countries in 2020 than in 2019. Our findings are consistent with other studies conducted by FAO for Asia and individual studies conducted in several Asian countries. COVID-19 disrupted small-scale fishery supply chains [Bassett *et al.*, 2021]. However, some supply chains, market segments, companies, small-scale actors, and civil society had shown initial signs of greater resilience than certain groups working in or dependent on the seafood sector [Love *et al.*, 2021].

FAO [2020b] reported that the pandemic shifted consumer preferences. While demand for fresh fish has waned, consumer demand for packaged and frozen products has grown as households look to stock up on non-perishable food. The hard lockdown affected fishers in the Davao Gulf of the Philippines through the reduced volume of their catch, increased fishing costs, food inadequacy, emotions, and low prices [Macusi *et al.*, 2022]. Partelow *et al.* [2023] found that COVID-19 has significantly changed seafood consumption patterns, reduced seafood consumption levels, and curtailed restaurant eating in Indonesia's West Nusa Tenggara province. A mixed scenario was reported for Bangladesh. Small-scale marine fishers of Bangladesh showed resilience during the 65-day fishing ban [Bhowmik *et al.*, 2021]. The pandemic severely affected food security and livelihoods in Bangladesh due to movement restrictions, reduced purchasing power, and further impacted on the most vulnerable small-scale fishers and associated people [Sunny *et al.*, 2021] via increased fish prices and reduced frequency and quantity of fish consumption [Mandal *et al.*, 2021].

7.5 Challenges in Asian Capture Fisheries

7.5.1 *Overexploitation of Fish Stocks Beyond Biologically Sustainable Levels*

Overexploitation is a significant challenge. An analysis of FAO data on the achievement of sustainable development goals (SDGs) indicates that only a few countries have their fish stocks within biologically sustainable levels. In 2018, the proportion of fish stocks within biologically sustainable levels (not overexploited) was only 16.7% in Turkey, 23.5% in Indonesia, 47.4% in Malaysia, 87.5% in Cyprus, 71.4% in Japan, 74.4% in Qatar, and 85.2% in Kazakhstan. Several countries (Saudi Arabia (100%), the Philippines (100%), Iran (100%), Georgia (100%), and Yemen (100%)) have their fish stocks within biologically sustainable levels.

7.5.2 *Lack of Stock Assessment and Limited Capacity to Assess Marine Stock*

Accurate estimates of fish stocks are essential to know whether fish populations are overexploited or underexploited relative to their ability to support sustainable yields. A recent report by the Asia-Pacific Fishery Commission [FAO, 2021] stated that South and Southeast Asia are the sources of 48% of the global marine capture fisheries. The report added that despite the importance of fisheries to the Asian economies, scientific monitoring and management of capture fisheries are modest, with most stocks lacking modern scientific stock assessments. China, India, Indonesia, and Thailand are changing their approaches to improve the assessment of some of their important stocks [FAO, 2021]. However, a strong need remains for far more comprehensive monitoring of marine fish stocks in Asian countries. To this end, monitoring and assessment capacity development remain a pressing need for marine fishery management in the Asian region.

7.5.3 *Combating Illegal, Unreported, and Unregulated Fishing*

Illegal, unreported, and unregulated (IUU) fishing is a critical challenge in Asian fisheries. FAO [2016] as well as FAO and CSIRO [2020] identified 38 illegal fishing activity hot spots within or adjoining the exclusive economic zones of the Asia-Pacific Fishery

Commission member states. These studies estimated that IUU fishing ranged between 2.0 and 2.5 million tons of catch in 2015 and 6.6 million tons, valued at USD 23.3 billion, in 2019. Encroachment, breach of license conditions followed by non-compliant gear, and illegal transshipment were the most prevalent. In addition, IUU was carried out mainly by illegal foreign fishing vessels [FAO, 2016; FAO and CSIRO, 2020].

An analysis of FAO data on the achievement of SDGs reports the progress by countries in the degree of implementation of international instruments aiming to combat IUU fishing (level of implementation: 1, lowest to 5, highest). Cyprus, Indonesia, Japan, Maldives, Myanmar, Oman, Thailand, and Vietnam obtained the highest score of 5. It was followed by a score of 4 (India, the Philippines, Turkey, and the UAE) and 3 (Bangladesh, China, Georgia, Iran, Malaysia, and Pakistan). Two countries (Singapore and Yemen) received a score of 2, and two countries (Kuwait and Lebanon) obtained the lowest score of 1.

7.5.4 *Legal, Regulatory, and Institutional Framework*

Limited application of a legal, regulatory, policy, and institutional framework that recognises and protects access rights for small-scale fisheries in Asia is a major concern. FAO [2022b] reported the degree of application of a legal/regulatory/policy/institutional framework that recognises and protects access rights for small-scale fisheries (level of implementation: 1, lowest to 5, highest). The highest score of 5 was obtained by Bangladesh, Cambodia, Cyprus, Indonesia, Japan, Myanmar, Oman, the Philippines, Saudi Arabia, Thailand, Turkey, Uzbekistan, and Yemen. A score of 4 was received by India, Iran, Mongolia, Pakistan, Sri Lanka, the UAE, and Vietnam. On the other hand, Armenia, Bhutan, Kyrgyzstan, and Malaysia obtained a score of 3. Afghanistan, Azerbaijan, China, Maldives, South Korea, and Tajikistan received a meagre score of 2, while Georgia, Kazakhstan, and Nepal obtained the lowest score (1).

7.5.5 *Adverse Effects of Climate Change*

Climate change will significantly affect many economically important fish species in Asia. Global warming directly or indirectly affects marine species, including their growth [Rijnsdorp *et al.*, 2009; Okunishi *et al.*, 2012; Ji *et al.*, 2020], abundance [Cheung *et al.*, 2010; Barange *et al.*, 2014; Holsman *et al.*, 2020; Reum *et al.*, 2020; Whitehouse *et al.*, 2021], and spatial distribution [Kim *et al.*, 2012; Alabia *et al.*, 2016]. Rising ocean temperatures — which affect the rebuilding of fish stocks, geographic distributions of stocks, and species composition — will escalate disputes over shared stocks [Kroetz *et al.*, 2022].

Barange *et al.* [2014] predicted that climate change will decrease total productive potential in South and Southeast Asia, driven by a temperature increase of approximately 2°C by 2050, despite increased primary production by small phytoplankton. Fernandes [2018] reviewed the literature on climate change impacts, vulnerabilities, and adaptations in Southern Asian fisheries. The study observed that Pakistan, India, Bangladesh, Myanmar, and the Maldives are among the countries most affected by climate change and weather events. The study added that existing studies do not agree on the magnitude of change, given that they consider different numbers of drivers and uncertainties. However, there is much agreement on areas of impact, the direction of this impact, and key drivers (temperature, acidification, and hypoxia).

Li *et al.* [2022] observed that anchovy fluctuations in the Pan-Pacific occurred synchronously. They argued that large-scale climate forcing might activate synchronous fluctuations for anchovy populations at the basin scale. In contrast, local-scale environmental forces are also responsible for anchovy fluctuations in the "micro-environment". Dramatic fluctuations in the Japanese anchovy (*Engraulis japonicus*) population in the Kuroshio Current Ecosystem[2] have important economic, ecological, and social consequences.

Bang *et al.* [2022] projected a decrease in the anchovy habitat area in the summer and fall seasons up to 19.4% in the 2050s, compared with the historical period (2000–2015). The study added that a substantial decline (16.5–60.8%) is expected in summer in the East China Sea and the Yellow Sea — the main spawning habitat. The study added that a considerable decrease in the spawning habitat might contribute to a decline in the anchovy biomass, relocation of the spawning area, and changes in the reproduction timing in Korean waters. The authors suggested that seasonal variation of the anchovy habitat should be considered to ensure effective future management strategies for the effect of climate change on fisheries resources, particularly for environmentally sensitive species such as anchovy.

7.5.6 *Blind Spots in Visions of a "Blue Economy"*

'Blue foods' are aquatic foods captured or cultivated in marine and freshwater systems [Naylor *et al.*, 2021]. Oceans can significantly reduce global hunger and malnutrition and the food system's contribution to global environmental change [Farmery *et al.*, 2021]. Blue food and blue economy narratives currently provide a limited examination of the systems that link production and consumption. Concerns over the inability to achieve or

---

[2]More information about the Kuroshio Current is available in Nagai [2019].

maintain blue economic growth have been linked to failures to anticipate the impacts of adverse extrinsic events and drivers [Caswell *et al.*, 2020]. Farmery *et al.* [2021] identified three blind spots in visions of a "blue economy". The study found that food production and consumption considerations are underrepresented in the blue economy agenda (blind spot 1). They added that where such concerns are visible, the focus is limited to production (blind spot 2), particularly mariculture production (blind spot 3). They argued that the blind spots could risk and undermine the ocean's contribution to eliminating hunger and malnutrition, both individually and cumulatively. Therefore, addressing the current blind spots in the blue economy is essential to ensure that the voices of small-scale fishers and mariculturists are heard alongside all others.

7.5.7 *Chemical Wastes, Microplastics and Maritime Littering*

Uncontrolled discharge of chemical and hazardous wastes, microplastics, and maritime littering have been polluting water bodies and damaging fish habitats in Asia (like in other parts of the world). Due to the reduced dissolved oxygen levels from pollution, many river basins became inhabitable for fish and fishery resources. FAO [2021] mentioned that abandoned, lost, or otherwise discarded fishing gear in the oceans makes up approximately 10% (640,000 tons) of all marine litter in the world. Plastic pollution in freshwater and marine ecosystems, including microplastics smaller than 5 mm, has become an emerging global concern [Phuong *et al.*, 2022; Auta *et al.*, 2017]. Microplastics adversely affect fish and human health [Bhuyan, 2022] and threaten seafood safety [Garrido Gamarro *et al.*, 2020]. Wang *et al.* [2020] concluded that microplastic contamination could occur in almost all types of aquatic habitats around the globe.

Curren *et al.* [2021], after a review of 36 studies, revealed the presence of microplastics on beach and benthic sediments, seawater, and marine organisms in Southeast Asia. Southeast Asian countries have high levels of marine plastic pollution, with Indonesia (10%), the Philippines (6%), Vietnam (6%), Thailand (3%), and Malaysia (3%) estimated to cumulatively contribute almost a third (30%) of marine plastic pollution to the world's oceans [Jambeck *et al.*, 2015]. Reducing the problem of microplastics will require involving the public, the socio-economic sectors, tourism, and companies specialising in waste management. Harnessing microbes to degrade microplastics is a promising and environmentally safe option. Microbes can be used to manage microplastics without negative effects and eventually favour the natural cleaning of contaminated environments [Auta *et al.*, 2017].

7.5.8 *Consumption of Wild-Caught Fish*

Relative prices of wild-caught fish have increased and resulted in a decline in their consumption by low-income consumers. A decrease in the supply has reduced availability and increased the scarcity of captured fish. Shortage in supply has thus increased the prices of wild-caught fish species more than farmed species. Empirical studies revealed that wealthy consumers have a low willingness to pay for fish for nutrition because they obtain essential micronutrients from other sources [Cojocaru *et al.*, 2022]. In contrast, poor consumers have high willingness to pay for fish for nutrition because they are unable to get micronutrients from other items in their diets. Higher seafood prices have dubious implications. Higher prices increase incomes for small-scale fisheries and small-scale aquaculture but make seafood less affordable for low-income consumers. One possible policy solution is to promote technological innovations that bundle seafood attributes differently to separate high-valued export-oriented products (that support income) from low-valued products (that support nutrition in domestic markets) [Cojocaru *et al.*, 2022].

7.6 Future Prospects

Our analyses revealed that the total harvest from capture fisheries in Asia increased in recent years compared to three decades earlier. However, there was wide variation across countries. There was a deterioration in capture fisheries in many Asian countries and for many economically important species. Also, there was evidence and examples of success in managing floodplains, riverine and estuarine fisheries, and coastal fisheries. Based on the analyses and evidence in this chapter, we can conclude that the future directions for capture fisheries for food and nutrition security in Asian countries would depend on evidence-based decision and policymaking. With the business-as-usual case, harvests from capture fisheries will decline and pose severe threats to food and nutrition security in most Asian countries. On the other hand, affirmative actions and cooperation among nations will at least be able to arrest the decline in capture fisheries, if not a rise in capture fisheries harvest. Therefore, we firmly believe that the future direction of Asian capture fisheries for food and nutrition security will depend on us, the governments, policymakers, fishers, fish consumers, citizens, and the media. Our collective wisdom and actions will define the future of our capture fisheries — inland and marine. We can undertake the following measures to redesign the future of capture fisheries in Asia.

7.6.1 *Promotion of Best Management Practices*

Co-management has become a mainstream approach to small-scale fisheries management across the developing world. Some Asian countries (particularly Bangladesh, Thailand, the Philippines, and

Vietnam) have evidence of successfully managing fisheries through a community-based approach (Evans *et al.*, 2011). Community-based fish culture (CBFC) practice, introduced by WorldFish and various Asian governmental and non-governmental institutions, has the potential to manage fisheries in Asian floodplains sustainably. Several countries have been practicing the CBFC model in floodplains, most extensively in Bangladesh [Dey *et al.*, 2013; Freed *et al.*, 2020]. CBFC succeeded to equal representation of stakeholders, improved power distribution, conflict resolution, and a mechanism of accountability in the decision making on fish culture activities in public and privately owned floodplains [Dey *et al.*, 2005b; Sheriff *et al.*, 2010]. Fisheries co-management and CBFC delivered benefits to end-users in these countries [Haque *et al.*, 2011; Haque and Dey, 2017; Evans *et al.*, 2011].

Bangladesh's example of managing Hilsa Shad in riverine, estuaries, and marine ecosystems may be adopted by other Asian countries. Bangladesh successfully managed Hilsa fisheries through coordination and collaboration with national and international organisations, a science-based management system, co-management partnership with fishers and coastal communities, support for alternative income-generating activities, enacting new rules, policies and acts, and their strong implementation [DoF, 2008; WorldFish, 2023; Islam *et al.*, 2020]. Tuna fisheries management in the Western Indian Ocean by the Maldives is an example of how we can manage our oceans sustainably. The Maldives have successfully involved fishers, government agencies, fish processors, and all stakeholders in tuna fisheries' sustainable management and harvest. The country predominantly uses pole and line gear technology, producing a high-quality catch with minimal environmental impact and discarding, and involving women workers in post-harvest operations [Jaleel and Smith, 2022].

7.6.2 *Actions to Reduce Illegal Fishing*

FAO and CSIRO [2020] made some recommendations, which could support efforts to reduce illegal fishing in the Asia-Pacific Fisheries Commission region. These are: (1) Establishment of a transparent, repeatable, and cost-effective approach to benchmarking illegal fishing and the effects of interventions in the region; (2) Development of guidance for countries in legal and regulatory reform, particularly addressing structural alignment between industry and regulation; (3) Capacity building for enforcement agencies, aimed at increasing knowledge of fishery regulations and embedding a view of fishery violations as serious crimes meriting action; (4) Information sharing to support cost-effective technological innovation in monitoring and surveillance by members; (5) Development of a platform for sharing monitoring information near borders that facilitates cooperation and reduces barriers to information sharing; (6) Focused effort to increase monitoring, surveillance, and enforcement activities aimed at fish buyers.

7.6.3 *Use of an Integrated Seafood System Approach*

Production in commercial capture fisheries, subsistence fisheries, and aquaculture is interdependent. Capture fisheries and aquaculture have a complementary role in increasing fish availability and access and, therefore, must be promoted in ways that support measurable nutrition and health gains [Thilsted *et al.*, 2016]. Harnessing the diversity of small-scale actors is crucial to the future of aquatic food systems [Short *et al.*, 2021].

7.6.4 *Strengthening Collaboration and Cooperation*

Strengthening collaboration and cooperation among countries and agencies within the country for managing interconnected water bodies and coordinating public investment strategies are essential. Strengthening transboundary fisheries management through collaboration and joint programs (such as by Bangladesh, India, and China in the Ganges-Brahmaputra River Basin; Bangladesh, India, and Myanmar in the Bay of Bengal, Eastern Indian Ocean; Indonesia, Sabah, Malaysia, and the Philippines in the Sulu-Sulawesi Marine Ecoregion, etc.) and implementation of an ecosystem approach with direct involvement of private sectors are important strategies for sustainable management of fisheries.

7.6.5 *Coordination in Data Generation, Management, and Sharing*

Coordination in data generation, management, and sharing for marine fisheries will enable better management of fisheries resources and deliver positive outcomes. For capture and recreational fisheries, data and technology can enhance governance largely by improving monitoring and enforcement [Cojocaru *et al.*, 2022]. Currently, more than 20% of fish harvested from capture fisheries are not documented under any species. They are just reported as "not included elsewhere (nei)" [FAO, 2021]. There is a lack of data on fish stocks within biologically sustainable levels in most Asian countries, including data on stock status, location, gear, species, length/weight, by-catch, and effort. We can strengthen our data-gathering and data-sharing efforts following the major marine fishing areas defined by the FAO of the United Nations. Artificial intelligence, like machine learning, will likely be the next frontier in fishery data collection and sharing.

7.6.6 *Research, Conservation, and Monitoring*

Well-articulated research, conservation strategies, and regular monitoring of capture fisheries are essential to stop the extinction and depletion of vulnerable species. To deal with the overexploitation of fisheries resources beyond the biological limit, countries must identify and protect fish breeding grounds and enact regulations to conserve threatened species. Identification of peak spawning season for commercially important species is essential. In addition, they should ban the harvest, transport, and sale of selected threatened fish species during breeding seasons. These will be beneficial for capture fisheries production.

7.6.7 *Information and Communication Technologies*

Information and communication technologies (ICTs) can play a critical role in collecting, analysing, and disseminating information for small-scale fisheries' sustainable management and development. Examples of innovative applications of ICTs for small-scale fisheries in Asian countries are available in FAO and WorldFish [2020].

Acknowledgment

Research support of Anindita Mandal and Hurunnahar Khusi is acknowledged.

Funding

This work was partly funded (some of Madan Dey and his research assistants' time) by the generous support of the American people provided by the Feed the Future Innovation Lab for Fish through the United States Agency for International Development (USAID). The contents are the responsibility of the authors and do not necessarily reflect the views of USAID or the United States Government. The Feed the Future Innovation Lab for Fish is managed by Mississippi State University through an award from USAID (Award

No. 7200AA18CA00030; M. Lawrence, PI) and provides support to Grant No. 193900.312455.03; M. Dey, PI.

References

Alabia, I. D., Saitoh, S. I., Igarashi, H., Ishikawa, Y., Usui, N., Kamachi, M., Awaji, T. and Seito, M. (2016). Ensemble squid habitat model using three-dimensional ocean data. *ICES Journal of Marine Science*, 73(7), pp. 1863–1874.

Auta, H. S., Emenike, C. U. and Fauziah, S. H. (2017). Distribution and importance of microplastics in the marine environment: a review of the sources, fate, effects, and potential solutions. *Environment International*, 102, pp. 165–176.

Bang, M. K., Sohn, D., Kim, J. J., Choi, W. K., Jang, C. J. and Kim, C. (2022). Future changes in the seasonal habitat suitability for anchovy (*Engraulis japonicus*) in Korean waters projected by a maximum entropy model. *Frontiers in Marine Science*, 9, p. 922020.

Barange, M., Merino, G., Blanchard, J. L., Scholtens, J., Harle, J., Allison, E. H., *et al.* (2014). Impacts of climate change on marine ecosystem production in societies dependent on fisheries. *Nature Climate Change*, 4(3), pp. 211–216.

Barange, M., Bahri, T., Beveridge, M. C. M., Cochrane, K. L., Funge-Smith, S. and Poulain, F., Eds. (2018). *Impacts of climate change on fisheries and aquaculture: synthesis of current knowledge, adaptation and mitigation options*. FAO Fisheries and Aquaculture Technical Paper No. 627. Food and Agriculture Organization.

Bartley, D. M., De Graaf, G. J., Valbo-Jørgensen, J. and Marmulla, G. (2015). Inland capture fisheries: Status and data issues. *Fisheries Management and Ecology*, 22(1), pp. 71–77.

Bassett, H. R., Lau, J., Giordano, C., Suri, S. K., Advani, S. and Sharan, S. (2021). Preliminary lessons from COVID-19 disruptions of small-scale fishery supply chains. *World Development*, 143, p. 105473.

Belton, B. and Thilsted, S. H. (2014). Fisheries in transition: Food and nutrition security implications for the global South. *Global Food Security*, 3(1), pp. 59–66.

Bhowmik, J., Selim, S. A., Irfanullah, H. M., Shuchi, J. S., Sultana, R. and Ahmed, S. G. (2021). Resilience of small-scale marine fishers of Bangladesh against the COVID-19 pandemic and the 65-day fishing ban. *Marine Policy*, 134, p. 104794.

Bhuyan, M. (2022). Effects of microplastics on fish and in human health. *Frontiers in Environmental Science,* 10, p. 827289.

Caswell, B. A., Klein, E. S., Alleway, H. K., Ball, J. E., Botero, J., Cardinale, M., Eero, M., Engelhard, G. H., Fortibuoni, T., Giraldo, A., Hentati-Sundberg, J., Jones, P., Kittinger, J. N., Krause, G., Lajus, D. L., Lajus, J., Lau, S. C. Y., Lescrauwaet, A., MacKenzie, B. R., McKenzie, M., Ojaveer, H., Pandolfi, J. M., Raicevich, S., Russell, B. D., Sundelöf, A., Thorpe, R. B., zu Ermgassen, P. S. E. and Thurstan, R. H. (2020). Something old, something new: Historical perspectives provide lessons for blue growth agendas. *Fish and Fisheries*, 21(4), pp. 774–796.

Curren, E., Kuwahara, V. S., Yoshida, T., and Leong, S. C. Y. (2021). Marine microplastics in the ASEAN region: A review of the current state of knowledge. *Environmental Pollution*, 288, p. 117776.

Cojocaru, A. L., Liu, Y., Smith, M. D., Akpalu, W., Chávez, C., Dey, M. M., Dresdner, J., Kahuiyy, V., Pincinatozz, R. B. M. and Tran, N. (2022). The "seafood" system: aquatic foods, food security, and the Global South. *Review of Environmental Economics and Policy*, 16(2), pp. 306–326.

Dey, M. M., Rab, M. A., Paraguas, F. J., Piumsombun, S., Bhatta, R., Ferdous Alam, M., and Ahmed, M. (2005a). Fish consumption and food security: a disaggregated analysis by types of fish and classes of consumers in selected Asian countries. *Aquaculture Economics & Management*, 9(1–2), pp. 89–111.

Dey, M. M., Prein, M., Mahfuzul Haque, A. B. M., Sultana, P., Cong Dan, N. and Van Hao, N., (2005b). Economic feasibility of community-based fish culture in seasonally flooded rice fields in Bangladesh and Vietnam. *Aquaculture Economics & Management*, 9(1–2), pp. 65–88.

Dey, M. M., Garcia, Y., Praduman, K., Piumsombun, S., Haque, M., Li, L., Radam, A., Senaratne, A., Khiem, N. T. and Koeshendrajana, S. (2008). Demand for fish in Asia: a cross-country analysis. *Australian Journal of Agricultural and Resource Economics*, 52(3), pp. 321–38.

Dey, M. M., Alam, M. F. and Paraguas, F. J. (2011). A multistage budgeting approach to the analysis of demand for fish: An application to inland areas of Bangladesh. *Marine Resource Economics*, 26(1), pp. 35–58.

Dey, M. M., Spielman, D. J., Haque, A. M., Rahman, M. S. and Valmonte-Santos, R. (2013). Change and diversity in smallholder rice-fish systems: Recent evidence and policy lessons from Bangladesh. *Food Policy*, 43, pp. 108–117.

DoF (Department of Fisheries). (2008). *Jatka conservation, alternate income generation for the jatka fishers and research project*. Department of Fisheries, Ministry of Fisheries and Livestock, Government of Bangladesh.

Evans, L., Cherrett, N. and Pemsl, D. (2011). Assessing the impact of fisheries comanagement interventions in developing countries: A meta-analysis. *Journal of Environmental Management*, 92(8), pp. 1938–1949.

FAO. (2016). *APFIC Regional Review of Illegal, Unregulated and Unreported Fishing by Foreign Vessels*. Information document presented to the 34th Session of the Asia-Pacific Fishery Commission, Colombo, Sri Lanka, 12–14 February 2016, APFIC/16/INF 07, 175p.

FAO. (2018). *The State of World Fisheries and Aquaculture: Meeting the Sustainable Development Goals*. http://www.fao.org/3/i9540en/I9540EN.pdf

FAO. (2020a). *Fishery and Aquaculture Statistics. Food Balance Sheets of Fish and Fishery Products 1961–2017 (FishstatJ)*. https://www.fao.org/fishery/en/statistics/software/fishstatj

FAO. (2020b). *The Effect of COVID-19 on Fisheries and Aquaculture in Asia*. http://www.fao.org/3/ca9545en/CA9545EN.pdf

FAO. (2021). *Overview of and Issues on Fisheries in the Asia-Pacific Fishery Commission region*. Asia-Pacific Fishery Commission Thirty-fifth Session [Virtual], Thailand, 5–7 May 2021.

FAO. (2022a). *Fishery and Aquaculture Statistics. Global Production by Production Source 1950–2020 (FishStatJ)*. https://www.fao.org/fishery/en/statistics/software/fishstatj

FAO. (2022b). *Sustainable Development Goals, Goal 14*. https://www.fao.org/sustainable-development-goals/goals/goal-14/en/

FAO and CSIRO. (2020). *A Review of IUU Fishing Related Issues and Progress in the APFIC Region 2020*. https://doi.org/10.4060/cb2640en

FAO and WorldFish. (2020). *Information and Communication Technologies for Small-Scale Fisheries (ICT4SSF) — A Handbook for Fisheries Stakeholders*. https://doi.org/10.4060/cb2030en

Farmery, A. K., Allison, E. H., Andrew, N. L., Troell, M., Voyer, M., Campbell, B., Eriksson, H., Fabinyi, M., Song, A. M. and Steenbergen, D. (2021). Blind spots in visions of a "blue economy" could undermine the ocean's contribution to eliminating hunger and malnutrition. *One Earth*, 4(1), pp. 28–38.

Fernandes, J. A. (2018). Chapter 13: Climate change impacts, vulnerabilities and adaptations: Southern Asian fisheries in the Arabian Sea, Bay of Bengal and East Indian Ocean. In Barange *et al.* (Eds.), *Impacts of Climate Change on Fisheries and Aquaculture: Synthesis of Current Knowledge, Adaptation and Mitigation Options*. Food and Agriculture Organization.

Freed, S., Barman, B., Dubois, M., Flor, R. J., Funge-Smith, S., Gregory, R., Hadi, B. A., Halwart, M., Haque, M., Jagadish, S. V. and Joffre, O. M. (2020). Maintaining diversity of integrated rice and fish production confers adaptability of food systems to global change. *Frontiers in Sustainable Food Systems*, 4, p. 207.

Funge-Smith, S. (2018). Review of the state of the world fishery resources: Inland fisheries. *FAO Fisheries and Aquaculture Circular No. C942*.

Garrido Gamarro, E., Ryder, J., Elvevoll, E. O. and Olsen, R. L. (2020). Microplastics in fish and shellfish–a threat to seafood safety?. *Journal of Aquatic Food Product Technology*, 29(4), pp. 417–425.

Golden, C. D., Seto, K. L., Dey, M. M., Chen, O. L., Gephart, J. A., Myers, S. S., Smith, M., Vaitla, B. and Allison, E. H. (2017). Does aquaculture support the needs of nutritionally vulnerable nations?. *Frontiers in Marine Science*, 4, p. 159.

Gregory, R., Guttman, H. and Kekputhearith, T. (1996). *Poor in all but fish: A study of the collection of rice-field foods from three villages in Svay Teap district, Svay Rieng*. Working Paper 5, AIT Aqua Outreach, Bangkok, Asian Institute of Technology.

Haque, A. B. M, Visser, L. E. and Dey, M. M. (2011). Institutional arrangements in seasonal floodplain management under community-based aquaculture in Bangladesh. *Asian Journal of Agriculture and Development*, 8(1), pp. 1–18.

Haque, A. M. and Dey, M. M. (2017). Impacts of community-based fish culture in seasonal floodplains on income, food security and employment in Bangladesh. *Food Security*, 9, pp. 25–38.

Holsman, K. K., Haynie, A. C., Hollowed, A. B., Reum, J. C. P., Aydin, K., Hermann, A. J., *et al.* (2020). Ecosystem-based fisheries management forestalls climate-driven collapse. *Nature Communications*, 11, p. 4579.

Islam, M. M., Nahiduzzaman, M. and Wahab, M. A. (2020). Fisheries comanagement in hilsa shad sanctuaries of Bangladesh: Early experiences and implementation challenges. *Marine Policy*, 117, p. 103955.

Jaleel, A. and Smith, H. D. (2022). The Maldives tuna fishery: an example of best practice. *Ocean Yearbook Online*, 36(1), pp. 314–345.

Jambeck, J., Geyer, R., Wilcox, C., Siegler, T. R., Perryman, M., Andrady, A., Narayan, R. and Law, K. L. (2015). Plastic waste inputs from land into the ocean. *Science*, 347, pp. 768–771.

Ji, F., Guo X. and Takayama, K. (2020). Response of the Japanese flying squid (*Todarodes pacificus*) in the Japan Sea to future climate warming scenarios. *Climatic Change*, 159, pp. 601–618.

Kawarazuka, N. and Béné, C. (2010). Linking small-scale fisheries and aquaculture to household nutritional security: an overview. *Food Security*, 2(4), pp. 343–357.

Kamonrat, W. (1996). *Spatial genetic structure of Thai silver barb Puntius gonionotus (Bleeker) populations in Thailand*. Ph.D. thesis submitted to Dalhousie University, Nova Scotia.

Kim, J. J., Min, H. S., Kim, C. H., Yoon, J. H. and Kim, S. A. (2012). Prediction of the spawning ground of Todarodes pacificus under IPCC climate A1B scenario. *Ocean and Polar Research,* 34(2), pp. 253–264.

Kroetz, K., Nøstbakken, L. and Quaas, M. (2022). The future of wild-caught fisheries: Expanding the scope of management. *Review of Environmental Economics and Policy,* 16(2), pp. 241–261.

Li, H., Zhang, X., Zhang, Y., Liu, Q., Liu, F., Li, D. and Zhang, H. (2022). Climate-driven synchrony in anchovy fluctuations: a Pacific-wide comparison. *Fishes*, 7(4), p. 193.

Love, D. C., Allison, E. H., Asche, F., Belton, B., Cottrell, R. S., Froehlich, H. E., Gephart, J. A., Hicks, C. C., Little, C. C., Nussbaumer, E. M., da Silva, P. P., Poulain, F., Rubio, A., Stoll, J. S., Tlusty, M. F., Thorne-Lyman, A. L., Troell, M. and Zhang, W. (2021). Emerging COVID-19 impacts, responses, and lessons for building resilience in the seafood system. *Global Food Security*, 28, p. 100494.

Macusi, E. D., Siblos, S. K. V., Betancourt, M. E., Macusi, E. S., Calderon, M. N., Bersaldo, M. J. I. and Digal, L. N. (2022). Impacts of COVID-19 on the catch of small-scale fishers and their families due to restriction policies in Davao Gulf, Philippines. *Frontiers in Marine Science*, 8, p. 770543.

Mandal, S. C., Boidya, P., Haque, M. I. M., Hossain, A., Shams, Z. and Mamun, A. A. (2021). The impact of the COVID-19 pandemic on fish consumption and household food security in Dhaka city, Bangladesh. *Global Food Security*, 29, p. 100526.

Nagai, T. (2019). The Kuroshio Current: Artery of Life. https://eos.org/editors-vox/the-kuroshio-current-artery-of-life

Naylor, R. L., Kishore, A., Sumaila, U. R., Issifu, I., Hunter, B. P., Belton, B., Bush, S. R., Cao, L., Gelcich, S., Gephart, J. A., Golden, C. D., Jonell, M., Koehn, J. Z., Little, D. C., Thilsted, S. H., Tigchelaar, M. and Crona, B. (2021). Blue food demand across geographic and temporal scales. *Nature Communications*, 12(1), p. 5413.

Okunishi, T., Ito, S. I., Hashioka, T., Sakamoto, T. T., Yoshie, N., Sumata, H., *et al.* (2012). Impacts of climate change on growth, migration and recruitment success of Japanese sardine (Sardinops melanostictus) in the Western North Pacific. *Climatic Change*, 115(3), pp. 485–503.

Partelow, S., Nagel, B., Paramita, A. O. and Buhari, N. (2023). Seafood consumption changes and COVID-19 impact index in West Nusa Tenggara, Indonesia. *PloS One*, 18(1), p. e0280134.

Phuong, N. N., Duong, T. T., Le, T. P. Q., Hoang, T. K., Ngo, H. M., Phuong, N. A., ... and Sempere, R. (2022). Microplastics in Asian freshwater ecosystems: Current knowledge and perspectives. *Science of The Total Environment*, 808, p. 151989.

Reum, J. C. P., Blanchard, J. L., Holsman, K. K., Aydin K., Hollowed, A. B., Hermann A. J., *et al.* (2020). Ensemble projections of future climate change impacts on the Eastern Bering Sea food web using a multispecies size spectrum model. *Frontiers in Marine Science*, 7, p. 00124.

Rijnsdorp, A. D., Peck, M. A., Engelhard, G. H., Möllmann, C. and Pinnegar, J. K. (2009). Resolving the effect of climate change on fish populations. ICES *Journal of Marine Science*, 66(7), pp. 1570–1583.

Sheriff, N., Joffre, O., Hong, M. C., Barman, B., Haque, A. B. M. M., Rahman, F., Zhu, J., van Nguyen, H., Russell, A., van Brakel, M., Valmonte-Santos, R., Werthmann, C. and Kodio, A. (2010). *Community-based Fish Culture in Seasonal Floodplains and Irrigations Systems*. CPWF Final Project Report. Project Number CP35. Challenge Program on Water and Food. http://www.worldfishcenter.org/resource_centre/CBFC/CP35_Final%20Project%20Report_v7.pdf.

Short, R. E., Gelcich, S., Little, D. C., Micheli, F., Allison, E. H., Basurto, X., Belton, B., Brugere, C., Bush, S. R., Cao, L., Crona, B., Cohen, P. J.,

Defeo, O., Edwards, P., Ferguson, C. E., Franz, N., Golden, C. D., Halpern, B. S., Hazen, L., Hicks, C., Johnson, D., Kaminski, A. M., Mangubhai, S., Naylor, R. L., Reantaso, M., Sumaila, U. R., Thilsted, S. H., Tigchelaar, M., Wabnitz, C. C. C. and Zhang, W. (2021). Harnessing the diversity of small-scale actors is key to the future of aquatic food systems. *Nature Food*, 2(9), pp. 733–741.

Sunny, A. R., Sazzad, S. A., Prodhan, S. H., Ashrafuzzaman, M., Datta, G. C., Sarker, A. K., Rahman, M. and Mithun, M. H. (2021). Assessing impacts of COVID-19 on aquatic food system and small-scale fisheries in Bangladesh. *Marine Policy*, 126, p. 104422.

Thilsted, S. H., Thorne-Lyman, A., Webb, P., Bogard, J. R., Subasinghe, R., Phillips, M. J. and Allison, E. H. (2016). Sustaining healthy diets: The role of capture fisheries and aquaculture for improving nutrition in the post-2015 era. *Food Policy*, 61, pp. 126–131.

UN Comtrade. (2022). *Fish and Fishery Products*. UN Comtrade Database. https://comtrade.un.org/data/

Wang, W., Ge, J. and Yu, X. (2020). Bioavailability and toxicity of microplastics to fish species: A review. *Ecotoxicology and Environmental Safety*, 189, p. 109913.

Welcomme, R. L., Cowx, I. G., Coates, D., Béné, C., Funge-Smith, S., Halls, A. and Lorenzen, K. (2010). Inland capture fisheries. *Philosophical Transactions of the Royal Society B: Biological Sciences*, 365(1554), pp. 2881–2896.

Whitehouse, G. A., Aydin, K. Y., Hollowed, A. B., Holsman, K. K., Cheng, W., Faig, A., *et al.* (2021). Bottom–up impacts of forecasted climate change on the Eastern Bering Sea food web. *Frontiers in Marine Science*, 8, p. 624301.

WorldFish. (2023). WorldFish Center Website. https://worldfishcenter.org/

https://doi.org/10.1142/9789811278297_0008

Chapter 8

The Future of Livestock and Livestock Production Systems in Asia's Food Security Landscape

Robyn Alders[1,2], Ruwani Kalupahana[3], Hung Nguyen-Viet[4], Habibar Rahman[5], Fred Unger[6] and Iain Wright[4]

[1]*Development Policy Centre and Institute for Climate, Energy and Disaster Solutions, Australian National University, Australia*
[2]*Global Health Programme, Chatham House, London, UK*
[3]*Department of Veterinary Public Health and Pharmacology, Faculty of Veterinary Medicine and Animal Science, University of Peradeniya, Sri Lanka*
[4]*International Livestock Research Institute (ILRI), Nairobi, Kenya*
[5]*Regional Representative for South Asia, International Livestock Research Institute (ILRI), New Delhi, India*
[6]*International Livestock Research Institute (ILRI), Hanoi, Vietnam*

8.1 Introduction

Asia, the world's largest continent, is home to a rich diversity of livestock and livestock production systems, many of which are integral components of local cultures and economies. Moving forward, the projected growth in demand for animal-sourced food in Asia must be balanced with the global push for sustainable food systems, especially in relation to greenhouse gas emissions and the loss of biodiversity and agrobiodiversity. At the same time livestock systems in Asia will need to adapt to future climate change.

A landscape approach has been proposed as a useful lens for addressing livestock, food security, climate change and agricultural biodiversity conservation in an integrated way [GIZ, 2014]. This approach draws attention to how people have managed natural resources in such a way that their multiple needs for food, fibre, fodder, fuel, medicinal products and drinking water are satisfied. It also takes into account changes in human societies, tenure arrangements, labour availability, access to markets and economic growth, as well as cultural traditions and political strategies that have shaped landscapes over centuries.

Focusing on Asia and through a landscape lens, this chapter explores livestock and their role in food and nutrition security, responsible terrestrial animal source food production, livestock as part of circular and sustainable livestock bioeconomies and recommendations for regional and national policy and value chain actions by 2030 and by 2050.

8.2 Livestock and their Role in Food and Nutrition Security

8.2.1 *Food and Nutrition Security*

In 2011, the importance of nutrition security was incorporated into the food and nutrition security definition by the Committee on World Food Security, CFS (Box 8.1). Additionally, over the past decade there has been increasing recognition of the complexity of food security as evidenced by recommendations to increase the number of pillars that contribute to it [HLPE, 2020] (Box 8.2).

Box 8.1 Food and Nutrition Security Definition

"Food and nutrition security exists when all people at all times have physical, social and economic access to food of sufficient quantity and quality in terms of variety, diversity, nutrient content and safety to meet their dietary needs and food preferences for an active and healthy life, coupled with a sanitary environment, adequate health, education and care." [CFS, 2012]

Box 8.2 Food Security Pillars

Availability of food relates to the supply of food through production, distribution, and exchange.

Access to food refers to the affordability and allocation of food, as well as the preferences of individuals and households.

Utilisation of food refers to both household and individual utilisation and metabolisation of nutritious and safe diets.

Stability in food availability and accessibility, and resilience in adapting to economic or environmental shocks or changes.

Box 8.2 (*Continued*)

Agency refers to the capacity of individuals or groups to make their own decisions about what foods they eat, what foods they produce, how that food is produced, processed and distributed within food systems, and their ability to engage in processes that shape food system policies and governance.

Sustainability refers to the long-term ability of food systems to provide food security and nutrition in a way that does not compromise the economic, social and environmental bases that generate food security and nutrition for future generations. [HLPE, 2020]

8.2.2 *Ongoing Human Malnutrition in Asia*

In the Asian region, food and nutrition security remain a significant concern in most countries. Food systems in the region were not efficiently supporting food and nutrition security prior to the COVID-19 pandemic [FAO, 2018] and the pandemic has exacerbated the situation [FAO, 2020]. Less than 50% of Asian countries are on course to meet the global target for stunting among children under 5 years of age, and less than one-third are meeting targets for wasting among children under 5 years of age [Development Initiatives, 2021]. According to UNICEF [2019], only 25% of children in South Asia are being fed much needed nutrients from livestock-derived foods. Not a single country in the region is on course to meet the targets for anaemia in women of reproductive age (15 to 49 years) [Development Initiatives, 2021].

8.2.3 *Livestock-Derived Foods in Human Diets*

Livestock-derived foods (LDFs) are high in macro- and micronutrients, most notably protein, iron, vitamin B12, vitamin A, zinc, and riboflavin [de Bruyn *et al.*, 2020]. Animal proteins contain a balanced complement of essential amino acids and have high bioavailability for humans. In addition, LDFs contain a variety of micronutrients in forms more readily absorbed and used by the human body than those found in plant-sourced foods.

The nutritional composition of food products from many traditional livestock species, breeds and production systems in Asia has not been studied and, therefore, most national food composition tables use data for commercial species and breeds raised under more intensive production systems. This is often borrowed from data generated in non-Asian countries [de Bruyn *et al.*, 2016]. National-level data would assist countries to more accurately determine the required daily intake of LDFs and overall livestock population and production levels required to meet national demand.

8.2.4 *Food and Nutrition Security Policy Issues in a Changing Region*

With expanding population and increasing incomes, urbanisation and retail sectors are contributing to rising meat consumption in Asia [Baltenweck *et al.*, 2020]. However, Ahuja and Staal [2013] remind us that "economic growth is a necessary, but not sufficient, condition for reducing poverty and hunger" as "the poor do not always benefit from economic growth either because of the nature and sectoral composition of growth or because of social, political and economic barriers in accessing productive assets, skills and services."

Meeting the food and nutrition security needs in Asia is an important development objective of policymakers but this cannot happen without a strong focus on the inclusive identification and implementation of national and international policies in support of livestock production systems that work in harmony with local ecosystems, are economically sustainable, achieve good animal welfare outcomes and deliver nutrient-dense LDF products [Alders *et al.*, 2021a].

8.3 Livestock Production Systems and Responsible Livestock-Derived Food Production

8.3.1 *Livestock Production Systems*

Livestock are raised under many different production systems in Asia and these systems are associated with the range of roles played by livestock [Devendra, 2007]. In general, Asian livestock production systems fall into one of three categories: i) "landless"; ii) crop-based; and iii) rangeland-based (Figure 8.1). It is only in the recent past, i.e., since the middle of the 20th century, that intensive livestock production (especially poultry and pigs) has increased significantly. Prior to that, most livestock were raised under extensive and semi-intensive systems and these systems remain common across most Asian countries, especially in those with significant areas of rangeland. Both ruminants and non-ruminants can be part of crop-animal systems depending on the local agroecological conditions and the synergistic interactions support both ecological and economic sustainability [Devendra, 2007]. Pastoral and transhumance systems (where people and their livestock move across the landscape in line with the seasons and pasture availability) continue to be practiced largely in China and South and Central Asia, despite the encroachment of sedentary agriculture into traditionally pastoral areas. In many Asian countries, such as Bangladesh, livestock production systems frequently have an interdependency with crop production in mixed farming systems [Hamid, 2017–2018].

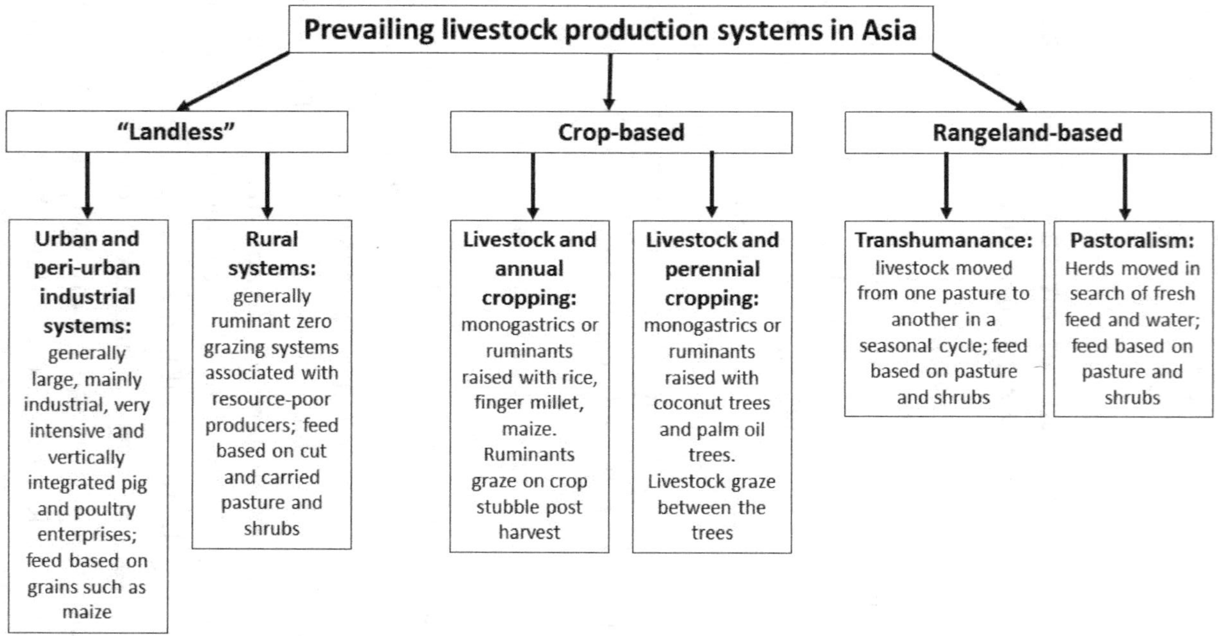

Figure 8.1 The three overarching livestock production systems in Asia together with an indication of the feed sources used in each. Adapted from Devendra [2007].

8.3.2 *Food-Feed Competition*

The responsible use of available nutrient resources has become a key issue over the past decade as nutrient resources have to meet the needs of increasing numbers of humans, livestock and companion animals [Alders *et al.*, 2021a]. With the intensification of livestock and aquaculture production and the globalisation of food systems, competition between humans and aquatic and terrestrial animals for human-edible crops has increased. Berners-Lee *et al.* [2018] argue that there is no nutritional case for feeding human-edible crops to animals and that a failure to heed this message will require a 119% increase in edible crops grown by 2050. Indeed, it is estimated that livestock, principally those raised in intensive systems, consume one-third of global cereal production requiring approximately 40% of arable land [Mottet *et al.*, 2017]. It is also reported that globally, 1 kg of meat requires 2.8 kg of human-edible feed for ruminants and 3.2 kg for monogastrics [Mottet *et al.*, 2017], although this figure varies considerably across production systems. It is projected that by 2030, the Southeast Asian region is to become the fastest growing importer of soybean meal (typically used in intensively raised pig and poultry feed), surpassing the European Union as the largest importer by 2022 [Lee and Hansen, 2019]. The production of soy for livestock feed is considered a major contributor to land clearing in the Amazon Basin, contributing significantly to climate change and biodiversity loss. Such environment factors should be taken into account when conducting a full life cycle analysis of food products [Prudêncio da Silva *et al.*, 2010].

Contrastingly, feed sources for extensive livestock production systems use little to no food suitable for human consumption, with Mottet *et al.* [2017] noting that at a global level 86% of biomass consumed by livestock is not edible by humans. Pastoralism (i.e., the herding of animals, often domesticated livestock such as cattle, sheep and goats, across landscapes in line with seasonal availability of feed and water) remains common on vast tracts of rangeland in Asia despite encroachment of sedentary agriculture and other developments on rangelands over the past few decades [Köhler-Rollefson and Kishore, 2021]. For centuries, pastoralism has been important for crop cultivation and long-term soil fertility. This service is provided as the animals distribute manure directly on the fields where they walk and are penned overnight. In India, manure is actually the main source of income for herders, as farmers compensate pastoralists for this service in cash or in kind. It is estimated that the nitrogen, phosphorus and potassium supplied by this manure contribute a massive 45 billion US dollars a year to the Indian economy [Köhler-Rollefson and Kishore, 2021].

With modest improvements in feed conversion ratios, further expansion of arable land dedicated to animal feed production could be prevented [Mottet *et al.*, 2017]. In support of sustainable development, it is vital that each country considers how best to use the food-feed resources at their disposal and implement any transitions required as efficiently and equitably as possible. Such deliberations require a holistic, systems-based approach taking a range of issues into account, including trade-offs associated with higher-quality animal feed (such as perennial pastures) contributing to climate change mitigation [Dass *et al.*, 2018; Sanderman *et al.* 2013] and the greenhouse gas emissions linked to feed production [Ritchie, 2019].

8.3.3 *Responsible Utilisation of Livestock Carcass Components*

The responsible utilisation of livestock carcass components is commonplace in much of Asia where all human-edible animal source food and other products are used, reducing pre-consumer losses in agri-food value chains. The consumption of offal minimises the number of animals required to meet nutrient requirements by providing highly nutritious bioavailable nutrients such as iron, vitamins A and B12 and zinc from products such as liver [Morrison, 2020; Wingett *et al.*, 2019]. Additional benefits include decreased greenhouse gas emissions and conservation of vulnerable rangeland and other resources due to increased yield per head of livestock [Wingett *et al.* 2019; Xue *et al.*, 2019].

8.3.4 *Environmental Stewardship and Planetary Boundaries*

Livestock production, especially ruminant production, has been facing widespread criticism concerning greenhouse gas emissions as an important driver of climate change. In addition, unsustainable livestock production systems are also affecting other Earth processes negatively including emerging infectious diseases, environmental degradation, loss of biodiversity and chemical pollution [Alders *et al.*, 2021a; van Zanten *et al.*, 2019]. Earth processes, or planetary boundaries , include biosphere integrity, global freshwater use, chemical pollution and climate change [Rockström *et al.*, 2009]). However, it is important to recognise that the impact of livestock production on Earth processes varies across the different systems [Alders *et al.*, 2021a]. For example, welfare-friendly livestock production practices can enhance plant and animal biodiversity and ecosystem function. Agroecological/regenerative livestock management systems can reduce net greenhouse gas emissions and improve overall soil health. There is significant opportunity for the vast rangelands of Asia to contribute to greenhouse gas emissions reduction and soil carbon sequestration. The Food and Agricultural Organization of the United Nations Office for Asia and The Pacific Region has detailed a range of climate-smart livestock solutions that focus on the efficient use of natural resources that deliver higher yields, improved water use efficiency, efficient use of low-carbon energy, and the reduction of waste along the value chain [FAO, 2021].

Moving beyond climate change mitigation, it is also crucial that sustainable livestock production systems adapt to the rapidly changing conditions caused by climate change. The selection of livestock for heat tolerance, efficient water use [Carabano *et al.*, 2019] and reduced susceptibility to livestock pests and diseases [Greeff and Karlsson, 2006] is vital. Conservation of indigenous livestock breeds can also support the adaptation process due to their robust traits [ILRI, 2019]. For example, a Chinese indigenous zebu cattle breed, the Dehong, is recognised for heat tolerance and genomic studies suggest that genes associated with heat shock, oxidative stress response, coat colour, feed intake and reproduction may all play a role in their heat adaptation [Li, 2020].

8.3.5 *Livestock and Health Security*

Livestock raising has accompanied human development over the centuries because of the net benefits they have contributed to human health and wellbeing [Alders *et al.*, 2021b]. However, since the middle of the 20th century, the increasing number of livestock raised — especially under intensive conditions — has contributed to an increase in the incidence of emerging infectious diseases of animal origin (i.e., zoonotic diseases such as highly pathogenic avian influenza H5N1, brucellosis and leptospirosis), foodborne pathogens of animal origin, an increase in antimicrobial resistance due to inappropriate use of antimicrobials, and concentration of heavy metals in certain LDFs [Alders *et al.*, 2021a; Yam *et al.*, 2019]. Livestock, especially intensive production systems, contribute to animal faecal waste which can lead to environmental degradation and human exposure to antimicrobial residues and waterborne pathogens, a key route through which these hazards enter food systems [Penakalapati *et al.*, 2017].

Moving forward, countries in Asia will need to decide which livestock production systems are contributing positively to human, animal and environmental health and which systems may need to be discontinued or more closely regulated. Many of these problems can be controlled via improved on-farm biosecurity and other management measures (e.g., Good Agriculture or Animal Husbandry Practices [Nguyen *et al.*, 2020]), including the effective use of vaccines that reduce the need for veterinary medicines — including antimicrobials — and pesticides, grazing management, selection of livestock breeds with robust immune systems, and organic fertilisers and soil amendments on land used to grow fodder. The environmental and health impacts of animal waste in some intensive livestock systems can be safely managed with an integrated approach that help to close the nutrient cycle and promote disease prevention [Nguyen-Viet, *et al.*, 2021]. In relation to LDF value chains, the risk of foodborne diseases linked to traditional, informal and wet markets can be reduced through capacity building, incentives that bring change and an inclusive policy process [Alonso Alvarez *et al.*, 2021].

Because of the interconnected nature of the problems, a One Health approach that "mobilises multiple sectors, disciplines, and communities at varying levels of society to work together to foster well-being and tackle threats to health and ecosystems, while addressing the collective need for healthy food, water, energy, and air, taking action on climate change and contributing to sustainable development" [One Health High Level Expert Panel, 2022] will assist with achieving optimal livestock production systems that contribute to landscape health in Asia.

8.3.6 *Wildlife Hunting and Farming, Foods and Health Risks*

From a food security perspective, wild animal farming and hunting of wild animals for food is a common practice in many parts of the world, in particular in Southeast Asia and China. In 2016, Chinese wildlife farms employed 14 million workers [IPBES, 2020] and supplied live mammals to cities across China [Xiao *et al.*, 2021]. At the start of the 21st century in Vietnam, it was estimated that the total volume of wildlife and wildlife meat consumed in and exported from Vietnam was around 3,050 tonnes per year; around half was reported to be consumed domestically [Nguyen, 2003]. Annual revenues and profits from illegal wildlife trading in Vietnam are estimated to be USD 66.5 million and USD 21 million, respectively [Pham *et al.*, 2021]. Hunting, farming and consumption of wild animals might present a risk in relation to disease transmission and spillover between animals and humans. For example, in response to the COVID-19 outbreak, China closed the Huanan wet market on 1 January 2020 following the emergence of the disease in late 2019 in Wuhan. It also banned all trade and consumption of wildlife for food on 26 January 2020. Vietnam banned wildlife imports and ordered the closure of illegal wildlife markets to protect human health and ecological balance in July 2020. In 2021, the World Health Organization (WHO), in conjunction with the World Organisation for Animal Health and the United Nations Environment Program, released guidance notes for reducing public health risks associated with the sale of live wild animals of mammalian species in traditional food markets [WHO *et al.*, 2021].

8.4 Evolution of Circular and Sustainable Livestock Bioeconomies

A circular bioeconomy minimises the leaks of energy and materials from the system by recirculating them through the production cycle

[FAO, 2021]. By employing sustainable and circular bioeconomy principles, Van Zanten *et al.* [2019] have proposed that livestock production systems that convert by-products from the food system and grass resources into valuable food and manure can contribute significantly to human food supply, while simultaneously reducing the environmental impact of the entire food system. Climate-smart livestock solutions that promote better livestock integration include the use of manure and animal traction (which generally has a lower carbon footprint than vehicles powered by fossil fuels) for increased crop productivity, nutrient recycling and in energy generation through biogas [FAO, 2021]. One example of a circular livestock bioeconomy is the Thailand Department of Livestock Development Green City project which was launched in 2015. The project subsidised the construction of biogas digesters and the promotion of wastewater treatment systems on pig farms to reduce greenhouse gas emissions and air and water pollution.

8.5 The Social Dimensions of Livestock Production and Utilisation

In Asian societies, livestock, especially traditional breeds, are frequently associated with multiple sociocultural and religious beliefs [Alders *et al.*, 2021b]. In the Hindu religion, for example, the cow is considered a sacred symbol of life to be protected and revered. In some Asian cultures, sacrificing animals to God or deities is performed to obtain blessings or favours. In southern Bhutan, for instance, it is reported that poultry play an important role in the worship of deities. Local beliefs indicate that certain deities require animals be offered in pairs; a chicken, duck, or pigeon can be paired with a large animal or offered in the place of a goat or pig. Farmers in Bhutan believe that the offerings will ensure that there will be no sickness in their household [Hilmi *et al.*, 2011]. In general, the carcasses of animals offered as sacrifices will be consumed by the household or community involved. In Timor-Leste, research has revealed that animal source food consumption is closely linked with the number of cultural ceremonies conducted and this has the potential to make a significant difference to household diets where maternal and child malnutrition is high [Wong *et al.*, 2018]. In Vietnam, people believe that certain animal organs such as pig heart, kidney and brain are suitable for infants and elderly people whereas other offal should not be given because they are unsafe or not nutritious [Nguyen-Viet *et al.*, 2019]. Consumers believed that the heart, brain, loin, hock, ham and spareribs were the most nutritious part of a pig. On the other hand, the most delicious were considered to be heart, stomach, loin, hock, ham, spareribs, belly slices and spare rib roast. Other parts such as bones, nose, tail, intestines, and liver were considered less nutritious and less delicious.

8.6 Conclusions

Livestock, and small livestock such as family poultry and small ruminants in particular, have been reported to contribute directly to 12 of the 17 Sustainable Development Goals (SDGs). Under appropriate management systems, they can also contribute to sustainable food systems. Moving forward, the quest is to identify and promote livestock systems that enhance environmental and human health and well-being as well as animal welfare. For this approach to deliver positive economic, environmental and social outcomes at the landscape scale, it will be essential for the livestock sector to work in close collaboration with the human health, environmental health, finance, land use planning and other key food system actors at the local and national levels. To achieve positive outcomes in Asia in the long term, effective coordination and collaboration between regional economic communities and with the relevant global institutions is critical.

8.6.1 *Recommendations for Policies to be Implemented by 2030*

In the period leading up to the 2030 SDGs, the following are action items to be considered for implementation in order to assure the sustainable contribution of livestock to Asian food security:

- Encourage the formation of One Health committees at local, national and regional levels.
- Enable animal health and public health communities to work together to study the nutritional properties and life cycle analysis of locally available foods and accompanying health promotion and behaviour change activities to improve utilisation of nutritious food.
- Incentivise the selection of livestock breeds and parent stock within breeds with low greenhouse gas emissions, efficient water use and robust immune systems.
- Encourage livestock production systems that minimise the use of human-edible foodstuffs, promote landscape regeneration, effective use of all livestock products and maximise recycling of resources through circular bioeconomies.
- Facilitate alignment of institutes within and between countries to further understanding and use of molecular epidemiology, spatial distribution and genetic evolution for sustainable livestock development.
- Ensure the adequate funding of livestock health systems — the introduction and use of risk-based approaches — so that zoonotic diseases and diseases of economic importance are efficiently

prevented, and disease outbreaks are detected and managed quickly through effective disease surveillance and response systems.

- Identify feasible (e.g., low-cost) incentives and innovations to support behaviour and practice change of livestock keepers and other LDF actors.
- Support livestock production systems and value chains that regenerate landscapes and promote equitable practices.
- In collaboration with producers, introduce and refine carbon and biodiversity credit schemes for small-, medium- and large-scale livestock producers.
- Conserve indigenous livestock species and breeds.
- Urgent policy action is required to support restoration of grasslands that are invariably in very poor state. In this context, there is an urgent need for improving rangelands, enhancing fodder production from problem soils and village common property lands.
- Urgent policy action needed to make provision of dedicated fodder marketing chains a priority with increased interactions among buyers and sellers, including value addition of dry fodder, use of straw-based feed blocks, creation of storage systems on-farm as well as en route to distant markets.

8.6.2 *Recommendations for Policies to be Implemented by 2050*

Longer-term action is recommended as follows:

- Sustainable and circular livestock bioeconomies established and monitored.
- High-risk livestock production systems phased out with transition packages available for owners and workers as appropriate.

In order to develop and implement safe and sustainable livestock food systems in the 21st century, the importance of effective and efficient collaboration between the livestock, public health and environmental sectors cannot be underestimated. Asia, with its consensus-building skills and ancient philosophies recognising the interconnectedness of the elements of life, has an opportunity to contribute to and drive discussions on this most strategic topic of global importance.

Acknowledgements

We thank our colleagues at the International Livestock Research Institute (ILRI), the Food and Agriculture Organization of the United Nations (FAO), in particular Vinod Ahuja, the FAO Representative to Mongolia, and also the veterinarians, extension specialists, researchers, traders, and farmers in Asia who have given freely of their time and expertise over the years.

References

Ahuja, V. and Staal, S. (2013). Poverty, Food Security, Livestock and Smallholders: Issues and Options for the Asia and Pacific Region. In V. Ahuja (Ed.), *Asian Livestock: Challenges, Opportunities and the Response*, pp. 97–106. Food and Agriculture Organization.

Alders, R. G., Campbell, A., Costa, R., Guèye, E. F., Hoque, M. A., Perezgrovas-Garza, R., Rota, A. and Wingett, K. (2021b). Livestock across the world: diverse animal species with complex roles in human societies and ecosystem services. *Animal Frontiers,* 11(5), pp. 20–29.

Alders, R. G., Chadag, M. V., Debnath, N. C., Howden, M., Meza, F., Schipp, M., Swai, E. S. and Wingett, K. (2021a). Planetary boundaries and veterinary services. *Revue Scientifique et Technique,* 40(2), pp. 439–453.

Alonso Alvarz, S., Grace, D. and Nguyen-Viet, H. (2021). Informal food markets: what it takes to make them safer. *The Conversation*, June 4, 2021. https://theconversation.com/informal-food-markets-what-it-takes-to-make-them-safer-161601

Baltenweck, I., Enahoro, D., Frija, A. and Tarawali, S. (2020). Why is production of animal source foods important for economic development in Africa and Asia? *Animal Frontiers*, 10(4), pp. 22–29.

Berners-Lee, M., Kennelly, C., Watson, R. and Hewit, C. N. (2018). Current global food production is sufficient to meet human nutritional needs in 2050 provided there is radical societal adaptation. *Elementa: Science of the Anthropocene*, 6, p. 52.

Carabano, M. J., Ramón, M., Menéndez-Buxadera, A., Molina, A. and Díaz, C. (2019). Selecting for heat tolerance. *Animal Frontiers*, 9(1), pp. 62–68.

CFS. (2012). *Coming to Terms with Terminology: Food Security, Nutrition Security, Food Security and Nutrition, Food and Nutrition Security*. Committee on World Food Security. 39th Session, 15–20 October 2012, Rome. https://www.fao.org/3/MD776e/MD776e.pdf

de Bruyn, J., Bagnol, B., Chan, H., Grace, D., Mitchell, M., Nunn, M., Wingett, K., Wong, J. T. and Alders, R. G. (2020). The role of animal-source foods in sustainable, ethical, and optimal human diets. In: A. A. Adenle, M. R. Chertow, E. H. M. Moors and D. J. Pannell (Eds.), *Science, Technology, and Innovation for Sustainable Development Goals: Insights from Agriculture, Health, Environment, and Energy*, pp. 344–363. Oxford University Press.

de Bruyn, J., Ferguson, E., Allmann-Farinelli, M., Darnton-Hill, I., Maulaga, W., Msuya, J. and Alders, R. (2016). Food composition tables in resource-poor settings: exploring current limitations and opportunities, with a focus on animal-source foods in sub-Saharan Africa. *British Journal of Nutrition*, 116, pp. 1709–1719.

Development Initiatives. (2021). Asia. 2021 *Global Nutrition Report: The State of Global Nutrition*. Development Initiatives Poverty Research

Ltd. https://globalnutritionreport.org/resources/nutrition-profiles/asia/

Devendra, C. (2007). Perspectives on animal production systems in Asia. *Livestock Systems*, 106, pp. 1–18.

FAO. (2018). *Asia and the Pacific Regional Overview of Food Security and Nutrition 2018 — Accelerating Progress Towards the SDGs*. https://www.fao.org/3/ca0950en/ca0950en.pdf

FAO. (2020). *Impacts of Coronavirus on Food Security and Nutrition in Asia and the Pacific: Building More Resilient Food Systems*. http://www.fao.org/3/ca9473en/CA9473EN.pdf

FAO. (2021). *Climate-smart Livestock Production: A Practical Guide for Asia and the Pacific Region*. https://doi.org/10.4060/cb3170en

FAO. (2022). *Member Countries in Asia and the Pacific*. https://www.fao.org/asiapacific/countries/en/

GIZ. (2014). Landscape approaches: addressing [sic] food security, climate change and biodiversity conservation in an integrated way. German Federal Ministry for Economic Cooperation and Development. *Deutsche Gesellschaft für Internationale Zusammenafbeit (GIZ) GmbH*. https://www.landportal.org/library/resources/landscape-approaches-adressing-food-security-climate-change-and-biodiversity

Gomez San Juan, M. and Bogdanski, A. (2021). *How to Mainstream Sustainability and Circularity into the Bioeconomy? A Compendium of Bioeconomy Good Practices and Polices*. https://doi.org/10.4060/cb5798en

Greeff, J. C. and Karlsson, L. J.-E. (2006). Breeding for worm resistance — whole farm benefits. *International Journal of Sheep and Wool Science*, 54(2), pp. 102–108.

HLPE. (2020). *Food Security and Nutrition: Building a Global Narrative Towards 2030*. https://www.fao.org/3/ca9731en/ca9731en.pdf

ILRI. (2019). *Climate Change Adaptation in Livestock Systems. Brief 5: Animal Breeding and Genetics*. https://cgspace.cgiar.org/bitstream/handle/10568/101609/climateChangeBrief5.pdf

Intergovernmental Science-Policy Platform on Biodiversity and Ecosystem Services (IPBES). (2020). *IPBES Workshop on Biodiversity and Pandemics: Workshop Report*. https://doi.org/10.5281/zenodo.4147317

Lee, T. and Hansen, J. (2019). Southeast Asia's growing meat demand and its implications for feedstuffs imports. *USDA Economic Research Service*. https://www.ers.usda.gov/amber-waves/2019/april/southeast-asia-s-growing-meat-demand-and-its-implications-for-feedstuffs-imports/

Li, R., Li, H., Chen, R., Chong, Q., Xiao, H. and Chen, S. (2020). Genome-wide scan of selection signatures in Dehong humped cattle for heat tolerance and disease resistance. *Animal Genetics*, 51, pp. 292–299.

Mottet, A., de Haan, C., Falcucci, A., Tempio, G., Opio, C. and Gerber, P. (2017). Livestock: On our plates or eating at our table? A new analysis of the feed/food debate. *Global Food Security*, 14, pp. 1–8.

Nguyen-Viet, H., Dang-Xuan, S., Pham-Duc, P., Roesel, K., Huong, N. M., Luu-Quoc, T., Hung, P. V., Nga, N. T. D., Lapar, L., Uunger, F., Häsler, B. and Grace, D. (2019). Rapid integrated assessment of food safety and nutrition related to pork consumption of regular consumers and mothers with young children in Vietnam. *Global Food Security*, 20, pp. 37–44.

Nguyen, L. T., Nanseki, T. and Chomei, Y. (2020). The impact of Viet-GAHP implementation on Vietnamese households' pig production. *Environment, Development and Sustainability*, 22, pp. 7701–7725.

Nguyen-Viet, H., Pham-Duc, P., Nguyen, V., Tanner, M., Odermatt, P., Vu-Van, T., Hoang, M. V., Zurbrüg, C., Schelling, E. and Zinsstag, J. (2021). A one health perspective for integrated human and animal sanitation, nutrient recycling and climate change. In J. Zinsstag, E. Schelling, L. Crump, M. Whittaker, M. Tanner and C. Stephen (Eds.), *One Health: The Theory and Practice of Integrated Health Approaches* (Second Edition), pp. 157–169. CAB International.

Nguyen, S. V. (2003). Wildlife trading in Vietnam: why it flourishes. EEPSEA Research reports, Tanglin, Singapore. pp. 1–75. https://econpapers.repec.org/paper/eepreport/rr2003111.htm

OECD/FAO. (2021). *OECD-FAO Agricultural Outlook 2021–2030*. https://doi.org/10.1787/19428846-en

One Health High-Level Expert Panel (OHHLEP), Adisasmito, W. B., Almuhairi, S., Behravesh, C. B., Bilivogui, P., Bukachi, S. A., *et al.* (2022). One Health: A new definition for a sustainable and healthy future. *PLoS Pathogens*, 18(6), p. e1010537.

Otte, J., Pica-Ciamarra, U. and Morzaria, S. (2019). A comparative overview of the livestock-environment interactions in Asia and Sub-saharan Africa. *Frontiers in Veterinary Science*, 6, p. 37.

Penakalapati, G., Swarthout, Delahoy, M. J., McAiley, L., Wodnik, B., Levy, K. and Freeman, M. C. (2017). Exposure to animal feces and human health: a systematic review. *Environmental Science & Technology*, 51(20), pp. 11537–11552.

Pham, T. T., Tran, Y. L., Nguyen Thị, K. N., Tang Thị, K. H. and Dang, H. P. (2021). *The Economic Value of the Wildlife Trade in Vietnam*. CIFOR. https://doi.org/10.17528/cifor/008098

Prudêncio da Silva, V., van der Werf, H. M. G., Spies, A. and Soares, S. R. (2010). Variability in environmental impacts of Brazilian soybean according to crop production and transport scenarios. *Journal of Environmental Management*, 91(9), pp. 1831–1839.

Rabobank. (2016). *Asia-Pacific: Agricultural Perspectives*. https://economics.rabobank.com/publications/2016/february/asia%2Dpacific%2Dagricultural%2Dperspectives/

Rockström, J., Steffen, W., Noone, K., … and Foley, J. (2009). Planetary boundaries: exploring the safe operating space for humanity. *Ecology and Society*, 14(2), p. 32.

UNICEF. (2019). *The State of the World's Children 2019. Children, Food and Nutrition: Growing Well in a Changing World*. https://www.unicef.org/media/106506/file/The%20State%20of%20the%20World%E2%80%99s%20Children%202019.pdf

Van Zanten, H. H. E., Van Ittersum, M. K. and de Boer, I. J. M. (2019). The role of farm animals in a circular food system. *Global Food Security*, 21, pp. 18–22.

WHO, OIE, UNEP. (2021). *Reducing Public Health Risks Associated with the Sale of Live Wild Animals of Mammalian Species in Traditional Food Markets: Interim Guidance*. https://www.who.int/publications/i/item/WHO-2019-nCoV-Food-safety-traditional-markets-2021.1

Wingett, K., Allman-Farinelli, M. and Alders, R. (2019). Food loss and nutrition security: reviewing pre-consumer loss in Australian sheep meat value chains using a Planetary Health framework. *CAB Reviews,* 13, p. 033.

Xiao, X., Newman, C., Buesching, C. D., *et al.* (2021). Animal sales from Wuhan wet markets immediately prior to the COVID-19 pandemic. *Scientific Reports,* 11, 11898.

Xue, L., Prass, N., Gollnow, S., Davis, J., Scherhaufer, S., Östergren, K., Cheng, S. and Liu, G. (2019). Efficiency and carbon footprint of the German meat supply chain. *Environmental Science & Technology*, 53(9), pp. 5133–5142.

Yam, E. L. Y., Hsu, L. Y., Yap, E. P-H., Yeo, T. W., Lee, V., Schlundt, J., Lwin, M. O., Limmathurotsakul, D., Jit, M., Dedon, P., Turner, P. and Wilder-Smith, A. (2019). Antimicrobial resistance in the Asia Pacific region: a meeting report. *Antimicrobial Resistance and Infection Control,* 8, p. 202.

https://doi.org/10.1142/9789811278297_0009

Chapter 9

China's Food (In)Security: Current Status, Emerging Challenges and Future Prospects in the Post-COVID-19 Era

Hongzhou Zhang[1], Genevieve Donnellon-May[2,3] and Cecilia Tortajada[4]

[1]*S. Rajaratnam School of International Studies, Nanyang Technological University, Singapore*
[2]*Department of Geography and the Environment, University of Oxford, UK*
[3]*Oxford Global Society, UK*
[4]*School of Social and Environmental Sustainability, University of Glasgow, UK*

9.1 Introduction

The world is experiencing a global food crisis. According to the World Food Programme, as of June 2022, as many as 828 million people went to bed hungry every night. A total of 50 million people in 45 countries are teetering on the edge of famine [World Food Programme, 2022]. Additionally, domestic food price inflation remains high globally with record-high food prices driving millions more into extreme poverty, magnifying hunger and malnutrition. The number of acute food-insecure people increased to 345 million in 82 countries in 2022, a shocking jump from 135 million in 2019 [World Food Programme, 2022]. This ongoing global food crisis is triggered and continues to be fuelled by several key factors, most notably climate shocks, armed conflicts, and government trade-distorting policies.

Amid the worsening global food crisis, notwithstanding the domestic and international concerns regarding the country's food security, the People's Republic of China (China), the world's second most populous country and largest food importer, has been relatively successful in terms of maintaining a stable food supply at the macro level [Zhang *et al.*, 2022]. Against a backdrop of rising global food prices and worsening food insecurity, it should be noted that food prices in China, except for pork, have remained largely stable. For instance, in November 2022, food prices in China had risen 3.7% compared to 2021, a decrease from the 7% increase seen in October, while pork prices saw a significant surge of 34.4% [China Daily, 2022]. Indeed, according to the Global Food Security Index, China ranked as the 25th most food-secure country in the world in 2022, ahead of developed countries such as South Korea, Italy, and Singapore, and a significant improvement as compared to 2020, when China was ranked 39th [The Economist Intelligence Unit, 2023]. How the world's most populous country and the largest importer managed to safeguard the country's food security amid the COVID-19 pandemic, climate shocks, and global armed conflicts remains an important question and could potentially offer important lessons for the rest of the world.

This chapter thus aims to provide a comprehensive assessment of the current status, policy responses, emerging challenges, and future prospects of China's food security. The rest of the chapter is organised as follows. Section 9.2 reviews the political importance of food security in China and summarises China's achievements in terms of agricultural development. Section 9.3 then examines the supply and demand balances of China's key food products, focusing on rice, wheat, corn and soybeans and new threats to the country's food security. Following this, Section 9.4 touches on the measures adopted by the country to safeguard its food security. In the final section, the prospects of China's food security will be discussed along with the global implications of these prospects.

9.2 Beijing's Strong Food Security Focus and Past Accomplishments

In many ways, China's history can be characterised by concern for food and famine [Li, 2007; Yang, 1996]. Given the importance of food in the country's culture, politics, religion, and medicine, food security has always been a key priority for the country's leaders [Cui and Shoemaker, 2018; Kung and Lin, 2003; Zhang, 2018]. In recent years, the importance of food security has risen to new heights, having been considered as important as energy and financial security in the face of an increasingly complex global environment. Furthermore, China's top leaders, including President Xi Jinping, have publicly emphasised the importance of safeguarding food security for the country, while the Minister of Agriculture and Rural Affairs, Tang Renjian, emphasised seeds and cultivated land as key components of China's food security. This continued focus on food security is further reinforced by the inclusion of food security in China's national and domestic five-year plans, such as the 14th Five-Year Plan [State Council of China, 2021a] and other key Chinese Communist Party (CCP) party documents, including Xi Jinping's 20th Party Congress Report [Xi, 2022a].

Due to the strong political commitment and policy support for domestic grain and food production, China's agricultural sector has achieved phenomenal development in the past decades. The agricultural production of key food products in China has significantly increased since the late 1970s. Notably, grain production increased by 100% between 1978 and 2020. Additionally, meat production increased six-fold from 1978 to 2011, while milk production rose from 13.6 million tonnes in 1978 to 28 million tonnes in 2020 [National Bureau of Statistics of China, 1979; 2021].

To reassure China's public and international community that the country will not face imminent grain security risks, the Chinese government has publicly pointed to its bumper grain harvests and massive grain reserve systems. For instance, in his 2023 New Year Address, Xi Jinping declared, "Despite a global food crisis, we have secured a bumper harvest for the 19th year in a row, putting us in a stronger position to ensure the food supply of the Chinese people" [Xi, 2022b].

At present, China holds significant quantities of the world's grain reserves, with the country's rice, wheat, and corn reserves having steadily grown in recent decades. According to a December 2021 report in *Nikkei Asia* which cited statistics from the U.S. Department of Agriculture (USDA), China is expected to hold 69% of the world's corn reserves, 60% of its rice, 51% of the world's wheat, and 37% of its soybeans [Watanabe and Munakata, 2021]. While this claim was denied by China's foreign ministry [Global Times, 2022a], an official from the country's National Food and Strategic Reserves Administration noted in November 2021 that supply in the domestic grain market is "fully guaranteed" while grain reserves are at a "historical high level". Given that China's rice and wheat imports only represent a smaller proportion of its overall consumption and with the country holding the world's largest rice and wheat reserves, China does not seem to have major concerns in the near term regarding staple supplies.

9.3 China's Main Food Security Challenges and New Threats

Despite these remarkable achievements in its agricultural production, China's food security still appears to face numerous challenges. Chief among the main challenges facing China's food security is the growing demand and supply imbalance of the country's feed supply and the structural imbalance of its staple supply.

9.3.1 *China's Feed Shortages*

The most significant risk to China's food security lies in its feed supplies, particularly its soybean supplies. Although the country was the world's largest soybean producer and a net soybean exporter between 1949 and the mid-1990s [Yan *et al.*, 2016], World Trade Organisation accession negotiations with the U.S. resulted in Beijing being forced to lower its overall agricultural tariffs and domestic agricultural support level. Due to the greater competitiveness of cheap soybean imports compared to domestically grown soybeans, China's domestic production of soybeans quickly shrank. Driven by a booming feed sector and declining domestic production [Ghose, 2014], China's soybean imports have since soared, increasing from 1 million tonnes in 1996 to 96.5 million tonnes in 2021 [Gu and Patton, 2022]. Today, China is by far the largest importer of soybeans in the world, accounting for over 60% of the world's total exports, with soybean imports now making up 85% of the country's soybean consumption [USDA, 2023].

The genetically modified (GM) soybean imported by China is mainly processed to produce oil for cooking and soybean meal for animal feed. In contrast, the country's local non-GM soybeans are used mainly to produce food (e.g., tofu, soybean milk, and soy sauce). While food consumption has increased, consumption of edible oils and soybean meal has grown even faster [Gale *et al.*, 2019]. Both the consumption of edible oils and soybean meal are expected to experience further increases as rising consumer income and urbanisation continue to change consumption habits. There has been growing demand for soybeans, brought on by growth in livestock, soybean-based foods, and nutritional supplement consumption. By 2028/2029, China's imports of soybeans are expected to reach as much as 126 million tonnes [USDA, 2019a].

Corn is another important component of China's food security. There is a growing fear that China's corn supply would experience a similar fate to that of its domestically produced soybeans as China seeks to modernise its animal husbandry sectors by replacing backyard pig farming with modern, large-scale industrial production. Over the past decade, demand for corn for feed has rapidly increased, prompting fears of large domestic corn shortages [Gu and Patton, 2020; Hansen and Gale, 2014]. In response to production deficits, China has significantly increased corn imports by several folds. In 2021, China had to import 28.35 million metric tons of corn, up 152% from the previous record of 11.3 million tonnes in 2020 [Reuters, 2022]. Although the decrease in U.S. corn imports in recent years can be attributed to the China-U.S. trade war, China has also sought out other corn suppliers, such as Ukraine, from whence China imports a considerable quantity of corn [Sizov, 2019]. In 2020, China was Ukraine's largest single-nation trading partner, with its agricultural exports becoming increasingly crucial for China [Ukrainian State Statistics Service, 2021]. Combined with potential labour shortages and rising gas and fertiliser prices, the Russia-Ukraine war and subsequent disruptions to shipments to China will create significant inflationary pressure. Due to lingering China-U.S. tensions and the Ukraine-Russia conflict, the continued diversification of corn imports from other countries, like Brazil, remains important [Ribeiro and Hirtzer, 2022; Zhou, 2022].

9.3.2 *Structural Imbalance of China's Staple Supplies*

In China, rice and wheat are the main staples; rice is predominately consumed in southern China while wheat is mainly consumed in northern China. While ensuring adequate supply has always been a top priority for Chinese leaders, the importance has continued to grow in recent years with President Xi Jinping referring to rice as the "rice bowl" on several occasions to further emphasise its significance. Despite previously being self-sufficient in rice production and a major rice exporter, in 2013, China became the world's leading rice importer and has since then remained one of the world's largest importers. In addition to official rice imports, research suggests that large quantities of rice have been smuggled into China, with some suggesting that the smuggled quantity of rice is possibly even more than the volume of legally imported rice. For example, between 2014 and 2017, approximately three million tonnes of rice were smuggled into China each year through the land borders with Vietnam and Myanmar [Zhang, 2019]. Furthermore, a USDA report stated that China's overall informal border trade, including rice smuggled from Myanmar, Vietnam, and Thailand, could be as high as 10 million tonnes [USDA, 2019b].

This means that when both formal and informal imports are taken into account, China likely remains the world's largest rice importer. Despite achieving consecutive bumper harvests, as President Xi has publicly pointed out (e.g., Global Times, 2022b; Xinhuanet, 2020a], China's rice supply is also facing structural imbalances, including an oversupply of Japonica rice and a shortage of high-quality Indica rice. In this context, Indica rice from Southeast Asia and South Asia is therefore crucial in addressing these structural imbalance issues in China's rice supply [Tortajada and Zhang, 2021].

Other factors also play a role in influencing China's rice supply and imports. Notably, intensive farming practices, overuse of fertilisers and pesticides, and industrial pollution have caused serious soil erosion and environmental pollution in China, negatively impacting its rice production [Guo, 2016]. A 2011 report stated that 10% of China's annual rice production is contaminated with heavy metals, making it unsafe for consumption. In 2013, a Guangdong Province report found that 44% of rice samples in the province had excessive levels of cadmium, leading to the term "cadmium rice" becoming well known in China [Tatlow, 2014]. In response to these interlinked concerns, President Xi Jinping announced at the 19th Party Congress in October 2017 that measures would be taken to strengthen the control of soil pollution, restore polluted soil, and improve rural living environments [Xi, 2017]. As China implements rice field restoration programs and reduces rice production on certain areas of land, domestic rice production may decline, thereby leading to a greater reliance on imports [Zhang, 2018].

To meet its increasing demand for rice, China will likely look to Southeast and South Asian countries along the Maritime Silk Road. Officials and scholars have suggested that China should focus on developing rice production in Southeast Asia to establish the region as an "offshore rice granary" [Han, 2014; Ministry of Agriculture Agricultural Trade Promotion Center, 2016]. However, the global rice trade is relatively small, with international rice trade volume at about 46 million tonnes or less than 10% of global rice output and about one-third of China's annual rice consumption [Zhang, 2018]. Additionally, global rice exports are dominated by a few Southeast Asian and South Asian countries. Thus, China seeks to increase regional rice production through the Belt and Road Initiative (BRI) using direct investment, technology transfer, and infrastructure development [Zhang, 2021]

Compared with rice, the importance of wheat as the second most important staple in China is often overlooked. China is the largest wheat-producing country, producing over 17% of the global total. The country is also reported to have the largest wheat reserves, accounting for over half of the worldwide wheat stock in 2022 [Watanabe and Munakata, 2021]. In recent years, however, the effects of climate change, including extreme weather-related disasters like droughts, have put domestic production of wheat and other grain crops at risk and caused production deficits. According to Zhou *et al.* [2017] and the World Resources Institute [2021], climate change-driven seasonal drought could cause significant losses of nearly 8% by 2030 in yields of the three main crops — rice, wheat, and corn — even if water-saving techniques are adopted.

Despite its enormous domestic production and massive wheat stock, China is the world's biggest wheat consumer and a leading wheat importer, having purchased nearly 10 million tonnes of wheat in 2021 [USDA, 2021]. The obvious reason for this is the large gap between domestic and international wheat prices, but the second and more important factor is the structural imbalance in China's wheat supply: for decades, China's wheat policies have focused on quantity rather than quality. To a certain extent, wheat quality is often sacrificed in favour of quantity. With rising income and shifting food preferences, however, the country now faces a shortage of high-protein wheat [Bloomberg News, 2022; Chen, 2019].

9.3.3 *New Threats*

Further exacerbating matters such as global instability, regional tensions and extreme climate events present China with enormous challenges.

Currently, Beijing finds itself in an increasingly complex geopolitical environment, facing growing geostrategic rivalry with the U.S. Complicating matters, the ramifications of an unstable environment exacerbate China's existing internal and external long-term challenges relating to food security. To add to this worsening scenario, the arrival of new threats has significantly impacted China's food security. One of the most significant new threats to ensuring China's food security was the COVID-19 pandemic and concomitant zero-COVID policy and lockdowns, which have, at times, impacted the country's ability to import food and prevented farmers to work in the fields from 2020 until the removal of the policy in late 2022.

Yet the COVID-19 pandemic has not been the only new challenge to the country's food security. Another emerging new threat is undoubtedly the Ukraine-Russia war (2022 —) due to the conflict's immediate and long-term effects on the country's imports. One of the most noticeable repercussions is the rise of food protection which has resulted in fewer countries exporting certain agricultural products. As part of broader efforts to reduce reliance on the U.S. and amid worsening ties between China and Western countries, Beijing has, in recent years, sought to diversify its food and fertiliser import sources. In particular, BRI countries in Central Asia and Eastern

Europe have been considered by Beijing as viable alternatives for key imports such as wheat, soybeans, and corn [Tortajada and Zhang, 2021; Zhan, 2022]. However, the ongoing war and sanctions on Russia have affected import routes, resulting in reduced supplies of fertiliser, wheat, and animal feed transported from these regions to China. So far, China has remained mostly unscathed by the war and its far-reaching consequences, unlike other countries, partly due to Beijing's stockpiling and willingness to buy large quantities of grain.

Nonetheless, a prolonged war between Ukraine and Russia, two agricultural powerhouses, could complicate matters by impacting China's ability to safeguard its food security. Notably, China would likely face greater competition for limited supplies (such as wheat), simultaneously further contributing to already-inflated food prices globally. Due to these many concerns, Beijing has consequently been forced to rethink how its national food security goals can be achieved. The response to growing food insecurity fears from Beijing has been to implement a range of strong policy measures, including executing national campaigns addressing food waste, introducing a series of legislative and technological measures, increasing agricultural investment and market reform, and pushing for greater domestic production [Huang and Yang, 2017; Tortajada and Zhang, 2021]. Nevertheless, it remains to be seen if these measures are sufficient to safeguard China's food security in the long term.

9.4 Beijing's Dual Food Security Strategy and Coping Measures

9.4.1 *Boosting Domestic Grain Production*

Grain security, an integral part of safeguarding China's food security, has been the government's main concern in the past several decades.

Indeed, "food security" (*liang shi an quan*) literally translates as "grain security" in Chinese. Until the mid-1990s, the Chinese central government's overarching goal was to achieve complete self-sufficiency in grain. However, given China's land and water constraints and growing food demand, the grain self-sufficiency target level since 1996 has been reduced to 95% or higher [Wang, 2019; Wong and Huang, 2012]. To encourage the domestic production of grains, Beijing has put forward various policies and plans to support farmers and the modernisation of farming in China. Since 2003, the Chinese government has implemented a policy of "four reductions and four subsidies" to encourage grain production [Kuteleva, 2016, p. 5; Wang, 2019], while various taxes (such as an agricultural tax and livestock tax) have been removed. To support domestic grain production, China has also undertaken enormous political and fiscal efforts alongside spatio-temporal changes in the country's grain production patterns to strengthen its grain production. And these efforts have, to some extent, paid off. Between 2003 and 2013, China's domestic grain production rose from 430 million metric tons to over 600 million metric tons, much of which came from the country's grain baskets — the mid-and-lower Yangtze River region, the Northeast China Plain, and the North China Plain [Lu *et al.*, 2020].

Although self-sufficiency remains at the core of China's food security strategy, the focus has shifted from achieving that goal in grains (rice, wheat, corn, soybean, and root tubers such as potatoes and coarse grains) to ensuring basic self-sufficiency in cereals (wheat, rice, and corn) and absolute security in staples (rice and wheat). Since 2014, the overriding objective of China's food security has been to safeguard the country's rice and wheat supplies [State Council Information Office of China, 2019]. This is further reflected in the Chinese central government's national plans. For instance, under the MARA Five-Year Agricultural Plan (2021–2025) on crop farming, China will seek to stabilise its annual grain production, to exceed a target of 700 million tonnes by 2025 to ensure grain security, and also increase domestic soybean production to 23 million tonnes by 2025 [MARA, 2021]. To support these aims, the plan sets out grain farmland and planting acreage targets for rice, wheat, and corn. For example, China will aim to keep its grain farmland above 1.75 billion *mu* (approximately 117 million hectares) while planting acreage of grains, and staple grains must stay above 1.4 billion *mu* (93.8 million hectares) and over 800 million *mu* (53.6 million hectares), respectively [State Council of China, 2022a].

To achieve these goals, the Chinese central government has implemented various policies. In 1990, China established national grain stockpiles, which "coordinate central state reserves and local reserves and complement government and corporate inventories with each other" [Wang, 2021]. Since then, China has continued undertaking various policies to safeguard food security. For example, from 2015 all provincial governors have been required to take full responsibility for food security. Further, in December 2020, food security was also listed as a major priority at the Central Economic Work Conference. This meeting, attended by President Xi, referred to food security as a "problem of seeds and arable land" and emphasised that the key to ensuring food security lies in storing grain [Global Times, 2020; Xinhuanet, 2020b]. Aside from recognising the need to safeguard the supply of grain and agricultural products and to protect China's so-called "red line" of 1.8 billion *mu* of arable land (equivalent to 120 million hectares), the meeting reiterated the importance of preventing the "non-agriculturalisation" of arable land in the management of grain reserves. It also pointed out the importance of creating a national food security and industrial belt to safeguard national food security [China Daily, 2021a].

The outcomes of the Central Economic Rural Conference from December 2020 were supported also by the State Council and CCP Central Committee's policy statement which focused solely on food security in February 2021. This statement demanded that the provincial authorities maintain a minimum national level "red line" of 120 million hectares of cultivated farmland to protect limited land resources by avoiding further land degradation. In addition, Beijing has established a National High-Standard Farmland Construction Plan (2021–2030) to increase the amount of arable land for farming and increase crop yields per acre. The plan aims to reach a national target of 71.75 million hectares of "high-standard farmland" by 2025, then 80 million hectares by 2030 [China Daily, 2021b; State Council of China, 2021c].

9.4.2 *China's Global Food Policy*

Internationally, China has adopted a global agricultural policy made up of four key aspects to meet the rising domestic demand for food. Firstly, Beijing plans to import more agricultural products, including grains, from the international market. Secondly, as its agricultural and food imports soar, China continues to diversify its agricultural trade routes, modes, markets, and imported food products. In particular, the Chinese government's emerging "Food Silk Road" aims to diversify food imports from many regions [Tortajada and Zhang, 2021; Zhan, 2022], including Africa and Latin America. To date, Beijing has signed over 100 agricultural cooperation agreements with BRI countries and appears keen to continue to seek alternative markets for food imports. Thirdly, Beijing aims to expand its agricultural operations overseas, exerting control over all stages of global food supply chains. In this light, China has become a significant player in overseas agricultural investment and related infrastructures, particularly under the BRI. Lastly, China plans to have a more significant role in shaping global food governance. Notably, in the country's 2019 Food Security White Paper, Beijing stated that it would actively engage in international and regional food security governance [State Council of China, 2019].

9.4.3 *Additional Measures*

China has taken a wide range of additional policy measures to safeguard its food security in the face of numerous challenges.

Firstly, greater emphasis has been placed on stressing food security as a political responsibility for both central and local governments. Following the outbreak of COVID-19 in late 2019 in China and growing food insecurity concerns, the Chinese central government put forward a number of policy responses. After the implementation of the 'six stabilities' (stability of employment, stability of financial markets, stability of foreign trade, stability of foreign investment, stability of investment, and stability of expectations) in 2020, the Politburo, the decision-making body of the CCP, released its 'six guarantees' (guarantee of employment for citizens, guarantee of people's basic livelihoods, guarantee of the mainstay status of the market, guarantee of food and energy security, guarantee of stability of the production and supply chains, and guarantee of basic operations) [China Daily, 2020; Ministry of Commerce of China, 2021]. In response to growing socio-economic inequalities brought on by the pandemic, global supply chain issues, and rising food prices, one of the 'six guarantees' was food security [Ministry of Commerce of China, 2021]. In another demonstration of emphasising food security to the public, the Politburo released the new

National Security Strategy (2021–2025), which includes food security [State Council of China, 2021b].

Secondly, the role of President Xi in promoting efforts to safeguard food security should not go unnoticed. In 2021, he emphasised that China's challenges and risks should be addressed with the country's strategic needs in mind while also calling for more robust measures to guarantee stable agricultural production and supply and steady growth in both the industry and in rural areas. "The food of the Chinese people must be made by and remain in the hands of the Chinese," he was quoted as saying by state broadcaster China Central Television [People's Daily, 2021]. President Xi has also called for efforts to safeguard grain area and protect farmland to encourage domestic production. In December 2021, amid growing concerns about the continued impacts of COVID-19 on the country's food supply and deteriorating relations with major economic partners, President Xi emphasised the importance of ensuring a secure supply of primary products and the responsibility of party and government officials in safeguarding the nation's food security [Xu, 2021].

Thirdly, China is seeking to reduce food waste and food demand. Although the country has seen consecutive bumper harvests, its leaders have frequently pointed out the necessity of preventing food waste to reduce undernourishment and generate economic gains for retailers and consumers. To reduce domestic food demand and wastage, in 2013 and 2020, President Xi launched nationwide campaigns against food waste, aided by the 2021 national "Anti-Food Waste Law" [CGTN, 2021; NPC, 2021] and, soon, a new national food security law.

Fourthly, the Chinese central government has also demonstrated growing interest in "future foods", including alternative protein (such as lab-grown meat) to bolster self-sufficiency. In December 2021, MARA released the Five-Year Agricultural and Rural Science and Technology Development Plan (2021–2025) [State Council of China, 2022b] which included a section on "creating future foods" for the first time. This section referred to lab-grown meats and plant-based eggs as examples of future foods that will be part of China's blueprint for food security. In March 2022, President Xi encouraged agricultural officials to seek protein sources outside of the traditional livestock industries to help safeguard China's food supply, noting that innovation is key to the country's food security and sustainable development [Xinhuanet, 2022]. Although regulatory approval for the commercial sale of cultivated meat in China has not yet been given, other alternatives like plant-based meat are already produced and sold in China. Furthermore, China has sought to improve both crop technology and mariculture (or marine ranching). In 2021, MARA announced that technological services and advanced technology could be promoted to help farmers increase production. As part of this, five provinces — Hebei, Shanxi, Shandong, Henan, and Shaanxi — are set to receive technical guidance from the ministry. At the same time, online training courses have been offered to over 800,000 people through the National Agricultural Technology and Education Cloud Platform [MARA, 2022].

Lastly, confronted with rising demand for high-quality animal proteins, growing feed challenges and acute farmland and water shortages, China has also embraced the concept of "Blue Granary", which aims for better utilisation of the "blue territories", primarily marine fishery and mariculture. In November 2017, MARA promulgated the "National Mariculture Development Plan (2017–2025)" under which China will build 178 national-level demonstration marine ranches. The target was raised to 200, according to the 14th Five-Year Plan for Fishery Development released in 2022 [MARA, 2022]. However, unless the fish feed issue is resolved, the rapid development of China's "Blue Granary Plan" could continue to exert pressure on the wild fish stocks of the country and beyond [Cao *et al.*, 2015; Zhang *et al.*, 2020].

9.5 Conclusion

Concerns over the country's food security are developing in China as a result of the sharp rise in food costs worldwide. Nevertheless, thanks to the strong political emphasis on the importance of agricultural development and food security in China, massive investment by the Chinese government in agricultural infrastructure, agricultural research and technology and its global food policy, China has achieved remarkable success in boosting domestic food production while ensuring resilience of its external food supply. Thanks to its enormous food reserve system and its relative lack of exposure to the world market, there is little risk in the medium term regarding the present food crisis. However, as more developing nations experience food crises, China will unavoidably come under intense international pressure and criticism. As global food shocks will also boost domestic food costs, primarily through feed supply, China's efforts to stockpile food will likely continue to receive criticism, having already been considered (partly) responsible for the global increases in food prices [Minter, 2022; Watanabe and Munakata, 2021].

In the longer term, there are both longstanding challenges and new threats, such as more frequent climate shocks and growing geopolitical instability to the country's food security. In response,

China has taken various initiatives to safeguard the country's food security. In addition to signs that the top leaders are concerned by food insecurity (such as by emphasising the significance of China controlling its own rice bowl), they are simultaneously attempting to diversify the nation's imports amid ongoing disruptions to global supply chains brought on by the COVID-19 pandemic and geopolitical rivalries. Ultimately, the success of these initiatives will determine China's food security. Currently, there are doubts about the effectiveness of China's food security measures. The effectiveness of some initiatives, such as the "red lines" for farmland to increase domestic agricultural production, which rely on local governments' assistance, are within the central government's power. However, strategies to increase food security at home are far less certain due to interlinked problems. In this context, Beijing's goals for food security will continue to be tested by climate change-related extreme weather events which have greatly harmed China's agricultural output in the past, much like many other nations around the world.

Chinese efforts to address its food security challenges are not only crucial for the 1.4 billion Chinese people but also have significant worldwide effects because it is the largest agricultural producer, leading agricultural importer, and major agricultural exporter. Regardless of its success or failure, China's approach to agricultural modernisation will influence the worldwide conversation on agrarian reform. The acceptance of GM foods in China may have significant international repercussions. The global food markets will be significantly shaped by changes in China's domestic food output, and efforts by China to diversify its agricultural imports are reorganising the world's food supply chains.

References

Bloomberg News. (2022, January 18). China's growing fondness for bread will help boost wheat imports. *Bloomberg*. https://www.bloomberg.com/news/articles/2022-01-18/bread-s-switch-from-snack-to-staple-boosts-china-s-wheat-imports

Brown, L. R. (1996). Who will feed China?. *The Futurist*, 30(1), p. 14.

Cao, L., Naylor, R., Henriksson, P., Leadbitter, D., Metian, M., Troell, M. and Zhang, W. (2015). China's aquaculture and the world's wild fisheries. *Science*, 347(6218), pp. 133–135.

CGTN (China Global Television Network). (2021, April 29). *China passes anti-food waste-law.* https://news.cgtn.com/news/2021-04-29/China-passes-anti-food-waste-law-ZQGMk1FYME/index.html

Chen, M. (2019). 加快推进我国农业食物营养转型发展. *Food and Nutrition in China*, 25(1), pp. 5–9.

China Daily. (2020, June 23). *每日一词 | 六保 ensure security in the six areas*. https://cn.chinadaily.com.cn/a/202006/23/WS5ef15ba9a310a859d09d3a76.html

China Daily. (2021a, January 5). *China to advance work related to agriculture, rural areas, farmers with concrete efforts*. https://global.chinadaily.com.cn/a/202101/05/WS5ff3c2dda31024ad0baa0770.html

China Daily. (2021b, September 23). *High-standard farmland can improve food security*. https://global.chinadaily.com.cn/a/202109/23/WS614bbba1a310cdd39bc6ad54.html

China Daily. (2022, December 9). *China's consumer inflation eases to eight-month low*. http://global.chinadaily.com.cn/a/202212/09/WS63929011a31057c47eba389f.html

Chunlai., L., Aimin, L., Yu, X., Xiaojie, L., Gaodi, X. and Shengkui, C. (2020). Changes in China's grain production pattern and the effects of urbanisation and dietary structure. *Journal of Resources and Ecology*, 11(4), pp. 358–365.

Cui, K. and Shoemaker, S. P. (2018). Public perception of genetically-modified (GM) food: a nationwide chinese consumer study. *NPJ Science of Food*, 2(1), p. 10.

Gale, F., Valdes, C. and Ash, M. (2019). Interdependence of China, United States, and Brazil in soybean trade. *US Department of Agriculture's Economic Research Service (ERS) Report*, pp. 1–48.

Ghose, B. (2014). Food security and food self-sufficiency in China: from past to 2050. *Food and Energy Security*, 3(2), pp. 86–95.

Global Times (2020, December 18). *China vows to solve seeds, arable land issues: top meeting*. https://www.globaltimes.cn/content/121035

Global Times (2022a, May 27). *China can ensure domestic grain supply without hoarding from international market: Chinese FM*. https://www.globaltimes.cn/page/202205/1266735.shtml

Global Times (2022b, September 28). *Bumper harvest forecast for 2022: top Chinese economic planner*. https://www.globaltimes.cn/page/202209/1276302.shtml

Gu, H. and Patton, D. (2020, September 1). China's looming corn shortage fans food security unease. *Reuters*. https://www.reuters.com/article/uk-china-food-security-corn-idUKKBN25S6EL

Gu, H. and Patton, D. (2022, January 14). China 2021 soybean imports slip 3.8% on falling margins, weak demand. *Reuters*. https://www.reuters.com/markets/us/china-2021-soybean-imports-slip-38-vs-2020-customs-2022-01-14/

Guo, J. (2016, March 3). 习近平"藏粮于地、藏粮于技"传递啥新理念?. *People.cn*. http://opinion.people.com.cn/n1/2016/0309/c1003-28184747.html

Han, J. (2014). *中国粮食安全与农业走出去战略研究*. China Development Press.

Hansen, J. and Gale, F. (2014). China in the next decade: Rising meat demand and growing imports of feed. *Amber Waves:The Economics of Food, Farming, Natural Resources, and Rural America*, 3, p. 1.

Huang, J. and Yang, G. (2017). Understanding recent challenges and new food policy in China. *Global Food Security*, 12, pp. 119–126.

Jamet, J. P. and Chaumet, J. M. (2016). Soybean in China: adapting to the liberalisation. *OCL*, 23(6), p. D604.

Kung, J. K. and Lin, J. Y. (2003). The causes of China's great leap famine, 1959–1961. *Economic Development and Cultural Change*, 52(1), pp. 51–73.

Kuteleva, A. (2016). China's food security situation: key issues and implications for Canada. *University of Alberta, China Institute. Occasional Paper Series*, 3(1), pp. 1–24.

Li, L. M. (2007). *Fighting Famine in North China: State, Market, and Environmental Decline, 1690s-1990s*. Stanford University Press.

MARA (Ministry of Agriculture and Rural Affairs of China). (2017, November 20). *农业部关于印发《国家级海洋牧场示范区 建设规划（2017–2025年）》的通知*. http://www.moa.gov.cn/nybgb/2017/201711/201802/t20180201_6136235.htm

MARA (Ministry of Agriculture and Rural Affairs of China). (2021). *农业农村部关于印发《"十四五"全国种植业发展规划》的通知 [2/29/2021]*. http://www.moa.gov.cn/govpublic/ZZYGLS/202201/t20220113_6386808.htm

MARA (Ministry of Agriculture and Rural Affairs of China). (January 7, 2022). *The 14th Five-Year Plan for national fishery development issued.* http://english.moa.gov.cn/news_522/202201/t20220110_300772.html

MARA (Ministry of Agriculture and Rural Affairs of China). (February 15, 2022). *China ramps up farming technology support to ensure harvest.* http://english.moa.gov.cn/news_522/202202/t20220215_300793.html

Ministry of Agriculture Agricultural Trade Promotion Center. (2016). *粮食安全与"非必需进口"控制问题研究*. http://www.agri.cn/V20/SC/myyj/201608/t20160816_5240166.htm

Ministry of Commerce of China. (2021, March 1). *《商务部印发围绕构建新发展格局做好稳外资工作的通知》* Shāngwù bù yìnfā wéirào gòujiàn xīn fāzhǎn géjú zuò hǎo wěn wàizī gōngzuò de tōngzhī [The Ministry of Commerce issued a notice on stabilising foreign investment around the establishment of a new development pattern]. http://www.mofcom.gov.cn/article/ae/ai/202103/20210303041579.shtml

Minter, A. (2022, January 5). One reason for rising food prices? Chinese hoarding. *Bloomberg*. https://www.bloomberg.com/opinion/articles/2022-01-05/one-reason-for-rising-food-prices-chinese-hoarding

National Bureau of Statistics of China. (1979). 2020 China statistical abstract.

National Bureau of Statistics of China. (2021). 2021 China statistical abstract.

NPC (National People's Congress). (2021). *中华人民共和国反食品浪费法*http://www.npc.gov.cn/npc/c30834/202104/83b2946e514b449ba313eb4f508c6f29.shtml

People's Daily. (2021, September 25). *中国人的饭碗牢牢端在自己手上* [The rice bowl of the Chinese people is firmly in their hands]. http://politics.people.com.cn/n1/2021/0925/c1001-32235942.html

Reuters. (November 18, 2021). *China's Politburo reviews national security strategy for 2021–2025*. https://www.reuters.com/article/china-security-politburo-idUKB9N2R902L

Reuters. (2022, January 18). *China's corn import soar to new record in 2021*. https://www.reuters.com/markets/asia/chinas-grain-pork-sugar-imports-december-2022-01-18/

Ribeiro, T. V. and Hirtzer, M. (2022, December 5). China ramps up corn purchases from Brazil as US exports decline. *Bloomberg*. https://www.bloomberg.com/news/articles/2022-12-05/china-ramps-up-corn-purchases-from-brazil-as-us-exports-decline

Sizov, A. (2019, August 14). *Ukraine to fill China's corn needs, replacing U.S. product*. Successful Farming. https://www.agriculture.com/

markets/your-world-in-agriculture/ukraine-to-fill-chinas-corn-needs-replacing-us-product

State Council of China. (2019). *Full Text: Food Security in China.* http://www.scio.gov.cn/zfbps/32832/Document/1666228/1666228.htm

State Council of China. (2021a, March 13). *中华人民共和国国民经济和社会发展第十四个五年规划和2035年远景目标纲要.* http://www.gov.cn/xinwen/2021-03/13/content_5592681.htm

State Council of China. (2021b, November 18). *中共中央政治局会议审议《国家安全战略（2021－2025年）》《军队功勋荣誉表彰条例》和《国家科技咨询委员会2021年咨询报告》 习近平主持.* http://www.gov.cn/xinwen/2021-11/18/content_5651753.htm

State Council of China. (2021c, September 16). *High-standard farmland gets push over next decade.* http://english.www.gov.cn/policies/latestreleases/202109/16/content_WS6142db85c6d0df57f98e0431.html

State Council of China. (2022a, January 13). *China aims at grain output of 700b kg by 2025.* http://english.www.gov.cn/statecouncil/ministries/202201/13/content_WS61dfcc42c6d09c94e48a3937.html

State Council of China. (2022b, January 7). *农业农村部关于印发《"十四五"全国农业农村科技发展规划》的通知* [Notice of the Ministry of Agriculture and Rural Affairs on Printing and Distributing the "14th Five-Year Plan"]. http://www.gov.cn/zhengce/zhengceku/2022-01/07/content_5666862.htm

Tatlow, D. K. (2014, April 25). After "cadmium rice," now "lead" and "arsenic rice." *Sinosphere Blog.* https://sinosphere.blogs.nytimes.com/2014/04/25/after-cadmium-rice-now-lead-and-arsenic-rice/

The Economist Intelligence Unit. Global Food Security Index (2023). https://impact.economist.com/sustainability/project/food-security-index/

Tortajada, C. and Zhang, H. (2021). When food meets BRI: China's emerging Food Silk Road. *Global Food Security*, *29*, p. 100518.

Ukrainian State Statistics Services. (2021). За 2020 рік товарообіг України склав $103,4 млрд [In 2020, Ukraine's turnover amounted to $103.4 billion]. https://customs.gov.ua/en/news/novini-20/post/za-2020-rik-tovaroobig-ukrayini-sklav-1034-mlrd-294

USDA (United States Department of Agriculture). (2019a). *USDA agricultural projections to 2028.* https://www-usda-gov.libproxy1.nus.edu.sg/oce/commodity/projections/USDA_Agricultural_Projections_to_2028.pdf

USDA (United States Department of Agriculture). (2019b). *Corn Prices Rise Amid Unprecedented Supply and Demand Shocks.* https://apps.fas.usda.gov/newgainapi/api/report/downloadreportbyfilename?filename=Corn%20Prices%20Rise%20Amid%20Unprecedented%20Supply%20and%20Demand%20Shocks_Beijing_China%20-%20Peoples%20Republic%20of_7-2-2019.pdf [Accessed January 12 2023].

USDA (United States Department of Agriculture). (2020). *Grain and Feed China Report.* USDA.

USDA (United States Department of Agriculture). (2021). *China wheat imports reach highest level in more than two decades.* https://www.ers.usda.gov/data-products/chart-gallery/gallery/chart-detail/?chartId=102088

USDA (United States Department of Agriculture). (2023, March 1). *Record U.S. FY 2022 agricultural exports to China.* https://www.fas.usda.gov/data/record-us-fy-2022-agricultural-exports-china

Wang, Y. S. (2019). The challenges and strategies of food security under rapid urbanisation in China. *Sustainability*, 11(2), p. 542.

Wang, O. (2021). China food security: why is it important and what caused November's panic buying? *The South China Morning Post.* https://www.scmp.com/economy/china-economy/article/3154982/china-food-security-why-it-important-and-what-caused

Watanabe, S. and Munakata, A. (2021, December 23). China hoards over half the world's grain, pushing up global prices. *Nikkei Asia.* https://asia.nikkei.com/Spotlight/Datawatch/China-hoards-over-half-the-world-s-grain-pushing-up-global-prices

Wong, J. and Huang, Y. (2012). China's food security and its global implications. *China: An International Journal*, 10(1), pp. 113–124.

World Resources Institute (2021, July 27). *《农业系统应对气候变化'渐进性适应还远远不够》*. Nóngyè xìtǒng yìngduì qìhòu biànhuà, jiànjìn xìng shìyìng hái yuǎn yuǎn bùgòu [Agricultural systems respond to climate change, incremental adaptation is not enough]. https://wri.org.cn/insights/hungry-change

World Food Programme (2022). A global food crisis. https://www.wfp.org/global-hunger-crisis

Xi, J. (2017, November 4). Full text of Xi Jinping's report at 19th CPC National Congress. *China Daily*. http://www.chinadaily.com.cn/china/19thcpcnationalcongress/2017-11/04/content_34115212.htm

Xi, J. (2022a, October 25). 习近平：高举中国特色社会主义伟大旗帜 为全面建设社会主义现代化国家而团结奋斗——在中国共产党第二十次全国代表大会上的报告. *State Council of China*. http://www.gov.cn/xinwen/2022-10/25/content_5721685.htm

Xi, J. (2022b, December 31). Full Text: 2023 New Year Address by President Xi Jinping. *China Daily*. https://www.chinadaily.com.cn/a/202212/31/WS63b02f89a31057c47eba7225.html

Xinhuanet. (2020a, July 22). *Xi Focus: How China secured bumper summer grain harvest despite COVID-19*. http://www.xinhuanet.com/english/2020-07/22/c_139232739.htm

Xinhuanet. (2020b, December 18). *China to safeguard food security by addressing seeds, farmlands problems: key meeting*. http://www.xinhuanet.com/english/2020-12/18/c_139601147.htm

Xinhuanet. (2022, March 7). *Xi visits CPPCC members in sectors of agriculture, welfare and social security*. https://english.news.cn/20220307/e98039b53ab8418e9684c0c5847e943c/c.html

Xu, W. (2021, December 27). Xi emphasizes steps to ensure food security. *China Daily*. https://www.chinadaily.com.cn/a/202112/27/WS61c8f379a310cdd39bc7d816.html

Yan, H., Yiyuan, C. and Bun, K. H. (2016). China's soybean crisis: The logic of modernization and its discontents. *The Journal of Peasant Studies*, 43(2), pp. 373–395.

Yang, D. L. (1996). *Calamity and Reform in China: State, Rural Society, and Institutional Change Since the Great Leap Famine*. Stanford University Press.

Yu, S., Zhu, Y. G. and Li, X. D. (2012). Trace metal contamination in urban soils of China. *Science of the Total Environment*, 421, pp. 17–30.

Zhan, S. (2017). Riding on self-sufficiency: Grain policy and the rise of agrarian capital in China. *Journal of Rural Studies*, 54, pp. 151–161.

Zhan, S. (2022). *China and Global Food Security*. Cambridge University Press.

Zhang, H. (2018). *Securing the 'Rice Bowl': China and Global Food Security*. Palgrave Macmillan.

Zhang, H. (2019). When Food Crosses Borders: Paradigm Shifts in China's Food Sectors and Implications for Vietnam. In J. Ehlert and N. K. Faltmann (Eds.), *Food Anxiety in Globalising Vietnam*, pp. 267–299. Springer.

Zhang, H. (2021). China's Global Quest for Food and the Belt and Road Initiative. In J. C. Liow, H. Liu and G. Xue (Eds.), *Research Handbook on the Belt and Road Initiative*, pp. 65–75. Edward Elgar Publishing.

Zhang, W., Liu, M., de Mitcheson, Y. S., Cao, L., Leadbitter, D., Newton, R., Little, D. C., Li, S., Yang, Y., Chen, X. and Zhou, W. (2020). Fishing for feed in China: Facts, impacts and implications. *Fish and Fisheries*, 21(1), pp. 47–62.

Zhang, Y., Xu, T. and Xiao, J. (2022). How has China maintained domestic food security amid global food crises? *World Economic Forum*. https://www.weforum.org/agenda/2022/11/china-domestic-food-stability-amid-global-food-crises/

Zhou, J. (2022). Chapter 7: Prospects for Agri-Food Trade Between Russia and China. In S. K. Wegren and F. Nilssen (Eds.), *Russia's Role in the Contemporary International Agri-Food Trade System*, pp. 195–223. Springer.

Zhou, S., Zhou, W., Lin, G., Chen, J., Jiang, T. and Li, M. (2017). Adapting to climate change: Scenario analysis of grain production in China. *China Agricultural Economic Review*, 9(4), pp. 643–659.

https://doi.org/10.1142/9789811278297_0010

Chapter 10

India's Food Security: Challenges and Prospects

Rajeev Malhotra[1] **and Manas Pathak**[2]

[1]*Senior Fellow Prime Ministers Museum and Library, Teen Murty House, New Delhi and Indian School of Business, Hyderabad and Mohali, India*

[2]*Manas Pathak, Jindal School of Government and Public Policy (JSGP), O.P. Jindal Global University, Sonipat, Delhi, India*

10.1 Introduction

The concept of food security is a complicated one, be it at the global, national, local or at a household level. It requires several dimensions to be simultaneously navigated to build an adequate understanding, especially for an effective policy response to address the issue. Indeed, when juxtaposed against India's economic, social, and political context, the concept acquires unwonted complexity. Apart from the obvious economic basis of food availability and a person's access to it, India's social and political economy has typically influenced food security in the contemporary understanding of the concept. This has happened in both positive and negative manners. Social attitudes, rooted customary practices and inequality in terms of income and social attainments while contributing to food security, in some instances, have also undermined aspects of it, especially in the rural and backward areas and for some communities. At the same time, economic policies initiated to strengthen the agricultural production economy in a specific context but persisted for far too long, even as they lost some of their relevance, may have contributed to weakening of practices that have traditionally supported nutrition security at the household level. Similarly, over the past five decades, India's political economy has greatly contributed to building the country's food security, especially food availability, but it has perhaps held back or delayed taking some measures that could have strengthened the sustainability of the country's food system, beyond the immediate concerns of food production to distribution and accessibility of people to adequate nutrition.

This chapter, while providing a brief overview of the state of food security in India along its various dimensions, focuses essentially on the challenges that India confronts in sustaining its food security, at both macro (or national) and micro (or household) levels, and the nature of the policy response required. Section 10.2 traces the evolution of the concept of food security in India and globally, establishing the issues therein that India has or needs to prioritise. This is followed by an assessment of India's food security in Section 10.3. Based on that analysis, Section 10.4 identifies the challenges and emerging concerns that policymakers must address.

10.2 Food Security in India: Evolution of Concept and Practice

The notion of food security has evolved over time, reflecting the technical complexity of the concept and success or failure of policy measures pursued to seek the desired social outcomes. Indeed, the successive definitions of food security adopted at the international level from 1974 to 1996, along with those reflected in official Food and Agriculture Organization (FAO) and World Bank documents in the mid-1980s, show substantive changes in the conceptual and operational focus on the issue. Indeed, they are milestones in the journey to understand food security as a problem of national and international responsibility, and the considerations shaping the policy response.

Food security as a concept originated in the international discussions in the mid-1970s, at a time of global food crisis. Famine, hunger, and general food scarcity in several parts of the world formed the backdrop of these discussions Thus, the initial focus on the issue, not surprisingly, was on food supply concerns — of assuring the availability and to some extent price stability of food at the national and international levels. This process led to the World Food Conference in 1974, which defined food security as: "availability at all times of adequate world food supplies of basic foodstuffs to sustain a steady expansion of food consumption and to offset fluctuations in production and prices" [United Nations, 1975]. This concept was expanded by the FAO to include the access of vulnerable people to available supplies, thereby creating a focus to balance the demand and supply side of the food security equation by adding: "ensuring that all people at all times have both physical and economic access to the basic food that they need" [FAO, 1983].

In 1986, the World Bank in its report "Poverty and Hunger" brought into focus the temporal dynamics of food insecurity. It made a distinction between chronic food insecurity, associated with problems of continuing or structural poverty and low incomes, and transitory food insecurity, involving periods of stress caused by natural disasters, economic collapse, or conflict. This thinking was elaborated to view food security in terms of: "access of all people at all times to enough food for an active, healthy life" [World Bank, 1986].

By the mid-1990s food security was recognised as a significant concern that spanned from an individual, at the local level, to the global level. The access to food now meant sufficient food, indicating an emphasis on protein-energy malnutrition. The definition was broadened to incorporate food safety and nutritional balance, reflecting concerns about food composition and minor nutrient requirements for an active and healthy life. Social and cultural determinants of food preferences also became a consideration. This brought in a considerable degree of context specificity to the concept, adding to the complexity in addressing its practice.

UNDP Human Development Report 1994, in promoting the concept of human security, highlighted the importance of food security (among six other securities) in the process of bringing in the human rights perspective into the concept [UNDP, 1994]. This thinking benefited from the seminal work of Amartya Sen [Sen, 1981] and Drèze and Sen [1989] where the notion of entitlements[1] related the importance of consumption, the demand side, and the issues of access of vulnerable people to food for shaping the concept of food security.

---

[1] Sen [1981] refers to entitlements as a set of alternative commodity bundles that a person can command in a society using totality of rights and opportunities that s/he faces. A person's entitlement includes his/her endowments, what s/he owns and what s/he can exchange that for, or his/her exchange entitlement. Unlike Nozick's [1974] theory of entitlement guaranteeing liberties equally to all but rejecting equality or any end patterning of outcomes, Drèze and Sen [1989] argue that entitlements can be ensured through right to use some commodities (*viz*. government food stocks for public distribution and consumption, and protecting traditional rights such as access to common resources) without owning them outright, thus creating a scope for affirmative action for improving a person's entitlements and for socially desired outcomes.

Building on this body of work, spread over 25 years, a comprehensive definition of food security was negotiated in the course of international consultations leading up to the World Food Summit (WFS) in November 1996, where it was highlighted that: "Food security, at the individual, household, national, regional, and global levels is achieved when all people, at all times, have physical and economic access to sufficient, safe and nutritious food to meet their dietary needs and food preferences for an active and healthy life" [FAO, 1996]. The State of Food Insecurity 2001 reiterated this formulation by suggesting that: "Food security is a situation that exists when all people, at all times, have physical, social and economic access to sufficient, safe and nutritious food that meets their dietary needs and food preferences for an active and healthy life" [FAO, 2001]. It is apparent from this articulation of the concept that there are four major dimensions of food security:

- **Food availability**: The availability of sufficient quantities of food of appropriate quality, made available through domestic production or imports (including food aid).
- **Economic and physical access to food**: Access by individuals to adequate resources (entitlements) for acquiring appropriate foods for a nutritious diet.
- **Utilisation:** Utilisation of food through adequate diet, clean water, sanitation, and health care to reach a state of nutritional wellbeing, where all physiological needs are met. Sufficient energy and nutrient intake by individuals are a result of good hygiene and feeding practices, food preparation, diversity of diet and intra-household distribution of food. This, combined with efficient biological utilisation of food consumed, determines the nutritional status of individuals. Thus, non-food inputs

and these other considerations are equally important in ensuring food security, especially so in the poor communities and regions.

- **Stability:** To be food secure, a population, household or an individual must have access to adequate food, at all times. They should not risk losing access to food due to sudden shocks (*viz.* an economic or climatic crisis) or cyclical events resulting in price volatility (*viz.* seasonal food insecurity or on account of business cycle contraction in economic activity). The notion of stability is therefore related to the availability and access dimensions of food security. Frequent fluctuations in global commodity prices, mainly food and fuel, economic disruptions due to pandemics, wars and downturns in economic activity have brought this dimension of food security to fore in recent times.

All these four dimensions must be fulfilled simultaneously to realise the food security goal. Importantly, food security is a layered concept where global, national, local, and household level facets are distinct, but related. Adequacy in food availability at the global or national level does not necessarily ensure economic and physical access to food at the household level, nor is household security a sufficient condition for food utilisation. Similarly, although the stability dimension of food security is a function of availability and accessibility to food, there are invariably other precipitating factors that influence it. Indeed, at each of those levels there are different policy concerns and often distinct policy drivers, as is highlighted in the analysis on India's food security concerns. Household food security, which is the ultimate objective of food security in any country context, or for that matter of the international interest, is the application of this multifaceted concept at the family level, with individuals within households as the focus of concern. Finally, food insecurity exists when people do not have adequate physical, social, or economic access to food as defined above.

Even as there is general acceptance of a broad-based conceptualisation of food security and the implied national and international responsibilities, it often does not find commensurate expression in the articulated policies or in the policy conduct across countries. Thus, for all practical purposes, policy response has a narrower focus and simpler objectives around which public action is organised in most countries where food security remains an active concern. Indeed, the declared primary policy objective is increasingly the reduction and elimination of poverty or halving of the number of hungry or undernourished people by 2015 as proposed by the WFS [FAO, 1996], or as in the case of Millennium Development Goals or Sustainable Development Goals subsequently.

The motivation to recall the evolution of the concept and the practice to address food security in the work of international agencies, which otherwise is well documented in the literature (see, for instance, Chapter 2 in FAO [2003]), is simply to highlight that India's approach to food security since the late 1960s closely mirrors these developments. Apart from the top priority accorded to producing enough food to meet its needs by focusing on the agricultural production economy in the late 1960s and 1970s, India has sought to address each of the four dimensions of food security almost continuously, although not always effectively or with adequate coverage of the population. The supply constraints on availability of food were addressed through a reasonably successful implementation of the Green Revolution and the agricultural pricing policy; access and stability issues were addressed through a range of programmes including maintaining buffer stocks, an extensive public distribution system (PDS) and regulation of food prices, besides development initiatives to create livelihood opportunities; and a gradual expansion of social security coverage of the vulnerable population. The utilisation dimension has been targeted through public health measures, supply of public goods, and social mobilisation efforts at the local level. While India's journey in that regard is elaborated in subsequent sections, it is instructive to note here that India has tracked three interrelated measures — poverty, hunger, and malnutrition (often confused with each other in the popular discourse) — in the pursuit of its food security objective, even as the concept of food security was acquiring its contemporary comprehensiveness of construct internationally.

The issue of poverty is at the heart of India's development discourse including in the context of its food security concerns. India's poverty has not just been about people who are hungry, rather it is also about people who are malnourished, acutely prone to health vulnerabilities and illness, unemployed or underemployed with poor productivity levels, homeless and invariably living an insecure life. It is about households that are poorly endowed, have a high dependency burden, are situated in habitats with limited, if any, coverage of civic amenities (public goods) and constantly threatened by environment sustainability concerns. It relates to population groups that are powerless, socially marginalised and can be easily disempowered and dispossessed of their entitlements because of their peculiar circumstances. It is also about certain regions that continue to be underdeveloped and poorly governed. All this adds up to the complexity of the issue, poverty as well as food security, and to the policy challenges in addressing it sustainably [Malhotra, 2014].

In tracking the magnitude of poverty, hunger and malnutrition over time, it is often pointed out that despite the country having attained national self-sufficiency in food production for nearly three decades and has been carrying large stocks of publicly procured foodgrains at any point of time over the past three decades, the high (higher than poverty head count ratio) and sticky incidence of malnourishment (measured, for instance, by underweight children under the 'weight for age' criterion) is an issue of national shame (Figure 10.1). Indeed, these are three distinct concepts — hunger, poverty and malnutrition — defined differently and entail distinct policy emphasis. While all three of them have an underpinning of some measure of food inadequacy, involving a comparison of the actual food intake to the recommended level, the norms involved are different.

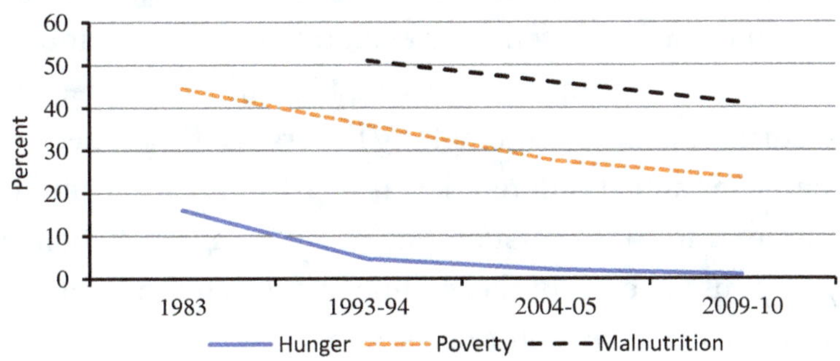

Figure 10.1 India's incidence of hunger, poverty and malnutrition: 1983–2010. Source: Malhotra [2014], estimated from proportion of households reporting adequate food intake throughout the year based on the National Sample Survey Office Reports No 415, 512 and 547 of the respective rounds on hunger; data on poverty are based on the Lakdawala estimates provided by the Planning Commission; and data on malnutrition relates to underweight children in the age group 1–47 months for 1993–94 and 2004–05 (National Family Health Survey) and underweight children up to 72 months for 2009–10 (from the Integrated Child Development Programme data reported in February 2011). It is strictly not comparable with other data on malnutrition but reveals broad trends for periods for which the other two estimates were available on a consistent basis.

The required level is defined in terms of frequency of 'square meals' in a day (proportion of households getting two square meals a day) for estimating the incidence of hunger and recommended dietary allowance in case of poverty (daily calorie adequacy norm) and malnutrition (a proportion of the recommended daily calorie norm, or the outcome-oriented anthropometric measures that reflect the cumulative consequences of food inadequacy among children). This comparison of the three measures underscores the point made earlier, namely that the four identified dimensions of food security must be seen in totality and simultaneously to get an adequate assessment of food security in a country. A good performance on one dimension does not necessarily indicate a good performance on the other. Human wellbeing requires food security to be sustainably met in its broadest sense, as elaborated in this section. Therefore, it sets the grounds for tracking the different dimensions of food security separately and making the assessment collectively on all dimensions and at different levels — national, local, and household. Importantly, it necessitates an analysis of the challenges and policy response at each of those dimensions and the level at which food security needs remain to be secured.

10.3 Food Security Attainments and Gaps

10.3.1 *Food Availability*

India has come a long way since the mid-1960s when it was living from "ship to mouth", with food aid from the U.S. (under the Public Law 480 programme) contributing a significant proportion to food availability in the country. Successful implementation of the Green Revolution in the northwest of India led to the country becoming self-sufficient in food at the national level in a short period of time. Indeed, after remaining a food-deficit country for about two decades after independence in 1947, the attainment of self-sufficiency in food grains has been one of the country's major achievements in the post-independence period. Foodgrain (cereal and pulses) production in the country increased from about 50 million tonnes in 1950–51 to over 315 million tonnes in 2020–21. Although the long-term growth rate of foodgrains has been around 2.5% per annum between 1951 and 2000, there is a marginal increase to around 3.2% in the two decades since then. The production of oilseeds, sugarcane, fruits, vegetables, milk, poultry, fish and marine products have all increased appreciably. Thus, for instance, production of milk has increased from 17 million tonnes in 1950–51 to 221 million tonnes in 2020–21. Over the same period, production of (poultry) eggs in number increased from about 2 billion to 130 billion and that of fish and marine products from 750 thousand tonnes to over 16 million tonnes [Ministry of Finance, 2022–23].

There has hardly been any foodgrain imports after the mid-1970s, with India becoming a net agriculture exporter and the largest rice exporter globally. According to the World Trade Organization, India's share in the total global export of agricultural products increased from 0.8% in 1990 to 2.6% in 2012. Between 2010 and 2022, India's share in world food grain market increased 3.38% to 7.89% (Director General of Commercial Intelligence and Statistics, Government of India). The country's export of agriculture and allied products in value terms increased from 644 million USD to over 50 billion USD amounting to 2% average annual growth from 1970–71 to 2021–22. During the same period, exports of fish and marine products increased from 40 million USD to nearly 8 billion USD, meat and meat products from 4 million USD to over 3 billion USD, and that of fruits and vegetables from about 16 million USD to over 2 billion

USD [Ministry of Finance, 2022–23]. This magnitude of growth in exports has been realised even as the domestic demand for fine cereal (wheat and rice, relative to traditional millets) and non-cereal food items (animal proteins, fruits, and vegetables) has grown significantly, with improvement in average living standards. This is reflected in the changing food consumption pattern for people, both in rural and urban India.

Much of the improvement in domestic availability has come about due to improvement in crop yields, for some crops more than others, with productivity increase in pulses and oilseeds being significantly less than for cereals, wheat and rice (Figure 10.2). This shows up in the trend in per capita net availability of cereal and pulses; while there has been improvement in the former, it has stagnated for the latter (Figure 10.3). It may be noted that with a majority of the Indian population being vegetarian, pulses are an important part of the diet for meeting protein needs. In the case of oilseeds, although production has increased along with some improvement

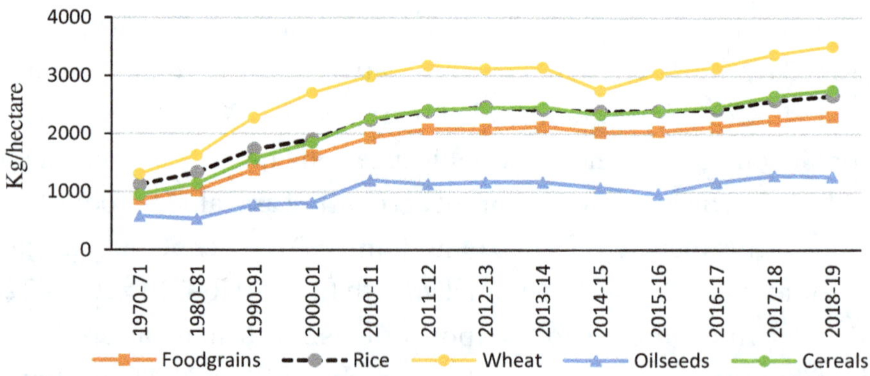

Figure 10.2 Yield of various crops (kg/hectare). Source: Agriculture Statistics at a Glance, various years, Department of Agriculture, Cooperation & Farmers Welfare, Government of India.

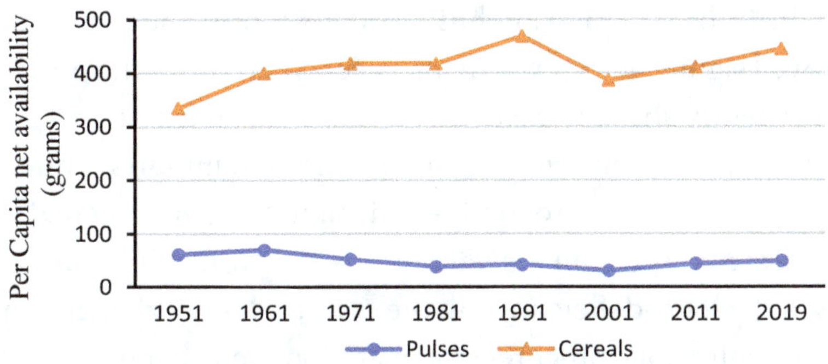

Figure 10.3 Per capita net availability of foodgrains — cereals and pulses. Net availability = Net production + Net imports − Changes in government stocks. Source: Directorate of Economics & Statistics, Department of Agriculture, Cooperation & Farmers Welfare, Government of India.

in yield, there is a considerable gap between domestic availability and demand. As a result, India is importing more than half of its edible oil consumption and about 15–20% of pulses consumption from global markets. This increases consumer vulnerability to global price fluctuations, especially for edible oils, thereby impacting stability of household food security.

Despite being a net agricultural exporter, India's rice and wheat trade policy is highly cautious and regulated. The agrarian economy being largely rain dependent, with over 50% of gross cropped area and 40% of the rice planting area rainfed, nearly 45% of population dependent on agriculture for sustenance and in all more than 1.4 billion people to feed, including the highest number of the global poor, the decision to open trade of staple crops, like rice and wheat, is politically sensitive and requires extreme caution. Not surprisingly, the government has always tried to meet first the domestic consumption needs and maintain adequate buffer stocks before letting the "residual" be traded.

Overall, India's food availability dimension of food security has improved significantly; even in instances where domestic production is consistently short of the demand (*viz.* for edible oils and pulses), the country has been bridging the gap through imports. Thus, India enjoys national or macro food security and has strengthened it over time. Moreover, the management of food from the food-surplus areas to the food-deficit areas in the country has worked reasonably well through public procurement operations and channelising stocks through countrywide PDS, and now freedom on foodgrain movement, but there are issues that need policy attention. However, the same is not true of household food security, both on account of lack of adequate economic and occasionally physical access, and inadequate utilisation of food in the absence of complementary non-food inputs that aid food utilisation.

10.3.2 *Household Food Security — Access, Utilisation and Stability*

India's battle to secure food security at household level is far from over. While the complicated problem of creating food self-sufficiency in India of the 1960s could be solved to a large extent, and rapidly so, by deploying the Green Revolution technology, supported by a conducive agriculture pricing policy regime and social mobilisation of farmers, the challenge of improving food access, economic as well as physical, and food utilisation has been a complex one. It requires significant structural changes in the economy — the way economic activity is organised, the nature and growth of livelihood opportunities, eradication of poverty, expansion in the supply and quality of public goods, and determined social mobilisation on issues that have a bearing on food security at the household level, including intra-household inequalities in consumption and social attainments. Entitlements of people, especially for the vulnerable and the marginalised, must improve, mediated by growth of markets and directly through public action where required. There has been progress in all these aspects reflected, for instance, in average increase in per capita income, in food consumption and its quality reflected in changes in consumption patterns, in both rural and urban areas, expansion and better targeting of the PDS and programmes to extend nutritional support to the most vulnerable segments of the population, such as school-going children, would-be and young mothers, and the elderly.

India's per capita income in current USD has increased from USD 83 in 1960 to USD 2,389 in 2022. In terms of constant 2017 Purchasing Power Parity international dollars, this increase has been from 1,819 in 1990 to 7,096 in 2022 [World Bank, 2022]. The average per capita consumption estimates capture the access dimension of food security somewhat better than per capita income estimates, at least in developing countries. This is because there is smoothening of impact of income fluctuations in consumption levels; non-monetised transactions are included in personal consumption which could be considerable in a poor developing country; consumption spending reflects the influence of public goods and services on an individual's entitlements and his/her consumption; and unlike income, consumption is a direct measure of access to food. India's inequality adjusted average, real per capita monthly consumption expenditure, between 1983 and 2010 at the all-India level (based on National Sample Survey Household Consumer Expenditure Surveys estimated in page 217 of Malhotra [2014]) recorded an increase of 32.7% in rural areas or an average annual growth of about 1.1%, and an increase of 39.2% in urban areas or an annual average growth of 1.35%. Although modest and varying across Indian provinces/states (*viz.* for the state of Kerala these were 2.96% and 3.12% per annum for rural and urban areas, respectively), these growth rates are adjusted for inequality, which has deteriorated over time, especially in urban areas. Moreover, as noted earlier, the consumption pattern of people in both rural and urban areas has changed in favour of finer cereals from coarse cereal or millets, and from cereals to non-cereal food items and animal proteins. The country's 'white revolution' brought about a sharp increase in milk production, 'red revolution' in the production of meat and tomatoes, 'silver revolution' increased the production of poultry eggs, and 'blue revolution' improved aquaculture, all of which contributed to nutritional security at the household level. The improved availability of these food items also contributed to addressing the stability dimension of food security.

India's efforts to address the absorption dimension of food security to secure nutritional wellbeing for its people have been directed at promoting an adequate diet, along with improved civic amenities and public healthcare. Indeed, as a part of the country's planned development process since independence, the focus has been to improve the supply of relevant public and merit goods to secure adequate food and nutritional balance at household level. Interventions have included both demand-side measures (improving purchasing power and social security coverage), and supply-side interventions (agricultural and food policies, trade policies and public distribution policies). At the micro level there have been measures for food fortification and supply through PDS, such as providing micronutrients to the children below five years of age through the Integrated Child Development Programme (ICDS), and mid-day meals to school-going children; improving access to potable water, sanitation, and developing infrastructure; creating awareness on public and personal hygiene; social mobilisation on specific issues; and institutionalisation of an approach to manage transitory food insecurity, including on account of natural calamities and volatility in the food market [Malhotra, 2014].

There has been all-round progress in implementing these interventions, although not adequately and uniformly across the Indian provinces/states. It is difficult to establish an unequivocal causality between the measures taken and outcomes attained to secure improved utilisation of available food and its efficient absorption by the human body for nutritional wellbeing. It is therefore instructive to look at the trends in some anthropometric indicators to get a sense of progress on this dimension of food security (Table 10.1). Anthropometric indicators reflect outcomes of food insecurity in terms of availability, access, and utilisation of available food for children at household level. In fact, it could be argued that if children in any household fare poorly on their anthropometric scores, that household is very likely facing serious food insecurity. No household, no matter how disadvantaged, would allow their children to go hungry and nutritionally starved.

Prolonged periods of inadequate food intake and poor diet, especially in combination with low birth weights and high rates of infection, can result in stunted and underweight children. Underweight assesses weight for age, stunting height for age, and wasting weight for height. Undernourished children are those more than two standard deviations below the median of the international reference population, recommended by the World Health Organization.[2] The most extreme manifestation of persisting hunger and malnutrition is mortality. In the case of India, there is evidence to

[2] The malnourishment norms for India are sometimes contested due to racial, cultural or climatic differences between the Indian and the reference international population used by the World Health Organization, but this aspect is not discussed here.

Table 10.1 India's anthropometric indicators at state level (1993–94 to 2019–20). Source: Various rounds of National Family Health Surveys corresponding to the indicated years. Data for 1998–99 relate to age 1–35 months, data for 1993–94 and 2005–06 relate to age 1–47 months.

	Stunted					Underweight					Wasted				
State	1993–94	1998–99	2004–05	2015–16	2019–20	1993–94	1998–99	2004–05	2015–16	2019–20	1993–94	1998–99	2004–05	2015–16	2019–20
Andhra Pradesh		38.6	42.7	31.4	31.2	49.1	37.7	32.5	31.9	29.6	NA	9.1	12.2	17.2	16.1
Arunachal Pradesh	53.9	26.5	43.3	29.4	28.0	39.7	24.3	31.9	19.5	15.4	11.2	7.9	15.3	17.3	13.1
Assam	52.2	50.2	46.5	36.4	35.3	50.4	36.0	36.5	29.8	32.8	10.8	13.3	13.7	17.0	21.7
Bihar	60.9	53.7	55.6	48.3	42.9	62.6	54.4	55.9	43.9	41.0	21.8	21.0	27.1	20.8	22.9
Chhattisgarh		57.9	52.9	37.6	34.6		60.8	47.1	37.7	31.3		18.5	19.5	23.1	18.9
Goa	32.5	18.1	25.6	20.1	25.8	35.0	28.6	25.0	23.8	24.0	15.3	13.1	14.1	21.9	19.1
Gujarat	48.2	43.6	51.7	38.5	39.0	50.1	45.1	44.6	39.3	39.7	18.9	16.2	18.7	26.4	25.1
Haryana	46.7	50.0	45.7	34.0	27.5	37.9	34.6	39.6	29.4	21.5	5.9	5.3	19.1	21.2	11.5
Himachal Pradesh	NA	41.3	38.6	26.3	30.8	47.0	43.6	36.5	21.2	25.5	NA	16.9	19.3	13.7	17.4
Jammu & Kashmir	40.8	38.8	35.0	27.4	26.9	44.5	34.5	25.6	16.6	21.0	14.8	11.8	14.8	12.1	19.0
Jharkhand		49.0	49.8	45.3	39.6		54.3	56.5	47.8	39.4		25.4	32.3	29.0	22.4
Karnataka	47.6	36.6	43.7	36.2	35.4	54.3	43.9	37.6	35.2	32.9	17.4	20.0	17.6	26.1	19.5
Kerala	27.4	21.9	24.5	19.7	23.4	28.5	26.9	22.9	16.1	19.7	11.6	11.1	15.9	15.7	15.8

Madhya Pradesh	NA	51.0	50.0	42.0	35.7	57.4	55.1	60.0	42.8	33.0	NA	19.8	35.0	25.8	19.0
Maharashtra	48.5	39.9	46.3	34.4	35.2	54.2	49.6	37.0	36.0	36.1	20.2	21.2	16.5	25.6	25.6
Manipur	33.6	31.3	35.6	28.9	23.4	30.1	27.5	22.1	13.8	13.3	8.8	8.2	9.0	6.8	9.9
Meghalaya	50.8	44.9	55.1	43.8	46.5	45.5	37.9	48.8	29.0	26.6	18.9	13.3	30.7	15.3	12.1
Mizoram	41.3	34.6	39.8	28.0	28.9	28.1	27.7	19.9	11.9	12.7	2.2	10.2	9.0	6.1	9.8
Nagaland	32.4	33.0	38.8	28.6	32.7	28.7	24.1	25.2	16.8	26.9	12.7	10.4	13.3	11.2	19.1
Orissa	48.2	44.0	45.0	34.1	31.0	53.3	54.4	40.7	34.4	29.7	21.3	24.3	19.5	20.4	18.1
Punjab	40.0	39.2	36.7	25.7	24.5	45.9	28.0	24.9	21.6	16.9	19.9	7.1	9.2	15.6	10.6
Rajasthan	43.1	52.0	43.7	39.1	31.8	41.6	50.6	39.9	36.7	27.6	19.5	11.7	20.4	23.0	16.8
Sikkim		31.7	38.3	29.6	22.3		20.6	19.7	14.2	13.1		4.8	9.7	14.2	13.7
Tamil Nadu	NA	29.4	30.9	27.1	25.0	48.2	36.7	27.7	23.8	22.0	NA	19.9	22.2	19.7	14.6
Tripura	46.0	40.4	35.7	24.3	32.3	48.8	42.6	39.6	24.1	25.6	17.5	13.1	24.6	16.8	18.2
Uttar Pradesh	59.5	55.5	56.8	46.3	39.7	59.0	51.7	42.4	39.5	32.1	16.1	11.1	14.8	17.9	17.3
Uttaranchal		46.6	44.4	33.5	27.0		41.8	38.0	26.6	21.0		7.6	18.8	19.5	13.2
West Bengal	NA	41.5	44.6	32.5	33.8	56.8	48.7	38.7	31.6	32.2	NA	13.6	16.9	20.3	20.3
India	**52**	**45.5**	**48**		**30.1**	**53.4**	**47**	**42.5**		**32.1**	**17.5**	**15.5**	**19.8**		**19.3**

suggest that chronic food inadequacy, especially among children, impair their health through increased vulnerability to diseases, especially the communicable diseases. This in turn leads to a higher mortality rate for children (number of deaths per 1,000 in the specified age group). Therefore, mortality rate can be seen as an important symptom of hunger, undernourishment as well as malnourishment. It is obvious that not all child mortality can be likened with food inadequacy, though it may be an important contributor to the higher mortality rates in some areas as against others [Malhotra, 2014]. Table 10.1 presents malnutrition based on anthropometric indicators at state level for India (1993–94 to 2019–20).

It is striking that India attained national food self-sufficiency for the past few decades, yet the incidence of malnutrition (and even child/infant mortality rate)[3] remains high, and the pace of moderation compares unfavourably with some of the neighbouring countries in South Asia. Child stunting has been shown to be associated with impaired early motor and cognitive development, with potentially life-long consequences for the individual and society. Child wasting is the most immediate, visible, and life-threatening form of malnutrition, resulting from the failure to prevent malnutrition among the most vulnerable children. Child mortality, as noted, reflects that death is the most serious consequence of undernourishment, and children are the most vulnerable.[4] While there is a declining trend

[3] India's infant mortality rate (number of deaths by age 1 per 1,000 live births) has declined from 105 in 1980 to 28 in 2020, although with considerable variation across states (Compendium of India's Fertility and Mortality Indicators, 1971 to 2013, and Sample Registration System Bulletin May 2022, Registrar General of India).

[4] The other category of malnutrition relates to overweight, obesity and diet-related non-communicable diseases.

in the incidence of underweight children (though not a monotonic decline, except for a few states), the same is not true of the incidence of stunted or wasted children. Moreover, there is wide variation at state level in these indicators. States that have better economies, higher per capita incomes, surplus food production and a faster decline in poverty incidence are not necessarily doing as well in addressing malnutrition. It appears contextual factors rooted in the larger social and cultural ethos of communities and regions may have some role in explaining the performance on these measures. They also reflect consequences of instability (price volatility and economic stress) that afflict food security from time to time, especially at local level. Thus, addressing malnutrition due to macro- (protein, carbohydrates, and fats) and micronutrient (vitamins and minerals) deficiencies largely due to inadequate food consumption and poor food utilisation of an average Indian remains a complex ask.[5]

10.4 Some Challenges and Policy Suggestions

It appears that undernourishment and the resulting incidence of malnutrition in India is a far more serious issue than the incidence of poverty, narrowly defined. The task of improving access to food, efficient body utilisation of the available food, and stability of food

[5] It is not surprising that India does not fare well on the Global Hunger Index (GHI), given that the index reports hunger on four component indicators (undernourishment, child stunting, child wasting, and child mortality) that reflect deficiencies in calories as well as in micronutrients. These, as noted earlier, could result from a range of underlying factors, including household food insecurity; inadequate maternal health or childcare practices; or inadequate access to health services, safe water, and sanitation. GHI is currently a joint project of Germany-based *Welthungerhilfe* and the Irish non-governmental organisation *Concern Worldwide*, accessed at https://www.globalhungerindex.org.

systems against price volatility and other exogenous shocks requires continued policy attention for meeting the country's food security objectives. This, however, does not imply that improving food availability and progress on poverty eradication could be set aside as issues of secondary policy importance, even as the public interventions are more squarely directed at addressing undernourishment. Indeed, strengthening and diversifying India's food production economy and eradication of poverty, defined more broadly in terms of multiple socio-economic deprivations (multidimensional poverty), is the principal pathway to ensure sustainable food and nutritional security in India. There is a need to do more of what has been done in the past for food security, but perhaps with a differentiated strategy and a geographic focus.

India's agricultural production, despite its remarkable performance in bringing about national food security in the past few decades, is challenged on multiple grounds. To begin with, the focus of improving food availability has been largely confined to the two cereal crops of wheat and rice and to the irrigated surplus-growing states of Punjab, Haryana, and western Uttar Pradesh in the northwest region of India, although for good reasons — rooted in India's geopolitics and the socio-economic context of the time. Intensive cultivation based on the Green Revolution package coupled with supportive pricing policy for these two crops have created imbalances vis-à-vis other food crops (*viz.* millets, fruits, vegetables, and poultry for which demand is gradually rising as average living standards improve) and other regions of the country. The productivity (yield) gains in this region are stagnating and excessive use of ground water has impacted soil fertility, increasing environmental stress. Attempts to gradually shift wheat and (the water-guzzling) rice cultivation to the central (*viz.* states of Madhya Pradesh, Chhattisgarh, and some parts of Uttar Pradesh) and the water-abundant eastern region (Bihar, Jharkhand, Odisha, West Bengal, and Assam), respectively, has gained momentum from around 2010 with the launching of the second Green Revolution in that region. The country is already reaping the resulting early gains in production and productivity in these two crops in the central-eastern region. This needs to be further deepened. It has opened up the possibility of using the irrigated northwest region of the country to diversify crops with income elasticity of demand, thus making efficient use of resources to secure sustainable food security for India.

Furthermore, it could be argued that the rainfed area of the country (central, parts of western India and the deccan or the peninsular region) has not been given the required attention in the food security planning of the country, although some signs of change have become visible in the past decade.[6] Rainfed areas have a very diverse ecosystem, with about 34 varieties of crops (which include different kinds of millets) being grown as against only three to four varieties of crops in the irrigated regions [Government of India, 2011]. The millets grown in this region require much less water and other inputs (chemical fertilisers and pesticides), thus involving low carbon and organic farming, and for centuries have provided food and nutritional support to the local people. They also provide sufficient fodder, which helps farmers to maintain livestock.[7] Despite there being no significant policy support, millets grown in rainfed areas have shown tremendous growth potential and their incremental productivity improvement since the turn

[6] Rainfed agriculture supports an estimated 40% of India's population and has a large share of cropped area under rice (over 40%), pulses (about 75%), oilseeds (more than 65%) and millets (85%).

[7] India has the largest cattle population in the world currently.

of the century has exceeded that of rice. This indicates the potential of rainfed agriculture to contribute to national food and nutritional security, and livelihood opportunities for the population residing in that area and this must be fully tapped, including through technological breakthroughs in the cultivation of crops suited to this region [Malhotra, 2014]. Importantly, the demand for millets is picking up, due in parts to their nutritional attractiveness and a growing domestic policy focus to strengthen the millet economy.[8]

The other very good reason to concentrate on the policy environment to advance the second Green Revolution in the central-eastern region of India and improve the policy support for rainfed agriculture is for India to renew its attack on poverty eradication. The gains in production and productivity are critical, equally important, if not more, in improving the economic access to food or addressing the demand side of the food security equation. In the past couple of decades, India's rural poverty is getting increasingly concentrated in the said region, and among specific social groups, including scheduled tribes, scheduled castes (in both rural and urban areas),[9] Muslims in urban areas and Christians in rural areas (mainly Odisha), asset-less labour and women. There is also evidence to suggest that interpersonal, rural-urban, and across-state inequalities in per capita consumption and in some socially valued human development outcomes have increased in recent years, though not uniformly [Malhotra, 2014].

---

[8] The United Nations has declared the year 2023 as the international year of millets, largely at India's behest.

[9] The Scheduled Castes and Scheduled Tribes are officially designated groups of people and among the most disadvantaged socio-economic groups under the Constitution of India.

Historically, it has been seen that a step-up in agriculture growth is the most effective solution to address rural poverty, especially so if agriculture uses more intensively the most abundant resource available to the poor — labour. Growth is most effective in reducing poverty when it is accompanied by a decline in inequality [Ravallion, 2004; Malhotra, 2018]. Importantly, the production gains in agriculture can be consolidated rapidly if tenancy reforms could be carried out (at the state level) with a view to make the market for agriculture land work efficiently. This would incentivise consolidation of operational land parcels for cultivation to optimal size, which otherwise are too small to allow surplus production for the market and adequate returns for most of the households engaged in agriculture.[10] Besides measures like development of modern technologies and practices like multiple cropping, intercropping and integrated farming systems, developing location-specific varieties and technologies for enhancing the production and productivity of farm holdings along with financial support (credit interest subvention) and crop insurance, the tenancy reforms can go a long way in addressing supply-side as well as demand-side concerns of the food economy.

Sustaining gains in agricultural production requires investment in infrastructure, including for irrigation, dissemination of agriculture credit, agriculture extension, efficient storage, decentralisation of agriculture wholesale markets (local food *mandis*) cold-chains, agro-processing industries, transportation, and organised retail. Public investment in these areas is seen to 'crowd-in' private investment. In all these areas, the government has stepped up efforts to

[10] The average size of operational holdings has decreased from 2.28 hectares in 1970–71 to 1.84 hectares in 1980–81, to 1.41 hectares in 1995–96 and to 1.08 hectares in 2015–16 (Agriculture Census, Government of India, 2020).

bridge the gaps, sometimes not effectively, especially in the absence of adequate stakeholder participation in the process of undertaking reforms; nevertheless, there has been some progress in the last two decades.

To contribute to household food security, there is a need to focus on urban poverty which is becoming more widespread than rural poverty and is likely to increase as the pace of urbanisation picks up in India in the coming decades. This requires a renewed policy focus on generating non-farm livelihood opportunities as well as improving the quality and coverage of social security. Ultimately, India needs to make decisive progress in completing its structural transformation. It needs to bring down the dependence of people on agriculture/rural economy from over 40% of its population at present to about 15% in the next 10–15 years, moving them to the industrial and the service sectors. This would help in raising the returns of the farming households, while providing the basis for improving average living standards in the country. This is a task easier said than done, with employment growth being severely anaemic for the better part of the last two decades, notwithstanding the various shocks faced by the economy, including COVID-19. India's labour market is predominantly informal (or unorganised, accounting for nearly 90% of the workforce) and overwhelmingly populated by micro- and small-sized firms that face various constraints on their growth and scaling up. While labour market reforms have been initiated by several state governments and industrialisation is being prioritised both at the central and state government levels, there is a long way to go to absorb the pool of unemployed and under-employed, besides keeping pace with the addition to the country's labour force. This discussion is beyond the scope of this chapter.

The food policy in India targets both the availability and the access aspect of food security. It has sought to moderate food prices in the open market and attain self-sufficiency in foodgrains, along with measures for maximising procurement from surplus areas [Dev and Sharma, 2010; Dev *et al.*, 2003]. The three main instruments of the food security system and agricultural price policy are: procurement prices, minimum support prices (MSP) and issue prices; buffer stocks; and the PDS. The government's intervention in domestic markets of wheat and rice (and some other crops) ranges from providing farmers with price support under MSP, procuring grains from *mandis* (grain wholesale markets) or through millers under compulsory levies on rice, to buffer stocking and distributing the procured grains at an issue price (generally below the economic cost of procurement and maintaining buffer stocks) through the PDS. Despite the huge costs of market intervention, including the carrying costs of large food buffer stocks, it is difficult to foresee a withdrawal of any of these interventions for fear of risking price volatility, which affects the food security of the vulnerable sections of society and is of course politically expedient.

PDS helps in improving food security at the household level. A public agency, Food Corporation of India, is the nodal agency that procures, stores, and distributes grains to state governments, which in turn distribute it to the identified beneficiaries under the various food-based welfare schemes. The scope and coverage of the PDS has expanded under the National Food Security Act (NFSA) 2013, which brings in a rights-based approach to address the food and nutritional security of people in India. It combines and expands some existing food-based welfare schemes, and a conditional cash transfer scheme called the Direct Benefit Transfer (DBT), making it the biggest programme of its kind globally, reaching more than 800 million people, with an annual, legally enforceable distribution commitment of over 61 million metric tons of grains sold at highly subsidised prices (with almost 90% subsidy). After a slow start, the fact that this system worked remarkably well during the COVID-19-led lockdown and the subsequent economic slowdown by delivering a certain level of food security to the targeted population in difficult circumstances, vindicates its relevance for the country. By creating a legal entitlement, the NFSA 2013 has contributed to the accountability and efficiency of the PDS, besides creating awareness among the intended beneficiaries of the benefits they are entitled to and promoting stability of food security. The use of JAM trinity (Jan Dhan accounts, Aadhar and Mobile) or the trinity of financial inclusion, digital identity and mobile network has contributed to the effectiveness of DBT with better targeting and efficient transfer of subsidies. As long as there is poverty in India and the pace of livelihood creation lags behind the demand for work, India's food policy and food security apparatus, as described, would remain relevant, although efforts to improve its operational efficiency cannot be over-emphasised.

Moreover, public interventions to reach and address the food and nutritional security needs of most vulnerable population groups like children (mid-day meals in schools or the ICDS programme for pre-school children), the elderly, and mothers especially in the first 1,000 days of a child's life remain relevant until such times as the anthropometric measures of malnourishment improve sufficiently. Policies to tackle undernourishment need dovetailing of the longer-term perspective, in the form of empowering of the poor and improving their entitlements through investment in human capital and direct provisioning through social protection measures, where required. As noted earlier, access to a diverse food basket alone may not help in overcoming malnutrition. There is scope for well-implemented government programmes so that access to sanitation (*viz.* the Swatch Bharat Mission), potable water and public health facilities, in a timely manner, helps in the consolidation of gains from improved entitlements to food and nourishment. In India, virtually all public programmes at the central and state levels have some elements of poverty and hunger eradication. Therefore, it is important that at the state and district levels there is an integrated and coordinated approach to the implementation of the public programmes. In regions where there is a large burden of malnourishment and undernourishment, the focus must be on involving the local community in service delivery and oversight. Synergy and convergence between different programmes at the grassroots level can ensure a more holistic and result-driven approach to eradication of undernourishment on a sustainable basis [Malhotra, 2014]. Some of these measures have been strengthened, have gained momentum and others need to be followed up to their logical end.

While the role and scope for public action remains paramount in securing and sustaining food security in a populous country like India, with a heavy burden of poor and nutritionally insecure population, sustainability of food security also requires ushering in market efficiency wherever it is feasible, without compromising on the equity considerations of the food economy. The need for tenancy reforms to create a market for agricultural land and promote optimally sized operational holdings was highlighted. Similarly, there is scope for selectively liberalising agriculture trade to improve returns for farmers, without compromising on the basic food security of the country. This will usher in efficiency in the overall resource use of the economy, provide an impetus to establish modern food supply chains, food safety standards and improved choice for the consumers in the country [Gulati *et al.*, 2019].

Finally, there is the politically difficult idea of exploring the creation of food security at the regional level in the Asia-Pacific region. The region comprises two of the biggest food producers and consumers in India and China, apart from other countries like Thailand, Indonesia, Malaysia, and Sri Lanka that are significant producers of certain food commodities like rice, edible oil, topical spices, vegetables and fruits, cocoa, tea, and marine products. Besides, there is Australia with its huge expanse of land that can be potentially cultivated to augment the supply of the required food in the region in an environmentally sustainable manner.

10.5 Conclusions

The idea of food security is complicated conceptually and in practice. It requires a multifaceted approach to address the issue, especially in India. Apart from securing and sustaining national food security, the ultimate objective is to ensure food security at the household level, which makes the task complex for India. India is food secure at the national level, but it is far from being food secure at the household level. The issue of food supply or food availability has been largely addressed, although there is an aspect of food availability linked to average living standards, which evolves with time and requires continued policy attention: the demand side of the food security that relates to access — economic and physical — utilisation and stability dimensions of food security remains a major challenge for India.

The issue of poverty is at the heart of India's food security concerns. India's poverty has not just been about people who are undernourished, rather it is about people who are acutely prone to health vulnerabilities and illness, are unemployed or underemployed, poorly endowed, with limited access to critical civic amenities (public goods), are powerless, socially marginalised and can be easily disempowered and dispossessed of their entitlements because of their peculiar circumstances. Importantly, food systems involve different stakeholders — people and institutions, as well as the socio-political, economic, technological and natural environments in which the activities to create food security take place. All this adds up to the complexity of policy challenges in addressing food security concerns sustainably.

Going forward, even as public interventions are being refined, made effective, and more squarely directed at the issues to address under-nourishment and malnutrition, it is argued that improving food availability through diversification of food crops and the cropping regions, and progress on poverty eradication, remains the principal path to secure and sustain food security in India. Although this journey continues to be difficult, India is well placed to attain its food security objectives in the not-too-distant future.

References

Dev, S. M. and Sharma, A. N. (2010). Food security in India: performance, challenges and policies. *Oxfam India Working Paper Series VIII.*

Dev, M., Kanan, K. P. and Ramachandran, N. (Eds.) (2003). *Towards a Food Secure India.* Institute for Human Development.

Drèze, J. and Sen, A. (1989). *Hunger and Public Action.* Clarendon Press.

FAO. (1983). *World Food Security: A Reappraisal of the Concepts and Approaches.* Director General's Report.

FAO. (1996). Rome Declaration on World Food Security and World Food Summit Plan of Action. World Food Summit 13–17 November 1996.

FAO. (2002). *The State of Food Insecurity in the World 2001.* https://www.fao.org/publications/card/es/c/62e4c9ae-f1e7-508e-8207-ff283a65d9ec/

FAO. (2003). *Trade Reforms and Food Security: Conceptualising the Linkages*. https://www.fao.org/3/y4671e/y4671e06.htm

Government of India. (2011). *Report of the XII Plan Working Group on Natural Resource Management and Rainfed Farming*. http://www.indiaenvironmentportal.org.in/content/344791/report-of-the-xii-plan-working-group-on-natural-resource-management-and-rainfed-farming/

Gulati, A., Kapur, D. and Bouton, M. M. (2019). *Reforming Indian Agriculture*. Center for the Advanced Study of India and the Indian Council for Research on International Economic Relations.

Malhotra, R. (2014). *India Public Policy Report 2014 — Tackling Poverty, Hunger, and Malnutrition*. Oxford University Press.

Malhotra, R. (2018). Economic Policy and Human Rights: Is Globalisation a Meeting Ground. In A. G. Dastidar, R. Malhotra and V. Suneja (Eds.), *Economic Theory and Policy amidst Global Discontent*. Routledge.

Ministry of Finance. (2022–23). *Economic Survey*. Government of India, New Delhi.

Nozick, R. (1974). *Anarchy, State and Utopia*. Basic Books.

Ravallion, M. (2004). Pro-poor growth: a primer. *World Bank Policy Research Working Paper* No. 3242.

Sen, A. (1981). *Poverty and Famines*. Clarendon Press.

United Nations. (1975). *Report of the World Food Conference, Rome 5–16 November 1974*. https://digitallibrary.un.org/record/701143?ln=en

UNDP. (1994). *Human Development Report 1994*. Oxford University Press.

World Bank. (1986). *Poverty and Hunger: Issues and Options for Food Security in Developing Countries*. https://digitallibrary.un.org/record/110631?ln=en

World Bank. (2022). *World Development Indicators*. https://data.worldbank.org/indicator/NY.GDP.PCAP.PP.CD?locations=IN

Issues in Technology

https://doi.org/10.1142/9789811278297_0011

Chapter 11

The Role of Digital Technologies in Food Supply Chains

Jose Ma. Luis Montesclaros

S. Rajaratnam School of International Studies, Nanyang Technological University, Singapore

11.1 Introduction

The notion of digitalised agriculture may appear oxymoronic at first glance. Agriculture has for the past decades been seen as a subsistence and uncapitalised sector with limited capital investment per person [Lewis, 1954]. This owes partly to the long-established view of food and agricultural products as "inferior goods" in economic terms, in the sense that as individuals' incomes increase, there is a tendency towards greater consumption of higher-valued manufactured products as opposed to food and agricultural products [Chakrabarty and Hildenbrand, 2009; Engel, 1857].

Moreover, the average education attainment within agriculture-related jobs (ranchers, farm managers) is generally lower compared to other jobs. Within Southeast Asia, for instance, the countries with the larger shares of employment in agriculture were also the ones with lower net enrolment ratios in secondary education [ASEAN, 2022]. In contrast, digital technologies are mostly associated with sectors where there are higher levels of education, including information and communications technology and other business-related jobs.

Despite these challenges, there has been growing investment in developing novel digital technologies for the agricultural sector globally. According to the venture capital firm AgFunder [2022] which presents annual reports of agrifoodtech investment globally, over USD 18.2 billion in private sector venture capital was invested in high-tech upstream agriculture technologies in 2021 alone, including farm management software, farm robotics and equipment, as well as biotechnologies. A further USD 32.1 billion was invested in downstream e-commerce applications such as e-groceries and online sales. This has grown from a total of only USD 2.7 billion in 2014. Asia has been the second largest with more than USD 15 billion invested in 2021 alone.

This chapter elucidates the rationale behind the adoption of digital technologies in agriculture in Asia, and provides a simple framework for categorising digital technologies in food production. It also discusses the critical challenges faced in further improving the adoption of these technologies, and presents some prospects for addressing these challenges in the long term.

11.2 Productivity-Enhancing Technologies to Meet Future Requirements for Food Security

The technical definition of food security is "a situation that exists when all people, at all times, have physical, social and economic access to sufficient, safe and nutritious food that meets their dietary needs and food preferences for an active and healthy life" [Food and Agriculture Organization (FAO), 2001: 51].

Broadly, this means having sufficient food to meet the growing consumption needs of populations, to enable them to live healthy lives. In this regard, food availability is a critical component of food security, in terms of having sufficient food production to meet the growing consumption needs. Asia, in fact, remains a net food trade deficit region, in the sense that it imports more food than it exports, with a food trade deficit of more than USD 240 million [FAO, 2022].

An earlier study by the Consortium of International Agricultural Research Centers for instance showed that in the case of rice as the top consumed food commodity in Asia, an additional 166 million tonnes of rice needs to be produced by 2035 to meet growing demand, relative to 2010 levels [GRISP, 2013]. Majority of the additional demand is anticipated to come from Asia. An earlier study by the Intergovernmental Panel on Climate Change (IPCC) notes that overall agricultural production will need to increase by over 50% from 2012 to 2050 to meet growing demand [Mbow *et al.*, 2019: 5.1].

An important challenge in this regard is the negative impact of climate change on agricultural productivity, the latter being measured in terms of tonnes of food produced per hectare farmed. More food needs to be grown even if the land available for farming cannot be indefinitely expanded. Worse yet, climate change is also leading to rising sea levels that contributes to "permanent submergence of land", coastal erosion, and salinisation of soils, which altogether further reduce the suitable viable land for agricultural production [Oppenheimer *et al.*, 2018: 4.1.3].

This can lead to increasing food scarcity, which makes food less affordable especially for poorer populations. A bleak but nonetheless realistic scenario of "stratified societies" was identified in another report by the FAO, which involves "exacerbated inequalities in terms of income, earning opportunities and access to essential goods and services across countries and layers of societies" [FAO, 2018a: 25]. This scenario anticipates that the share of undernourished individuals in the world population would increase from 10% in 2020 to approximately 12% in 2030 and remain at this level heading up to 2050. Given a growing global population, this means that the number of undernourished would increase from approximately 780 million in 2020 to close to 1.25 billion in 2050.

These forecasts are by no means an exaggeration, since as early as 2014, the FAO's annual State of Food Insecurity in the World report already reflected an increase in global undernourishment from 10.7% in 2014 to 10.8% in 2016 [FAO, 2018b]. Across Asia's subregions, undernourishment increased in Southeast Asia from 9.7% in 2014 to 9.9% in 2016, which translates to an additional three million people falling into hunger [Montesclaros, 2021a]. The share of undernourished also increased in Western Asia from 10.4% in 2014 to 11.1% in 2016, which represents an additional 2.65 million people falling into undernourishment. While the shares of undernourishment have been steady in other areas in Asia, the absolute numbers of undernourished have nonetheless increased by two hundred thousand people in Central Asia.

Therefore, the problem of undernourishment presents a clear rationale for the adoption of technologies to boost the productivity of agriculture. This is a critical imperative if the growing consumption needs of Asia's population are to be met with increasing production capacity amidst the impacts of climate change on agriculture.

11.3 Digital Technologies for Climate-Smart Food Production

A myriad of digital technologies is available today which can allow Asia to meet its growing food consumption requirements. This section presents a categorisation of such technologies to better introduce their potential contributions to boosting food productivity in the continent.

One compilation of digital technologies was presented in an earlier report by the Organisation for Economic Cooperation and Development [OECD, 2019]. Their categorisation is further tailored in this regard across the supply chain of agriculture, with a focus on climate-smart food production. The logic behind these technologies generally follows the concept of **precision agriculture**, which focuses on only experimental designs for crop nutrient management [Fisher, 1935]. In the presence of digital technologies, the definition of precision agriculture has since evolved into "the science of improving crop yields and assisting management decisions using high technology sensor and analysis tools" [Singh *et al.*, 2020: 121].

An extension of precision agriculture has occurred over the recent decade with the advent of the Fourth Industrial Revolution (IR) as previously noted by Klaus Schwab [2017], the founder of the World Economic Forum. He distinguished this from the First IR (water and steam power for mechanising tools); the Second IR (electrical power for mass production); and the Third IR (electronics and information technology to automate production). The Fourth IR reflects "a fusion of technologies that is blurring the lines between the physical, digital, and biological spheres" [Schwab, 2017: 2].

In this regard, a further evolution of precision agriculture amidst the advent of the Fourth IR is through the automated implementation of recommendations from precision agriculture, better known today as the "**Internet of Things**" (IoT) in agriculture [Montesclaros *et al.*, 2019]. Three key technologies are implied by the IoT in agriculture, namely, data collection technologies, data analysis technologies, and the automated implementation of the recommendations of data analysis. These are summarised in Figure 11.1, and further described in the remainder of this section.

11.3.1 *Data Collection Technologies*

Data collection technologies are typically used for tracking environmental factors/changes that can influence crop growth. They are used for monitoring purposes, to capture changes in crop growth alongside environmental factors/changes so that farmers can adjust their farming practices accordingly. A related important concern which these technologies can assist farmers with is the presence of pests and diseases, as these can easily spread to the rest of the farms. In Southeast Asia, for instance, pests and diseases have impacted close to one thousand hectares of rice and maize lands in 2022 alone [AFSIS, 2022].

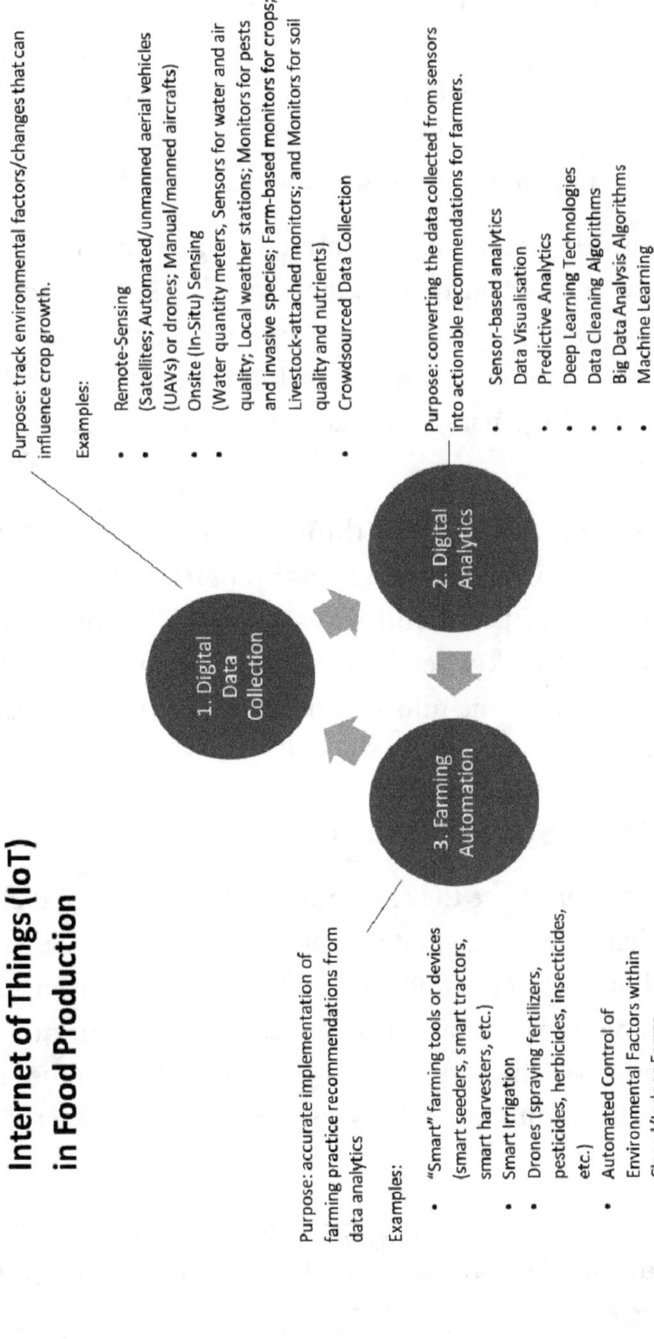

Figure 11.1 Internet of Things (IoT) in food production.

Data collection technologies are divided into three. The first are **remote-sensing technologies** which leverage satellites, automated/ unmanned aerial vehicles or drones, and manual/manned aircrafts. Apart from remote-sensing technologies, there are also **onsite-sensing** ["*in situ*"] **technologies** which allow for on-ground monitoring of further conditions that cannot be gathered remotely.

In situ monitoring technologies include water quantity metres, sensors for water and air quality, local weather stations, monitors for pests and invasive species, farm-based monitors for crops, livestock-attached monitors, and monitors for soil quality and nutrients. Data from agriculture using precision agriculture are also included among these.

The third type of technology is through **crowd-sourced data collection**, whereby farmers can use their mobile phones to directly report instances of pests and diseases. Such reports are then uploaded to a network whereby thousands of farmers are able to almost instantly draw the information to be able to act on them in a timely manner.

11.3.2 *Data Analytics Technologies*

Not all farmers may have the capability of analysing digital data. As such, a further technology that complements digital data collection is data analytics, which **converts the data collected from sensors into actionable recommendations for farmers**. For example, **sensor-based analytics** help visualise the data drawn from the sensors and convert them into more digestible information from the viewpoint of farmers.

Data analytics technologies are important given the rather lower average education level of farmers relative to other jobs/sectors, as noted earlier. Not all farmers are agronomists by training, so upon receiving data from the sensors, most farmers will need additional assistance in answering the "so what" question.

Similarly, not all farmers are meteorologists by training. They are unable to immediately convert weather data on air pressure, wind speed/direction, and humidity into projections on droughts and floods, as well as on expectations for rainfall. Such weather projections, which can be drawn from **predictive analytics**, are critical to farmers who are planning their crops for each planting season.

To process data from sensors, data analytics technologies leverage a sub-category of technologies, namely, **deep learning technologies**. These include **data-cleaning algorithms** which remove irrelevant data and also help identify measurement errors (including outlier values) to increase the accuracy of the data-gathering methodologies. Data cleaning also involves standardising the programming languages so that the data can be used by other applications. It can also be used to translate the table headings into vernacular languages which farmers can understand [Pathak, 2023].

Equally important are **big data analysis algorithms**, which allow for combining data from the multiple types of sensors cited under data collection technologies. For instance, the benefits of remote-sensing data are significantly improved when combined with on-site data. Alternatively, there may be further disruptions which have not yet been encoded as environmental factors to be tracked by both remote-sensing and on-site data; in these cases, the direct inputs from farmers are invaluable in introducing factors of importance for future monitoring and yield growth optimisation purposes.

Machine learning technologies, in this regard, can improve the way in which the ever-changing environments for farming are captured and understood by computers. They can also be complemented with crowd-sourced applications for sorting and labelling data.

11.3.3 *Automation of Farming*

The third technology category which was not captured in the OECD's [2019] original categorisation of technologies, but which completes the proposed trilogy of climate-smart agriculture, is the automation of farming. In particular, this refers to the automated implementation of data analytics recommendations. As earlier noted, this is a key feature of the IoT-enabled agriculture which distinguishes it from the previous notions of precision agriculture.

The purpose of this third group of technologies is to allow for more accurate implementation of the farming practice recommendations from data analytics technologies. Examples include adjusting transplanting schedules, timely application of pesticides, and more even application to make for more efficient uses of farming inputs.

The origins of automated implementation of data analytics recommendations lies in the mechanisation of agricultural processes. This includes the use of tractors for tilling the soil, seeders for transplanting seedlings, harvesters for harvesting crops, among others. A key difference, amidst the Fourth IR, is how the same tools are being retrofitted to turn them into **"smart" farming tools or devices**, whose repetitive operations are relegated to computers/machines instead of relying solely on manual efforts. This builds on **global positioning systems** so that the said machines can be programmed to go in particular locations/directions, in line with recommendations from the data analytics technologies.

During the 2017 World Agricultural Forum hosted by the S. Rajaratnam School of International Studies (RSIS), Nanyang Technological University, Singapore, Rangsit Poosiripinyo shared "a call for a paradigm shift from using traditional agricultural methods that are land and labour intensive to knowledge intensive agriculture methods, which includes precision farming, green technology, commercial farming and entrepreneurship support" [RSIS, 2017]. Poosirpinyo shared this in her capacity then as Deputy Secretary General, Office of Agricultural Economics, and on behalf of the Ministry of Agriculture and Cooperatives, Thailand, then the 2017 Country Chair of the ASEAN Ministers of Agriculture and Forestry.

As such, data analytics recommendations are fed into "**smart harvesters**", "**smart seeders**" **and** "**smart tractors**" to allow these to be automatically implemented in fields with minimum manual farmer intervention [Montesclaros, 2021b]. Apart from machinery, there are also practices of "**smart irrigation**" which allow for minimising water loss through evaporation/evapotranspiration within plants, thus increasing water efficiency. For example, Jain, an Indian company, has released a smart irrigation control product which allows farmers to know how much they are spending on water, and to also adjust accordingly to optimise plant growth [Reynolds, 2023].

A further improvement, which has resulted from the increasing use of drones or unmanned aerial vehicles, is in using **drones** to take over tasks which farmers previously conducted manually. Such tasks include **spraying chemical farming inputs like fertilisers, pesticides, herbicides and insecticides** on crops, as noted earlier by the FAO and the International Telecommunications Union (ITU) [Sylvester, 2018].

A yet further improvement to the traditional precision agriculture is the automated **control of environmental factors within closed/indoor environments**. These factors include the temperature, air pressure and humidity, which together with irrigation and crop nutrition allow for shorter growing cycles (i.e., faster growing periods) for crops. These also allow for overcoming the seasonality of production schedules which are a common limiting factor [Montesclaros *et al.*, 2019]. Within indoor environments, farmers are further able to grow crops on multiple tiers or layers, thus providing a significant increase in food production potential.

Therefore, in combination, the use of data collection technologies, data analytics technologies, and automated implementation of data analytics technologies, allow for IoT-enabled agricultural production. These allow for developing "climate-smart" agricultural practices, in which farming practices can eventually be tailored automatically according to changing environmental conditions. These can be further complemented by crowd-sourced information so that the data which sensors are designed to collect correspond to the key threats which farmers face.

It is important to note that this framing of digital technologies in food production is not encompassing, as there are further technologies which present partial approaches in relation to the IoT in agriculture. For instance, **digital farmer advisory services** provide farmers with advice on how to optimise their crop-growing practices in an offline mode [Grow Asia, 2022]. Such services do not require the automation of food production. Moreover, rather than building on complex data analytics, such advice can build on expert consultation by the company or individual providing this service.

11.4 Digital E-Commerce: Enabler for Digital Production

The digitalisation of the food production sector alone may not be sufficient in food systems, however, since further problems include farmer's access to consumers/buyers as well as farmers' access to inputs. For example, farmers have a tendency to lose a significant share of the value of what they produce (also known as farmers' "marketing margins"), as this goes to food processors and distributors/traders [Dawe *et al.*, 2008]. In this regard, digital **e-commerce** allows for improving the income of farmers by providing a direct link to their consumers. The key technologies involved, as well as their enablers, are described in Figure 11.2 and further discussed below.

11.4.1 *Distributed Ledger Technologies/Blockchain*

E-commerce builds on **distributed ledger technologies (DLT)** which are defined in an introductory publication by the FAO and for this technology as "a decentralized system for recording transactions with mechanisms for processing, validating and authorizing transactions that are then recorded on an immutable ledger" [Sylvester, 2019: 1]. Another popular term for DLTs is **blockchain** in the sense that the data for each transaction are put into groups ("blocks"). Data is then linked together using cryptography to ensure that the transaction's data is secure [Hayes, 2022: 1].

DLTs/blockchain technologies allow farmers to sell their products directly to consumers, during which the transactions are monitored by a third party in the form of the DLT. For instance, the payments by consumers are not transferred immediately to the farmers, until the consumers verify that they have received the food items in good

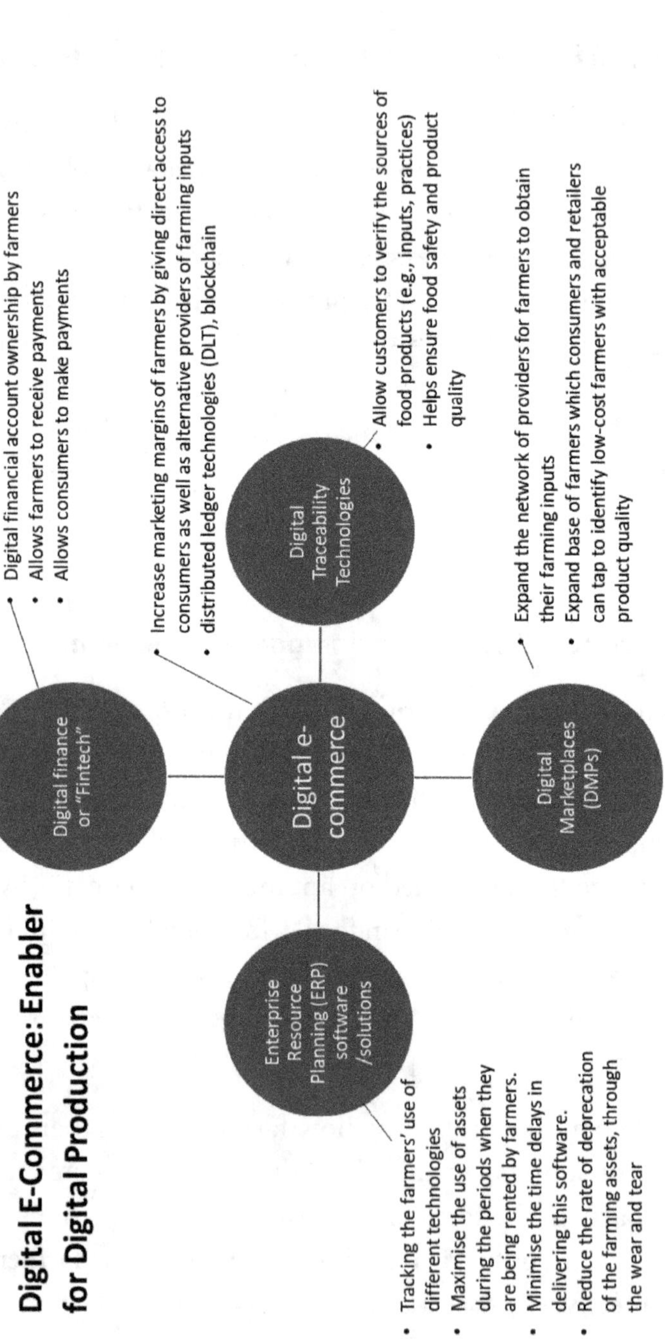

Figure 11.2 Digital e-commerce: enabler for digital production.

condition. Another benefit of these technologies is in allowing farmers access to a greater range of technology providers for digital data collection and analysis, as well as automation technologies. These also provide farmers with flexible financing options for paying for these technologies.

11.4.2 *Digital Finance (Fintech)*

A further pre-requisite for these technologies is that farmers and consumers have sufficient access to **digital finance**. In particular, farmers and consumers need to have internet identities and accounts which are connected to their bank accounts or financial accounts, which they can use to receive/send money accordingly, dubbed as "**fintech**" by the United Nations Economic and Social Commission for Asia and the Pacific [UN ESCAP, 2022].

Even if e-commerce is a potential enabler of IoT approaches in agriculture, a number of issues need to be resolved before e-commerce can lift off. In Southeast Asia, for instance, 44% of adults are still unbanked according to the United Nations Capital Development Fund [UNCDF, 2020]. A further pre-requisite is the **presence of efficient logistics systems**, including roadways, and access points for dropping off/picking up the food items, as well as **stable and reliable internet access** in Asia's rural areas.

11.4.3 *Digital Traceability Solutions*

A further future avenue to allow farmers to expand their digital e-commerce customer base and, in turn, their revenue base is through **digital traceability technologies**. These technologies allow customers, and governments as well, to verify the sources of food products, including the inputs used. For example, the

Indonesia-based private company Koltiva has a "KoltiTrace" software which uses geolocation and mapping features to trace the transactions that occurred before a food product reached a consumer, including the seeds/chemicals used, practices applied, and the transport paths taken [Koltiva, 2023].

11.4.4 *Digital Marketplaces*

Once farmers are able to show where their farming inputs are sourced and ensure that their food products are produced in a manner that aligns with regulatory requirements for consumer safety, farmers will be able to significantly expand their consumer base through **digital marketplaces (DMPs)**. DMPs complement e-commerce by providing a broader network for farmers to obtain their farming inputs, as well as for consumers and retailers to identify low-cost farmers with acceptable product quality. For example, in 2015, the NINAYO application was launched to serve as a DMP for agricultural products in Tanzania. This application allows farmers to not only sell their products digitally, but to also obtain fertilisers and other technology inputs at fairer market prices, through loans which are repaid once crops are harvested [World Food Programme, 2020].

11.4.5 *Enterprise Resource Planning Software/Solutions*

To support the adoption of multiple technologies within farms, a further technology complement lies in **enterprise resource planning (ERP) software/solutions** for farmers. This technology solution allows for tracking the farmers' use of different technologies which the farmer will likely rent for the purpose of the farm. It then uses data analytics to help optimise the scheduling of the use of this equipment. Such approaches can have manifold benefits. Firstly,

ERP solutions can maximise the use of assets during the periods when they are being rented by farmers. Secondly, they can minimise the time delays in delivering this software. Thirdly, they can potentially reduce the rate of deprecation of the farming assets through wear and tear.

11.5 Addressing Key Issues in Scaling Up Internet of Things in Asian Agriculture

Recent trends show that there has been greater private venture capital investment in downstream industries relative to upstream industries, a trend which will likely continue heading into 2030 (Figure 11.3). The 2022 AgFunder report noted that e-grocers,

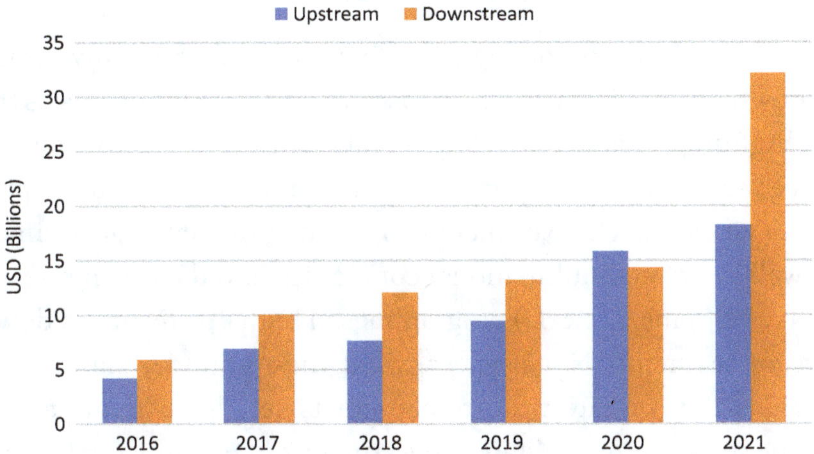

Figure 11.3 Annual global venture capital financing in upstream and downstream Agrifoodtech, in USD (billions). Source: Compiled by author from various AgFunder Reports. Note: Years are the report's reference years; for example, the 2022 AgFunder Report's reference year is 2021. Interpolation was applied to fill in missing data.

which are a form of downstream e-commerce in supply chains, saw the fastest investment growth of 188% growth from 2020 to 2021. This reflects consumers' greater desire for convenience in food consumption, and the private sector's desire to cater to this desire.

Given finite resources to invest in agricultural technologies (agtech), the trend of greater investment in downstream industries can only come at the expense of investments in IoT and related upstream technologies for boosting farmer resilience amidst climate change. The slow liftoff of IoT-enabled agriculture in Asia can be seen in slowing productivity growth in upstream agriculture in recent decades. This reveals growing vulnerability of Asian farmers to the impacts of climate change [Montesclaros and Teng, 2021]. In 2022, for instance, Southeast Asia lost over 709,000 hectares of land for its key crops, namely, rice, maize, sugarcane, soybean and cassava to floods and droughts [AFSIS, 2022].

A caveat to the AgFunder figures, which showed greater investment in downstream industries as opposed to upstream industries, is that the AgFunder database covers neither funding recipients beyond agtech start-ups, nor funding sources beyond private venture capital. Other types of such investment include investments by government as well as private/multinational companies into their own research and development (R&D) programmes in both upstream and downstream segments. Nonetheless, what the AgFunder statistics do show is that private venture capitalists see downstream agtech segments as more profitable investment opportunities relative to upstream opportunities.

One explanation for this is a perception that farmers are less bankable relative to the users of downstream technologies, including supermarkets and consumers. This is partly justified since 87% of smallholder farmers globally are in Asia. These farmers typically grow food on plots of land sized two hectares or smaller, and commonly have little access to financing [Hazell and Rahman, 2014]. Moreover, across countries in East Asia and the Pacific, it has been shown that poverty in rural areas is four times the poverty in urban areas [Rigg *et al.*, 2016].

In contrast, the technologies which compose IoT are of a **highly capital-dependent nature** [Montesclaros *et al.*, 2019]. As such, a key challenge to scaling up the adoption of the IoT in agriculture in Asia is that farmers are ill-equipped to afford them. There are likewise infrastructure gaps, including electricity access. For instance, it is estimated that approximately 130 million individuals in Southeast Asia lack access to electricity [The Renewable Energy Support Programme for ASEAN (RESP) Team, 2013]. As such, the **affordability of IoT technologies and availability of supporting infrastructure in food production** are key constraints to farmers' adoption of these technologies.

If smallholder farmers are less bankable from the private venture capitalists' viewpoint, then states may need to step up their support to upstream agtech developers which cater to farmers' need for upstream technologies. One potential initiative is to develop a funding database of investments by governments and private funders beyond venture capital, and in a manner that distinguishes between private sector investment as well as between upstream and downstream. This could potentially allow for ascertaining the size of the financing gap faced by upstream agtech, paving the way for public intervention to bridge these gaps.

States can also potentially play more active roles in bringing farmers closer to the upstream IoT technologies, through measures such as the **nationalisation or state ownership** of these resources. For instance, in 2017, China National Chemical Corporation (Chinachem), which is among China's biggest state-owned conglomerates, bought over Syngenta, a Swiss-owned multinational [Shields, 2017]. This allowed the Chinese government to deploy further measures to increase the access of the country's farmers to the agtech of modern seeds, pesticides and fertilisers, thus plugging important technology gaps in its agricultural sector [Wang, 2021].

Alternatively, states can provide **funding to support private sector entities** which wish to either bring in foreign technologies, or to develop these domestically. This also involves **interventions in the education system** to draw interest by the youth into this sector, as well as equip early-career individuals with the needed skills to enter this sector. Singapore, for instance, has an active "Singapore Food Story" R&D programme which provides funding support to develop the country's own agri-food-tech ecosystem into a "globally respected, future-ready food safety system that ensures a continual supply of safe food for Singapore and supports the growth of the agri-tech and food sector" [Singapore Food Agency, 2020].

11.6 Potential Future Issues: The Vanishing Farmer?

In the long term, a further issue is the **potential future displacement of farmers**, assuming that the IoT in agriculture/farming were to lift off as an easily **replicable modular process**. Private venture capital in agriculture has grown significantly from USD 2.36 billion in 2014 [AgFunder, 2014] to USD 51.7 billion in 2021 alone [AgFunder, 2022]. The number of published investors has likewise increased significantly from 271 in 2014 to 4,570. In fact, the largest deal in 2021 amounted to USD 3 billion, which is larger than the total size of private venture capital investment in 2014.

An important concern is whether the average farmer will still find his or her place within the agricultural sector. If machines can grow crops better than human beings following an easily replicable modular process of farming, then the prospect emerges of totally replacing farmers, and displacing them from their current occupations.

Should such modular approaches be developed and scaled up, there is a further risk in that this could lead to a **corporatisation of the farming sector**. Such corporatisation is already happening in patches; for instance, Olam International is a Singapore-based company which acts as an aggregator of farming products from farmers. In certain crops, it likewise provides farmers with digital tools to boost their production capacity.

While the assistance provided by private businesses to agriculture is beneficial to farmers, it would be cause for worry should the corporatisation of farming further evolve into private or multinational companies playing an active role in the direct growing of crops, beyond companies' current supporting roles as aggregators or providers of advisory services. Should this occur, it could lead to declining bargaining powers of both farmer and consumers relative to big companies, as earlier noted in a scientific study commissioned by the European Parliament [EP *et al.*, 2019]. A further extension of this is in the vertical integration of companies within the agricultural sector, as this too could lead to similar capacities to influence input prices in their favour.

State intervention will be needed in addressing these risks, to curtail potentially monopolistic or oligopolistic price-setting mechanisms among big companies for agricultural products. State regulation of land markets, including the transfers of ownership of farms to larger companies, will thus be a potential forward-looking policy to explore in Asia should the IoT technologies in agriculture lift off. Moreover, it will be in states' interest to ensure that the corporate governance practices of large companies are aligned with the public good, to prevent unfair practices from ensuing. These may include having either state or farmer representatives with significant shareholder powers to be parts of the boards of these companies.

11.7 Conclusion

Asia today faces an important challenge of a large and growing food trade deficit, as it is a net importer of food products. The region also faces significant challenges, including poverty, which prevents its populations from having sufficient access to affordable food that meets their daily nutritional requirements. Climate change further adds to these challenges by making the farming process more toiling for farmers, as it reduces the amount of food which can be harvested for every hectare of land.

The development of digital technologies in agriculture, within the framework of IoT, allows for potential improvements in this regard to make the farming process "smarter" and less risky for farmers, amidst climate change. As the IoT technologies for agriculture have been developed amidst the Fourth IR in the recent decade, the next frontier is in allowing for greater adoption of these technologies.

A key challenge is in bringing about a parallel transformation of IoT adoption in the agricultural sector, alongside modern industrial sectors where the Fourth IR is already taking place. It also calls for addressing the growing gap in private venture financing between upstream and downstream technologies, favouring the latter. Addressing this challenge requires bridging the capital gaps to technology adoption by smallholder farmers. Two examples have been presented, namely, a strongly state-led approach to technology acquisition as in the case of China, and an approach where the state plays a more supporting role in developing the domestic ecosystem for these technologies as in the case of Singapore.

Furthermore, food production technologies also need to be complemented by digital e-commerce. The latter allows farmers to increase their revenues by allowing them to sell their products to consumers directly, so that they retain a larger share of their profits. It further broadens the range of technology providers that farmers can access, and increases the range of flexible financing options for farmers. However, this requires improving digital financial access among farmers and consumers alike, and improving the connectivity infrastructure as well in terms of efficient logistics and stable internet connectivity.

Moving forward, a potential challenge relates to the future control of food production should the IoT movement in agriculture reach phenomenal adoption across states. It could potentially trigger a corporatisation of the farming sector that goes beyond private companies providing support, but rather into them playing more active roles in the production process itself.

Assuming IoT technologies allow for transforming food production into a modular process, this could lead to a questioning of the place of farmers in food production in the future, in the case that digital technologies are able to replace them. This potentially brings the risk that farmers, and states as a whole, may lose control of their food sectors to larger business interests.

Potential solutions have likewise been raised, including an organised effort by states to curtail potentially monopolistic or oligopolistic price-setting mechanisms among big companies for agricultural products or inputs. This may also require state regulation of land markets to be informed of transfers of ownership of farms to larger companies. Finally, states can ensure corporate governance practices of large companies are aligned with the public good, to prevent unfair practices from ensuing.

References

AgFunder. (2014). *AgriFoodtech Investment Report.* https://agfunder.com/research/agtech-investing-report-2014/

AgFunder. (2022). *AgriFoodtech Investment Report.* https://agfunder.com/research/2022-agfunder-agrifoodtech-investment-report/

ASEAN. (2022). *ASEAN Statistical Yearbook 2021.* https://www.aseanstats.org/publication/asyb-2021/

ASEAN Food Security Information System (AFSIS). (2022). *ASEAN Agricultural Commodity Outlook* No. 29 December 2022. https://aptfsis.org/uploads/normal/ACO%20Report%201/ACO%2028/ACO%20No.28.pdf

Chakrabarty, M. and Hildenbrand, W. (2009). Engel's law reconsidered. *Bonn Econ Discussion Papers*, No. 22/2009.

Dawe, D. C., Moya, P. F., Casiwan, C. B. and Cabling, J. M. (2008). Rice marketing systems in the Philippines and Thailand: Do large numbers of competitive traders ensure good performance?. *Food Policy*, 33(5), pp. 455–463.

Engel, E. (1857). Die Productions- und Consumtionsverhaltnisse des Kdnig- reichs Sachsen. *Zeitschrift des Statistischen Buireaus des K. Sach- sischen, Ministerium des Innern*, 8(9), pp. 1–54.

European Parliament, Directorate-General for Parliamentary Research Services, Daheim, C., Poppe, K. and Schrijver, R. (2019). *Precision agriculture and the future of farming in Europe: scientific foresight study.* https://op.europa.eu/en/publication-detail/-/publication/40fe549e-cb49-11e7-a5d5-01aa75ed71a1

FAO. (2001). *The State of Food Insecurity in the World 2001.* https://www.fao.org/publications/card/en/c/62e4c9ae-f1e7-508e-8207-ff283a65d9ec/

FAO. (2018a). *The Future of Food and Agriculture: Alternative Pathways to 2050.* https://www.fao.org/global-perspectives-studies/resources/detail/en/c/1157074/

FAO. (2018b). *The State of Food Insecurity in the World 2018.* https://www.fao.org/documents/card/en/c/I9553EN

FAO. (2022). *UN FAOStat database.* Accessed 1 December 2022, https://www.fao.org/faostat/en/#data

Fisher, R. A. (1935). *The Design of Field Experiments.* Oliver and Boyd.

GRiSP (Global Rice Science Partnership). (2013). *Rice Almanac,* 4th edition. International Rice Research Institute.

Grow Asia. (2022). Agritech business model showcase, part 1: farmer advisory. https://www.growasia.org/farmer-advisory

Hayes, A. (2022). Blockchain facts: what is it, how it works, and how it can be used. *Investopedia.* https://www.investopedia.com/terms/b/blockchain.asp

Hazell, P. B. and Rahman, A. (Eds.) (2014). *New Directions for Smallholder Agriculture.* Oxford University Press.

Koltiva. (2023). KoltiTrace, an integrated multi crop platform for the responsible businesses. https://www.koltiva.com/koltitrace

Lewis, W. A. (1954). Economic development with unlimited supplies of labour. *The Manchester School of Economic and Social Studies*, 22(2), pp. 139–191.

Mbow, C., Rosenzweig, C., Barioni, L. G., Benton, T. G., Herrero, M., Krishnapillai, M., Liwenga, E., Pradhan, P., Rivera-Ferre, M. G., Sapkota, T., Tubiello, F. N. and Xu, Y. (2019). Food Security.

In P. R. Shukla, *et al.* (Eds.), *Climate Change and Land: an IPCC special report on climate change, desertification, land degradation, sustainable land management, food security, and greenhouse gas fluxes in terrestrial ecosystems*. Intergovernmental Panel on Climate Change.

Montesclaros, J. M. L. (2021a). Changing the narrative of ASEAN progress in addressing hunger: 'snoozing' the alarm for SDG #2?. *Food Security*, 13, pp. 1283–1284.

Montesclaros, J. M. L. (2021b). The 'Internet of Things' in agriculture: pitfalls and opportunities. *THINK*, Issue 9, pp. 18–27.

Montesclaros, J. M. L. and Teng, P. (2021). Agriculture and Food Security in Asia. In J. M. Pulhin, M. Inoue and R. Shaw (Eds.), *Climate Change, Disaster Risks, and Human Security,* pp. 137–168. Springer.

Montesclaros, J. M. L., Babu, S. C. and Teng, P. (2019). IoT-enabled farms and climate-adaptive agriculture technologies: investment lessons from Singapore. *IFPRI Discussion Paper* 1805. International Food Policy Research Institute.

OECD. (2019). Digital innovations and the growing importance of agricultural data. In *Digital Opportunities for Better Agricultural Policies*. https://doi.org/10.1787/571a0812-en

Oppenheimer, M., Glavovic, B., Hinkel, J., van de Wal, R., Magnan, A. K., Abd-Elgawad, A., Cai, R., *et al.* (2019). Sea level rise and implications for low lying islands, coasts and communities. In H.-O. Pörtner, *et al.* (Eds.), *IPCC Special Report on the Ocean and Cryosphere in a Changing Climate*, pp. 321–445. Cambridge University Press.

Pathak, A. (2023). Data cleaning in data science: process, benefits and tools. *KnowledgeHut*. https://www.knowledgehut.com/blog/data-science/data-cleaning

Reynolds, L. (2023). Jain releases smart irrigation product. *Irrigation Today*. https://irrigationtoday.org/news/jain-releases-smart-irrigation-product/

Rigg, J., Albert, S. and Thompson, E. C. (2016). The puzzle of East and Southeast Asia's persistent smallholder. *Journal of Rural Studies*, 43, pp. 118–133.

S. Rajaratnam School of International Studies (RSIS). (2017). *World Agricultural Forum 2017, Singapore: Summary of Conference Proceedings*. https://www.rsis.edu.sg/WAF2017/Summary%20of%20Conference%20Proceedings_RSIS.pdf

Schwab, K. (2017). *The Fourth Industrial Revolution*. Currency Books.

Shields, M. (2017). ChemChina clinches landmark $43 billion takeover of Syngenta. *Reuters*. https://www.reuters.com/article/us-syngenta-ag-m-a-chemchina-idUSKBN1810CU

Singapore Food Agency (SFA). (2020). Singapore Food Story R&D Programme. *SFA*. https://www.sfa.gov.sg/food-farming/singapore-food-story/r-and-d-programme

Singh, P., Pandey, P. C., Petropoulos, G. P., Pavlides, A., Srivastava, P. K., Koutsias, N., Deng, K. D. K. and Bao, Y. (2020). Hyperspectral remote sensing in precision agriculture: Present status, challenges, and future trends. In P. C. Pandey, *et al.* (Eds.), *Hyperspectral Remote Sensing*, pp. 121–146. Elsevier.

Sylvester, G. (2018). *E-Agriculture in Action: Drones for Agriculture*. FAO and ITU.

Sylvester, G. (2019). *E-Agriculture in Action: Blockchain for Agriculture*. FAO and ITU.

The Renewable Energy Support Programme for ASEAN (RESP) Team. (2013). *ASEAN Guideline on Off-Grid Rural Electrification Approaches*. https://aseanenergy.org/asean-guideline-on-off-grid-rural-electrification-approaches/

UNCDF. (2020). Measuring progress 2020: financial inclusion in selected ASEAN countries." *UNCDF*. https://www.uncdf.org/article/6456/measuring-progress-2020-financial-inclusion-in-selected-asean-countries

UN ESCAP. (2022). *Policy Guidebook: Harnessing Digital Technology for Financial Inclusion in Asia and the Pacific*. https://www.unescap.org/kp/2022/policy-guidebook-harnessing-digital-technology-financial-inclusion-asia-and-pacific

Wang, O. (2021). China food security: Syngenta buyout shows Beijing's haste to plug technology gap with foreign expertise. *South China MorningPost*. https://www.scmp.com/economy/china-economy/article/3139417/china-food-security-syngenta-buyout-shows-beijings-haste-plug

World Food Programme. (2020). NINAYO: Increasing incomes and improving access with digital tools. https://innovation.wfp.org/project/ninayo

https://doi.org/10.1142/9789811278297_0012

Chapter 12

Genetic Modification and Gene Editing of Crops to Assure Asian Food Security

Rhodora Romero-Aldemita

International Service for the Acquisition of Agri-biotech Applications Inc. (ISAAA Inc.), Los Banos, Philippines

12.1 Introduction

Advancements in science and technology shape a country's roadmap to economic recovery and food sustainability. A country that is frequently hungry and chronically poor must take immediate action to minimise and completely stop dependency on foreign aid and dole-outs. Capacity building that allows scientific discovery enables scientific research to thrive and leads to useful technology needed for food, and environmental sustainability is one of the important action points. These are the main drivers for scientists to continuously seek scientific solutions to the various agricultural problems that affect food sustainability.

In order to improve the traits of organisms essential for food and agriculture, variation should be introduced through breeding followed by selection and testing. Natural processes also cause sequence variation in nature, and that variation is fundamental for evolution and life. Food producers learned this process through trial and error, and such a convenient way of generating variation takes a long period of time, effort, and funds, but this can be expedited using innovative tools called genetic modification and gene editing.

Genetic modification (GM) and gene editing are two of the most revolutionising technologies developed in the last four and two decades, respectively. Genetic modification of organisms is the introduction of genes from related and non-related species through molecular biology and genetic engineering tools. Termed recombinant DNA technology, this allows the introduction of foreign/related (trans) and endogenous (cis for overexpression) genes to the genome of the recipient organism to improve yield, resistance to biotic and tolerance to abiotic stresses in crops, animals, and microbes.

Since 1996, the first year of GM crop commercialisation, there have been 439 GM events approved for commercial release as food, feed, and propagation with eight traits in 29 crops and by 45 countries [ISAAA, 2023]. AquAdvantage salmon is the only GM fish commercialised in 2017 (Canada) and 2018 (USA) [Aquabounty, 2018]. GM has also been used in soil and water remediation, pharmaceuticals, and biofuel production.

Gene editing is the use of an organism's inherent capacity to identify, break and repair damaged DNA sequences using the cell's own machinery. Following this sequence, scientists make targeted single- or double-stranded breaks at an identified location in the DNA, and then let the cell's natural mechanisms repair the break. Through the process, alterations are made precisely in a target gene to effect specific desired/undesired (addition/deletion) traits. It is thus a directed and accelerated means of generating sequence diversity.

Target changes may be on the scale of a few base pairs and easily repaired to effect a loss of function/knockout or gain in function, repaired without a template. This is called SDN-1 or single-directed nuclease. If the repair involves a template, it is called SDN-2. Insertions of new and useful genes called SDN-3 ("trans" genes originating elsewhere) make a transgenic organism as described above [Horvarth, 2021]. Improvement of crops, animals and microbes through gene editing has been found to be more precise, not costly (less regulatory cost), and fast. Gene-edited high oleic acid soybean Calyno, developed by Calyxt Inc., was the first gene-edited product commercialised in 2019. This was followed by Japan's GABA tomato in 2021 [ISAAA, 2021a].

These new breeding innovations have been uniquely effective at achieving the goal of long-lasting resistance crops and animals to pest and diseases, and their products are widely recognised as safe [ISAAA, 2021a].

This chapter will expound on the current situation in the Asian region and how the mentioned innovative tools can contribute to economic recovery and food sustainability.

12.2 No More "Business as Usual" for Asian Food and Agriculture Needs

The Asian region, composed of developing and developed countries with increasing populations, is still reeling from the economic, trade, and health-related problems brought about by the COVID-19 pandemic, followed by the Ukraine/Russian war, and the uncharacteristic slowdown in China.

The rapid population growth is one of the key challenges in the effort to combat hunger and malnutrition for sustainable development

[Rubaiyath Bin Rahman and Zhang, 2022]. Asia is the most populated region in the world, with a population of 4.75 billion (60% of the world population), with China and India contributing 60% as of 2022. Asia also consumes 90% of the world's rice production. Current findings show that the production of rice in developed regions will remain stagnant or fall slightly. Rice cultivation area is also expected to decline in Asian countries, for example, China, Vietnam, Thailand, and others, despite their production increase through yield improvements. The trend in rice price will continue to increase until 2023, then the price is expected to decline to US$476/tonnes. The demand for rice consumption will significantly increase, mainly in countries in West Asia and sub-Saharan Africa. Thus, the high population rate in Asia has a tremendous impact on food insecurity within the region.

Increased population also contributes to human-induced climate change and widespread disruption of nature, affecting the lives of billions of people around the world. This is on top of the increasing heatwaves, droughts, and floods, which already exceed plant and animal tolerance thresholds, driving mass mortalities among all living organisms. People and ecosystems least able to cope in Africa, Asia, Central, and South America, on small islands, and in the Arctic become more vulnerable to acute food and water insecurity that are increasingly difficult to manage [IPCC, 2022a].

An International Monetary Fund (IMF) publication [IMF, 2022] indicates that the Asia-Pacific region was able to rebound economically in 2021 with 6.5% growth, an expected moderate increase of 4% in 2022, and an estimated 4.3% economic growth in 2023. There is also recurring inflation as an effect of global financial tightening, the expected slowdown of external demand, and rising public debts. The COVID-19 crisis brought with it deaths as well as lower investment, unemployment, and lessened productivity growth. FAO

Food Price Index reached its highest level since its inception in 1990 and warned that the cascading impact of the war in Ukraine could further exacerbate global food prices since Russia and Ukraine are dominant players in highly concentrated global grain markets. Russia is the largest exporter of wheat worldwide, while Ukraine is the fifth largest. China's growth in 2022 of 3.2%, its second-lowest level since 1977, has a spillover effect on the Asian region through trade and financial links.

International organisations have continuously called for vigilant actions to prevent food crises and climate catastrophes. The Intergovernmental Panel on Climate Change (IPCC) report released on April 4, 2022, indicated that the average annual global greenhouse gas emissions have slowed down. Various options were offered for all sectors to mitigate emissions in transportation and industry and strategic land use to at least halve emissions by 2030 [IPCC, 2022b].

The Food and Agriculture Organization (FAO) of the United Nations and the United Nations World Food Program (WFP) issued a blunt notice about multiple risk factors that could push the present food crisis into a future food availability crisis. These include conflict, climate shocks, the pandemic, public debt burdens, and further intensified by the war in Ukraine, pushing food and fuel prices to accelerate in many countries worldwide. Climate shocks continue to drive acute hunger, indicating that a "new normal" has started where droughts, flooding, hurricanes, and cyclones repeatedly devastate farming and livestock rearing, drive population displacement, and push millions to the brink in countries around the world [FAO-WFP, 2022].

Among the recommended actions endorsed by FAO Director General Qu Dongyu was the scaling up of emergency agricultural assistance, investment in infrastructure for farming and storage, prioritising investment in science and innovation, and reducing food loss and waste [FAO, 2022]. Moreover, FAO was a part of four initiatives enumerated below that were launched by the Egyptian Presidency at COP27.

- Food and Agriculture Sustainable Transformation aimed at supporting climate action in agri-food systems;
- Initiative on Climate Action and Nutrition to support member states in implementing policies for improved access to nutritious and healthy diets from sustainable food systems;
- Action for Water Adaptation and Resilience to address better management of water for climate adaptation and resilience; and
- Waste management in Africa to treat and recycle at least 50% of the solid waste produced in Africa by 2050.

12.3 Three Decades of GM Crop Commercialisation

In the face of the unwavering challenges mentioned above, the global scientific community has been highlighted to play a significant role in attaining the 2030 Agenda and its Sustainable Development Goals (SDGs). It must be emphasised that its role is to encourage investment in science and innovation and find ways to reduce food waste. Moreover, FAO Director Qu Dongyu highlighted the importance of academic and research institutions in building stronger, more strategic partnerships with civil society organisations, parliamentarians, indigenous peoples, academia and research institutions, and the private sector, especially with the youth [FAO, 2022b].

Nearly four decades ago, scientists acknowledged that feeding the world cannot be solved by "business as usual" food production strategies. Research in molecular biology led to the development of innovative technologies termed biotechnology which, after nearly three decades, have delivered safe, nutritious, high-yielding, and dependable biotech products. The World Economic Forum [2022] puts a spotlight on genetic engineering as one of the tools used by scientists to adapt to climate change. Improved varieties of rice, maize, and wheat have been developed to withstand extended drought periods and wetter monsoon seasons. Extreme temperatures also contribute to more fungal and pest attacks and, thus, experts have used biotech or GM technology to make cassava, potatoes, and cacao disease resistant. Aside from these efforts, GM tools for climate change adaptation are currently used for mitigation.

ISAAA Inc. reported that from 1996 to 2019, the accumulated area planted for biotech crops reached 2.7 billion hectares, with 190.4 million hectares planted in 2019 alone. A total of 72 countries adopted biotech crops, 29 countries planted and 43 additional countries imported [ISAAA, 2020].

The contribution of biotech/GM crops was reported by Graham Brookes [2022a]. Firstly, the economic impact of GM crops at the farm level increased by US$261.3 billion from 1996 to 2020. This is equivalent to a US$112 per hectare average farm income gain, majority of which (72%) were due to an increase in yield, while the remaining 28% was attributed to cost savings [Brookes, 2022a].

In another part of the same report, Brookes [2022c] expounded in detail on the environmental impact of biotech/GM crops, including the parameters that contribute to climate change. Through the widespread adoption of biotech/GM crops, pesticide application (herbicide and insecticide) has declined by 748.6 million kg (–7.2%) of the active ingredient. This reduction has an accompanying reduced environmental impact, as measured by the Environmental Impact Quotient, of a more significant 17.3% between 1996 and 2020.

Greenhouse gas and carbon emissions have been associated with extensive agriculture, accounting for one-third of global greenhouse emissions [United Nations, 2021]. Thus, food production systems are contributory to pollution and climate change. With the widespread adoption of GM crops, a significant decrease in on-farm fuel use helped farmers move from plow-based systems to reduced or no-tillage systems. This resulted in a yearly reduction in carbon emissions, equivalent to taking 15.6 million cars off the road in 2020 [Brookes, 2022b].

12.4 Biotech/GM Crop Developments in Asia

Biotech/GM crop adoption in highly populated India and China has flourished since 1996. They are the two highest adopters of insect-resistant, herbicide-tolerant, and stacked trait cotton at 11.9 million hectares and 3.2 million hectares, respectively. And, together with Pakistan and Myanmar, who planted 2.5 million hectares and 300,000 hectares, respectively, have made Asia the largest producer of biotech cotton, surpassing the area planted in the USA by 2019 at 5.3 million hectares [ISAAA, 2020]. However, the commercialisation of other biotech/GM crops has not been so successful.

12.4.1 *India's Biotech Mustard is for Immediate Release, with High Hopes for Bt Eggplant*

After years of successful biotech/GM cotton commercialisation in India, news on the possible commercialisation of Bt eggplant and GM Indian mustard has not surfaced in a few years. Surprisingly,

India's Genetic Engineering Appraisal Committee (GEAC) of the Ministry of Environment, Forest and Climate Change, chaired by Shri Naresh Pal Gangwar, recommended the environmental release of GM mustard in the country on October 18, 2022. The transgenic mustard DMH-11 uses parental lines bn 3.6 carrying barnase and bar genes, and modbs 22.99 containing barstar and bar genes. The committee states that the environmental release of mustard hybrid DMH-11 for its seed production and testing followed the Indian Council of Agricultural Research regulations, and the approval is for a limited period of four years from the date of issue of the approval letter and is renewable for two years at a time based on the compliance report (GEAC Appraisal Committee, 2022).

The GM Mustard DMH-11 has been field tested against national check Varuna and zonal check RL1359 in confined field trials at multiple locations in India. The field trials were conducted to assess the impact on human health and the environment according to the stipulated guidelines and applicable rules. Results showed that DMH-11 yielded 28% more than the national check and 37% more than the zonal checks. Moreover, extensive studies carried out on toxicity, allergenicity, compositional analysis, field trials, and environmental safety studies of GM mustard lines vs. their non-transgenic comparators have provided evidence that they are safe for cultivation and for food and feed use [Indian Express, 2022]. The renewed focus on GM mustard by the Indian regulatory bodies could lead to its eventual commercialisation. Farmers in India are still waiting for another Bt eggplant regulatory review that could lead to its commercialisation.

Another important staple in India is chickpeas. Researchers from India evaluated chickpea lines that were improved to combat the gram pod borer, one of the major pests of the crop, and reached promising results.

This is an important development considering there is no complete-resistance source that has been identified in the chickpea gene pool. The study conducted that cmVip3Aa can be an effective option for insect resistance management in chickpeas [Singh *et al.*, 2022].

12.4.2 *China's Approval Process and Transgenic Research has Progressed*

In a report by Xhiao and Kerr [2022], delays in the commercialisation of GM crops in China are caused by the government's effort to balance interests and conflicts. Specifically, the delay in commercialisation can be attributed to the country's goal of keeping social stability. Biotech critics have affected public perception of biotechnology, and their efforts have gained widespread acceptance among interest groups and have been adequate to advance the threat of social instability. Such delays affect not just the country's food production but could also impact food security.

Notwithstanding this occurrence, China continues to conduct recombinant DNA innovations for food security. Some of the developments are the conduct of field trials for insect-resistant and herbicide-tolerant soybean and maize. Herbicide-tolerant soybean requires only one spray to attain 95% weed control, decrease cost by 50%, and boost yield by 1% [Global Agricultural News, 2022]. Soybean with resistance to cyst nematode has also been developed and is already in the final stages of testing. Results showed that host-induced silencing of essential SCN genes could enhance broad-spectrum SCN resistance in stable transgenic soybean plants without negatively impacting agronomic performance.

The GM corn varieties reached 85% to 95% resistance to fall armyworms, without the use of pesticides [Yimeng, 2022].

Another insect-resistant (against corn borers) maize, Ruifeng 125, has been developed in Zhejiang University which can provide corn borer control to as high as 96%, and maize yield can increase by 5% to 10% compared to conventional maize [ZJU News Agency, 2022].

Field trials of drought-tolerant sugarcane developed by Guangxi University have also been conducted in Guangxi province. Results showed an increase of as much as 41.9% in yield and 44.4% in the number of ratooned seedings. There was no reduction in the sucrose content, gravity, purity, and other major quality trials in transgenic sugarcane despite the water deficit. The drought-tolerant sugarcane hopes to address the use of marginalised soil prone to drought and to sustain China's position as one of the top sugar-producing, albeit a high sugar-consuming, country as well [Xiao *et al.*, 2022].

By mid-2022, China had streamlined its approval process. With the remarkable results in the pilot testing of GM maize and soybeans mentioned above, Chinese agriculture ministry officials released statements that those developed by the China National Seed Group, a unit of Syngenta Group, and a herbicide-tolerant variety produced by Hangzhou Ruifeng Bio-Tech Co. Ltd will be approved for commercialisation in the country [Reuters, 2022].

Following this development was the approval of drought-tolerant HB4 soybeans by Bioceres Crop Solutions Corporation on April 29, 2022. The approval is for the import and use of soybean as a raw material produced using Bioceres' proprietary drought tolerance technology. It is worth noting that Argentina approved HB4® soybeans for growth and consumption in 2015, with the unrestricted commercialisation of HB4® soybean seeds in Argentina subject to Chinese import approval. HB4® soybeans are now approved for unrestricted growth and commercialisation in the United States, Canada, Brazil, Argentina, Paraguay, representing roughly 85% of the global soybean trade [Bioceres Crop Solutions, 2022].

12.4.3 *Philippines' Golden Rice and Bt Eggplant Soon to be in Farmers' Hands*

The Philippines has proven to be a model country in GM crop adoption and regulation in Southeast Asia. With over 21 years of cultivation, the country planted nearly 900,000 hectares of GM corn in 2019 [ISAAA, 2020]. GM corn is one of the viable options to help meet food security and income needs in emerging economies. It has been proven over the years that this success rests mainly on the high level of political support, enabling policies and continued investment in biotechnology; adoption and evolution of science-based regulations; partnership for GM maize testing; information, education, and communication strategies for public awareness; and ensuring sustainable benefits [APAARI, 2021].

In the past two years, the Philippines made a mark on biotech crop approval and regulation. Simultaneous regulatory approvals were granted for commercialisation to Golden Rice (beta-carotene-enriched rice) [IRRI, 2021] and for food and feed and processing to Bt eggplant in 2021 [ISAAA, 2021]. Golden Rice is a rice variety, genetically engineered to contain additional levels of beta-carotene, converted into vitamin A by the human body. It was intended to be a complementary intervention to vitamin A deficiency, the most common cause of childhood blindness and a contributing factor to a weakened immune system. Golden Rice has been assessed to be as safe as conventional rice in five countries, the Philippines included, with the added benefit of beta-carotene in the grains.

By May 2022, the Philippine Rice Research Institute started the deployment of Golden Rice to farmers and ramped up its seed production operations. The Department of Agriculture (DA) Secretary William Dar led the ceremonial handover of the Golden Rice seeds to seed growers and producers at the PhilRice Central Experiment Station in Munoz, Nueva Ecija. Seed workers and producers participated in the expanded Golden Rice seed production in the wet season planting in the Philippines. Regional DA research and experimental stations in the provinces of Ilocos Norte and Isabela also received seeds a week prior [PhilRice, 2022]. Seven provinces that have records of high cases of stunting among infants and children ages five years and below planted Golden Rice in 2022. These include Maguindanao, Quirino, Samar, Antique, Lanao del Norte, and Agusan del Norte [Manila Times, 2022].

In a similar vein, in 2022, the Philippines Department of Agriculture Bureau of Plant Industry (DA-BPI) gave its approval for the commercial cultivation of insect-resistant Bt eggplant in the country. With this approval, the Philippines becomes the second country in the world, after Bangladesh, to allow the commercial propagation of borer-resistant Bt eggplant. Bt eggplant, an insect-resistant crop, contains a natural protein from the soil bacterium *Bacillus thuringiensis* (Bt), making it resistant to eggplant fruit and shoot borer (EFSB), the crop's most devastating insect pest. This Bt protein is highly specific to EFSB and is safe for humans, animals, and other non-target insects. Previously conducted *ex ante* socio-economic studies in the Philippines estimated that the cultivation of Bt eggplant will incur lower production costs and ultimately result in up to three-fold higher net farm incomes due to the combined effects of significantly reduced pesticide use and increased marketable fruit yields [UPLB College of Agriculture and Food Science, 2022].

12.4.4 *Australia's 20 years of GM Crop Benefits Boost New GM Crop Adoption*

Australia has cultivated GM canola and cotton since 1996 and safflower starting in 2018, with a total GM area of 600,000 hectares [ISAAA, 2020]. A report of a commissioned review on GM crops containing multiple herbicide-tolerant traits indicated impacts on herbicide use, herbicide tolerance, and herbicide resistance management issues in Australia. The report stated that long-term sustainable use of GM and non-GM herbicide tolerance traits within Australia provide flexible crop rotation choices. The report also identified a need and opportunity for improved strategic regulatory guidance on crop herbicide-tolerant stewardship for volunteer crop control. The options highlighted the broadening role of existing strategic expert stewardship groups; establishing a new commodity-specific or related cross-industry strategic expert stewardship group; risk management options for stacked trait herbicide-tolerant crop volunteers; assessment of trade and market access issues arising from herbicide residues on stacked GM and non-GM herbicide-tolerant crops; and chemicals used to control volunteer crops [Office of Gene Technology Regulation (OGTR), 2022a].

The increasing global demand for palm oil substitutes combined with the war in Ukraine has left a gap in the market for specialist oils, as Ukraine is one of the world's largest global producers of high oleic sunflower oil. This gave a significant increase in the demand for Australia's GM high oleic acid safflower oil, as reported by the Agricultural Biotechnology Council of Australia as market preferences and access to resources shifted globally in mid-2022 [GRDC Ground Cover, 2022].

OGTR approved the commercial release of GM Indian mustard (DMH-11 with herbicide tolerance) on October 13, 2022. The GM

Indian mustard and products derived from it may enter general commerce, including use in human food and animal feed [OGTR, 2022b].

Food Safety Australia and New Zealand (FSANZ) also granted approval for foods derived from HB4® wheat to enter the market as imported food products. FSANZ stated that no public health and safety concerns were identified and that food derived from wheat line IND-00412-7 is considered as safe for human consumption as food derived from conventional non-GM wheat cultivars. The wheat line IND-00412-7 has been genetically modified for tolerance to drought and to the herbicide glufosinate. The approval allows the food derived from wheat line IND-00412-7, which includes flour, bread, pasta, biscuits, and other baked products, to be sold and used for food. Labelling requirements dictated by the Australia New Zealand Food Standards Code will be applied to these products [FSANZ, 2022].

12.4.5 *Bangladesh's Years of Bt Eggplant Benefits Opened up Bt Cotton Adoption*

Commercialisation of Bt eggplant in Bangladesh has had a significant impact on the lives of resource-poor farmers and their families in Bangladesh, according to a study conducted by the Bangladesh Agricultural Research Institute. Bangladesh planted some 50,000 hectares of Bt eggplant in 2019 [ISAAA, 2020], and is projected to increase in the coming years. The farmers garnered a six-fold increase in net returns compared to planting non-Bt brinjal and have 61% pesticide cost savings. In another survey conducted by the International Food Policy and Research Institute, the results showed that Bt brinjal exhibited excellent control of EFSB, a 51% increase in yield, 128% growth in net revenues, 37.5% reduction in pesticide costs, and 11.5% decrease in pesticide poisonings

[Shelton, 2022]. Bangladesh also approved the second GM crop in the country, cotton. Two Bt cotton varieties were approved that would yield over four tonnes per hectare. Aside from increased yield, farmers can save pesticide costs against bollworms [Fibre-2Fashion, 2022].

12.4.6 *Indonesia's new GM Sugarcane Trait and a New Focus on GM Soybean*

Indonesia is gearing up toward the commercialisation of another GM sugarcane trait after the drought-tolerant sugarcane commercialised in 2019. A GM sugarcane that over-expresses sucrose-phosphate synthase was evaluated under field trial conditions and was found to perform better than its non-transgenic counterparts without affecting bacterial diversity and soil rhizosphere. The field trials will help in the selection of transgenic lines best suited for specific agro-climatic conditions to identify a variety with increased sugar yield intended for sustainable agriculture [Suherman *et al.*, 2022].

The cultivation of GM soybean is also being considered in Indonesia. The Indonesian government issued a statement encouraging farmers to use superior GM soybean varieties to maintain national food security. The statements come after Indonesia's soybean production continued to decline, and the President was said to have given directions to improve the country's situation and become less dependent on imports. Using GM soybeans can increase the production per hectare from 1.6–2 tons per hectare to 3.5–4 tons per hectare, which is consistent with the country's goal to increase production from 1.5 tons per hectare to 3–4 tons per hectare [Cabinet Secretariat of the Republic of Indonesia, 2019].

12.5 Future Prospects of GM Crops Commercialisation and Acceptance in Asia

Acceptance and adoption of GM crops rest on innovation, trends in the agri-food industry, and acceptance by society. A review study was conducted to investigate the bibliographic trend from 543 journal articles published in multi-languages between 1981 and 2021. Researchers found a strong link between GM research with agriculture and food science technology. The majority of the research publications were linked to developed nations, with Europe and the United States being the first region and country, respectively, in terms of the number of active institutions that produced research.

Moreover, publishing research results about GM foods is important because public support increases when the potential benefits are communicated through clear messages. These are reinforced when communicated by the media, which in turn increases people's trust in the government and science. These findings are especially important as governments in different countries have regulatory policies to ensure the safety of the technologies' beneficiaries and the environment.

It was also recommended that for GM food research, regulatory frameworks and testing protocols must be harmonised among countries and regions, and safety assessments must be conducted based on scientific studies. These will ensure the safety of humans and the environment, help address socio-political concerns, bridge the communication gap between researchers and public opinion on GM food and safety, and foster innovation in GM research. For transparency with agri-food industries, disclosing critical technical details, compliance to food safety standards and product labelling, and enabling a traceability feature promote public awareness of safer and healthier foods. Acceptance of GM crops by society should be based on science rather than opinion-based misperceptions, which also encourages awareness of food safety protocols and labelling, as well as an informed decision-making process on producing and consuming GM foods [Sendhil *et al.*, 2022].

Upcoming trends in GM research and development focus on the industry, especially the development of renewable resources and less wastage. These include the increasing acceptance of non-browning potatoes and apples and technologies to develop biodegradable products. Smart packaging from corn extends food shelf life. The packaging material was developed through the electrospinning of zein from corn, together with the antimicrobial compounds cellulose and acetic acid. The biodegradable material can potentially help cut down the amount of plastic waste and serve as an environmentally friendly alternative to petroleum-based polymer used in commercial food packaging [Nanyang Technological University, 2021].

12.6 The Promise of Gene Editing For Food Security in Asia

Gene-editing technologies have gained applications in various organisms in less than a decade. During the pandemic, its applications in health, especially the biomedical segment, vaccine production, and COVID-19 diagnostic tests, had increased, having a positive impact on the market. North America dominates the CRISPR market and is expected to continue till 2027. Market growth drivers include increasing government and private funding, rising demand and adoption of CRISPR, and other technological advancements [Report Linker, 2022].

Thus, the CRISPR Global Market was estimated to have increased by 24% in March 2022. The global CRISPR technology market was projected to increase from US$1,064.91 million in 2021 at a compound annual growth rate (CAGR) of 24.6%. The primary reason for the market expansion is the resumption of operations of the companies using CRISPR after recovering from the impact of the COVID-19 pandemic. By 2026, the CRISPR technology market is expected to reach US$3,112 million at a CAGR of 23.7% [Report Linker, 2022].

There is mounting evidence suggesting that the potential contributions of gene editing to increased yield, enhanced nutrition, and greater environmental sustainability can help attain the top three SDGs. Applications of gene editing in crops and animals contribute by promoting more environmentally sustainable agriculture, ending hunger, and achieving food security, which are components of SDG 2, Zero Hunger. Gene editing contributes to increased sustainability through the improvement of water- and nitrogen-use efficiency of crops, reduction in environmental footprint in agricultural production, and enabling the production of more food using less or the same amount of resources as conventional crops and livestock.

Applications of gene editing can also directly improve human health through the development of foods that can help prevent specific diseases while increasing the nutritional values of food. Some examples are the GABA tomato, tomato with increased lycopene, and wheat that produces less asparagine. These gene-edited foods help promote SDG 3, Good Health and Well-Being. Gene editing can also help attain SDG 1, No Poverty. The adoption of gene-edited crops increases yield and reduces input costs, which results in higher farm and household incomes. Increased income also provides a better opportunity for higher levels of education for the farmers' children [Smyth, 2022].

It is noteworthy that the public accepts products of gene editing. A case in point is Japan's approval for the commercialisation of two CRISPR-edited fishes and GABA tomato [ISAAA, 2023]. GABA tomato contains high amounts of gamma-aminobutyric acid and has been sold directly to consumers in Japan by Tokyo-based Sanatech seed. GABA can help support the lowering of blood pressure and promote relaxation [ISAAA, 2021]. The CRISPR-edited tiger puffer had its leptin receptor gene disrupted, resulting in the fish's increased appetite and rapid weight gain. The CRISPR-edited red sea bream had its myostatin protein disabled. This causes the fish to grow larger than the conventional counterpart using the same amount of feed. This will likely lead to reduced farm production costs [Murakami *et al.*, 2022].

In China, gene editing is being used extensively in improving rice. Researchers from Yangzhou University in China improved the eating and cooking quality of rice using gene editing and targeting grain storage protein glutelin. The research team used CRISPR-Cas9 to knock out the genes coding for glutelin. This led to rapidly produced lines with down-regulated grain protein content and enhanced eating and cooking quality [Yang *et al.*, 2022].

The intolerable amount of cadmium in rice has also been solved through gene editing. Cadmium is a highly toxic heavy metal produced by industries. Reducing cadmium contamination in rice plants is vital to protect human health. China Agricultural University scientists successfully generated low-cadmium rice germplasm using CRISPR-Cas9 gene editing. *OsLCD* gene has been linked to cadmium accumulation in rice. CRISPR-Cas9 was used to generate *oslcd* single mutants from indica and japonica rice cultivars. *Osnramp5* single mutants and *oslcd osnramp5* double mutants in the indica background were also developed. It was found that when grown in cadmium-contaminated paddy soils, all *oslcd* single mutants accumulated less cadmium than the wild types. Furthermore, *oslcd* single mutants grown in cadmium-contaminated hydroponic culture accumulated significantly less cadmium in the shoots as compared to the wild types. This decrease in accumulation probably resulted from the reduction of cadmium translocation under cadmium stress. *OsLCD* knockout could thus be used to generate low-cadmium rice germplasms [Chen *et al.*, 2022].

Gene editing has also been used in fishery and aquaculture in China. Scientists from the Huazhong Agricultural University and the Chinese Academy of Sciences were able to produce the first generation of spineless fish by knocking out the main genes that control bone growth in sea bream, grass carp, and pond crucian carp. The amino acid and fatty acid content in the fish meat were not significantly different from ordinary fish, and the fish meat quality remained the same. The scientists intend to develop spineless breams and carps. The first generation of these spineless fish is currently being investigated. The investigation will continue until the third generation of spineless fish to determine the stability of the genetic trait [Huazhong Agricultural University, 2021].

Finally, one of the main benefits of gene editing, in crops and other organisms, is that it can deliver improved varieties to smallholder farmers faster. Past studies have shown that genome editing has cut the development phase of improved varieties by about two-thirds while significantly decreasing, if not eliminating, the linkage drag caused by non-elite residual genes from the donor parent. As gene editing has now become the tool for improving living organisms that would contribute to food sustainability, scientists collated an analysis of the top concerns and risks associated with gene-edited crops. These are comparable to the risks associated with accepted, past, and current breeding methods [Pixley *et al.*, 2022].

Reproduced as published in this section are the top seven risks concerning gene-edited crops and addressed one by one:

- *Non-target edits lead to mutations that compromise safety or the crop's agronomic performance.* This is addressed by continuous improvement of gene-editing tools and techniques to mitigate and reduce the likelihood of non-target edit occurrence.
- *Gene editing breaks natural protective barriers to prevent some mutations from occurring in nature.* Extensive field evaluations are conducted to select crops more superior to current varieties and deliver them to farmers.
- *Inadequate stewardship.* Molecular tools can be used to show that the transgenic intermediate has been resolved in the lab and greenhouse before field trials, with country-appropriate stewardship for edited crops.
- *Enhanced inequity between multinational corporations and large-scale farmers, and smallholder farmers.* Ensure that the gene-editing technology remains accessible to those who will use it to democratise its benefits, especially for resource-poor farmers and consumers.
- *Lack of transparency.* Create an easily accessible registry on which technology developers can disclose the use of gene-editing technologies and meet the public's interest in how specific foods are produced.
- *Lack of resolution about intellectual property ownership.* Identify and follow models that advance new varieties through national agricultural research programs and local and global seed companies that cater to smallholder farmers.
- *Inadequate public sector institutional infrastructures to support the use of gene-editing technologies.* Innovation for infrastructure

varies significantly, depending on institutional frameworks. Projects, institutes, strategic alliances, and explicit biotech and bioeconomy policies can help overcome some of the environmental factors that limit the full-scale use of gene-edited crops.

12.7 Concluding Remarks

Since 2010, ISAAA Inc. has started to monitor the approvals for planting and imports of GM crop events globally. The database was henceforth developed and maintained with high integrity and accuracy and has become the top resource at the ISAAA Inc. website. The number of countries that granted approval for planting has always been lower than the number of countries that granted approvals for food, feed, and processing. For instance, the latest data published in 2020 indicated that of the 72 countries that adopted GM crops, 43 were for imports for food, feed, and processing, while 29 countries planted. This result implies the following:

a. Products of genetic improvement have been extensively traded globally in various forms other than seeds;
b. Some governments allow the importation but not the cultivation of GM crops, such as Japan, South Korea, and Singapore, to name a few, due to non-scientific reasons;
c. The dominant GM products commercialised globally as imports are corn, soybean, and canola, which are primarily consumed as feeds for animals and secondarily as human food;
d. Political will is a strong force to move the adoption of biotech crops and their products, with or without regulation, such as in Bangladesh and Brazil.

The source for global importation of the four biotech crops, corn, soybean, cotton, and canola for food, feed, and fibre, is concentrated in the five big biotech crop producers, the USA, Brazil, Argentina, Canada, and India. These countries possess not only optimum regulatory oversight but also high consumer acceptance of biotech crops and products. It is thus imperative that with the increased number of planting/cultivating countries, the many variable traits introduced into an increasing number of crops through the years, the potential contribution to food sustainability and other pressing food security issues such as climate change, food availability and access, reduced waste, and many others will be greater.

It is also worth mentioning that, similar to crops, biotechnology can also be used to improve animals and fish. The overwhelming acceptance of GM AquAdvantage salmon in the USA and Canada, gene-edited slick cattle in Argentina and Brazil, and gene-edited red sea bream and puffer fish in Japan are manifestations of how biotechnology products can change consumer acceptance when they are produced through innovation following science-based regulation. We expect more GM and gene-edited organisms to contribute to food sufficiency and environmental sustainability in the Asian region.

Biotechnology, therefore, has much remaining potential to help meet the multifarious challenges to crops and animals in Asia. While the technology has an impeccable record of safety for humans and the environment, the reluctance of some countries to exploit the potential of this technology appears to be short-sighted and not based on science. As Asian demand for food quantity and diversity increases, it is hoped that rational policymakers will weigh the benefits to be derived versus the unproven, speculative risks from this technology.

References

APAARI. (2021). *Adoption of GM maize in emerging economies: Economic and policy lessons from the Philippines.* https://www.apaari.org/policy-paper-on-scaling-up-the-adoption-of-gm-maize-in-emerging-economies-economic-and-policy-lessons-from-the-philippines/

Aquabounty Website. (n.d.). https://aquabounty.com/

Bioceres Crop Solutions. (2022). Bioceres Crop Solutions announces regulatory approval of HB4 in China. https://investors.biocerescrops.com/news/news-details/2022/Bioceres-Crop-Solutions-Announces-Regulatory-Approval-of-HB4-Soy-in-China/default.aspx

Brookes, G. (2022a). Farm income and production impacts from the use of genetically modified (GM) crop technology 1996–2020. *GM Crops & Food*, 13(1), pp. 171–195.

Brookes, G. (2022b). Genetically modified (GM) crops use 1996–2020: Impacts on carbon emissions. *GM Crops & Food*, 13(1), pp. 242–261.

Brookes, G. (2022c). Genetically modified (GM) crop use, 1996–2020: Environmental impacts associated with pesticide use change. *GM Crops & Food*, 13(1), pp. 262–289.

Cabinet Secretariat of the Republic of Indonesia. (2019). Government pushes for improved domestic soybean productivity. https://setkab.go.id/en/govt-pushes-for-improved-domestic-soybean-productivity/

Chen, H., Ye, R., Liang, Y., Zhang, S., Liu, X., Sun, C., Li, F. and Yi, J. (2022). Generation of low-cadmium rice germplasm via knockout of *OsLCD* using CRISPR/Cas 9. *Journal of Environmental Sciences*, 126, pp. 138–152.

FAO. (2022a). A statement by FAO Director General Qu Dongyu. Global food security ministerial call to action. https://www.fao.org/director-general/speeches/detail/en/c/1513186/

FAO. (2022b). Innovative partnerships key to global food security FAO Director General says. https://www.fao.org/newsroom/detail/

innovative-partnerships-key-to-global-food-security-fao-director-general-says/en

FAO and World Food Prize. (2022). FAO-WFP early warnings on acute food insecurity. https://www.fao.org/3/cc0364en/cc0364en.pdf

Fibre2Fashion. (2022). Bangladesh regulators approve introduction of 2 Bt cotton varieties. https://www.fibre2fashion.com/news/textile-news/bangladesh-regulators-approve-introduction-of-2-bt-cotton-varieties-281429-newsdetails.htm

FSANZ. (2022). Food derived from drought-tolerant wheat line IND-00412-7. www.foodstandards.gov.au/code/applications/Documents/A1232%20Approval%20Report.pdf

GEAC Appraisal Committee. (2022). Minutes of the 147th meeting of the Genetic Engineering Appraisal Committee held on 18.10.2022. www.geacindia.gov.in/Uploads/MoMPublished/MoMPublishedOn20221025200345.pdf

Global Agricultural News. (2022). China has made great strides in GMO soybean and corn projects, ministry officials says. https://tittlepress.com/world/1419390/

GRDC Ground Cover. (2022). Australia's GM safflower demand on the rise. https://groundcover.grdc.com.au/innovation/industry-insights/australias-gm-safflower-demand-on-the-rise

Horvarth, D. (2021). ISAAA Blog. https://www.isaaa.org/blog/entry/default.asp?BlogDate=3/31/2021

Huazhong Agricultural University. (2021). Hzau makes breakthroughs in spineless fish. https://www.hzau.edu.cn/info/1138/15572.htm

Indian Express. (2022). GM mustard hybrids yield more than 28% more than national check: Minister in Raiya Sabha. https://indianexpress.com/article/india/gm-mustard-hybrid-yield-28-national-check-minister-8314254/

IMF. (2022). IMF launches regional economic outlook report for Asia and Pacific: sailing into headwinds. https://www.imf.org/en/News/Articles/2022/10/26/pr22362-imf-launches-regional-economic-outlook-report-for-asia-and-pacific-sailing-into-headwinds

IPCC. (2022a). Climate change: a threat to human well-being and health of the planet. https://www.ipcc.ch/report/ar6/wg2/resources/press/press-release/

IPCC. (2022b). The evidence is clear: the time for action is now: we can halve emissions by 2030. https://www.ipcc.ch/report/ar6/wg3/resources/press/press-release/

IRRI. (2021). Philippines becomes first country to approve nutrient-enriched "Golden Rice" for planting. https://www.irri.org/news-and-events/news/philippines-becomes-first-country-approve-nutrient-enriched-golden-rice

ISAAA. (2020). *Global Status of Commercialized Biotech/GM Crops in 2019*. https://www.isaaa.org/resources/publications/briefs/55/

ISAAA. (2021a). *Breaking Barriers with Breeding: A Primer on New Breeding Innovations for Food security*. https://www.isaaa.org/resources/publications/briefs/56/default.asp

ISAAA. (2021b). Philippines approves Bt eggplant for direct use as food, feed, or for processing. https://www.isaaa.org/blog/entry/default.asp?BlogDate=7/23/2021

ISAAA. (2023). GM crop approval database. Retrieved Mar. 28, 2023, https://www.isaaa.org/gmapprovaldatabase/countrylist/default.asp

Murakami, Y., Ando, M., Futamata, R., Horibe, T., Ueda, K., Kinoshita, M. and Kobayashi, T. (2022). Targeted deletion of *ecto-5'-nucleotidase* results in retention of inosine monophosphate content in postmortem muscle of medaka *Oryzias latipes*. *Scientific Reports*, 12, p. 18588.

Nanyang Technological University. (2021). Scientists from NTU Singapore and Harvard University develop smart and sustainable food packaging that keeps harmful microbes at bay. www.ntu.edu.sg/docs/default-source/corporate-ntu/hub-news/ntu-and-harvard-scientists-develop-sustainable-food-packaging-that-kills-harmful-microbesdaf6e3a8-07bf-4ccd-b360-c34fac7f0b6b.pdf?sfvrsn=262d8380_1

OGTR. (2022a). Commercial release of Indian Mustard genetically modified for herbicide tolerance (RF3). https://www.ogtr.gov.au/gmo-dealings/dealings-involving-intentional-release/dir-190

OGTR. (2022b). Genetically modified organism herbicide tolerance review. https://www.ogtr.gov.au/news/announcement/release-genetically-modified-organism-herbicide-tolerance-trait-review

PhilRice. (2022). Golden Rice expanded seed production. https://www.philrice.gov.ph/golden-rice-expanded-seed-production-underway/

Sumangil, F. (2022). Seven provinces to produce Golden Rice. *Manila Times*. https://www.manilatimes.net/2022/05/27/news/regions/7-provinces-to-produce-golden-rice/1845154

Reuters. (2022). China to approve more GM maize varieties. https://www.agriculture.com/markets/newswire/china-to-approve-more-gmo-corn-varieties-agriculture-ministry

Report Linker. (2022). CRISPR Technology Market — Growth, Trends, COVID-19 Impact, and Forecasts (2022–2027). https://www.reportlinker.com/p06271886/CRISPR-Technology-Market-Growth-Trends-COVID-19-Impact-and-Forecasts.html?utm_source=GNW

Rubaiyath Bin Rahman, A. N. M. and Zhang, J. (2022). Trends in rice research: 2030 and beyond. *Food and Energy*, 12(2), p. e390.

Pixley, K. V., Falck-Zepeda, J. B., Paarlberg, R. L., Phillips, P. W. B., Slamet-Loedin, I. H., Dhugga, K. S., Campos, H. and Gutterson, N. (2022). Genome-edited crops for improved food security of smallholder farmers. *Nature Genetics*, 54, pp. 364–367.

Sendhil, R., Nyika, J., Yadav, S., Mackolil, J., Prashat, R., Workie, E., Ragupathy, R. and Ramasundaram, P. (2022). Genetically modified foods: bibliometric analysis on consumer perception and preference. *GM Crops & Food*, 13(1), pp. 65–85.

Singh, P., Sujayanand, G. K., Thakur, S., Rathore, M., Verma, O. P., Singh, N. P. and Das, A. (2022). Evaluation of transgenic chickpea harboring codon-modified Vip3As against gram pod borer (*Helicoverpa armigera* H). *PLoS ONE*, 17(6), p. e0270011.

Shelton, A. (2022). Bt eggplant: A personal account of using biotechnology to improve the lives of resource-poor farmers. *American Entomologist*, 67(3), pp. 52–59.

Smyth, S. S. (2022). Contributions of genome editing technologies towards improved nutrition, environmental sustainability, and poverty reduction. *Frontiers in Genome Editing*, 4, p. 863193.

Suherman, S., Wijayanto, I., Anur, R. M., Neliana, I. R., Dewanti, P. and Sugiharto, B. (2022). Field evaluation on growth and productivity of the transgenic sugarcane lines overexpressing sucrose-phosphate synthase. Sugar *Tech*, 24, pp. 1689–1698.

United Nations. (2021). Food systems account for over one-third of global greenhouse gas emissions. https://news.un.org/en/story/2021/03/1086822

UPLB College of Agriculture and Food Science. (2022). Philippine government approves Bt eggplant commercial cultivation. https://cafs.uplb.edu.ph/bt_news/philippine-govt-approves-bt-eggplant-for-commercial-cultivation/?fbclid=IwAR27wJaeiEFEPTnFkJWc3-waXuk9OVY01DWkEhCRTZcyB_vtmogBaCnyx_A

World Economic Forum. (2022). Explained: How engineered crops can fight climate change. https://www.weforum.org/agenda/2022/07/engineered-crops-can-fight-climate-change/

Xhiao, K. and Kerr, W. (2022). The political economy of China's GMO commercialization dilemma. *Food and Energy Security*, 11, p. e409.

Xiao, S., Wu, Y., Xu, S., Jiang, H., Hu, Q., Yao, W. and Zhang, M. (2022). Field evaluation of TaDREB2B-ectopic expression sugarcane (*Saccharum* spp.hybrid) for drought tolerance. *Frontiers in Plant Science*, 13(1), p. 963377.

Yang, Y., Shen, Z., Li, Y., Xu, C., Xia, H., Zhuang, H., Sun, S., Guo, M. and Yan, C. (2022). Rapid improvement of rice eating and cooking quality through gene editing toward glutelin as target. *Journal of Integrative Plant Biology*, 64(10), pp. 1860–1865.

Zhao, Y. (2022). GM corn, soybean, earn safety approval after pilot program. *China Daily.* https://global.chinadaily.com.cn/a/202201/12/WS61de3494a310cdd39bc80870.html

ZJU News Agency. (2022). Transgenic maize 'Ruifeng 125' is remarkably resistant to corn borers. https://www.zju.edu.cn/english/2022/0329/c19573a2511524/page.htm

https://doi.org/10.1142/9789811278297_0013

Chapter 13

Novel Technologies to Enhance Nutrition Security and their Evolving Benefits and Concerns

Shaun Yong Jie Sim[1], Jie Hong Chiang[1], Darel Wee Kiat Toh[1], Xin Yi Hua[1], Ruo Rou Lee[1] and Christiani Jeyakumar (CJK) Henry[1,2]

[1]*Clinical Nutrition Research Centre (CNRC), Singapore Institute of Food and Biotechnology Innovation (SIFBI), Agency for Science, Technology and Research (A*STAR), Singapore 117599*

[2]*Department of Biochemistry, Yong Loo Lin School of Medicine, National University of Singapore, Singapore 117596*

13.1 Introduction

In Southeast Asia, nearly a quarter of the total population suffers from malnutrition [ASEAN *et al.*, 2021]. This has been described as a triple burden with the co-existence of undernutrition, micronutrient deficiencies and overweight/obesity. With 46% of the more than 600 million people lacking access to a healthy diet, there is dire need to recognise this eminent crisis and develop countermeasures to prevent it from spiralling out of control [ASEAN *et al.*, 2021].

Food and nutrition security, as defined by the InterAcademy Partnership, refers to an "access for all to a healthy and affordable diet that is environmentally sustainable and culturally acceptable" [Fears and Meulen, 2019]. Achieving food and nutrition security relies on four critical factors: (1) accessibility, (2) availability, (3) stability and (4) utilisation [Thorndike *et al.*, 2022].

Accessibility is primarily determined by the affordability of a nutritious diet relative to household income and resources. Its influence on nutrition security is aptly demonstrated by the direct association between socioeconomic status (SES) and diet quality [Wright *et al.*, 2022]. Notably, low SES households have greater price sensitivity and are more likely to compromise on healthier food selections and dietary diversity in favour of empty-calorie foods, satiating food choices (e.g., high sugar/starch, high fat) and staple-heavy diets. Augmented by the higher cost of nutritious foods over contemporary selections, these collectively contribute to the nutritional disparity and align with the observed socioeconomic gradient in diet and nutrition [Gaupholm *et al.*, 2022; Love *et al.*, 2018].

Availability describes the ease of obtaining nutritious foods. This can be highly contextual and dependent on factors including the geographical location and rural-urban divide. Rural communities are challenged by spatial and environmental barriers, with numerous small retailers offering an abundance of poor nutritive value convenience foods, and a sparse distribution of fresh markets. Due to limitations in transportation and mobility, this disproportionately burdens the more vulnerable sub-populations, widening the aforementioned socioeconomic dietary gap [Blankenship and Blancato, 2022; Houghtaling *et al.*, 2022]. On the contrary, the globalisation of highly palatable, low-cost, easy foods laden with refined carbohydrates, fat and salt have also increasingly threatened the local dietary patterns and food ecosystems of urban environments. In Southeast Asia, the rapid expansion of these foods was driven to a large extent by infrastructural developments, trade policy liberalisations and the gradual transition in population density to urban areas [ASEAN *et al.*, 2021; Popkin *et al.*, 2020].

Stability refers to the establishment of sustainable food ecosystems that are resilient to future challenges including climate change, political instabilities and global pandemics. Emphasis is often centred on the development of mitigating measures that can buffer against these adverse risks. As evidenced by the COVID-19 pandemic, this is imperative especially amongst high-risk sub-populations (e.g., low SES, vulnerable minority groups) that were hit especially hard by the crisis [Picchioni *et al.*, 2021]. Measures taken may include the reduction of food wastage from farm to fork as well as a more efficient management of agricultural land systems through agrobiodiversity which will be elaborated on in a later section. Promoting underutilised native crops with high nutritive value for example offers exceptional promise to establish not only a more robust agricultural system but also serve as a platform to introduce greater diversity into consumer diets [Fears *et al.*, 2019; Wright *et al.*, 2022].

Utilisation describes the period between consumer access to food, up until the point in which nutrients and other phytochemicals consumed are bioavailable. With the tremendous selection readily available in today's supermarkets, consumers are susceptible to misinformed selections due a lack of nutritional literacy and the influence of fictitious health and nutrition-related beliefs [Bernstein and Munoz, 2012; Thorndike *et al.*, 2022]. Furthermore, subsequent food-handling methods (e.g., transportation and transfer, storage, preparation and cooking) and the eventual degree of physiological uptake and assimilation have also evolved into key concerns that may threaten nutritional security. For example, disease- and age-related deteriorations in gastrointestinal function, increased adoption of long-term medications and polypharmacy can adversely impair bioaccessibility. Moreover, older adults are also susceptible to sensorial loss and difficulties in mastication and swallowing which further limits food selection and diversity [Bernstein and Munoz, 2012; Ingram, 2020].

While it is recognised that nutritional security is a multifaceted challenge and must be tackled on various fronts — policy, industry, socioeconomic, governmental, etc. — the objective of this chapter is to present a scientific view on a range of "novel technologies" as tools used to enhance nutritional security. We will begin by exploring commercially available modern food processing technologies that can reduce postharvest losses, improve the shelf-life and availability of foods, and enhance their nutritional quality. To strengthen food resilience and stability, there has been a drive towards alternative proteins and controlled-environmental agriculture. But are they truly a panacea for our nutritional needs? We will therefore examine the nutritive profile of these novel foods and produce grown in such advanced agricultural systems. It is also crucial to note that we usually eat whole foods and not individual ingredients; hence, we will also need to consider other components, beside alternative proteins, that make up foods. We will comment on utilising underexploited sources of carbohydrates and lipids as alternative ingredients. Finally, we will discuss some evolving concerns and pitfalls that may arise if these novel technologies and solutions are blindly embraced without careful deliberation.

This chapter will commence by describing what "novel technologies" are, followed by its applications along the supply chain from post-harvest to consumption. Using case examples, the chapter will showcase how modern technologies can be used to reduce postharvest losses, improve shelf-life, and enhance nutritional quality. The nutritive properties of novel foods (e.g., plant-based foods, cultured meats) and local produce grown in advanced agricultural systems (e.g., indoor hydroponics and vertical farming) will also be discussed. Next, given that rice is the most extensively consumed carbohydrate staple and edible oils remain an expensive resource, we recommend utilising underexploited sources of carbohydrates and lipids (e.g., tubers, seeds, piths) to meet the dietary needs of the burgeoning ASEAN population. The chapter will also highlight the importance of considering the nutritional and food security needs of those at the apex and the base of the societal pyramid and the imperative to develop low-cost innovations. Finally, the unintended consequences of embracing modern technologies blindly for both food security and nutrition will be discussed.

13.2 Applications of Modern Technologies to Enhance Nutrition Security and Case Examples

Conventional food processing techniques have been proven to create safe products. However, the quality of the final product is sometimes significantly poorer than the unprocessed version as flavour, aroma, texture, and nutritional value are affected considerably. There is growing interest in developing and using novel thermal and non-thermal food processing tools for fresh-tasting, high-quality, healthy, and safe products throughout the food supply chain. Novel technologies such as pulsed electric field (PEF), high-pressure processing (HPP), cold plasma, microwave, and ohmic heating are among the most promising. For instance, compared to retort sterilisation, microwave-assisted thermal sterilisation at 915 MHz is found to be more effective in eradicating pathogens including bacterial spores and improving shelf-life, yet not affecting the nutritive and sensory qualities of food products [Soni *et al.*, 2020]. Likewise, cold plasma has the potential to inactivate bacterial spores, enzymes and reduce toxins/allergens [Gavahian and Khaneghah, 2020; Sruthi *et al.*, 2022]. In this section, the application of two innovative and modern commercial technologies, HPP and PEF, will be highlighted.

13.2.1 *High-Pressure Processing to Enhance the Shelf-Life and Nutritional Properties of Foods*

HPP is a non-thermal processing method whereby food placed in flexible packaging is subjected to high hydrostatic pressures (300–600 MPa) and held for a short period of time (3–5 min) at cold temperatures. All food components experience the same pressure quasi-instantaneously. This technique allows for the cold pasteurisation and shelf-life extension of foods. This is achieved through the pressure inactivation of pathogenic and spoilage vegetative organisms or enzymes [Balasubramaniam *et al.*, 2016]. The low temperatures enable the preservation of colour, taste, aroma, and heat-labile nutrients. One of the earliest commercial examples include guacamole [Alañón *et al.*, 2022]. The technology has since expanded to improve the shelf-life of juices, fruits and vegetables, meats and seafoods, soups and sauces, dairy products, baby foods and ready-to-eat meals [Houška *et al.*, 2022; Huang *et al.*, 2017; Roobab *et al.*, 2022; Sánchez *et al.*, 2020].

Beyond shelf-life extension, HPP can also be used to improve the nutritional properties of foods or to create new types of nutritious foods. For example, HPP can create unique varieties of protein gel structures [Gharibzahedi and Smith, 2021; Sim *et al.*, 2019; Sim and Moraru, 2020] to be used in plant-based yogurts [Sim *et al.*, 2020] and to improve protein digestibility [Sim *et al.*, 2021; Wang *et al.*, 2022]. However, some challenges for using HPP include the high equipment cost and the need for chilled storage, which reduces its viability for some countries. Fortunately, there are increasing numbers of toll facilities worldwide where food manufacturers can pay-per-use without purchasing their own equipment. Additionally, there is active research to develop shelf-stable foods [Al-Ghamdi *et al.*, 2020; Aldrete-Tapia and Torres, 2021; Evelyn and Silva, 2019; Inanoglu *et al.*, 2022] that do not require cold chain management. These efforts are anticipated to boost nutritional security by improving the availability and utilisation of foods.

13.2.2 *Pulsed Electric Field Processing to Reduce Post-Harvest Loss*

PEF technology involves short-duration pulses (from nanoseconds to milliseconds) at a high electrical voltage from 100–300 V/cm to 10–80 kV/cm. During this process, cell membranes of microorganisms, plant materials, or animal products are disrupted [Barba *et al.*, 2015; Leong *et al.*, 2018; Parniakov *et al.*, 2022]. PEF technology comprises an impulse generation system and a treatment chamber operating at high electric fields (>20 kV/cm), which can be used to modify the microstructure of plant and animal tissues, enhancing the extraction yield and quality of bioactive compounds, and inactivating microorganisms (e.g., pasteurisation of fruit juices) [Barba *et al.*, 2015; Leong *et al.*, 2018; Toepfl *et al.*, 2014]. PEF can easily be incorporated into existing processing lines due to its continuous operability with quick processing times [Toepfl *et al.*, 2014].

Potatoes are one of the world's most-produced food crops, and the market size for potato processing was estimated to be around US$24.83 billion in 2018, with an annual growth rate of 5.2% [Parniakov *et al.*, 2022]. It constitutes an essential part of the human diet, providing carbohydrates, minerals, proteins, fibres and vitamins [Moens *et al.*, 2021]. However, potatoes are prone to respiration, water loss, and starch hydrolysis, which alters the textures of potatoes during storage [Pinhero and Yada, 2016]. As such, potatoes must be properly stored after harvest for consumption all year round. This includes having specific storage temperatures, ventilation systems, and sprout suppressants to reduce sprout growth and disease development [Moens *et al.*, 2021].

In recent years, PEF technology has garnered interest from food manufacturers, especially in the potato industry, for producing French fries and potato chips [Leong and Oey, 2022]. It is an intermediary step before cutting/slicing, blanching, pre-drying, and frying [Abduh *et al.*, 2021; Leong *et al.*, 2022]. In the past, preheaters were used to soften raw potatoes, making them processable for French fry production. This process resulted in high energy and water consumption, with longer start-up and shutdown times [Hill *et al.*, 2022]. The first PEF system was installed in the potato processing industry in 2010 [Hill *et al.*, 2022] and has been shown to be effective in softening potato tuber tissues. This improved the textural qualities of the potatoes, resulting in a smoother cutting surface, reduction in starch loss and oil uptake, and lowered acrylamide formation, in addition to more uniform colour development during frying [Abduh *et al.*, 2021; Fauster *et al.*, 2018; Lee *et al.*, 2022; Schouten *et al.*, 2020].

Ignat *et al.* [2015] and Lee *et al.* [2022] investigated the effects of PEF pre-treatments (ranging from 0.5 kV/cm to 2.50 kV/cm electric field) on potatoes before deep-fat frying of French fries. Control samples were prepared by either dipping or blanching the freshly cut potatoes to simulate conventional operations used by the industry. The PEF-treated potato cubes exhibited lower peak force during textural analysis than the dipped control, possibly due to electroporation causing a partial loss in turgor pressure. This could have impaired the firmness of the plant tissue, resulting in a texture change [Ignat *et al.*, 2015; Pereira *et al.*, 2009]. Upon frying, PEF-treated potato cubes showed a more uniform and brighter colour. However, dipped potato cubes had uneven darker colours with brown edges, which could be due to the amount of sugars participating in the Maillard reaction [Ignat *et al.*, 2015; Lee *et al.*, 2022]. Lee *et al.* [2022] reported that reducing sugar content decreased by half when increasing PEF electric fields, with glucose, fructose, and low-molecular substrates involved in the Maillard reaction being released [Janositz *et al.*, 2011; Parniakov *et al.*, 2022]. This could potentially lower the acrylamide content in French fries [Zhang *et al.*, 2021]. In conclusion, this work demonstrated the use of PEF technology as an alternative to the typical thermal blanching process for French fry production. The application of PEF provides a broad spectrum of quality and processing benefits to obtain excellent and superior food products.

13.3 Nutritive Properties of Novel Foods and Local Produce

13.3.1 *Plant-Based Foods*

Plant-based foods refer to food products made from vegetables, fruits, grains, legumes, seeds, and nuts to replace foods of animal origins such as meat, fish, dairy and eggs [Ostfeld, 2017]. There has been increased demand for plant-based foods as consumers are motivated to turn to these alternative products for health, environmental and ethical reasons [Reipurth *et al.*, 2019]. However, plant-based foods may not necessarily have superior nutritional profiles and bioavailability when compared to traditional foods [McClements and Grossmann, 2021], and may even contain larger amounts of undesirable nutrients such as saturated fat and sodium [Tso and Forde, 2021]. The following is a survey of some common plant-based food categories.

Plant-based meat analogues are constructed using macronutrients from plant sources, such as soy and pea, to parallel the sensorial properties of animal meat [Sha and Xiong, 2020]. Impossible Foods and Beyond Meat are two notable companies that have commercialised comminuted meat analogue products including burger patties, sausages and nuggets [McClements and Grossmann, 2021]. However, the bigger challenge in the production of plant-based meat analogues lies in the matching of nutritional profile to that of the original meat. Plant-based proteins from cereal and legume sources are commonly used in the formulation of meat analogues. However, they have lower protein quality because of their incomplete amino acid profiles and typically lower digestibility due to indigestible cell walls and the presence of antinutrients such as polyphenols that inactivate proteases [Shaghaghian *et al.*, 2022].

Meat is also a valuable source of iron, zinc and vitamin B in highly bioavailable forms [McClements and Grossmann, 2021]. While plant-based meat analogues can be fortified with the lacking nutrients, bioavailability remains largely unknown [Bryngelsson *et al.*, 2022]. For instance, iron found in meat is present in the haem form which is more easily absorbed than iron from plants; anti-nutrients present in legumes also impedes the bioavailability of iron [Bryngelsson *et al.*, 2022]. Furthermore, plant-based meat analogues often contain numerous additives for stabilisation and preservation purposes that are not normally found in meat. Some meat analogues, as noted earlier, may even contain high saturated fat and sodium content [Sha and Xiong, 2020] to mask undesirable flavours and improve mouthfeel.

Among the other categories of plant-based foods, milk alternatives produced from a variety of sources such as soy, oat, almond and pea, are the most frequently consumed [McClements and Grossmann, 2021]. However, it is important to note that the nutritive properties of plant-based milk are generally inferior to that of cow's milk, in both macro- and micro-nutrient quality. While soy milk and cow's milk have similar protein content, protein digestibility and amino acid bioavailability in soy milk is lower than in cow's milk since plant protein sources are generally of lower quality and are less digestible [Martínez-Padilla *et al.*, 2020]. Additionally, the amount of calcium present in soy milk is only a fifth of cow's milk [Sethi *et al.*, 2016]. Hence, calcium is often added during the production of plant-based milks either as calcium carbonate or tricalcium phosphate salts [Sethi *et al.*, 2016]. Calcium carbonate-fortified soy milk was previously found to have similar bioavailability to cow's milk while tricalcium phosphate-fortified soy milk was lower [Zhao *et al.*, 2005].

Various plant-based eggs such as those produced by JUST Egg are currently available on the market. Chicken eggs are naturally rich in various vitamins and minerals that are not present in plants; therefore the nutritional profile of plant-based eggs are often lacking [McClements and Grossmann, 2021] and require fortification like other plant-based foods.

13.3.2 *Cultured Meat*

Cultured meat is produced in a bioreactor using the *in vitro* cultivation of animal cells in a growth medium [Treich, 2021] which aims to possess similar sensorial and nutritional properties to traditional meat [Fraeye *et al.*, 2020]. The Singapore Food Agency was the first in the world to approve the commercial sale of cultured meat products in December 2020 [Ong *et al.*, 2021]. Some examples of these products that are currently available or close to available include bite-sized chicken nuggets from Eat Just, crustaceans from Shiok Meats and beef patties from Mosa Meat.

Traditional meats, as mentioned previously, are important sources of vitamins, minerals and quality proteins of high digestibility and complete amino acid profile. However, the majority of the compounds present in muscle cells that contribute to their sensorial and nutritional properties are derived from metabolic processes carried out by non-muscle organs [Fraeye *et al.*, 2020]. For example, vitamin B_{12} is produced by gut bacteria and is present solely in foods of animal origin [Kadim *et al.*, 2015]. Therefore, these extracellular nutrients need to be specifically supplied to the cells. While the nutrients can be added into the growth medium, the actual amount of nutrients taken up and retained by the cells has yet to be established [Balasubramanian *et al.*, 2021].

13.3.3 *Microbial Protein*

Quorn is a commercial mycoprotein that is produced via the fermentation of *Fusarium venenatum*, a natural fungus, to obtain a texture similar to meat [Denny *et al.*, 2008]. Mycoprotein typically has a high protein and fibre content of 45% and 25%, respectively [Finnigan *et al.*, 2019]. While its protein content might be lower than meat, 41% of the proteins present in mycoprotein is made up of essential amino acids, which is higher than other typical plant proteins [Ahmad *et al.*, 2022; Finnigan *et al.*, 2019]. Protein digestibility and bioavailability of mycoprotein were also found to be comparable to milk protein [Ahmad *et al.*, 2022]. In addition to having a low fat content, the fatty acid profile of mycoprotein is also favourable as it contains predominantly monosaturated and polyunsaturated fatty acids [Ahmad *et al.*, 2022]. Furthermore, the saturated fat content in mycoprotein is low, which is beneficial for cardiovascular health [Ahmad *et al.*, 2022].

Like plant-based meat analogues, iron and vitamin B_{12} levels in mycoprotein are also lower than those of red meat. Due to the presence of purines in ribonucleic acid, there may also be concerns of gout due to the accumulation of uric acid when consumed in excess. However, heat treatment is often applied to mycoproteins after harvest to reduce ribonucleic acid content via the activation of endogenous RNAse enzymes [Denny *et al.*, 2008].

13.3.4 *Hybrid Foods*

Hybrid foods refer to products that include a blend of both animal- and plant-based ingredients to provide a healthier and more sustainable alternative to pure meat products. Compared to pure plant-based products, hybrid foods allow consumers to gradually shift their consumption behaviour [Neo, 2022], increasing the acceptance of foods made from plant-based materials. Chicken Plus™ hybrid nuggets by Perdue Farms® is an example of a hybrid food that is made using a blend of chicken breast, chickpea, and cauliflower. Advantageously, the nutritional profile of hybrid foods can be tailored by the combination of animal- and plant-based ingredients like traditional flexitarian diets.

13.3.5 *Indoor Hydroponics and Vertical Farming*

To build a resilient food supply, Singapore aims to produce up to 30% of its nutritional needs locally by 2030. Yet Singapore, like many urban and developing cities, faces the challenge of land and resource scarcity, making traditional agriculture unfeasible [Kyaw and Ng, 2017]. Vertical farming, community farming and rooftop farming are examples of urban farming, of which vertical farming requires lower land and water use [van Delden *et al.*, 2021] while community and rooftop farming maximise the potential of underutilised spaces in commercial and residential areas [Xi *et al.*, 2022]. The close proximity between farms and consumers also reduces transportation costs, food spoilage and wastage during transportation [Xi *et al.*, 2022]. As such, urban farming is seen as a potential solution to overcome these challenges and increase local food production.

Indoor vertical farming systems allow for high, uniform yields and the production of seasonal crops throughout the year [Rouphael *et al.*, 2018] as it enables precise control over the environmental factors that influence the growth characteristics of plants. Sterile hydroponic growing mediums, coupled with hygiene control, reduce contamination and the occurrence of pests and diseases [van Delden *et al.*, 2021].

The quality of crops grown is dependent on the interplay of environmental factors which can be tailored in hydroponics to meet the specific needs of each plant species and the consumers. For instance, when the amount of photosynthetically active photons that reaches the crop surface per unit time is higher, photosynthesis increases [van Delden *et al.*, 2021]. In response to light stress, the production of compounds such as carotenoids, anthocyanins and vitamin C are induced, altering the nutritional profile of the crops [van Delden *et al.*, 2021].

While nutrient content and anti-nutrient concentrations in the growing medium can be easily modified, it is important to note that nutritional value of the crops does not increase indefinitely since bioavailability is determined by a myriad of factors in the food matrix [van Delden *et al.*, 2021].

13.4 Underexploited Sources of Carbohydrates and Lipids to Feed a Growing ASEAN Population

In Asia, rice is a staple food and the main source of carbohydrates. However, major environmental issues such as droughts and agricultural water shortages could affect rice yield and production. In addition, pandemic events such as COVID-19 could disrupt trade, leading to volatility in rice imports and prices [Tansuchat *et al.*, 2022]. This is especially detrimental for countries such as Philippines and Malaysia, where rice production for consumption is not enough for domestic demand [Tansuchat *et al.*, 2022]. With a burgeoning ASEAN population, there is a need to explore underexploited and non-traditional sources of carbohydrates. Asia is home to a wide range of fruits that are known for large-scale commercial cultivation, including papaya, jackfruit and longan. While these fruits are often processed to form end-products such as dried goods, jams and juices, their seeds are often thrown away [Raihana *et al.*, 2015]. Yet, many of these fruit seeds are good sources of carbohydrates and/or oil that can be exploited for food. In this section, we will survey a list of potential alternative carbohydrate and lipid sources.

Jackfruit seeds are an alternative to rice as a staple and carbohydrate source. The jackfruit (*Artocarpus heterophyllus*) is the largest edible fruit in the world and each fruit can contain up to 500 seeds, making up around 15% of the total weight. Jackfruit seeds measure about 2–4 cm and 1–2 cm in length and diameter, respectively [Suzihaque *et al*., 2022]. Although jackfruit seeds are widely used in Asian culinary preparation, or boiled and eaten as a snack, they are usually discarded [Swami *et al*., 2012; Zhang *et al*., 2016]. This is likely due to their short shelf-life because of the seed's high carbohydrate (60–80% on dry basis) and protein (8% on dry basis) content. Hence, starch from jackfruit seeds is usually extracted first, and then used in various food applications [Zhang *et al*., 2016]. In Asian countries, jackfruit seed flour has been incorporated in baked, extruded and traditional food products as alternatives with higher nutritional value [Suzihaque *et al*., 2022].

Another non-traditional alternative source of starch is longan seeds. The longan (*Dimocarpus longan* Lour.) is a fruit widely grown in Asia. Thailand and Vietnam are two of the largest longan-producing countries, while the oversupply of longan has led to the decrease in its price [Hong-in *et al*., 2021]. Due to its short shelf-life, the longan is usually preserved in the dried form [Hong-in *et al*., 2021]. As such, most of its starch-containing seeds are discarded as waste. The starch content of longan seeds ranges from 49.5% to 59.4% w/w [Kittipongpatana *et al*., 2021]. Kittipongpatana *et al*. [2021] suggested that the drying and incubation process of longan to produce black longan that is traditionally used in Chinese medicine can affect the granular arrangement of starch in the seeds, causing changes in its thermal, functional and digestibility properties. Indeed, the authors found that the resistant starch content in seeds of black longan was four-fold higher than those extracted from seeds of fresh longan [Kittipongpatana *et al.*, 2021]. They attributed this to the starch inclusion complexes formed due to interactions between components in the seeds during the incubation period. Given the abundance of longan in Asia and the possible health benefits of black longan seed starch, there is great potential for its application in new food products.

Lastly, the kithul palm (*Caryota urens*) is an underutilised palm tree that belongs to the Arecaceae family [Sudheesh *et al.*, 2019]. Although not a fruit, kithul palm is commonly found in some ASEAN countries such as Myanmar and Malaysia where its sap, roots and cabbage are used for culinary and medicinal purposes [De Silva *et al.*, 2022]. Kithul flour from the palm trunk contains more than 60% starch [Sudheesh *et al.*, 2019]. Ng and Henry [2020] reported that kithul flour had good gelling properties and significantly lower starch digestibility than other unconventional starches used in Asia, namely red rice flour, sago, water chestnut and sweet potato starches. Wijesinghe *et al.* [2015b] also reported a decent amount of potassium (59.5 mg/100 g), calcium (70.1 mg/100 g), iron (14.0 mg/100 g) and magnesium (66.6 mg/100 g) present in kithul flour. Currently, kithul flour is widely used in Sri Lanka to make rice cake (kawum), porridge (kenda) and flatbread (rotee) [Wijesinghe *et al.*, 2015a]. Given its positive nutritional and functional properties, there is strong potential for kithul flour to be used in ASEAN food products.

Other than carbohydrates, oil is another essential component of the human diet as a concentrated energy source [Raihana *et al.*, 2015]. The guava (*Psidium guajava* L.) is a pear-shaped fruit containing many hard white seeds that are 2–3 mm in diameter, embedded in the white or pink edible flesh [Sherazi *et al.*, 2019]. Thailand is the world's third largest guava cultivator and most of it are exported to other ASEAN countries like Singapore, Malaysia and Myanmar [Suwanwong and Boonpangrak, 2021]. In the beverage industry, guava is the top processed crop and its seeds are the main bulk of waste post-processing [Kumar *et al.*, 2022]. Yet, guava seed is still a highly nutritive by-product. Guava seeds contain around 10–15% oil [Kumar *et al.*, 2022]. In a study by Kapoor *et al.* [2020], it was reported that guava seed oil (GSO) contains around 76% polyunsaturated fatty acids, 11% monounsaturated fatty acids and 14% saturated fatty acids. The authors also found that GSO is relatively stable due to its low peroxide value of 0.62 meq/kg. In addition, GSO also contains a considerable amount of tocopherol (654 ppm) and carotenoids (19.24 ppm) that could provide oil stability as they function as antioxidants against lipid peroxidation [Kapoor *et al.*, 2020]. More importantly, it has been reported to be non-toxic and safe for human consumption [Kumar *et al.*, 2022].

Mango (*Mangifera indica* L.) is a popular tropical fruit largely produced in Thailand and Indonesia. It is estimated that 35–60% of the fruit is considered as waste after processing [Sultana and Ashraf, 2019]. However, mango seed oil can be extracted from mango seed kernel (that is enclosed in the seed), which represents around 15–20% of post-processing waste. Mango seeds are a good and safe source of oil (11% fat on average) that can be substituted for any solid fat without adverse effects [Karunanithi *et al.*, 2015]. Oleic and stearic acid are the main constituents in mango seed oil. Mango seed oil has garnered increasing attention due to its physical and chemical properties that are like cocoa, illipe and sal butter [Jahurul *et al.*, 2015]. Particularly, there is limited use of cocoa butter in tropical countries due to challenges in tempering. Nevertheless, Jahurul *et al.* [2014] reported that blends of mango seed fat and palm stearin can form temperature-resistant hard butter and be used as cocoa butter replacers without significantly affecting the product's physical and chemical properties.

Finally, papaya (*Carica papaya* L.) is an important tropical fruit that is native to ASEAN countries such as Malaysia, Indonesia and Philippines [Wadekar *et al.*, 2021]. Papaya seeds account for around 15% of the weight of the fruit. They are unpalatable as they taste peppery and pungent [Raihana *et al.*, 2015]. Although most of the seeds are discarded as agricultural waste, they are still highly nutritive with a considerable lipid content (28–31%) [Zhang *et al.*, 2019]. Papaya seed oil is high in oleic acid (69.8–72.0%) and triacylglycerol and has nutritional and functional properties similar to olive oil. Its rich oleic acid content may confer oxidative stability to be used as a frying oil [Tan, 2019]. However, there is a lack of studies investigating the toxicology and safety of papaya seed oil [Tan, 2019]. Thus, there is a need to assess its suitability for use as cooking oil before further applications in foods.

13.5 Evolving Concerns from Embracing Modern Food Solutions

Historically, food processing methodologies such as drying, canning and fortifications have revolutionised the diets of man. The same can be said in today's context where a strategic integration of modern science, technology and innovation can likewise yield tremendous promise to address the evolving food and nutrition insecurities in Southeast Asia and the rest of the world. However, while it is important to embrace these novel technologies, we should continue to be mindful of and not disregard any of the four key pillars that are at the foundation of food and nutrition security.

With the growing income gap in the ASEAN region and beyond, accessibility and affordability become key limitations for novel technologies that are too costly, restricting their potential outreach. While strategies including HPP enhance supply yield and nutrient stability (e.g., shelf-life extension, nutrient and phytonutrient retention), it is imperative to conduct a critical evaluation of the cost-benefit analysis in all aspects of food and nutrition security to ensure an effective and successful application.

In this aspect, a resourceful use of low-cost raw materials that may include a range of underutilised native crops as well as the valorisation food wastes/side streams can address some of these evolving concerns. However, while many of these alternative foods can be nutritionally promising alternatives, we need to continue to be mindful of its potential pitfalls. For example, food side-streams including seeds and pomace contain innately higher concentrations of anti-nutrients such as phytates, saponins and tannins. These further limit nutrient bioavailability and unintendedly place an individual at a greater risk of malnutrition. While this may be alleviated with the use of modern techniques that can degrade these compounds, a meticulous selection is necessary to strike a careful balance between its health effects and escalating costs.

In recent years, the food and nutrition industry has witnessed unprecedented advances. Yet, successful application is often held back by the skewed target market that favours the affluent. Hence, an important priority moving forward should therefore focus on the development of affordable nutrition solutions that cater to the large base of the socioeconomic pyramid that is very often neglected. This is crucial to address not only the growing nutritional insecurities globally, but also attenuate any longer-term implications on public healthcare, labour productivity and our future generations.

13.6 Conclusion

In this brief review, we have attempted to highlight both the challenges and opportunities to meet the food security needs of this region. It is ironic that in a region that has over 400 edible plant species, our current focus is on no more than five staples (rice, wheat, corn, potato, and cassava). The exploitation of underutilised plants in concert with valorisation of waste will become a critical part of our food story. The present focus on "alternative proteins" serves as an example of the need to separate the pursuit of pure economic benefits over its real nutritional contribution. Such an analysis should also be conducted on the various "novel technologies" discussed above and how it influences nutritional security. Finally, in a region that has many of its people earning less than 3 USD a day, could there be room for low-cost "village-level" technologies that can deliver nutritious foods?

References

Abduh, S. B., Leong, S. Y., Zhao, C., Baldwin, S., Burritt, D. J., Agyei, D. and Oey, I. (2021). Kinetics of colour development during frying of potato pre-treated with pulsed electric fields and blanching: effect of cultivar. *Foods, 10*(10), p. 2307.

Ahmad, M. I., Farooq, S., Alhamoud, Y., Li, C. and Zhang, H. (2022). A review on mycoprotein: History, nutritional composition, production methods, and health benefits. *Trends in Food Science and Technology*, 121, pp. 14–29.

Al-Ghamdi, S., Sonar, C. R., Patel, J., Albahr, Z. and Sablani, S. S. (2020). High pressure-assisted thermal sterilization of low-acid fruit and vegetable purees: Microbial safety, nutrient, quality, and packaging evaluation. *Food Control,* 114, p. 107233.

Alañón, M. E., Cádiz-Gurrea, M. L., Oliver-Simancas, R., Leyva-Jiménez, F. J., Arráez-Román, D. and Segura-Carretero, A. (2022). Quality assurance of commercial guacamoles preserved by high pressure processing versus conventional thermal processing. *Food Control,* 135, p. 108791.

Aldrete-Tapia, J. A. and Torres, J. A. (2021). Enhancing the inactivation of bacterial spores during pressure-assisted thermal processing. *Food Engineering Reviews, 13*(3), pp. 431–441.

ASEAN, UNICEF and WFP. (2021). *ASEAN Food and Nutrition Security Report 2021* (Vol. 1). https://asean.org/wp-content/uploads/2022/04/Digital_ASEAN_FNSR_Volume-1_21-4-2022_FINAL.pdf

Balasubramaniam, V., Barbosa-Cánovas, G. V. and Lelieveld, H. (2016). *High Pressure Processing of FOOD: Principles, Technology and Applications.* Springer.

Balasubramanian, B., Liu, W., Pushparaj, K. and Park, S. (2021). The epic of *in vitro* meat production — A fiction into reality. *Foods,* 10(6), p. 1395.

Barba, F. J., Parniakov, O., Pereira, S. A., Wiktor, A., Grimi, N., Boussetta, N., . . . Vorobiev, E. (2015). Current applications and new opportunities for the use of pulsed electric fields in food science and industry. *Food Research International,* 77, pp. 773–798.

Bernstein, M. and Munoz, N. (2012). Position of the Academy of Nutrition and Dietetics: Food and nutrition for older adults: promoting health and wellness. *Journal of the Academy of Nutrition and Dietetics,* 112(8), pp. 1255–1277.

Blankenship, J. and Blancato, R. B. (2022). Nutrition security at the intersection of health equity and quality care. *Journal of the Academy of Nutrition and Dietetics,* 122(10), pp. S12–S19.

Bryngelsson, S., Moshtaghian, H., Bianchi, M. and Hallström, E. (2022). Nutritional assessment of plant-based meat analogues on the Swedish market. *International Journal of Food Sciences and Nutrition,* 73(7), pp. 889–901.

De Silva, G., Diddeniya, I., Dahanayake, J. and Perera, P. (2022). Traditional medicinal benefits of Caryota urens: A review article. *Sri Lanka Journal of Indigenous Medicine (SLJIM)*, 7(01), pp. 582–591.

Denny, A., Aisbitt, B. and Lunn, J. (2008). Mycoprotein and health. *Nutrition Bulletin*, 33(4), pp. 298–310.

Evelyn and Silva, F. V. M. (2019). Heat assisted HPP for the inactivation of bacteria, moulds and yeasts spores in foods: Log reductions and mathematical models. *Trends in Food Science and Technology*, 88, pp. 143–156.

Fauster, T., Schlossnikl, D., Rath, F., Ostermeier, R., Teufel, F., Toepfl, S. and Jaeger, H. (2018). Impact of pulsed electric field (PEF) pre-treatment on process performance of industrial French fries production. *Journal of Food Engineering*, 235, pp. 16–22.

Fears, R. and Meulen, V. (2019). Scientific opportunities for nutrition security. *The Lancet*, 393(10187), p. 2200.

Fears, R., ter Meulen, V. and von Braun, J. (2019). Global food and nutrition security needs more and new science. *Science Advances*, 5(12), pp. 4–5.

Finnigan, T. J. A., Wall, B. T., Wilde, P. J., Stephens, F. B., Taylor, S. L. and Freedman, M. R. (2019). Mycoprotein: The future of nutritious nonmeat protein, a symposium review. *Current Developments in Nutrition*, 3(6), p. nzz021.

Fraeye, I., Kratka, M., Vandenburgh, H. and Thorrez, L. (2020). Sensorial and nutritional aspects of cultured meat in comparison to traditional meat: Much to be inferred. *Frontiers in Nutrition*, 7, p. 35.

Gaupholm, J., Papadopoulos, A., Asif, A., Dodd, W. and Little, M. (2022). The influence of food environments on dietary behaviour and nutrition in Southeast Asia: A systematic scoping review. *Nutrition and Health*, 29(2), 231–253.

Gavahian, M. and Khaneghah, A. M. (2020). Cold plasma as a tool for the elimination of food contaminants: Recent advances and future trends. *Critical Reviews in Food Science and Nutrition*, 60(9), pp. 1581–1592.

Gharibzahedi, S. M. T. and Smith, B. (2021). Effects of high hydrostatic pressure on the quality and functionality of protein isolates, concentrates, and hydrolysates derived from pulse legumes: A review. *Trends in Food Science and Technology*, 107, pp. 466–479.

Grace, N. C. F. and Jeyakumar Henry, C. (2020). The physicochemical characterization of unconventional starches and flours used in Asia. *Foods*, 9(2), p. 182.

Hill, K., Ostermeier, R., Töpfl, S. and Heinz, V. (2022). Pulsed Electric Fields in the Potato Industry. In J. Raso, V. Heinz, I. Alvarez and S. Toepfl (Eds.), *Pulsed Electric Fields Technology for the Food Industry: Fundamentals and Applications*, pp. 325–335. Springer.

Hong-in, P., Punyoyai, C., Sriyab, S., Neimkhum, W. and Chaiyana, W. (2021). Enhanced antioxidant activity of pericarp extract from black Dimocarpus longan Lour. *Asia-Pacific Journal of Science and Technology*, 27(02), p. APST-27.

Houghtaling, B., Greene, M., Parab, K. V and Singleton, C. R. (2022). Improving fruit and vegetable accessibility, purchasing, and consumption to advance nutrition security and health equity in the United States. *International Journal of Environmental Research and Public Health*, 19(18), p. 11220.

Houška, M., Silva, F. V., Evelyn, Buckow, R., Terefe, N. S. and Tonello, C. (2022). High pressure processing applications in plant foods. *Foods*, 11(2), p. 223.

Huang, H.-W., Wu, S.-J., Lu, J.-K., Shyu, Y.-T. and Wang, C.-Y. (2017). Current status and future trends of high-pressure processing in food industry. *Food Control*, 72, pp. 1–8.

Ignat, A., Manzocco, L., Brunton, N. P., Nicoli, M. C. and Lyng, J. G. (2015). The effect of pulsed electric field pre-treatments prior to deep-fat frying on quality aspects of potato fries. *Innovative Food Science and Emerging Technologies*, 29, pp. 65–69.

Inanoglu, S., Barbosa-Cánovas, G. V., Sablani, S. S., Zhu, M.-J., Keener, L. and Tang, J. (2022). High-pressure pasteurization of low-acid chilled ready-to-eat food. *Comprehensive Reviews in Food Science and Food Safety*, 21(6), pp. 4939–4970.

Ingram, J. (2020). Nutrition security is more than food security. *Nature Food*, 1, p. 2.

Jahurul, M. H. A., Zaidul, I. S. M., Ghafoor, K., Al-Juhaimi, F. Y., Nyam, K.-L., Norulaini, N. A. N., . . . Mohd Omar, A. K. (2015). Mango (Mangifera indica L.) by-products and their valuable components: A review. *Food Chemistry,* 183, pp. 173–180.

Jahurul, M. H. A., Zaidul, I. S. M., Nik Norulaini, N. A., Sahena, F., Abedin, M. Z., Mohamed, A. and Mohd Omar, A. K. (2014). Hard cocoa butter replacers from mango seed fat and palm stearin. *Food Chemistry,* 154, pp. 323–329.

Janositz, A., Noack, A. K. and Knorr, D. (2011). Pulsed electric fields and their impact on the diffusion characteristics of potato slices. *LWT — Food Science and Technology,* 44(9), pp. 1939–1945.

Kadim, I. T., Mahgoub, O., Baqir, S., Faye, B. and Purchas, R. (2015). Cultured meat from muscle stem cells: A review of challenges and prospects. *Journal of Integrative Agriculture*, 14(2), pp. 222–233.

Kapoor, S., Gandhi, N., Tyagi, S. K., Kaur, A. and Mahajan, B. V. C. (2020). Extraction and characterization of guava seed oil: A novel industrial byproduct. *LWT — Food Science and Technology,* 132, p. 109882.

Karunanithi, B., Bogeshwaran, K., Tripuraneni, M. and Krishna Reddy, S. (2015). Extraction of mango seed oil from mango kernel. *International Journal of Engineering Research and Development,* 11(11), pp. 32–41.

Kittipongpatana, N., Wiriyacharee, P., Phongphisutthinant, R., Chaipoot, S., Somjai, C. and Kittipongpatana, O. S. (2021). Resistant starch contents of starch isolated from black longan seeds. *Molecules,* 26(11), p. 3405.

Kumar, M., Kapoor, S., Dhumal, S., Tkaczewska, J., Changan, S., Saurabh, V., . . . Jyoti Bhuyan, D. (2022). Guava (Psidium guajava L.) seed: A low-volume, high-value byproduct for human health and the food industry. *Food Chemistry,* 386, p. 132694.

Kyaw, T. Y. and Ng, A. K. (2017). Smart aquaponics system for urban farming. *Energy Procedia*, 143, pp. 342–347.

Martínez-Padilla, E., Li, K., Blok Frandsen, H., Skejovic Joehnke, M., Vargas-Bello-Pérez, E. and Lykke Petersen, I. (2020). *In vitro* protein digestibility and fatty acid profile of commercial plant-based milk alternatives. *Foods*, 9(12), p. 1784.

McClements, D. J. and Grossmann, L. (2021). A brief review of the science behind the design of healthy and sustainable plant-based foods. *NPJ Science of Food*, 5(1), p. 17.

Moens, L. G., Van Wambeke, J., De Laet, E., Van Ceunebroeck, J.-C., Goos, P., Van Loey, A. M. and Hendrickx, M. E. G. (2021). Effect of postharvest storage on potato (Solanum tuberosum L.) texture after pulsed electric field and thermal treatments. *Innovative Food Science and Emerging Technologies*, 74, p. 102826.

Neo, P. (2022). Step-by-step: Hybrid products 'steady strategy' for alt protein industry to convert consumers — experts. *Food Navigator.* https://www.foodnavigator-asia.com/Article/2022/02/21/hybrid-products-steady-strategy-for-alt-protein-industry-to-convert-consumers

Ong, K. J., Johnston, J., Datar, I., Sewalt, V., Holmes, D. and Shatkin, J. A. (2021). Food safety considerations and research priorities for the cultured meat and seafood industry. *Comprehensive Reviews in Food Science and Food Safety*, 20(6), pp. 5421–5448.

Ostfeld, R. J. (2017). Definition of a plant-based diet and overview of this special issue. *Journal of Geriatric Cardiology*, 14, p. 315.

Lee, S.-H., Shahbaz, H., Jeong, S.-H., Hong, S.-Y. and Lee, D.-U. (2022). Effect of pulsed electric field treatment on cell-membrane permeabilisation of potato tissue and the quality of French fries. *Italian Journal of Food Science,* 34, pp. 13–24.

Leong, S. Y., Bremer, P., Silcock, P. and Oey, I. (2018). Pulsed electric field technology offers new potential for New Zealand potato processing and wine making industries. *Food New Zealand,* 18(4), pp. 21–23.

Leong, S. Y. and Oey, I. (2022). Application of novel thermal technology in foods processing. *Foods,* 11(1), p. 125.

Leong, S. Y., Roberts, R., Hu, Z., Bremer, P., Silcock, P., Toepfl, S. and Oey, I. (2022). Texture and in vitro starch digestion kinetics of French fries produced from potatoes (Solanum tuberosum L.) pre-treated with pulsed electric fields. *Applied Food Research,* 2(2), p. 100194.

Love, P., Whelan, J., Bell, C., Grainger, F., Russell, C., Lewis, M. and Lee, A. (2018). Healthy diets in rural Victoria — Cheaper than unhealthy alternatives, yet unaffordable. *International Journal of Environmental Research and Public Health*, 15(11), p. 2469.

Parniakov, O., Lebovka, N., Wiktor, A., Alles, M., Hill, K. and Toepfl, S. (2022). Applications of pulsed electric fields for processing potatoes: Examples and equipment design. *Research in Agricultural Engineering*, 68, pp. 47–62.

Pereira, R. N., Galindo, F. G., Vicente, A. A. and Dejmek, P. (2009). Effects of pulsed electric field on the viscoelastic properties of potato tissue. *Food Biophysics,* 4(3), pp. 229–239.

Picchioni, F., Goulao, L. F. and Roberfroid, D. (2021). The impact of COVID-19 on diet quality, food security and nutrition in low and middle income countries: A systematic review of the evidence. *Clinical Nutrition*, 41(12), pp. 2955–2964.

Pinhero, R. G. and Yada, R. Y. (2016). Chapter 10 — Postharvest Storage of Potatoes. In J. Singh and L. Kaur (Eds.), *Advances in Potato Chemistry and Technology* (Second Edition), pp. 283–314. Academic Press.

Popkin, B. M., Corvalan, C. and Grummer-Strawn, L. M. (2020). Dynamics of the double burden of malnutrition and the changing nutrition reality. *The Lancet*, 395(10217), pp. 65–74.

Raihana, A. R. N., Marikkar, J. M. N., Amin, I. and Shuhaimi, M. (2015). A review on food values of selected tropical fruits' seeds. *International Journal of Food Properties,* 18(11), pp. 2380–2392.

Reipurth, M. F. S., Hørby, L., Gregersen, C. G., Bonke, A. and Perez Cueto, F. J. A. (2019). Barriers and facilitators towards adopting a more plant-based diet in a sample of Danish consumers. *Food Quality and Preference, 73,* pp. 288–292.

Roobab, U., Abida, A., Afzal, R., Madni, G. M., Zeng, X.-A., Rahaman, A. and Aadil, R. M. (2022). Impact of high-pressure treatments on enzyme activity of fruit-based beverages: an overview. *International Journal of Food Science and Technology*, 57(2), pp. 801–815.

Rouphael, Y., Kyriacou, M. C., Petropoulos, S. A., De Pascale, S. and Colla, G. (2018). Improving vegetable quality in controlled environments. *Scientia Horticulturae*, 234, pp. 275–289.

Sánchez, L., Pérez, M. D. and Parrón, J. A. (2020). Chapter 11 — HPP in Dairy Products: Impact on Quality and Applications. In F. J. Barba, C. Tonello-Samson, E. Puértolas and M. Lavilla (Eds.), *Present and Future of High Pressure Processing*, pp. 245–272. Elsevier.

Schouten, M. A., Genovese, J., Tappi, S., Di Francesco, A., Baraldi, E., Cortese, M., . . . Romani, S. (2020). Effect of innovative pre-treatments on the mitigation of acrylamide formation in potato chips. *Innovative Food Science and Emerging Technologies*, 64, p. 102397.

Sethi, S., Tyagi, S. K. and Anurag, R. K. (2016). Plant-based milk alternatives an emerging segment of functional beverages: a review. *Journal of Food Science and Technology*, 53(9), pp. 3408–3423.

Sha, L. and Xiong, Y. L. (2020). Plant protein-based alternatives of reconstructed meat: Science, technology, and challenges. *Trends in Food Science and Technology*, 102, pp. 51–61.

Shaghaghian, S., McClements, D. J., Khalesi, M., Garcia-Vaquero, M. and Mirzapour-Kouhdasht, A. (2022). Digestibility and bioavailability of plant-based proteins intended for use in meat analogues: A review. *Trends in Food Science and Technology*, 129, pp. 646–656.

Sherazi, S. T. H., Mahesar, S. A., Arain, A. and Sirajuddin. (2019). Guava (Psidium guajava) Oil. In M. F. Ramadan (Ed.), *Fruit Oils: Chemistry and Functionality*, pp. 541–559. Springer.

Sim, S. Y., Srv, A., Chiang, J. H. and Henry, C. J. (2021). Plant proteins for future foods: a roadmap. *Foods*, 10(8), p. 1967.

Sim, S. Y. J., Hua, X. Y. and Henry, C. J. (2020). A novel approach to structure plant-based yogurts using high pressure processing. *Foods,* 9(8), 1126.

Sim, S. Y. J., Karwe, M. V. and Moraru, C. I. (2019). High pressure structuring of pea protein concentrates. *Journal of Food Process Engineering,* 42(7), p. e13261.

Sim, S. Y. J. and Moraru, C. I. (2020). High-pressure processing of pea protein–starch mixed systems: Effect of starch on structure formation. *Journal of Food Process Engineering,* 43(2), p. e13352.

Soni, A., Smith, J., Thompson, A. and Brightwell, G. (2020). Microwave-induced thermal sterilisation- A review on history, technical progress, advantages and challenges as compared to the conventional methods. *Trends in Food Science and Technology,* 97, pp. 433–442.

Sruthi, N. U., Josna, K., Pandiselvam, R., Kothakota, A., Gavahian, M. and Mousavi Khaneghah, A. (2022). Impacts of cold plasma treatment on physicochemical, functional, bioactive, textural, and sensory attributes of food: A comprehensive review. *Food Chemistry*, 368, p. 130809.

Sudheesh, C., Sunooj, K. V., George, J., Kumar, S., Vikas, and Sajeevkumar, V. A. (2019). Impact of γ– irradiation on the physico-chemical, rheological properties and in vitro digestibility of kithul (Caryota urens) starch; a new source of nonconventional stem starch. *Radiation Physics and Chemistry,* 162, pp. 54–65.

Sultana, B. and Ashraf, R. (2019). Mango (Mangifera indica L.) Seed Oil. In M. F. Ramadan (Ed.), *Fruit Oils: Chemistry and Functionality*, pp. 561–575. Springer.

Suwanwong, Y. and Boonpangrak, S. (2021). Phytochemical contents, antioxidant activity, and anticancer activity of three common guava cultivars in Thailand. *European Journal of Integrative Medicine,* 42, p. 101290.

Suzihaque, M. U. H., Zaki, N. A. M., Alwi, H., Ibrahim, U. K., Abd Karim, S. F. and Anuar, N. K. (2022). Jackfruit seed as an alternative replacement for starch flour. *Materials Today: Proceedings,* 63, pp. S451–S455.

Swami, S. B., Thakor, N. J., Haldankar, P. M. and Kalse, S. B. (2012). Jackfruit and its many functional components as related to human health: a review. *Comprehensive Reviews in Food Science and Food Safety*, 11(6), pp. 565–576.

Tan, S. S. (2019). Papaya (Carica papaya L.) Seed Oil. In M. F. Ramadan (Ed.), *Fruit Oils: Chemistry and Functionality*, pp. 615–626. Springer.

Tansuchat, R., Suriyankietkaew, S., Petison, P., Punjaisri, K., and Nimsai, S. (2022). Impacts of COVID-19 on sustainable agriculture value chain development in Thailand and ASEAN. *Sustainability,* 14(20), p. 12985.

Thorndike, A. N., Gardner, C. D., Kendrick, K. B., Seligman, H. K., Yaroch, A. L., Gomes, A. V., ... Schwartz, M. B. (2022). Strengthening US food policies and programs to promote equity in nutrition security: a policy statement from the American Heart Association. *Circulation*, 145(24), pp. e1077–e1093.

Toepfl, S., Siemer, C., Saldaña-Navarro, G. and Heinz, V. (2014). Chapter 6 — Overview of Pulsed Electric Fields Processing for Food. In D.-W. Sun (Ed.), *Emerging Technologies for Food Processing* (Second Edition), pp. 93–114. Academic Press.

Treich, N. (2021). Cultured meat: Promises and challenges. *Environmental and Resource Economics*, 79(1), pp. 33–61.

Tso, R. and Forde, C. G. (2021). Unintended consequences: Nutritional impact and potential pitfalls of switching from animal- to plant-based foods. *Nutrients*, 13(8), p. 2527.

van Delden, S. H., SharathKumar, M., Butturini, M., Graamans, L. J. A., Heuvelink, E., Kacira, M., Kaiser, E., Klamer, R. S., Klerkx, L., Kootstra, G., Loeber, A., Schouten, R. E., Stanghellini, C., van Ieperen, W., Verdonk, J. C., Vialet-Chabrand, S., Woltering, E. J., van de Zedde, R., Zhang, Y. and Marcelis, L. F. M. (2021). Current status and future challenges in implementing and upscaling vertical farming systems. *Nature Food*, 2(12), pp. 944–956.

Wadekar, A. B., Nimbalwar, M. G., Panchale, W. A., Gudalwar, B. R., Manwar, J. V. and Bakal, R. L. (2021). Morphology, phytochemistry and pharmacological aspects of Carica papaya, an review. *GSC Biological and Pharmaceutical Sciences,* 14(3), pp. 234–248.

Wang, W., Yang, P., Rao, L., Zhao, L., Wu, X., Wang, Y. and Liao, X. (2022). Effect of high hydrostatic pressure processing on the structure, functionality, and nutritional properties of food proteins: A review. *Comprehensive Reviews in Food Science and Food Safety,* 21(6), pp. 4640–4682.

Wijesinghe, J., Wicramasinghe, I. and Saranandha, K. (2015a). Deviation of chemical properties of kithul (Caryota urens) flour obtained from five different growing areas in Sri Lanka. *International Journal on Innovations in Research and Technology,* 2(2), pp. 67–76.

Wijesinghe, J., Wicramasinghe, I. and Saranandha, K. (2015b). Kithul flour (Caryota urens) as a potential flour source for food industry. *American Journal of Food Science and Technology*, 3(1), pp. 10–11.

Wright, O. R. L., Sivakumar, D., Sultanbawa, Y. and Netzel, M. E. (2022). Editorial: Food and nutrition security: underutilized plant and animal-based foods. *Frontiers in Nutrition*, 8, p. 821388.

Xi, L., Zhang, M., Zhang, L., Lew, T. T. S. and Lam, Y. M. (2022). Novel materials for urban farming. *Advanced Materials*, 34(25), p. 2105009.

Zhao, Y., Martin, B. R. and Weaver, C. M. (2005). Calcium bioavailability of calcium carbonate fortified soymilk is equivalent to cow's milk in young women. *The Journal of Nutrition*, 135(10), pp. 2379–2382.

Zhang, C., Zhao, W., Yan, W., Wang, M., Tong, Y., Zhang, M. and Yang, R. (2021). Effect of pulsed electric field pre-treatment on oil content of potato chips. *LWT — Food Science and Technology,* 135, 110198.

Zhang, W., Pan, Y.-G., Huang, W., Chen, H. and Yang, H. (2019). Optimized ultrasonic-assisted extraction of papaya seed oil from Hainan/ Eksotika variety. *Food Science and Nutrition,* 7(8), 2692–2701.

Zhang, Y., Zhu, K., He, S., Tan, L. and Kong, X. (2016). Characterizations of high purity starches isolated from five different jackfruit cultivars. *Food Hydrocolloids,* 52, pp. 785–794.

https://doi.org/10.1142/9789811278297_0014

Chapter 14

Effective Communication Strategies for Stakeholder Acceptance of New Technologies in Agri-food Systems

Mahaletchumy Arujanan[1,2]

[1]*BioTrust Global-ISAAA, Malaysia*
[2]*Malaysian Biotechnology Information Centre, Malaysia*

14.1 Introduction: The "What and Why" of Science Communication

Just like any communication which is meant to transfer information from one party to another, science communication is the transfer of science-related information. The question is from whom to whom and why is it needed? Since science is perceived to be complex, esoteric and not accessible easily to the public, this information transfer was initially a linear process from the scientific community to society. This gave rise to the deficit model — that society is deficit of scientific knowledge and that scientists fill this gap. However, with the advent of citizen participation and availability of resources, this model has been challenged and now there are many models or a hybrid of models. The newer models involve two-way communication, dialogues, public participation and expression of lay expertise. However, every model has its advantages and disadvantages.

Although communicating science to the wider public is as old as science itself, the emergence of modern science communication dates back to only about 60 years. It is a field that is extremely fluid as there are no restrictions on the communication approaches, the types of audience and communicators, and the reasons to communicate.

Science communication is increasingly picking up momentum as science permeates every facet of our lives. The recent COVID-19 pandemic saw the rise of conspiracy theories, fake news and pseudo-science, and glaring non-science statements from politicians, social media influencers and even a divided scientific and healthcare community that led to public confusion, rejection of vaccines and flip-flops in policies and guidelines. The rapid advancement of science and technology also causes transformative and disruptive effects in our lives where citizen participation and informed decision-making skills are critical. This is the case for agriculture and food production; healthcare, nutrition; and sustainable development.

Science communication enhances public awareness of science, increases enjoyment and interest in science, technology and engineering, and informs public understanding or opinion of scientific endeavours [Burns *et al.*, 2003]. All these aspects address the dwindling interest among students to pursue science education and career; support enabling policies, regulations and funding ecosystem that in turn support commercialisation of research; encourage technopreneurship; enable the public to distinguish science from pseudo-science; and include citizen participation in the science and technology direction a country takes.

It is also time to take stock of past communication strategies and evaluate their successes and failures, develop new messaging that is more suited to the changing consumer behaviour, regulatory landscape and evolving technologies. The chapter will discuss past and present communication strategies, accomplishments and mistakes, and the enablers of and constraints on effective science communication.

14.2 Science Communication in Agri-food Systems

One sector that is in dire need of effective science communication strategies is that of agri-food systems. The agri-food system is a complex system with many stakeholders and is influenced by culture, history, politics, taste, nutrition, aesthetic values, health conditions, economy, personal preference, marketing, and fads and myths, besides science. This sector goes all the way to the beginning of civilisation that provides one of the basic human needs. It is also one that is infused with disruptive and emerging technologies. It is a sector that is ever evolving but unlike any other sector, emerging technologies in this sector are often scrutinised way more than others. Consumers want to feel good and safe about the food they put in their bodies and with affluence there is emotional and sentimental values attached to foods. However, impression is created by technology critics that our foods are tampered with, monopolised by corporate companies and safety is compromised.

The Food and Agriculture Organization (FAO)'s projections indicate that world food demand may increase by 70% by 2050 [FAO, 2009], and this requires all the tools in the farmers', scientists', breeders' and manufacturers' toolkits. A growing population is not the only challenge for this sector. Increase in production must be achieved while battling with emerging crop pests and diseases, shrinking arable land, growing freshwater scarcity, ageing farmers, lack of farm workers, and crises such as war, pandemic and political instability.

There is yet another major challenge to increasing agriculture productivity — sustainability. This comes from the "green lobby" or activists creating propaganda against modern agribiotechnology. Many newer technologies such as genetic modification and gene editing require approval from regulatory agencies. However, regulatory approvals do not translate into adoption as successful commercialisation is dependent on social licensing or public approvals. Social license is described as the privilege of operating with minimal formalised restrictions (legislation, regulation or market requirements) based on building and maintaining public trust [Charlebois and Sterling, 2016]. To build this social licensing, the public has to be engaged in emerging technologies and kept updated so that the public court of opinion accepts these technologies based on science and not widespread misinformation.

For emerging technologies to be adopted, effective communication strategies are crucial, and this requires concerted efforts at various levels. Capacity building to develop a pool of science communicators, incentives for scientists to engage with wider public and financial resources for communication activities, lay abstracts for journal papers, and creating science communication offices in all universities and research institutes are a few timely strategies.

This section will use case studies to illustrate situations in which science communication has led to improved acceptance of new technologies. While science communication has been receiving much attention, the failures to attain social licensing for emerging technologies in agri-food systems is still poorly understood by scientists and effective approaches are not optimally practiced. A few case studies are presented to dissect real success in handling diverse issues related to agri-food systems and factors that led to better engagement with relevant stakeholders.

14.2.1 *Case Study I: Making Churches Say "Yes" to Genetically Modified Crops in the Philippines*

Bt corn or the insect-resistant corn was first approved in the Philippines in 2002 and in 2003, a total of 10,000 hectares were planted with this corn [Panopio and Navarro, 2011]. In 2019, the total area of genetically modified (GM) corn in the Philippines was 0.9 million hectares [ISAAA, 2019]. This success did not come without any resistance from the public. In fact, the churches were one of the biggest opponents in the early years. This was a huge challenge to the scientists as religious leaders are considered as highly credible sources of information not just by the public but also by policymakers.

In early 2000, many church leaders were reluctant to support Bt corn as they feared the risk to human, animal and environmental safety, and there were concerns about corporate greed and profiteering. The technology was also seen as "playing God" in creating new plant types. It was a clear case where technical issues were downplayed and the focus was on moral, cultural and/or ideological concerns, according to Panopio and Navarro [2011]. During the height of Bt corn adoption, it was common for farmers and priests to jointly protest against the cultivation of the biotech crop. In one such gathering, organised by the Social Action Center of the Archdiocese of Jaro, Iloilo, these two stakeholder groups demanded the public to individually and collectively oppose the sale and propagation not only of Bt corn but all GM programmes [Today, 2003]. The gravity of resistance around the country caused by protests by a top influencer group is a perfect recipe to derail the biotechnology agenda.

The resistance to the Bt corn plantings triggered the need for government agencies to collaborate with academics, and all other stakeholders, and to rally together to determine a common response. The stakeholders included the SEARCA Biotechnology Information Centre, International Service for the Acquisition of Agribiotech Applications (ISAAA), Department of Science and Technology, Department of Agriculture, industry players, University Philippines (UP) Los Banos, UP Diliman, UP Mindanao, Biotechnology Coalition of the Philippines, and the Philippine Council for Agriculture Aquatic and Natural Resources Research and Development, among others. Their pioneering coordinated approaches not only silenced the protests but created more champions even among the churches. One such champion was Rev. Father Emmanuel 'Noli' Alparce from the Roman Catholic Church, who remains a strong spokesperson even today.

The result was strong statements from the leaders in the churches. Reverend Father Noli had this to say: "Biotechnology is moral because it addresses problems of poor farmers and it has a lot of potential in positively impacting humanity" [Panopio, 2009].

Workshops, popular communication materials, comics, research papers, media interviews, board games, websites, country-wide consultations, grassroots activities, roundtable discussions and exhibitions were among the multifaceted initiatives undertaken by biotechnology advocates to create a favourable environmental for adoption of GM corn.

Lessons learnt from the Philippines:

1) It is helpful to build allies and champions among the critics;
2) A strong multisectoral coalition among biotechnology advocates is needed to stage a concerted outreach effort; and
3) A combination of outreach programmes, ranging from the serious science-based events to children's activities, is essential.

14.2.2 *Case Study II: Spiritual Leader on 100-day, 30,000 km Motorbike Ride to Save Soil*

While this story may not be directly related to agribiotechnology, it is about a successful campaign to create awareness and call for action on the need to conserve soil health, a major element in ensuring food security, and closely associated with climate change mitigation.

The campaign was not initiated by someone with scientific background nor driven by government. It was the brainchild of an Indian spiritual leader, fondly known as 'Sadhguru'. With a following of 8.8 million on Instagram, 5.3 million on Facebook and 4 million on Twitter, Jaggi Vasudev (his real name) was a perfect champion to bring attention to this cause from all over the world, including world leaders.

Sadhguru even added some antics to his campaign — solo motorbike ride from London to India, across 27 countries, and jingles and dance to make the entire campaign lively and engaging for all age groups [Turns, 2022]. He founded the "Conscious Planet" global movement that seeks to bring concerted and conscious response to mitigate soil extinction [www.consciousplanet.org]. Conscious

Planet has country chapters around the world made up of volunteers and professionals of all ages. Celebrities, scientists, politicians, students, and the general public thronged to all the meetings and events as he stopped at major cities to deliver his resonating speech on the current state of soil health and the need to regenerate it. Memoranda of Understanding (MoUs) were signed along the way with world leaders and institutes.

Sadhguru spoke about reversing desertification, soil-friendly agricultural policies and practices and the role of soil in regulating planet temperature, food security and conserving water [The Petri Dish, 2022]. He is a great storyteller linking soil health to loss of livelihood, and conflict and migration, but did not fail to add some light science. He aligned his campaign with Sustainable Development Goal 15 which calls to protect, restore and promote sustainable use of terrestrial ecosystems, sustainably manage forests, combat desertification, halt and reverse land degradation and halt biodiversity loss. His messages included: Poor soil health leads to reduced nutrition in foods and demands higher use of fertilisers which leaves environmental footprint; lack of water retention ability of soil causes water scarcity, drought and flood; when carbon dioxide sequestration is reduced, there is more greenhouse gas emission that accelerates climate change.

As climate change, carbon sequestration and greenhouse gas emissions are all terms that are still abstract to most people, and also not their immediate concern, Sadhguru related failing to restore soil health to everyone's daily life. His strong message was that neglecting soil health will lead to food shortages, volatility and increases in food prices that eventually will affect public health and political stability, which are everyday worries for ordinary folks.

The 'Save Soil Movement' turned out to be a successful environmental campaign with 74 countries inking MoUs with his organisation and policy documents prepared for 198 countries [Times of India, 2022]. Whether this will transform into actions, policies and improved sustainable agriculture practices is yet to be seen. However, the campaign managed to create awareness of the current condition of soil and its importance in our lives.

Often, he was asked who he is fighting against and his answer on his Twitter was, "The Save Soil movement is a love affair with the land and life around us, not a fight with anyone."

Lessons from the 'Save Soil' campaign:

1) Engage a strong influencer with clout to resonate with the audience;
2) Hold campaigns where the element of fun is infused to show it is not a fight but a personal affair that is related to everyone;
3) Leverage on the strength of social media; and
4) Create a global pool of supporters.

14.2.3 *Case Study III: Genetically Modified Cowpea in Nigeria*

The government of Nigeria approved in 2019 GM cowpea that is resistant to an insect, the *Maruca vitrata* pod borer. It was developed by Nigeria's Institute for Agricultural Research at Ahmadu Bello University in Zaria in collaboration with American and Australian researchers. It took decades for the improved crop to reach the hands of farmers who are now seeing an increase of yields by as much as 80%. Being a staple crop in most parts of West Africa, it is expected to improve food security and livelihoods of millions of farmers and consumers.

How did Nigeria cross all the hurdles and barriers to get this crop to the farm? The main approach is achieving public enlightenment, said Prof Celestine Aguoru, president of Nigeria's National Biotechnology and Biosafety Consortium to the Alliance of Science (AfS) [Isaac, 2022]. Policymakers, rural populace and farmers were the focus. Yet, Aguoru admitted mistakes were made — public education started late "that created a vacuum that technology opponents used to sow the seeds of doubt in the hearts of many". This is a common mistake that scientists and technology developers make. Communication and public engagements are not often proactive but reactive. It is often firefighting when concerns are blown out of proportion. This is when the "mental noise" of the opponents is strong and confirmation bias is already formed against the technology, products and the developers.

Confirmation bias is the usual tendency to search for information that supports and validates any pre-existing belief when this belief is confronted with opposing concepts. Naturally, those who have negative perceptions of biotechnology will search for information from sources that criticise this technology to reinforce their belief. Early engagements offer opportunities to change the attitude and positions of biotechnology-averse audiences as there is then considerable flexibility in their beliefs.

Speaking the same language as the intended audience is another key lesson from the Nigerian experience. Cowpea is known as "beans" in Nigeria. So, when scientists kept referring it to cowpea, the public could not relate to it, and this gave an opportunity to the opponents to come out with conspiracy theories.

Dr Rose Gidado, country coordinator of the Open Forum on Agricultural Biotechnology, Nigeria chapter, told AfS that it is important to engage the critics, listen to them, "put ourselves in their shoes and make them understand" [Isaac, 2022].

Nigeria today tells her neighbouring countries in West Africa on how to engage their stakeholders to adopt GM cowpea.

Lessons from Nigeria:

1) Communication should be proactive and not reactive — Start before the opponents reach the audience;
2) Speak the same language as the audience; and
3) Have empathy, listen, and engage.

14.2.4 *Case Study IV: Tackling the Sensitivities Among Muslim Scholars*

During the mid-2000s there was much discussion on the permissibility of GM foods for Muslims among Islamic scholars and agencies in Asia. This includes Malaysia and the Philippines. The Malaysian Ministry of Health was contemplating a zero threshold for imported GM grains in their Amended Food Safety Act. The Fatwa Council in the Philippines was arguing about the permissibility of GM foods. To infuse science into these deliberations, the Malaysian Biotechnology Information Centre (MABIC) organised a dialogue among local and international scientists and officers from Malaysian Islamic authorities and state agencies in 2009. The dialogue collapsed before reaching any consensus. This was due to the highly controversial nature of the topic and its sensitivities, but the main reason was that the religious representatives were middle management officers. These officers were not confident enough in both areas — science and Islam. This was coupled with a lack of local champions who could handle the sensitivities and were bold enough to address the issues. All these shortcomings led to the suspicion among the officers that they were being 'hoodwinked' to make statements favouring a new technology. Their limited knowledge in both areas (Islam and biotechnology) created a fear of the unknown and of moving into uncharted waters.

MABIC attempted another dialogue for the second time in 2010, but this time with higher ranking international *ulama* and an organisation that has clout and credibility in the area of Islam, the International Halal Integrity Alliance. The workshop was tied to the World Halal Forum, which gave more prominence as well. Consensus was achieved that GM foods are halal as long as there are no genes from forbidden sources like porcine. This success was followed by another workshop in late 2010 involving international *ulama* and scientists where a resolution was developed to support GM foods and its research for food security [MABIC and ISAAA, 2010].

Lessons from religious discourse:

1) Religion is a contentious topic, and it must be handled by high-ranking and knowledgeable experts in that area;
2) Partner with more credible organisations to ride on their credibility; and
3) One-off engagement will not yield the desired results for topics of such magnitude and sensitivities.

14.3 Learning from the Opponents: Their Winning Tactics

Opponents of technologies do well in engaging the public and wining their trust, while scientists pale in comparison. They use some common approaches and tactics to support their cause. This section provides an analysis of some of these tactics that are found to be highly effective in shaping and influencing public opinion. Although some of these approaches might not be suitable for science-based discourses, understanding their tactics allows scientists to develop strategies to win over science-averse audiences.

14.3.1 *Fallacy Over Facts*

While scientists frame their messages to hit the brain of their audiences, the opponents outsmart the scientists as their messages are targeted to touch their audiences' hearts [Olson, 2009]. Science is downplayed, while emotions are triggered by the tactics of the opponents, which results in resistance to and fear of the technology.

This does not mean that scientists have to do the same. Scientists should acquire the skills of storytelling to gain the attention and trust of their audience. Storytelling in science communication is not all about fallacy and fiction but data that have soul. The impact of a scientist's research on anyone (patients, farmers, industry players, etc.) and how it can offer life-changing experiences are the real stories that can be combined with facts and figures to weave science into stories. Storytelling changes the narrative and is a powerful tool and approach to engage and capture audiences.

14.3.2 *Enculturation of Science*

Failing to understand the role of moral values in contentious debates explains why public discourses sometimes fail [Waldhof and Pies, 2020]. Scientists are often fixated with facts and data, and fail to incorporate moral values and cultural beliefs. This alienates them from their audience. Scientists also commonly do not connect their research to everyday life. The research is made to look very remote and abstract, and that creates the fear factor.

Enculturation of science is important as any research area can be made relevant to the public. Science and technology can be communicated with cultural references that connect with the target audience. This helps build a relationship between the communicator and the audience and opens doors for discussion even if there are opposing views of a technology. These engagements also help elicit more interactions, actions from the audience and social licensing. For example, genetic modification could be introduced through cheese making instead of crop improvement to gain approval. Cheese is connected to many cultures and the traditional process of making cheese requires enzymes from the stomach lining of calves. Showing how GM technology helped save calves from being slaughtered might resonate well with cultures where cheese is an important part of their cuisines, or even with vegans and vegetarians.

14.3.3 *Shoot the Message, not the Messenger*

Scientists who support technologies that are commercialised by industry players are often accused of collaborating with industry or receiving industry funding. Opponents of such technologies disregard them as untrustworthy source of information. Scientists resort to disassociating themselves from industry players to avoid any such unpleasant experience that jeopardises their credibility. This, however, does not solve the problem. The public must be made to understand that many biotechnology critics are also supported by the industry such as the organic farming industry and makers of organic personal care products among others. Many social media influencers who are opponents of biotechnology are even either selling their own products or endorsing brands that pay them.

Scientists should start educating the public that most innovations which play a crucial role in all aspects of our lives are from the industry. The public must be empowered to evaluate the technology based on science and to address issues through the lens of science and stop demonising the industry. It is also time to stop the age-old defence mechanism used by scientists where they confess of not receiving any money from the industry. Instead, they should explain to the public the role of industry in all other technological areas, the responsible practices in corporate sectors, and the need for collaborations.

14.4 The Long Road to Victory

Experience has shown that there is no shortcut to change public attitude and trust, and to build political will. Scientists have been staying in the ivory tower and refusing to change their narratives for too long. It is time for scientists to step out from their comfort zone and engage with the public and be the spokesperson for science. This was how Neal Lane, former National Science Foundation director and science advisor to President Clinton, described a civic scientist: "A 'civic scientist' to me is a true scientist who uses his or her knowledge, accomplishments, and analytical skills to help bridge the gap between science and society" [Lane, 1999].

For this to happen, scientists must first realise their role as communicators and not just as researchers or educators. Here are some recommendations to make this happen:

- Develop national policy on science communication and public engagement
    - This will be the top-down approach to ensure funding, human resource, capacity building and incentives are in place to support science communication;

- Establish science communication offices in all universities and research institutes
  - Dedicated science communicators are hired to support scientists in their public and media engagement roles, conduct science communication trainings, and develop science communication strategies for the institute;
  - This is different from the role of Public Relations and Corporate Affairs office as they are focused on branding the institute;
- Introduce science communication modules in all STEM programmes in the universities
  - It is important to instil science communication skills and aspiration before scientists start their careers;
  - Early training will also create industry players, regulators, policymakers, teachers and any other STEM professionals who are good science communicators;
- Include layperson abstract in all journals
  - This will allow research papers to be understood by non-technical stakeholders;
  - It will also be important training for scientists to express the work in layperson language;
- Allocate a small percentage of research grants for science communication/society engagement
  - This is an obligation for scientists to allocate their time for public engagement;
- Training for scientists on science communication
  - To help develop a pool of science communicators among scientists as most are not familiar with this area;
- Incentives for civic scientists
  - Incentives in the form of professional growth just like how journal papers and patents are used as key performance indicators.

Science has to be made fashionable. As much as we need a science-literate public, we also need public-literate scientists — scientists who have empathy towards the non-technical audience; who speak their language; who infuse culture, traditional values and beliefs, and furthermore, those who relate science to everyday aspects of life. The interest in science must be ignited and made infectious.

14.5 Conclusion

According to the FAO, the undernourished population in Asia increased from 361 million to 418 million between 2019 and 2020 and the COVID-19 pandemic escalated this [Schipper *et al.*, 2022]. Prior to the pandemic, Asia was already battling with climate change, volatile world food prices [Carrasco and Zhang, 2022], an ageing farming community, and lack of home-grown agribiotechnology and supporting regulatory frameworks, all of which contributed to its food insecurity. While issues related to the macro economy cannot be addressed through science and technology, the development and adoption of technologies that support agriculture could be elevated through public-private and multilateral research cooperation, regulatory harmonisation, investment and public acceptance of such technologies. All these require effective communication strategies as they involve building political will to support emerging technologies, development of science-based policies and regulations by experts such as regulators, scientists and policymakers, and social licensing from the public.

It must be realised that emerging technologies in agriculture require strong and effective communication strategies for research and development to reach the consumers as the fear of the unknown is prevalent among the public as well as policymakers. Adoption, approval and public acceptance of foods from modern agribiotechnologies involve a complex network of stakeholders with diverse views and backgrounds. These stakeholders require customised messages and regular engagements, making science communication an integral part of efforts to achieve food security.

References

Arujanan, M. (2022). What's with that 'Save the Soil' campaign of Sadhguru? *The Petri Dish.* https://thepetridish.my/2022/06/15/whats-with-that-save-the-soil-campaign-of-sadhguru/

Burns, T. W., O'Connor, D. J. and Stocklmayer, S. M. (2003). Science communication: a contemporary definition. *Public Understanding of Science*, 12, pp. 183–202.

Carrasco, B. and Zhang, Q. (2022). Confronting Asia's triple threat: climate change, biodiversity loss, food insecurity. *ADB Blog*. https://blogs.adb.org/blog/confronting-asia-s-triple-threat-climate-change-biodiversity-loss-and-food-insecurity

Conscious Planet. (n.d.). https://consciousplanet.org/

FAO. (2009). High level expert forum — how to feed the world in 2050. https://www.fao.org/fileadmin/templates/wsfs/docs/Issues_papers/HLEF2050_Global_Agriculture.pdf

ISAAA. (2019). *Global Status of Commercialized Biotech/GM Crops in 2019: Biotech Crops Drive SocioEconomic Development and Sustainable Environment in the New Frontier.* https://www.isaaa.org/resources/publications/briefs/55/

Isaac, N. (2022). Nigeria: learn from our experience with GM crops. *Alliance for Science.* https://allianceforscience.org/blog/2022/07/nigeria-learn-from-our-experience-with-gmo-crops/

Lane, N. (1999). *The Civic Scientist and Science Policy*. AAAS Science and Technology Policy Yearbook.

MABIC and ISAAA. (2010). *International Workshop for Islamic Scholars on Agribiotechnology: Shariah Compliance*. Georgetown, Penang, Malaysia (1–2 December 2010). http://bic.org.my/wp-content/uploads/2019/07/penang.pdf

Olson, P. (2009). *Don't Be Such a Scientist: Talking Substance in an Age of Style*. Island Press.

Panopio, J. (2009). Fr. Emmanuel Alparce: The Morality of Genetic Engineering. In M. J. Navarro (Ed.), *Communicating Crop Biotechnology: Stories from Stakeholders*, pp. 134–136. International Service for the Acquisition of Agri-biotech Applications (ISAAA).

Panopio, J. and Navarro, M. J. (2011). Drama and Communication Behind Asia's First Commercialized Bt Corn. In M. J. Navarro and R. A. Hautea (Eds.), *Communication Challenges and Convergence in Crop Biotechnology*. International Service for the Acquisition of Agri-biotech Applications (ISAAA).

Schipper, S., Crowley, S. and Firshan, K. (2022). Millions are going hungry in post pandemic Asia: Here's how to respond. *ADB Blog*. https://blogs.adb.org/blog/millions-are-going-hungry-in-post-pandemic-asia-here-s-how-to-respond

Times of India. (2022). Sadhguru, Karnataka CM Basavaraj Bommai to sign MoU today on 'saving soil'. https://timesofindia.indiatimes.com/city/bengaluru/sadhguru-karnataka-cm-basavaraj-bommai-to-sign-mou-today-on-saving-soil/articleshow/92311271.cms

Today. (2003). Illoilo. Farmers, Priests Support Anti-Bt Corn Hunger Strike. Media release, May 18, 2003.

Turns, A. (2022). Indian mystic Sadhguru on 100-day motorbike mission to save soil. *The Guardian*. https://www.theguardian.com/environment/2022/mar/19/indian-mystic-sadhgurus-19000-mile-trip-to-save-soil-aoe

Waldhof, G. and Pies, I. (2020). Conflicting values in the German GMO debate? Leibniz-*Institut für Agrarentwicklung in Transformationsökonomien (IAMO)*. https://www.iamo.de/fileadmin/user_upload/iamo2020_en_c8.pdf

https://doi.org/10.1142/9789811278297_0015

Chapter 15

Private Sector Investments in Agrifoodtech to Improve Food Security

Rob Hulme

CEO and Group Director, The Boralis Group Pty. Ltd., Sydney, Australia

15.1 Introduction

The private sector has a crucial role in helping to address global challenges around food security by raising food production, enhancing efficiency, and lowering costs by investing in infrastructure, commercialisation, and research and development (R&D) [FAO, 2020].

Many private sector players participate in different stages of the food system, such as input supply, production, processing, retail, and consumption. These organisations exist in both the formal and informal sectors. They can be small, medium, or large agricultural farms, food value chain businesses, individual entrepreneurs, family-owned companies, cooperatives, social enterprises, or large corporations [Ligot and Deau, 2016]. Recently, non-traditional sector actors like water and energy companies, tech companies, pension and private funds, and insurance companies have become more involved [Reardon and Timmer, 2012].

Over the past decade, the agrifoodtech sector has experienced an unprecedented increase in investment, signalling growing confidence in the potential of technology to transform food production. Key macro drivers include population growth and urbanisation, climate change and water scarcity, requiring significant improvements in food production efficiency and productivity [FAO *et al.*, 2023].

Investing in the agrifoodtech sector can be rewarding and profitable, but it comes with challenges and risks. The sector has a complex and unpredictable regulatory landscape, and investors must navigate technological obsolescence and market adoption barriers. To make informed decisions, investors need a comprehensive understanding of the sector and the inherent risks associated with food production, which typically has long production lead times and complex supply chain structures. This requires patient capital that matches the cyclical nature of agricultural production.

Private investors can be incentivised to bring capital, energy, modern technology, and management experience to improve supply chain efficiency and reduce losses [Kopicki, 2011]. In this context, the private sector brings unique resources, innovation, and scale-up capabilities, making it a key contributor to addressing food security challenges.

15.1.1 *Resources*

Developing new agricultural technologies is a capital-intensive process that requires significant investment to drive research, development, and market penetration strategies. Private companies have the necessary resources and expertise to invest in R&D activities to improve agricultural practices, develop new technologies, and enhance crop productivity. By conducting R&D

efforts, the private sector can contribute to develop innovative solutions that increase food production and improve agricultural efficiency.

15.1.2 *Innovation*

Innovation is pivotal in agrifoodtech as companies constantly strive to enhance efficiency, yield, and sustainability through new technologies and practices. In creating something new that adds value, keeping up with these innovations is essential for investors seeking promising opportunities. At the same time, it's important to recognise that investment in innovation in fast-moving technological sectors can also pose risks such as obsolescence. What may seem revolutionary today could become outdated in only a few years.

Private companies often invest in and have access to cutting-edge innovative technologies and possess the necessary expertise to apply these technologies to the agricultural sector. This expertise includes advances in synthetic chemistry, precision agriculture, biotechnology, smart decision-making algorithms, and digital platforms, which can significantly improve crop and animal productivity, resource utilisation, and overall efficiency in food production.

15.1.3 *Scale*

Private companies typically excel at commercialising innovative products and technologies as catalysts to scale commercially viable solutions. Their ability to bring products to market efficiently and at scale can accelerate the adoption of new agricultural practices, increase the availability of improved seeds and fertilisers, and facilitate the dissemination of advanced farming techniques.

15.2 Drivers for Private Investment

Identifying and aligning with the private sector's key drivers of investments in agrifoodtech is critical for improving solutions' development, adoption, and scaling. These typically include the following.

15.2.1 *Profit*

Return on investment to shareholders primarily occurs when investments in technologies and practices help improve profitability, reduce costs, increase revenue, and improve market share and brand equity, which drives private companies. The private sector helps foster an entrepreneurial culture encouraging innovation, risk taking, and adaptation to market dynamics. Agrifoodtech incubator and accelerator programmes have been established by venture capital groups and multinational corporations seeking to make early-stage investments, often in conjunction with sovereign wealth capital.

15.2.2 *Capital*

The private sector has significant financial resources that can be used to improve food security through research, development, and technology implementation. These resources include investments in agricultural startups and scaleups, innovative technology development, and infrastructure projects that enhance food production, processing, storage, and distribution efficiency. Vital infrastructure, such as insurance, public utilities, public works, transportation, and research facilities is also crucial for agricultural development [Post *et al.*, 2021].

15.2.3 *Reputation*

Many private companies believe they are responsible to their shareholders to help address global challenges such as food insecurity. The "triple bottom line" approach incorporating People, Planet, and Profit is often referenced by companies seeking to validate corporate credentials, acknowledging the public sentiment's important role in a company's valuation. In recent times, publicly listed corporations have been increasingly focused on the social impacts of climate change and meeting carbon emission targets as drivers of environment, social, and governance (ESG) performance metrics.

15.2.4 *Regulation*

Governments increasingly regulate the food sector to ensure food safety, protect the environment, and promote sustainable agricultural practices. These regulations create new opportunities for private companies to engage with government regulators and align with investment priorities in food security. A good example is Singapore, where the government actively provides regulatory support to encourage the rigorous safety of products before the market entry of new protein production categories, including precision fermentation-based products (cellular agriculture).

15.3 Private Capital Sources in Food and Agriculture

With an increasing focus on sustainable development and emerging technologies, investors will continue to channel capital into innovative solutions that address pressing global challenges. The Asia-Pacific region is well positioned to attract significant private investments due to the increasing population base and resulting demand for food. Sources of private capital in the food and agriculture sectors include the following.

15.3.1 *Banks*

Banks traditionally provide debt financing and credit facilities to food production, processing, distribution, and retail businesses. They provide specialised financing options to meet the unique requirements of agricultural enterprises, such as short-term working capital loans for seasonal operations, long-term loans for land acquisition and infrastructure development, and trade finance products to ease cross-border trade [FAO, 2017]. Some prominent banks involved in financing food and agriculture activities include Rabobank, ANZ Bank, Commonwealth Bank of Australia, National Australia Bank, Westpac Banking Corporation, Agricultural Bank of China, Asian Development Bank, and Industrial & Commercial Bank of China.

15.3.2 *High Net-Worth Individuals*

High net-worth individuals are another valuable source of private capital in the food and agriculture industries. These wealthy investors often diversify their portfolios by investing in different asset classes, such as farmland or agribusinesses, to achieve higher returns and mitigate risk. A study by Global AgInvesting [2020] revealed that high net-worth individuals had shown increased interest in allocating more assets to agriculture-related investments due to factors like growing global demand for food, attractive returns on investment, portfolio diversification benefits, and opportunities for positive social impact. For example, Australian billionaire Andrew Forrest has invested over USD 100 million into agricultural innovation projects such as carbon farming techniques through his Minderoo Foundation.

15.3.3 *Private Equity*

Private equity firms also contribute significantly to the flow of private capital into food and agriculture ventures. These firms typically provide funding through equity investments or buyouts with a medium- to long-term horizon, partnering with companies at various life cycle stages, from startups to mature businesses seeking expansion or exit strategies. In recent years, the Asia-Pacific region has witnessed a surge in private equity deals within the agrifood sector.

Some noteworthy examples include PAG Asia Capital's acquisition of Golden Foods Group from Primavera Capital Group in 2020, Proterra Investment Partners' acquisition of Emerald Grain in 2014, and KKR's investment in Sundrop Farms in 2014.

15.3.4 *Venture Capital*

Venture capital funds represent a critical component of the private capital landscape for food and agriculture enterprises. AgrifoodTech represents a relatively nascent sector [Montesclaros and Teng, 2018], driven by new enabling technologies, and requires patient capital, typically in a 7- to 10-year investment cycle, much longer than the Silicon Valley approach. These funds primarily focus on early-stage investments in high-growth startups, offering financial capital, strategic guidance, and industry connections. In the Asia-Pacific region, numerous venture capital firms have demonstrated interest in backing food tech and agritech innovations that address food security, sustainable farming practices, and efficient supply chain management. Some notable examples include IDG Capital's investment in China's Pinduoduo[1] and Temasek Holdings' participation in a funding round for India-based agribusiness DeHaat.[2] Mike Cannon-Brookes, an Australian billionaire and co-founder of software company Atlassian, continues to invest in a range of clean energy investments through his company Grok Ventures.

---

[1] Pinduoduo: https://pinduoduo.com/en/

[2] Dehaat: https://agrevolution.in/

15.3.5 *Family Offices*

Family offices constitute another essential source of private capital for the food and agriculture sectors. These entities manage investments for wealthy families or individuals with significant assets, often seeking long-term growth opportunities while preserving wealth across generations. Many family offices are increasingly attracted to the food and agriculture space due to its potential for providing stable returns and aligning with their values-driven investment approach. For example, Singapore-based Blue Planet Environmental Solutions raised $25 million from the Neev Fund, a joint venture between the State Bank of India and the UK's Department for International Development, and other investors, including family offices.

15.3.6 *Pension Funds*

Pension funds represent another substantial investor group within the food and agriculture sector. With significant pools of capital available for long-term deployment, pension funds often seek low-risk investments capable of generating steady cash flows over extended periods. Consequently, they find agricultural assets like farmland or timberland appealing due to their relatively stable return profile and inflation-hedging qualities. In recent years, some prominent pension funds have made sizeable allocations to agriculture-related investments in the Asia-Pacific region, such as Australia's First State Super acquiring a stake in New South Wales almond farms.

15.4 Investment Themes in Agrifoodtech

The potential within the farming industry is immense, ranging from startups inventing revolutionary equipment and software to established companies driving sustainable agricultural practices forward. However, seizing the appropriate opportunity requires a understanding of this sector and what is required to deliver potential return on investment.

In the agrifoodtech industry, innovation serves as a powerful catalyst. Companies continuously strive to enhance efficiency, productivity, and sustainability by developing novel technologies and methods. Staying updated on these advancements to invest in this sector effectively can uncover fruitful prospects. What may be regarded as groundbreaking today could quickly become outdated within a short time.

The private sector continues to invest in critical areas of R&D, infrastructure, capability, and capacity building, all of which contribute to improved food security. In addition to their in-house R&D programmes, private companies allocate significant resources to agricultural research institutions, universities, and other collaboration partners to develop new farming techniques, crop varieties, and sustainable agricultural practices. These investments improve crop yields, enhance disease and pest resistance, and establish climate-resilient farming methods.

Several critical areas of agrifoodtech investment focus for the private sector include the following.

15.4.1 *Advanced Breeding*

Genetic modification was first recorded 10,000 years ago in Southwest Asia, where humans first bred plants through artificial selection and selective crossbreeding [Santra *et al.*, 2017]. This conventional process typically takes many years and has a high associated cost, often producing variable results where unwanted traits appear alongside desired characteristics.

Biotechnology and genetic engineering offer innovative solutions to enhance crop characteristics, improve biotic resistance to pests and diseases, and increase resilience to extreme environmental conditions such as drought and flooding. These crops can be developed and launched in a reduced timeframe, helping farmers manage risk and deliver stable and reliable food production even in challenging climates.

Genetically Modified Organisms (GMOs, or transgenic crops) include genetically engineered crops launched in the mid-1990s. These crops provided farmers with additional agronomic tools to improve yield and rotations by exhibiting tolerance to certain insect pests, diseases, and weeds while reducing applications of synthetic agrochemicals [Raman, 2017]. Transgenic crops offer farmers greater flexibility in managing crops, increased productivity, and environmental benefits by reducing the use of pesticides [Post *et al.*, 2021]. Today, over 90% of the corn, soybeans, and sugar beets available globally come from GMOs. An essential reason that large companies are the sole providers of GMO crops is that they are costly to develop and carry substantial risk in terms of deregulation. Complex requirements must be established before a GMO can be approved, so only the most prominent companies can afford to comply [Zeigler, 2019].

In 2012, Emmanuelle Charpentier and Jennifer Doudna developed a new method for editing genes called CRISPR-Cas9 (Clustered Regularly Interspaced Short Palindromic Repeats). This technology precisely cuts DNA and allows natural DNA repair processes, resulting in high-precision genome editing. Gene editing is a relatively new technology that offers accurate and precise plant and animal breeding improvements. It also speeds up the component processes at a reduced cost. This gene editing technology is significantly more cost effective for crop breeding programmes, making it accessible to a broader range of seed companies, breeders, farmers, and consumers [Charpentier, 2020]. Gene editing can enhance the value of overlooked crops and underutilised species, often making them nutritious and adapted to challenging environments [Ray *et al.*, 2017].

In traditional wheat breeding, the uniformity of lines derived from a breeding population is developed through repeated breeding from the F1, which can take up to ten years. Doubled haploid technology, a relatively recent plant breeding technique, utilises androgenesis and embryo culture to significantly reduce cultivar development and launch timelines [Santra *et al.*, 2017].

Submergence stress from monsoonal rains and flooding is estimated to cause annual (rice crop) losses of up to US$1 billion in Asia, adversely impacting around 20 million hectares of crops. Modern rice varieties adapted to these conditions help farmers minimise yield impacts. A specific gene (Sub1A) confers submergence tolerance in lowland rice that dampens ethylene production, allowing rice to recover after flooding [Fukao *et al.*, 2006].

Crop breeding has traditionally focused on enhanced tolerance to biotic (pests, diseases) and abiotic (temperature, moisture) stresses that can impact yield potential. The recent development of dual-purpose wheat and canola varieties has allowed extended livestock grazing without impacting grain yield at harvest, reducing reliance on hay and silage production.

15.4.2 *Precision Fermentation*

Precision fermentation is a type of synthetic biology that has existed for many years. It involves engineering the gene sequence of a specific protein into a bacterium or yeast strain, which is then grown in large-scale fermenters to produce the desired protein. This technology has been used in biotechnology for decades, previously known as "recombinant protein production". It has been adopted for various vaccines and drugs, including insulin [Wood and Tavan, 2022].

Cheese production relies on chymosin, a genetically modified source of enzymes required to coagulate milk. Initially, this enzyme was derived from calves' stomachs [Wood *et al.*, 2023]. Precision fermentation also allows for the creation of new plant proteins. Impossible Foods,[3] for example, has developed heme as an iron-containing molecule that provides the look and smell of red meat when cooked in plant-based burgers. Heme was initially extracted from soybean plants, but it is now produced more efficiently through precision fermentation using a genetically engineered yeast containing the soy leghemoglobin gene.

Recently, many companies have focused on creating cell-based meats with the help of private sector investments. They aim to produce meat without slaughtering animals. When Singapore approved the first global deregulation of cultured chicken breast in December 2020, it piqued significant interest. Eat Just GOOD Meat, now one of the most well-funded cultivated meat companies at $465 million, received approval for sale in Singapore. Singapore-based fund Temasek has invested in companies that work with precision fer-

[3] Impossible Foods: https://impossiblefoods.com/

mentation and cell-based foods, such as Upside Foods, The Every Company, and Perfect Day. Although the industry has had a promising start, it faces significant challenges, such as high scaling costs in large bioreactors, significant volumes of complex media, and post-production processing and quality control processes.

15.4.3 *Plant-Based Meat*

The plant-based meat industry has gained popularity recently due to its potential to address human health, animal welfare, and climate change issues. Plant-based meat alternatives are typically derived from soybean, pea protein or mycoprotein isolates, with companies such as Impossible Foods, Beyond Meat,[4] V2Food,[5] Quorn,[6] Green Rebel Foods[7] and Fable Foods,[8] all attracting significant investment and market attention, particularly in high-income countries. However, perceptions of over-processing and consumer acceptance remain challenging for future growth, where price, taste, and convenience are the primary drivers of consumer purchase behaviours compared to animal-based proteins.

15.4.4 *Precision Agriculture*

Private sector investments in precision agriculture technologies revolutionise farming practices by incorporating data-driven decision making and precision application of resources. Precision agriculture solutions greatly rely on hardware and software components,

---

[4] Beyond Meat: https://www.beyondmeat.com/en-US/

[5] V2Food: https://v2food.com/

[6] Quorn: https://www.quorn.com.au/

[7] Green Rebel: https://greenrebelfoods.com/

[8] Fable Food: https://fablefood.co/

as they serve as the foundation that gathers data for analytics. This crucial information aids farmers in making informed decisions.

Additionally, these platforms leverage artificial intelligence (AI) technology to offer predictive analytics capabilities. Precision agriculture tools — including sensors, drones, robotics, and satellite imagery — enable farmers to monitor real-time data, including soil conditions, weather patterns, crop and animal health, pest and disease infestation and irrigation needs, efficiently and effectively. These technologies provide farmers with valuable insights for informed decision making, delivering cost savings while improving returns. Examples of privately funded Australian agtech companies making advances in this area include remote monitoring solutions from Farmbot,[9] which has reduced labour costs and hours manually checking livestock watering systems, and remote monitoring of livestock location and animal productivity solutions from CeresTag.[10]

Digital technologies and data analytics revolutionise agricultural practices by providing farmers access to market information, financial services, and tools for supply chain optimisation. Digital platforms connect farmers to market information, helping them make informed decisions about crop selection, pricing, and market trends. Additionally, these platforms enable access to financial services, empowering farmers with cent and expansion. CropIn[11] is an Indian agtech startup that utilises data analytics, AI, and remote sensing technologies to enable precision agriculture. Their platform offers real-time crop monitoring, pest management solutions, and

[9] Farmbot: https://farmbot.com.au/

[10] CeresTag: https://cerestag.com/

[11] Cropin: https://www.cropin.com/

personalised agronomic advice. CropIn's solutions have significantly improved crop productivity, reduced input costs, and optimised resource utilisation for farmers in India.

The use of big data analytics and AI in agriculture allows for the processing and analysis of large volumes of data. The application of satellite imagery combined with weather, crop yield and soil data enable farmers to have more accurate insights for crop management decisions. These insights allow users to reallocate human resources dedicated to 4D (dirty, dangerous, dull and dumb) tasks, often highly precarious, menial and with a high risk of repetitive strain injury and focus more on value-adding activities involving innovation, insight, and intuition [Frison, 2016]. Objective data-driven insights provide decision support, help optimise production processes, forecast market demand more accurately, and improve overall production and processing efficiency. The result is less post-harvest losses, food waste, and timely produce delivery to consumers, enhancing food security. The Climate Corporation, a Bayer subsidiary, uses AI and machine learning algorithms to provide farmers with data-driven insights and recommendations for optimal crop management, helping them increase productivity and sustainability.

15.4.5 *Supply Chain*

Investing in infrastructure and supply chains has become essential for adequate food production, storage, and distribution. Private companies invest in storage facilities, warehouses, and cold chain logistics to reduce post-harvest losses and improve food safety. In 2022, JBS Foods (Canada) partnered with New Zealand-based Scott Technology for a US$71 million automation project to develop a fully automated warehousing system for the Brooks facility. Previous investments have also resulted in robotic processing innovations [Oatman, 2022], enabling the efficient handling, preservation, and transportation of perishable food products, extending their shelf-life, and maintaining their nutritional value.

Adequate storage facilities help maintain the quality and freshness of agricultural produce, extending its market availability and reducing waste. Innovations in food packaging can preserve the quality, safety, and nutritional value of food products, meet consumer needs and preferences, reduce food loss and waste, and lower the cost of nutritious foods, especially across longer supply chains. Recent developments in shelf-life extension treatments, such as Apeel,[12] have helped improve saleable produce and reduce waste, enhancing the profitability of farmers and wholesalers. Circular packaging solutions can include redesigning packaging formats and delivery models, introducing reusable packaging, and improving the economics and quality of recycled plastic materials [Oatman, 2022].

Nanotechnology shows potential for food processing innovations. Companies are now using nanotechnology to develop intelligent packaging systems that regulate gas composition, temperature, and humidity within food packaging, reducing spoilage and preserving freshness [Singh *et al.*, 2017]. Nanosensors and nanocoatings can detect and prevent microbial contamination, extending the shelf-life of perishable products and improving food safety, quality, and nutritional value. Nanoparticles can also enhance the bioavailability of nutrients, addressing malnutrition and micronutrient deficiencies. Blockchain and other technologies enhance transparency and traceability in the food supply chain. Investing in these technologies can improve efficiency and meet the growing consumer demand for

---

[12] Apeel: https://www.apeel.com/

transparency. Escavox[13] provides track-and-trace technology for food supply chains, providing real-time visibility to reduce rejections and waste.

15.4.6 *Digital Marketplaces*

Private sector investments in digital platforms connect farmers to markets, enabling them to access buyers and receive fair prices for their produce. Online marketplaces, mobile applications, and e-commerce platforms streamline the agricultural value chain, providing farmers with market information, access to financial services, and direct market linkages. TaniHub[14] is an Indonesian startup connecting smallholder farmers with markets and financial services through a digital platform. With total private funding of $94.5 million, TaniGroup's initiatives have empowered farmers in Indonesia by increasing their income, reducing post-harvest losses, and improving market access.

Blockchain technology offers unprecedented transparency and traceability in the food supply chain, where secure and decentralised recording of transactions enables stakeholders to track the journey of food products from farm to fork. This transparency enhances food safety, ensures fair trade, and reduces fraud and counterfeiting. In Asia, the Golden Agri-Resources Group has implemented blockchain technology to trace the palm oil supply chain, providing consumers and stakeholders with visibility into the sourcing and sustainability of palm oil, promoting responsible practices, and mitigating environmental and social risks. The DCX Group[15]

[13] Escavox: https://www.escavox.com/

[14] TaniHub: http://www.tanihub.com

[15] DCX Group: https://www.dcx.group/

established Rice Exchange, backed by lead investor Wavemaker,[16] to establish a transparent global marketplace for rice trade and other agricultural commodities.

15.4.7 *Training and Extension*

Building capacity and capability in food production requires a practical yet effective knowledge extension platform, empowering farmers and agribusinesses to adopt new technologies and practices. Limited awareness and knowledge about new technologies can impede their adoption by farmers. Resistance to change and scepticism among farmers can hinder the extension and adoption of new technologies. Private sector investments should include awareness campaigns, training programmes, and knowledge-sharing platforms to educate farmers about the benefits and proper use of innovative solutions. Collaboration with agricultural extension services, farmer organisations, and academic institutions can help disseminate information and build capacity among farmers. Demonstrations and field trials can also provide practical insights into the effectiveness and advantages of technology adoption.

Training and extension programmes that empower farmers with knowledge, skills, and technology adoption are critical for sustainable and efficient food production. These programmes provide farmers with in-field demonstrations and essential information on improved agronomic techniques, climate-smart practices, and sustainable resource management, helping build the capability and capacity required to drive productivity and resilience. These initiatives include digital connectivity and skills to effectively utilise

---

[16] Wavemaker: https://wavemaker.vc/

precision agriculture tools, digital platforms, and other technological innovations.

Nestlé's Nescafé Plan[17] is a sustainable coffee-sourcing initiative that supports smallholder coffee farmers in Vietnam. The programme focuses on training farmers in sustainable coffee cultivation practices, improving coffee quality, and providing fair prices. By participating in the Nescafé Plan, smallholder coffee farmers in Vietnam have experienced increased productivity, higher incomes, and improved livelihoods.

The Olam Farmer Information System (OFIS)[18] is a comprehensive digital platform that provides smallholder farmers access to agricultural inputs, training, and market information. OFIS is active in multiple countries across Asia, including India, Vietnam, and Indonesia. The initiative has empowered smallholder farmers by equipping them with knowledge, improving their productivity and income, and providing them with fair market access.

15.4.8 *Climate-Smart Technologies*

Climate-smart technologies focus on developing innovative solutions that enhance agricultural resilience to climate change, conserve natural resources, and reduce greenhouse gas emissions.

Climate-resilient crop varieties exhibit enhanced tolerance to biotic (pests and diseases) and abiotic (climatic-related) stresses

---

[17] Nestlé Nescafé Plan: www.nestle.com/media/pressreleases/allpressreleases/sustainable-coffee-Nescafe-plan-2030

[18] OFIS: https://www.ofi.com/innovation/digital-technology-and-tools/olam-farmer-information-system.html

that can impact yield potential. The development of rice varieties tolerant to submergence during monsoonal flooding in tropical systems.

The recent increase in dual-purpose wheat and canola crops has allowed extended livestock grazing without impacting grain yield at harvest. Farmers can mitigate the negative impacts of extreme weather events by cultivating climate-resilient crops and ensuring a stable food supply even under challenging conditions.

Improved land management and carbon sequestration practices, such as conservation agriculture, agroforestry, intensive grazing, and perennial intraspecies planting, can help to enhance soil health, conserve water, and mitigate greenhouse gas emissions, contributing to a more sustainable and resilient food system. Private sector investment in companies developing carbon sequestration and offsets has increased significantly recently. Loam Bio[19] was founded in 2019 and has developed microbial seed treatments that, when inoculated onto the seed, help plants sequester soil carbon. Loam Bio has raised AUD 155 million from three funding rounds, initially backed by Horizon Ventures[20] led by Australian billionaire Mike Cannon-Brookes.

Investing in agricultural companies that promote renewable energy can yield significant benefits. The increased prevalence of technologies such as solar panels, heat transfer pumps, geothermal, wind turbines, and bioenergy systems helps lower carbon emissions and offers long-term cost savings. In the face of the growing global emphasis on sustainability, farms implementing renewable energy

[19] Loam Bio: https://www.loambio.com/

[20] Horizon Ventures: https://www.horizonsventures.com/

solutions could gain a competitive edge, making it an attractive investment opportunity.

In recent years, investing in companies that manage and extract value from agricultural waste has increased as part of a circular economy focus. New technologies to valorise excess and graded whole-crop waste into value-added snack foods offer new market opportunities for otherwise discarded produce. Processing and food waste traditionally fed to livestock or sent to landfills can be further utilised to extract water, nutrients, ingredients, and organic materials.

One company, Botanical Water Technologies,[21] is extracting water from fruit, vegetable, and sugarcane processing waste, which can be used for drinking water, diverted into environmental flows, or recharging of aquifers. This approach helps farmers reduce waste and earn extra income while promoting sustainability, making waste-transforming technologies a potential investment opportunity.

15.4.9 *Controlled Environment Agriculture*

Controlled environment agriculture encompasses numerous intensive crop production technologies, including hydroponics, aeroponics, and aquaponics, typically applied in indoor (vertical farms) or outdoor (greenhouse) typologies. Vertical farming enterprises such as Plenty, Aerofarms,[22] Kalera[23] and Sustenir[24] have attracted significant investment over the last decade in short-season, leafy vegetable and micro-herb production concentrated in

[21] Botanical Water Technologies: https://www.wegrowwater.com/

[22] Aerofarms: https://www.aerofarms.com/

[23] Kalera: https://kalera.com/

[24] Sustenir: https://sustenir.com/

urban environments. This technology is highly productive and uses significantly less water than conventional farming systems, but it is also energy intensive as temperature, humidity, and lighting are artificially created. It requires significant capital, dedicated facilities, and specialised crop varieties. By comparison, hybrid greenhouse operations like ComCrop[25] in Singapore and Perfection Fresh[26] in Australia utilise natural light augmented with artificial light derived from renewable energy sources, and mainstream plants are often grown hydroponically. These systems generally offer more attractive unit economics and lower operating costs.

15.5 Agrifoodtech Investment Trends

15.5.1 *History*

From 1990 to 2014, private spending on agricultural R&D worldwide more than tripled, with companies based in high-income countries accounting for 88% of global private agricultural R&D spending but still focused on a relatively small number of commodities [Fuglie, 2016].

Traditionally, private sector investments by multinationals in food and agriculture have been reported at up to 15% of net revenue. Here, resources are allocated to internal R&D programmes to generate proprietary innovation. Bayer CropScience reported 2022 R&D investments comprising 7,000 employees and €2.6 billion. At approximately 10% of revenue, this is consistent with other major manufacturers such as Syngenta, Corteva, and BASF, where investments focus on biotechnology (seed trait development), digital

[25] ComCrop: http://comcrop.com/

[26] Perfection Fresh: https://www.perfection.com.au/home

farming tools, and crop protection active ingredients (synthetic and biological) [Bayer Annual Report, 2022].

For the 11 years from 2012 to 2022, an estimated $196 billion was invested across the agrifoodtech sector. This investment peaked in 2021, when venture capital and private equity firms' ability to access cheap money at historically low interest rates, combined with inflated technology valuations, helped drive a record-breaking $53.2 billion investment in agrifoodtech funding (Figure 15.1).

Then, in 2022, the market crashed due to war in Ukraine, inflation, higher interest rates, and continued supply chain disruptions. Investor sentiment fell sharply, with a 44% year-over-year decline to $29.6 billion in total investment and a 19% decline in deals closed. The result was a significant contraction and consolidation in the Vertical Farming, Cellular Agriculture and Alternative Protein segments, except for Plenty ($400 million Series E), Upside Foods ($400 million Series C) and Vow ($49.2 million Series A). Conversely, funding increased in agricultural biotech, bioenergy,

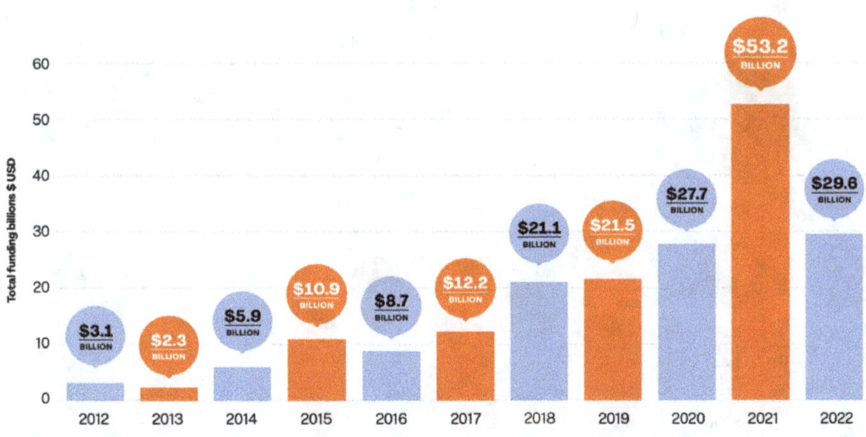

Figure 15.1 Global agrifoodtech investment by year. Source: AgFunder [2023].

biomaterials, farm management software and Internet of Things (IoT), and novel farming systems [AgFunder, 2023].

15.5.2 *Regional Investment*

Investment capability and supporting ecosystems for agrifoodtech vary by region. While some regions, such as the Asia-Pacific and Europe, have seen significant investment in agrifoodtech ventures, others, such as Latin America, have historically been underfunded.

Generally, most of the private sector investment in agrifoodtech continues to be led by North America ($13.6 billion), Asia ($8.6 billion), and Europe ($5.1 billion), representing over 90% of the total invested (Figure 15.2) [AgFunder, 2023].

North America has seen a steady stream of funding over the last decade, reaching a record high of $51.7 billion in global

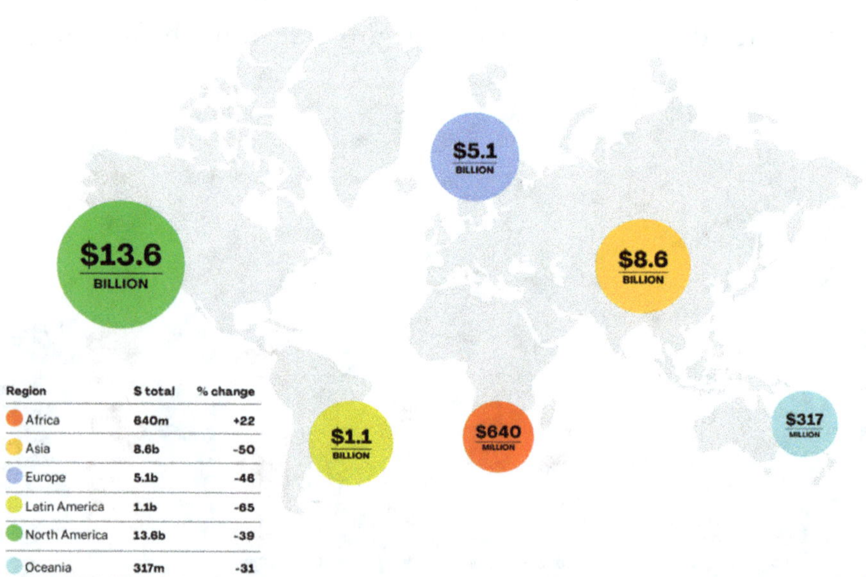

Region	$ total	% change
Africa	640m	+22
Asia	8.6b	-50
Europe	5.1b	-46
Latin America	1.1b	-65
North America	13.6b	-39
Oceania	317m	-31

Figure 15.2 2022 agrifoodtech funding by region. Source: AgFunder [2023].

investments in 2021. According to a report by Howarth in 2022, the agtech market in North America is currently valued at more than $9 billion, over twice the value of any other region. It is expected to grow to $14 billion by 2025, thanks to advancements in precision agriculture, livestock monitoring, indoor farming, and aquaculture development.

Europe has also seen significant investments in agrifoodtech ventures, with $9.2 billion in 2021. However, investors mostly backed online grocery ventures and other asset-light downstream technologies, with European e-grocery startups raising $4.2 billion, representing 43% of Europe's total agrifoodtech investment capital and a 1,300% year-over-year jump [Agfunder, 2022a].

Meanwhile, Asia-Pacific has seen significant investment in agrifoodtech startups, with $15.2 billion in 2021 accounting for 30% of global foodtech and agtech funding. However, investment flows of $5.3 billion in the first half of 2022 indicate a significant slowdown, in line with the worldwide venture capital slowdown. India is also experiencing growth in agrifoodtech funding, with $2.7 billion of investment recorded in the first half of 2022 [AgFunder, 2022b].

Latin America, on the other hand, has historically been underfunded, only receiving 5% of what is called "global agrifoodtech" venture capital investment in 2022. In recent years, there has been an increased focus on adopting small-scale solutions that address unique challenges in the region while contributing to considerable agricultural advancements. Despite the importance of agriculture in the region and the need for solutions that allow Latin American farmers to deliver on the rising demand for agricultural production, investment opportunities in agrifoodtech are being overlooked in Latin America.

15.5.3 *Future Trends*

The agtech market worldwide is currently valued at around $20 billion. However, experts predict that by 2030, it will grow at a compound annual growth rate (CAGR) of 10.2%, reaching a value of $43.37 billion. The Asia-Pacific region is expected to lead this growth, with countries such as India, China, Australia, and Japan adopting agricultural AI at an increasing rate. China's agtech market is projected to grow at a CAGR of 27% from 2020 to 2030 [Howarth, 2022].

15.5.3.1 *Consolidation*

In 2023, the prevalence of cheap money, high valuations and oversubscribed funding are replaced by a more moderate investment approach, where investors are mindful of higher interest rates, market uncertainty, failed investments, and realistic valuations. Down rounds will affect plant-based proteins, and consolidation will continue among digital agriculture tools, particularly those with no apparent value proposition to users [AgFunder, 2023].

15.5.3.2 *Climate Tech*

The recent focus on sustainability, ESG, and climate-tech investments will continue to attract significant interest from private sector investors who prioritise more than just financial gains and value the overall influence of their assets. There is a natural association between climate tech and agrifoodtech, where agriculture and food production represent significant global greenhouse gas emissions but also have the potential for positive disruption.

Within the agtech industry, this includes evaluating environmental contributions, social impacts, and management practices. In the case of climate change mitigation, the number of emerging technologies involved in carbon sequestration continues to increase. Access to effective carbon baseline measurement, validation, and reporting technologies will be critical for companies looking to deliver emission target commitments.

The increased focus on crop, processing, and food waste solutions will also drive investment into circular economy projects, including processing innovation and extracting organic materials, water, and nutrients from traditional waste streams.

15.5.3.3 *Vertical Integration*

Continued shifts away from interconnected global supply chains towards locally sourced food and vertically integrated domestic value-added processing activities will continue to drive private sector investment. This investment will help address the persistent issues driving global inflation across food commodities (e.g., rice, sugar, and flour) and energy.

15.5.3.4 *Artificial Intelligence*

In line with the release of ChatGPT and multiple associated AI integrations, the use of AI in backend agrifoodtech applications will increase significantly. The critical focus areas include data capture, analytics and insights, computer vision, decision support, and robotics.

15.5.4 *Investment Potential*

In assessing an investment opportunity, the assessment criteria include the following.

15.5.4.1 *Market Size*

The accessible market size must be substantial enough to facilitate company expansion while consistent and sustainable revenue growth proves favourable. Additionally, weighing in on technology adoption rates becomes significant as it indicates future growth opportunities and profitability.

15.5.4.2 *Intellectual Property Rights*

Intellectual property rights include patents, trademarks, and copyrights that give the company a competitive edge by preventing competitors from copying their innovations. In evaluating agtech companies, the strength of their intellectual property portfolio is another crucial measure.

15.5.4.3 *Management Team*

The management team of the agrifoodtech company is a crucial aspect for potential investors, where attributes such as expertise, resilience, and past performance, along with their vision and strategy for future growth, are essential. A capable and seasoned management team can significantly enhance the probability of success for the company.

15.5.4.4 *Financials*

Evaluating the company's financial health is crucial to gauging its overall performance and potential for growth. Investors must carefully analyse the management accounts, including balance sheets, incomes, and cash flow statements. These records can offer valuable insights into aspects like profitability, liquidity, and solvency of the company in question. These are also critical in positioning the company for various capital-raising activities.

15.5.4.5 *Regulation and the Market*

Understanding the regulatory landscape and market trends is crucial to grasp the regulatory obligations imposed on a company's product or service and assess its competitive positioning and potential disruptive factors within the market.

15.5.4.6 *Ability to Scale*

This is about establishing a compelling product and service offering that addresses a key challenge and can gain market traction and grow, ideally across different markets and geographies.

15.6 Challenges for Private Sector Agrifoodtech Investment

Several challenges and limitations hinder the effective participation of the private sector in promoting food security. Understanding and addressing these challenges is crucial in unlocking opportunities and creating an enabling environment that maximises the potential of private sector involvement in achieving sustainable food security.

15.6.1 *Regulatory Frameworks*

Policies and associated regulations can pose challenges for private sector investments in food security. The regulatory landscape often needs help to keep pace with rapid technological advancements. Complex and lengthy approval processes for innovative agricultural products, such as genetically modified crops, can discourage private sector investments in R&D.

Governments must strive to streamline regulatory frameworks to balance safety, environmental sustainability, and innovation. Collaborative efforts between private sector entities, government agencies, and research institutions can create a more efficient and supportive regulatory environment.

15.6.2 *Ethics*

Using emerging technologies in agriculture raises ethical considerations, including concerns about genetic modification, data privacy, and environmental impacts. Private sector investments must prioritise technology's responsibility and ethics by adhering to established guidelines and engaging in transparent practices. Collaboration with regulatory bodies, research institutions, and civil society organisations is crucial to addressing these concerns and establishing stakeholder trust. For instance, industry-led initiatives can develop voluntary codes of conduct and certification programmes to ensure the ethical use of technologies.

15.6.3 *Public-Private Partnerships*

Public-private partnerships are crucial for maximising the impact of private sector investments in food security. They may increase private sector investment in poorly performing agricultural value chains [Post *et al.*, 2021]. Private investors may perceive less risk if the initiative has public funding. Policymakers should create platforms for dialogue and partnership between government agencies, private sector entities, farmer organisations, and civil society groups. Public-private consultative bodies help facilitate public-private joint ventures and encourage knowledge-sharing platforms.

15.6.4 *Business Environment*

A deficient enabling environment has deterred private sector agricultural investment [Bruce and Costa, 2019]. The degree to which a country's business environment invites or discourages private investment has a critical effect on triggering and sustaining economic growth [WEF, 2020]. This area includes access to talent and capital, combined with an environment of good governance and stable government. Corruption in countries creates an ethical divide that hinders effective public administration [Downe *et al.*, 2016]. The prevalence of inherent corruption challenges private sector investment, mainly where the companies are publicly listed. Here, the fiduciary risk for companies, for both brands and reputation, provides binding constraints prohibiting further investment in competitive markets, efficient supply chains, and improved sector productivity.

Government incentives that encourage a positive business environment typically include tax offsets, grants and matched funding, and subsidies to incentivise private sector entities to invest in R&D, technology adoption, and sustainable agricultural practices. They are essential in attracting private sector investment in food security, where financial support mechanisms can offset the initial costs of implementing new technologies and encourage investment in long-term sustainable solutions.

Government policies can influence the level of risk associated with private sector investments. For instance, investing in a fixed rice processing facility that needs a minimum break-even flow of farm products to make a profit is directly tied to government policies such as imports, tax subsidies, grants, and land incentives. Agricultural investments are riskier than industrial manufacturing due to market and climate variability, regardless of favourable policy environment [WEF, 2020].

15.6.5 *Safety, Data Security, and Environmental Considerations*

Technologies that enhance productivity and sustainability should not compromise food safety, biodiversity, or ecosystem health. Compliance with internationally recognised standards and certifications, such as Good Agricultural Practices and organic certifications, is essential to maintain consumer trust and promote responsible agricultural practices. Private sector entities can invest in R&D of environmentally friendly technologies, such as biomimicry, biological pest control methods, and precision application of inputs, to minimise any adverse environmental impacts.

Policymakers should prioritise developing and implementing policies promoting sustainable agriculture practices, including incentives for adopting climate-smart technologies and agroecological approaches and supporting the transition to regenerative agriculture. Policies should also encourage sustainable resource management, including water conservation, soil health improvement, and biodiversity conservation.

Data security has become a significant concern as IoT devices and data analytics increase. A possible system breach could have an adverse impact on both the company and the farmers who depend on these technologies.

15.6.6 *Intellectual Property Rights*

Significant research and innovation are frequently involved in advancing new technologies within the agtech industry. It is essential to safeguard these innovations through patents or other forms of intellectual property protection; however, this process can be intricate and expensive. Failing to secure proper intellectual property rights may risk a particular technology's innovation and competitive advantage.

15.6.7 *Investment Model*

The increasingly high valuations experienced in recent years, fed by ready access to capital and high expectations for shorter-term growth and profitable initial public offering (IPO) exits often associated with the fintech sector, have contributed to several high-profile startup failures. Some companies with emerging technology pursuing relatively new food and agriculture market subsegments, particularly vertical farming, robotics, cellular agriculture, and biologicals, have encountered significant challenges in company valuation, fuelled by lower gross margins and higher marginal costs, including Plenty, Impossible Foods, Aerofarms, and Blue River Technology[27] (acquired by John Deere[28] in 2017). Indigo Ag,[29] a sustainable agriculture company founded in 2014 with a carbon-sequestering biologicals portfolio and a disruptive closed-loop marketplace model, reportedly raised a new funding

[27] Blue River Technology: https://bluerivertechnology.com/

[28] John Deere: https://www.deere.com/en/

[29] Indigo Ag: https://www.indigoag.com/

round in 2023 led by the Unic-Tech Fund at a valuation of just $200 million, a 94% drop from the $3.5 billion at which it was valued in 2021 [Auslender, 2023].

Thomas (2023) highlights the trap of positioning companies involved in agriculture as tech companies instead of tech-enabled agricultural companies, which often have more moderate valuations that reflect the long development cycles, complex supply chains, and inherent production risk from climate and market variability. Further, he identifies the chance of positioning a company with many different business units rather than dominating a niche, which requires large amounts of resources and capital. Indigo Ag has raised $1.2 billion since forming [Cruchbase 2023]. Advanced technologies, such as synthetic chemistry, precision agriculture tools, and biotechnology, have the potential to improve productivity and sustainability significantly. However, these technologies also have high development costs and a runway to launch. Nolet [2023] reports that "there are venture-scale impact and return opportunities in agrifood, and unlocking them will take an industry-specific approach, not a copy/paste of what's worked for venture capital investment in other industries".

15.6.8 *Smallholder Farmer Adoption*

Smallholder farmers in Asia and Africa comprise a wide-ranging group of food producers who require specific investments to improve their productivity and overall livelihoods. These family farms are responsible for around 80% of the world's food production in value, with farms less than 2 hectares producing about 35%. It is, therefore, imperative to enhance farm productivity and income in rural areas, improve market access for small-scale producers, and promote connectivity to enable smoother exchanges of goods, services, and information between rural and urban areas [FAO *et al.*, 2023].

Farmers are traditionally risk averse; adopting and scaling new technologies can take time and effort. Meanwhile, the private sector continues to weigh the market reality of attempting to accommodate a diverse farming demographic, from smallholder farmers to large corporate farms, often with nuances in language, culture, farm management, and business practices.

These solutions encompass customised agricultural practices, inputs, and advisory services that address smallholders' needs and constraints. Service providers who engage directly with smallholder farmers through government plant protection agronomists, cooperatives, contractors, and agribusiness retailers play an increasingly significant role in extending good agricultural practice for smallholder farmers to scale efficiently.

Companies increasingly focus on developing cost-effective and scalable solutions to make advanced technologies more affordable and accessible to resource-limited farmers, particularly smallholder farmers. Activities can include technology-enabling solutions such as leasing or rental schemes, financing and joint purchasing arrangements, and knowledge-sharing platforms that allow farmers to pool resources and share the costs of acquiring and utilising innovative technologies such as drones, hybrid seeds, and machinery.

Access and affordability are significant barriers that need to foster private sector investments in food security. Connectivity is one of the considerable challenges in bridging the digital divide in rural, regional, and remote communities, limiting internet and digital infrastructure access to smallholder farmers' adoption of digital technologies. In collaboration with governments and international organisations, private sector initiatives must prioritise expanding digital connectivity and providing training on digital literacy to ensure equal access to information and technology and establish rural broadband networks and mobile-based agricultural information systems.

15.7 Conclusion

Private sector investment in agrifoodtech can present a complex yet rewarding venture in food security, bringing a unique combination of resources, innovation, and scale-up capabilities to address key food security challenges among banks, high net-worth individuals, private equity firms, venture capital, family offices, and pension funds.

Agrifoodtech offers immense potential for startups and established companies to develop innovative solutions to improved efficiency, productivity, and sustainability, driven by investment in key areas, including advanced breeding, precision agriculture, controlled environment agriculture, robotics, and data analytics.

However, it is a sector with inherent investment risk, driven by long development cycles, complex supply chains, volatile commodity markets and climate variability. In recent years, high valuations, fed by ready access to capital, high expectations for shorter-term growth, and profitable IPO exits often associated with the fintech sector, have contributed to several high-profile startup failures. Patient capital is required, where investors are focused on active industry participation and long-term value creation.

The Asia-Pacific region is attracting significant private investments in the agriculture sector due to its growing population and demand for food. Building a vibrant ecosystem that connects investors, innovators, industry, and governments is critical to achieving sustainable growth and security.

References

Agfunder. (2022a). *AgFunder Europe AgrifoodTech Investment Report 2022.* https://agfunder.com/research/europe-2022-agrifoodtech-investment-report/

Agfunder. (2022b). *AgFunder APAC AgrifoodTech Investment Report 2022.* https://agfunder.com/research/europe-2022-agrifoodtech-investment-report/

AgFunder. (2023). *AgFunder AgrifoodTech Investment Report.* https://agfunder.com/research/AgFunder-global-agrifoodtech-investment report-2023/

Auslender, V. (2023). Indigo AG's valuation was down 94% to $200 million in the latest funding round. *CTech News.* https://www.calcalistech.com/ctechnews/article/syswxgjph

Bayer Annual Report. (2022). www.bayer.com/en/investors/integrated-annual-reports

Bruce, K. and Costa, H. (2019). Enabling environment for PPPs in agricultural extension projects: policy imperatives for impact. *Journal of Rural Studies*, 70, pp. 87–95.

Charpentier, E. (2020). Facts. *NobelPrize.org.* https://www.nobelprize.org/prizes/chemistry/2020/charpentier/facts/

Crunchbase. (2023). Indigo profile. https://www.crunchbase.com/organization/indigoag

Downe, J., Cowell, R. and Morgan, K. (2016). What determines ethical behaviour in public organizations: is it rules or leadership?. *Public Administration Review,* 76(6), pp. 898–909.

Economist Impact and JP Morgan. (2022). AgTech in Latin America: Small-scale solutions in a large-scale transformation. https://privatebank.jpmorgan.com/gl/en/insights/investing/

agtech-in-latin-america-small-scale-solutions-in-a-large-scale-transformation#20

Food and Agriculture Organization of the United Nations (FAO). (2020). *The Role of the Private Sector in Food Security and Nutrition.* https://www.alliance2015.org/wp-content/uploads/2019/12/DEF_summary_Private_A4-resized.pdf

FAO, IFAD, UNICEF, WFP and WHO (2023). *The State of Food Security and Nutrition in the World 2023.* https://doi.org/10.4060/cc3017en

Frison, E. A. and IPES-Food. (2016). *From Uniformity to Diversity: A Paradigm Shift from Industrial Agriculture to Diversified Agroecological Systems.* https://hdl.handle.net/10568/75659

Fuglie, K. (2016). The growing role of the private sector in agricultural research and development worldwide. *Global Food Security*, 10, pp. 29–38.

Fukao, T., Xu, K., Ronald, P. and Bailey-Serres, J. (2006). A variable cluster of ethylene response factor–like genes regulates metabolic and developmental acclimation responses to submergence in rice. *The Plant Cell Online*, 18, pp. 2021–2034.

Global AgInvesting. (2020). *Global Aginvesting Rankings & Trends Report2019.*https://www.globalaginvesting.com/wp-content/uploads/2020/04/HQP20_AGINV_RT_RPT_FNL.pdf

Haugen, H. M. (2020). The UN Development on Peasants' Rights (UNDROP): Is article 19 on seed rights adequately balancing intellectual property rights and the right to food? *The Journal of World Intellectual Property,* 2020, pp. 1–22.

Howarth, J. (2022). Global AgTech market size, growth, & trends (2023–2030). *Exploding Topics.* https://explodingtopics.com/blog/agtech-market

Kopicki, R. (2011). *Trusting Trade and the Private Sector for Food Security in Southeast Asia.* World Bank. https://doi.org/10.1596/978-0-8213-8626-2

Ligot, J. and Deau, R. (2016). *Promoting Private Sector Contribution to the Climate Change Response in Cambodia.* General Secretariat of National Council for Sustainable Development.

Montesclaros, J. M. L. and Teng, P. (2018). Singapore's nascent urban farming: potential future regional centre. *RSIS Commentary CO18195*. https://www.rsis.edu.sg/rsis-publication/nts/singapores-nascent-urban-farming-potential-future-regional-centre/#.XVZE0MzaM8.

Nolet, S. (2023). Is Silicon Valley still killing agtech? *LinkedIn*. https://www.linkedin.com/pulse/silicon-valley-still-killing-agtech-sarah-nolet

Oatman, R. (2022). JBS Canada partners with Scott Technology on $71 million automation system. *Sosland Publishing Company*. https://www.meatpoultry.com/articles/26901-jbs-canada-partners-with-scott-technology-on-71-million-automation-system

Post, L., Schmitz, A., Issa, T. and James, O. (2021). Enabling the environment for private sector investment: impact on food security and poverty. *Journal of Agricultural & Food Industrial Organization*, 19(1), pp. 25–37.

Raman, R. (2017). The impact of Genetically Modified (GM) crops in modern agriculture: A review. *GM Crops Food*, 8(4), pp. 195–208.

Ray, A., Panda, D. and Sarkar, R. K. (2017). Can rice cultivar with submergence tolerant quantitative trait locus (SUB1) manage submergence stress better during reproductive stage?. *Archives of Agronomy and Soil Science*, 63(7), 998–1008.

Reardon, T. and Timmer, C. P. (2012). The economics of the food system revolution. *Annual Review of Resource Economics*, 4(1), pp. 225–264.

Santra, M., Wang, H., Seifert, S. and Haley, S. (2017). Doubled Haploid Laboratory Protocol for Wheat Using Wheat-Maize Wide Hybridization. In P. L. Bhalla and M. B. Singh (Eds.), *Wheat Biotechnology*, pp. 235–249. Springer.

Singh, T., Shukla, S., Kumar, P., Wahla, V., Bajpai, V. K. and Rather, I. A. (2017). Application of nanotechnology in food science: perception and overview. *Frontiers in Microbiology*, 18, p. 1501.

Thomas, S. (2023). Indigo Ag: Analyzing what went into their $3.5 billion valuation and what went wrong. A deep dive on the dynamics of the business of Indigo Ag. *Upstream Ag*. https://www.upstream.ag/p/indigo-ag-analyzing-what-went-into

Wood, P., Thorrez, L., Hocquette, J. F., Troy, D. and Gagaoua, M. (2023), "Cellular agriculture": current gaps between facts and claims regarding "cell-based meat". *Animal Frontiers,* 13(2), pp. 68–74.

Wood, P. and Tavan, M. (2022). A review of the alternative protein industry. *Current Opinion in Food Science*, 47, p. 100869.

Zeigler, R. (2019). Plant sciences, public policies, and food security. *Outlook on Agriculture*, 48(3), pp. 220–228.

https://doi.org/10.1142/9789811278297_0016

Chapter 16

Agricultural Extension to Improve Food Production

Rosana P. Mula[1], Mary Grace M. Nidoy[2], Moo C. Rodriguez[1] and Karen Eloisa T. Barroga[2]

[1]*Agricultural Training Institute, Department of Agriculture, Philippines*
[2]*Philippine Rice Research Institute, Munoz, Philippines*

16.1 Introduction

This chapter highlights the strategies in extension and advisory services (EAS) that contribute to the overall development of the agriculture and fishery sector. Cases are provided by the Agricultural Training Institute (ATI) and its partner agencies. ATI is the Philippine government's training and extension arm under the Department of Agriculture (DA). It acts as the capacity builder, knowledge bank, and catalyst of agriculture and fishery extension in the Philippines.

Research and extension systems are key components of innovation and technology transfer in the agriculture and fishery sector. However, the linear transfer of technology model has been observed and cited as inadequate in comprehending the causes of and solutions to the increasingly complex current situations [Kalaitzandonakes *et al.*, 2018].

The Global Forum of Rural Advisory Services calls for the need for new capacities for EAS to address complex challenges while situating the role of EAS within the agricultural innovation system (AIS) in the "New Extensionist" paradigm [Sulaiman and Davis, 2012]. The AIS method stresses the diversity of factors influencing innovation generation and spread, recognising that innovation develops from a network of actors and their interactions [Kalaitzandonakes *et al.*, 2018]. With this, the DA-ATI has been subscribing to this paradigm proposed by the Global Forum of Rural Advisory Services which highlights the importance of reskilling and strengthening core competencies. It aims to focus on addressing individual needs and challenges at the organisational and system levels to guarantee that extension makes a substantial contribution to the development of the agriculture and fishery sector [Department of Agriculture, 2022b; Sulaiman and Davis, 2012].

Agricultural extension in Asia faces both challenges and opportunities. A transformative change in the agriculture and fishery sector is necessary to achieve developmental goals. ATI's stakeholders suggest that EAS strategies consider challenges and opportunities, as in Table 16.1, to be more effective.

This section analyses the prevalent issues in AIS's socio-cultural, economic, environmental, and policy aspects by highlighting the agriculture and fishery sector's challenges and opportunities.

16.1.1 *Socio-Cultural Issues*

Despite recent progress and technological advances, major socio-cultural issues persist. Poverty remains a rural phenomenon, where small farmers have weak bargaining power and political voices [Baig and Aldosari, 2013; Sulaiman and Hall, 2005]. The ballooning population in the region puts pressure on the agriculture and fishery

Table 16.1 Challenges and opportunities confronting EAS in Asia.

Issues	Challenges	Opportunities
Socio-cultural	Demographics – Growing and aging population – Decreasing land area and depleting resources – Increasing poverty	Increasing efforts towards: – Farm consolidation and clustering – Youth engagement in agriculture – Use of information and communication technologies for development
Economic	Globalisation	Rural farm tourism
Environmental	– Climate change – Global health crisis – Lack of resilience of agricultural livelihoods from shocks (transboundary diseases, conflicts)	– Sustainable agri-technologies for climate change adaptation and mitigation
Policy and Governance	– Weak extension policies – Weak research-extension-farmer linkages – Limited access to new farming technologies – Non-prioritisation of agriculture in the programs of local government units – Low reward/incentive system	– Convergence initiatives – More active private sector engagement, i.e., public-private partnership

sector to supply enough food, aggravated by decreasing land area and depleting natural resources [FAO, 2017; DA-ATI, 2019].

Additionally, farmers in Asia are aging, with 28.5% being over 55 [Heide-Ottosen *et al.*, 2014]. Older farmers have been noted to need more financial resources to buy additional inputs, have inadequate skills (e.g., literacy), and have low energy to invest in adopting new practices; hence, agricultural innovations are not readily adopted [FAO, 2017]. Extension must disseminate technologies effectively to increase productivity while considering issues of accessibility, affordability, and poverty reduction. Farm consolidation and clustering address these socio-cultural challenges by allowing EAS to aid in empowering farmers and fisherfolk. It increases production levels, improves income, and enhances access to resources, technologies, and markets. EAS can also take advantage of the growing number of youths in food systems by establishing an enabling environment or incentivising them to increase their involvement. Additionally, maximising EAS in agriculture will make extension initiatives more efficient since technology transfer can be made swifter with good infrastructure and effective in a situation of quality databases and information.

16.1.2 *Economic Issues*

There are also pressing economic issues affecting the region. Despite making goods and services more available, globalisation has negatively affected less competitive sectors, especially smallholder farmers who, more often, cannot compete and benefit from regional and world trade [DA-ATI, 2019]. International food commodity prices have reached an all-time high due to market conditions and high costs of energy, fertilisers, and other agricultural services, further exacerbated by the Ukraine-Russia conflict [FAO Council, 2022]. High commodity prices have led some Asian countries to resort to protectionist policies, further aggravating food security concerns [Montesclaros and Caballero-Anthony, 2022]. These issues highlight the need for EAS to make farmers and fisherfolk competitive with global market standards, which would contribute to food security. Rural farm tourism addresses economic issues as it increases rural income and employment and promotes innovative technologies.

16.1.3 *Environmental Issues*

Environment-related issues include climate change, transboundary diseases, conflict, and the COVID-19 pandemic, which add to the challenges faced by EAS. First, climate change continues to be a threat multiplier with cross-cutting impacts [Caballero-Anthony, 2022]. Developing and least-developed countries in many sub-regions in Asia are more heavily affected by climate change and will experience a higher decline in food productivity [Ancog *et al.*, 2018]. Secondly, as more people, animals, plants, and agricultural goods traverse international boundaries, and as animal production methods become more intensive, there is a rising risk of transboundary animal illnesses. These diseases cause a high mortality rate and spread quickly across borders due to their high contagiousness. The increase in transboundary pests and diseases is also a result of climate change altering pest population dynamics. Third, conflicts impair access to food, healthcare, and social safety nets while reducing the food supply [FAO, 2017]. Lastly, COVID-19's effects on the food and agriculture industry have shown weaknesses in the agri-food supply chain. Constraints faced by smallholders are worsened due to a lack of access to credit and training programs, while food supply chain disruptions hinder access to markets and finance [Fan *et al.*, 2021]. Hence, EAS must build the resilience of farmers and fisherfolk to shocks.

16.1.4 *Policy and Governance-Related Issues*

Policy and governance-related issues in Asia's EAS, such as weak extension policies and research-extension-farmer linkages, limited access to new technologies, and the low or non-prioritisation of agriculture and fishery, are significant issues that must be addressed. Most extension departments in Asia, according to Baig and Aldosari [2013], struggle with the following issues: insufficient funding and resources; a lack of qualified and experienced extension staff; poor, deteriorating infrastructure; ineffective coordination and functional links with other institutions in the public and private sectors; the absence of quality control and impact assessment mechanisms; and unclear extension mandates and job descriptions for extension staff. Agricultural Extension Workers (AEWs) are key players that make any extension system a success, highlighting the need to professionalise and provide them with proper incentives. Convergence initiatives and promoting pluralism through public-private partnerships would further strengthen extension policies and meet the needs of the farmers and fisherfolk [Baig and Aldosari, 2013].

EAS in Asia must constantly evolve to enable farmers, fisherfolk, agribusinesses, and even whole nations to cope with, compete against, and survive in the face of the myriad of complicated problems [World Bank, 2012]. The challenges and opportunities have established the need for innovations and their scaling to increase their impact. This has necessitated the need to view EAS under the context of the "New Extensionist Paradigm" and innovation systems.

Various strategies must be explored for disseminating and promoting technologies, considering EAS's pluralistic, participatory, and demand-driven nature. This includes examining strategies for building players' capacity and the enabling policy environment for innovations and their scaling, along with the required monitoring and evaluation process.

The following section examines Asia's EAS strategies, particularly in the Philippines. In 2021, the agency reached almost 150,000 beneficiaries through its experiential and season-long training, and other related extension activities [PSA, 2022]. The next part cites these initiatives.

16.2 Strategies in Extension and Advisory Services

The strategies outlined in the following sections enable the creation of a more responsive extension service where stakeholders must collectively participate in and provide the necessary resources. Such strategies guide extension service activities in agriculture and fishery to improve food production. EAS must be able to capacitate and engage the various players along the value chain to adopt techniques and technologies that are productive, inclusive, and sustainable. The performance of EAS depends on the players' technical skills and how they behave or interact with clients and others in the agriculture innovation system, thereby contributing knowledge and expertise to the innovation process [Sulaiman and Davis, 2012].

16.2.1 *Professionalisation of the Sector Through Agricultural Extension Workers*

Since AEWs are at the frontline in providing extension services, they must fulfil their function of ensuring that technologies are promoted and taught effectively to the different farmers and fisherfolk in their communities. Despite the important role that AEWs play, Baig and Aldosari [2013] noted that due to their poor status or positions, lack of perks, and limited prospects for career advancement compared with other professions, extension professionals in Asia lack the technical expertise and enthusiasm to carry out their duties. In the Philippines, AEWs in the local government are underpaid and have no assurance of security of tenure, with AEWs in poorer sixth-class municipalities having an average monthly salary of PhP 10,274.00 (US$188) [DA-ATI, 2016]. The lack of training to pursue professional development and proper incentives lead AEWs in the Philippines to have low morale and confidence to fulfil their duties.

Hence, professionalising AEWs is a vital aspect of improving the extension system. Olorunfemi *et al.* [2021] define professionalisation in extension as "expertise in terms of knowledge and skills combined with integrity and ethics resulting in a competent, highly capable, committed, responsive, and accountable extension practitioner". They added that this enhances EAS's image, promotes credibility and accountability, regulates extension personnel's professional conduct, and ensures extension agents' competence.

Professionalisation of EAS entails supporting career development and continuous professionalisation of AEWs by providing the necessary capability-building functions and incentives to perform their duties, functions, and responsibilities properly. Under the AIS, functional and technical competencies must be part of the framework for professionalisation. The World Bank [2012] emphasised that technical skills must be complemented with functional expertise as AIS require a range of skills, such as scientific, technical, managerial, and entrepreneurial skills and other skills and routines related to partnering, negotiating, building consensus, and learning. Other factors of professionalisation include acquiring the appropriate educational preparation for the job, possessing a license to practice one's profession, and exercising integrity and commitment to the job. Therefore, incentives such as scholarships for degree and non-degree courses and other reward systems should be offered to empower and motivate AEWs. ATI and its partner agencies have taken the necessary steps to pursue this endeavour.

16.2.1.1 *Specialist Training Courses*

One of the effects of limited funding for extension systems is that AEWs are compelled to address all agriculture-related issues in their respective localities, transforming them from commodity or subject matter specialists into generalists [Ani and Correa, 2016 as cited in DA-ATI, 2019]. While generalists play a crucial role in extension, they must be supported by specialists with expertise in various subject matters [Sulaiman and Davis, 2012]. Offering specialist training courses to AEWs enables the development of a cadre of appropriate specialists required in and aligned with the system. Such pursuit also makes AEWs more credible as resource persons in addressing specific problems on the farm and training the next generation of AEWs. This ensures quality knowledge and expertise are passed on from one AEW to another.

16.2.1.2 *Training of Trainers*

Training of trainers (TOT) courses engage master trainers in coaching and mentoring new trainers to deliver a particular topic or demonstrate a skill, and manage a training course (Case A). In TOT, the participant can watch and observe how an experienced trainer delivers and facilitates exercises and activities and practice their teaching skills. This prepares future trainers to present information effectively, respond to participant questions, and lead activities that reinforce learning. Simultaneously, this allows the development of a pool of competent trainers who can be tapped to deliver and manage training sessions, effectively expanding the reach and impact of EAS [DA-ATI, 2022d].

16.2.1.3 *Scholarships*

The provision of scholarships to AEWs contributes to professionalisation. As an incentive, it encourages AEWs to develop their careers and become more competent in their field. Moreover, scholarships ensure that AEWs have the proper standard of education required for their duties, help pass the necessary qualifying exams, meet the minimum experience level, and attain the pre-requisite licenses to practice their profession [Olorunfemi *et al.*, 2021].

Case A Ladderised Training Program in the Philippines to Capacitate and Professionalise AEWs

DA-ATI's [2022b] report showed 32,382 AEWs in the Philippines, with 9,977 positioned in the local government units. These AEWs are strategically designated in national and local governments, non-governmental organisations, and the private sector. Their professionalisation is done through a ladderised approach. ATI uses the approach in its human capital development framework. It is composed of three levels: basic training, which intends to build knowledge, skills and attitude on the fundamentals of extension; advanced training, which aims to scale up the knowledge, skills and attitude acquired during the basic training; and specialised training, which focuses more on the enhancement of knowledge, skills and attitude in more specific specialisations. The AEWs' staff development programs ensure the competency and upscaling of the professionalised Philippine EAS to deliver quality services to clients. Specifically, about 572 capability-building activities were participated in by 12,486 AEWs which included ladderised courses, TOT, retooling/refresher courses on financial literacy, business planning, project development and management, among other topics along the value chain [DA-ATI, 2022a].

ATI and its partner agencies offer commodity-specific training courses to aid in technology transfer. For example, the Agricultural Development Officers of the Community (AgRiDOC) course seeks to develop a new breed of rice extension experts by providing rice-related training programs with transformational leadership as its foundation. As of 2017 data, 21 season-long trainings of this course have been conducted all over the country, and 618 have graduated. There are also specialist courses on Integrated Crops Management for high-value crops where graduates conduct season-long TOTs for AEWs and selected farmer-leaders. The latter will conduct farmer field schools in their respective municipalities. ATI also provides specialists training courses on technical topics, such as the Participatory Guarantee System for quality assurance initiatives.

Some of the well-sought TOTs are the following: season-long TOT for high-value crops development program, season-long TOT on ICM[1] in corn, TOT on good agricultural practices for fruits and vegetables, TOT on farm and fisheries clustering and consolidation program, corn-based farmer-scientist RDE[2] training program, TOT on the management of fall army worm, climate-resilient farm business school TOT, sustainable corn production in sloping areas, site specific nutrient management/nutrient expert in maize, skills training in corn and cassava processing, training course on good agricultural practices, code of practice on the prevention and reduction of mycotoxin in corn grits, and labelling and packaging.

[1] https://icminc.com/

[2] https://www.usep.edu.ph/rde/about-rde/

ATI offers various reward systems and incentives for AEWs to empower them with opportunities for career development. In particular, the Educational Grants for Extension Workers and the Thesis and Dissertation Assistance for AEWs program incentivise AEWs to pursue educational opportunities. These programs aim to enhance their roles as extension providers by capacitating them to provide excellent and competitive extension delivery services. Subsequently, these programs produce research in agriculture, fishery, and related fields that could be useful in addressing prevailing issues in the sector. Likewise, the Institute achieved the accreditation of training activities to continuously upgrade AEWs' professional licenses (Case B).

Additionally, ATI has made efforts towards the legislation of the Magna Carta for AEWs, which acknowledges and strengthens the importance of the AEWs' contribution to agricultural development and modernisation. This is by affirming their rights and privileges, providing an enabling work environment and support system, strengthening a mechanism for career development and professionalisation, and instituting appropriate compensation through a viable evaluation and reward system. The proposed bill promotes and ensures that AEWs in the government are accorded appropriate positions and parenthetical titles, with equivalent salary compensation and opportunities for promotions. It also further encourages career development and professionalisation by directing the ATI and other relevant national government agencies to continue to develop and implement training programs for AEWs. It has provisions for additional allowances, incentives, and benefits for AEWs. The bill is a legislation in progress.

Case B Continuing Professional Development (CPD) Accreditation for AEWs in the Philippines

One of ATI's current initiatives is providing CPD training programs for licensed agriculturists. The agency applies for the accreditation of its trainings to the CPD Council of Agriculture through the CPD Accreditation System. This aids in the professionalisation of AEWs since it allows AEWs to renew their licenses.

For 2021, the Professional Regulations Commission, as CPD Provider for Agriculture, accredited seven of the Institute's operating units. These are the International Training Center on Pig Husbandry, Regional Training Centers in IV-A, V, VIII, X, XII, and the central office. There were about 82 training courses conducted in 2021 that allowed the participants to earn CPD points equivalent to the courses they completed [DA-ATI, 2022a].

16.2.2 *Strengthening Farmers' and Fisherfolk's Capabilities*

There are many approaches in delivering extension support to farmers and fisherfolk. These are categorised into two: top-down and participatory approaches [Olayemi *et al.*, 2021]. Traditional top-down extension methods have been criticised for failing to account for users, discriminating against women, emphasising production and technology over markets, and focusing on general recommendations that ignore the variety of farm household conditions [World Bank, 2012].

On the other hand, group-based and participatory approaches emphasise farmer participation and more tailor-made services, including facilitating access to financial services and markets. It is decentralised, where key stakeholders are involved in problem solving and implementation [Olayemi *et al.*, 2021]. Modern and pluralistic extension approaches also consider innovations in communications and their effects on farmers having an increasing range of sources of knowledge. To be effective, adopting some other supportive approaches must be considered [Abdel-Maksoud, 2019].

Specific approaches include training and visiting, farmer-to-farmer extension programs, farmer field schools (FFS), and extension programs through information and communication technologies [Kusnandar *et al.*, 2021].

16.2.2.1 *Training and Visiting*

This top-down approach to extension promoted by the World Bank in the mid-1970s as a national public extension system [Naanwintome and Millar, 2013, as cited in Olayemi *et al.*, 2021] has still much relevance to this date. Experience has it that extension workers, especially those with access to technology generated by research and development institutions, consider training and visiting as one of the most efficient approaches since this can be interspersed during trainings. However, it has been criticised as too rigid, labour intensive, and expensive [Olayemi, 2021].

16.2.2.2 *Farmer-to-Farmer Extension Programs*

According to Kusnandar *et al.* [2021], farmer-to-farmer extension programs are participatory and involve trained farmers (as senders) transferring knowledge to other farmers (as receivers). The AEWs and external parties train senders to conduct field experiments and share the knowledge they obtained with other farmers in their area. This has been noted to be effective in considering the local context regarding extension and innovation. However, the challenge is ensuring local farmers have the necessary skills and motivation to integrate this knowledge into their host programs. A case in point is the Learning Site for Agriculture, or referred to as a farm school in the case of the Rice Competitiveness Enhancement Fund extension program (Cases C1 and C2, respectively).

Case C1 Learning Sites for Agriculture (LSA) as Partners in Farmer-to-Farmer Training in the Philippines

The certification of LSA aims to contribute to the improvement in productivity and profitability of the less developed but resource-rich farming/fishing communities and the non-farming rural community members engaged in agri-processing enterprises by utilising the farmer-to-farmer extension approach. LSAs have two categories: the farming LSA and the agri-processing LSA. The former practices diversified and integrated farming systems, specialised farming in a sizable production volume, or utilises a specialised technology in agriculture. The latter practices and promotes agri-processing. Certified LSAs serve as a demonstration area in their communities for hands-on learning. LSAs provide lectures/orientations to on-site training participants, visiting groups, ATI's scholarship grantees, youth trainees, and others [DA-ATI, 2022d].

In 2021, 326 LSAs were certified under the ATI's regular banner program, while 80 LSAs were certified under the Rice Competitiveness Enhancement Fund-Rice Extension Services Program (RCEF-RESP). ATI is one of the implementing agencies of

RCEF-RESP along with its partner agencies, such as the Philippine Rice Research Institute (PhilRice), Philippine Center for Postharvest Development and Mechanization, and Technical Education and Skills Development Authority.

The LSAs can be scaled up as Extension Service Providers. This expands not only the livelihood opportunities of farmers but also their chance to serve more farmers and other agri-enthusiasts [DA-ATI, 2022a]. This demonstration and training process encourages sharing technologies with fellow farmers/agri-processors in their local area, thereby increasing the adoption of innovations to help improve food security in local farming communities.

Case C2 Farm Schools for Farmer-Level Training in the Rice Competitiveness Enhancement Fund-Rice Extension Service Program (RCEF-RESP)

Farm schools under RCEF-RESP are essential in the dissemination and advocacy process in scaling innovations on rice and promoting sustainability. The RCEF-RESP utilises the participatory, season-long FFS model to conduct training activities on rice. Farm schools under this program are strengthened by allowing their owners, managers, and staff to enhance inbred rice and seed production, mechanisation, and knowledge and technology transfer. In turn, they improve the capabilities of farmers in their communities by educating them on new farming techniques, including the use of new farm machinery, and facilitating the sharing of farming experiences.

In 2021, 63 farm schools were established, while 54 were enhanced [DA-ATI, 2022a]. Since the implementation of RCEF-RESP in 2019, there have been 107,504 farmers who have graduated from various farm schools. Graduates are expected to act as the critical mass who will lead in sharing the knowledge and values they learned from FFS with their fellow farmers, creating a ripple effect of impacts in farming communities. As part of the implementing agencies' commitment, monitoring is being undertaken to ensure the continuous operation of the FFS even after program termination.

16.2.2.3 *Farmer Field Schools*

Another participatory approach is the season-long FFS model. This participatory learning method, technology development, and dissemination are based on adult-learning principles, such as experiential learning. It is specifically developed for field studies, where hands-on management skills and conceptual understanding are required. Its defining characteristics are discovery learning, farmer experimentation, and group action. The approach is an interactive and practical method of training that empowers farmers to be technical experts on major aspects of their farming system. Farmers perform research, identify and evaluate issues, create solutions, and share knowledge with others [World Bank, 2012]. Among the challenges in FFS implementation, as cited by Olayemi *et al.* [2021], include the lack of coordination of FFS activities at the national level, gender inequalities, inadequate exposure of research and extension staff to FFS concepts and procedures, competition and conflicts of interest between donor agencies, sharing of proceeds from the school approach, and low participation and involvement of policymakers.

Similar to the FFS model is the farm business school. This non-traditional extension modality seeks to enhance knowledge and skills in entrepreneurship and marketing to improve their income.

This entails helping farmers learn about their business in their locality and how to make it more profitable. The farm business school is an extension modality institutionalised across the ATI's network of training centres to assist farmers in coping with the demand of a market-driven environment and help them manage their farms as business units with stronger market linkages. From the 75 activities conducted, 1,606 farmers were able to participate [DA-ATI, 2022a].

16.2.2.4 *Digital Agriculture*

Information and communication technologies (ICTs) have three broad functions in rural advisory services. First, ICTs address the need for localised and customised information; store information for future reference; and facilitate the creation of networks [World Bank, 2012]. Recent ICT innovations promoted the development of e-extension programs. These programs have the potential to provide a means for effective and efficient knowledge sharing. Challenges for ICT include the farmers' limited digital skills and poor ICT infrastructure in rural farming areas [Kusnandar *et al.*, 2021]. Notable initiatives in digital agriculture in the Philippines include the Digital Farmers Program (DFP), the Digital Agriculture Course (DAC) for RCEF, and other digital applications and platforms. A brief discussion on these is presented in Case D, which highlights the potential of ICT-mediated platforms in extension delivery systems.

Case D Digital Agriculture Initiatives in the Philippines

The DFP is an ICT-based capacity development program that aims to help Filipino farmers access information online to make better farming decisions, improve efficiencies and skills using digital technologies, expand and tap a wide network of market opportunities, increase resiliency, and enhance their livelihood. The program employs a three-course digital literacy sequence and covers basic digital tools such as smartphones and social media to more complex services such as e-commerce and online payment systems. In addition, the program provides an avenue to promote and maximise the use of existing agriculture-focused digital tools and applications developed by both governmental and private institutions.

It starts with DFP 101, where topics on the smartphone, internet, and social media are taught. All DFP 101 finishers move up to the second level of the program — DFP 102 — which covers more complex services, such as online payment systems and various applications in agriculture, like the Smarter Pest Identification Technology mobile app for digital identification and remote monitoring of pests and diseases and the Plant Doctor Online application which serves as a tool for the identification of plant diseases, among others. A total of 1,741 clients benefitted from the 80 trainings under the program, equipping more clients to use technologies in farming. The 18th Philippine Quill Awards, organised by the International Association of Business Communicators Philippines, awarded DFP the Excellence Award. The program received the Best Extension Project award during the 2021 Philippine Extension Advisory Services Network Biennial Extension Symposium [DA-ATI, 2022a].

The DAC for RCEF is complementary to RCEF-RESP FFS as it aims to capacitate and prepare FFS to implement digital literacy training for farmers or their children in their respective areas. The DAC 101 course covers smartphone use, internet access, mobile applications such as Facebook, Google, and YouTube, internet safety and security lessons, basic agri-ICT applications, and an introduction to social media marketing using Facebook. The DAC 102 course incorporates rice-related agriculture applications such as the Rice Crop Manager, Agricultural Development Officers of the Community, Binhing Palay, Rice Doctor, and the Pinoy Rice Knowledge Bank, among others.

The International Rice Research Institute [2021] defines Rice Crop Manager as a blended digital agriculture platform grounded in robust scientific research to generate the most appropriate nutrient and crop management recommendation specific to an individual farmer's field. On-farm trials have indicated that Rice Crop Manager increased yields by an average of 392 kg/ha/cropping season and provided an average additional net income of US$122/ha/cropping season.

PhilRice, one of ATI's partners in implementing EAS, has also developed digital applications to help farmers access timely and relevant information that would enable them to make informed decisions on their farms. But even before the pandemic, PhilRice had been using ICTs since the early 2000s through the Open Academy for Philippine Agriculture, which paved the way for technologies such as DA-PhilRice Text Center and the Pinoy Rice Knowledge Bank. Recent applications and information systems that PhilRice developed include the Rice Seed Information System; *Binhing Palay*, which helps farmers access rice varietal information; *Binhi e-padala*, a digital voucher system for seeds; Minus One-Element Technique and Leaf Color Chart, both of which guide farmers on nutrient management; and the eDamuhan app, which enables farmers to identify weeds in the farm. The agency also tapped big data analytics through its RiceLytics, an online data analytics dashboard that contains information on the status of the Philippine rice industry [PhilRice, 2022]. Such information is valuable for policymakers in creating policies grounded on timely data.

The positive impact of digital platforms on technology adoption, yield, and income highlights the need for extension services and enabling policies to increase their adoption to reach an even wider scale. These expanded information sources became even more relevant during the onslaught of the COVID-19 pandemic when most, if not all, of the initiatives went digital. The extension system must accommodate these new technologies to keep up and cope with the changing agricultural landscape.

16.2.3 *Harnessing Extension Intermediaries*

Intermediaries constitute a significant part of the AIS due to the systemic perspective of enhancing the interaction among various actors. They also function as facilitators or brokers. In technology transfer, they serve more than just a linking role. They also help transform the ideas and knowledge being transferred. Intermediaries may also include actors and organisations that bridge and link players within a technological system.

These intermediaries are facilitators or brokers who aim to develop shared meaning and language between dialogue partners to stimulate change and develop innovative solutions [Kalaitzandonakes *et al.*, 2018]. As the public extension is only one important intermediary actor among the many other actors in the AIS, its comparative advantage lies in its transformation as a "bridging" organisation, linking the different bits of knowledge held by different actors by promoting platforms and networks, and facilitating their application and use, thereby fostering innovation [Howells, 2006]. The public extension is one intermediary actor that can bridge and link knowledge held by different actors and promote these through platforms and networks, facilitating their application and use [Sulaiman and Davis, 2012].

16.2.3.1 *Farmer Leaders, Local Farmer Technicians, and Youth*

Apart from conventional intermediaries like AEWs, farmer leaders and local farmer technicians aid in facilitating and brokering technologies to the farmers in their respective localities. In the case of DA, local farmer technicians are tapped to complement the public AEW workforce. Local farmer technicians are model farmers who provide extension services to the rice farmers in their communities. Local farmer technicians are capacitated with various capability-building activities by ATI to ensure that they have the proper competencies to fulfil their functions and provide them with up-to-date information on new technologies. On the other hand, the youth (Cases E and F) can also be used as intermediaries, especially for digital technologies and ICT.

Case E Philippine Youth Internship Program in Japan and Taiwan

ATI has been implementing youth development programs in partnership with different countries directed at out-of-school youth in the Philippines. The Young Filipino Farm Leaders Training Program in Japan (YFFLTPJ) and the Filipino Young Farmers Internship Program in Taiwan are notable programs borne out of the partnerships with the governments of Japan and Taiwan. These two programs aim to develop deserving young Filipino farmers to become farmer leaders and empowered agricultural entrepreneurs. It consists of acquiring skills and knowledge through exchanging modern agricultural and fishery techniques, marketing strategies and mechanisms, cooperative management, and enhancement of competencies, discipline, and values.

The Young Filipino Farm Leaders Training Program in Japan is a commitment of the Japanese government to the ASEAN regions through the Japan Agricultural Exchange Council and the Japan Ministry of Agriculture Forestry and Fisheries. It started in 1986 under the leadership of the ATI for five years. In 1991, the program was managed by the National Agricultural and Fishery Council as a result of the rationalisation initiative. Since its inception, 592 participants have completed the program. Completers of the program receive a grant of P50,000 (US$917) each to fund their agri-entrepreneurship projects. Their projects usually showcase technologies of their interests that are relevant in their area.

On the other hand, the Filipino Young Farmers Internship Program in Taiwan is a partnership between the Manila Economic and Cultural Office and the Taipei Economic and Cultural Office in the Philippines. In 2021, 29 interns graduated from this program.

Successful graduates serve as resource persons in their expertise to fellow farmers and host farmers during the Home Stay Module of the succeeding trainings. Graduates are deputised as local farm technicians and provide other extension work to intensify the dissemination of modern farming techniques.

Case F Youth and Agriculture: The Infomediary Campaign in the Philippines

Another youth initiative from PhilRice is the Infomediary Campaign, which engaged young people in rice farming to serve as infomediaries. They are mobilised to read publications, send queries, or search for information on rice which is subsequently shared with their farmer-parents or any farmer in the community. The campaign, conducted from 2012–2017, had more than 200 high schools serving as infomediaries for farmers who accessed ICT platforms, such as PhilRice Text Center and the Pinoy Rice Knowledge Bank. Results of the campaign showed that engaging students helped reduce the ICT anxiety of farmers. To help inculcate the importance of agriculture in the youth sector, PhilRice recommends including agriculture lessons in the high school curriculum and the continuous training of AEWs on the latest ICTs [PhilRice, 2021].

This is a program closely participated in by PhilRice, DA, and the CGIAR Research Program on Climate Change, Agriculture, and Food Security, including the Department of Education, a partner in the campaign implementation.

16.2.3.2 *The School-On-the-Air Smart Rice Agriculture Program in the Philippines*

The School-On-the-Air Smart Rice Agriculture (SOA-SRA) is a continuing radio-based distance learning program for farmers and local intermediaries nationwide on rice and rice-based farming systems. PhilRice developed its content, and the delivery of the SOA programs is simultaneously conducted by the DA-Regional Field

Offices, with DA-ATI and aired by DWDA,[1] Philippine Broadcasting Service, Philippine Information Agency, and members of the Philippine Federation of Rural Broadcasters. SOA broadcasters are provided with a syllabus containing ready-to-be-aired scripts in modular format, radio plugs, jingles, and canned interviews.

The SOA-SRA helps catalyse agriculture modernisation through the massive and sustained education of smallholder farmers and local intermediaries on modern and innovative technologies and approaches to smart rice production. The program shares cutting-edge technologies and innovative approaches to help maximise rice productivity in medium- and low-yield provinces through radio, amplifying the limited reach of AEWs. Radio is one of the traditional media that is still being used in rural areas. Through the program, farmers who do not have access to the internet are still reached, ensuring that EAS uses all available channels to bring information to farmers. There are now 18,439 farmers who have benefitted from the said program.

16.3 Extension Policies, Assessment, and Monitoring and Evaluation

An enabling policy environment primarily determines the capacity of the system to innovate and the efficacy of technology transfer in the AIS. Without an enabling environment, EAS will not be effective and sustainable [Sulaiman and Davis, 2012]. This entails providing policy support, strengthening the planning, monitoring, and evaluation mechanisms such as assessment and tracer studies, determination of return of investment, and result and impact

[1] A radio station owned and controlled by the Philippines Department of Agriculture.

evaluation; human resource management; budget; infrastructure and facilities. An enabling policy environment ensures the sustainability of strategies and agenda for extension and technology transfer towards nutrition-sensitive agriculture and ensures food security.

Effective EAS must have a legal foundation and a mission, as well as effective links with research and farmer organisations, state financial support, well-trained and motivated AEWs, ongoing in-service trainings to fill knowledge gaps, incentives for AEWs to keep them motivated, and political backing to improve extension work [Baig and Aldosari, 2013]. Key reforms include pluralism, decentralisation, devolution, cost recovery, commercialisation, and privatisation. However, extension strategies need to be led from the inside, guided by understanding what works and what does not by the specifics of the local circumstances and environment [Sulaiman and Hall, 2005].

For the scaling of technologies to occur, policies must support innovation. Farmers and businesses, according to the World Bank [2012], would not take the risk of inventing under unfavourable conditions, and researchers would not engage in long-term activities that are not aligned with the regulatory structure. With complementing expenditures to establish a conducive environment, innovation and business development can occur.

Complementary to enabling policy environment is monitoring and evaluation (M&E). This is essential for technology transfer and AIS for assessment and prioritisation, as they allow insights into impact and change [World Bank, 2012]. Integrating lessons learned through monitoring and evaluation as the process evolves is integral in scaling. Appropriate indicators for process, outputs, and outcomes (immediate, intermediate, and ultimate) should be developed. With monitoring and evaluation, lessons learned from the pilot can be used to scale up the model to create more significant socioeconomic and developmental impacts [Anandajayasekeram, 2016]. Monitoring and evaluation can also provide insights on extension approaches and strategies, further ensuring that it is demand driven and responsive to the needs of the beneficiaries.

The DA has key extension policies, guidelines, and programs towards improving agriculture, including the fishery production system. The following policies, guidelines, and programs in the Philippines provide the principles and paradigms to beef up the agriculture and fishery extension system and address needs in the value chain — from agricultural production (including processing/value addition) to marketing. These include the Province-led Agriculture and Fisheries Extension System; One Research for Development and Extension Agenda and Programs; National Agriculture and Fisheries Modernization Plan 2021–2030; Philippine Action Plan for Family Farming, among others.

16.3.1 *Province-led Agriculture and Fisheries Extension System*

The Province-led Agriculture and Fisheries Extension System [DA-ATI, 2022b, 2022c] is an institutional arrangement in pursuing the full devolution of agriculture and fishery extension services to local government units, integrating the implementation of agriculture and fishery programs and related support services at the provincial level. It includes capacity building of local government units to plan and implement multiple agriculture and fishery programs. The province thus becomes the centre for operations. It strengthens the research-extension-farmer linkages in the provinces, improves institutional capabilities of local government units in agriculture and fishery extension, creates sustainable co-financing arrangements in agriculture and fishery extension and, in turn, enhances rural livelihoods and increases household income.

16.3.2 *OneDA Research for Development and Extension*

With the AIS approach, the DA is undergoing a significant transformation toward a unified and integrated agri-fishery Research for Development and Extension (OneDA R4DE) system. The R4DE continuum (Figure 16.1) was developed in response to the fragmentation of the R4DE system in the Philippines. This framework seeks to harmonise the programs and activities of the research and extension agencies of the DA, namely the Bureau for Agricultural Research and the DA-ATI, while also serving as a guide for key actors in technology development until the technology transfer and scaling process. Hence, the DA's Unified R4DE Agenda and Programs institutionalised modes of R4DE convergence, specifically co-development, co-financing, co-implementing, institutional arrangements for lead agencies, and local and network-based governance.

The National Agriculture and Fishery Modernization and Industrialization Plan 2021–2030 (NAFMIP) serves as a Directional Plan to steer sector-wide growth over the next decade. It will guide the trajectory of more detailed and operations-oriented agri-fishery development plans such as the commodity system roadmaps,

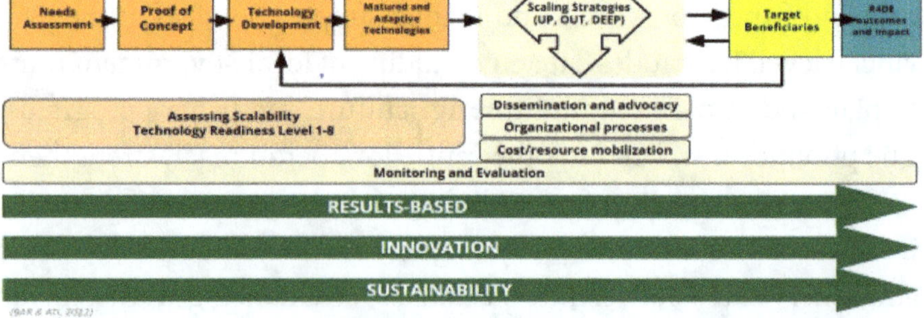

Figure 16.1 The R4DE continuum concept.

provincial commodity investment plans, and comprehensive land use plans. Thus, NAFMIP is more policy- and strategy-oriented but less detailed than previous iterations. The NAFMIP introduces several key innovations in planning and plan implementation, such as ICT-supported transformative planning, transformative performance indicators, commodity systems approach, a highlight on urban agriculture, and multi-sector consultations. NAFMIP utilises the AIS concept that aims to enhance research, development, and extension by incentivising the capacity of the agri-fishery sector to innovate and create novelty throughout value chains. NAFMIP will adopt e-marketing and other disruptive technologies to benefit smallholder farmers and fisherfolk [Department of Agriculture, 2022a].

16.3.3 *Philippine Action Plan for Family Farming*

The Philippine Action Plan for Family Farming is a ten-year plan with an overarching goal of prioritising two of the 17 Sustainable Development Goals to mobilise the whole nation, government, and civil society to end poverty and hunger among family members by 2028. It has three strategic action areas: an enabling policy environment, organised family farmers, and functional multi-stakeholder partnerships to address the root causes of family farmers' problems. In the Philippines, the concept of family farming is culture-based and family managed, highlighting the significant roles and needs of family farmers, small fishers, women, and the youth; the support for the transformation of family farming tenants and farmworkers into owner-cultivators based on existing asset reform laws; the government's thrust of clustering into production groups; and its contribution to sustainable management of land, soil, and water resources towards the achievement of just, inclusive, and sustainable development [DA-ATI, 2021]. This is also in conjunction with the Philippine Development Plan of 2023–2028 where the emphasis is on social transformation and inclusive economic growth by building an environment that allows for equal opportunities.

16.4 Conclusion

This chapter highlights the relevance of EAS in ensuring that small farmers have access to new technologies and the pressing socio-cultural, economic, environmental, and policy issues and challenges that EAS faces. Yet such challenges also paved the way for various opportunities that led to rethinking and creating new EAS strategies as outlined in the case studies. Lessons learned from these case studies established the need for AIS to have a plethora of complementary and need-based strategies to bring innovations and accelerate their adoption or adaptation. The promotion of climate-resilient inbred rice varieties, for instance, emphasises that all extension players must work together to harmonise and complement their efforts because the challenges hounding the agriculture and fishery sector are complex.

Strategies must also be grounded on relevant issues, timely data, and practical solutions that help the agriculture and fishery sector achieve food security. Relevant issues include demand-driven ideas that require immediate action. The sector's volatility and uncertainty need timely data for farmers to cope with the effects of climate change. Digital platforms, for instance, provide up-to-date information to guide farmers in altering their cropping calendar. Lastly, practical solutions such as training programs, scholarships, and internships continue to entice the youth to engage in agriculture, allowing them to see the sector as a viable career path.

While it has been established that innovations foster economic efficiency, transparency, and productivity, it is worth noting that these must be cognizant of other equally important factors that constitute agricultural life, such as social, cultural, spiritual, and psychological. Behind every strategy in extension, the farmers and fisherfolk must be put front and centre in the development process.

References

Abdel-Maksoud, B. M. (2019). The effective agricultural extension approach. *Asian Journal of Advanced Research and Reports*, 4(3), pp. 1–8.

Ancog, R. C., Ticsay, M. V. and D. Ruzol, C. (2018). Status of Climate Change Adaptation in Agriculture Sector in Asia. In M. Alam, J. Lee and P. Sawhney (Eds.), *Status of Climate Change Adaptation in Asia and the Pacific*, pp. 183–209. Springer.

Anandajayasekeram, P. (2016). *Scaling Up and Scalability: Concepts, Frameworks, and Assessment*. Vuna. https://beamexchange.org/resources/1166/

Ani, P. and Correa, A. (2016). Agricultural extension policies in the hilippines: towards enhancing the delivery of technological services. *Food and Fertilizer Technology Center for the Asian and Pacific Region (FFTC)*. https://ap.fftc.org.tw/article/1092

Baig, M. B., and Aldosari, F. (2013). Agricultural extension in Asia: constraints and options for improvement. *The Journal of Animal & Plant Sciences,* 23(2), pp. 619–632.

Caballero-Anthony, M. (2022). Non-Traditional Security Threats to Peace and Security in the Indo-Pacific. In V. A. Manhit (Ed.), *Beyond the Crisis: A Strategic Agenda for the Next President*, pp. 57–80. Stratbase Albert Del Rosario Institute for Strategic and International Studies.

Department of Agriculture. (2022a). *National Agriculture and Fisheries Modernization and Industrialization Plan 2021–2030: Transforming the Philippine Food System Together*. https://www.bswm.da.gov.ph/download/national-agriculture-and-fisheries-modernization-and-industrialization-plan-2021-2030/

Department of Agriculture. (2022b). One Research for Development and Extension Agenda and Programs.

Department of Agriculture — Agricultural Training Institute (DA-ATI). (2016). *National Extension Agenda and Programs (NEAP) 2017–2022.*

Department of Agriculture — Agricultural Training Institute (DA-ATI). (2019). Challenges and Opportunities Confronting the Philippine Agriculture and Fisheries Extension. In *Philippine Agriculture and Fisheries Extension Strategic Plan 2020–2022*, pp. 8–16. https://www.studocu.com/ph/document/city-college-of-el-salvador/export-marketing/ati-2019-enhanced-philippine-afe-strategic-plan-2020-2022-compressed/51520833

Department of Agriculture — Agricultural Training Institute (DA-ATI). (2021). *Philippine Action Plan for Family Farming 2019–2028.* https://ati2.da.gov.ph/ati-main/content/publications/pamela-mappala/philippine-action-plan-family-farming-2019-2028

Department of Agriculture — Agricultural Training Institute (DA-ATI). (2022a). *2021 Annual Accomplishment Report.* https://ati2.da.gov.ph/ati-4a/content/publications/maridelle-g-jaurigue/cadence-annual-accomplishment-report-2021

Department of Agriculture — Agricultural Training Institute (DA-ATI). (2022b). *Competency Assessment of Agricultural Extension Workers at the Local Government Units.*

Department of Agriculture — Agricultural Training Institute (DA-ATI). (2022c). PAFES Manual of Operations. https://ati.da.gov.ph/archives/ati-main/?q=content/pafes-manual-operations

Department of Agriculture - Agricultural Training Institute (DA-ATI). (2022d). ATI Operations Manual.

Fan, S., Teng, P., Chew, P., Smith, G. and Copeland, L. (2021). Food system resilience and COVID-19 — lessons from the Asian experience. *Global Food Security*, 28, p. 100501.

Food and Agriculture Organization of the United Nations (FAO). (2012). Impact of the Ukraine-Russia conflict on global food security and related matters under the mandate of the Food and Agriculture Organization of the United Nations (FAO). *FAO Hundred and Seventieth Council Session*. https://www.fao.org/3/nj164en/nj164en.pdf

Food and Agriculture Organization of the United Nations (FAO). (2017). *The Future of Food and Agriculture — Trends and Challenges*. https://www.fao.org/policy-support/tools-and-publications/resources-details/en/c/472484/

Heide-Ottosen, S., Vorbohle, T. and O'Neill, K. (2014). *The Ageing of Rural Populations: Evidence on Older Farmers in Low and Middle-Income Countries*. HelpAge International.

Howells, J. (2006). Intermediation and the role of intermediaries in innovation. *Research Policy*, 35, pp. 715–728.

International Rice Research Institute (IRRI). (2021). *Rice Crop Manager Harnessing Digital Agriculture: Lessons from the Philippines*. http://books.irri.org/RCM-Case-Study.pdf

Koutsouris, A. (2018). Role of Extension in Agricultural Technology Transfer: A Critical Review. In N. Kalaitzandonakes, E. G. Carayannis, E. Grigoroudis and S. Rozakis (Eds.), *From Agriscience to Agribusiness*, pp. 337–359. Springer.

Kusnandar, K., van Kooten, O. and Brazier, F. M. (2021). COCREATE: a self-directed learning approach to agricultural extension programmes. *Development in Practice*, 31(5), pp. 636–639.

Montesclaros, J. M. L. and Caballero-Anthony, M. (2022). Ukraine war and food security: how should ASEAN respond? *RSIS Commentaries, 053-22*. https://www.rsis.edu.sg/rsis-publication/nts/ukraine-war-and-food-security-how-should-asean-respond/

Olayemi, S., Ope-Oluwa, A. and Angba, C. (2021). Evolution of agricultural extension models in sub-saharan Africa: a critical review. *International Journal of Agricultural Extension and Rural Development Studies*, 8(1), pp. 29–51.

Olorunfemi, O. D., Oladele, O. I. and Olorunfemi, T. O. (2021). Perceived effects of professionalization of extension services by public and private agents in South West Nigeria. *Journal of Agricultural Extension*, 25(1), pp. 59–72.

Philippine Development Plan 2023–2028. https://pdp.neda.gov.ph

PhilRice. (2021). Farmers to benefit more from ICTs through infomediaries. https://www.philrice.gov.ph/farmers-to-benefit-more-from-icts-through-infomediaries/

PhilRice. (2022). Digital transformation: our next chapter. https://www.philrice.gov.ph/digital-transformation-our-next-chapter/

Philippine Statistics Authority (PSA). (2022). *Agricultural Indicators System 2017–2021*. https://psa.gov.ph/system/files/main-publication/2-%2528ons-cleared%2529_FO-4_AIS-Agricultural-Resources-ao-29July_ONS-signed.pdf

Sulaiman, R. and Hall, A. (2005). Extension policy at the national level in Asia. *Plant Production Science*, 8(3), pp. 308–319.

Sulaiman, R. and Davis, K. (2012). *The "New Extensionist": Roles, Strategies, and Capacities to Strengthen Extension and Advisory Services*. Global Forum for Rural Advisory Services. https://www.g-fras.org/en/activities/the-new-extensionist.html

World Bank. (2012). *Agricultural Innovation Systems: An Investment Sourcebook*. https://openknowledge.worldbank.org/handle/10986/2247

Issues in Increasing Available Food

https://doi.org/10.1142/9789811278297_0017

Chapter 17

The Dynamics of Food Production and Trade to Achieve Food Security

Rolando T. Dy, Senen U. Reyes, Marie Annette Dacul, Ditas R. Macabasco and Joy Kristel L. Orzales

Center for Food and Agri Business, University of Asia and the Pacific, Philippines

17.1 Introduction

Food production and trade are key factors that affect food security. In fact, one of the main pillars of food security which is food availability specifically points to "the existence of enough quantities of food of adequate quality, supplied through domestic production or imports".

Food security is part of the sustainable development goals (SDG) identified by the United Nations. In particular, SDG 2 seeks to end hunger and all forms of malnutrition by 2030, achieve food security and improved nutrition, and promote sustainable agriculture.

In Asia, which is home to about 4.7 billion people or more than half of the world's population, some progress has been made towards SDG 2. But food security remains a critical issue in the region. Some 9% (424.5 million) of its population suffered from hunger in 2021 [Food and Agriculture Organization (FAO) of the United Nations, 2022]. Further, an average of 9.5% (439.2 million) of the Asian population faced severe food insecurity from 2019–2021 while 23.9% (1.1 billion) faced moderate or severe food insecurity during the same period. The affected population represented at least half of the global prevalence — 10.7% (830.2 million) and 28.1% (2.2 billion), respectively, during the comparable period.

Food security is a complex matter. Achieving it will require addressing a host of issues such as climate change, the growing scarcity of land and water resources, consumption shifts, population growth, and rising input and commodity prices. The situation is exacerbated by the COVID-19 pandemic and the Russia-Ukraine war, which have caused major disruptions in global supply chains. Further, the current high food prices could evolve into a food availability crisis in 2023 if no actions are taken.

By 2050, Asia's population from 48 countries is projected to hit 5.3 billion. Considering such magnitude of people to feed, this chapter will basically address the question: "Does Asia produce an adequate quantity of basic commodities or is it import dependent?" It will present the current food security situation in the region, analyse what has been accomplished to address the issues especially in relation to the enablers and constraints, and discuss future prospects.

17.2 The Current State of Food Production and Trade in the Context of Food Security

17.2.1 *Food Availability*

17.2.1.1 *Production*

Availability of food is often the prioritised dimension of food security. It can be measured in terms of agricultural production and trade. In Asia, rice is a staple food, and its production is of primary value since it is the most consumed cereal crop. The region produced about 451.30 million tons of rice in 2020 (Table 17.1), which contributed 89% of world production. Next to rice in importance are maize and wheat, which are also significantly produced in Asia. In 2020, maize production in the region amounted to 365.31 million tons, which accounted for 31% of global output. In the same year, wheat production reached 347.92 million tons or 46% of world production. China is the major producer of the three commodities, accounting for 44% of total output in Asia.

Table 17.1 Selected commodity production, Asia (million tons). Source: UN FAO (2022). FAOSTAT Statistical Database: Production. Accessed 15 November 2022. https://www.fao.org/faostat/en/#data/QCL

Commodity	2016	2017	2018	2019	2020
Rice	440.06	448.86	454.39	449.17	451.30
Maize	358.92	359.52	363.14	360.77	365.31
Wheat	328.62	333.69	325.78	336.89	347.92
Soya beans	28.61	30.69	29.42	34.11	33.56
Meat of pig	66.49	66.75	66.51	54.45	53.26
Meat of chicken	36.96	39.94	42.15	43.25	43.49
Meat of cattle	14.11	14.49	14.89	15.14	15.31

Notes: Rice, paddy (rice milled equivalent); Meat of cattle and pig with bones, fresh or chilled; Meat of chicken, fresh or chilled.

For plant-based protein, the region produced 9% of overall soya bean production in 2020. In terms of sources of protein from animals, Asia is a major producer of pig meat. In 2020, pig meat production totalled 53.26 million tons or 48% of global output. Chicken and cattle meat are two other vital animal-based protein sources produced in the region. During the same period, the region produced 36% and 23%, respectively, of world meat production. China (mainland) contributed 56% of the total selected meat production in Asia.

17.2.1.2 *Trade*

Food trade is an essential part for Asia in assuring food supply to meet dietary needs. It also helps the region generate jobs and alleviate poverty, thereby boosting the economy [Lin *et al.*, 2022]. Although rice production mainly caters to domestic demand, the region exported on average twice the amount it imported over the five-year period, 2016–2020 (Table 17.2). In contrast, the region relies on imports to meet domestic demand of maize, wheat, and soya beans.

For meat, the region is a net importer of pork, chicken, and beef. The region nevertheless exports meat products, which reached a total of 1.56 million tons in 2020 or about 7% of world exports. The preference of the region for chicken meat to other meat is indicated by an increase in quantity imported in the last years. Pig meat imports more than doubled in 2020 after outbreaks of African swine fever in the region.

17.2.1.3 *Self-Sufficiency Ratio*

The self-sufficiency ratio (SSR) is the share of food produced to food consumed at the domestic level. A ratio greater than 100% indicates a production surplus. It shows the extent to which one region can

Table 17.2 Selected commodity trade, Asia, 2016–2020 (million tons). Source: UN FAO (2022). FAOSTAT Statistical Database: Trade. Accessed 15 November 2022. https://www.fao.org/faostat/en/#data/TCL

Commodity	2016	2017	2018	2019	2020
		IMPORTS			
Rice	15.32	18.43	19.71	17.85	17.61
Maize	64.42	53.09	71.59	78.57	84.07
Wheat	73.27	78.04	73.72	75.30	85.48
Soya beans	105.47	118.96	112.94	115.47	127.56
Meat of pig	1.51	1.26	1.18	1.79	3.53
Meat of chicken	5.22	5.12	5.23	5.64	6.38
Meat of cattle	0.38	0.45	0.54	0.61	0.67
		EXPORTS			
Rice	30.93	37.66	36.72	33.72	35.55
Maize	1.87	2.36	2.32	2.81	4.37
Wheat	5.04	5.03	8.57	6.26	6.57
Soya beans	0.57	0.60	0.47	0.38	0.33
Meat of pig	0.20	0.20	0.09	0.07	0.04
Meat of chicken	1.47	1.52	1.71	1.55	1.43
Meat of cattle	0.06	0.05	0.07	0.07	0.08

Notes: Rice, paddy (rice milled equivalent); Meat of cattle and pig with bones, fresh or chilled; Meat of chicken, fresh or chilled.

satisfy its food demand from its own production. It gives an insight of the self-capacity of the region to produce food. However, food self-sufficiency does not ensure food security in an area.

In Asia, most grains have relatively high SSR with at least 80% of the demand requirement being produced in the region (Figure 17.1). The rice ratio is more than 100% which means production is in large surpluses in the region. Soya beans recorded the lowest ratio with 21%, on average, from 2016 to 2020. Meat products registered high ratios with at least 90% of the demand requirement being produced in the region.

17.2.1.4 *Import Dependency Ratio*

Asia's relatively high SSR for most grains is related to its import dependency ratio (IDR), which indicates the extent to which an area's supply of commodities came from imports. A high ratio implies greater dependency on importation. Its focus on grains and food staples as in the rest of the world can be seen in its large production volumes led by rice in the last five years. Its import dependency is low, ranging from 3–4% (Figure 17.2) despite being host to the most populous countries (China, India, Indonesia, Pakistan) and top rice-importing countries (China, Philippines). This is somehow offset as the region is also host to the top rice-exporting countries (India, Vietnam, Thailand, Pakistan). However, Asia's import dependency in maize and wheat is still considerable at a fifth of its demand while it practically relies on imports for its soybean requirement. Except for rice, the region is a net importer of the other grain crops.

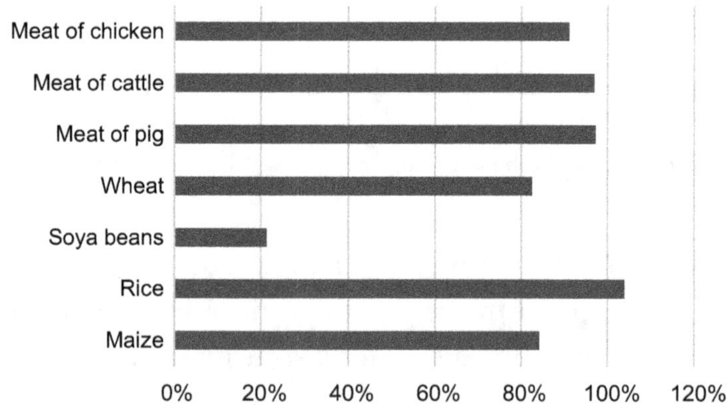

Figure 17.1 Self-sufficiency ratios for selected food commodities, Asia, 2016–2020. Notes: SSR = Production / (Production + Imports – Exports) ×100. Rice, paddy (rice milled equivalent); Meat of cattle and pig with bones, fresh or chilled; Meat of chicken, fresh or chilled. Source of basic data: UN FAO (2022). FAOSTAT Statistical Database: Production and Trade. Accessed 15 November 2022.

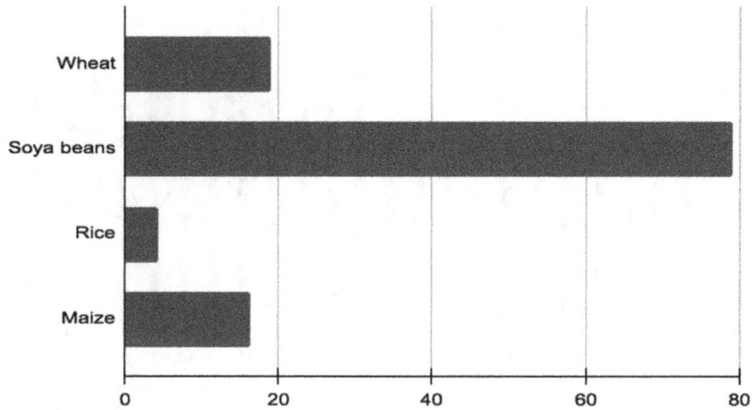

Figure 17.2 Import dependency ratios (in %) for selected grain crops, Asia, 2016–2020. Note: IDR = Imports / (Production + Imports – Exports) × 100. Source of basic data: UN FAO (2022). FAOSTAT Statistical Database: Production and Trade. Accessed 15 November 2022.

17.2.2 *Affordability*

Affordability of food measures the ability of consumers to purchase food to meet their nutritional requirements. It can be assessed using the food consumer price index (CPI) and food price inflation. The prevalence of moderate or severe food insecurity is also presented.

FAO defines CPI as "the price change between the current and reference periods of the average basket of goods and services purchased by households". Meanwhile, food price inflation is "annual year-over-year inflation or percentage change over corresponding month of the previous year".

Food CPI continued to increase over the period in Asia and reached its peak at 147.39 at the end of 2021 (Figure 17.3). There has also been a significant increase in food price inflation in the region since December 2019 because of the impact of the COVID-19 pandemic.

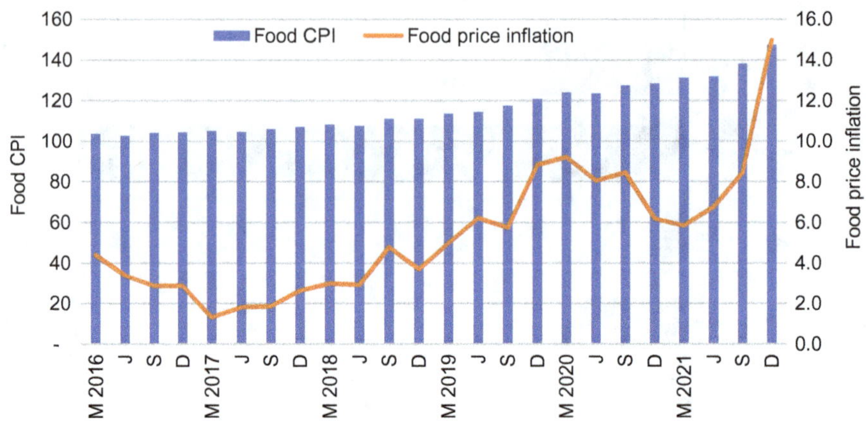

Figure 17.3 Food CPI and food price inflation (in %), Asia, 2016–2021 (2015 = 100). Source: UN FAO (2022). FAOSTAT Statistical Database: Prices. Accessed 15 November 2022. https://www.fao.org/faostat/en/#data/CP

The rise in prices which can be translated to the decline of purchasing power over time slowed down in the third quarter of 2020 to the first quarter of 2021 but began to soar up to 14% in December 2021 and more after. The price spikes are brought about by internal and external factors such as climate variability, production volatility, and market instability [Lin *et al.*, 2022].

The state of food insecurity in the region reveals that despite the availability of food in the region, affordability counts in ensuring food security. The prevalence of moderate or severe food insecurity in Asia rose during 2016 to 2020, and peaked in 2020 when 25.8% or about 1.2 billion people experienced food insecurity (Figure 17.4). It was exacerbated by the COVID-19 pandemic that led to high food prices. A slight improvement was recorded in 2021 when it dropped to 24.6%.

Striking a balance in the demand and supply of food is key in the pursuit for food security. It is not just about having food but making

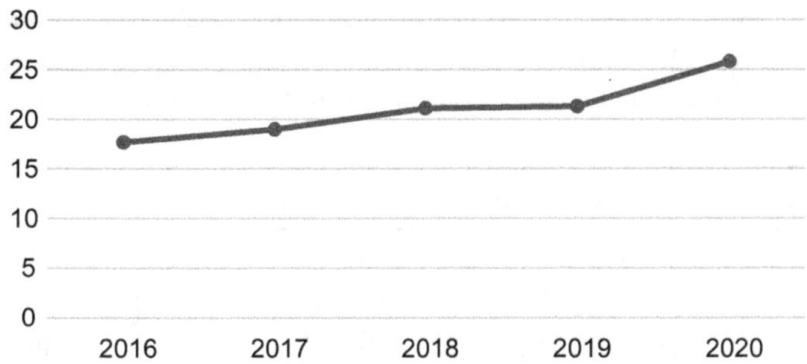

Figure 17.4 Prevalence of moderate or severe food insecurity (in %), Asia, 2016–2020. Source: UN FAO (2022). FAOSTAT Statistical Database: Food Security and Nutrition. Accessed 15 November 2022. https://www.fao.org/faostat/en/#data/FS

it affordable and available. In many Asian countries, strategies like farm consolidation, mechanisation and logistics are proven approaches to achieve economies in production. Furthermore, it is also crucial to consider the other two pillars of food security — ensuring food quality and safety, as well as minimising the susceptibility to climate and natural resources risks. Food quality and safety becomes even more important especially at this challenging time, wherein eating healthy and keeping healthy have become a precept. So is coping with the risks related with climate change as it impacts on food production [Dy, 2021].

17.2.3 *Major Players in the Asian Food System*

17.2.3.1 *Food Producers*

The major players in agricultural production in Asia are China and India (Table 17.3). China led with 71% share (260.7 million tons) of Asia's maize production, soya bean with 54% (19.6 million tons) and rice with 31% (141.3 million tons). It is also a major producer of meat, accounting for 77% of meat of pig (41.1 million tons), 39%

Table 17.3 Major country players by commodity, 2020 (in tons and %). Source: UN FAO (2022). FAOSTAT Statistical Database: Trade — Crops and Livestock Products. Accessed 18 November 2022. https://www.fao.org/faostat/en/#data/TCL

Commodity	Production	Exports	Imports
Rice	China* (141.3 M, 31%)	India* (14.5 M, 41%)	China* (2.9 M, 17%)
Maize	China (260.7 M, 71%)	India (1.8 M, 41%)	Japan (15.8 M, 19%)
Soya beans	China (19.6 M, 58%)	China (0.79 M, 24%)	China* (100.3 M, 79%)
Wheat	China* (134.3 M, 39%)	Kazakhstan (5.2 M, 79%)	Indonesia* (10.3 M, 12%)
Meat of cattle	China (6.0 M, 39%)	Pakistan (0.67 M, 80%)	China* (0.30 M, 44%)
Meat of chicken	China (15.1 M, 35%)	Turkey (0.52 M, 37%)	China* (1.5 M, 24%)
Meat of pig	China* (41.1 M, 77%)	Hong Kong (0.18 M, 44%)	China* (3.2 M, 92%)

*Also the leading global exporter.

of meat of cattle (6.0 million tons), and 35% of meat of chicken (15.1 million tons).

In the case of India, it produced 26% (118.9 million tons) of Asia's rice production, 34% (11.2 million tons) of soya bean production and 31% (107.6 million tons) of wheat production in 2020.

17.2.3.2 *Food Importers*

The top importer in Asia in 2020 was also China. It was the biggest importer of rice even if it also dominated its production. Its other leading imports were soya beans accounting for 79% (100.3 million tons) of the commodity imports in Asia, rice 17% (2.9 million tons), meat of pig 92% (3.2 million tons) and meat of cattle 44% (297,000 tons). Aside from China, Japan was also big in maize imports accounting for 19% (15.8 million tons) of the volume.

17.2.3.3 *Food Exporters*

For exports, the biggest in Asia in 2020 was India. India accounted for 41% each of Asia's total exports of maize (1.8 million tons) and rice (14.5 million tons). Other leading exporters in the region include Kazakhstan for wheat with a share of 79% (5.2 million tons), China (0.79 million tons) and Turkey (0.78 million tons) for soya beans (24% each), Turkey for meat of chicken with 37% (0.52 million tons), Pakistan for meat of cattle with 80% (0.66 million tons), and Hong Kong for meat of pig with 44% (0.19 million tons).

17.2.4 *Food Balance Sheets*

The food balance sheet shows the comprehensive picture of food supply during a specific reference period. It shows the data of the commodities' supply and utilisation, where the utilisation is categorised into human consumption, exports and non-human consumption (e.g., feeds, seeds, other non-food uses) [FAO, n.d.].

Rice and products (539.8 million tons) have the highest food supply availability in Asia in 2019, followed by wheat and products (297.2 million tons). For meat products, notable were pig meat (71.4 million tons), poultry meat (48.5 million tons), and bovine meat (22.7 million tons) (Table 17.4). Maize dominated in terms of usage as feeds.

Food utilisation of rice and rice products accounted for 83.9% of the total domestic supply in 2019. The region also exported 7.3% of the commodity while 4.4% was used as feeds. Per capita

Table 17.4 Food balance sheet of selected commodities, Asia, 2019 (million tons). Source: UN FAO (2022). FAOSTAT Statistical Database: Food Balances. Accessed 27 October 2022. https://www.fao.org/faostat/en/#data/FBS

	Rice and products	Wheat and products	Maize and products	Soya bean	Pig meat	Poultry meat	Bovine meat
Domestic supply	643.1	376.6	445.9	135.8	71.5	48.7	23.0
Feeds	28.4	41.9	291.7	6.1	—	—	25
Food	539.8	297.2	47.6	8.3	71.4	48.5	22.7
Processing	9.9	1.7	11.9	116.7	a	a	.014
Other uses (non-food)	18.7	5.3	73.4	0.3	—	—	—
Seed	16.2	12.4	3.5	1.7	—	—	—
Food supply*	118	65	10	2	16	11	5

*kg/capita/year.

a — less than 1,000 tons.

food supply stood at 118 kg/year, which increased by only 0.5% since 2015.

For wheat and products, domestic supply was mostly used as food accounting for 78.9% (297.2 million tons). It has the second highest per capita consumption in 2019 with 65 kg/year, which increased only by 0.3% on average from 2015. From 2015–2019, wheat production increased by 1.4% per year, imports by 4.2% per annum and feed utilisation by 4.3% yearly.

Meat commodities (pig, poultry and bovine) were also mainly used as food in the region in 2019. Annual per capita consumption in 2019 were at 16 kg, 11 kg, and 5 kg, respectively. Pig meat has the highest domestic supply, followed by poultry meat and bovine meat. Production of pig meat fell by 17.9% in 2019 due to the African swine fever that resulted in increased imports by 10.5%.

For maize, about 65% of the total domestic supply was used as feeds in 2019, which increased by an average of 5.6% from 2015. Food supply was at 10.7% while other uses (non-food) accounted for 16.5%. Maize in the region is being utilised as non-food, mainly as feeds.

The region relies on imports to meet domestic demand for certain products. This is especially true for wheat, soya beans and maize. Imports of soya beans were high, representing 85% of the domestic supply imported in 2019. Soya beans were mainly processed, accounting for about 86% of the total domestic supply.

17.3 Asian Action to Address Food Security Issues

Generally, approaches to addressing the issues on food security have been focused on grains and/or food staples under country-specific policies and programs. The FAO [FAO *et al.*, 2022] noted that "national food security policies were designed with the aim of ensuring national food availability, particularly for cereals". This allowed countries to be able to provide and meet the daily dietary energy requirement though the same FAO document noted that the average share of the cost of staple foods is only 15% of the total cost in a healthy diet.

17.3.1 *China*

China for instance released "The Number 1 Document" in February 2022 whose first stipulation is to "Make every effort to do a good job in grain production and supply of important agricultural products" followed by the second point to "Strengthen the basic support of modern agriculture". It seeks to ensure self-sufficiency in grains with an output of 1.3 trillion kg coming from its own production of Chinese grain. This is supported with measures to protect cultivated land which must be observed at 1.8 billion mu (120 million hectares). Furthermore, it is indicated that 100 million mu (6.7 million hectares) of high-standard farmland and 400 million mu (26.7 million hectares) of high-efficiency water-saving irrigation will be built in 2022. Its 14th Five-Year Plan included grain security.

The document includes an enabling mechanism to encourage grain production by way of a reasonable guarantee to give grain farmers a profitable income. This will be done through an increase in the minimum purchase price of rice and wheat, stabilising producer subsidies, covering insurance and increasing incentives.

Other programs and projects include the increase in the production of soybeans and oilseeds, guaranteeing supply of "vegetable basket" products, stabilising support policies and production of live pigs, expansion of beef, mutton and dairy production, stabilising the area for aquaculture and improving the quality of fishery development. Additional basic support services include the promotion of research on key agricultural technologies such as seed industry revitalisation and improvement in the research, development and application of agricultural mechanisation. Part of China's food security strategy is to make overseas investments in agriculture.

17.3.2 *India*

India has the National Food Security Act 2013 which provides for a public distribution system of food grains to identified sectors of the population. This entitles eligible households to receive 5 kg of food grains per person per month at subsidised prices or 35 kg of food grains per household per month at prices specified. Under the Act, the different branches of government of India have set objectives towards food and nutritional security. These objectives include the revitalisation of agriculture, related interventions on procurement, storage and movement of food grains, and access to related support such as drinking water, health care and adequate pensions.

The occurrence of the COVID-19 pandemic during the early part of 2020 brought forth additional issues on food security. To help address these issues, the Government of India has implemented the large-scale distribution of free food grain through the PM Garib Kalyan Anna Yojana. It is a food security welfare scheme for its poorest citizens which provides 5 kg of rice or wheat per person and 1 kg of dal to families with a ration card.

17.3.3 *ASEAN Plus 3*

The Association of Southeast Asian Nations (ASEAN) entity started with membership from ten ASEAN member states and subsequently evolved into the ASEAN Plus 3 entity. ASEAN Plus Three consist of ten ASEAN member states and the People's Republic of China, Japan and the Republic of Korea. Member states of the ASEAN formulated and implemented the ASEAN Integrated Food Security Framework from 2009–2020 and two Strategic Plans of Action on Food Security (SPA-FS) in 2009–2013 and 2015–2020. The Framework aims to ensure long-term food security and nutrition and improve the livelihood of farmers. The priority crops included are rice, maize, soybean, sugar and cassava.

This was extended to 2021–2025 and adopted by the ASEAN Ministers of Agriculture and Forestry in October 2020. The SPA-FS 2021–2025 has nine strategic thrusts with its own set of outputs, activities, deliverables, timeline, and identified agencies and partners. The first strategic thrust is to strengthen food security including emergency/shortage relief arrangement. A main item in this thrust is the country-specific implementation of the ASEAN Plus Three Emergency Rice Reserve agreement signed in October 2011 by the ASEAN member states together with China, Japan and South Korea. The agreement aspires to strengthen production, prevent postharvest losses, promote labour opportunities and provide rapid response to supply shortages in emergencies in any signatory country.

The participation of Japan and South Korea in the agreement may be seen as a means for the two food import-dependent countries to have secure access to rice which is its major staple. Both are, however, committed to be rice self-sufficient and already have a high self-sufficiency rate. The Japanese government has also started the review of the Basic Law on Food, Agriculture and Rural Areas to strengthen the country's food security. Under the review, areas that can be explored are the expansion of grain production, provision of more subsidies, crop selection and prioritisation for domestic production, and strengthening ties with its major country food suppliers. The use of innovation and digital technologies is a key pillar in the Kishida government's food security plan. It aims to increase productivity and inspire young people to go into agriculture.

South Korea's 2021–2025 National Food Program provides for an increase in the public rice reserve, increase in the self-sufficiency in wheat and beans, and increase in the provision of agricultural and food vouchers for underprivileged citizens. The government created the National Institute of Crop Science in 2018 to increase domestic wheat production. The Ministry of Agriculture, Food and Rural Affairs indicated that to support the increase in the production of major grains, additional infrastructure will be built and expanded like production, storage and processing facilities.

Regional trade regimes such as the ASEAN Trade in Goods Agreement, Asia-Pacific Economic Cooperation, and ASEAN Free Trade Agreements with partner countries have paved the way for economic and trade cooperation in agriculture and food towards food security. The Regional Comprehensive Economic Partnership Agreement entered into force on January 1, 2022 among ten countries with South Korea joining a month later. It is expected that four other member states of the ASEAN will complete the RCEP to 15 countries.

17.4 Future Prospects

Food production remains the main base of food security. Across countries in Asia, performance is mixed. With food security in the region mainly focused on cereal crops especially rice, Asia actually presents a contrasting picture. On one hand, it boasts of hosting the world's biggest exporters of rice — India, Thailand, Vietnam and Pakistan — but on the other hand, it is also home to the world's biggest importers of the commodity — China and the Philippines. But overall, Asia is a surplus producer of rice. For other key cereal crops like maize and wheat, local production is short of demand, with imports accounting for about a fifth of supply. In terms of protein sources, Asia is able to produce at least 90% of its meat requirements but imports a substantial share of plant-based protein soya beans, as well as plant-based animal feed.

The role of imports in food security specially to address the lack of production or shortfalls in production cannot be understated. A case in point is Singapore which imports more than 90% of its food requirements and yet performs relatively well when it comes to food security. A key contributory factor is effective stock management, with supply coming from a diversified base, and the relatively high household food affordability. The Singapore case is a stark contrast to Indonesia, whose food security policy is anchored on food self-sufficiency. Indonesia focused on growing its own food to feed its people but rather than contributing to food security, the policy resulted in high food prices, food shortages and weak investments and innovation in agriculture [Springer, 2022]. Further, the country continued to import many commodities although the government limits importations through tariffs and quotas.

The overall food security picture in Asia is not very encouraging. In 2021, some 10.5% (484.5 million) of the population in the region suffered from severe food insecurity. More than double the number — 24.5% (1.1 billion) of the population — experienced moderate or severe food insecurity.

With the region's population projected to reach 5.3 billion by 2050, food production needs to increase by 60–70% in order to keep up with the growth in demand. As it is, Asia is already a booming market with various forces at work: huge population base, increasing middle class and rising incomes. Further, Asia's expanding middle class will shift demand towards poultry and livestock products which actually require more resources for their production.

Several pathways can be pursued to improve the food security picture: increasing local production and productivity, sustainable agriculture, climate change adaptation and resilience, investments in innovation and technologies, education, training and research for development and improving governance.

17.4.1 *Increasing Production and Productivity*

Increases in production can be realised through area expansion and higher productivity. But across countries in Asia, there are common constraints to increasing production such as climate change, sustainability, food wastage, industrialisation, urbanisation, shrinking farmlands and labour force, and aging farmers and fishers. Further, given the growing scarcity of land, water and other natural resources, there may be limited room to increase harvested areas.

But there is a lot of potential to increase yield levels especially given that many crops perform below par. This could be done through the use of better production technologies, seeds/breeds, mechanisation and more scale. Productivity can also be helped by reducing postharvest losses.

Diversification of production can also be pursued not only to boost income streams but also to provide for a wider choice of commodities for a healthier diet.

17.4.2 *Sustainable Agriculture*

Achieving a balance among economic, social and environmental aspects of agriculture will also be key to address food security. Production has to be made sustainable moving forward through adoption of improved agricultural practices that will protect the soil, conserve water, manage pests and diseases, among other things.

Perhaps a related concept is food sovereignty which also emphasises "ecologically appropriate production, distribution and consumption, social economic justice and local food systems as ways to tackle hunger and poverty and guarantee sustainable food security for all peoples" as cited in www.changeforchildren.org.

17.4.3 *Climate Change Adaptation and Resilience*

Climate change has been affecting the food production environment with the occurrence of more frequent and more intense weather disturbances that wreak havoc on agriculture areas. Talk about longer droughts, more intense typhoons, flooding, and forest fires.

Climate change can have impacts on production, infrastructure and livelihoods, cause market disruptions and lead to increases in commodity prices. In turn, these have repercussions to food security especially in the aspects of availability, accessibility and affordability. There is a need to climate-proof agriculture to cushion the impacts, for example, possibly through adopting varieties that are more tolerant to drought or water logging.

17.4.4 *Investments in Innovation and Technologies*

Innovation is crucial in order to remain relevant. The food production systems must evolve considering the challenges of the times — climate change, land and water scarcity, among others.

Digitalisation is an area worth investing in. There is a need to take advantage of information technology to improve processes across the whole supply chain from input sourcing down to markets. After all, food security is beyond just production. It encompasses the whole supply chain from input supply, production, processing, trading and to markets, including logistics.

17.4.5 *Education, Training and Research*

Educating people that each and every one has a role to play to help address food security is important. Food security is not just the job of the government. It requires collaborative effort and partnerships with the private sector and the general public/consumers.

Continuous research must be pursued to improve on inputs, products and processes. Equally important is human resource development/training to be able to effect changes.

17.4.6 *Governance*

While food security is a collaborative effort, the government's role is crucial especially in setting policy directions and pursuing interventions that are responsive to the needs of the time. Political commitment/will is key.

Addressing the food security issue becomes even more daunting especially in the light of climate change, growing scarcity of resources, distribution bottlenecks, changing consumption patterns, among others. More recent events such as the COVID-19 pandemic and the Russia-Ukraine war have put further pressure on production systems and global supply chains. They have resulted in trade constraints as the regular flow of agricultural, fishery and food products has been disrupted with export restrictions, trade sanctions, border controls and logistics problems.

The COVID-19 pandemic and the Russia-Ukraine conflict, which have impacted the world, somehow raise questions on the level of food self-sufficiency a country should have in order to maintain its food security. Can globalisation and trade liberalisation still be relied upon especially in emergency situations where a country can buy its food needs anywhere, anytime?

The dynamics of food production and trade towards food security is a complex matter especially in Asia, which is home to more than half of the world's consumers. The region is a major producer, importer and exporter of food with much potential to increase productivity. However, it still needs a diversified supply base to meet its food demand. National approaches to addressing the food security issue vary; there is no single solution for all. But certainly, fostering collaboration and cooperation across countries, governments and peoples towards the common goal will make a lot of difference.

References

ASEAN Secretariat. (2020). *ASEAN Integrated Food Security Framework.* https://asean.org/wp-content/uploads/2020/11/42-AIFS-Framework-SPAFS-Final-13-July-2020.pdf

Change for Children Learn & Teach Food Sovereignty Resources. (n.d.) Food security vs. Food Sovereignty: What's the difference? https://changeforchildren.org/wp-content/uploads/2016/06/Food-Security-vs-Food-Sovereignty.pdf

Debnath, D., Babu, S.C., Ghosh, P. and Helmer, M. (2017). The impact of India's food security policy on domestic and international rice market. *IFPRI Discussion Paper 1635.* http://ebrary.ifpri.org/cdm/ref/collection/p15738coll2/id/131151

Dy, R. T. (2021). Measuring food security across countries. Food and Agri Business Monitor, pp. 2–3.

Economist Intelligence Unit. (2022). *Global Food Security Index 2022.* https://impact.economist.com/sustainability/project/food-security-index

Food and Agriculture Organization (FAO) of the United Nations. (2022). https://www.fao.org/faostat/en/#data. Accessed November 15, 2022.

FAO. (n.d.). Food balance sheets. https://www.fao.org/economic/the-statistics-division-ess/publications-studies/publications/food-balance-sheets/en/

FAO, IFAD, UNICEF, WFP and WHO. (2022, various years). *The State of Food Security and Nutrition in the World.* https://www.fao.org/publications/home/fao-flagship-publications/the-state-of-food-security-and-nutrition-in-the-world/en

Goedde, L., Denis, N., Tanaka, M., Yamada, Y. and Nakada, K. (2017). Building a food security strategy for Japan in an age of global competition. *McKinsey.* https://www.mckinsey.com/featured-insights/asia-pacific/food-security-in-japan-building-a-strategy-in-an-age-of-global-competition

Lin, H.-I., Yu, Y.-Y., Wen, F.-I. and Liu, P.-T. (2022). Status of food security in East and Southeast Asia and challenges of climate change. *Climate 2022*, 10, p. 40.

Roy, A. (2022). China's food security strategy in the new era: policies and challenges. *Organisation for Research on China and Asia*. https://orcasia.org/2022/09/chinas-food-security-strategy-in-the-new-era-policies-and-challenges/

SG101. (2014). Key points on ensuring food security in Singapore. https://www.sg101.gov.sg/resources/current-topics/ensuring foodsecurityinsingapore

Springer, K. (2022). Australia has a solution to Indonesia's soaring food prices. *The Interpreter*. https://www.lowyinstitute.org/the-interpreter/australia-has-solution-indonesia-s-soaring-food-prices

The Gazette of India Extraordinary. (2013). *The National Food Security Act 2013*. https://nfsa.gov.in/portal/nfsa-act

US Department of Agriculture Foreign Agricultural Service. (2022). *PRC Emphasizing Grain and Food Security in 2022*. Global Agricultural Information Network, Report No. CH2022-0029. https://www.fas.usda.gov/data/china-prc-emphasizing-grain-and-food-security-2022

https://doi.org/10.1142/9789811278297_0018

Chapter 18

Urban Agriculture as a Mainstream Contributor to Food Security

Elyssa Kaur Ludher

ISEAS-Yusof Ishak Institute, Singapore

18.1 Introduction: The Need to Expand Urban Agriculture

Urban agriculture, consisting of home-based, community-based, commercial, and institutional farms, are already commonplace in many parts of Asia. From Ahmedabad to Zhuhai, households grow herbs and fruits in backyards and balconies, and cities reserve marginal spaces for community farms. Schools often teach horticulture, and some set aside land for food growing. Peri-urban farms provide fresh foods to markets and supplement incomes with recreational activities. Urban agriculture is recognised as a part of any green, sustainable, and liveable city. The movement controls and supply chain disruptions due to COVID-19 and the Russian invasion of Ukraine have further highlighted the need for more resilient food systems [Ben Hasan and El Bilali, 2022], which includes urban agriculture [Food and Agriculture Organization (FAO) *et al.*, 2022].

Yet "commonplace" is not enough. Urban agriculture needs to go beyond the 5–20% that it contributes to our food supply [Teng, 2020], to ensure that our future, both urban and rural, is more resilient and food secure.

By 2050, food production needs to increase by 70% from 2005 levels [FAO, 2009] to feed the expected population of 9.8 billion [UN, 2017], up from its current 8 billion. This is even as urbanisation has led to the loss of 1.5 million hectares (ha) of agricultural land annually [Akaeze and Nandwani, 2020].

Intensifying conventional agriculture in non-urban areas can only contribute to part of the solution. Relying on genetic modification, precision agrochemicals, and automation will increase yields; however, climate change may shift agricultural landscapes. Recent scientific reports have projected that more than 30% of global crop and livestock areas could become climatically unsuitable by 2100 in the worst-case scenario [IPCC, 2022].

With rapid urbanisation, it is also unrealistic and inequitable to rely on the dwindling rural population for food production. By 2030, three in five persons will live in cities, and by 2050, two in three [UN, 2020]. Between 2020 and 2050, the urban population is expected to rise by a further 20% in East Asia, 58% in Southeast Asia, and 81% in South Asia [Cabbanes *et al.*, 2022]. As food demand will continue to come mainly from cities, it is thus natural that cities should be involved in the production of food.

To seriously contribute to food security, urban agriculture must be part of a city's masterplan. Urban agriculture is well documented to contribute to social, environmental, and economic benefits (see Section 18.3), yet most cities do not give it the weight of other urban needs such as water, transport, or housing. Urban farmland is often developed into housing estates, townships, roads, commercial centres, and others. For urban agriculture to make a significant dent to food security, it needs to be given equal priority.

New technologies have made urban agriculture economically competitive in land-scarce cities. Food can now be grown indoors — on rooftops, on verges, underground and other marginal or unconventional spaces, using hydroponics, aquaculture or in containers. Other new technologies mean that food can also now be manufactured or grown in a lab from cells. Food production is thus no longer limited to large, fertile lands.

Few cities, however, have policies that comprehensively facilitate urban agriculture. According to a World Bank study, food policy has been a "blind spot" in many emerging Asian cities, due to being overwhelmed by the weighty challenges associated with unplanned growth — underdeveloped infrastructure, environmental pollution, education, health, etc. [Acharya *et al.*, 2021]. Yet Asia's rapid urbanisation is precisely the reason there is an urgency to address food resilience, before harmful policies are "locked in" for decades to come, creating needless setbacks and resulting in missed opportunities [Acharya *et al.*, 2021].

It is thus timely for cities to take steps to incorporate urban agriculture into city plans and policies. This chapter will thus delve into urban agriculture — how it is defined, what are its benefits, how it is being adopted in cities, and then identify facilitative actions to catalyse the expansion of urban agriculture so that it is a mainstream contributor to food security.

18.2 What is Urban Agriculture?

The FAO defines urban agriculture as "the practices that yield food and other outputs from agricultural production and related processes (among others transformation, distribution, marketing, recycling), taking place on land and other spaces within cities and surrounding regions, involving urban and peri-urban actors, communities, methods, places, policies, institutions, systems, ecologies and economies, largely using and regenerating local resources to meet changing needs of local populations while serving multiple goals and functions" [FAO *et al.*, 2022]. In short: "The production of food and other outputs and related processes, taking place on land and other spaces within cities and surrounding regions" [FAO *et al.*, 2022].

Based on the *Urban and Peri-Urban Agriculture Sourcebook*, urban agriculture can be broadly grouped into the types summarised below [FAO *et al.*, 2022].

18.2.1 *Home-Based Farming*

This is the most common form of urban agriculture. Outputs are vegetables, herbs, fish, or livestock. Production may be in front/backyards, balconies, window sills, rooftops, or indoor spaces. With small-scale "growlight" and hydroponic technologies increasingly available, home-based farms are no longer only grown in the ground, pots, or containers. Fish may also be grown in ponds or containers. Small-scale livestock farms of chicken, guinea pigs, goats or others may also contribute to household food security. Livestock could also be confined to the home or allowed to roam. Food produced is mostly for self-consumption.

18.2.2 *Community-Focused Farming*

These are often outdoor farms that could be situated in residential, recreational, educational, industrial, or commercial spaces in a city. Many urban farms are established due to their considerable community benefits (see Section 18.3). Farms can range from one or two square metres to hundreds. Spaces could be farmed collectively or in allotments. Participation is often open to the public, or could be run by a formal group, a cooperative, or a loose group of farmers. Similarly, the produce may be for individual use, the community, or welfare. Some farms may prefer more organic, regenerative, or traditional farming methods, while others may include irrigation or hydroponic systems, or be combined with livestock farming.

Community-based farms have had an important contribution in times of stress. During World War One and Two, "Victory Gardens" (Figure 18.1) were set up in public parks or private residences in the United States, United Kingdom, Canada, Australia, and Germany to supplement rations and to boost morale [Caves, 2004]. In 1943, of the 18 million victory gardens in the United States, 12 million were in cities [Caves, 2004].

18.2.3 *Commercial Farms*

These can be outdoor or indoor farms within the confines of the urban or metropolitan region. It can be for horticulture, fish, livestock or fungi farming. They can be grown on soil/land, in greenhouses, or indoors. Technologies adopted include hydroponics (or its derivatives — aeroponics or aquaponics), recirculating aquaculture systems, or others.

Commercial farms have always been part of cities — in fact most cities grow on and around prosperous farming communities

Figure 18.1 Victory gardens were planted in World War One and Two to supplement food rations and boost morale. Source: Wikimedia Commons.

[Bricas and Conaré, 2019]. Indeed, the historical growth of cities, especially in Europe, has been strongly influenced by the proximity to food sources [Steel, 2013]. With urbanisation, commercial farms have often been pushed to peri-urban areas [Bricas and Conaré, 2019]. However, the rise of technology and the ability to farm more intensively in small spaces have allowed commercial farms to be established in city centres, including on rooftops, underground, industrial spaces or even shop lots. In Seoul, a farm-to-retail facility was even found at a downtown Metro station (Figure 18.2).

18.2.4 *Institutional Farms*

These are food-growing facilities within institutions — schools, universities, prisons, hospitals, etc. — that cater to its community. Its purpose is typically for social benefits — health, education, interaction, etc.

Figure 18.2 A farm-to-retail concept at a metro station in Seoul with minimal labour. Source: Eugene Tay, reproduced with permission.

Beyond food, urban agriculture could also contribute to livestock feed, ornamental planting (such as flowers), or for enhancing biodiversity and providing ecological services (through pollination, habitat creation, ecological bridges and other benefits).

18.3 What are the Benefits of Urban Agriculture?

The benefits of urban agriculture can be grouped into four areas: food and nutritional security, environment and ecosystem services, economic benefits, and social benefits (Figure 18.3).

Urban agriculture provides food and nutritional security as fresh produce retains nutrition for longer. By harvesting on demand, yield over time may be higher, with less waste. Where farming uses organic and regenerative principles, produce may also be a better source of

Figure 18.3 Benefits of urban agriculture.

vitamins, micronutrients and proteins compared to conventionally farmed foods. Urban farms often also offer a variety of species to enrich diets; this diversity also increase resilience against disease.

Urban agriculture also supports environmental quality and ecosystem services by enhancing greenery in urban spaces — rooftops, balconies, road verges and vertical spaces. They may not only slow rainwater runoff, act as groundwater sinks and retain habitats for fauna, but also alleviate the urban heat island effect. Where farming utilises regenerative techniques such as companion cropping, no-till farming, or organic composting, farms may also protect and enrich soils, and sequester carbon. Participating in food growing often enhances environmental and ecological awareness. Urban and peri-urban forestry also improves air quality, mitigates urban warming, reduces erosion, and maintains biodiversity. One study found that urban agriculture provided ecosystem services that equate to approximately $33 billion annually [Clinton *et al.*, 2018].

Economically, urban agriculture allows income savings and moderates the effects of price volatility, thus it is an effective poverty alleviation tool [FAO, 2011]. It provides opportunities for social and economic integration of women, youth, and urban newcomers, as intensive horticulture units can provide between 10 and 40 jobs per hectare [FAO, 2011]. Beyond low-income communities, urban agriculture also benefits the wider public. Having short supply chains means food retailers may be less inclined to overstock as foods are more accessible. Urban agriculture has also created more liveable environments; urban farms have been known to improve property values; one study found that community gardens in New York City raised neighbouring property values by nearly 10% [Voicu and Been, 2008]. Urban farms have become an attractive urban design feature. Recognising this, a skyscraper in the middle of the central business district in Singapore incorporated a public urban farm on its rooftop (Figure 18.4).

Finally, urban agriculture contributes numerous social benefits, such as community cohesion, mental health improvement, and active lifestyles that improve physical fitness. A study in Singapore showed that those who are involved in community gardens reported higher levels of resilience and optimism than non-gardening control groups [Koay and Dillon, 2020]. Furthermore, those involved in

Figure 18.4 An urban farm on the 51st storey of a commercial building in the central business district of Singapore.

community gardening have higher levels of social empowerment and sense of belonging to the community [Booth *et al.*, 2018].

18.4 Expanding Urban Agriculture for Impact

Today, urban agriculture is a common facet in sustainable and liveable cities. A cursory analysis of some of the "most liveable cities" in 2021 (top ten and top five Asian cities, see Table 18.1), as defined by the Economist Intelligence Unit, shows that all cities had provisions for urban agriculture.[1] There is, however, a difference in

[1] Note: the EIU Global Liveability Ranking does not include presence of urban agriculture in its calculation. The EIU ranking was used merely to identify cities considered liveable.

extent — of type of urban agriculture, and how it is incorporated into policy (see Table 18.2 — a fuller description is in Annex 18.1).

Indeed, culture and tradition have entrenched urban farming in many Asian cities. This is especially true for cities in China and Japan, which pushed for urban agriculture programmes decades ago when urbanisation threatened the sector (see box story on Beijing).

Table 18.1 Top liveable cities based on EIU Global Liveability Ranking 2021.

Global	Top Asian Cities
1.Melbourne	15. Tokyo
2.Vienna	17. Osaka
3. Vancouver	46. Hong Kong
4. Toronto	49. Singapore
5. Adelaide	58. Seoul
6. Calgary	
7. Sydney	
8. Perth	
9. Auckland	
=10. Helsinki	
=10. Zurich	

Table 18.2 Urban agriculture in policy, and prevalence of each group, in top global liveable cities.[1]

	Urban agriculture part of general policy	Has standalone urban agriculture policy
Has community- and home-based gardens	**Adelaide**: part of state policy	**Auckland**: *Community Gardens Policy*

[1] Note: Due to lack of published data, this analysis is based on author's research in November–December 2022. Institutional urban agriculture is not included due to lack of information.

Table 18.2 (*Continued*)

	Urban agriculture part of general policy	Has standalone urban agriculture policy
Has home-, community-, and commercial-based agriculture, including vertical farms	**Vienna**: part of environmental policy **Vancouver**: part of city policy **Sydney**: part of city policy **Perth**: part of city's community gardens policy **Helsinki**: part of city policy **Zurich**: part of city and national policy **Tokyo, Osaka**: protected under national policy — *Special Provision of Farmland; Act on Promotion of Development of Community Farms; Urbanisation Promotion Area;* and *Productive Green Spaces*	**Melbourne**: *Urban Agriculture Policy* **Toronto**: *GrowTO Urban Agriculture Plan* **Calgary**: *CalgaryEATS! Food Action Plan* **Hong Kong**: *New Agriculture Policy* **Singapore**: *30by30 Policy* **Seoul**: *Act on Development and Support of Urban Agriculture*

One of the major motivations for urban agriculture is its contribution to poverty alleviation. For example, from 2008, Pune City Corporation in India worked with grassroots organisations on a City Farming project to encourage residents to grow crops in marginal spaces to supplement incomes and improve nutrition. Residents were given funding and training; eventually, numerous ventures arose that supported the ecosystem [Roy, 2017].

The 2008 Global Food Crisis led some cities to boost their food production. For example, Singapore, which imports 90% of its food, recognised its vulnerability and has since sought to increase its food production. It launched its "30by30" campaign (to have 30% of its nutrition needs grown locally by 2030) to achieve this [SFA, 2021].

Beijing: Encouraging Urban Farming Since the 1990s [Cai, 2014; Yang *et al.*, 2016]

Urbanisation resulted in Beijing losing 65,000 ha of agricultural land between 1992 and 2004. Subsequently, Beijing integrated urban agriculture into its development since the 1990s. Its municipal government launched "agro parks" for food, tourism, and education. Beijing designated five "zones" for agro parks (Figure 18.5):

- the "urban agricultural area/inner urban core": for gardening, landscaping, and exhibition
- the "inner peri urban agriculture/suburban plain": for recreational agriculture and high tech/precision agriculture;
- the "plain agriculture area/outer suburban plain": for modern, large-scale food production and processing;
- the "ecological mountain area": for special fruits and ecological protection; and
- the "regional cooperation" zone: where neighbouring communities and cooperatives work together to bolster food security and ensure import quality.

The focus on urban agriculture did not stop there. In 2004, the municipality introduced the "221 project" which provided comprehensive guidelines on how to improve urban agriculture in the five zones through understanding the market, the technology, and provide transparent data. The "221" information platform is managed and operated by the Beijing Rural Economic Research Center, which is also a one-stop shop for agro-related events and fairs.

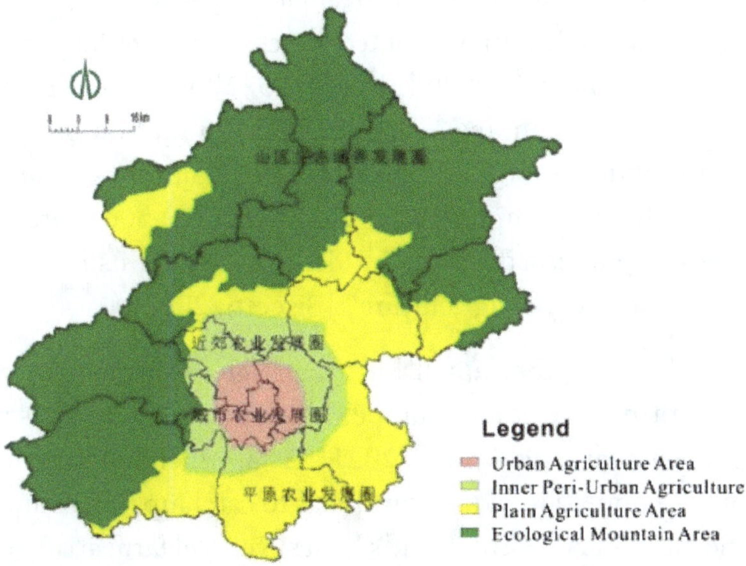

Figure 18.5 Five zones for urban agriculture in Beijing [Yang *et al.*, 2016].

The city continues to track and report performance in its annual statistical yearbook. According to the report, Beijing's urban agriculture contributed 340 billion yuan in 2012 through its 1,300 agro parks.

The COVID-19 pandemic has also catalysed support for urban agriculture. In Jakarta, for example, the Ministry of Agriculture formalised its support for urban farming through the *Pekarangan Pangan Lestari* (Sustainable Food Yard) programme. As a result, 735 urban farms are now located in Jakarta, including 175 which practice hydroponics [Lia and Kenzu, 2022].

However, a serious contribution to food security requires that commercial farms multiply. This had mainly been on a downward trend due to pressures of urbanisation. Fortunately, this is reversing.

Globally, venture capital into vertical farming reached $3 billion in 2020 [Biscotti, 2022]. In the United States, 74 indoor farming companies were founded in 2020 [Biscotti, 2022]. In 2022, one vertical farm — Plenty Unlimited — raised US$400 million in its latest funding round [Biscotti, 2022]. More than half of the investment was by Walmart, a supermarket chain with 10,500 stores in 24 countries; it purchased a stake in Plenty as part of its belief in the need for "a new era of agriculture" [Biscotti, 2022].

To move forward, the capital for urban agriculture needs to flow beyond North America and Europe, which currently captures nearly half of the global capital [N.A., 2021]. Asia, which holds more than half of the population of the world, has to catch up. There are some glimmerings. In 2022, the world's largest vertical farm at 30,000 m^2, ECO1, was opened in Dubai. The facility is expected to produce 900 tonnes of vegetables annually. It is one of 12 vertical farms in UAE occupying 7,600 m^2 of land [N.A., 2018]. Ezhou, a secondary city outside of Wuhan, China, just announced a new inaugural 26-storey intensive pig farm [N.A., 2022].

A supportive ecosystem is also crucial for the sustainability of a large-scale urban agriculture industry. E-commerce, online delivery systems, farmers' markets, skills training programmes, credit and insurance access, and agricultural land leasing programmes are some of the ecosystem services that support a viable industry, but this is commonly weak or lacking in most cities.

18.5 Facilitative Actions to Expand Urban Agriculture in Cities

Even though urban farms have become common, they still face challenges to growth. Whether community or commercial, their adoption is curtailed by frictions in land/space use, prohibitive zoning, stringent licencing, limited market options, underdeveloped cold chain, high cost of operation, lack of labour, and lack of/unaffordable water/electricity.

The following sections provide details of fundamental actions to facilitate the growth of urban agriculture.

18.5.1 *Facilitative Leadership, Governance, and Policy*

A survey of 170 Asian cities by the World Bank in 2019 found that most cities have policies relating to food, but three-quarters reported their policies were weak due to lack of prioritisation, mandate, capacity, funding or coordination with other governments [Acharya *et al.*, 2021].

Integration within national and statal programmes, i.e., within frameworks on urban planning, land/water management, waste, and product safety assurance, is crucial for the expansion of urban agriculture. South Korea's 2011 *Act on Development and Support of Urban Agriculture*, for example, established an urban agriculture programme nationwide. Seoul saw an increase in urban farmers from 45,000 in 2011 to 647,000 in 2019, and land used for urban farming increased from 29 ha to 202 ha in the same period [Lee, 2020; O'Callaghan, 2020]. Similarly in Cuba, the national government took the lead on land management and food safety which ensured urban agriculture was integrated into its urban landscape [McNamara, 2017].

Facilitative national policies could also be introduced with regard to taxes, licencing, or utility costs. The Netherlands, which is the second largest exporter of food by value in the world, adopted a range of measures to reduce costs of innovation in farm enterprises, including having 1) the Research and Development (Promotion) Act which is a tax scheme that compensates for wage costs in development of new products; 2) providing direct loans at low interests for high-risk innovation ideas, 3) providing loans for startups and small and medium enterprises at a low interest of 4.55% to create proof of concepts, and 4) providing an innovation box fiscal facility which allows lower tax rates for innovation [Netherlands Enterprise Agency, 2020]. These have continued to promote The Netherlands as an agriculture powerhouse and initiated numerous intensive agriculture enterprises.

Beyond national initiatives, local governments play a vital role in urban agriculture expansion. City governments are often better informed of local challenges, better connected with local stakeholders, and better able to measure and monitor effectiveness to deliver environmental, health and social goals. They are better placed to address the inevitable conflicts that may arise due to interpersonal disagreements, entrenchment, or privatisation of public spaces. It would also be able to integrate farming activities with local waste management initiatives, such as introducing preventative measures, recycling options, composting or bio-energy solutions.

18.5.2 *Preserving and Updating Land, Zoning, and Lease Policies*

Historically, cities have developed, often over centuries, on and around the most fertile of plains. Yet as cities urbanised, agricultural lands are often a casualty. The near irreversibility of agri-land conversion, and its implications on wider food security, requires national-level analysis [Acharya *et al.*, 2021]. Newly opened agriculture lands may take years or even decades to achieve similar yields. Eventually, agricultural lands and its soils may require the same protections as nature reserves.

Case Study: Baltimore [Halliday *et al.*, 2019; Peters, 2019; Garcia, 2021]

Baltimore in the United States is often seen as a model for urban agriculture expansion. In 2010, recognising that food was a complex, multifaceted issue, the City of Baltimore launched the *Baltimore Food Policy Initiative.* A Food Policy Director coordinated the actions across staff in four departments in Baltimore City Council — the Department of Planning, Office of Sustainability, Baltimore City Health Department, and Baltimore Development Corporation. Over the next decade, Baltimore opened up underutilised land and leasing opportunities for urban farms, updated its tax code to facilitate tax credits, updated its building and zoning codes, and set up regulations for soil and animals. As of 2019, Baltimore is home to more than 20 large urban farms (including Google-backed Bowery and Gotham Greens) and over a hundred community gardens.

Even when land or space suitable for urban agriculture do exist, it is often not permitted to do so under zoning or planning policies, often due to concerns of smell, noise, pest attraction, pollution, and sanitation. New technologies and protocols in urban agriculture may invalidate these concerns. Hydroponics, for example, make it possible for food to be grown in disused warehouses, underground spaces, rooftops or other otherwise inhospitable spaces. Thus, zoning and planning policies need to be updated to allow for these new activities. The City of Paris, through its 2016 *Parisculteurs* programme, has selectively expanded permitted uses on sites, resulting in 30 ha of space opened for agriculture, up from just 11 ha previously [Ville de Paris, n.d.]. The city is aiming to open up 100 ha, through rooftops, underground, parking lots and other marginal spaces, under the programme [Ville de Paris, n.d.].

Secured land should also consider how lease length will impact on sustainability of the urban farm. Short leases limit the viability of farms. For example, in Singapore, many of the farms have less than 10-year leases; however, these commonly require 5–12 years to break even [Dasarathy, 2021]. Thus, the leases need to be favourable to contribute to lasting food security.

Parks and verges can also be "opened up", where appropriate, for growing of fruit trees or other edible horticulture. Many cities have pledged to green environments and grow trees to satisfy carbon goals. Singapore, for example, has pledged to grow a million trees by 2030 [NParks, n.d.], yet most are ornamental due to concerns over higher maintenance requirements, fruit dropping, and attraction of pests. Leaving edibles out of the greening movement is a missed opportunity to develop food resilience. 'Adopt-a-tree/grove' programmes are one way of community ownership and reducing maintenance.

18.5.3 *Ecosystem Support, Funding, and Research and Development*

Centuries of agriculture have optimised it for conventional farming in rural settings; urban agriculture, however, differs. Growing spacings are smaller, inputs (seeds, fertiliser) may differ, and pests may be unique. It requires experimentation and innovation to improve the farmed output, all of which require time, capital and knowledge. These translate into need for funding, support from research and learning institutes, and provision of extension services and knowledge platforms to solve problems.

Governments and civil organisations often support some start-up costs of home or community farms; however, maintenance and continued education and support are often limited. Some cities have recognised this; San Francisco's Garden Resource Centre, for example, is a one-stop-shop where one can walk in with a diseased leaf and ask advice from volunteer "Master Gardeners" on standby [Sabatini, 2019]. Similarly, Seoul has multiple government-funded "Farming Support Centres" that provide advice, guidance, seeds, and organic compost.

To ramp up urban agriculture's contribution to food security, investment and research and development (R&D) in commercial farming are required. In Singapore, start-up costs for controlled environment agriculture are between $30,000 and $30 million (US$22,000 to US$22 million), with a median set-up cost of S$375,000 [Dasarathy *et al.*, 2021]. Furthermore, funds typically come from savings or private funds, as few are able to access bank loans due to perceptions of its high risk. In recognition of this, the Singapore government has allocated S$300 million (US$221 million) for its Singapore Food Story R&D programme to support the growth of its urban agriculture industry [CNA, 2022].

For now, profitability of urban farming is still uncommon. In a 2016 survey of urban farmers in the U.S., only one in three said they made a living from the farm [Nast, 2018]. A survey in Singapore echoed this lack of profitability; many farms found government grants inaccessible and mired in red tape [Darasathy *et al.*, 2021]. More targeted funding programmes may be needed to increase urban agriculture and support its move to profitability.

Beyond funds for production, a healthy urban agriculture industry would also be supported by a thriving ecosystem, which requires funding and R&D as well. Support could include agrifood innovation incubation, training programmes, nutritious food businesses, and entrepreneurship. Investing in market services — credit, e-commerce, cold chain facilities, and information platforms — also assist small farms to be sustainable.

Beyond funding, demand-support policies could aid the financial viability of urban farms. Urban farm produce is often priced higher due to diseconomies of scale, high start-up capital, vulnerabilities to disruptions, and lack of bargaining power with established retailers. Demand-enhancing policies could include public procurement, affordable food safety testing, branding, and providing market infrastructure.

18.5.4 *Nurturing Talent and Human Capital*

Globally, the average age of farmers is 60 as few young people turn to agriculture [FAO, 2014]. For example, in Indonesia which is largely an agricultural nation, only 23% of the 14.2 million youths in Indonesia are currently working in agriculture, forestry, and fishery sectors [Iswara, 2020]. Agriculture is perceived as low income, low skill, and low prospects.

Perceptions, however, can be changed. Associating urban agriculture with technical skills and respect could raise its attraction. Indeed, commercial agriculture involving aquaculture, hydroponics, and intensive livestock farming require sophisticated skills. The narrative on farming should be updated to highlight its future. Social media, educational exhibits, public events, and awards could assist in changing the perception of wider community towards food growing. Planting food should also be part of the education curriculum to accustom the public to the value of producing one's own produce, and of supporting local farms.

A thriving urban agriculture industry requires mainstream centres of learning to offer advanced short- and long-term education and training on biology, horticulture, technical skills, food hygiene and environmental management measures. Physical or virtual education spaces also encourage valuable informal knowledge exchange.

Furthermore, by 2050, people in Asia over the age of 65 will outnumber those under 15 [UNDESA, 2022]. Gardening has proven to support active aging and mental health [Elton and Cole, 2022].

18.5.5 *Safe Food Infrastructure*

The World Health Organization has highlighted food contamination as a global challenge, and value chains are susceptible to contamination [WHO, 2022]. In recent years, the risk of encountering antimicrobial resistance in bacteria, fungi, viruses, and other microorganisms in food supply has been increasing. Having shorter food chains improve food safety.

According to the World Bank, urban Asia is emerging as a hotspot in relation to food safety and accounts for nearly two-thirds of estimated productivity losses from unsafe foods [Acharya *et al.*, 2021]. Examples of concerning practices in urban agriculture include inappropriate use of agrochemicals, inadequate manure disposal by livestock farms, or biocontamination that may result in poisoning, soil, or water pollution.

The hazards associated with urban agriculture may be anticipated by appropriate government agencies, which may in turn take steps to introduce standards, safety protocols and hygiene practices, while balancing against obstructive regulation. These responsibilities could become mandates for relevant government agencies.

Services offered by governments seeking to facilitate urban agriculture could include affordable testing/self-testing, labelling and education. Familiarising consumers with farms raise trust levels and social accountability. In South Korea, for example, urban farm produce is sold at cooperatives where samples are tested daily, labelled with the name of the source, and packaged [Kim, 2017]. This differentiation often supports demand for local produce.

—

To achieve the above requires effective collaboration and coordination across various actors and stakeholders in society involved, such as civil organisations, private sector, educational institutions, and the government, to ensure successful development and implementation of urban agriculture.

18.6 Conclusion: Urban Agriculture is Crucial for City Sustainability

Urbanisation, climate change and population growth will continue to disrupt our current food system. Business as usual will result in increasingly frequent episodes of food shortages and empty shelves. Urban agriculture, in concert with rural agriculture, can contribute to alleviate this.

While urban agriculture in the form of home-based, community, commercial, and institutional agriculture is already present in many cities, it plays a relatively minor role in the global food supply. Urban agriculture needs to contribute more than its current 5–20% if it is to have a role towards a food-secure future.

Beyond contributing to food, urban agriculture creates a greener, more biodiverse city. Where residents are involved, it promotes social cohesion, mental and physical health. Furthermore, urban agriculture makes economic sense. Not only does it support low-income households and communities, but it is also projected to grow at a compound annual growth rate of 2.8% between 2021 and 2026 due to recognition of its growing importance [N.A., 2021].

Integrating food systems and infrastructure also alleviates pressures on other city systems. A megacity[2] requires at least 6,000 tonnes of food trucked in daily [FAO-SOFA, 1998]. Trucking food alone exacerbates traffic congestion, carbon emissions, air pollution, waste volumes and food safety. Of the 32 megacities globally, 20 are in Asia; thus, the problem is more acute in Asia.

Therefore, urban agriculture needs to be integrated into city masterplans to harness its benefits in the long term. Those cities which do not have the foresight to integrate food into plans now risk unintentionally adopting policies that exclude agriculture, resulting in needless setbacks and missed opportunities and, ultimately, a more food-insecure future.

Facilitating urban agriculture requires national, statal and local governments to enact facilitative governance structures and policies to overcome the systemic and antiquated obstructions constricting urban agriculture today. This includes updating land, zoning, and lease policies to conserve and promote urban farms. Other facilitative policies could include ecosystem support, funding, and R&D for the industry. Nurturing talents and skills for this nascent industry supports its sustainability; it requires the involvement of both educational and training institutions. Appropriate food safety infrastructure ensure that urban agriculture does not in turn become a liability.

On the path to urban agriculture, it is prudent to learn from the drawbacks of "modern agriculture" — its dependence on greenhouse

[2] A megacity is one that has a population of over 10 million.

gas-emitting fossil fuels for inputs, monopolisation by a handful of global conglomerates, loss of food diversity, the linear approach to food production and the commodification of foods which is prone to market manipulation.

There is a high cost of inaction. COVID-19 and the Russian aggression in Ukraine has shown only a glimpse of the food supply challenges facing society in the volatile future. Urgent action today will determine how many urban centres will survive.

References

Acharya, G., Cassou, E., Jaffee, S. and Ludher, E. K. (2021). *RICH Food, Smart City*. World Bank.

Akaeze, O. and Nandwani, D. (2020). Urban agriculture in Asia to meet the food production challenges of urbanization: A review. *Urban Agriculture & Regional Food Systems*, 5(1), p. e20002.

Barton, J. (2020). Seoul unveils plan to create 1m urban farmers. *CGTN*. https://news.cgtn.com/news/2020-10-24/Seoul-unveils-plan-to-create-1m-urban-farmers-UQG8jAGUY8/index.html

Biscotti, L. (2022). Old MacDonald's farm no more: Companies invest in vertical agriculture. *Forbes*. https://www.forbes.com/sites/louisbiscotti/2022/02/08/old-macdonalds-farm-no-more-companies-invest-in-vertical-agriculture/?sh=208ab18457c6

Booth, J. M., Chapman, D., Ohmer, M. L. and Wei, K. (2018). Examining the relationship between level of participation in community gardens and their multiple functions. *Journal of Community Practice*, 26(1), pp. 5–22.

Bricas, N. and Conaré, D. (2019). Historical perspectives on the ties between cities and food. *Field Actions Science Reports*, 20, pp. 6–11.

Cabbanes, Y., Prain, G. and van Veenhuizen, R. (2022). *Urban and Peri-Urban Agriculture for Strengthening Pro-Poor Resilience in Asian Cities: Investment Needs and Opportunities*. Asian Development Bank.

Cai, J. M. (2014). Urban agriculture makes China's cities more liveable. *China Dialogue.* https://chinadialogue.net/en/cities/7091-urban-agriculture-makes-china-s-cities-more-liveable/

Caves, R. W. (2004). *Encyclopedia of the City*. Routledge, p. 751.

Chan, O. (2021). Is urban food farming a priority? *Chinadailyhk*. https://www.chinadailyhk.com/article/254026#Is-urban-food-farming-a-priority?

City of Sydney. (2021, February 22). Decision — Highlighting the importance of urban agriculture in the city of Sydney | City of Sydney. *Council and committee meetings.* https://meetings.cityofsydney.nsw.gov.au/ieDecisionDetails.aspx?Id=2690

Clinton, N., Stuhlmacher, M., Miles, A., Uludere Aragon, N., Wagner, M., Georgescu, M., ... and Gong, P. (2018). A global geospatial ecosystem services estimate of urban agriculture. *Earth's Future*, 6(1), pp. 40–60.

CNA. (2022). Singapore to invest additional S$165 million in food security programme: DPM Heng. https://www.channelnewsasia.com/singapore/singapore-food-security-investment-dpm-heng-3026951

Dasarathy, A., Chai, D., Ong, J., Lee, D. and Lee, R. S. Y. (2021). Securing Singapore's 30-by30 goal: improving the viability of CEA farms. *LKYSPP*.

Elton, S. and Cole, D. (2022). Is a vegetable garden essential? Toronto gardens as culinary infrastructure. *Food, Culture & Society*, pp. 1–21.

FAO-SOFA. (1998). *The State of Food and Agriculture.* https://www.fao.org/documents/card/en/c/e6259450-e20e-5d8e-a776-969bd28761cb

FAO. (2009). *Global Agriculture towards 2050.* https://www.fao.org/fileadmin/templates/wsfs/docs/Issues_papers/HLEF2050_Global_Agriculture.pdf

FAO. (2011). *The Place of Urban and Peri-Urban Agriculture (UPA) in National Food Security Programmes.* https://www.fao.org/3/i2177e/i2177e00.pdf

FAO. (2014). Food security for sustainable development and urbanization: Inputs for FAO´s contribution to the 2014 ECOSOC

Integration Segment, 27–29. May 2014. https://www.un.org/en/ecosoc/integration/pdf/foodandagricultureorganization.pdf

FAO, Rikolto and RUAF (2022). *Urban and Peri-Urban Agriculture Sourcebook — From Production to Food Systems.* https://doi.org/10.4060/cb9722en

Garcia, S. (2021). Baltimore farmers are cultivating the city's first 'AgriHood,' heralded for its innovation. *Baltimore Sun.* https://www.baltimoresun.com/features/bs-fe-agrihood-urban-farm-park-heights-20210924-xnonds3wuzebldxrfyj6ooqxgy-story.html

Halliday, J., Platenkamp, L. and Nicolarea, Y. (2019). A menu of actions to shape urban food environments for improved nutrition. GAIN, MUFPP and RUAF.

Ben Hassen, T. and El Bilali, H. (2022). Impacts of the Russia-Ukraine war on global food security: towards more sustainable and resilient food systems?. *Foods*, 11(15), pp. 2301.

IFOAM Organics Europe. (n.d.). Feeding Vienna organically. https://euorganic2030.bio/initiatives/improve-inspire-deliver/feedding-vienna-organically/

IPCC. (2022). IPCC Sixth Assessment Report. https://www.ipcc.ch/assessment-report/ar6/

Iswara, M. A. (2020). A land without farmers: Indonesia's agricultural conundrum. *The Jakarta Post.* https://www.thejakartapost.com/longform/2020/08/13/a-land-without-farmers-indonesias-agricultural-conundrum.html

Kim, H. S. (2017). How farming practices have developed in Seoul, South Korea from 1960s to the 2010s: focusing on the Green Revolution Technology, Organic Farming and Urban Farming. Master's Thesis. https://aaltodoc.aalto.fi/bitstream/handle/123456789/27149/master_Kim_Hyesun_2017.pdf?sequence=1&isAllowed=y

Koay, W. I. and Dillon, D. (2020). Community gardening: Stress, well-being, and resilience potentials. *International Journal of Environmental Research and Public Health*, 17(18), p. 6740.

Lee, M. J. (2020). Seoul city aims to nurture 1 mln urban farmers by 2024. *Yonhap News Agency.* https://en.yna.co.kr/view/AEN20200923004300315

Lia, S. and Kenzu, T. (2022, July 19). Urban farming takes root among youth in south of Jakarta. *Antara News.* https://en.antaranews.com/news/240141/urban-farming-takes-root-among-youth-in-south-of-jakarta

McNamara, T. (2017). Crisis of urban agriculture: case studies in Cuba. *Tropical Resources Bulletin*, 36.

N.A. (2018). Dubai government agrees on deal to start up 12 vertical farms in the city. *The National.* https://www.thenationalnews.com/uae/environment/dubai-government-agrees-on-deal-to-start-up-12-vertical-farms-in-the-city-1.748247

N.A. (2021). Urban farming market — forecast (2022–2027). *Industry Arc.* https://www.industryarc.com/Report/15491/urban-farming-market.html

N.A. (2022). China's 26-storey pig skyscraper ready to slaughter 1 million pigs a year. *The Guardian.* https://www.theguardian.com/environment/2022/nov/25/chinas-26-storey-pig-skyscraper-ready-to-produce-1-million-pigs-a-year

Nast, C. (2018). Big data suggests big potential for urban farming. *WIRED.* https://www.wired.com/story/big-data-suggests-big-potential-for-urban-farming/

Netherlands Enterprise Agency. (2020). Subsidies and programmes. https://english.rvo.nl/subsidies-programmes

NParks. (2021). *Annual Report 2020–2021.* https://www.nparks.gov.sg/portals/annualreport/theme/default/document/NParks_Annual_Report_2020_21_Annual_Report.pdf

NParks (n.d.). OneMillionTrees movement. https://www.nparks.gov.sg/treessg/one-million-trees-movement

O'Callaghan, L. (2020). Seoul's ambitious urban farming goal. *Fruitnet.* https://www.fruitnet.com/asiafruit/seouls-ambitious-urban-farming-goal/183324.article

Peters, A. (2019). Bowery opens its largest indoor farm in Baltimore. *AGRITECTURE*. https://www.agritecture.com/blog/2019/11/8/bowery-opens-its-largest-indoor-farm-in-baltimore

Roy, P. (2017). Hydroponic gardening program: Love for science among young students. *Science Times*. http://www.sciencetimes.com/articles/15488/20170519/hydroponic-gardening-program-love-for-science-among-young-students.htm

Sabatini, J. (2019). SF plans to launch an urban agriculture resource center for community gardeners. *San Francisco Examiner*. https://www.sfexaminer.com/news/sf-plans-to-launch-an-urban-agriculture-resource-center-for-community-gardeners/article_3b7f8c39-9f9b-5427-a0f0-adee7ad67f2d.html

SFA. (2021). *Annual Report 2020–2021*. https://www.sfa.gov.sg/docs/default-source/publication/annual-report/sfa-ar-2020-20212c7b8b52e3e84fd193c56d53f42fe607.pdf

Steel, C. (2013). *Hungry City*. Vintage Books.

Teng, P. (2020). Urban agriculture — the future of farming. *SciDevNet*. https://www.scidev.net/asia-pacific/opinions/urban-agriculture-the-future-of-farming/

UN. (2017). World population projected to reach 9.8 billion in 2050, and 11.2 billion in 2100. https://www.un.org/en/desa/world-population-projected-reach-98-billion-2050-and-112-billion-2100

UN. (2020). Cities. https://www.un.org/sustainabledevelopment/cities/

UN DESA. (2022). *World Population Prospects 2022*. https://population.un.org/wpp/

Ville de Paris. (n.d.). Parisculteurs in a nutshell | About | The Parisculteurs. https://www.parisculteurs.paris/en/about/parisculteurs-in-a-nutshell/

Voicu, I. and Been, V. (2008). The effect of community gardens on neighboring property values. *Real Estate Economics*, 36(2), pp. 241–283.

WHO. (2022). *Food Safety*. https://www.who.int/news-room/fact-sheets/detail/food-safety

Yang, Z., Hao, P., Liu, W. and Cai, J. (2016). Peri-urban agricultural development in Beijing: Varied forms, innovative practices and policy implications. *Habitat International*, 56, pp. 222–234.

Annex 18.1 List of "liveable" cities and urban agriculture prevalence.

City and Liveability Rank (2021)	Urban Agriculture (UA) Policies	Description on Urban Agriculture (UA)	Examples of Commercial Intensive Farms
1. Melbourne	UA is part of its *Urban Agriculture Policy* and *Food Policy*.	• Melbourne's metropolitan area is governed by multiple municipalities, many of which have UA policies.	• SkyFarm (rooftop farm)
2. Vienna	UA is part of its environmental policy.	• UA covers 5,900 ha (17%) of Vienna's city area, dedicated to organic farming [IFOAM Organics Europe, n.d.] • The OkoKauf (Ecobuy) programme incentivises purchase of organic food for public kitchens, etc.	• Billa • Vertical Farm Institute (advises on vertical farming)
3. Vancouver	UA is part of its city policy.	• Vancouver's urban farming is largely driven by civil organisation Vancouver Urban Farming Society and its associated urban farmers.	• Verticrop (rooftop farm) • UP Vertical Farms
4. Toronto	*GrowTO Urban Agriculture Action Plan* was introduced in 2012 to expand UA.	• Toronto is seen as a model for UA globally due to its comprehensive literature and experience.	• Living Earth • Elevate • We the Roots
5. Adelaide	UA is protected under the state's *Environment and Food Production Areas* policy.	• Low-density Adelaide city has many backyard and community gardens.	• Fruit farms and vineyards in Adelaide metropolitan areas

City and Liveability Rank (2021)	Urban Agriculture (UA) Policies	Description on Urban Agriculture (UA)	Examples of Commercial Intensive Farms
6. Calgary	UA is part of *CalgaryEATS! Food Action Plan* in 2012.	• City bylaws were amended to allow food growing in indoor and industrial spaces.	• NuLeaf Farms • NewRoots vertical farm • Sunspring
7. Sydney	UA is supported in the form of community gardens, footpath and verge gardens.	• Sydney is reviewing its UA policies to increase self-sufficiency in food [City of Sydney, 2021].	• Urban Green
8. Perth	UA is mainly in the form of community gardens policy.	• Low-density Perth has many home-based and community gardens.	• Eden Towers
9. Auckland	UA is part of the *Community Gardens Policy*, and in the *Auckland Climate Plan*.	• Auckland Council owns 1,500 ha of agri-land. • Home-based and community farms are popular but there are restrictions on sales of produce.	• n/a
=10. Helsinki	UA is indirectly promoted through the city's Culinary Culture Strategy.	• Helsinki has urban farms that date back to more than a hundred years.	• iFarm • Arctic Farming • Robbe's Little Garden
=10. Zurich	UA has been part of city policy. The city has bought land to safeguard city green spaces and agriculture.	• Agriculture is part of Swiss culture and agricultural land is conserved.	• YASAI AG, (total cultivation area: 585 m^2, started in January 2022)

City and Liveability Rank (2021)	Urban Agriculture (UA) Policies	Description on Urban Agriculture (UA)	Examples of Commercial Intensive Farms
15. Tokyo	UA is protected by the 1993 *Act on Special Provision of Farmland*, the *Act on Promotion of Development of Community Farms*, and more recently the *Urbanisation Promotion Area* and *Productive Green Spaces*.	• Most of the *Productive Green Spaces* have 30-year leases and were recently extended for another 10 years.	• InFarm (in supermarkets) • Pasona (institutional)
17. Osaka		• Urban farms are often also disaster evacuation sites.	• VegetaFarm • Spread (outside city boundaries in Nara)
46. Hong Kong	UA is supported under the *New Agriculture Policy* (2016) and funded by the Sustainable Agriculture Development Fund.	• Hong Kong has 50 m^2 of agriculture land (4.5% of its land) [Chan, 2021].	• Farm66 (Aquaponics) • Rooftop Republic • Sustenir • Growgreen
49. Singapore	UA is supported by the *30by30* policy to gain 30% food self-sufficiency by 2030.	• Singapore has 265 licenced urban farms and more than 1,700 community gardens [NParks, 2021; SFA, 2021].	• ComCrop • Citiponics • Vertivegies • Kalera • Blue Aqua (aquaculture)
58. Seoul	UA is promoted under the *Act on Development and Support of Urban Agriculture* (2011).	• Seoul has 200 ha of urban farmland and has a goal of adding a further 40 ha by 2024. It also wants to develop one million urban farmers [Barton, 2020].	• Metrofarm/Farm8 • NextOn (outside Seoul) • N.Thing • ALGA Farmtech

https://doi.org/10.1142/9789811278297_0019

Chapter 19

Opportunities and Challenges in Meeting the Demands for Fish in Asia with Intensive Aquaculture

C. W. Lee[1,2], S. Padmanabhan[1] and D. Chan[1]

[1]*Aquaculture Innovation Centre, Temasek Polytechnic, Singapore*
[2]*Centre for Aquaculture Research, Innovation and Education, Nanyang Technological University, Singapore*

19.1 Introduction

Asia is a major producer of food fish from both wild fisheries and aquaculture, and accounts for a significant portion of global production in these sectors. According to the Food and Agriculture Organization (FAO), Asia was responsible for 92% of the total live weight volume of aquaculture products in the world in 2017, which includes fish, shellfish, seaweeds, and other aquatic organisms. China is the world's largest aquaculture producer and has been at the forefront of the industry's growth and development. Other major aquaculture producers in Asia include India, Vietnam, and Bangladesh, which are also important players in the industry and have seen significant growth in recent years.

The aquaculture industry has emerged as an important player in addressing food security in many countries, particularly in Asia. It is also the source of livelihood of millions of coastal and inland farmers. However, many of the aquaculture farms in Asia are still traditional, small-scale operations that are limited by the lack of capital to adopt technology and improve their operations. Most of these farms are land-based and typically range from 0.5 to 1 hectare in size. Freshwater finfish aquaculture is the dominant type of inland aquaculture in all regions of Asia, with species such as carp and tilapia being the main species cultured. For sea-based aquaculture farms, traditional open net-cage culture is widely practised, with farms being made up of wooden frame structures floated by high-density polyethylene drums. These farms are often limited by their lack of access to technology and capital to mitigate environmental risks and improve productivity.

The challenges faced by traditional farms are numerous and varied. One of the primary challenges is their vulnerability to adverse external environmental factors such as plankton blooms, oil spills, and low dissolved oxygen, which can have severe impacts on fish health and productivity. Poor water quality, climate change, and the lack of control over the spread of diseases are also major constraints that traditional farms face. Moreover, traditional farms are also constrained by various development-related challenges. These include the lack of good quality seeds and feed, low technical capacity, poor market and value addition, inadequate extension services and materials, poor management of culture systems, low capacity in disease diagnostics and biosecurity, and competition from cheaper fishery products. Additionally, traditional farms face challenges in accessing various financial instruments and support. While new technologies and innovations are being developed to ensure high-quality and consistent supply of farmed fish to the market, the impact and scalability of their uptake are slow and inadequate to achieve the transformational change envisaged in the "Blue Revolution" [Swaminathan, 2004]. The Blue Revolution is a global movement aimed at transforming the fisheries and aquaculture sector to ensure sustainable food security, income generation, and environmental protection.

The Technology Acceptance Model by Davis [1989] provides a valuable framework for understanding why smallholder farmers in Asia may not adopt new aquaculture technologies. By emphasising the importance of perceived ease of use and perceived usefulness, the model highlights the need for technology providers to consider the needs and limitations of smallholder farmers. This could involve tailoring new technologies to meet the specific needs of smallholder farmers, providing adequate training and support to help farmers adopt and implement the technology, and promoting the benefits of technology adoption. It is also important to understand the local context and the factors that may influence farmers' decisions to adopt new technologies. Hence the future research, extension, and education programmes should focus on problems of practising aquaculture in resource-limited environments as well as social and cultural factors such as tradition and local knowledge. By taking these factors into account, technology providers and extension services can work to overcome barriers to technology adoption in a way that is relevant to smallholder farmers.

19.2 Biosecurity Issues in Small-Scale Aquaculture Affecting the Livelihood of Farmers

Biosecurity in aquaculture context can be defined as a set of management and physical measures designed to reduce the risk of pathogen introduction, establishment and spread of animal diseases, and infections to, from and within an animal population. Therefore, in this chapter, we prioritise the discussion of biosecurity issues that fish farmers confront and explore the measures that can be adopted to safeguard aquaculture operations.

The World Organisation for Animal Health (WOAH) had set the framework for developing international standards for protection of sanitary and phytosanitary standards for trade in animals and animal products, including for aquatic animals. These WOAH standards are recognised by the World Trade Organisation as reference international sanitary rules. WOAH also sets international guidelines for aquatic animal health and disease control. Government agencies are also in the best position to coordinate international practices for control of aquatic animal diseases and to facilitate the safe trade of aquaculture products. However, it is not easy for small-scaled farmers in developing and developed countries to adopt and comply to these standards, despite their majority proportion. They still face many challenges at the farm implementation level in maintaining aquatic animal health, following biosecurity guidelines and food safety measures. Infectious diseases are constraining the development and sustainability of the aquaculture sector through direct production losses and increased operating costs and, indirectly, through restrictions on trade and impact on biodiversity. Among the various attributing factors of disease outbreaks, intensification of aquaculture practices and transboundary spread of animal diseases associated with animal movement are of major concern [Kyule-Muendo *et al.*, 2022].

Epidemiology and aetiology of aquaculture diseases are complex dynamics involving several factors including fish species, pathogen virulence, movement behaviour and environment conditions, making it difficult to predict and analyse without proper biosecurity measures in place. Regionally, countries have different generic national guidelines and regulations at commodity and farm levels addressing disease prevention and control, farm management practices, strategies on animal health and the environment, movement of live animals and emergency response measures.

Biosecurity plans need to be fit for purpose and balance practicality, affordability, and regulatory requirements. Government support is critical in improvement of biological, operational, and economic performance of the farms, and ability to achieve the desired outcomes. Biosecurity plans should be viewed as insurance, and in essence require both financial and intellectual investment. It involves three levels *viz.* entry, internal and exit operations in risk analysis, identification, assessment, and management [Perera *et al.*, 2008]. Transmission routes onto, within and from the farms involve people, equipment, vehicle, water, feed, and waste management. A paradigm shift in the aquaculture development policies is currently needed to remodel the fragmented and uncoordinated clusters of smallholder aquaculture farmers and develop strategically community-based coordination and support frameworks.

19.2.1 *Limited Farmer Awareness in Biosecurity*

There is a paucity of knowledge on aquaculture biosecurity and implementation among the small-scale farming industry sector, which presents a serious threat to the productivity and sustainability of aquaculture. It is important that all farmers have a clear understanding of their responsibilities to maintain farm biosecurity. Appropriate biosecurity induction training programmes should be instituted enabling them to recognise signs of ill health; be aware of the major routes of disease transmission; understand the farm biosecurity plan and their responsibilities for its implementation;

and be familiar with work practices and standard operating procedures that support the farm biosecurity plan [Ragasa *et al.*, 2022]. Moreover, post-training support needs to be extended to assist them in applying their learning in risk assessment, general farm management, record keeping, emergency procedures, monitoring and periodical audit of the biosecurity plans.

19.2.2 *Lack of Access to Basic Aquatic Health Services*

Aquaculture is a highly complex industry involving various species, different habitats, unique food habits, customised production systems and production practices. Predicting fish disease dynamics is important when preventing and combating fish diseases. The results of such predictions may facilitate the management process and inform the aquaculture industry, and also help combat the spread of diseases by applying actions such as through vaccinations or removal of the pathogens. Biosecurity would be a constraint if the cost of implementation on the farm's bottom line was exorbitant. Individual farm circumstances determine to what extent biosecurity is considered as essential for profitability rather than an option when considering past incidents and expected future threats. Aquaculture biosecurity is, therefore, a collective responsibility in maintaining/improving aquaculture's image in the eyes of consumers and other stakeholders, who are increasingly aware of, and have growing concerns regarding, the ecological impacts of aquaculture operations and the food safety of farmed products.

It is necessary for farms to have access to local laboratory services for aquatic animal health and to make these affordable; this then helps to inculcate awareness and discipline to take greater responsibility for biosecurity at the farm level. Early detection and treatment can prevent a disease from spreading through the farm.

Understanding disease transmission and life cycle of pathogens helps to implement necessary biosecurity measures. Setting up of a national or regional information exchange between farmers and responsible parties including specialists, veterinarians, researchers, and regulatory agencies is important to reduce the risk of disease transmission, prevention, and control. Besides applying all these strategies, surveillance for diseases and having sensitive and specific diagnostic tests are invaluable to assure healthy fish. Compliance to health certification and integrating quarantine measures as part of a national biosecurity framework for live animal movement are necessary to prevent diseases from entering a country. Emerging issues in aquaculture operations should be communicated and made available to the local farm sector, not limited to responsible use of chemotherapeutics in aquaculture, climate change and disease ecology, fish welfare and fish health, improving and strengthening farmer-veterinarian dialogue and cooperation, and certification of aquatic animal health service providers.

19.2.3 *Lack of Affordable Disease Diagnostic Kits*

Emerging diseases pose a serious challenge to the local aquaculture industries with limited knowledge of pathogens and their effect on fish stock, and the economic losses due to disease outbreaks are worrisome. Farm-level biosecurity measures involve the application of a combination of activities which includes strict quarantine measures, sanitation of equipment, disinfection of eggs, traffic control, water treatments, clean feed, and appropriate waste disposal. It is imperative to have a rapid screening tool for quarantine of potential production diseases in the local aquaculture context. Correct diagnosis of disease should then be followed by treatment with efficacious agents for the appropriate period. Inappropriate use of antibiotics will lead to development of antibacterial resistance.

A wide range of immunodiagnostic and molecular technologies are available for aquaculture disease diagnosis. Nonetheless, several constraints including user friendliness, affordability and sophisticated infrastructure dependence have made these tools out of reach of most farmers. Innovative technologies that address the above concerns and are cost effective, rapid and sensitive should be able to provide valuable diagnostic tools to aquaculture end-users.

19.3 State Extension Services

19.3.1 *Origin of Extension Services*

Agriculture extension traditionally refers to the application of scientific research and new knowledge to agricultural practices through farmer training and education. It originated at least 2,000 years ago in China with the creation of agricultural policies to disseminate advice to farmers and ensure food security. Modern extension services began in Ireland in 1847 during the great famine, where "practical instructors" were sent to rural areas to teach small farmers alternative crop cultivation [Boydell and McDonagh, 2013; Brosnan, 1985]. The term "university extension" was first used in 1867 by the Universities of Cambridge and Oxford to describe teaching activities that extended the institution's work beyond the campus to provide knowledge and skills to non-enrolled individuals. Today, it has evolved into continuing education for adults.

19.3.2 *Industry Development Via Extension Services*

Extension services for aquaculture in Asia refer to a range of services and support provided to aquaculture farmers to help them improve their operations and increase their productivity and profitability. Some of the key extension services for aquaculture include:

a. **Technical Assistance:** This is a key part of extension services and can play a critical role in helping farmers increase their competitiveness and improve their aquaculture practices. By providing farmers with access to the technical expertise and skills they need, extension services can help to support the growth and development of the sector. Immediate technical assistance needed are training in best practices for feed management, disease control, water and waste management, just to name a few.

b. **Knowledge Transfer:** This is a critical component of extension services, as it involves the dissemination of information and knowledge from researchers, experts, and other sources to farmers. The goal of knowledge transfer is to provide farmers with the information and resources they need to make informed decisions about their aquaculture practices and increase their competitiveness. Knowledge transfer is an ongoing process, and extension services must continuously adapt and evolve to meet the changing needs of farmers and communities.

c. **Technology Transfer:** This is to bring new and improved technologies from research institutions to farmers, with the expectation that these technologies will increase productivity, efficiency, and competitiveness. In addition, we have to ensure that these technologies are able to be effectively adopted and used by farmers. Technology transfer has been used successfully in agriculture in developing countries, to increase agricultural productivity and competitiveness. However, it can also be criticised for being a one-size-fits-all approach that does not consider the specific needs and context of different regions or communities.

d. **Research and Development:** Extension services can also provide support for research and development in aquaculture, including the development of new technologies, breeding programs, and disease management strategies, etc.

e. **Access to Market Information:** Extension services may provide farmers access to market information on market trends, prices, and demand, to help them better understand the market and make informed decisions about their aquaculture production and marketing.

f. **Access to Financing:** Small-scale farmers often have limited access to financing, which limits their ability to invest in new technology and equipment, expand their operations, and manage financial risks. Extension services can help farmers access financing for their operations, including loans, grants, and other forms of financial assistance.

g. **Networking and Collaboration:** Extension services can provide opportunities for farmers to network with other farmers, researchers, and industry experts, which can help them share information and best practices, collaborate on projects and build stronger relationships with key stakeholders.

h. **Regulatory Compliance:** Extension services can help farmers understand and comply with regulations related to aquaculture, including environmental regulations and food safety standards. Small-scale farmers may struggle to comply with these regulations, which can limit their ability to operate their farms.

i. **Manpower Sharing and Transfer:** This is an important aspect of extension services, as it helps to ensure that farmers have access to the technical expertise and support they need to improve their aquaculture practices and increase their competitiveness. Activities include attachment of experts, farmer-to-farmer extension, joint training and demonstration.

Overall, extension services can play a critical role in supporting the development and growth of aquaculture in Asia, by providing farmers with the resources, knowledge, and support they need to build sustainable and profitable operations.

19.3.3 *Extension Problems in Asian Countries*

In many extension organisations, the planning of extension programs is weak due to a lack of analysis of why farmers make certain decisions. This often results in the provision of recommendations that farmers have already determined to be unprofitable or unsuitable for their situation [Baidu-Forson *et al.*, 1997; Chambers, 1997; Davis and Wiggins, 2004]. Additionally, the extent to which extension should educate farmers to increase their competence as farm managers or provide them with information is not always clear.

For effective agricultural extension, there needs to be cooperation among farmers, extension agents, and researchers to develop suitable production technologies for each unique situation. This approach involves offering a variety of opportunities that can be tested in different contexts rather than just transferring predetermined technologies. It also requires a joint learning process, where farmers, extension agents, and researchers collaborate and learn from each other. Innovative farmers can be a valuable source of information, particularly for new farming systems. To adopt a participatory approach to extension, the staff at all levels in the extension organisation must have a high level of competence.

In addition to the participatory approach, it is essential to establish a platform for communication between farmers and extension service agents using digital technologies. Such a platform would enable farmers to seek information and promote farm-farm communication.

For example, satellite images or photos taken by drones with analyses of the situation of their fishponds can be shared instantly between farms and extension service agents. Ultimately, the effectiveness of agricultural extension depends on the farmers' confidence in the competence and motivation of the extension agents to help them realise their goals.

19.4 Policies for Engagement

Government agencies play a crucial role in promoting the growth and success of the aquaculture industry by establishing national standards and regulations. They are responsible for ensuring the health and welfare of aquatic animals, protecting the environment, and maintaining food safety. By setting standards and regulations, government agencies can help to prevent the spread of diseases, promote best practices in aquaculture, and encourage the growth of a sustainable industry. In addition to setting standards and regulations, government agencies can also provide technical and financial support to aquaculture farmers to help them adopt sustainable practices and improve their operations. This can include providing training and education programs, as well as funding for research and development initiatives.

Sustainability is another major challenge facing the aquaculture industry. The hurdles include higher impact of disease due to intensification of production, environment degradation due to nutrient and chemical pollution, habitat alteration at aquaculture sites, and over-reliance on antibiotics. It is important for government agencies to play a leading role in addressing these challenges by implementing positive governance of the aquaculture agenda to ensure long-term sustainability. This includes planning for sustainable aquaculture sites, safeguarding environment and biodiversity resources, developing national surveillance platforms for major aquatic animal diseases, and coordination of aquaculture research needs, all of which should be supported by strong science and technology, as well as excellent veterinary care and management.

The continued success of the aquaculture industry requires the participation and collaboration of multiple stakeholders and the implementation of sound policies. To achieve the goal of delivering a world-class aquaculture industry, a strong public-private partnership involving the industry, research institutions, and government agencies is essential. Such a partnership can support the future growth of the industry through transparent collaboration, with each stakeholder playing synergistic roles to support a sustainable aquaculture sector.

19.5 Production Challenges Faced by Most Asian Aquaculture Industries

19.5.1 *Inaccessibility to Freshwater Supply*

The availability of freshwater is a concern for in-land aquaculture development. Freshwater is a limited resource. The use of freshwater in aquaculture can compete with other uses of water, such as human consumption and agriculture, and this can create challenges for the development and expansion of the sector. One way to address this challenge is to focus on developing aquaculture in areas where alternative sources of water are available. This could include coastal and offshore locations, where seawater is readily available and less likely to be subject to overuse, or areas where other sources of water, such as recycled water or brackish water, can be used. In-land aquafarming could be reserved for high-value activities that require specific conditions or controlled environments, such as breeding, hatchery, nursery, and high-value species.

19.5.2 *Unavailability of Affordable Quality Feed*

Aquafeed is a critical input in the development and production of aquaculture. The cost and availability of feed ingredients, particularly proteins and oils, can be a significant constraint on the growth and profitability of aquaculture industries, especially in urbanised countries. However, there are opportunities to develop new and innovative sources of feed ingredients, including through the use of urban food waste.

The use of food waste as a source of aquafeed ingredients has several potential benefits. First, it can help to reduce the environmental impact of food waste by diverting it from landfills and incinerators. Second, it can provide a local source of high-quality feed ingredients, reducing the reliance on imported feed and improving the economic viability of aquaculture production. Third, it can help to improve the sustainability of aquaculture by reducing the use of wild-caught fish and other feed ingredients that are associated with environmental and social concerns. However, it is important to note that the use of food waste as a feed ingredient requires careful management and processing to ensure that it is safe and nutritionally appropriate for use in aquafeed. This can include processes such as fermentation, hydrolysis, and enzymatic digestion, which can help to break down the food waste into usable components and remove potential contaminants.

19.5.3 *Energy Issues*

The rapid growth of aquaculture production has required a huge power demand, which is estimated to be about 40% of the total energy cost. Energy dependence was related to aquaculture production intensity [Tyedmers and Pelletier, 2007], which can go up to 10 kWh/kg for land-based intensive culture systems. However, it is possible to reduce this expense using alternatives such as renewable energy (i.e., solar energy) instead of non-renewable energy. Solar energy is one of the cleanest energy sources and is touted as a potential renewable energy source for the world with benefits such as reducing CO_2 emissions, reversing global warming by being eco-friendly, and bringing innovation to sustainable aquaculture. Furthermore, it is important to implement energy management practices that help to minimise energy use and to reduce energy costs and carbon footprint.

19.5.4 *Shortage of Skilled Workforce*

The shortage of skilled workforce in the aquaculture industry is a major challenge that is affecting the growth and development of the sector. This shortage can be due to several factors, such as lack of education and training opportunities, aging workforce, attractiveness of other industries, lack of recognition of the importance of skilled personnel, and complexity of modern aquafarming systems within system(s). Furthermore, Industry 4.0 itself also imposed new sets of specialised skills that are currently lacking. Hence to address the shortage of skilled workforce in the aquaculture industry, it is important to invest in education and training programs, provide attractive working conditions and benefits, and work with schools and universities to promote the industry as a career choice. Additionally, the industry can work to retain existing workers by offering ongoing training and development opportunities, and by promoting a positive working environment.

19.5.5 *Competing for Space*

Land shortage is a major constraint to aquaculture expansion globally, especially in highly urbanised and densely populated areas. To overcome this challenge, super intensification and vertical expansion are potential solutions that can help to increase the productivity and profitability of aquaculture in land-scarce countries. Both super intensification and vertical expansion methods have potential benefits and drawbacks. It is important to ensure that these methods are implemented in a way that is environmentally sustainable and socially responsible, considering factors such as water and energy use, waste management, and labour conditions.

19.6 Opportunities of Asian Aquaculture Industries

World fish production, consumption and trade are expected to increase. Total fish production (aquaculture plus wild capture) is expected to expand from 179 million tonnes in 2018 to 201 million tonnes in 2030. Aquaculture production is projected to reach 109 million tonnes in 2030, an increase of 32% (26 million tonnes) over 2018. Asia will continue to dominate the aquaculture sector and will be responsible for more than 89% of the increase in production by 2030.

With increasing environmental risks, unpredictable weather and with no possibility of increasing land area, one solution is to intensify land-based production, and intensification is becoming a growing trend in aquaculture worldwide. This trend provides opportunities in developing low-cost, energy-efficient, intensive recirculatory aquaculture systems for small stakeholders as most farms in Asia regions are in the range of 1 to 2 hectares.

Rapid progression in science, combining with data and predictive analytics, created opportunities for technology owners to provide farmers with better decision-making tools while supporting practices that eliminate wastes, improve animal health, and propel economic productivity. The following are some key areas for both technical and business development.

19.6.1 *Nutrition, Feeds and Feeding*

Feed has a major impact on aquaculture as it constitutes nearly 40–50% of total expenditure of intensive aquaculture systems. Out of this total feed cost, 95% of money goes to buying energy- and protein-constituting feed ingredients. The rest of the money goes into minerals, vitamins and feed additives. Furthermore, during farming, irregularity or shortage of feed supplies add to risks and may jeopardise operations. Opportunities to mitigate risk include using urban food wastes and feed ingredients and culturing omnivore/herbivore finfish and crustaceans where total replacement of fishmeal have been possible.

19.6.1.1 *Nutritional Formulation*

As aquaculture production continues to grow and evolve, there is a need for ongoing research and development to ensure that feed formulations are optimised for the specific nutritional requirements of different species and life stages. In addition, the use of nutrigenomics to understand the evolving nutritional requirements of genetically selected strains of aquaculture species can also play an important role in improving feed formulations and optimising production systems. By combining expertise in nutritional formulation and nutrigenomics research, it is possible to develop highly customised and optimised feed formulations that can improve the growth, health, and sustainability of aquaculture production.

19.6.1.2 *Availability of Ingredients*

Fishmeal and fish oil, including the major use of omega-3 fatty acids such as eicosapentaenoic acid and docosahexaenoic acid, are considered the most nutritious and most digestible ingredients for farmed fish. However, their inclusion rates in compound feeds for aquaculture have shown a clear downward trend, largely because of cost as a result of supply shortages due to increased demand from the aquafeed industry. They are increasingly used selectively at specific stages of production, such as for hatchery, broodstock and finishing diets. The decreased incorporation of fishmeal and fish oil in grower diets has affected the growth performance of livestock. Because of the variability of fishmeal and fish oil production and associated price variations, commercial opportunities arise from seeking alternative sources of proteins and polyunsaturated fatty acids. These include insect meals, plant-based proteins and oils, aquatic plants, single-cell organisms such as bacteria and microalgae, zooplanktons and by-products from the food industry, etc. However, there are technical and practical challenges regarding the processing of these raw materials such as poor digestibility, high enzyme load that affects the stability of raw ingredients used, high content of certain minerals such as fluoride (in shellfish), presence of anti-nutritional compounds and a no-optimal amino acid profile (in plant-based proteins), etc. Therefore, stable supply of complementary key ingredients for feed formulation and development of novel and specialty ingredients within each country are essential for self-sustainability in feed ingredients for local aquaculture production.

19.6.1.3 *Feed Manufacturing Technology and Methods*

Practical feed manufacturing capabilities for pelleting, extrusion, microencapsulation and other formats are essential for development of feed production protocols. Advanced feed manufacturing technology capabilities such as microencapsulation, nano grinding, and novel feed formats (semi-moist, etc.) are needed to move up the manufacturing value chain. In addition to large-scale extrusion there is also a need for small-scale and pilot feed mills to supply local markets and develop commercial quantities of novel feed formulations to minimise logistics disruption.

19.6.2 *Disease and Husbandry*

19.6.2.1 *Water Management Solutions and Resource Usage in Intensive Farming Systems*

At moderate and high production levels, the inputs of nutrients and organic matter to culture units may exceed the assimilative capacity of the ecosystems. The result is deteriorating water quality which stresses the culture species, and stress leads to poor growth, greater incidence of disease, increased mortality and low production. Furthermore, the effluents from aquaculture systems can cause pollution to the environment and consequently affect food quality and safety. The objective in aquaculture should be to optimise profits and reduce risks instead of maximising production. Unfortunately, many farms seem to equate high production with good profits. Although this is true within a certain range of production, the cost in maintaining water quality is inevitably increased as production increases. Hence in land-based high-intensity recirculating aquaculture systems, the water quality will be more critical and will need to be better managed than any other culture system.

The approaches and opportunities for improving water quality in land-based aquaculture systems include: (i) ensure water supply of adequate quality, (ii) control of suspended solids in incoming and recirculating water, (iii) control of water pH, (iv) regulation of stocking and feed rates, (v) better control of feed quality and feeding techniques, (vi) improvement of dissolved oxygen concentrations/budgets, (vii) improved hydrodynamics of water circulation, (viii) minimisation of water exchange, (ix) cost-effective treatment of effluents and solid wastes, (x) management of water microbiome and effective use of pre- and probiotics, and (xi) novel application of plant extracts, organic and inorganic compounds as therapeutants, disinfectants, oxidants and chelators, etc., for enhancement of water quality.

19.6.2.2 *Smallholder Farms' Economically Viable Systems*

The majority of the farm enterprises in Asia are resource limited and, for the most part, use traditional farming methods which are increasingly unproductive and inadequate in light of national food security. To ameliorate this situation, technologies which could take advantage of existing on-farm resources to improve productivity and environmental sustainability need to be developed. However, to develop new technologies for smallholder farms one must understand that, among other things, the perceived ease of use or simplicity of the technology is more crucial than just the potential for fish production.

Amalgamation to form larger holdings is one possible scenario for future aquaculture in most countries to overcome the social economic constraints (e.g., lack of investment capital and social-levelling mechanisms) of these smallholders to adopt novel technologies. Another is creating integrated farming systems, i.e., from feed to fish or from farm to fork. Nevertheless, in land-scarce countries such as Singapore, the future farming enterprises are unlikely to be merged into a few mega farms. It is possible that most high-tech farms in Singapore will remain as smallholders but operate as part of the community and not as standalone single-commodity enterprises.

The success of intensive aquaculture is heavily dependent on the efficiency of the environmentally friendly recirculating aquaculture systems (RAS). There are several critical potential bottlenecks in RAS as the production intensifies: (i) denitrification efficiency to prevent the accumulation of nitrate, (ii) nitrification efficiency to reduce the volume biofiltration systems, and (iii) sludge balance to achieve negligible amounts of waste for disposal and water loss, etc. RAS was originally developed to provide a solution to the environmental problems generated by the traditional pond and flow-through aquaculture systems, since it enables the treatment of polluted water within a closed loop, offers improved control of effluent discharge, and allows complete environment control. Moreover, RAS confers ecological and economic advantages in that it facilitates a reduction in the amounts of water and energy required and reduces land use. In addition, it provides growers with the geographical freedom to set up aquaculture systems in "non-traditional" farming areas.

19.6.2.3 *Regenerative Integrated Multitrophic Intensive Aquaculture Systems*

Integrated multitrophic intensive aquaculture (IMTIA) is the co-cultivation of fed species (such as fish or shrimp) together with extractive species, such as suspension-feeding (e.g., mussels and oysters) and deposit-feeding (e.g., sea cucumbers and sea urchins) invertebrates and seaweeds, which feed on the organic and inorganic effluents generated by the fed species. By establishing such integrated cultivation systems, the sustainability of aquaculture may be increased and so will the biomass. However, for IMTIA to be economically viable, each of the individual components must be marketable, or adding value through accounting for the ecosystem services that extractive species provide.

The integrated farming of vastly different organisms with different needs is complex. Challenging also is the optimisation of how the extractive species get exposed by the waste products of the fed species. This is especially so if the IMTIA is applied to offshore aquaculture due to great variability, both spatially and temporally, in hydrodynamic conditions, pelagic primary productivity, water seston concentrations, farm waste characteristics, etc., among sites which will affect the outcome and success of the IMTIA system.

IMTIA has been most widely adopted in countries with well-established aquaculture industries and strong government support for sustainable aquaculture practices, such as Norway, Canada, and China. In Norway, for example, IMTIA has been applied in salmon farming operations, where salmon are grown alongside seaweed and shellfish to reduce the environmental impact of salmon farming and improve overall production efficiency.

19.6.3 *Genetics, Seeds and Hatchery*

19.6.3.1 *Tropical Species Diversity and Diversification in Production*

The great diversity of climatic and environmental conditions in locations across the world where aquaculture is practised has given rise to a rich and diverse number of species utilised in different types of aquaculture production systems using freshwater, brackish water and marine water. This is especially so in the tropical environment, and provides potentially "unlimited" growth prospects for this industry. In addition, diversifying aquatic farmed species can be of importance for long-term performance and viability of the sector with respect to sustaining food production under changing conditions. In contrast, selection and focus on only a limited number of species can lead to rapid improvements in terms of production and profitability.

Aquaculture, like all agriculture sectors, is vulnerable to exogenous shocks that affect production. Generally, when production is distributed more evenly between species from different groups, one would expect that it reduces the risks related to production failure from, for example, disease or weakening markets, at least at a national level [Gephart *et al.*, 2017]. Thus, a broad and diverse aquaculture portfolio of a country should be more resilient to future perturbations, although much depends on the type, severity and duration of disturbance. In addition, it is noteworthy that commercial diversification and competitiveness can, theoretically, also drive species diversification of the industry. Therefore, social, environmental and economic aspects should be in line with political willingness to facilitate diversification for achieving sustainable development for future aquaculture [FAO, 2016].

19.6.3.2 *Breeding Programmes for Tropical Species of Interest*

Genetic improvement programmes that enhance traits such as growth rate, survival, stress and disease resistance, sexual maturation, product quality and feed efficiency will have the potential and ability to:

- modify the animal to suit a purpose or environment,
- provide greater food security by increasing productivity, reliability and consistency to achieve permanent gain,

- offer solutions to existing or emerging pathogens, and to environmental challenges,
- provide a favourable return on investment,
- fill the gap between demand and supply without a negative environmental impact, and
- assist in managing inbreeding in the intensive production system.

However, information about phenotypic and genetic parameters of economically important traits are quite limited for most of the species farmed in Asia. Therefore, there is a great need to run breeding experiments in order to get reliable estimates of genetic parameters for economically important traits in the most important farmed species. This will drive demand for other genetics-related activities, as well as grow-out and disease challenge testing. Top of the list of skills required are in breeding techniques (such as artificial insemination, eliminating Genotype x Environment interactions effects, broodstock rearing, etc.), breeding methods (such as monosex, breeder lock and polyploidy, etc.), and fish reproductive biology, with attention given to quantitative genetics and breeding strategy.

19.6.3.3 *Genomics Technologies*

The application of genomic selection over traditional aquatic breeding programmes offers significant advantages through being able to accurately predict complex polygenic traits including disease and stress resistance; increasing rates of genetic gain; minimising inbreeding; and negating potential limiting effects of genotype by environment interactions. Further practical advantages of genomic selection are conferred through the use of large-scale communal mating that favour intensive rearing systems.

19.6.3.4 *Hatchery Technologies*

The supply of juveniles from hatcheries is one of the primary constraints in expanding aquaculture. Hence having a local supply of quality seedstock in each country is essential for the development of the sector for both research and commercial production. The following points need to be considered in developing hatchery knowhow and technology:

- There are no standard larviculture methods suitable for all species;
- Variable, unpredictable survival rates hinder planning, production and profitability;
- Nutrition requirements during the early development stages of most commercially important fish species are not well understood;
- The importance of broodstock nutrition on larvae microbiome;
- Microbiome and manipulation of microbiological control of the environment must be at the top of the list of research topics to be addressed; and
- Developing a sophisticated RAS for hatcheries could be a solution in managing and controlling the aqua-rearing environment.

19.6.3.5 *Aquaculture Engineering, Hardware and Supplies*

The systems and technology used in aquaculture have developed rapidly in the past 50 years. They vary from very simple facilities (e.g., mud ponds for domestic consumption) to high-technology systems (e.g., intensive closed systems for export production). However, these high-tech systems are very complex and may not be economically viable on a commercial scale if the increase in capital expenditure outstrips the profitability. Nevertheless, a greater understanding of complex interactions between water, microbiome and cultured organisms, together with advances in hydrodynamics applied to pond and tank design, have enabled the development of closed culture systems, such as RAS. The RAS has the advantage of isolating the aquaculture systems from natural aquatic systems, thus minimising the risk of disease or genetic impacts on the external systems.

There is a need to develop capabilities for aquaculture engineering for on-shore, in-shore and off-shore facilities by leveraging on oil and gas offshore engineering or rig construction. In parallel, it is advocated to develop expertise in aquaculture engineering of indoor vertical culture systems in flatted factory type of infrastructure. Opportunities can also be found in process, structural and system engineering of aquaculture operations (e.g., mass balance and mass transfer engineering, process engineering, hydrological engineering of pond systems, water treatment systems engineering, and energy optimisation).

19.6.3.5.1 Robotics and Automation

Aquaculture technologies, such as robotics, sensors, internet of things (IoT), and artificial intelligence, have advanced significantly in recent decades, supporting the growing scale of production and reducing costs and risks. However, many aquaculture practices are still labour intensive, requiring humans to maintain infrastructure, care for species, and perform tasks like harvesting and processing. Intense resource and environmental pressures, as well as biological needs, are driving the development of intensive farming systems that increase costs, especially those associated with human labour. This presents an excellent opportunity to introduce various forms of automation to improve efficiency and cost effectiveness in aquaculture but taking cognisance of the potentially increased costs. Areas for progress include innovations in low-power computation, sonar technologies, computer vision systems, sensors, batteries, IoT-based farm management, big data analysis, autonomy software, remotely operated vehicles, autonomous underwater vehicles, and more.

19.6.3.5.2 Sustainability and Traceability Systems

Poor regulation and mislabelling have been longstanding issues in the aquaculture industry. In order to address these challenges, there is a growing need for greater transparency and traceability in seafood supply chains. This can be achieved through the implementation of various technologies, such as blockchain, which can enable the tracking of seafood products from the farm or fishery to the end consumer. Additionally, there is a need for stronger regulations and enforcement to ensure that seafood products are accurately labelled and sustainably produced.

Blockchain technology has the potential to provide a secure and efficient traceability solution for the seafood industry, allowing for better transparency and accountability throughout the value chain (from feed to food). To build a traceability system using blockchain technology, a cloud-based infrastructure would be necessary to store and manage the data. An IoT-based peripheral would be required to collect the relevant data from the various stakeholders in the seafood value chain. By providing a shared, decentralised platform for the collection and sharing of this information, blockchain technology would benefit not only the seafood industry, but also consumers and the regulatory agencies concerned with the safety and sustainability of seafood production.

A recent United Nations report [Blaha and Katafono, 2020] states that "while the potential exists for the use of blockchain technology to enhance seafood trade, there are a number of challenges that need to be overcome". From an operations perspective, the biggest challenges are still on the operational management and the field data collection fronts as collecting accurate and timely data from various sources in the seafood supply chain can be challenging.

The aquaculture industry has come a long way since the 1970s and is well on its way to making fish one of the most sustainable and safest food sources, particularly protein. However, those advantages only matter if everyone from regulators to consumers can trust that they are not being misled. Embedding trust throughout the ecosystem can help to ensure a more sustainable food fish supply, both now and in the future.

19.7 Conclusion

Intensification is becoming a growing trend in aquaculture worldwide as a response to increasing demand for animal protein, environmental risks, and limited land availability. The contribution of aquaculture to global food fish availability is anticipated to increase in importance, concomitant with increased global demand for fish as a healthy protein and in the light of increased effects from climate change on wild fisheries. Intensification can provide opportunities to develop low-cost, energy-efficient, and intensive recirculatory aquaculture systems that can benefit small-scale farmers, especially in regions like Asia where most farms are relatively small. The use of modern technology, including data and predictive analytics, can also help farmers make better decisions and improve practices that can eliminate waste, improve animal health, and boost economic productivity. These technologies can help farmers optimise production and reduce waste, while also supporting sustainable and responsible practices that can help ensure the long-term success of the industry. Overall, intensification and the adoption of modern technologies and best practices in aquaculture can open the gate for success and prosperity for farmers, while also helping to produce enough protein for a growing population.

Acknowledgements

The authors are grateful to Enterprise Singapore and Temasek Polytechnic for providing funding and operation support to Aquaculture Innovation Centre. And to many friends and colleagues for their insightful inputs and valuable contributions during the preparation of this manuscript.

References

Ayalew, A. and Abunna, F. (2018). Maintenance of fish health in aquaculture: review of epidemiological approaches for prevention and control of infectious disease of fish. *Veterinary Medicine International*, 2018, p. 5432497.

Baidu-Forson, J., Ntare, B. R. and Waliyar, F. (1997). Farmer participatory research in resource-poor environments: A case of cowpea in the semi-arid tropics of West Africa. *Experimental Agriculture*, 33(04), pp. 513–521.

Blaha, F. and Katafono, K. (2020). Blockchain application in seafood value chains. *FAO Fisheries and Aquaculture Circular No. 1207*.

Boydell, S. and McDonagh, J. (2013). *Agricultural Extension in Ireland: A Review of its History, Structure and Function*. Teagasc.

Brosnan, T. (1985). *An Irish Agrarian History: A Survey of Irish Agriculture from the Middle Ages to the 1980s*. Gill and Macmillan.

Chambers, R. (1997). *Whose Reality Counts?: Putting The First Last.* Intermediate Technology Publications.

Davis, F. D. (1980). Perceived usefulness, perceived ease of use, and user acceptance of information technology, *MIS Quarterly*, 13, pp. 319–340.

Davis, K. E. and Wiggins, S. (2004). Agricultural Extension: Changing Institutional Environments and Options for Reform. In *Agricultural Extension, Rural Development and the Food Security Challenge,* pp. 11–28. Food and Agriculture Organization.

FAO. (2016). *Planning for Aquaculture Diversification: The Importance of Climate Change and Other Drivers.* http://www.fao.org/3/a-i7358e.pdf

Gephart, J., Deutsch, L., Pace, M. L., Troell, M. and Seekell, D. A. (2017). Shocks to fish production: identification, trends, and consequences. *Global Environmental Change*, 42, pp. 24–32.

Kyule-Muendo, D., Elick Otachi, E., Fonda Awour, F., Ogello, E., Obiero, K., Abwao, J., Muthoni, C. and Munguti, J. (2022). Status of fish health management and biosecurity measures in fish farms, cages and hatcheries in Western Kenya. *CABI Agriculture and Bioscience*, 3, pp. 18–28.

WOAH. (2022). *Manual of Diagnostic Tests for Aquatic Animals 2022.* https://www.woah.org/en/produit/manual-of-diagnostic-tests-for-aquatic-animals-2021/

Perera, R. P., Jones, B., Beers, P., Kleeman, S. and McGladdery, S. (2008). Maintaining Biosecurity in Aquaculture Systems: A Constraint or a Challenge. In M. G. Bondad-Reantaso, *et al.* (Eds.), *Diseases in Asian Aquaculture VI. Fish Health Section*, pp. 3–20. Asian Fisheries Society.

Ragasa, C., Amewu, S., Agyakwah, S. K., Mensah, E. T.-D. and Asmah, R. (2022). Impact of aquaculture training on farmers' income: Cluster randomized controlled trial evidence in Ghana. *Agricultural Economics*, 53, pp. 5–20._

Swaminathan, M. S. (2004). *Fisheries and Aquaculture: Towards the Blue Revolution.* FAO Fisheries Department.

Tyedmers, P. and Pelletier, N. (2007). Biophysical Accounting in Aquaculture: Insights from Current Practice and the Need for Methodological Development. In *Comparative Assessment of the Environmental Costs of Aquaculture and Other Food Production Sectors: Methods for Meaningful Comparisons*, pp. 229–241. Food and Agriculture Organization.

Van den Ban, A. W. (1999). Problems of Agricultural Extension in Developing and Former Communist Countries. In B. S. Hansra, *et al.* (Eds.), *Globalising Indian Agriculture: Policies and Strategies*, pp. 115–122. Classical Publishing Company.

https://doi.org/10.1142/9789811278297_0020

Chapter 20

Alternative Proteins — Challenges and Opportunities within the Asian Context

Wong Min Hao

*Agency for Science, Technology & Research (A*STAR), Singapore*

20.1 Introduction

Within Asia and the developing South, the issue of food supply is expected to be increasingly acute. Global demand for meat has increased three-fold over the last 50 years [Chen *et al.*, 2022], with 574 million metric tons of meat, seafood, dairy, and eggs consumed in 2020 [Boston Consulting Group, 2021]. The change in meat consumption has been the most pronounced in areas experiencing economic growth such as Asia. This pattern is also mirrored in meat production, with 40–45% of meat production in 2018 attributable to Asia [Chen *et al.*, 2022].

Over the period 2000–19, global protein consumption grew by around 45%, rising from 166 million tonnes in 2000 to around 242 million tonnes in 2019. This is equivalent to an increase from around 73 grams in 2000 to 85 grams per person per day in 2019. Five countries in Asia drove the vast majority of this growth — around

63% of the overall increase — with China (26%) and India (14%) displaying the largest growth among individual countries. Despite the rapid recent growth in protein demand, there is still much room for growth given that most of these countries are still significantly below the global average of protein consumption [Food Industry Asia and AlphaBeta, 2021].

Conventional meat production is land and resource intensive (Sim *et al.*, 2021), raising concerns about its long-term sustainability, in terms of environmental, ethical and health aspects.[1] Therefore, transformational changes, rather than incremental enhancements, are necessary to meet the future demand for protein [Chen *et al.*, 2022].

This chapter shall seek to explore novel foods — a category of food or food formats that hitherto has not been consumed by the mainstream population — as a potential (partial) solution to the increasing demand on the world's food supply. Specifically, we will explore three main categories of novel foods; plant-based, microbe-based, and cell-based proteins. While such a survey is by no means exhaustive, we will focus particularly on emerging technologies within these three categories that have the potential to be transformative, if successful. Where relevant, these technologies are contextualised to Asia.

20.2 The Case for Novel Foods

Beyond ecological benefits, novel foods and their associated production systems could contribute to food and nutrition resilience

---

[1] However, in some cases, animals convert what humans cannot eat (e.g., grass) into food. Hence it is arguable that livestock contributes to food security where it is not practical to grow crops (McClements and Grossman, 2022). Nevertheless, novel foods could have the potential to contribute to food security.

that is applicable to Asia's context. Food resilience benefits could arise in two key pillars: (1) operating in closed systems, hence reducing risk exposure, and (2) utilising modular systems and decentralising food networks [Tzachor *et al.*, 2021].

1) Operating in closed systems

   a. Some novel foods can be produced in closed loop, stackable systems, which are largely unaffected by environmental issues that plague the traditional farming systems [Tzachor *et al.*, 2021]. For example, microbial protein and cultured meat production systems aim to provide optimised, stable conditions to ensure consistent yields.
   b. Alternative proteins which substitute animal protein also avoid bacterial and faecal matter contamination, thus aiming to mitigate the risk of supply disruptions from contamination. This may be of relevance to Asia's context where, in certain regions, sanitary practices may still be lacking.

2) Utilising modular systems and decentralisation of production

   a. The modular design of many novel foods production systems often allows a level of adaptability and control, to react nimbly to abrupt changes in demand and supply. Modular systems can contain possible contamination to the production unit, without spreading throughout the entire production system.
   b. Novel foods can decentralise and democratise production, compared to traditional farming which tends to be concentrated, e.g., in factory farming. Production could be located closer to isolated communities, where nutrition insecurity is prevalent. This diversifies the geography of

farming and mitigates volatility and variability arising from changes in demand and supply. For example, this could alleviate the contagion effect of international blockages, and also allow tapping into the crop mix available in Asia (in the case of plant-based proteins).

20.3 Current and Emerging Technologies

In general, innovation for novel foods should create products with physiochemical, functional and sensory properties to mimic their conventional animal-based counterparts. Additionally, innovation should also aim to create products with reduced costs, clean labels and raw materials with a reliable, abundant supply and consistent performance [McClements and Grossman, 2022]. Finally, to encourage consumer adoption in Asia, innovation should be tailored to localised Asian cooking habits and cultural norms.

Here, we outline the key current and emerging technologies across three alternative protein types — microbial, plant-based, and cultivated meat.

20.3.1 *Microbial Proteins*

Asia's use of fermentation dates back centuries, and has more recently been applied to the pharmaceuticals sector. However, using microorganisms as food sources has recently come into the limelight [Ciani *et al.*, 2021], particularly in view of food security and the sustainability agenda.

Innovation in fermentation can broadly be applied to two categories:

1. Biomass fermentation leverages the fast growth and high protein content of many microorganisms to efficiently produce large quantities of protein. The microbial biomass

itself can serve as an ingredient, with the cells intact or minimally processed — for example, the cells can be broken open to improve digestibility or enrich for even higher protein content.

2. Precision fermentation uses microbial hosts as 'cell factories' to produce specific functional ingredients such as lipids, vitamins, flavouring and colourants to improve sensory and functional aspects of finished food products [Chai *et al.*, 2022]. Microbial protein production can be more efficient than conventional production methods such as bulk extraction or organic synthesis [Chai *et al.*, 2022] due to the optimal use of inputs and stable growth parameters. Production is generally under optimal conditions in bioreactors, which vary depending on the organism, e.g., hydrogen-oxidising bacteria, methanotrophic bacteria, fungal microbial protein and microalgae [Ciani *et al.*, 2021]. Examples include Perfect Day's dairy proteins, Clara Foods' egg proteins, and Impossible Foods' heme protein.

As long as inputs can be obtained, high-risk or non-agricultural regions can generate high-quality proteins [Good Food Institute, 2021] for both food and feed, which could ultimately contribute to food security in Asia.

20.3.1.1 *Emerging Technologies in Fermentation*

Despite fermentation's long history, there remains a range of opportunities for innovation across the value chain to enable scale-up and widespread adoption. The key areas of innovation can be summarised as follows:

(i) *Target selection and design:* For precision fermentation, one of the most basic challenges is target selection and design, to determine which molecules contribute to the specific desired quality in question. This is a non-trivial endeavour, as often the chemicals that precision fermentation seeks to replace have their own supply chains and ingrained regulatory process. Choosing the appropriate targets is hence particularly important.

(ii) *Strain development:* The diverse range of fungi, bacteria and microalgae offer the opportunity to discover and develop species for optimised yields and other production traits. This could utilise the latest tools in biotechnology and other breeding strategies. Within this space, start-ups and companies often employ genetic engineering and codon optimisation techniques to increase the titre values, and also to encourage the secretion of proteins extracellularly. These genetic toolboxes can include multi-copy cloning within a single strain, and various other codon optimisation techniques that are suited for mammalian, *Escherichia coli*, or yeast cells. By genetically engineering cells to express proteins extracellularly, downstream processing unit operations may be dramatically simplified.

(iii) *Feedstock optimisation:* Although feedstock represents a major cost driver for production, most feedstock remains sugar-based. Feedstocks are a major cost driver for most fermentation processes. At present, the majority of fermentation relies on fairly standardised, refined, sugar-based feedstocks.

(iv) *Bioprocess design:* Current production facilities offer limited opportunity to tailor to the needs of novel organisms or novel applications. Current innovation includes continuous production, accommodating denser or more viscous cultures, enhanced nutrient and air exchange at higher volumes and energy efficiency, novel harvesting methods, and downstream purification.

20.3.1.2 *Alternatives for Sugar-Based Feedstock*

Although feedstocks are a major cost driver for the production process, fermentation's resilience and adaptability can be attributed to the flexibility offered by its feedstock raw material inputs. Currently, fermentation is largely dependent on refined, sugar-based feedstock, which is well established in the food and biotechnology sectors. For example, *Fusarium venenatum,* which is commercially available as *Quorn,* utilises glucose for fermentation. However, glucose is associated with considerable arable land requirements [Upcraft *et al.*, 2021]. Therefore, more sustainable and lower-cost substrates from a more diverse range of sources are required.

Current research involves exploring alternative substrates, such as the conversion of by-products and waste streams. For example, a recent LCA/TEA report proposed that lignocellulosic plant materials (e.g., agricultural residue) could be used for mycoprotein production, where a key benefit was the minimal arable land requirement [Upcraft *et al.*, 2021]. In this study, Upcraft *et al.* [2021] extracted glucose from rice straw residue, noting that crude mycoprotein past products could be producing for \$40.04 per kg-protein, with scope to reduce the price further. The LCA also validated the associated environmental impact, with less than 14% GHG emissions compared to protein from beef [Upcraft *et al.*, 2021].

Innovations like these could enable Asia to exploit the significant amount of underutilised cellulose resources, simultaneously alleviating the burden on arable land, albeit involving additional processing steps. Similar technologies may be applicable to Asia, with its potentially large source of cellulosic waste, e.g., oil palm waste, rice straw.

Additionally, alternatives to sugar substrates have been applied to biomass fermentation, utilising a range of agrifood side streams, e.g., date waste [Reihani and Darani, 2018], potato protein liquor [Sar *et al.*, 2022], orange, pineapple, banana, watermelon and cucumber waste [Oshoma and Eguakun-Owie, 2018]. Other start-ups have also explored using malt as the starting feedstock for fermentation. Given that malt has been extensively used in breweries and that the germination process of barley to release enzymes (i.e., malting) is fairly well understood, this may be an attractive alternative to glucose feedstock in some instances.

20.3.1.3 *Plant Molecular Farming*

Rather than using microbes as hosts, one emerging technology is the use of plant molecular farming using plants to produce ingredients such as animal proteins and other ingredients to enhance functionality and sensory properties [Watson, 2022]. Similar to microbial precision fermentation, plant molecular farming could also serve as an enabler for the plant-based protein and cultured meat segments. Table 20.1 compares common approaches in various synthetic biology approaches to protein engineering.

There are some natural advantages and disadvantages of plant molecular farming, which is due to the differing characteristics of plant cells, as summarised in Table 20.2.

Table 20.1 Common approaches in protein engineering.

	Transient expression in plants	Cell suspension cultures (plants)	Transgenic plants	Cell suspension cultures (other microbials)	Chemical approaches (non-synbio)
Overview	Insertion of promoters and genetic sequences into plant nuclei for transient expression	Isolation of genetically modified plant cell cultures in bioreactors for subsequent fermentation	Generation of parental lineages with permanently transformed genotype	Use of fungal, bacterial, mammalian cell types for precision fermentation	Chemical production of target molecules without use of biological processes
Advantages	Short development timelines Able to use different hosts Low resistance to adoption/ less regulatory risk	Adapted to particular processes (e.g., glyco-optimisation)	Highly scalable Adapted towards oral vaccines	Strains such as *E. coli* are well studied with regulations established	Scalable Tend to have short cycle times Able to use harsh, non-biological conditions for processing
Limitations	Transfection efficiency and protein yields tend to be low (enhanced with transplastomic means) Scalability needs to be proven Non-permanence may be a limitation Downstream processing (plants tend to secrete other proteins into media)	Generally more costly (require aeration, C1-C6 media, etc.) Plant protein yields tend to be low (typical plant cell ~1,000 times larger than a CHO cell and ~10,000 times larger than a bacterial cell) Downstream processing	Long development time Specific to crop type Regulatory hurdles	Generally more costly Require external C1-C6 source	Less sustainable (typically uses high temperatures, harsh chemistry) Typically generates significant waste streams

Table 20.2 Comparison of cell types in plant molecular farming. Comparison of the characteristics among plants cells, microbes and mammalian cells in bioprocess development.

Characteristics	Plant cells	Mammalian cells	Bacteria
Shape	Spherical/ cylindrical	Spherical	Spherical
Size	20–200 μm	10–50 μm	<1 μm
Cell wall	Yes	No	Yes
Doubling time	20–100 h	20–48 h	Less than 2 h
Cell aggregation or Dumping	Aggregated to form cell clusters over 2 mm	Not aggregated	Not aggregated
Shear sensitivity	High	Extremely high	Low
Oxygen uptake rate	5–10 mmol/L h	0.05–5 mmol/L h	10–90 mmol/L h
$K_L\alpha$ required in bioreactor operation	10–50/h	0.25–10/h	100–1000/h
Protein yields	0.01–200 mg/L	1–10 g/L	<1 g/L
Protein localisation	Intracellular/ secreted	Secreted	Usually intracellular
Scale-up capacity	Medium	Medium	High

Due to the differences above, poor cell growth and low protein production have been reported when plant cell cultures were scaled up in bioreactors. Two distinctive properties of plant cell culture that require special consideration in bioreactor process development include large cell size and complex morphology. Plant cells are much larger than other commonly used microbial platforms like yeast and bacteria, with a large intracellular vacuole accounting for up to 90% of the cell volume. Plant cells also typically have a rigid, inflexible cellulose-based cell wall. These factors make plant cells susceptible to shear stresses, limiting the mechanical agitation techniques available to meet oxygen demands for cell growth. This is a challenge particularly with scaled-up volumes where there may be more dead zones or uneven rheology within the fermentation tank. Companies and labs have generally tried to address this challenge through alternative bioreactor designs (e.g., pneumatic or single-use reactors).

Further, suspension-cultured plant cells tend to form aggregates ranging from two to thousands of cells (from <100 μm to over 2 mm) and sometimes even display cellular differentiation. The formation of aggregates may sometimes confer positive benefits such as protecting the shear-sensitive plant cells from shear damage and enhancing sedimentation rates of the cultured cells. However, cell aggregates tend to adhere to reactor surfaces forming extensive wall growth, and effective mass transfer to inner plant cells may be hindered, resulting in adverse effects on cell growth and foreign protein production from stress.

Assuming some of the technology limitations can be addressed, the use of plant molecular farming can be potentially applied to the production of flour with functional egg and dairy proteins, with reduced need for downstream processing [Good Food Institute, 2021]. Companies such as Moolec Science are developing genetically engineered beans and peas, but with porcine and bovine proteins. They are targeting proteins from the blood and muscles of animals to improve the nutritional and sensory properties of meat analogues, including the possibility of replacing methyl cellulose, as well as combining the matrix of plant and animal proteins [Watson, 2022].

20.3.2 *Plant-Based Proteins*

Whilst Asia has long produced and consumed plant-based foods such as tofu, tempeh and seitan, they did not closely resemble the characteristics of animal-based foods. This chapter focuses on next-generation plant-based products that aim to imitate the characteristics of their animal-based counterparts [Dass, 2022]. Although some plant-based protein products are already on the market and are arguably the most mature of the three novel food types analysed in this chapter, there remains significant room for innovation. Some emerging technologies are highlighted below.

20.3.2.1 *Raw Material and Inputs*

Optimising crops for plant-based protein products: Plant-based products today are typically made of soy or beans. Other crops such as pea and potato have become more popular as ingredients in plant-based meats. However, these crops have largely been optimised for starch yields (or oil seed crops, in the case of soy), rather than for properties that are useful for plant-based meats. Current research explores crop breeding techniques that are optimised for plant-based protein products, such as higher protein content, improved sensory characteristics or more efficient fractionation. Companies active in this space include Equinom, Benson Hill Biosystems, etc.

Further, the different types of plant-based foods require different combinations of ingredients to achieve different characteristics [McClements and Grossman, 2022]. However, most crops have not been explored for alternative protein applications. This means that novel foods producers have a narrow range of sources of ingredients to choose from, with implications to food resilience. Tools such as high-throughput screening, computational or machine learning can be used to explore novel protein sources and learn about how growing conditions influence the ingredients' characteristics. For instance, companies such as Agrematch claimed to have developed a unique artificial intelligence-based predictive system called AI4AI: artificial intelligence for active ingredients. The system combines multi-layered machine learning and deep learning algorithms with a proprietary database and validation pipeline to efficiently discover and develop products. Another company, Prose Foods, focused on the utilisation of predictors for intrinsically disordered proteins towards the identification of alternative (plant) sources of casein. It builds on a heuristic model based on an understanding of the molecular grammar of casein, as well as an artificial intelligence-based classification algorithm, to identify plant proteins that may be functionally similar to casein. Overall, there have been significant developments in recent years on the prediction of three-dimensional structures of proteins from their amino acid sequences. AlphaFold is a programme with a deep learning-based approach to protein structure prediction, for instance, and has demonstrated remarkable success in independent assessments of prediction accuracy.

20.3.2.2 *Texturisation, End-Product Formulation and Manufacturing*

Product formulation includes texture and sensory aspects and nutritional attributes. To produce a finished product with the desired texture and forms, processes such as extrusion, shear cell processing, stretching, kneading, press forming, folding, layering, and 3D printing are often used. One commonly used processing method is extrusion, to produce the fibrous structure of meat. However, a number of challenges exists: capital costs and energy requirements for extrusion are high and subject to significant quality control issues. High temperatures and pressures can cause differential breakdown in amino acids, adversely impacting nutritional quality. Current innovation for texturisation and forming includes new manufacturing methods like 3D printing and shear cell technology to improve energy requirements, lower capital costs and produce whole-cut products (rather than the commercially available minced products). Non-extrusion methods such as chemical or biological processes could help to avoid high capital costs in developing regions of the world. Software can also be used to help with systems analysis and predictive capabilities, particularly during the extrusion process.

One interesting texturisation technology that has emerged is the use of directional freezing to create texturised meat products. This cold processing technology is based on formulated hydrocolloids, which are able to directionally freeze and create ice-filled channels of the desired size. Subsequent thawing and diffusion of soluble proteins into the hydrocolloids then enable the formation of layered muscle tissue. This technique further enables tunability, as flavours, colours, etc., can also be introduced into the channels easily and at scale. Companies such as New School Foods have since announced products based on directional freezing.

20.3.2.3 *Nutritional Enhancement of Plant-Based Foods*

For widespread adoption, it is important that plant-based meats are considered nutritious and healthy. This means containing the appropriate macronutrients and micronutrients (and their interactions), dietary fibres, impacts on metabolism and the gut microbiome [McClements and Grossman, 2022]. This is particularly important in Asia, where one of the key drivers for plant-based protein adoption is health [Food Industry Asian and AlphaBeta, 2012; Neo, 2021]. For example, in 2016, the Ministry of Health in China detailed guidelines to halve meat consumption [Neo, 2021]. Some plant-based foods may be lacking in their nutritional profiles, i.e., macronutrients, micronutrients (e.g., vitamin B12, vitamin D, iron, zinc, and calcium), dietary fibres and nutraceuticals [McClements and Grossman, 2022].

Many of the current generation of plant-based meats may not be optimised for nutrition and health, containing considerable amounts of sugar, salt, fat and calories, which tend to be digested and absorbed quickly. Therefore, much research on the health and nutrition aspects of plant-based foods is required. There are two main ways to improve the healthfulness of plant-based foods, namely fortification and reformulation.

Some emerging technologies involve the replacement of the sensory and functional properties provided by fat, using lipids with lower calories, such as SALATRIM. Food-grade particles that scatter light such as proteins of indigestible carbohydrates (with different glycaemic indices) can help to imitate the creamy appearance of fat droplets, whilst hydrocolloids or other food-grade particles can imitate the textural characteristics of fat. Further, plant proteins can have considerable salt levels as they are produced using salting-out methods. Plant-based products can also contain high levels of salt as they are used for flavourings or for formulation. To reduce the amount of salt required, some strategies include the use of hollow salt crystals, or to trap salts in small particles, allowing a reduction in salt usage, but with the same perceived saltiness [McClements and Grossman, 2022].

20.3.3 *Cultivated Meat*

Cultured meat is gaining the attention of governments, scientists, investors and entrepreneurs alike. However, much innovation is required to overcome challenges in costs, scalability, safety, consumer acceptance and nutrition [Domigan *et al.*, 2022]. Innovation throughout the value chain is required, from cell sourcing and banking, cell culture process, bioprocessing and scale-up to product formulation, nutrition and sensory properties.

20.3.3.1 *Cell Culture Media*

Cell culture media is widely considered to be a significant cost driver for cultured meat production, forming up to 80% of the production costs in some instances. Currently, cell culture media typically contains fetal bovine serum, which is associated with high costs and high bioloical variability. Besides technical challenges, there are also ethical and sustainability concerns arising from the serum extraction. Although there has been some innovation to optimise media formlations over time, the key composition of basal cell culture media has not changed significantly [Good Food Institute, n.d.]. Some serum-free media formulations have been developed within the medical field, but largly feature animal-derived ingredients, and are typically too expensive for scaling up cultured meat production [Chen *et al.*, 2022].

Emerging technologies in this space focus on solutions which utilise serum-free media and non-animal-derived serum components. Whilst Upside Foods had previously found non-animal-derived components as substitutes for the key components in cell culture media, they have recently announced a "biological breakthrough, where the remaining components are also non-animal-derived, and the cell media is now entirely free from animal-derived components" [Watson, 2021]. Typically, compound screening libraries are used to develop optimised serum-free cell culture. Thousands of molecules are screened for the desired effect, with the hopes of serendipitously landing on at least one moledule. Mark Post and team have adopted a targeted approach, using RNA sequencing and differential expression analysis to understand the molecular changes in cell surface receptors during myogenic differentiation. They were able to induce myogenic differentiation without utilising animal serum, by targeting the receptors of interest, whose expression were altered, with known ligands. This research was focused on bovine cells, and furture research could be extended to other cultured products such as chicken and pork [Domigan *et al.*, 2022].

Other technologies have involved exploring the use of plants of microbial fermentation to derive ingredients. For example, corn steep solids, yeast, or soy extracts could offer essential nutrients for cell growth, and may hold promising solutions for the replacement of serum. However, there are likely to be challenges in variability in the final product, and the presence of cytotoxic impurities. Here, future research could include the application of such media formulations to support cell culturing for longer periods and with greater consistency [Chen *et al.*, 2022]. Also, besides knowing what the required components are for cells to proliferate, and producing this in a cost-effective, animal-free method, further research is required about the timing in which specific components are introduced in the process [Watson, 2021]. For example, the timing of adding specific growth factors, if optimised, may enable significant cost savings.

20.3.3.2 *Taste and Texture of Cultured Meat*

To enable widespread adoption of cultured meat, current research is exploring the taste and texture in addition to its production. Taste is affected by the amino acid composition of meat; amino acids can evoke complex tastes, namely an amalgamtion of sweetness, sourness, saltiness, bitterness and umami. For example, in a study by Joo *et al.* [2022], the composition of amino acid- and nucleotide-related compounds, and taste characteristics of cultured meat tissue obtained by culturing satellite cells isolated from chicken and cattle, were investigated and compared to those of traditional meat [Joo *et al.*, 2022]. Using an electronic tongue system, the study found that some taste characteristics differed such as the umami, bitterness and sourness of cultured meat tissue were less intense than those of their conventional meat counterparts, but the astringency in cultured meat tissues was higher than their traditional meat counterparts [Joo *et al.*, 2022]. These results implied the need to adapt the composition of the growth media to affect the umami and bitterness levels of the cultured meat, to arrive at a taste profile similar to that of conventional meat [Joo *et al.*, 2022].

In addition to taste, some studies are exploring the mechanical properties and textural behaviour of cultured meat. For example, Paredes *et al.* [2022] have used texture profile analysis and rheology tests for determining cultured meat properties. This research is significant for Asia, which is home to a vast array of cuisines. Taste and nutrition requirements could be tailored to the unique needs of individual geographical regions. Kamalapuram, Handral and Choudhury propose that in order to tailor cultured meat ingredients and products to the Indian consumer, it is necessary to delineate the signatures of molecular interactions associated with the taste appeal of native cuisine [Kamalapuram *et al.*, 2021]. Continued research to understand the drivers for taste, as well as in technologies that can modulate and control the taste and textural behaviour of cultured meat, would be critical for its adoption in future.

Significant progress has been made in terms of cultivating whole muscle mass to resemble that of conventional meat. Recently, TissenBioFarm debuted a whole cut meat prototype that weighed in excess of 10 kg [TissenBioFarm, 2023]. While the prototype is understood to primarily utilise bioink and currently may contain a relatively low percentage of cells, it is clear that the industry has made significant advances since the first cultivated burger was introduced by Mark Post in 2013 [Post, 2014].

20.4 Conclusion

Any investment and research into novel foods must necessarily appreciate that food is a deeply cultural subject. Insects, seen as a delicacy in some parts of Asia and Africa, evoke repulsion in many Western nations. The turkey, which is an integral part of Thanksgiving within the United States, is largely not on the menus of people in North and South Asia. For religious reasons, pork is typically not consumed in Arab and Muslim countries while beef is not consumed in Hindu and Buddhist nations. These cultural constraints and preferences manifest themselves in the different proportions of proteins consumed within each country. Any businesses within the food industry would need to fully grasp the cultural diversity within different regions of the world to achieve success at scale.

Interestingly, a recent study by Euromonitor [Chehtman, 2023] categorised consumer responses into a few key types — (1) in need of alternatives; where consumers have low brand loyalty and high price sensitivity, (2) affluent but disengaged; where consumers may change to competing brands and alternative products, (3) unworried and loyal; where consumers continue to purchase brands that they are familiar with due to high perceived value, and (4) looking for emotional comfort; where consumers continue to buy a brand as a token of emotional comfort. For companies launching novel food products in this space, targeting the marketing towards the relevant segment of consumers would be critical.

Beyond ingrained cultural norms, dietary preferences also evolve with time from changing perceptions of what constitutes "healthy", "sustainable" or "tasty" food. Consumers used to be concerned with genetically modified organisms, but at present appear to be a lot more accepting of them in alternative proteins. As more and more companies offer products in this space, the synthetic biology field is gaining significantly more experience at offering complex protein products for the consumer market. Independent of whether these proteins dominate the market or not, the next set of companies that propose proteins as replacement for various materials will be bolstered from these efforts. In this light, emerging technologies for novel foods will likely remain relevant for a long time to come.

Acknowledgement

The author wishes to acknowledge Priscilla Wettasinghe for her contributions in the writing of this chapter.

References

Boston Consulting Group. (2021). Food for thought: the protein transformation. https://www.bcg.com/publications/2021/the-benefits-of-plant-based-meats

Chai, K. F., Ng, K. R., Samarasiri, M. and Chen, W. N. (2022). Precision fermentation to advance fungal food fermentations. *Current Opinion in Food Science*, 47, p. 100881.

Chehtman, A. (2023). How consumers and businesses are reacting to food price inflation. *Euromonitor*. https://euromonitor.com/article/how-consumers-and-businesses-are-reacting-to-food-price-inflation/

Chen, L., Guttieres, D., Koenigsberg, A., Barone, P. W., Sinskey, A. J. and Springs, S. (2022). Large-scale cultured meat production: Trends, challenges and promising. *Biomaterials*, 280, p. 121274.

Ciani, M., Lippolis, A., Fava, F., Rodolfi, L., Niccolai, A. and Tredici, M. R. (2021). Microbes: food for the future. *Foods*, 10(5), p. 971.

Dass, C. (2022). The future of Asian food is plant-based, according to Growthwell Foods' Manuel Bossi. *Tatler Asia*. https://www.tatlerasia.com/dining/digest/growthwell-foods-manuel-bossi-plant-based-food-industry-asia

Domigan, L. J., Feisst, V. and Ogilve, O. J. (2022). Recipes for cultured meat. *Nature Food*, 3(1), pp. 9–10.

Food Industry Asia and AlphaBeta. (2021). The future of proteins in Asia. https://foodindustry.asia/hubfs/The%20Future%20of%20Proteins%20in%20Asia.pdf

Good Food Institute. (2021). *State of the Industry Report, Fermentation: Meat, Seafood, Eggs, and Dairy*. https://gfi.org/wp-content/uploads/2022/04/2021-Fermentation-State-of-the-Industry-Report.pdf

Good Food Institute. (n.d.). Deep dive: Cultivated meat cell culture media. https://gfi.org/science/the-science-of-cultivated-meat/deep-dive-cultivated-meat-cell-culture-media/

Joo, S. T., Choi, J. S., Hur, S. J., Kim, G. D., Kim, C. J., Lee, E. U., Bakhsh, A. and Hwang, Y. H. (2022). A comparative study on the taste characteristics of satellite cell cultured meat derived from chicken and cattle muscles. *Food Science of Animal Resources*, 42(1), pp. 175–185.

Kamalapuram, S. K., Handral, H. and Choudhury, D. (2021). Cultured meat prospects for a billion! *Foods*, 10(12), p. 2922.

McClements, D. J. and Grossmann, L. (2022). *Next-Generation Plant-based Foods: Design, Production, and Properties*. Springer, p. 263.

Neo, P. (2021). Plant-based innovation in Asia: Localisation, health, taste and affordability top drivers of industry growth and evolution. *Food Navigator Asia*. https://www.foodnavigator-asia.com/Article/2021/07/19/Plant-based-innovation-in-Asia-Localisation-health-taste-and-affordability-top-drivers-of-industry-growth-and-evolution-Growth-Asia-panel

Oshoma, C. E. and Eguakun-Owie, S. O. (2018). Conversion of food waste to single cell protein using *Aspergillus niger*. *Journal of Applied Sciences and Environmental Management*, 22(3), pp. 400–405.

Paredes, J., Cortizo-Lacalle, D., Imaz, A. M., Aldazabal, J. and Vila, M. (2022). Application of texture analysis methods for the characterization of cultured meat. *Scientific Reports*, 12, p. 3898.

Post, M. (2014). Cultured beef: medical technology to produce food. *Journal of the Science of Food Agriculture*, 94(6), pp. 1039–1041.

Reihani, S. S. F. and Darani, K. K. (2018). Mycoprotein production from date waste using *Fusarium venenatum* in a submerged culture. *Applied Food Biotechnology*, 5(4), pp. 243–352.

Sar, T., Larsson, K., Fristedt, R., Underland, U. and Taherzadeh, M. (2022). Demo-scale production of protein-rich fungal biomass from potato protein liquor for use as innovative food and feed products. *Food Bioscience*, 47, p. 101637.

Sim, S. Y. J., Akila, S. R. V.,Chiang, J. H. and Henry, C. J. (2021). Plant proteins for future foods: a roadmap. *Foods*, 10(8), p. 1967.

TissenBioFarm. (2023). The future of cultivated meat. http://www.tissenbiofarm.com/en/index.jsp

Tzachor, A., Richards, C. E. and Holt, L. (2021). Future foods for risk-resilient diets. *Nature Food*, 2, pp. 326–329.

Upcraft, T., Tu, W. C., Johnson, R., Finnigan, T., Hung, N. V., Hallett, J. and Guo, M. (2021). Protein from renewable resources: mycoprotein production from agricultural residues. *Green Chemistry,* 23, pp. 5150–5165.

Watson, E. (2021). 'A biological breakthrough...' Upside Foods has animal-component-free cell media for cell cultured (aka cultivated) meat. *Food Navigator*. https://www.foodnavigator-usa.com/Article/2021/12/09/A-biological-breakthrough-UPSIDE-Foods-hails-animal-component-free-cell-media-for-cell-cultured-aka-cultivated-meat

Watson, E. (2022). 'Proudly genetically modified...' Moolec 'molecular famring' co gears to launch meat proteins from GM crops. *Food Navigator.* https://www.foodnavigator-usa.com/Article/2022/04/25/Proudly-genetically-modified-Moolec-molecular-farming-co-gears-up-to-launch-meat-proteins-from-GM-crops

https://doi.org/10.1142/9789811278297_0021

Chapter 21

The Importance of Plant Health in Asia's Food Security

Serge Savary[1,2,3]

[1]*GB Pant University of Agricultural Research and Technology, Pantnagar, India*
[2]*University of California, Davis, USA*
[3]*University of Twente, The Netherlands*

21.1 Introduction

Plant health seldom features in texts dealing with major themes in current science such as food security or climate change. This is because plant health, with all its bacteria, viruses, oomycetes, nematodes, and ascomycetes is often seen as too complex. This is also because plant health is only seen as a consequence of major forces that shape our current world but the fact is that plant health is an important factor of agrosystems' performances and sustainability and, therefore, of food security.

This chapter offers albeit a narrow view of plant health affecting food security in Asia from the angle of diseases caused by pathogens, and does not include diseases of abiotic causes.

21.2 Plant Diseases Affect All Components of Food Security

Several frameworks have been devised to define the components of food security. While the FAO Policy Brief of June 2006 [FAO, 2006] lists four components (food availability, access, stability, and utilisation), the FAO-IFAD-WFP Report on Food Insecurity [FAO, 2013] considers six components (availability, physical access, economic access, stability exposure, stability shocks, utilisation); and the ASEAN Food Security Thought and Issue Paper [Desker *et al.*, 2013] defines six components (primary production, vulnerability of stocks and stocks, physical access and supply chains, economic access, stability of production and supply, and the utility, quality, and nutritive value of food). Savary *et al.* [2017] developed a synthesis of these categories, considering six (non-overlapping) components of food security (Table 21.1): (1) primary production, (2) availability (including the national or local production, imports, and stocks), (3) physical access and value chains, (4) economic access, (5) stability of supply, and (6) safety, quality, and nutritional value of food.

Using this framework, Savary *et al.* [2017] surveyed the literature on major plant diseases worldwide. They found that every component of food security may be affected, sometimes very seriously, by plant diseases (Table 21.1). This is because plant diseases cause much more than just crop yield reductions. For example, the potato late blight epidemic of the 19th century in Ireland, in addition to causing a massive reduction of production, also led to depleted food stocks, affected supply chains, created an instability of production for decades, and decreased the food quality of whatever potato was left for the poor. Wheat rusts (leaf, stripe, and stem rusts) currently

Table 21.1 Examples of impacts of plant disease on food security components. Adapted from Savary *et al.* [2017].

	Examples of plant disease epidemics, past and current					
Components of food security	**Potato late blight (Ireland, 19th century)**	**Wheat rusts (world's main wheat production areas, today)**	**Fusarium head blight (U.S. Mid-west, today)**	**False smut of rice (Asia, today)**	**Brown spot of rice (South Asia, today)**	**Coffee rust (Central America, today)**
1. Availability, primary production	Very large	Large	Strongly impacted	Large	Large	Not affected
2. Availability, import, stocks	Large	Strongly impacted	Strongly impacted	Impacted	Strongly impacted	Impacted
3. Access, physical and supply chains	Impacted	Impacted	Impacted	Not affected	Strongly impacted	Impacted
4. Access, economical	Not affected	Impacted	Impacted	Impacted	Strongly impacted	Large
5. Stability of food availability	Impacted	Impacted	Impacted	Impacted	Large	Not affected
6. Safety, quality, nutritive value	Impacted	Not affected	Very large	Large	Strongly impacted	Not affected

are a major cause for yield losses worldwide, with dramatic consequences where wheat is a primary food crop (e.g., in West Asia, North Africa, and Ethiopia). These diseases also strongly affect the stocks of major wheat-exporting regions (North America, Europe, Russia, Ukraine, Australia, and the Southern Cone of South America). They, therefore, have long-term consequences on economies and in turn on infrastructure. Plant diseases have pernicious long-term impacts on food prices and some immediate "spike" effects (as shown by the Arab Spring). Plant disease epidemics further create uncertainty on the cereal markets. Yield and production reductions are not only at stake; grain quality, value, and safety are also affected by plant diseases. Fusarium head blight on wheat has for example massive consequences because of the mycotoxins produced in infected grains that make them unsuitable for food or feed. This disease occurs in some of the major world granaries: North America, Western Europe, and the Northern Plains of China, with serious economic consequences spreading over all food security components. Rice false smut also leads to mycotoxin production. Once a minor disease of marginal concern in rice [Ou, 1985], false smut now affects several components of food security (Table 21.1) across Asia. Brown spot, a disease of rice that has been associated in the past with major famines in today's Bangladesh and East India [Padmanabhan, 1973], reduces both yield and grain quality, and thus affects all components of food security. Brown spot must now be considered as a chronic, yet poorly recognised, yield reducer in the regions of Asia which are the most vulnerable to food insecurity: the Indo-Gangetic Plain and large swaths of Indo-China, across Myanmar and Thailand.

Plant diseases have consequences on food security even when they do not concern food crops. A good example is that of coffee rust in

Central America [Avelino *et al.*, 2015], where serious economic downturn mostly affected the poor (small holders and farm workers), as a result of successive epidemics in the past decade, which led to the launching of food aid programmes even in countries with reputedly stable economies. A disease that affects a crop with export purpose or industrial use can gravely damage the livelihoods of both rural and urban communities.

21.3 Assessing the Impact of Plant Diseases on Plant Health

The impacts of plant diseases, expressed through crop losses — that is to say, losses in both crop yield and quality [FAO, 1981] — are hard to assess. Although this distinction is somewhat arbitrary (both may occur simultaneously), it is useful to distinguish quantity and quality crop losses.

21.3.1 *Loss in Quantity*

The reason for the difficulty in measuring quantity (yield) loss (i.e., losses in quantities harvested) is simple: it obviously is difficult to quantify the production that could have taken place, but did not materialise. Over the decades, a range of methodologies have been designed to produce reliable, verifiable, and falsifiable estimates of yield losses caused by diseases, as well as by animal pests (nematodes, arthropods, mammals, and birds) and weeds. Since the pioneering work of Chiarappa [1981], Zadoks [1967, 1985], and Teng [1983, 1987], these methods have been reviewed in several instances [Savary *et al.*, 2006; Esker *et al.*, 2013]. The available methods include combinations of field surveys, field experiments, statistical modelling, and process-based simulation modelling. These methodological advances make such assessments theoretically possible and reliable, but such assessments are extremely costly — their cost actually increases as trained field expertise becomes rare and more expensive. Yield loss assessment is very data hungry. Disease and crop data must be collected in large samples of fields by well-trained teams of experienced observers. Irrespective of the technology deployed, no reliable yield loss assessment is possible without accurate field observations using standardised, formal methods.

21.3.2 *Loss in Quality*

Measuring losses in quality caused by plant diseases is difficult too, but for entirely different reasons. There too, proper sampling is required, which may be challenging especially when agricultural systems have poor infrastructure. The main problem, however, is that the range of possible reductions in quality is bewildering. This includes reductions in nutrient contents (e.g., protein content in cereals), or the production of an array of mycotoxins with variable toxicity potentials and diverse molecular structures, or again the consequences of conventional plant protection methods: pesticide residues. A large number of countries in the world, especially in the Global South, do not have the infrastructure, the equipment, or the funding — and critically, do not have the qualified personnel to conduct proper and regular quality control on harvests and stocks. This has very grave consequences on local, often rural, populations, on the rural and urban poor, and also on economies; contamination by toxicants is a major cause for blockage of exports and trade.

As a result of these difficulties, the information which is available for the international scientific community is extraordinarily heterogeneous in format and detail, and it is patchy [Savary *et al.*, 2019]. Roughly, yield losses to diseases may be ascribed to a baseline of about 10% of the attainable yield (that is to say, 10% of the yield that would be achieved in absence of diseases). This round number, however, ignores tremendous geographical disparities, differences in technological and economic contexts, and the irregularity in occurrence of plant disease epidemics.

21.4 Types of Plant Disease Epidemics

Using a terminology derived from public (human) health, one may distinguish three epidemic patterns: chronic, acute, and emerging [Savary *et al.*, 2011]. These tree types affect major food crops of Asia. Table 21.2 displays a small set of examples in rice, wheat, and miscellaneous crops such as potatoes and vegetables.

21.4.1 *Chronic Epidemics*

Chronic epidemics occur regularly in a given agricultural landscape, causing persistent attrition in crop production, even though variation may occur, for instance, when caused by unusual climatic events. An example is the brown spot epidemic in rice which occurred at the end of the 1940s [Padmanabhan, 1974] as typhoons hit the Bay of Bengal. Weather, rice disease, and the socio-economic and political context interacted in causing a famine. Obviously, however, crop losses would not have taken place had it been for a plant pathogen, which had been carefully quantified [Padmanabhan, 1974].

Brown spot is still omnipresent today in South Asia and large swaths of rice-growing areas of Southeast Asia, where drought stresses are frequent and soils are poor with a potassium-nitrogen imbalance [Ou, 1986]. Sheath blight also occurs whenever crop canopies are dense, dark, and humid, often as a result of high seeding rates and/

Table 21.2 Types of plant disease epidemics in Asia.

	Type of epidemics			
Examples	**Chronic**	**Acute**	**Emerging**	**Remarks**
Epidemics on rice	Brown spot; Sheath blight	Leaf blast; Neck blast; Bacterial leaf blight; Rice tungro disease	False smut; Rice black-streaked dwarf (fijivirus); Ragged stunt virus disease	Brown spot is enhanced by climate change; False smut induces mycotoxin production
Epidemics on wheat	Spot blotch; Brown (leaf) rust	Yellow (stripe) rust; Fusarium head blight (scab)	Wheat blast	Spot blotch is enhanced by climate change; Wheat blast (Bangladesh) seems to taper off; Fusarium head blight induces mycotoxin production
Miscellaneous (food) crops	Potato late blight; Brown rot (bacterial wilt)		Potato cyst nematode	Potato late blight seems chronic in China and Northern India, but has an acute pattern in Europe; Brown rot affects a large number of horticultural crops and is expanding; Potato cyst nematode (*Globodera rostochiensis*) is emerging in India

or excessive (nitrogen) fertiliser inputs [Castilla *et al.*, 1996]. Spot blotch is the wheat equivalent of brown spot in rice; it especially is frequent where wheat crops suffer from poor nutrition and water stress [Sharma, 2004]. Late blight occurs wherever potato is cultivated in Asia, and on tomato under cool Asian environments. *Ralstonia solanacearum*, the soilborne bacterial pathogen, is also omnipresent in peri-urban horticultural crops, causing brown rot and massive losses on a host of different crop plants, especially *Solanaceae* species.

21.4.2 *Acute Epidemics*

Acute epidemics increase in intensity at the field scale and expand over a landscape. Over one or a few growing seasons, the epidemic reaches a maximal spatial extent and then recedes, and either disappears or becomes chronic. Acute epidemiological patterns may occur as a result of management mistakes such as the deployment of exceedingly susceptible crop varieties (e.g., the male cytoplasmic maize cultivars deployed in the U.S. mid-west in the 1970s [Zadoks and Schein, 1979]). Disruptions in crop establishment patterns (e.g., because of failing irrigation systems), inadequate access to proper seed, and shifts in the genetic make-up of plant pathogen populations are other causes for acute epidemics. The latter cause is especially important and frequent: many plant pathogens may rapidly adapt and overcome resistance genes that are deployed against them in crop cultivars.

Blast typifies acute epidemics on rice in Asia [Ou, 1986; Teng, 1998; Luo *et al.*, 1998; Zeigler *et al.*, 1994]. The leaf blast form of rice blast destroys young foliage, wiping out newly established crop stands, and jeopardising future harvests in susceptible varieties. The neck (and panicle) form of blast is cause for large losses on older stands after flowering. Bacterial (leaf) blight also leads to acute epidemics in rice. The seedling, 'kresek', form of bacterial leaf blight that affects recently transplanted seedlings is the worst, destroying entire stands within days. Bacterial blight used to be the main rice disease in much of Southeast Asia. Were it not for host plant resistance (HPR), no rice cultivation in large parts of the lowland 'rice bowls' of Asia would be possible today (T. W. Mew, personal communication). Stripe rust is the type for acute epidemics on wheat in China.

21.4.3 *Emerging Epidemics*

Emerging plant disease epidemics regularly appear on the headlines of scientific and wide-audience journals. Recent examples include the stem rust epidemics or the wheat blast epidemic in Bangladesh. These epidemics are commonly driven by factors of both chronic or acute epidemics: rapid pathogen evolution and adaptation, sudden climatic events, and abrupt technology shifts. Pathogen introductions fuelled by trade, global exchanges, and human movement can have disastrous consequences in agriculture [GPHA, 2022], and is a specific factor at play in emerging epidemics.

Emerging epidemics are currently occurring in Asia (e.g., rice false smut and several virus diseases on rice, several diseases on potato and vegetables; Table 21.2; [GPHA, 2022]). The wheat blast outbreak of recent years is another example of an emerging epidemic.

21.5 Plant Health and its Impacts

Plant disease epidemics depend on a number of elements: the nature of the causing pathogen and its life cycle (which may involve secondary hosts, propagules of different types, survival structures, the host range of the pathogen, the ability of the pathogen to genetically evolve, and the nature of plant tissues that the pathogen infects). These elements of the life cycle and their succession in turn depend on numerous factors, biological or physical. The latter are, to a large extent, influenced by humans in cultivated crop stands. The status of plant health thus depends on an array of biophysical and human-made factors, which are studied in plant disease epidemiology.

The impacts of poor plant health on crop performances, which may lead to impacts on food security, depend on a completely different set of elements, such as: the trophic behaviour of the pathogen on the host and the nature of the physiological injury caused, the nature of the plant organs affected (e.g., roots, vascular system, foliage, fruits or storage organs), the ability of a crop stand to compensate for pathogen injury, and the crop development stage when infection takes place. These elements of the host-pathogen interaction involved in disease impacts depend, in turn, on a range of factors: physiological and biological, as well as physical, the latter being influenced by the many diverse human management interventions to minimise disease impacts. Among these, pesticide applications are often singled out. There are many more possible actions, however. For instance, Egyptian wheat farmers counteract the yield-reducing effects of leaf rust by applying an additional round of (gravitational) irrigation water: this is an effective method, because it alleviates the exacerbated evapotranspiration in the wheat-infected plants.

The elements involved in, and the influencing factors of, plant disease epidemics and of plant disease impacts are therefore profoundly different. Some of the processes of epidemics and impacts take place at common scales: the plant and the crop stand; however, epidemiological processes also take place at the landscape and even at the regional scales. Some of the factors, such as weather, are common to the two types of processes, epidemiological or crop performance reduction. These common factors, however, absolutely do not act in the same ways, because they do not influence the same process elements. This is why it is critically important to distinguish two separate aspects through which plant diseases affect plant health: one aspect is epidemiological; the other aspect, which depends on the former, is plant- and crop-physiological.

In what follows, plant health and impacts are therefore treated separately. To achieve this, following the approach of the Global Plant Health Assessment [GPHA, 2022], symbols are used, with different colours for status over the past 30 years (red: 'bad'; orange: 'poor'; yellow: 'fair'; light green: 'good'; dark green: 'excellent') and different arrow directions for trends in the past 10 years (down: 'declining'; level: 'stable'; up: 'improving').

21.6 State and Evolution of Plant Health in Asia

The state of plant health on four major sources of food crops (rice, wheat, potato, and vegetables) is summarised in Table 21.3, which is extracted from the Global Plant Health Assessment [GPHA, 2022].

21.6.1 *Rice Plant Health*

In Southeast Asia, the many diseases of rice may be considered under reasonable control. HPR has been, and still is, the key instrument for this, especially for the two lead diseases, bacterial leaf blight and blast. Sheath blight, a third key disease, is indirectly and progressively controlled by direct seeding [Willocquet *et al.*, 1997], which becomes dominant in many rice landscapes due to lack of manpower [Savary *et al.*, 2005]. Direct seeding reduces the aerial spread of the

Table 21.3 State and evolution of plant health, and its impact on food provisioning in Asia (Global Plant Health Assessment, simplified excerpt).

Rice					
Plant Health					
Eco-region	**State of plant health**	**Evolution of plant health**	**Assessment: state and evolution**	**Level of assessment confidence**	**References**
Southeast Asia	Many diseases — viral, bacterial and fungal. These have been brought under acceptable control mainly through HPR.	Strong dynamics between production contexts and disease patterns have taken place. Overall, rice health has been sustained.	→	reasonably confident	Savary *et al.*, 2000; Savary *et al.*, 2014; Cabauatan *et al.*, 2009; Cuong *et al.*, 1997.
East Asia	Two dominant diseases, blast and bacterial blight, have long dominated rice health, and been controlled through HPR. Rice sheath blight has become more serious.	Major new issues have emerged. A monsoon-driven regional epidemic system has been established, enabling long-distance spread of grave viral diseases.	↘	reasonably confident	Savary and Mew, 1996; Willocquet *et al.*, 2000; Zhou *et al.*, 2013; Fang *et al.*, 2001; Okuta, 2013; Cho *et al.*, 2015; Wang *et al.*, 2008; Matsumura and Sanada-Morimura, 2010; Li *et al.*, 2015; Huang *et al.*, 2011.

South Asia (Indo-Gangetic Plains)	As in East Asia, two dominant diseases, blast and bacterial blight, have been controlled through HPR. Brown spot remains a major unresolved challenge.	False smut has become a serious concern, both in terms of yield quantity and quality (mycotoxins). Climate change enhances brown spot epidemics.	↘	reasonably confident	Nagarajan, 1994; Gnanamanickam *et al.*, 1999; Nagarajan, 1989; Barnwal *et al.*, 2013; Reddy *et al.*, 2011; Fan *et al.*, 2016; Han *et al.*, 2020.
		Impact on the Provisioning of Food			
Southeast Asia	Excellent progress of rice production across the region despite disease losses.	Stabilisation of food production at the cost of a drop in total factor productivity, and serious environmental costs.	→	reasonably confident	Savary *et al.*, 2014.
East Asia	Major productivity achievements have been performed through science. This has ensured the nutrition of one of the most populated eco-regions of the world.	Crop performances are maintained and food production, as a service, remains stable. Major challenges will have to be addressed in the future, which will involve plant diseases.	→	reasonably confident	Peng *et al.*, 2009; 2010; Hu *et al*, 2016;

(Continued)

Table 21.3 (*Continued*)

Rice					
Plant Health					
Eco-region	**State of plant health**	**Evolution of plant health**	**Assessment: state and evolution**	**Level of assessment confidence**	**References**
South Asia (Indo-Gangetic Plains)	Rice production has progressively increased, averting a major food crisis. Rice diseases are a clear reducer of system performances, but not a cause for system disruption.	Climate change, insufficient use of integrated pest management, and challenges in training and education bring about an actual impact on plant diseases. Sustaining the performance of the rice wheat system will become even more challenging.	↘	reasonably confident	Chauhan *et al.*, 2012; Barnwal *et al.*, 2013; Sharma *et al.*, 2007; Timsina and Connor, 2001; Erenstein and Thorpe, 2011.

Wheat					
Plant Health					
Eco-region	**State of impacts of diseases on food provisioning**	**Evolution impacts of diseases on food provisioning**	**Assessment: state and evolution**	**Level of assessment confidence**	**References**
East Asia (China)	Numerous and very diverse, serious plant pathogens.	Many different diseases; massive, networked efforts; breeding, monitoring, forecasting	↗	reasonably confident	Cock *et al.*, 2016; Guo *et al.*, 2019

		systems. Considerable improvement through modern technology. Strong reliance on pesticides.			
South Asia (Indo-Gangetic Plains)	Several chronic diseases (leaf blight) over very large acreages; frequent epidemics (rusts).	Climate change (heat waves) documented to increase disease (leaf blight). Persistent epidemic threats (rusts).	↘	reasonably confident	Duveiller *et al.*, 1997; Duveiller *et al.*, 2007; Sharma *et al.*, 2007
		Impact on the Provisioning of Food			
East Asia (China)	Major wheat production centre for regional food security. Massive progress over 30 years.	Many different diseases; increasing concerns over quality (Fusarium head blight). Production is not directly threatened *per se*, but its environmental cost is a concern.	→	reasonably confident	FAOSTAT, 2020
South Asia (Indo-Gangetic Plains)	Major wheat production centre for regional food security. Steady progress over 30 years.	Emerging concerns on climate change-driven diseases (wheat blight), and sustainability of the system with a clear role of diseases.	→	reasonably confident	Chauhan *et al.*, 2012

(Continued)

Table 21.3 *(Continued)*

Potato					
Plant Health					
Eco-region	**State of plant health**	**Evolution of plant health**	**Assessment: state and evolution**	**Level of assessment confidence**	**References**
East Asia	Main yield reducers are potato early blight, late blight, rhizoctonia, as well as bacterial and fungal wilts. Control is difficult under shortage of healthy seed, fragmented and poor farms, and absence of rotations.	Demand drives susceptible varieties. Access to resource (seed) and knowledge to manage disease are difficult. Pesticides are a main recourse. Plans to strengthen research and development are underway.	↘	reasonably confident	Huang and Liu, 2016a; 2016b; Jing *et al.*, 2018
Impact on the Provisioning of Food					
East Asia	China is the largest potato producer in the world despite insufficient research and development investment in potato health for poor, fragmented farming systems.	Steps are being taken to improve plant health: improved seed health, healthy seed multiplication, consideration of soil-borne pathogens and rotations.	→	reasonably confident	FAO, 2022

Peri-Urban Horticultural Systems and Household Gardens					
Plant Health					
Eco-region	**State of plant health**	**Evolution of plant health**	**Summary**	**Level of assessment confidence**	**References**
South Asia	Many diseases in very diverse systems. Introduced plants (tomato) severely diseased. Large differences in vulnerability among crops.	Climate change-induced temperatures enhancing virus transmissions. Effective breeding programs (HPR), microbial biological control, grafting, and chemical pesticides.	↗	reasonably confident	Nagendran *et al.*, 2019; Gautam *et al.*, 2013; Ali *et al.*, 2010; Bhattacharya *et al.*, 2014; Chowdappa, 2013; Raj *et al.*, 2010;
Southeast Asia	Many diseases in extremely diverse systems. Many different production systems involving a range of technologies. Large differences in vulnerability among crops.	Major (soil-borne) diseases still prevail. New races existing pathogens, better adapted, more aggressive, or with expanding ranges. Inoculum build-up (soil), and poor seed health.	↘	reasonably confident	Jansen *et al.*, 1995; Kenyon *et al.*, 2014; Mishra *et al.*, 2019; Schreinemachers *et al.*, 2012;

(Continued)

Table 21.3 (*Continued*)

Impact on the Provisioning of Food					
Plant Health					
Eco-region	**State of plant health**	**Evolution of plant health**	**Summary**	**Level of assessment confidence**	**References**
South Asia	Despite the exploding urban population, sustained food provisioning. This is attributable at least in part to dynamic plant breeding progress against diseases.	Innovative breeding biotechnology leading to disease-resistant plant material; bio-pesticides deployment.	↗	reasonably confident	Uppala *et al.*, 2010; Chowdappa, 2013; Mishra *et al.*, 2019
Southeast Asia	Despite pressure, food provisioning has grown apace with that of Southeast Asia's cities.	Evolution similar to that of South Asia: innovative breeding biotechnology leading to disease-resistant plant material; bio-pesticides deployment.	→	reasonably confident	Schreinemachers *et al.*, 2012

sheath blight pathogen from infected rice plant to healthy rice plant [Willocquet *et al.*, 2000]. Over successive growing seasons this leads to a polyetic [Zadoks and Schein, 1979] reduction of (soil-borne) primary inoculum, and to an overall disease reduction. East Asia, however, shows a different path in rice plant health status and evolution. There, too, major diseases have been brought under control through, mostly, HPR. However, major issues have emerged, especially in the form of viral arthropod-vectored disease epidemics, which are involved in a regional system. Monsoon rains and typhoon of the rainy season enable crop establishment from the Philippines to Vietnam, Southern, Central and North China, Korea and Japan. This happens as viruliferous vectors are transported by wind currents in their Northwest-ward progress.

As crops are being established, they rapidly are infected by inbound viruliferous vectors, serving as stepping stones for further vector transport and new infections. This system seems fairly new and now constitutes an immediate threat for rice production in East Asia. A critical challenge in rice production in China is its over-reliance on pesticides in a country where plant disease is now recognised as the main factor to address unsatisfactory yield levels [GPHA, 2022]. East Asia is also confronted with flower diseases in small cereals. Such flower diseases are Fusarium head blight in wheat and, in rice, false smut and multiple Fusarium flower infections [Huang *et al.*, 2011]. A key feature of these flower diseases is their consequences on yield quality; the infected grain is contaminated with mycotoxins, some of which are dangerous to humans and animals. Why this surge in flower diseases occurs is hard to explain. A common element is that breeding processes (towards hybrids in particular) have led to plant material in which the flowering stage has been artificially expanded, leaving flowers exposed for a longer time to contamination by pathogen propagules. In South Asia, blast and bacterial leaf blight have also been brought under overall control through HPR. Brown spot of rice, on the other hand, has been ignored by genetic improvement. HPR in brown spot is a very challenging goal [Barnwal *et al.*, 2013]. Thus, rice brown spot remains a chronic, persistent, and potentially growing cause for yield attrition, especially under less favourable growing environment under climate change: poor rice farmers therefore bear the brunt of this burden. All over Asia, furthermore, the threat of false smut has emerged in the past decades. It does seem that the emergence of the disease has been associated with the deployment of new germplasm, especially hybrids, at least in India [Reddy, 2011]. New rice germplasm, especially germplasm used for hybrid production, is necessarily associated with a longer duration of flower opening, paving the way towards flower infections (T. W. Mew, personal communication).

21.6.2 *Wheat Plant Health*

Wheat health in East Asia involves a large number of different diseases [GPHA, 2022], where rusts (yellow and brown) dominate. Over the years, however, a very strong network of universities and institutes, involving pathologists and breeders, has developed effective forecasting systems. These provide support to variety deployment (as in yellow rust), although disease management remains highly reliant on pesticides. Wheat health in South Asia is dominated by a chronic disease (spot blotch) and an acute one (yellow rust), the latter causing serious but irregular epidemics whenever host-pathogen compatibility and disease-conducive weather jointly occur. Plant breeding for resistance in spot blotch (as in rice brown spot) is very difficult [Neupane *et al.*, 2007]: as in brown spot of rice, the wheat spot blotch pathosystem involves (1) polygenic, partial-effect HPR with many quantitative trait loci; (2) a genetically flexible pathogen; and (3) very strong genotype-environment interactions (the disease is enhanced by abiotic stress generated by water shortage and imbalanced mineral nutrition). This is why spot blotch in wheat, as in brown spot in rice, should be expected to become a dominant wheat disease as climate change unfolds over the region [Sharma *et al.*, 2007; Barnwal *et al.*, 2013].

21.6.3 *Potato Plant Health*

Potato health in East Asia is unsatisfactory in several respects. Late blight and early blight cause chronic epidemics, as does black shank, given the survival capability of its causal bacterial pathogen(s) in soils. Another grave problem is potato seed health and the carry-over and spread of multiple viruses [GPHA, 2022]. Informal and uncontrolled (health-wise) seed carry-over (within farms) and exchanges (between farms) seem to take place, which maintain, amplify, and spread multiple viral seed infections. The current state of potato health is necessarily connected with a most common production situation in China: small farms where crop rotation is difficult and crop investments (healthy seed) are beyond farmers' reach; hilly or mountain areas with poor roads, making access to field scouts and information exchange harder; poor soils and cold, rainy conditions; difficult access to information, advice from extension services, agricultural inputs, and markets — making farmers poorer. Strangely, while China is the largest potato producer worldwide, potato research has long been considered secondary to research on small grains [GPHA, 2022] in the national policy. This seems to be changing.

21.6.4 *Plant Health in Urban Horticultural Systems*

Vegetable production in peri-urban agricultural systems has accomplished the feat to keep up with the urban explosion of Asia's population. This is despite major plant health challenges which are described in the Global Plant Health Assessment [GPHA, 2022] for South and Southeast Asia. The lead common vegetable of South Asia, tomato, is grown in a wide range of contexts, where a number of oomycete, fungal and viral diseases occur. Exotic introduced varieties are especially vulnerable. However, a range of management tools, including improved cultivars (HPR), microbial biological control, grafting, and chemical pesticides have been deployed to achieve acceptable control; compared to field agricultural systems, peri-urban agriculture can be highly technological. Peri-urban agricultural systems are even more diverse in Southeast Asia, with a considerable diversity of local vegetable species. This diversity, along with their local co-evolution with pathogens, may explain in part the good performance of these systems, health-wise. All peri-urban agricultural systems nevertheless are vulnerable to many soil-borne pathogens (including nematodes), among which brown rot (*Ralstonia* spp.) is a keystone species. Agricultural intensification, exceedingly fast turnover of crops (on very expensive land), fallow periods measured not in weeks but days or even hours, and increasing genetic similarity of plants (e.g., *Solanaceæ*) cultivated on the same plot are permanent and increasing structural weaknesses, health-wise, of these systems.

21.7 Impacts of Plant Health on Asia's Food Security: Yield (quantity) Losses

Rice is the icon for a global food crop. 90% of the world's rice production takes place in Asia, where it also is consumed by, roughly, three-fifths of the current world population [Zeigler and Savary, 2009]. Contrary to wheat, maize, or potato, no rice is ever grown for animal feed, biofuel, or industrial purpose: rice is grown for human consumption, and this has been so for millennia. The history of rice coincides with that of the many and diverse societies that Asia has known, and still knows today. In short, rice is more strongly linked with national food security and food sovereignty than any other food crop grown in Asia. Yield losses caused by rice diseases therefore have special meaning for Asian culture, daily life, markets, and policies.

21.7.1 *East and Southeast Asia*

In East and Southeast Asia, a new step following the progress achieved by the Green Revolution needs to be accomplished. This is because the stabilisation, or the marginal progress, in limiting yield losses to diseases (and other yield reducers including animal pests and weeds), is coming at massive costs in chemical inputs — fertilisers and pesticides. While irrigation in rice and methane production is pointed at in rice production, seldom is the large energy (and CO_2 emission) cost of fertiliser production [Smil, 2000] considered. In Southeast Asia [Savary *et al.*, 2022], yield losses have been maintained in the range of 20–30% (overall, all yield reducers included; 5–20% for plant diseases) under production situations where fertiliser inputs have increased, as well as pesticide use. In 1980 the median for fungicide usage per rice field per season was zero: the norm was no fungicide use. In the decade 2000–2010, this median became 1.0: for the first time ever, at least one application of a fungicide had become the norm. This is a major departure from the management strategy where HPR is dominant, and pesticide is secondary. In East Asia (China in particular), rice disease control has been declared a government priority to achieve yield increases. Rice yields have reached a ceiling since at least ten years ago, despite a very large increase in (energy costly, environmentally harmful, and soil impoverishing) mineral fertiliser inputs, and a near-continuous pesticide blanket. Major progress in HPR is required in breeding programmes. These programmes now must also address the adaptation of rice to climate change (including the highly vulnerable rice anthesis stage to excessive temperature), water scarcity, and possibly growing industrial and urban air pollution too. Strongly organised and well-trained public extension systems also constitute a prerequisite.

21.7.2 *South Asia*

In South Asia, the gains from the Green Revolution have stabilised. Unlike in East Asia, rice diseases are not to be considered as cause for potential system disruption *per se*; they nevertheless constitute a very strong challenge, because they are cause for chronic performance attrition, and therefore systems unsustainability. This happens in the context of unfavourable environmental conditions and infrastructural decline. Climate change will bring about more frequent and more severe heat waves, and it is causing increasing disruptions in the vital monsoon onset, intensity, regularity, and duration. In a region where agriculture is to a very large extent rainfed, climate change also brings about a shortage of freshwater, which is amplified by ever-intensifying irrigation and often by poorly maintained irrigation systems; this in turn brings about soil salinisation risks and a competition between urban and rural communities towards water. The once very effective and well-trained and -manned public extension system is under pressure, as a result of competition with the private sector (the fertiliser, seed, and pesticide industry); and even the mid- and high-level system of public education in agriculture is facing competition with private institutions with short-term, benefit-oriented objectives. Most of the children of Indian farmers do not want to be farmers themselves. Costs of transportation and the often inadequate road system hamper direct contacts between farmers and advisors — information technology does help, but nothing replaces a discussion in the field. All this has direct consequences on crop performances, and indirect but important consequences on epidemics and their impacts: extension officers, too, have to learn from farmers. Brown spot, once dubbed 'the poor rice farmer's disease', is on the rise, with little or no ways to suppress its yield-reducing effects. So is wheat spot blotch. Potato crops in the Indo-Gangetic Plains suffer heavily from late blight with losses in excess of 40%, and much more is lost during storage to multiple bacterial infections. Storage systems are notoriously ineffective in South Asia. Massive efforts to design farmer-acceptable, effective, and environmentally sustainable disease management are required. This will unfortunately be confronted with previously unsuccessful attempts — and farmers have long memories, especially of setbacks. New, innovative approaches for technology development and transfer are needed; these require direct farmers' involvement, and close links with effective educational systems; and human relations, not information technology alone, will need to be brought to the front. Human relations imply employment of well-trained, strongly motivated field personnel.

21.8 Impacts of Plant Health on Asia's Food Security: Quality Losses

The increasing importance of quality losses in food crop production deserves specific mention. Quality losses include loss of nutritional value, presence of pesticide residues, and presence of pathogen-associated toxins, in particular the latter. In rice, false smut is a key quality issue [Koiso *et al.*, 1998]. Research that addresses the extremely complex life cycle of the pathogen (with several forms of propagules, some being sclerotia able to survive in soil for a decade [Fan *et al.*, 2016]), the entry point in this cycle where HPR might act, the quantitative trait loci or genes that could be employed, the cycle stages where non-chemical control could be implemented, is necessary. The multiple *Fusarium* spp. infections observed in rice in East Asia [Huang *et al.*, 2011], leading to mycotoxin accumulation in grain, requires close scrutiny. Fusarium head blight of wheat is the other major mycotoxin concern. Here, progress that has been made elsewhere, especially in plant breeding, should be deployed in breeding programmes.

21.9 Impacts of Plant Heath on Asia's Food Security: Food Scares

Food scares must be avoided at all costs. I believe that this cannot come from the suppression of news regarding possible risks, but that it instead depends on accurate, transparent, and verifiable public information. The latter, however, must be based on the best possible science. Examples of epidemics that did not occur on a large scale in Asia include the rice tungro disease in the Indo-Gangetic plains [Nagarajan, 1989], or stem rust (Ug99) in South Asia in the 2000s [Nagarajan, 2014]. The recent wheat blast epidemic may be another example.

21.10 Conclusion: Issues that Threaten Plant Health

21.10.1 *Emerging and Re-emerging Diseases*

Emergences and re-emergences of plant diseases are bound to increase as long as international trade (imports) increases. Customs and quarantines can play a very effective role in controlling introductions. Research on potential invasions can be very useful, as long as the 'ecological niches' considered are not simplistically climatical only, and the impacts — potential crop losses — properly modelled. Modelling potential management intervention post-invasion are also most desirable.

21.10.2 *Climate Change*

Climate change affects all agrosystems of Asia, which evolve under its influence. This evolution will accelerate. In the dryer agrosystems, wheat is likely to be replaced by nutritious, heat- and drought-resistant, but low-yielding millets, and rice will disappear, replaced by other crops. This will entirely change the state of health of agrosystems. New agrosystems will emerge, which will need to be made climate and disease resilient in order to be sustainable. These systems will also have to ensure food security in Asia. This is a major undertaking at the Asian scale, which would require very strong national and international research.

21.10.3 *Mycotoxins*

Mycotoxin issues are increasing in Asia. The warning of the danger of the wheat-maize association [Zadoks and Schein, 1979] regarding fusarium polyetic epidemic build-up was not heard; short-term benefits at the farm scale, and the need of maize grain for the meat industry, prevailed. Breeding against mycotoxin production, a very complex trait in the pathogen under control of multiple — many unknown yet — host plant effectors, and other — mainly misunderstood — environmental factors, is very hard. Changes in crop types, and even in cropping systems, might be a better option than plant breeding. To the best available knowledge, chemical control and detoxification are not current or likely options.

21.10.4 *Pesticide Residues*

Very little data exist on pesticide residues. These should be collected systematically, and be made available to scientists and the public. This mainly concerns vegetables that are produced in peri-urban agricultural systems, where far too much pesticide is used [Schreinemachers *et al.*, 2020]. Urban agricultural systems deserve very strong policy and research support, being a prime source of nutrients for the urban poor, and of income for small farmers. Integrated pest management in these systems is challenging, but possible. An array of technology exists. Integrated pest management will make these systems more resilient; and a by-product of integrated pest management is pesticide use reduction.

21.10.5 *Education in Agriculture*

Young professionals — farmers, advisors, technicians, scientists — must be trained. A new generation of such professionals is long awaited, and a generation gap is building up, especially in South Asia. Education by and for agriculture has been downplayed for too long, too often; it needs revival so that a new generation of professionals can address the upcoming challenges of agriculture and of plant health in agricultural systems.

21.10.6 *Public Extension Systems and Training of Field Extensionists*

A key issue in implementing policies at the landscape scale, and of strategies at the farm and field scales within landscape, is a strong, well-trained, sufficiently manned, and well-respected public extension system. In many Asian countries, these systems have been in regular decay for decades. In medicine, the physician who makes a diagnostic does not also sell the medicines: this would obviously be a conflict of interest. Similarly, in plant health, diagnostic and disease management instruments must be in different hands. The privatisation of extension and technical support to farmers is a present and grave danger, as evidenced by the false smut crisis in India. This calls for urgent policy decisions to be made across Asia.

21.10.7 *"Eyes in the Fields"*

Multiple infections by different pathogens are commonplace in farmers' fields. A tomato plant in the suburbs of Bangkok may for instance be infected by three or more viruses, two or three fungi, one oomycete, and one or several nematodes at the same time. Multiple infections are frequently combined with signs of abiotic stresses (drought, salinity, nutrition deficiencies, or water excess), which are bound to occur more often as climate change progresses. Surprises will become the rule rather than the exception. Artificial intelligence is not prepared for surprises, or the unusual — by design, it simply cannot be. Artificial intelligence will only repeat with what it already "knows", without understanding it, and be lost. It takes instead trained, experienced, and professional human eyes to take accurate observations in the field. The decades to come will see an increased need for experienced field scouts to generate the data required for proper diagnostics, assessments, and predictions so that effective and timely disease management [McRoberts *et al.*, 2003] is implemented.

References

Ali, I., Malik, A. H. and Mansoor, S. (2010). First report of Tomato leaf curl Palampur virus on bitter gourd in Pakistan. *Plant Disease,* 94, p. 276.

Avelino, J., Cristancho, M., Georgiou, S., Imbach, P., Aguilar, L., Bornemann, G., Läderach, P., Anzueto, F., Hruska, A. J. and

Morales, C. (2015). The coffee rust crises in Colombia and Central America (2008–2013): impacts, plausible causes and proposed solutions. *Food Security*, 7(2), pp. 303–321.

Barnwal, M. K., Kotasthane, A., Magculia, N., Mukherjee, P. K., Savary, S., Sharma, A. K., Singh, H. B., Singh, U. S., Sparks, A. H., Variar, M. and Zaidi, N. (2013). A review on crop losses, epidemiology and disease management of rice brown spot to identify research priorities and knowledge gaps. *European Journal of Plant Pathology*, 136(3), pp. 443–457.

Bhattacharya, I., Dutta, S., Mondal, S., *et al.* (2014). Clubroot disease on Brassica crops in India. *Canadian Journal of Plant Pathology*, 36, pp. 154–160.

Cabauatan, P. Q., Cabunagan, R. C. and Choi, I. R. (2009). Rice Viruses Transmitted by the Brown Planthopper Nilaparvata lugens Stål. In K. L. Heong and B. Hardy (Eds.), *Planthoppers: New Threats to the Sustainability of Intensive Rice Production Systems in Asia*, pp. 357–368. International Rice Research Institute.

CABI. (2020). Crop protection compendium. https://www.cabi.org/cpc

Castilla, N. P., Leano, R. M., Elazhour, F. A., Teng, P. S. and Savary, S. (1996). Effects of plant contact, inoculation pattern, leaf wetness regime, and nitrogen supply on inoculum efficiency in rice sheath blight. *Journal of Phytopathology*, 144(4), pp. 187–192.

Ceresini, P. C., Castroagudín, V. L., Rodrigues, F. Á., Rios, J. A., Eduardo Aucique-Pérez, C., Moreira, S.I., Alves, E., Croll, D. and Maciel, J. L. N. (2018). Wheat blast: past, present, and future. *Annual Review of Phytopathology*, 56, pp. 427–456.

Chauhan, B. S., Mahajan, G., Sardana, V., Timsina, J. and Jat, M. L. (2012). Productivity and sustainability of the rice–wheat cropping system in the Indo-Gangetic Plains of the Indian subcontinent: problems, opportunities, and strategies. *Advances in Agronomy*, 11, pp. 315–369.

Cho, S. Y., Jeong, R. D., Yoon, Y. N. Shin, D, Kang, H. W. and Lee, B. (2015). A nationwide survey and genetic analysis of rice stripe virus in South Korea during 2012–2013. *Journal of General Plant Pathology,* 81, pp. 390–398.

Chowdappa, P. (2013). Disease Management in Urban and Peri-Urban Horticulture. In H. P. Sumangala, S. K. Malhotra and P. Chowdappa (Eds.), *Urban and Peri-urban Horticulture: A Perspective,* pp. 35–42. Confederation of Horticulture Associations of India.

Cock, M. J. W., Tang, R., Liu, Z. and Wang, H. (2016). The main agricultural insect and disease pests of China and implications for the use of remote sensing for their management. *CAB Reviews*, 11, p. 014.

Cruppe, G., Cruz, C. D., Peterson, G., Pedley, K., Asif, M., Fritz, A., Calderon, L., Lemes da Silva, C., Todd, T., Kuhnem, P. and Singh, P. K. (2020). Novel sources of wheat head blast resistance in modern breeding lines and wheat wild relatives. *Plant Disease,* 104(1), pp. 35 – 43.

Cuong, N. L., Ben, P. T., Phuong L. T., Chau, L. M. and Cohen, M. B. (1997). Effect of host plant resistance and insecticide on brown planthopper *Nilaparvata lugens* (Stål.) and predator population development in the Mekong Delta, Vietnam. *Crop Protection*, 16(8), pp. 707–715.

Desker, B., Caballero-Anthony, M. and Teng, P. (2013). Thought/issues paper on ASEAN food security: towards a more comprehensive framework. ERIA Discussion Paper Series [ERIA-DP-2013- 20].

Devaux, A., Goffart, J., Petsakos, A., Kromann, P., Gatto, M., Okello, J., Suarez, V. and Hareau, G. (2020). Global Food Security, Contributions from Sustainable Potato Agri-Food Systems. In H. Campos and O. Ortiz (Eds.), *The Potato Crop: Its Agricultural Nutritional and Social Contribution to Humankind*, pp. 3–36. Springer.

Duveiller, A., Dubin, E., Reeves, H. J. and McNab, A. (Eds.) (1997). Helminthosporium blights of wheat: spot blotch and tan spot. Proceedings of an International Workshop; El Batan, Texcoco (Mexico); 9-14 Feb 1997, CIMMYT, Mexico.

Duveiller, E., Singh, R. P. and Nicol, J. M. (2007). The challenges of maintaining wheat productivity: pests, diseases, and potential epidemics. *Euphytica,* 157(3), pp. 417–430.

Erenstein, O. and Thorpe, W. (2011). Livelihoods and agro-ecological gradients: A meso-level analysis in the Indo-Gangetic Plains, India. *Agricultural Systems*, 104(1), pp. 42–53.

Esker, P. D., Savary, S. and McRoberts, N. (2013). Crop loss analysis and global food supply: focusing now on required harvests. *CAB Reviews*, 7, pp. 1–14.

Fan, J., Yang, J., Wang, Y. Q., Li, G.B., Li, Y., Huang, F. and Wang, W. M. (2016). Current understanding on *Villosiclava virens*, a unique flower-infecting fungus causing rice false smut disease. *Molecular Plant Pathology*, 17(9), pp. 1321–1330.

Fang, S., Yu, J., Feng, J., Han, C., Li, D. and Liu, Y. (2001). Identification of rice black-streaked dwarf fijivirus in maize with rough dwarf disease in China. *Archives of Virology,* 146, pp. 167–170.

FAO. (1981). Crop Loss Assessment Methods. Supplement N°3.

Food and Agricultural Organisation (FAO), Agriculture and Development Economics Division (ESA). (2006). *Food Security.* http://www.fao.org/forestry/13128-0e6f36f27e0091055bec28ebe830f46b3.pdf

Food and Agricultural Organisation (FAO), International Fund for Agricultural Development (IFAD) and World Food Programme (WFP) (2013). *The State of Food Insecurity in the World 2013.* http://www.fao.org/docrep/018/i3434e/i3434e.pdf

FAO. (2022). FAOSTAT. http://www.fao.org/faostat

Gautam, H. R., Bhardwaj, M. L. and Kumar, R. (2013). Climate change and its impact on plant diseases. *Current Science,* 105, pp. 1685–1691.

Gnanamanickam, S. S., Priyadarisini, V. B., Narayanan, N. N., Vasudevan, P. and Kavitha, S. (1999). An overview of bacterial blight disease of rice and strategies for its management. *Current Science,* 77(11), pp. 1435–1444.

Guo, L.-M., He, J., Li. J., Chen, J.-P. and Zhang, H.-M. (2019). Chinese wheat mosaic virus: A long-term threat to wheat in China. *Journal of Integrative Agriculture,* 18, pp. 821–829.

GPHA. (2022). Global Plant Health Assessment. https://www.isppweb.org/about_gpha.asp

Han, Y., Li, D., Yang, J., Huang, F., Sheng, H. and Sun, W. (2020). Mapping quantitative trait loci for disease resistance to false smut of rice. *Phytopathology Research,* 2(1), pp. 1–11.

Huang, C. and Liu, W. (2016a). Occurrence characteristics and monitoring advice of potato late blight in China in recent years (in Chinese). *China Plant Protection,* 42(5), pp. 142–147.

Huang, C. and Liu, W. (2016b). Occurrence characteristics and monitoring strategies of potato diseases and pests (in Chinese). *China Plant Protection,* 36(6), pp. 48–52.

Huang, S. W., Wang, L., Liu, L. M., Tang, S. Q., Zhu, D. F. and Savary, S. (2011). Rice spikelet rot disease in China–1. Characterization of fungi associated with the disease. *Crop Protection*, 30(1), pp. 1–9.

Hu, X. F., Cheng, C., Luo, F., Chang, Y. Y., Teng, Q., Men, D. Y., Liu, L. and Yang, M. Y. (2016). Effects of different fertilization practices on the incidence of rice; pests and diseases: A three-year case study in Shanghai, in subtropical, southeastern China. *Field Crops Research,* 196, pp. 33–50.

Jansen, H. G. P., Midmore, D. J., Binh, P. T., Valasayya, S. and Tru, L. C. (1995). Peri-urban vegetable production in Ho Chi Minh city, Vietnam (Shanhua, Tainan: AVRDC), p. 65. http://worldveg.tind.io/record/23547/files/eb0171.pdf

Jing, R., Li, H., Hu, X., Shang, W., Shen, R., Guo, C., Guo, Q. and Subbarao K. V. (2018). Verticillium wilt caused by *Verticillium dahliae* and *V. nonalfalfae* in potato in Northern China. *Plant Disease,* 102(10), pp. 1958–1964.

Kenyon, L., Tsai, W.-S., Shih, S.-L. and Lee, L.-M. (2014). Emergence and diversity of begomoviruses infecting solanaceous crops in East and Southeast Asia. *Virus Research*, 186, pp. 104–113.

Koiso, Y., Morisaki, N., Yamashita, Y., Mitsui, Y., Shirai, R., Hashimoto, Y. and Iwasaki, S. (1998). Isolation and structure of an antimitotic cyclic peptide, ustiloxin F: chemical interrelation with a homologous peptide, ustiloxin B. *The Journal of Antibiotics,* 51(4), pp. 418–422.

Li, S., Hao, W. J., Lu, G. H., Huang, J. L., Liu, C. H. and Zhou, G. H. (2015). Occurrence and identification of a new vector of rice orange leaf phytoplasma in South China. *Plant Disease,* 99, pp. 1483–1487.

Luo, Y., Teng, P. S., Fabellar, N. G. and TeBeest, D. O. (1998). The effects of global temperature change on rice leaf blast epidemics: a simulation study in three agroecological zones. *Agriculture, Ecosystems and Environment*, 68(3), pp. 187–196.

Matsumura, M. and Sanada-Morimura, S. (2010). Recent status of insecticide resistance in Asian rice planthoppers. *JARQ-Japan Agricultural Research Quarterly*, 44, pp. 225–230.

McRobert, N., Hughes, G. and Savary, S. (2003). Integrated approaches to understanding and control of diseases and pests in field crops. *Australasian Plant Pathology*, 32(2), pp. 167–180.

Mishra, R. K., Parihar, A. K., Basvaraj, T., *et al*. (2019). Identification of new sources of resistance in Rajmash (*Phaseolus vulgaris* L.) against powdery mildew (*Erysiphe polygoni*) and stem rot (*Sclerotinia sclerotiorum*) diseases. *Legume Research,* 42(3), pp. 430–433.

Nagarajan, S. (1989). Plant protection problems in rice-wheat rotation system-a perspective. *Oryza*, 26(4), pp. 329–333.

Nagarajan, S. (1994). Rice Pest Management in India. In P. Teng, K. L. Heong and K. Moody (Eds.), *Rice Pest Science and Management: Selected Papers from the International Rice Research Conference*, pp. 43–52. International Rice Research Institute.

Nagarajan, S., Kogel, K. H. and Zadoks, J. C. (2014). Epidemiological analysis of the damage potential of Pgt-Ug99 in Central East, North East Africa, Iran and Punjab (India). *Indian Phytopathology*, 67, pp. 26–32.

Nagendran, K., Venkataravanappa, V., Chauhan, N. S., *et al.* (2019). Viral diseases: a threat for tomato cultivation in Indo-Gangetic eastern plains of India. *Journal of Plant Pathology*, 101, pp. 15–22.

Neupane, R. B., Sharma, R. C., Duveiller, E., Ortiz-Ferrara, G., Ojha, B. R., Rosyara, U. R., Bhandari, D. and Bhatta, M. R. (2007). Major gene controls of field resistance to spot blotch in wheat genotypes 'Milan/Shanghai# 7'and 'Chirya 3'. *Plant Disease*, 91(6), pp. 692–697.

Okuta, A. (2013). Migration of rice planthoppers and their vectored re-emerging and novel rice viruses in East Asia. *Frontiers in Microbiology,* 4, p. 309.

Ou, S. H. (1985). *Rice Diseases*, 2nd Edition. Commonwealth Mycological Institute.

Padmanabhan, S. Y. (1973). The great Bengal famine. *Annual Review of Phytopathology,* 11, pp. 11–26.

Peng, S. B., Tang, Q. Y. and Zou, Y. B. (2009). Current status and challenges of rice production in China. *Plant Production Science,* 12, pp. 3–8.

Peng, S. B., Buresh, R. J., Huang, J. L., Zhong, X. H., Zou, Y. B., Yang, J. C., Wang, G. H., Liu, Y. Y., Hu, R. F., Tang, Q. Y., Cui, K. H., Zhang, F. S. and Dobermann, A. (2010). Improving nitrogen fertilization in rice by site-specific N management. A review. *Agronomy for Sustainable Development,* 30, pp. 649–656.

Raj, S. K., Snehi, S. K., Khan, M. S., *et al.* (2010). First report of Pepper leaf curl Bangladesh virus strain associated with bitter gourd (*Momordica charantia* L.) yellow mosaic disease in India. *Australasian Plant Disease Notes,* 5, pp. 14–16.

Reddy, C. S., Laha, G. S., Prasad, M. S., Krishnaveni, D., Castilla, N. P., Nelson, A. and Savary, S. (2011). Characterizing multiple linkages between individual diseases, crop health syndromes, germplasm deployment, and rice production situations in India. *Field Crops Research*, 120(2), pp. 241–253.

Savary, S. and Mew, T. W. (1996). Analyzing Crop Losses due to *Rhizoctonia solani*: Rice Sheath Blight, A Case Study. In S. Baruch, S. Jabaji-Hare, S. Neate and G. Dijst (Eds.), *Rhizoctonia Species: Taxonomy, Molecular Biology, Ecology, Pathology and Disease Control*, pp. 237–245. Springer.

Savary, S., Willocquet, L. and Teng, P. S. (1997). Modelling sheath blight epidemics on rice tillers. *Agricultural Systems*, 55(3), pp. 359–384.

Savary, S., Willocquet, L., Elazegui, F. A., Teng, P. S., Du, P. V., Zhu, D., Tang, Q., Lin X., Singh H. M. and Srivastava R. K. (2000). Rice pest constraints in tropical Asia: characterization of injury profiles in relation to production situations. *Plant Disease*, 84, pp. 341–356.

Savary, S., Castilla, N. P., Elazegui, F. A. and Teng, P. S. (2005). Multiple effects of two drivers of agricultural change, labour shortage and water scarcity, on rice pest profiles in tropical Asia. *Field Crops Research*, 91(2–3), pp. 263–271.

Savary, S., Teng, P. S., Willocquet, L. and Nutter, F. W. (2006). Quantification and modeling of crop losses: a review of purposes. *Annual Review of Phytopathology*, 44, pp. 89–112.

Savary, S., Nelson, A., Sparks, A. H., Willocquet, L., Duveiller, E., Mahuku, G., Forbes, G., Garrett, K. A., Hodson, D., Padgham, J. and Pande, S. (2011). International agricultural research tackling the effects of global and climate changes on plant diseases in the developing world. *Plant Disease*, 95(10), pp. 1204–1216.

Savary, S., Esker, P. D., McRoberts, N. and Willocquet, L. (2014). Environmental interactions and multiple forcing leading to shifts and variability of crop yield losses. *Phytopathology*, 104(11), p. 150.

Savary, S., Bregaglio, S., Willocquet, L., Gustafson, D., Mason D'Croz, D., Sparks, A., Castilla, N., Djurle, A., Allinne, C., Sharma, M. and Rossi, V. (2017). Crop health and its global impacts on the components of food security. *Food Security*, 9(2), pp. 311–327.

Savary, S., Willocquet, L., Pethybridge, S. J., Esker, P., McRoberts, N. and Nelson, A. (2019). The global burden of pathogens and pests on major food crops. *Nature Ecology and Evolution*, 3(3), pp. 430– 439.

Savary, S., Willocquet, L., Castilla, N., Nelson, A., Shankar Singh, U., Kumar, J. and Teng, P. S. (2022). Whither rice health in the lowlands of Asia: Shifts in production situations, injury profiles, and yields. *Plant Pathology*, 71(1), pp. 55–85.

Schreinemachers, P., Schad, I., Tipraqsa, P., Williams, P. M., Neef, A., Riwthong, S., Sangchan, W. and Grovermann, C. (2012). Can public GAP standards reduce agricultural pesticide use? The case of fruit and vegetable farming in northern Thailand. *Agriculture and Human Values*, 29(4), pp. 519–529.

Schreinemachers, P., Simmons, E. B. and Wopereis, M. C. S. (2018). Tapping the economic and nutritional power of vegetables. *Global Food Security*, 16, pp. 36–45.

Schreinemachers, P., Grovermann, C., Praneetvatakul, S., Heng, P., Nguyen, T. T. L., Buntong, B., Le, N. T. and Pinn, T. (2020). How much is too much? Quantifying pesticide overuse in vegetable production in Southeast Asia. *Journal of Cleaner Production*, 244, p. 118738.

Sharma, R. C. and Duveiller, E. (2004). Effect of Helminthosporium leaf blight on the performance of timely and late seeded wheat under optimal and stressed levels of soil fertility and soil moisture. *Field Crops Research*, 89, pp. 205–218.

Sharma, R. C., Duveiller, E. and Ortiz-Ferrara, G. (2007). Progress and challenge towards reducing wheat spot blotch threat in the Eastern Gangetic Plains of South Asia: is climate change already taking its toll?. *Field Crops Research*, 103(2), pp. 109–118.

Singh, R. P., Singh P. K., Rutkoski, J., *et al.* (2016). Disease impact on wheat yield potential and prospects of genetic control. *Annual Review Phytopathology,* 54, pp. 303–322.

Smil, V. (2000). *Feeding the World — A Challenge for the Twenty-First Century.* The MIT Press.

Teng, P. S., Torres, C. Q., Nuque, F. L. and Calvero, S. B. (1990). Current Knowledge on Crop Losses in Tropical Rice. In P. S. Teng (Ed.), *Crop Loss Assessment in Rice*, pp. 39–53. International Rice Research Institute.

Teng, P. S. (1983). Estimating and interpreting disease intensity and loss in commercial fields. *Phytopathology,* 73, pp. 1587–90.

Teng, P. S. (Ed.) (1987). *Crop Loss Assessment and Pest Management.* APS Press.

Thomas-Sharma, S., Abdurahman, A., Ali, S., *et al.* (2016). Seed degeneration in potato: the need for an integrated seed health strategy to mitigate the problem in developing countries. *Plant Pathology,* 65, pp. 3–16.

Timsina, J. and Connor, D. J. (2001). Productivity and management of rice–wheat cropping systems: issues and challenges. *Field Crops Research,* 69(2), pp. 93–132.

Uppala, S., Beena, S., Chapala, M., *et al.* (2010). Bioefficacy of endophytes in the management of leaf blight disease of amaranth. In M. S. Reddy, S. Desai, R. Z. Sayyed, *et al.* (Eds.), *Plant Growth Promotion by Rhizobacteria for Sustainable Agriculture*, pp. 524–530. Scientific Publishers.

Wang, H. D., Chen, J. P., Zhang, H. M., Sun, X. L., Zhu, J. L., Wang, A. G., Sheng, W. X. and Adams, M. J. (2008). Recent rice stripe virus epidemics in Zhejiang province, China, and experiments on sowing date, disease-yield loss relationships, and seedling susceptibility. *Plant Disease,* 92, pp. 1190–1196.

Willocquet, L., Fernandez, L. and Savary, S. (2000). Effect of various crop establishment methods practised by Asian farmers on epidemics of rice sheath blight caused by *Rhizoctonia solani*. *Plant Pathology*, 49(3), pp. 346–354.

Zadoks, J. C. (1967). Types of losses caused by plant diseases. In *FAO Symposium on Crop Losses*, pp. 149–158. Food and Agriculture Organization.

Zadoks, J. C. and Schein R. D. (1979). *Epidemiology and Plant Disease Management*. Oxford University Press.

Zadoks, J. C. (1985). On the conceptual basis of crop loss assessment: the threshold theory. *Annual Review of Phytopathology,* 23, pp. 455–73.

Zeigler, R. S., Leong, S. A. and Teng, P. S. (Eds.) (1994). *Rice Blast Disease*. CABI-IRRI.

Zeigler, R. S. and Savary, S. (2009). Plant Diseases and the World's Dependence on Rice. In R. N. Strange and M. L. Gullino (Eds.), *The Role of Plant Pathology in Food Safety and Food Security*, pp. 3–9. Springer.

Zhou, G. H., Xu, D. L., Xu, D. G. and Zhang, M. X. (2013). Southern rice black-streaked dwarf virus: a white-backed planthopper-transmitted fijivirus threatening rice production in Asia. *Frontiers in Microbiology,* 4, p. 270.

https://doi.org/10.1142/9789811278297_0022

Chapter 22

Reducing Food Loss and Waste in Food Systems

Rosa S. Rolle

Food and Nutrition Division, Economic and Social Development Stream, Food and Agriculture Organization of the United Nations, Rome, Italy

22.1 Introduction: Issues of Concern

The Asian region is vast and diverse. It is home to some of the world's most developed countries, as it is to some of the least developed and most fragile [ESCAP, 2022]. Almost 60% of the world's population live in the region, and more than 80% of the world's smallholders and family farmers live off the land in the region.

Urbanisation is a defining megatrend across Asia. Projections are that nearly 55% of Asia's population will reside in urban areas by 2030 [FAO *et al.*, 2023]. These rapid urbanisation rates, coupled with rising living standards in urban centres, have contributed to shifting patterns of food consumption that are having profound impacts on the region's agrifood systems.

Smallholders, landless and marginal farmers and their families comprise the main category of rural self-employed in the region's agricultural sector and contribute significantly to the total value of agricultural output. Farming systems face a number of challenges from rising wages, a declining workforce due to aging farming populations, rural-to-urban migration along with increasing non-agricultural labour demand, climate change and water shortages [ADB, 2021]. Transboundary pests and diseases pose a challenge to food security trade and livelihoods, generating significant losses for farmers and threatening the region's food security.

The region also suffers keenly from the effects of climate change but is also a source of the problem in that it produces about half of the world's carbon dioxide emissions. Performance on climate action (Sustainable Development Goal (SDG) 13) is unequivocally worse than any other goal in the Asian region [ESCAP, 2023]. In 2020, Asia accounted for the highest total pre- and post-production emissions recorded globally at 3.09 Gt CO_2eq [FAO, 2023a]. Climate change threatens growth, livelihood productivity and wellbeing across all countries in the region.

Land resources for agriculture are declining and there is a growing scarcity of water resources. Rising prices for food, energy and production inputs — seed and fertiliser — floods, drought, water scarcity, and increasing climate-related disasters are currently driving food insecurity and malnourishment across the region.

An estimated 8.5% of Asia's population faces hunger [FAO *et al.*, 2023], while levels of food losses across the region remain high. Large quantities of food go to waste in dining establishments and in fresh produce markets in developing countries across the region, while household food waste predominates in the more developed countries of the region.

Progress towards all 17 of the SDGs in the region has been slow, increasing from 4.4% in 2017 to 14.4% in 2022 [ESCAP, 2023].

Regression has occurred on responsible consumption and production (Goal 12). No measurable progress has been made towards achieving SDG target 12.3 that seeks by 2030 to *halve per capita global food waste at the retail and consumer levels and reduce food losses along production and supply chains, including post-harvest losses* [ESCAP, 2023].

Prioritising the reduction of food loss and waste is critical to transforming the region's agrifood systems to make them more efficient, sustainable, inclusive and resilient, diminishing their impact on the natural resource base and the environment, while ensuring their contribution to improving food security and nutrition across the region.

22.2 Food Supply Systems in the Asian Region

Agrifood systems in Asia are currently in a phase of change driven largely by income growth and high urbanisation rates. Food procurement systems in developing countries across the region are increasingly seeking to respond to growing market opportunities through value chain development, and to reduce food losses and address food safety and quality issues in traditional supply chains. These traditional production-driven supply chains operate in the informal sector (Table 22.1) and continue to play an important role in supplying the food needs of the urban poor through food vendors and markets. They involve a large number of intermediaries and lack vertical coordination. Food losses in these traditional supply chains are high, and produce is of poor quality in their informal markets due to excessive handling.

Table 22.1 Characteristics of modern and traditional food supply chains in the Asian region.

Characteristics of value chains	Characteristics of traditional supply chains
• Consumer oriented	• Production oriented
• Focus on processes	• Fragmented production units
• Differentiated products	• Multi-layered channels
• Integrated systems	• Un-differentiated products
• High quality	• Minimal value added
• Grading and private labelling	• Predominance of wholesalers
• Attention to food safety	• Production push market
• Use of post-harvest technology	• High levels of post-harvest loss
• Value creation	
• Logistics as backbone	
• Information & communications technology as enabler	
• Consumer pull market	

22.3 Food Losses in the Asian Region

Food losses refer to the decrease in the quantity or quality of food resulting from decisions and actions by food suppliers in the food supply chain, excluding retail, food service providers and consumers [FAO, 2019]. The global percentage of food lost after harvesting at the farm, transport, storage, wholesale and processing levels was estimated at 13.3% in 2020 [FAO, 2022].

Food loss percentages across the Asian region are high, with East and Southeast Asia (15.1%), Central and South Asia (13.6%), North Africa and Western Asia (14.8%), and Australia and New Zealand (13.6%) [FAO, 2022]. High levels of food losses in Southeast Asia are largely due to high levels of losses in value chains for fruits and vegetables, when compared to Central and Southern Asia (13.6%) and Australia and New Zealand (13.6%) [FAO, 2022].

Major underlying causes of food losses in the region include the lack of, or inadequacy of, technology and infrastructure in the traditional chains that supply the bulk of food requirements to low-income consumers and the relatively weak knowledge base of smallholders who operate in these chains.

Inappropriate post-harvest management practices, inefficient technologies and the lack of understanding of the factors that affect grain quality are the main cause of post-harvest losses in rice [IRRI, n.d.]. Poor quality reduces the market price of milled rice by 10–30% thus affecting farmer income.

Losses in fresh fruits and vegetables across the region, on the other hand, are comparably higher than in the case of rice, owing largely to excessive handling, the high degree of perishability of fruits and vegetables under ambient conditions, and mechanical damage due to poor packaging.

Apart from reducing the quality, quantity and value of food, losses result in the wastage of resources, reduce returns to smallholder farmers, contribute to increased prices for consumers and add pressure to an already strained natural resource base as farmers try to compensate by increasing their production. Improvements in post-harvest technologies and the application of systemic management approaches, together with capacity development, will go a long way to reducing food losses in a sustainable manner in the agrarian countries of the region.

22.4 Food Waste in the Asian Region

Food waste refers to the decrease in the quantity or quality of food resulting from decisions and actions by retailers, food services and consumers. Food is wasted mainly in households, in the food service sector and in retail [UNEP, 2021].

Consumer households generate large quantities of food waste in the industrialised countries of the region (see box below), while increased dining in buffets is a major underlying cause of food waste in developing Asian countries [UNEP, 2021]. In a business-as-usual scenario, food waste in China, India and Southeast Asia is expected to increase on average by 24% in the next decade. Adopting best-in-class practices offers significant potential to reduce food waste in Asia [Huang and Sinha, 2021].

Food Waste in Developed Countries of the Asian Region

- In 2016–17, **Australia** produced **7.3 million tonnes** of food waste across the supply and consumption chain. Of this, 2.5 million tonnes (34%) was created in households, and 1.8 million tonnes (25%) in the manufacturing sector [Government of Australia, 2019].
- The estimated total amount of food loss and waste, excluding inedible parts generated in 2021, in **Japan** was approximately **5.23 million tonnes** (2.44 million tonnes from households and 2.79 million tonnes from businesses) [Government of Japan, 2023].
- Over **475 thousand tonnes** of food waste were recycled in **South Korea** in 2021, a significant increase from the previous year. This was also more than double that of 2019 [Statista Research Department, 2023].
- In 2022, the total amount of food waste generated in **Singapore** was about **813 thousand tonnes**. Food waste accounts for around 10% of the total waste generated in Singapore. In that same year, around 18% of the food waste generated was recycled [Statista Singapore, 2023].

22.5 Impacts of Food Loss and Waste on Food Security

Food security is the *raison d'etre* for sustaining agrifood supply and food system resilience [Fan *et al.*, 2021]. Food loss and waste currently exert a pressing challenge in the design of sustainable food systems and negatively affect the region's food security. They result in the wastage of human resources, energy, and inputs — fertilisers, seeds and water — used for production and all activities downstream in the supply chain and represent a lost opportunity to consume, sell or trade foods.

Food loss and waste tighten the food market by increasing food prices, affecting food access for consumers. They also have a longer-term effect on food security that results from the unsustainable use of scarce natural resources such as land and water, on which the future production of food depends [FAO, 2019].

Reducing food loss and waste across the food supply chain reduces the need to increase food production, protects the natural resource base, and reduces the pressure of increasing yields to meet food security goals [ADB, 2021; FAO, 2019]. Reducing food loss and waste across the region's supply chains would also contribute to retaining nutrients generated across the food system towards improving food and nutrition security [ADB, 2022].

Food loss reduction, in particular, has the potential to generate win-wins across all dimensions of hunger targets — by improving food availability, food access, and smallholder incomes — and offers an opportunity to enhance efficiency in the use of the region's scarce natural resources [United Nations Food Systems Summit, 2021].

22.6 Emissions, Climate Change and Impacts on Food Loss and Waste in Agrifood Systems

22.6.1 *Pre- and Post-Production Emissions Across Asia*

The Asian region produces about half of the world's carbon dioxide emissions. It is also home to four countries — China, Japan, Indonesia and India — with the highest global pre- and post-production carbon dioxide emissions per capita, as measured for the period 2018–2020 (Figure 22.1). Pre-production activities take place before the farm gate and include fertiliser manufacture, pesticide manufacture, and generation of electricity and heat used on farms. Post-production activities, on the other hand, cover activities after the farm gate, including food processing, packaging, food transport, food retail, food household consumption and agrifood systems waste disposal [Tubiello *et al.*, 2022; FAO, 2023a].

Of the top four Asian countries, China has the highest carbon dioxide emissions in food household consumption (0.45 Gt CO_2eq on average between 2018 and 2020) and agrifood systems waste disposal (0.21 Gt CO_2eq), highlighting the environmental impact of the country's large population and waste management challenges [FAO, 2023a]. India experiences substantial emissions from on-farm electricity use (0.16 Gt CO_2eq) and agrifood systems waste disposal (0.16 Gt CO_2eq), shedding light on the country's reliance on fossil fuels and inefficiencies in its agricultural sector [FAO, 2023a]. Food retail, food transport and food processing are the major contributors of carbon dioxide emissions in developed countries such as Japan.

Changing dietary habits with rapid urbanisation and dietary shifts towards the consumption of animal products will likely lead to

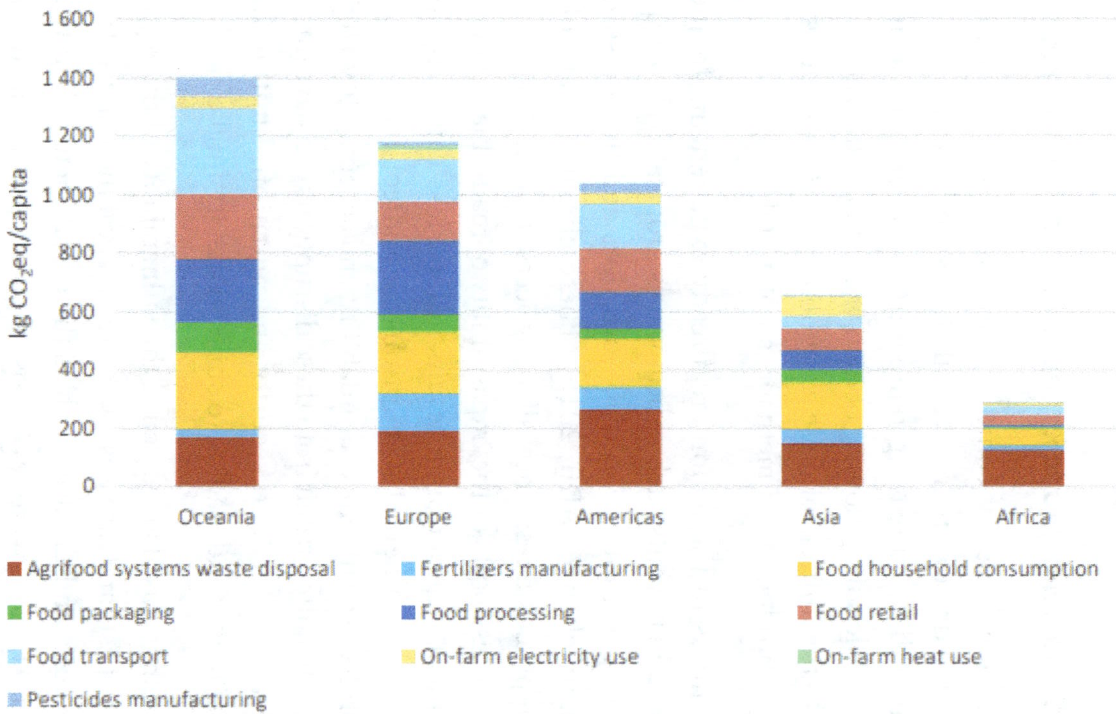

Figure 22.1 Pre- and post-production emissions per capita of the top 10 emitters globally (2018–2020). Source: FAO [2023a].

increased livestock farming in the region, contributing further to increasing emissions.

22.6.2 *Climate Change and its Impacts on Agrifood Systems*

Carbon dioxide emissions contribute to an unstable climate that is often prone to drastic environmental change and extreme weather events, including increasing temperatures or global warming, droughts and flooding. Rotting of food waste in landfills adds considerably to the impacts of these greenhouse gas (GHG) emissions through the production of methane, a potent GHG.

Many countries in the region are already experiencing frequent extreme weather events such as heat waves, tropical cyclones, prolonged dry spells, intense rainfall, tornadoes and thunderstorms from climate change [ADB, 2016]. These climate shocks often disrupt supply chain resilience, affecting access to food. The inability of ships to access ports or the impassability of roads due to flooding and inclement weather often results in food loss caused by food spoilage. Environmental disruptions also affect food security through shifts in availability, affordability, and acceptability. Higher food prices that often result from these disruptions can have important implications for food security and nutrition, limiting food purchasing power and leading to shifts in dietary intake.

Climate change has also worsened the vulnerability of the region's resources to pests and diseases and increased pest incursions. Transboundary pests and diseases such as the desert locust, Fall Armyworm and African swine fever pose a significant threat to food security, trade and livelihoods, generating significant field-level losses for farmers and threatening the region's food security [FAO, 2020]. Climate change increases the potential for infestations in stored crops and is projected to affect the nutritional quality of staple crops [Smith and Myers, 2018], reduce the yields of primary commodities (irrigated rice, wheat and soybeans) and increase the prices of these commodities, affecting nutrition [ADB, 2016].

Climate change also poses a threat to food safety. Changes in temperature, precipitation and environmental factors are expected to affect the geographic persistence of foodborne pathogens and parasites [FAO, 2022], increasing the potential for foodborne illness. Prolonged drought conditions can put stress on the availability and usage of water, affecting food-processing plants where food safety may be compromised to compensate for the lack of sufficient water. Rising soil temperatures are expected to facilitate the uptake of heavy metals by plants — for instance, arsenic in rice, a regional food staple crop known to accumulate heavy metals in plants as well as grains [FAO, 2020].

Reducing food loss and food waste serves as a key climate strategy by reducing GHGs as it helps countries and businesses to raise climate ambition, while conserving and protecting ecosystems and natural resources upon which the future of the region's food depends.

22.7 Reducing Food Losses in Asia

22.7.1 *Milestones Towards Addressing Food Loss Reduction*

A high-level regional multi-stakeholder consultation convened in 2013 prioritised awareness raising, capacity building and multi-disciplinary/multi-sectoral collaboration as requirements to address food loss and waste reduction in the region [FAO, 2014a]. Countries also highlighted the need for the development of national and regional strategies and policies to tackle the issues. A joint communique outlining actions to reduce food loss and waste was endorsed by country representatives, who pledged *to work together in the framework of a Regional Save Food Asia-Pacific Campaign launched at that event, "to reduce food losses along food supply chains and fight the growing problem of food waste"* [FAO, 2014a]. Some countries — notably Malaysia and Thailand — followed suit with the launch of national campaigns, while others opted to mainstream the issues through various ongoing programmes linked to agriculture, food security and nutrition.

The ADB's *Operational Plan for Agriculture and Natural Resources: Promoting Sustainable Food Security in Asia and the Pacific in 2015–2020* provides guidance for increasing emphasis on food security and agriculture productivity. The Plan focuses operations of the ADB Agriculture and Natural Resources sector in four priority areas: (i) increasing productivity and reducing pre- and post-harvest losses of food crops; (ii) improving market connectivity and value chain linkages; (iii) enhancing food safety, quality, and nutrition; and (iv) enhancing management and climate resilience of natural resources. These priority areas, including the key elements of the food value chain (production, processing, distribution, and consumption), are highly interconnected, requiring innovative and integrated multi-sector approaches and interventions to address food security in developing member countries more directly [ADB, 2015].

Signature of the 2030 Agenda by Governments in 2015 strengthened the regional focus on reducing food losses, with target setting by countries. Specific targets were set by Vietnam and the Philippines to reduce post-harvest losses in staple foods such as rice and corn, and in fishery and aquaculture products [APEC, 2018]. The Jinan

Initiative of the International Conference on Food Loss and Waste convened by China in 2021, among other issues, proposed four key areas for cooperation to prevent food losses: preventing food loss during harvest, preventing grain storage losses, preventing grain processing losses, and improving grain transport logistics systems [PR Newswire, 2021]. Malaysia also set a target to reduce food loss and waste by half by 2030.

22.7.2 *Core Requirements to Tackle Food Loss Reduction in the Region*

Reliable data is critical for informing actions to reduce food loss and waste and to increase supply chain efficiency. Target setting, data collection and evidence generation, followed by the scale-up of actions are critical needs and inputs to reduce food losses (qualitative and quantitative) at scale towards impacting national food loss indices in countries, generating economic, social and environmental benefits and contributing to food systems transformation.

22.7.2.1 *Building an Evidence Base to Reduce Food Losses, and Improve Quality and Safety in Traditional Horticultural Supply Chains*

Through the implementation of holistic, systemic approaches to underpin interventions to reduce food losses for prioritised crops in traditional horticultural supply chains, a replicable evidence base was built across South and Southeast Asian countries [Rolle, 2017; Rolle and Esguerra, 2018; FAO, 2018a–f; FAO field data — unpublished].

This involved the conduct of surveys with supply chain stakeholders, followed by the identification of critical loss points or hotspots in the supply chains and their underlying causes. These findings informed stakeholder discussions pertinent to the identification of context-appropriate solutions to reduce food losses and generate economic, social and environmental benefits. Losses were measured at critical loss points [Rolle and Esguerra, 2018]. Pertinent cost/benefit analyses of loss and waste reduction interventions and good practices were disseminated through training to support stakeholders in their decision making to adopt improved practices.

Implemented in collaboration with governments in the framework of technical cooperation projects, these initiatives have fostered regional networking through capacity building at all levels — trainer, extension officer, practitioner, academic, farmer leader — to support the diffusion and uptake of improved post-harvest handling practices, with the introduction of simple technologies. These simple technologies introduced — reusable plastic crates in lieu of plastic bags for the bulk packaging of produce during transportation, and the hot water treatment of mangoes and papayas to reduce pre-harvest pest and disease infestations — were widely adopted by value chain stakeholders as well as stakeholders engaged in cross-border, regional and international trade. Results achieved for highly perishable horticultural crops such as tomatoes (see box below) were replicable across a number of countries in the region, with no less than an 80% reduction in the levels of food losses with the introduction of good practice.

Awareness raising and the scaling up and scaling out of these successful replicable models offer considerable potential to accelerate the pace of actions to impact national food loss indices while generating beneficial nutritional impacts. Governments in some countries have incentivised the adoption of the good practice introduced. In others, supermarket chains have come on board as buyers of high-quality produce from these stakeholders, and have equipped them with reusable plastic crates to scale up the good practice introduced, in order to meet their requirements for specific produce items.

Reducing Food Loss and Waste in Tomato Chains in Bangladesh: Generating an Evidence Base towards Scaling up Actions

Through the piloting of systemic approaches to reduce food losses in traditional winter tomato supply chains, losses during transport, a critical loss point, were estimated at 17%, while more than 29% of the fruit underwent spoilage in retail markets within three days, due to decay. Mechanical damage caused by poor-quality packaging was the major underlying cause of this loss and waste. Switching from the 50 kg disposable plastic bags used to transport tomatoes to markets, to 25 kg rigid returnable plastic crates, with the introduction of simple good practice — sorting to remove damaged and decaying fruit, and washing of the fruit — a 100% reduction in losses was achieved. Better-quality tomatoes and a 98% reduction in food waste after three days was also achieved [Rolle and Esguerra, 2018]. By applying these simple practices to reduce food losses, win-wins were generated across all sustainability targets:

Economic benefit: that results from better-quality tomato fruits, reduced losses during transport, longer shelf life, and the diversified market opportunities that result from improved quality.

Social benefit: having access to better-quality tomatoes means reduced food waste in households and makes a significant difference for low-income consumers that shop in these markets.

Environmental benefit: With the introduction of reusable plastic crates, fewer plastics go into the environment and less waste goes to landfills.

22.7.2.2 *Building an Evidence Base to Reduce Food Losses in Micro-, Small and Medium Food Processing Enterprises*

Micro-, small and medium food processing enterprises (MSMEs) play an important role in countries at different stages of development across Asia, and contribute significantly to food security, nutrition, income and employment generation [Rolle, 2014]. Strong, dynamic and efficient MSMEs are, therefore, critical to ensuring sustainable, inclusive and broad-based economic and social development across the region.

Improvements in the food processing operations of MSMEs offer considerable potential to upgrade the quality and shelf life of their outputs, reduce food losses, build climate resilience in food supplies, and improve incomes for producers and processors.

An evidence base to underpin the measurement and reduction of food losses in the processing and distribution operations of MSMEs was developed through a country-wide survey conducted in 196 MSMEs across five sub-sectors [FAO, 2023b] — animal products, dairy products, fishery products, rice products and snack food products — in Thailand. Through the conduct of these qualitative surveys in 66 of the 77 provinces in Thailand, the main underlying causes of food loss and critical loss points in processing and distribution operations of MSMEs were identified. Good practice, together with simple innovations introduced in processing operations, measurably reduced quantitative losses at critical loss points, and qualitative losses at various stages of the processing and distribution operations [FAO, 2023b], resulting in products of improved quality.

The replication and scale up of the approaches, principles and good practice in reducing food losses in the processing and distribution operations of MSMEs will go a long way towards improving the quality and shelf life of their processed outputs and to the realisation of improved economic returns from wider market opportunities (FAO, 2023b).

22.7.2.3 *Improving Efficiency Across Supply Chains in the Region*

Poor road connections, the lack of post-harvest specific infrastructure — packing houses and cool and dry warehouses — are underlying causes of inefficiencies that result in food losses in the region's food supply chains. Investments to improve road connections and logistics systems, and collection centres for fresh produce in particular, would contribute significantly to reducing the levels of food losses in the supply chain.

The mechanisation of rice post-harvest operations; improved drying, storage infrastructure and milling of harvested paddy and secondary processing of rice to enhance consumer convenience; and vertical coordination and shortening of the rice value chain for improved efficiency present major opportunities for reducing losses [FAO, 2014b].

Digitalisation also offers considerable potential to improve overall efficiency across both modern and traditional supply chains across the region. The increased use of mobile apps by stakeholders in traditional supply chains across the region contributes to increasing their efficiency in marketing their crops, while reducing losses. Advances in sensor technologies have substantially increased the potential for real-time collection and the use of data for decision making, contributing to improving the quality and safety of perishables and reducing food losses across the value chain.

Internet of Things wireless sensors linked to cloud data consolidators measure and record temperature, humidity and location of fresh produce, allowing for real-time decision making pertinent to quality management as it moves across the cold supply chain or is kept in cool storage. This data can have direct implications for reducing food loss and waste by triggering actions (see box below) to stem the problem.

The Fresherator: An Innovative Cold Chain System in India

Superplum, an Indian-based startup near New Delhi, has developed an innovative cold chain solution for fresh fruit produce called the Fresherator. This container, which can attach itself to any 24 ft (8 m) truck, has the ability to transport 4–7 tonnes of fruit from the farm and keep it fresh up to four weeks at a stretch, apparently offering effective cold chain storage and a transport solution for India's fresh fruit market. Custom engineered from scratch, the Fresharator works like any refrigerated container. With a standard Internet of Things system, which operates through a cellular network, it can remotely control temperature, humidity, oxygen and ethylene levels.

Source: [Packaging Europe, 2022]

22.8 Approaches and Actions to Tackle Food Waste in Asia

Preventing and reducing food waste, rescuing surplus food that is fit for consumption and creating value from food waste, keeping food out of landfills and shifting towards more sustainable production and consumption are core priorities to be tackled across the region.

Developed countries like Australia and Japan have set targets to reduce food waste by 50% in alignment with the SDG 12.3 target, while Singapore's GreenPlan 2030 [Government of Singapore, n.d.] focuses on reducing the amount of food waste to landfill per capita per day by 30% and meeting 30% of Singapore's nutrition needs through locally produced foods. These countries have also put in place strategies, roadmaps and policy action plans and have invested in raising consumer awareness on food waste and its impacts, in research to improve efficiencies, and in building the infrastructural support base to support the reduction of food waste.

22.8.1 *Policies, Strategies, Regulations and Programmes to Manage Food Waste in Developed Countries Across the Region*

- **Australia** has developed a *National Food Waste Strategy* that provides a framework to support collective action towards halving Australia's food waste by 2030, as well as a roadmap that provides a clear path forward towards meeting that target. The roadmap documents the main steps and initiatives required and recognises the significant contributions of governments and the private sector to date.
- **Japan's** *Food Loss Act* [Government of Japan, 2021], which took effect on October 1, 2019, was part of the government's plans [Ministry of Environment, n.d.] for taking measures to reduce household food waste in response to SDG 12.3. The Act requires that national and local governments educate consumers and businesses. Moreover, national and local governments are required to take measures to facilitate activities of non-governmental organisations to collect usable food and to redistribute it [Global Legal Monitor, 2019].
- **Japan's** *Food Recycling Act* enacted in 2001 and amended in 2007 promotes reducing and recycling food wastes into fertiliser and feed. One provision of the Act obligates businesses

that generate large amounts of food waste to take measures to reduce and recycle the waste and report their food waste situation to the government periodically (Articles 7 and 9).

- **Singapore**'s *integrated solid waste management system* focuses on two key thrusts — waste minimisation and recycling, or simply the 3Rs (Reduce, Reuse, Recycle). In land-scarce Singapore, waste-to-energy incineration plants offer the best technical solution by reducing waste volume efficiently to conserve landfill space. The 3Rs play a crucial role by preventing waste generation at its source and bringing along numerous benefits.
- The "*pay as you throw*" law enacted in Seoul, **Republic of Korea** in 2013 requires that food waste is discarded in biodegradable bags, and a household fee is charged based on the weight of the waste [Yeong, n.d.].

22.8.2 *Policies, Regulations and Programmes Focused on Food Rescue and Recovery in Developing Countries Across Asia*

Across much of developing Asia, food waste reduction policies and programmes have focused largely on food rescue, recovery and redistribution.

- The *Anti Food Waste Law of the People's Republic of* **China** was enacted in 2021 [FAOLEX Database, 2021]. This Law, consisting of 32 Articles, enacted in accordance with the Constitution, aims to prevent food waste, guaranteeing grain security of the state, carrying forward traditional virtues of the Chinese nation, saving resources, protecting the environment, and promoting sustainable economic and social development.

Food waste mentioned in the Law refers to the failure to reasonably utilise safe, edible or drinkable food according to its functions and purposes, including abandonment or reduction in quantity or deterioration of quality of food due to unreasonable utilisation, among others.

- A *Disposal of Excess Food Regulation 2019* enacted by **Pakistan** requires that leftover food from restaurants and hotels is supplied to needy people, providing a reward system for restaurants and hotels that support this initiative [Punjab Food Authority, 2019].
- The *Food Donation Act (RA 9803, 2009)/Food Surplus Act (HB 2469)* of the **Philippines** encourages the donation of food for charitable purposes to reduce food waste and alleviate poverty. Food-related businesses are required to donate edible food wastes which are unadulterated to food banks [Republic of the Philippines, 2009].
- *Food Safety and Standards (Recovery and Distribution of Surplus Food) Regulations*, in **India**, came into force on the date of their publication (26 July 2019). These regulations specify the responsibility of the food donor and organisations that distribute surplus food to any person free of cost. Any food donor having surplus food may donate such food to any food distribution organisation in accordance with the provisions of these regulations [FAOLEX, 2019].

22.8.3 *Keeping Food Waste out of Landfills through Mobile Apps*

Across Asia, tech startups are channelling food otherwise destined for landfills and are providing discounted meals through mobile phone apps [Glass, 2022], as well as composting services to businesses and households. The emergence of food-sharing apps across the region has facilitated efficiency in food rescue as well as intelligent redistribution of surplus foods and foods nearing their expiration dates [Food Bank Singapore, n.d.; Glass, 2022]. Mobile applications also facilitate product traceability, and can facilitate consumers in meal planning, shopping as well as in accessing recipes for the use of leftovers towards reducing household food waste.

22.9 Moving Towards Agrifood Systems Transformation

High levels of food loss and waste in the face of hunger and food insecurity across the region clearly highlight the pivotal role of preventing and reducing food loss and waste in transforming the region's agrifood systems. Reducing food loss and waste is central to improving food security and nutrition, mitigating climate change, and enhancing the efficient use of the region's natural resources. Effectively tackling the reduction of food loss and waste in the region necessitates the prioritisation of targeted solutions by countries, and investing in their implementation at scale. Efforts and actions are also required to promote awareness on the issues at all levels, and to promote and foster behavioural change through widespread education and awareness-raising initiatives, with a concerted focus on youth.

Unlocking maximum value from agrifood systems in the region will necessitate shifting from the current linear take-make-use-discard model of current agrifood systems operations to circular systems. These are systems that prioritise the prevention and reduction of food loss and waste, followed by the rescue, recovery and redistribution of surplus or unsold/unmarketable food that is safe and suitable for consumption; then recycling and upcycling, with disposal as the final option. Composting is a widely practiced method of recycling food loss and waste to nourish soils and support further crop production.

Upcycling provides a good economic case for the reduction of food loss and waste with the generation of financial gains through value creation. An interesting example from the region is the production of non-alcoholic beverages from fruit and vegetable waste and loss such as fruit peels, seeds and rinds for local and export markets [Taylor, 2022]. Traditional food fermentation processes applied across Asia, such as the production of fish sauces and vinegars, are excellent examples of the upcycling of by-products that contribute significantly to diets across the region. Upgrading these processes with technological innovations to improve the efficiency of their operations, with attention to assuring the environmental sustainability of their practices, will also contribute significantly to food systems transformation.

The upcycling of food waste through treatment with the black soldier fly, *Hermetia illucens*, contributes to reducing a range of environmental problems such as GHG emissions and the generation of harmful substances associated with existing disposal methods including landfills and incineration [Kim *et al.*, 2021]. Black soldier fly larvae convert organic waste into high-quality nutrients for pet foods, fish and poultry feeds as well as residue fertiliser for soil amendment, using technologies of various levels and scales of operation [Siddiqui *et al.*, 2022]. Cultivating black soldier flies in Asian countries with adequate light and a mild climate offers small businesses the opportunity to generate high returns without high levels of investment [Kim *et al.*, 2021].

The circular economy offers potential to increase efficiency and profitability, and to reduce cost, drive innovations and create more sustainable business models [Boz and Robinson, 2021]. Shifting to circular approaches can help to address food security and promote sustainable production and consumption. Implementing innovative circular economy models, however, requires the development of new processes, necessitating investment, common motivation, and participation of food businesses, policymakers, non-governmental organisations, development agencies, consumers, and scientists.

Applying the circular economy and reducing food loss and waste towards meeting the SDG target 12.3 will maximise wins by contributing to achieving other SDGs — in particular SDG 2, SDG 8, and SDGs 13 and 14, thereby catalysing the transformation of agrifood systems.

References

ADB. (2015). *Operational Plan for Agriculture and Natural Resources: Promoting Sustainable Food Security in Asia and the Pacific in 2015–2020.* https://www.adb.org/sites/default/files/institutional-document/175238/op-agriculture-natural-resources.pdf

ADB. (2016). *Safe, Nutritious and Affordable Food for all.* https://dx.doi.org/10.22617/TCS178714

ADB. (2021). *Financing Sustainable Resilient Food Systems in Asia and the Pacific.* https://www.adb.org/sites/default/files/publication/749251/sustainable-resilient-food-systems-asia-pacific.pdf

ADB. (2022). *Unlocking Value from Agrifood Waste Streams.* https://development.asia/policy-brief/unlocking-value-agrifood-waste-streams

APEC. (2018). *APEC Survey on Feasible Solutions for Food Loss and Waste Reduction.* https://www.apec.org/publications/2018/09/apec-survey-report-on-feasible-solutions-for-food-loss-and-waste-reduction

Boz, Z. and Robinson, J. (2021). Moving toward a more circular system via upcycling. *Food Technology*, 75(9), pp. 53–55.

ESCAP. (2022). *Building Urban Economic Resilience During and After COVID-19.* https://www.unescap.org/kp/2022/building-urban-economic-resilience-during-and-after-covid-19-asia-pacific-regional-policy

ESCAP. (2023). *Asia and the Pacific SDG Progress Report 2023: Championing Sustainability Despite Adversities.* https://www.unescap.org/kp/2023/asia-and-pacific-sdg-progress-report-2023

Fan, S., Teng, P., Chew, P., Smith, G. and Copeland, L. (2021). Food system resilience and COVID-19 — Lessons from the Asian experience. *Global Food Security*, 28, p. 10050.

FAO. (2014a). *High-Level Multi-Stakeholder Consultation on Food Losses and Food Waste in Asia and the Pacific Region.* https://www.fao.org/3/i3657e/i3657e.pdf

FAO. (2014b). *A Regional Rice Strategy for Food Security in Asia.* https://www.fao.org/3/i3643e/i3643e00.htm

FAO. (2018a). *Low Cost, High Impact Solutions for Improving the Quality and Shelf Life of Mangoes in Local Markets.* https://www.fao.org/documents/card/ru/c/I8327EN/

FAO. (2018b). *Low Cost, High Impact Solutions for Improving the Quality and Shelf Life of Snap Beans in Local Markets.* https://www.fao.org/publications/card/ru/c/I7699EN/

FAO. (2018c). *Low Cost, High Impact Solutions for Improving the Quality and Shelf Life of Tomatoes in Local Markets.* https://www.fao.org/documents/card/ru/c/I7698EN/

FAO. (2018d). *Low Cost, High Impact Solutions for Improving the Quality and Shelf Life of Bananas in Local Markets.* https://www.fao.org/documents/card/fr/c/I7594EN/

FAO. (2018e). *Low Cost, High Impact Solutions for Improving the Quality and Shelf Life of Mandarins in Local Markets.* https://www.fao.org/documents/card/ru/c/I7694EN/

FAO. (2018f). *Low Cost, High Impact Solutions for Improving the Quality and Shelf Life of Cauliflower in Local Markets.* https://www.fao.org/documents/card/en/c/66327d23-061c-49f9-83a0-8aec196b510c/

FAO. (2019). *The State of Food and Agriculture Moving Forward on Food Loss and Waste Reduction.* https://www.fao.org/policy-support/tools-and-publications/resources-details/en/c/1242090/

FAO. (2020). *Climate Change: Unpacking the Burden on Food Safety.* https://doi.org/10.4060/ca8185en

FAO. (2022). *FAO SDG Indicators Portal.* https://www.fao.org/sustainable-development-goals/data/indicators/1231-global-food-losses/en

FAO. (2023a). *Greenhouse Gas Emissions from Pre- and Post-agricultural Production Processes. Global, Regional and Country Trends, 1990–2020.* https://www.fao.org/documents/card/en/c/cc5768en

FAO. (2023b). Developing capacity to reduce food loss and waste in Thailand. https://www.fao.org/3/cc4736en/cc4736en.pdf

FAO, IFAD, UNICEF, WFP and WHO. (2023). *The State of Food Security and Nutrition in the World 2023.* https://doi.org/10.4060/cc3017en

FAOLEX Database. (2019a). Food Safety and Standards (Recovery and Distribution of Surplus Food) Regulations, in India. http://faolex.fao.org/docs/pdf/ind194992.pdf

FAOLEX Database. (2019b). Food Safety and Standards (Recovery and Distribution of Surplus Food) Regulations, in India. http://faolex.fao.org/docs/pdf/ind194992.pdf

FAOLEX Database. (2021). Anti-food Waste Law of the People's Republic of China. https://www.fao.org/faolex/results/details/en/c/LEX-FAOC203240/

Food Bank Singapore (n.d.). Virtual food banking. https://foodbank.sg/virtual-foodbanking/

Glass, M. (2022). Apps turning restaurant leftovers into cheap meals. *Japan Times*. https://www.japantimes.co.jp/news/2022/08/13/business/tech/asia-food-waste-apps/

Global Legal Monitor. (2019). Japan: Diet passes new act aimed at reducing food loss. https://www.loc.gov/item/global-legal-monitor/2019-10-09/japan-diet-passes-new-act-aimed-at-reducing-food-loss/

Government of Australia. (2019). National food waste baseline. https://www.dcceew.gov.au/environment/protection/waste/food-waste#national-food-waste-baseline

Government of Australia. (2022). Tackling Australia's food waste. https://www.dcceew.gov.au/environment/protection/waste/food-waste

Government of Japan. (2021). Food Recycling Act. https://perma.cc/S5JD-8JWX

Government of Japan. (2023). MOE Japan discloses the estimated amount of Japan's food loss and waste generated in FY2021. https://www.env.go.jp/en/press/press_01833.htm

Government of Singapore. (n.d.). SG Green Plan. https://www.greenplan.gov.sg/

Huang, M. and Sinha, S. (2021). *No Time to Waste: Managing Food Waste in Asia's Food Retail and Food Service Channels*. Rabobank RaboResearch.

IRRI. (n.d.). Mechanization and postharvest. https://www.irri.org/mechanization-and-postharvest

Kim, C. H., Ryu, J., Lee, J., Ko, K., Lee, J., Park, K. Y. and Chung, H. (2021). Use of black soldier fly larvae for food waste treatment and energy production in Asian countries: a review. *Processes*, 9, p. 161.

Kwang, K. and Kim, Y. J. (2012). *Volume-based Waste Free System in Korea*. Korea Development Institute (KDI) School of Public Policy and Management.

Ministry of Environment, Japan. (n.d.). The 4th Fundamental Plan for Establishing a Sound Material-Cycle Society. https://perma.cc/RC5G-LM5T

Packaging Europe. (2022). IOT-based cold chain solution could reduce India's fruit distribution problems. https://packagingeurope.com/news/iot-based-cold-chain-solution-could-reduce-indias-fruit-distribution-problems/791

PRNewswire. (2021). First International Conference on Food Loss and Waste, Jinan, China. https://www.prnewswire.com/news-releases/the-first-international-conference-on-food-loss-and-waste-closes-with-10-consensus-on-food-loss-and-waste-301374795.html

Punjab Food Authority. (2019). Disposal of Excess Food Regulation approved by PFA board. https://cell.pfa.gop.pk/knowledge-base/disposal-of-excess-food-regulation-2019-approved-by-pfa-board

Republic of the Philippines. (2009). Act 9803. An act to encourage the donation of food for charitable purposes. https://www.officialgazette.gov.ph/2009/11/20/republic-act-no-9803/

Rolle, R. S. (2011). Toward Improved Packaging Practices for Post-Harvest Loss Reduction. In *Packaging in Fresh Produce Supply Chains in Southeast Asia*, pp. 1–3. FAO RAP Publication 2011/20.

Rolle, R. S. (2014). Policy Measures for Micro-, Small And Medium-, Food Processing Enterprises in the Asian Region. In *Policy Measures for Micro, Small and Medium Food Processing Enterprises in the Asian Region*, pp. 1–7. FAO RAP Publication 2014/27.

Rolle, R. S. (2017). *Policy Measures for Managing Quality and Reducing Post-Harvest Losses in Fresh Produce Supply Chains in South Asian Countries*. Food and Agriculture Organization.

Rolle, R. S. and Esguerra, E. B. (2018). *Case Studies on Managing Quality, Assuring Safety and Reducing Post-harvest Losses in Fruit and Vegetable Supply Chains in South Asian countries*. Food and Agriculture Organization.

Siddiqui, S. A., Ristow, B., Rahayu, T., Putra, N. S., Widya Yuwono, N., Nisa, K., Mategeko, B., Smetana, S., Saki, M., Nawaz, A. and Nagdalian, A. (2022). Black soldier fly larvae (BSFL) and their affinity for organic waste processing. *Waste Management*, 140, pp. 1–13.

Smith, M. R. and Myers, S. S. (2018). Impact of anthropogenic CO2 emissions on global human nutrition. *Nature Climate Change*, 8(9), pp. 834–839.

Statista Research Department. (2023). South Korea volume of household food waste recycled. https://www.statista.com/statistics/1380937/south-korea-volume-of-household-food-waste-recycled/

Statista Singapore. (2023). Volume of food waste generated in Singapore. https://www.statista.com/statistics/961794/volume-food-waste-generated-singapore/

Taylor, B. (2022). Brewed to perfection sustainably. *Waste Today Magazine*. https://www.wastetodaymagazine.com/news/crust-singapore-food-scraps-processing-brewery/

Tubiello, F., Karl, K., Flammini, A., Gutschow, J., Obli-Laryea, G., Conchedda, G., Pan, X., Qiu, S. Y., Heiðarsdóttir, H. H., Wanner, N., Quadrelli, R., Souza, L., Benoit, P., Hayek, M., Sandalow, D., Mencos Contreras, E., Rosenzweig, C., Rosero-Moncayo, J., Conforti, P. and Torero, M. (2022). Pre- and post-production processes increasingly dominate greenhouse gas emissions from agri-food systems. *Earth System Science Data*, 14(4), pp. 1795–1809.

UNEP. (2021). *UNEP Food Waste Index Report*. https://www.unep.org/resources/report/unep-food-waste-index-report-2021

UNEP DTU Partnership and United Nations Environment Programme. (2021). *Reducing Consumer Food Waste Using Green and Digital Technologies*. https://www.unep.org/resources/publication/reducing-consumer-food-waste-using-green-and-digital-technologies

United Nations Food Systems Summit. (2021). Achieving zero hunger by 2030. A review of quantitative assessments of synergies and trade-offs among the UN Sustainable Development Goals. https://doi.org/10.48565/scgr2021-2337

https://doi.org/10.1142/9789811278297_0023

Chapter 23

Yellow Biotechnology: Farmed Insects as a Source of Alternative Food and Feed

Christian Hermansen[1], Mahabubur Rahman Talukder[1], Till Röthig[2], Andreas Vilcinskas[2] and Melanie Weingarten[1]

[1]*Singapore Institute of Food and Biotechnology Innovation (SIFBI), Agency for Science, Technology and Research (A*STAR), Singapore*
[2]*Department of Bioresources, Fraunhofer Institute for Molecular Biology and Applied Ecology IME, Gießen, Germany*

23.1 Introduction

Yellow biotechnology, synonymous with insect biotechnology, is an emerging field in applied entomology. It encompasses biotechnological approaches to develop insects (or their molecules, cells, organs or associated microorganisms) into products and services facilitating or enabling specific applications in medicine (red biotechnology), agriculture (green biotechnology) and/or industry (white biotechnology) [Vilcinskas, 2013]. This includes applications in drug discovery, preclinical research, plant protection, industrial and food biotechnology. Yellow represents the mixed colour of the interfacing red, green and white biotechnology, and the colour of insect haemolymph, the insect analogue to blood (Figure 23.1).

Figure 23.1 Yellow biotechnology revolves around insects and interfaces with medicine (red biotechnology), agriculture (green biotechnology) and industry (white biotechnology). Illustration provided courtesy of Professor Andreas Vilcinskas, Fraunhofer IME [Vilcinskas, 2013].

Based on its wide application range, yellow biotechnology facilitates environmental, social and economic sustainability and therefore bioeconomy on a global scale. In the context of food security, insects are a promising resource to valorise biogenic sidestreams to nutritious food and feed, thereby minimising waste, facilitating food security and a sustainable circular economy [van Huis *et al.*, 2021]. The United Nations have formulated 17 interlinked Sustainable Development Goals (SDGs) to foster peace and prosperity for people and the planet [FAO, 2019]. Insects as feed have been linked to directly support 5 SDGs [Dicke, 2018] and as food to 7 SDGs [Moruzzo *et al.*, 2021], underlining their sustainability potential.

In Asia, about 400 million people are estimated to be undernourished in 2020 and the COVID-19 crisis is furthering inequalities in access to food [FAO *et al.*, 2022]. This, in part, is caused by a food waste problem. Worldwide, approximately one-third of all produced food is lost or wasted, amounting to a staggering 1.3 billion tons in

2007 [FAO, 2013a], and estimated to almost have doubled to 2.5 billion tons in 2021 [WWF-UK, 2019]. Industrialised Asia (China, Japan and Republic of Korea), South and Southeast Asia together account for about 50% of the global food waste [FAO, 2013a]. This waste and its concomitant large carbon footprint contribute to climate change and further food insecurities [FAO, 2013a]. Insect farming allows upcycling of nutrients from biogenic side-streams and food waste into high-quality biomass, offering a toehold to tackle the food and waste crisis. Given a supportive legal framework, insect protein in particular can return into the food chain in a safe manner, bolster food security, sustainability, and create economic value in Asia [Yen, 2015].

23.2 Insects and Food Security

23.2.1 *Insects in Food*

There are currently more than 1 million described insect species, and millions more believed undiscovered. For humans, insects are valuable resources but also pests. Insects and certain microbiota they transmit can severely affect crop and human health [Deutsch *et al.*, 2018]. However, they are also invaluable pollinators for crops and a traditional, important food source in some parts of the world (i.e., Asia and Africa). Worldwide, around 2,000 insect species are edible and consumed by humans (entomophagy). Around 500 species of insects are consumed in Asia (Figure 23.2), and several have been proposed as flagship species to promote entomophagy [Yen, 2015]. Palm weevils (*Rhynchophorus ferrugineus*) from the Sago palm are popular across the continent and regionally a highly prized delicacy [Yen, 2015]. Demand for crickets, such as the two-spotted cricket (*Gryllus bimaculatus*) and locusts including

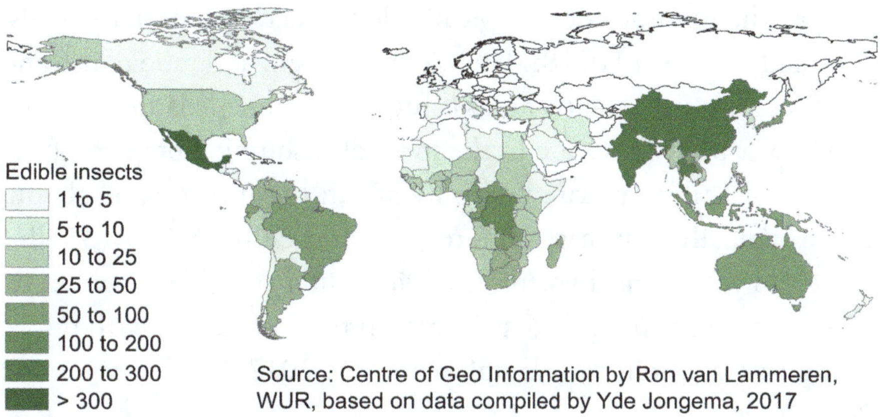

Figure 23.2 Global distribution of insect species diversity for human consumption. Illustration provided courtesy of Professor Ron van Lammeren, Wageningen University [Jongema, 2017].

the Bombay locust (*Patanga succincta*), outstrips natural supply in Thailand, necessitating their import and farming [Yen, 2015]. Moths and their larvae like Bogong moths (*Agrotis infusa*) and witjuti grubs (*Endoxyla leucomochla* and other species) are traditionally eaten in Australia, while the bamboo worm (*Omphisa fuscidentalis*) is popular in China, Thailand and Laos [Yen, 2015]. Aquatic insects such as the giant water bug (*Lethocerus indicus*) are eaten in several Asian countries [Yen, 2015]. Ants and termites, for example the weaver ant (*Oecophylla smaragdina*), are used as food, feed, medicine and a biological control agent [Yen, 2015].

Insects are nutritionally rich food, composed of protein, fat, carbohydrate and other micronutrients such as minerals and vitamins. Protein content is highly variable from 7% to 65% dry matter depending on the type and development stage [Nowakowski *et al.*, 2022]. Similarly, fat content ranges between 10% and 60% dry matter and depends mostly on species and life stage, with larvae being fattier. The lipid profile is typically dominated by C18 fatty acids, especially oleic acid (C18:1), while the content and ratio of n-6 and n-3 polyunsaturated fatty acids is highly variable [Adámková *et al.*, 2017]. Carbohydrates are in the form of insoluble fibre composed mainly of chitin, a structural polymer in the insect exoskeleton. Fibre typically comprises 8% to 27% and chitin 6% to 13% dry matter in yellow mealworm (*Tenebrio molitor*) and black soldier fly (BSF; *Hermetia illucens*), depending on their life cycle, with pupae being richer in chitin [Adámková *et al.*, 2017; Soetemans *et al.*, 2020].

Edible insects are a good source of minerals such as K, Na, Ca, Cu, Fe, Zn, Mn and P as well as B vitamins riboflavin, pantothenic acid and biotin, while farmed insects such as the yellow mealworm (*T. molitor*) and house cricket (*Acheta domesticus*) also contain cobalamin (vitamin B_{12}) and iron in similar or higher amounts than meat [Nowakowski *et al.*, 2022]. Other vitamins are typically low in insects, but can at least partially be fortified by supplying favourable insect feed (substrate). Insects are therefore able to replace meat and dairy products in a well-balanced human diet [Kouřimská and Adámková, 2016], and insects have traditionally been part of the human diet in many parts of the world [FAO, 2013b]. Insects are now being rediscovered as a sustainable source of alternative protein, and are globally receiving growing interest as novel foods [van Huis *et al.*, 2021].

23.2.2 *Insects in Feed*

Additional to direct consumption, insects can enter the human food chain as animal feed. Many animals include insects in their natural diet, like chicken, pigs and many fish species [Dicke, 2018]. However, current livestock farming employs species-specific and insect-free formulated feeds, especially in Europe and North America [Dicke, 2018]. For example, fed aquaculture, one of the fastest growing animal production sectors, relies on unsustainable fishmeal and fish oil with limited availability. Current substitutes including soy and animal by-products are also largely unsustainable or lack suitable nutritional properties [Röthig *et al.*, 2022]. However, insects like BSF (*H. illucens*), housefly (*Musca domestica*), yellow mealworm (*T. molitor*), lesser mealworm (*Alphitobius diaperinus*), house cricket (*A. domesticus*), banded cricket (*Gryllodes sigillatus*), Jamaican field cricket (*Gryllus assimilis*) and silkworm (*Bombyx mori*) have been successfully demonstrated to at least partly replace fishmeal and fish oil, especially for carnivorous fish [Henry *et al.*, 2015]. Insects like BSF and yellow mealworm are defatted to simplify feed formulation, processing and to optimise production rates in aquaculture species [Alfiko *et al.*, 2022]. To prevent potential deficiencies, certain micronutrients, for example lysine and methionine, are used as feed supplements [Henry *et al.*, 2015]. Importantly, initial trials using insects as sustainable feed ingredients for aquaculture demonstrate promising economic viability [Arru *et al.*, 2019; Rawski *et al.*, 2020]. In both aquaculture and for terrestrial animals, insect-based feed have been found to boost health and immunity [Lee *et al.*, 2022]. The potential of insects for feed applications are now being realised and thus there is much interest in safely scaling up and commercialising their production [Dicke, 2018].

23.2.3 *Insects and Microbes*

The goal of the food production chain is to produce safe and nutritious food. This includes the nutritional composition of the product and the absence of directly or indirectly harmful substances. In this context, it is important to consider that insects are holobionts that consist of the animal host and its associated microbial community including bacteria, fungi and viruses [Wilson and Duncan, 2015]. The microbial partners found both internally and externally, referred to as the microbiome, are essential for many processes, including nutrient availability and absorption, immunology, behaviour, fertility and mating preferences [Gupta and Nair, 2020]. Whereas many wild insects might contain pathogens (e.g., transmission of malaria-causing *Plasmodium spp.* via mosquitoes), insect species for industrial production are selected for their low potential to transmit pathogens. They often possess a high propensity to control pathogens or unwanted microbes, for example by expressing certain antimicrobial peptides, and some gut microbiota have been shown to degrade pesticides [Mikonranta *et al.*, 2014]. For consumers, the risk of insect-derived pathogens is generally regarded as low based on the insects' phylogenetic distance to humans [Hardy *et al.*, 2015]. However, substrate-supplied pathogens can be carried over and toxins, including heavy metals, can accumulate in most insects making stringent substrate regulations and monitoring essential [Diener *et al.*, 2015]. Such regulations are already in place in the European Union (EU Regulation (EC) No 178/2002).

23.2.4 *Insect Farming*

Only 2% of edible insect species are estimated to be farmed at any scale [Yen, 2015]. Insect farming practices vary widely depending on the species, scale of operation, and cultural background. For example, silk has been farmed in China at large scale for thousands of years, and crickets are traditionally reared in Asia by smallholder farmers as a delicatessen, and are now also farmed industrially in the West. Based on its high nutritional value, benefits for growth, health and immunity, low requirements of water and land area, low risk for the spread of disease and ability to grow efficiently on a very broad range of substrates, the FAO has identified BSF (*H. illucens*) as an excellent candidate for feed production. BSF is now well studied and reared commercially across the world [FAO, 2013b], with a projected global demand of half a million tons of insect protein by 2030 [van Huis, 2022].

The leading BSF companies by funding raised and their headquarters are InnovaFeed (France), Agronutris (France), BioFlyTech (Spain), Protix B.V. (Netherlands), NextProtein (France), Nutrition Technologies (Singapore), Entocycle (UK), Entogreen (Portugal), Enviroflight (USA) and Veolia (France). Nine of the ten companies are headquartered in the West, and they are pursuing large-scale intensive BSF farming with a high degree of automation in the production line. For example, Protix opened the world's largest BSF production facility in 2019 with 14,000 square meters of floor space, and state-of-the-art fully automated processing solutions [Bühler AG, 2019]. A standardised BSF larvae production concept developed by Bühler AG is illustrated in Figure 23.3.

In contrast to the West, Asia has a long history of entomophagy and rearing of insects such as silkworms (*B. mori* and *Antheraea pernyi*), crickets (*A. domesticus* and *G. bimaculatus*), and more recently flies (BSF and *M. domestica*) and mealworms (*T. molitor* and *A. diaperinus*) intended for feed applications [Raheem *et al.*, 2019; Yen, 2015]. Asia's commercial insect farming takes place in Australia, China, India, Indonesia, Malaysia, South Korea, Singapore, Thailand and Vietnam [Yen, 2015]. Some of the globally leading BSF companies (see above) are located in Asia as well as some smaller production sites including Entobel (Vietnam), Protenga (Malaysia) and Flylab (Thailand). In addition, there are numerous pilot-scale BSF operations looking to secure funding for scaling up to industrial production.

Figure 23.3 Standardised BSF larvae production in an insect protein plant designed by Bühler AG. Illustration provided courtesy of Bühler AG [Bühler AG, 2022].

The following section will describe the details of BSF farming in Asia, as BSF (*H. illucens*) is the leading insect species globally, the runner-up being the yellow mealworm (*T. molitor*). This allows for contrasting the Asian *status quo* with the global, industrialised state-of-the-art insect farming from both academic and industrial perspectives.

23.3 Black Soldier Fly Farming in Asia

23.3.1 *Black Soldier Fly Substrates*

For industrialised insect production, the utilisation of inexpensive and sustainable substrates enables insects to facilitate sustainable, circular economy in the food and feed sector. The key to scaling up are sources of suitable substrates at large volume, constant quality, low cost, year-round availability and near the factory. Some insects, such as BSF, are practically omnivorous and will grow well on substrates dedicated for waste treatment and not approved for animal feed in most countries, such as municipal organic waste, slaughterhouse waste, animal manure and faecal sludge. BSF are typically reared on various combinations of agro-industrial waste, food processing side-streams, food and restaurant waste. Common substrates widely available and permitted as animal feed, such as brewer's spent grain, industrial food waste and vegetable overproduction have been well studied (Figure 23.4) [Broeckx *et al.*, 2021; Ffoulkes *et al.*, 2021]. Substrate composition affects the insect

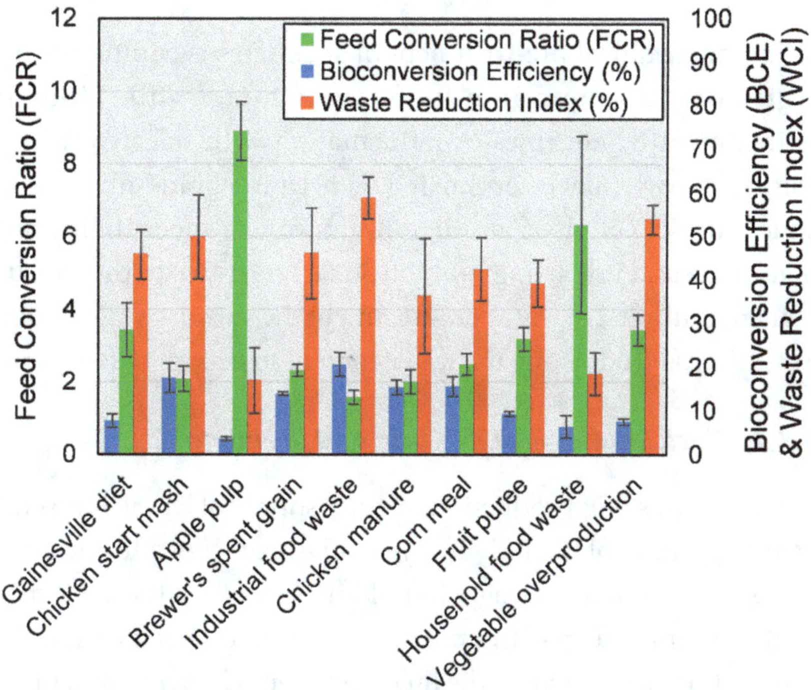

Figure 23.4 Feed conversion ratio, bioconversion efficiency and waste reduction index for BSF rearing on typical substrates [Broeckx *et al.*, 2021].

composition, quality and growth, and needs to be consistent [Broeckx *et al.*, 2021].

The amounts and compositions of available substrates are different in Asia, and some major side-streams are not commonly found in the West, including rice, soybean, banana, coconut and palm oil-related side-streams. These substrates are little studied for insect production and offer new opportunities [Foo, 2021; Kim *et al.*, 2021]. This also includes biogenic waste products that themselves pose current environmental or waste management problems at their production sites, like palm oil production waste [Mohd Hanafiah *et al.*, 2022]. However, process development is required to efficiently utilise new substrates, potentially necessitating physical, thermal, biological and chemical pre-treatment.

For BSF, mechanical pre-treatment of substrates is commonly done by grinding to 5 mm in a knife- or hammer-mill. Biological pre-treatment by enzymes or fermentation with selected microorganisms is particularly promising as it can degrade fibre such as hemicellulose, cellulose and lignin, improving digestibility, nutritional value and imparting probiotic characteristics to the substrate [Peguero *et al.*, 2022]. After pre-treatment the substrate is formulated by blending and adjusting the water content to maximise BSF growth.

23.3.2 *Black Soldier Fly Life Cycle and Breeding*

For continuous BSF production, regular supply of larvae is essential. At the beginning of the BSF life cycle, mating is typically performed in 12 × 2 m^3 wire mesh cage, but often as small as 1 × 2 × 2 m^3 for small-scale producers. In contrast to temperate regions such as Europe and the U.S. where the breeding cage is kept in a greenhouse or heated, in tropical Asia the breeding cage is air-conditioned to maintain a suitable temperature around 30°C [Chia *et al.*, 2018]. Natural light is rarely used; instead, light-emitting diodes with a daylight-like spectrum are employed. Relative humidity will typically be in the range of 50–70% in oftentimes air-conditioned rooms. Smelly attractants such as decaying organic matter are used to entice BSF to egg traps, typically in proprietary stackable egg traps, alternatively in cardboard stacks or wood blocks for smaller producers. Each BSF female lays around 500 eggs in the interstices in the egg trap. This is referred to as oviposition, for which BSF prefers interstices slightly wider than their 1 mm egg size and with a depth of 7–10 mm [Tomberlin *et al.*, 2002]. Shortly after ovipositioning the female BSF dies.

Egg traps are placed in or over a nursery container, and about 70% of the eggs will hatch over a period of about 4 days. The nursery container is typically replaced daily to ensure uniform age of larvae. Neonate larvae are reared in the nursery for 4–6 days. 2–5% of the neonates are utilised for breeding and the rest for production. Larval numbers are estimated by sample counts and weight. For breeding purposes, neonates are grown out to larvae for about two weeks in a dedicated nursery and continuously fed with high quality feed (e.g., chicken feed). The larvae stop feeding and migrate to a dry location to pupate over a period of 7–12 days. The pupae are transferred to environmentally controlled dark cages, where they start to emerge as adult flies 10 to 14 days after pupation. The adult BSF require light stimulation to move or mate and are attracted to and stimulated by the mating cage light. Adult BSF live for only 3–8 days, do not feed and subsist only on water and stored fat deposits acquired in their larval stage. Thus is the life cycle of BSF from egg to adult (Figure 23.5).

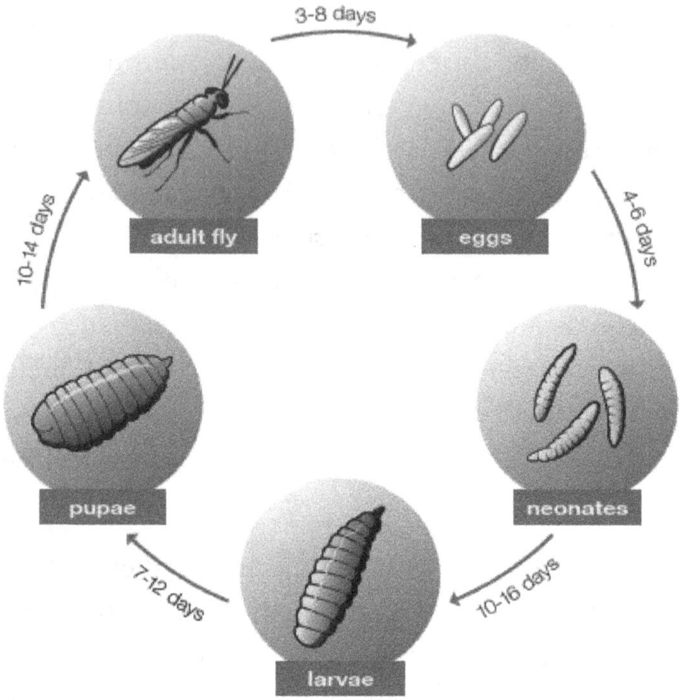

Figure 23.5 BSF life cycle from egg to neonate larva, pre-pupa larva, pupa and to adult fly. Illustration provided courtesy of Bühler AG [Bühler AG, 2022].

23.3.3 *Black Soldier Fly Larvae Production*

While some adult BSF are required for egg production, most larvae are harvested before pupation. In the main production facility neonates are grown to larvae using formulated substrate, as discussed previously. Typically, production is performed in stacked trays reminiscent of vertical farming setups and allowing for ventilation between trays (Figure 23.6). A common tray size is 40 × 60 × 17 cm suitable for 15 kg of wet substrate at about 80% moisture hosting 10,000 neonates, making for about 40,000 larvae per square meter tray area. Larger tray sizes enable scaling of substrate amounts and larvae, if appropriate ventilation, temperature,

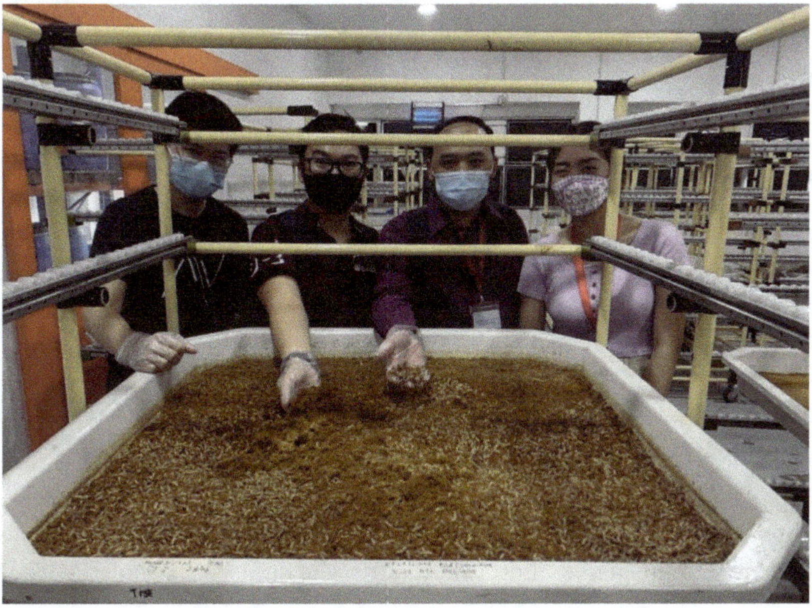

Figure 23.6 A pilot-scale BSF production facility located in Singapore. Illustration provided courtesy of Ento Industries.

humidity and other conditions can be maintained on process scale-up.

Adding to the starting substrate, additional feedings for example after 5 and 8 days may be required as thick substrate layer may affect the turnover. Depending on the facility, prior to harvesting around day 10, additional air circulation may be employed to lower temperature and reduce moisture content, thus allowing for easier separation of larvae and substrate.

23.3.4 *Black Soldier Fly Harvesting and Refining*

Harvesting is done by separating larvae and substrate on a rotating cylinder sieve or high-frequency shaking sieve with a recommended 5 mm to 6 mm gap or mesh size [Peng *et al.*, 2022]. In dry

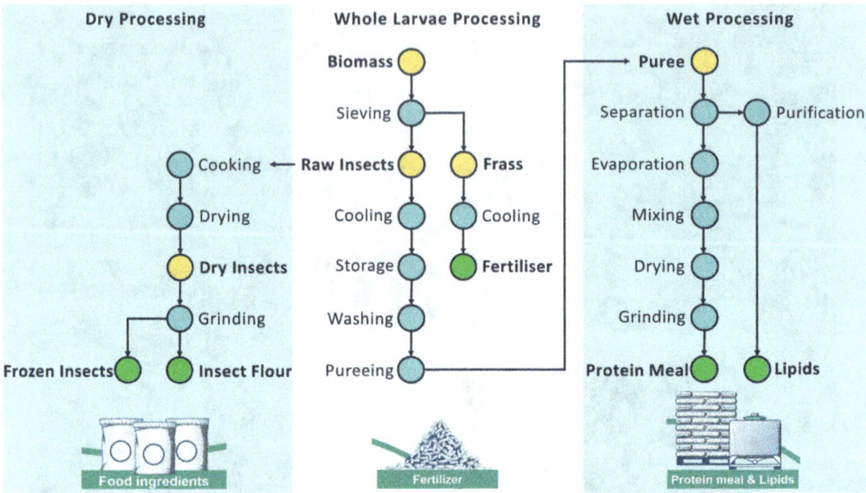

Figure 23.7 Examples of harvesting and refining process flows for insect production. Adapted from illustration courtesy of Bühler AG [Bühler AG, 2022].

processing, BSF larvae can be devitalised and sanitised for example in boiling water for 2 minutes, by oven drying or freezing. Typically, larvae are oven dried to reduce the moisture content below 10% or even below 5%, which allows for long-term storage. Final products are dried or frozen insects or flour (Figure 23.7).

BSF larvae contain about 30% fat, which can turn rancid on prolonged storage. Defatting can be performed by oil pressing, centrifugation or solvent extraction, resulting in an insect oil and insect protein fraction. During wet processing for oil extraction the larvae are pureed, then pasteurised, oil extracted, and the larval puree evaporated, dried and ground. Final products are insect lipids and protein meals (Figure 23.7).

23.3.5 *BSF Products and Applications*

Dried or frozen BSF larvae can be readily obtained with minimal processing and typically contain about 40% protein, 30% fat, 10%

carbohydrate, 10% ash and 10% moisture, depending on substrate, rearing conditions and post-processing [Shumo *et al.*, 2019]. Unprocessed dried BSF larvae are used for pet food and animal feed application, including chicken and pigs. Currently aquafeed and pet food are the largest target market for BSF larvae that provides sufficient margins according to the current scale and costs of BSF production [Niyonsaba *et al.*, 2021].

In order to formulate BSF as feed ingredient product, defatting and dosing the insect protein and oil fraction separately is a standard practice to avoid complications in the pelletisation process and simplify feed formulation. The insect oil extracted from BSF is high in saturated fatty acids (typically 60% to 80% of fats), especially lauric acid (typically 40% to 50% of fats) [Ewald *et al.*, 2020]. The oil has high gross energy content, high oxidative stability due to the high saturated fatty acid content, and also antibacterial and antiviral properties due to the lauric acid. While lauric acid gives an unpleasant taste for humans, the BSF oil is a suitable replacement of coconut or palm kernel oil in many other applications. The oil is used in feed applications, such as broiler chickens and piglets, but is not suitable as a replacement of fish oil, which is high in polyunsaturated fatty acids [Ewald *et al.*, 2020].

A by-product of BSF production is frass, the residue of the substrate remaining after rearing and separating the larvae consisting of insect faeces and exuviae. Depending on the substrate, frass composition and amounts vary between 200 and 700 kg per ton of substrate [Lopes *et al.*, 2022]. Total carbon is around 37%, nitrogen 3%, phosphorous 1–5% and potassium 0.5–4.1%, the latter two being more variable depending on the substrate [Lopes *et al.*, 2022]. The processing of BSF frass is highly variable between different suppliers, but typically consists of some degree of composting with natural

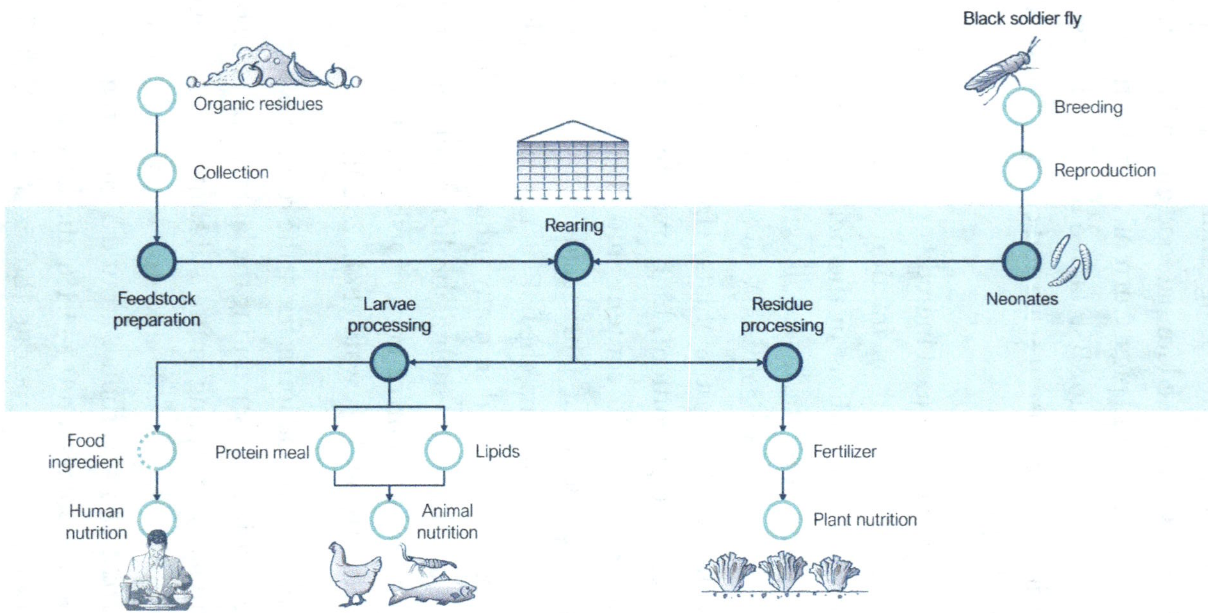

Figure 23.8 BSF inputs, processes and products. Illustration provided courtesy of Bühler AG [Bühler AG, 2022].

microbial flora, crushing, mixing, pelleting, drying, sieving and packaging. BSF frass is used as an organic fertiliser that generally performs similar or superior to commercial products [Lopes *et al.*, 2022]. Performance maxima are attributed to beneficial compounds or microorganisms derived from the substrate and insects, some of which have plant growth-promoting properties. For example, chitin from the exoskeleton is known to suppress plant-parasitic fungi and nematodes in soil [Lopes *et al.*, 2022]. BSF frass also contains potentially plant growth-promoting microorganisms, such as *Bacillus spp.*, *Lactobacillus spp.*, *Actinobacteria spp.* and *Pseudomonas spp.* [Lopes *et al.*, 2022]. It should be noted here that in November 2021 EU regulation 142/2011 was modified to require insect excrements, such as BSF frass, to be heated to 70°C for one hour before further utilisation, which is expected to heavily reduce viable microorganisms, both beneficial and pathogenic [Lopes *et al.*, 2022]. However, currently there are no such regulations in place in Asia, offering an opportunity to more economically develop frass as a high-value organic fertiliser including plant growth-promoting microorganisms.

Finally, a range of high-value food, cosmetic and pharmaceutical ingredients such as chitin, chitosan, melanin and antimicrobial peptides can be extracted from BSF [Khayrova *et al.*, 2020; Manniello *et al.*, 2021]. The extraction, purification, and application processes are mostly still at the research and development stage. An overview of BSF-derived products and applications is provided (Figure 23.8).

23.4 Future Prospects

23.4.1 *Yellow Biotechnology for Food Security in Asia*

The warm and humid tropical climate in most of Asia is ideal for insect rearing, as insects are naturally cold-blooded and increase their metabolic rate at higher temperatures. BSF larvae in particular have an optimum feeding temperature of 30°C and tolerate temperatures of up to 44°C [Chia *et al.*, 2018].

Asia contains about 60% of the world population and produces 40% of the worlds' meat [Ritchie *et al.*, 2017; Roser and Rodés-Guirao, 2013]. Demand for meat products in Asia is increasing, and large quantities of feed ingredients are imported, such as soybean, corn and wheat products [Lee and Hansen, 2019]. Asia, and predominantly China, is the world centre for aquaculture, with more than 90% of global production in 2020 [FAO, 2022]. An estimated 33 million tons of aquafeed was consumed in eight Asian countries with large aquaculture industries in 2020 [Merica, 2021]. Locally produced insects such as BSF and mealworms could reduce reliance on imports and unsustainable compounds and ensure the food security and sustainability of Asian aquaculture.

The long history of entomophagy and traditional farming of insects in Asia increases consumer acceptance of insects as a food compared to the West. Insects as food compared to insects as feed applications skips a trophic level and lowers required resources by a factor of two or more. There is an opportunity for technical advances in insect farming leading to higher efficiencies, lower costs and improved food security in the region. The main challenge for technological progress in the Asian insect farming industry is scale-up. Current practice of rearing in trays is labour intensive, and there are efforts to increase automation, especially in state-of-the-art facilities in the West. Technology providers now offer high-tech turn-key insect production plants, production lines and individual equipment for BSF and mealworm production and processing [Bühler AG, 2022]. In Asia, manpower costs are still relatively inexpensive for insect production facilities which hampers the automatisation progress. Thus, in Asia an alternative to intensive scale-up might be scale-out. Many relatively small and less capital-intensive insect farms in rural communities near substrate sources could become economically viable if an insect market arises with attractive prices for insect products, or if using non-approved substrates such as manure becomes feasible [Groeneveld *et al.*, 2021]. A circular economy concept using insects is presented which could be applied in Asia (Figure 23.9).

The cost of insect production must come down to realise this concept, as insects are still expensive compared to most animal and plant alternatives. One important avenue for further development is the identification of inexpensive substrates and pre-treatment

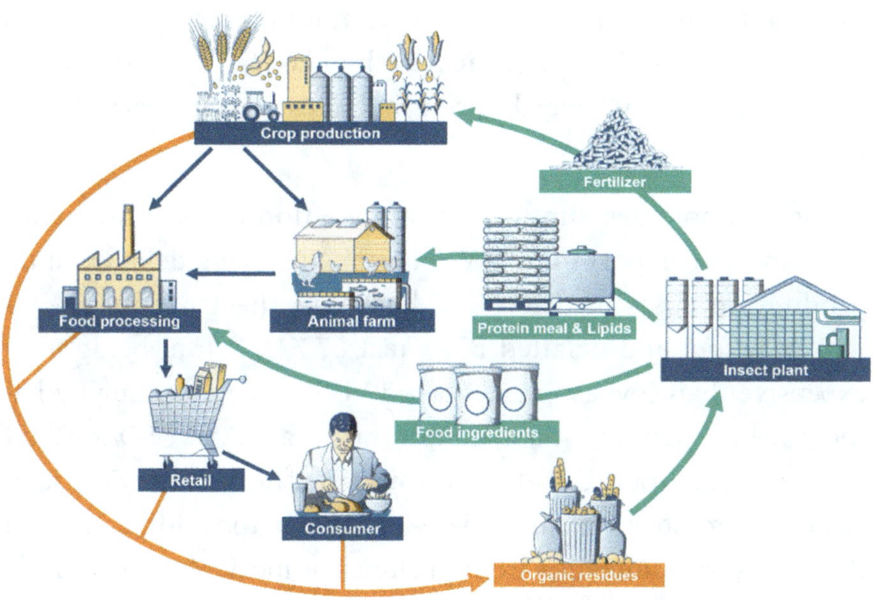

Figure 23.9 Circular economy concept utilising insects for conversion of organic residues to food ingredients, protein meals, lipids and fertilisers. Illustration provided courtesy of Bühler AG [Bühler AG, 2022].

technologies to develop high-yielding insect substrates. This is especially relevant for Asia, where widely available waste streams are less well studied. Inspiration can be taken from pre-treatment for biogas production which is also a biological digestion process and is better studied [Peguero *et al.*, 2022]. Genetic improvement of insects is another non-controversial avenue expected to lead to higher growth and yield, similar to what has been achieved in animal agriculture. Given the short generation time of insects, large improvements can be obtained quickly, for example 26% improvement in dry matter yield and 4% in feed conversion ratio was reported for BSF after 16 generations of artificial selection [Facchini *et al.*, 2022]. Genetic editing of insects and their microbiome is considered controversial compared to artificial selection but could greatly increase the productivity. Knocking out the prothoracicotropic hormone (*ptth*) that initiates the moulting signalling cascade resulted in a 20-fold increase in length of last larval stage and 2–3 fold increase in body weight prior to harvest in BSF [Barrett *et al.*, 2022].

These technologies aim to reduce operation costs and increase profitability. A report from WWF optimistically modelled that the production costs of dried BSF larvae in the UK could reach 750 USD/ton, and defatted BSF meal 675 USD/ton, being more expensive than soybean meal (ca. 550 USD/ton), but roughly half the price of soybean protein concentrate (ca. 1,250 USD/ton) and fishmeal (ca. 1,600 USD/ton) [Ffoulkes *et al.*, 2021]. This is an attractive proposition, and Asia is in a strong position to achieve this. Asia's predominantly tropical climate is ideal for insect farming and reduces energy costs for heating; labour costs are low, there are abundant high-quality and underutilised substrates available, and regulations are less strict allowing for employment of additional substrates and development of innovative products such as insects for human food or frass as biofertiliser. Additionally, possible future taxes on greenhouse gases including CO_2 will benefit the insect farming industry, as it diverts waste streams from composting or incineration processes generating CO_2 into insect products [Mertenat *et al.*, 2019]. Partial replacement of imported fish meal and soy meal in aquafeed and animal feed applications seems to be an ambitious yet achievable goal for the Asian insect farming industry.

23.4.2 *Consumer Acceptance*

Consumer acceptance is essential for the development of the growing and increasingly industrialised global insect production. Consumer acceptance is mostly driven by traditions, food processing/preparation, quality, price, background knowledge and availability [Arena *et al.*, 2020; Sogari *et al.*, 2019; Szendro *et al.*, 2020]. More than two billion people regularly consume insects in the Global South whereas in other parts of the world insects are largely considered as novel food [Feng *et al.*, 2018; Raheem *et al.*, 2019; Sogari *et al.*, 2019]. Insect feed is likely to be accepted more favourably provided that aroma, texture and price of the product are not compromised [Cunha and Ribeiro, 2019; Gasco *et al.*, 2019; Rumbos *et al.*, 2021]. Consumer acceptance can, however, be positively influenced by advertising the benefits of insect food and feed, including sustainability and health aspects [Cunha and Ribeiro, 2019; Gasco *et al.*, 2019].

23.4.3 *Legal Framework*

Alongside consumer acceptance, the success of insects as food and feed largely depends on the legal framework, which differs widely across global jurisdictions. For example, by 2022 the EU has permitted three insects (*T. molitor*, *Locusta migratoria* and *A. domesticus*) for human consumption and the application of eight insect species (BSF, *M. domestica*, *T. molitor*, *A. domesticus*, *G. sigillatus*, *G. assimilis*, *A. diaperinus* and *B. mori*) as feed ingredients for aquaculture, poultry and pig production. In the USA, insects as food have not yet officially been recognised and regulated and only BSF is an approved animal feed ingredient for limited application [Lähteenmäki-Uutela *et al.*, 2021]. Countries in Asia that traditionally endorse entomophagy employ more favourable legislatures. For example, China has novel food regulations similar to the EU, but since 324 species of insects have traditionally been used for food, feed and medicinal applications, these are not considered novel foods [Feng *et al.*, 2018; Lähteenmäki-Uutela *et al.*, 2021]. In Japan, grasshoppers (*Oxya japonica* and *yezoensis*), larvae and pupae of wasps (*Vespula lewisi*) and silkworm (*B. mori*) are traditionally consumed, and in addition novel foods do not require pre-market authorisation [Lähteenmäki-Uutela *et al.*, 2021]. Singapore is looking to approve 16 insect species for human consumption, while others could be approved following a novel food application to the Singapore Food Agency [SFA, 2022].

Particularly, insect substrates which contain faeces and municipal waste are of regulatory concern, as these materials can contain high levels of pathogens and harmful contaminants, such as microbial toxins, heavy metals, or prions potentially carrying over into the insects. Regulations in Asia regarding animal feeds are less strict than in the West, and typically not well defined for insect farming [Lähteenmäki-Uutela *et al.*, 2021]. Singapore recently drafted regulations that permit substrates that have undergone controlled fermentation, but does not permit manure, decomposing organic material, materials originating from diseased animals or fish, and materials of ruminant origin excepting deboned meat cuts and dairy (e.g., milk and cheese) products [SFA, 2022]. While comparably generous laws in Asia likely facilitate the regional development, the globally heterogeneous legislation hampers the industrialisation of insect production, as international producers must adhere to different regulations depending on production and customer locations.

23.5 Conclusion

The interest to use insects as food and feed is increasing exponentially on a global scale due to (a) the potential to be a suitable alternative protein source with respect to feeding a growing world population, (b) to become more independent on recent supply chain disruptions encountered during the COVID-19 pandemic, and (c) to deliver sustainable solutions for our planet [Dicke, 2018]. Insects have the tremendous advantage to be used as food and feed. The nutritional value of insects is comparable in many aspects to meat products [Kouřimská and Adámková, 2016]. Furthermore, insects have great potential to provide additional high-value products such as food, cosmetic and pharmaceutical ingredients.

However, mainly based on still immature production systems, insect products are relatively expensive. To lower the price, research should focus on developing pre-treatment solutions to high-yielding insect substrates, genetic improvement of insects, and high-efficiency automated and digitised production systems. BSF can thrive on many biogenic side-streams such as food waste and this contributes to a circular economy concept. However, food or agricultural waste employed as insect substrates requires close monitoring for chemical and biological contaminants (e.g., heavy metals, pesticides and mycotoxins). To valorise a broader range of waste, insect-microbe symbiosis poses a promising and presumably adjustable system. Traditional breeding of insects is non-controversially expected to lead to higher yields and growth rate, similar to what has been achieved in animal agriculture. Genetic modifications of insects and their microbiome are controversial but could greatly increase the productivity if accepted by consumers and regulatory bodies. We note that genetic modification of mosquitoes and related pathogens for pest control are increasingly accepted and implemented [Beech *et al.*, 2012]. Automation, digitalisation and continuous production systems are best developed in the West where manpower costs are high, and can be implemented in Asia when the technology is mature and the economic benefits are clear.

Most societies in the West are not accustomed to entomophagy, and strategies to increase consumer acceptance are necessary, for example by informing on hygienic safety, environmental sustainability, and palatability. Asia has a long history of using insects for food, feed and medicine, and face fewer consumer acceptance and regulatory barriers. The use of insects for animal feed applications is increasingly accepted and poses a well-developed market especially in the pet feed and aquaculture sectors.

The insect sector is developing fast, and is seeking to scale up rapidly in the next five years, which can only be achieved by close cooperation of all stakeholders. Industry and academia are engaged in developing competitive, healthy and safe insect products, and cooperating with governmental and legal entities to progress yellow biotechnology successfully.

References

Adámková, A., Mlček, J., Kouřimská, L., Borkovcová, M., Bušina, T., Adámek, M., Bednářová, M. and Krajsa, J. (2017). Nutritional potential of selected insect species reared on the island of Sumatra. *International Journal of Environmental Research and Public Health,* 14(5), p. 521.

Alfiko, Y., Xie, D., Astuti, R. T., Wong, J. and Wang, L. (2022). Insects as a feed ingredient for fish culture: Status and trends. *Aquaculture and Fisheries*, 7, pp. 166–178.

Arena, E., Mazzaglia, A., Selvaggi, R., Pecorino, B. and Fallico, B. (2020). Exploring consumer's propensity to consume insect-based foods. empirical evidence from a study in southern Italy. *Applied System Innovation*, 3(3), p. 38.

Arru, B., Furesi, R., Gasco, L., Madau, F. A. and Pulina, P. (2019). The introduction of insect meal into fish diet: The first economic analysis on European sea bass farming. *Sustainability*, 11, pp. 1–16.

Barrett, M., Chia, S. Y., Fischer, B. and Tomberlin, J. K. (2022). Welfare considerations for farming black soldier flies, Hermetia illucens (Diptera: Stratiomyidae): a model for the insects as food and feed industry. *Journal of Insects as Food and Feed,* 9(2), pp. 119–146.

Beech, C. J., Koukidou, M., Morrison, N. I. and Alphey, L. (2012). Genetically modified insects: science, use, status and regulation. *Collection of Biosafety Reviews*, 6, pp. 66–124.

Broeckx, L., Frooninckx, L., Slegers, L., Berrens, S., Noyens, I., Goossens, S., Verheyen, G., Wuyts, A. and Van Miert, S. (2021). Growth of black soldier fly larvae reared on organic side-streams. *Sustainability,* 13(23), p. 12953.

Bühler AG. (2019). Bühler congratulates Protix on opening the largest insect protein facility in the world. *Bühler Group.* https://www.buhlergroup.com/content/buhlergroup/global/en/media/media-releases/buehler_congratulatesprotixonopeningthelargestinsectproteinfacil.html

Bühler AG. (2022). Insects to feed the world. *Bühler Group*. https://www.buhlergroup.com/content/buhlergroup/global/en/industries/insect-technology.html

Chia, S. Y., Tanga, C. M., Khamis, F. M., Mohamed, S. A., Salifu, D., Sevgan, S., Fiaboe, K. K. M., Niassy, S., Van Loon, J. J. A., Dicke, M. and Ekesi, S. (2018). Threshold temperatures and thermal requirements of black soldier fly Hermetia illucens: Implications for mass production. *PLoS One*, 13, pp. 1–26.

Cunha, L. M. and Ribeiro, J. C. (2019). Sensory and Consumer Perspectives on Edible Insects. In G. Sogari, C. Mora and D. Mezonni (Eds.), *Edible Insects in the Food Sector*, pp. 57–71. Springer.

Deutsch, C. A., Tewksbury, J. J., Tigchelaar, M., Battisti, D. S., Merrill, S. C., Huey, R. B. and Naylor, R. L. (2018). Increase in crop losses to insect pests in a warming climate. *Science*, 361, pp. 916–919.

Dicke, M. (2018). Insects as feed and the Sustainable Development Goals. *Journal of Insects as Food and Feed,* 4, pp. 147–156.

Diener, S., Zurbrügg, C. and Tockner, K. (2015). Bioaccumulation of heavy metals in the black soldier fly, Hermetia illucens and effects on its life cycle. *Journal of Insects as Food and Feed*, 1, pp. 261–270.

Ewald, N., Vidakovic, A., Langeland, M., Kiessling, A., Sampels, S. and Lalander, C. (2020). Fatty acid composition of black soldier fly larvae (Hermetia illucens) — Possibilities and limitations for modification through diet. *Waste Management*, 102, pp. 40–47.

Facchini, E., Shrestha, K., Boer, E. Van Den, Junes, P. and Sader, G. (2022). Long-term artificial selection for increased larval body weight of Hermetia illucens in industrial settings. *Frontiers in Genetics*, 13, pp. 1–9.

FAO. (2013a). *Food Wastage Footprint: Impacts on Natural Resources.* https://www.fao.org/3/i3347e/i3347e.pdf

FAO. (2013b). *Edible Insects: Future Prospects for Food and Feed Security*. https://www.fao.org/fsnforum/resources/reports-and-briefs/edible-insects-future-prospects-food-and-feed-security

FAO. (2019). *The State of Food and Agriculture 2019: Moving Forward on Food Loss and Waste Reduction.* https://www.fao.org/policy-support/tools-and-publications/resources-details/en/c/1242090/

FAO. (2022). *The State of World Fisheries and Aquaculture 2022: Towards Blue Transformation.* https://doi.org/10.4060/cc0461en

FAO, IFAD, UNICEF, WFP and WHO. (2022). *The State of Food Security and Nutrition in the World 2022.* https://doi.org/10.4060/cc0639en

Feng, Y., Chen, X.-M., Zhao, M., He, Z., Sun, L., Wang, C.-Y. and Ding, W.-F. (2018). Edible insects in China: Utilization and prospects. *Insect Science*, 25, pp. 184–198.

Ffoulkes, C., Illman, H., O'connor, R., Lemon, F., Behrendt, K., Wynn, S., Wright, P., Godber, O., Ramsden, M., Adams, J., Metcalfe, P., Walker, L., Gittins, J., Wickland, K., Nanua, S. and Sharples, B. (2021). *WWF-UK and Tesco Development of a roadmap to scale up insect protein production in the UK for use in animal feed.* Technical Report prepared by ADAS and Michelmores for WWF-UK and Tesco.

Foo, Y. L. (2021). A primer on the black soldier fly market in Asia. *Mana Impact.* https://www.manaimpact.com/post/a-primer-on-the-black-soldier-fly-market-in-asia

Gasco, L., Biasato, I., Dabbou, S., Schiavone, A. and Gai, F. (2019). Quality and Consumer Acceptance of Products from Insect-Fed Animals. In G. Sogari, C. Mora and D. Mezonni (Eds.), *Edible Insects in the Food Sector*, pp. 73–86. Springer.

Groeneveld, I., Elissen, H., van Rozen, K. and van der Weide, R. (2021). The profitability potential of black soldier fly BSF) larvae raised on pig manure at farm level. *Wageningen University & Research.* https://doi.org/10.18174/549892

Gupta, A. and Nair, S. (2020). Dynamics of insect — microbiome interaction influence host and microbial symbiont. *Frontiers in Microbiology,* 11, p. 1367.

Hardy, A., Benford, D., Noteborn, H. P., Halldorsson, T. I., Schlatter, J., Solecki, R. A., Jeger, M., Knutsen, H. K., More, S., Mortensen, A., Naegeli, H., Ockleford, C., Ricci, A., Rychen, G., Silano, V. and Turck,

D. (2015). Risk profile related to production and consumption of insects as food and feed. *EFSA Journal*, 13, p. 4257.

Henry, M., Gasco, L., Piccolo, G. and Fountoulaki, E. (2015). Review on the use of insects in the diet of farmed fish: Past and future. *Animal Feed Science and Technology*, 203, pp. 1–22.

Jongema, Y. (2017). List of edible insects of the world. https://www.wur.nl/en/research-results/chair-groups/plant-sciences/laboratory-of-entomology/edible-insects/worldwide-species-list.htm

Khayrova, A., Lopatin, S. and Varlamov, V. (2020). Obtaining chitin / chitosan-melanin complexes from black soldier fly Hermetia illucens. *IOP Conference Series: Materials Science and Engineering*, 809, p. 012020.

Kim, C., Ryu, J., Lee, J., Ko, K., Lee, J.-Y., Park, K. Y. and Chung, H. (2021). Use of black soldier fly larvae for food waste treatment and energy production in Asian countries: a review. *Processes*, 9, p. 161.

Kouřimská, L. and Adámková, A. (2016). Nutritional and sensory quality of edible insects. *NFS Journal*, 4, pp. 22–26.

Lähteenmäki-Uutela, A., Marimuthu, S. B. and Meijer, N. (2021). Regulations on insects as food and feed: a global comparison. *Journal of Insects as Food and Feed,* 7, pp. 849–856.

Lee, J. H., Kim, T. K., Cha, J. Y., Jang, H. W., Yong, H. I. and Choi, Y. S. (2022). How to develop strategies to use insects as animal feed: digestibility, functionality, safety, and regulation. *Journal of Animal Science and Technology*, 64, pp. 409–431.

Lee, T. and Hansen, J. (2019). Southeast Asia's growing meat demand and its implications for feedstuffs imports. *USDA*. https://www.ers.usda.gov/amber-waves/2019/april/southeast-asia-s-growing-meat-demand-and-its-implications-for-feedstuffs-imports/

Lopes, I. G., Yong, J. W. and Lalander, C. (2022). Frass derived from black soldier fly larvae treatment of biodegradable wastes. A critical review and future perspectives. *Waste Managment*, 142, pp. 65–76.

Manniello, M. D., Moretta, A., Salvia, R., Scieuzo, C., Sgambato, A., Lucchetti, D. and Falabella, P. (2021). Insect antimicrobial peptides: potential weapons to counteract the antibiotic resistance. *Cellular and Molecular Life Sciences*, 78, pp. 4259–4282.

Merica, Z. (2021). Aquafeeds in 2019: Pulled by market demand. *Aquaculture Asia Pacific*. https://aquaasiapac.com/2021/05/05/aquafeeds-in-2019-pulled-by-market-demand/

Mertenat, A., Diener, S. and Zurbrügg, C. (2019). Black Soldier Fly biowaste treatment — Assessment of global warming potential. *Waste Managment*, 84, pp. 173–181.

Mikonranta, L., Mappes, J., Kaukoniitty, M. and Freitak, D. (2014). Insect immunity: oral exposure to a bacterial pathogen elicits free radical response and protects from a recurring infection. *Frontiers in Zoology*, 11, p. 23.

Mohd Hanafiah, K., Abd Mutalib, A. H., Miard, P., Goh, C. S., Mohd Sah, S. A. and Ruppert, N. (2022). Impact of Malaysian palm oil on sustainable development goals: co-benefits and trade-offs across mitigation strategies. *Sustainability Science,* 17, pp. 1639–1661.

Moruzzo, R., Mancini, S. and Guidi, A. (2021). Edible insects and sustainable development goals. *Insects*, 12, pp. 1–9.

Niyonsaba, H. H., Hohler, J., Kooistra, J., van der Fels-Klerx, H. J. and Meuwissen, M. P. M. (2021). Profitability of insect farms. *Journal of Insects as Food and Feed,* 7, pp. 923–934.

Nowakowski, A. C., Miller, A. C., Miller, M. E., Xiao, H. and Wu, X. (2022). Potential health benefits of edible insects. *Critical Reviews in Food Science and Nutrition*, 62, pp. 3499–3508.

Peguero, D. A., Gold, M., Vandeweyer, D., Zurbrügg, C. and Mathys, A. (2022). A review of pretreatment methods to improve agri-food waste bioconversion by black soldier fly larvae. *Frontiers in Sustainable Food Systems*, 5, pp. 1–9.

Peng, C., Zhou, T., Song, S., Sun, S., Yin, Y. and Xu, D. (2022). Design and experiment of black soldier fly frass mixture separation through a cylinder sieve with different rotation speeds. *Applied Science*, 12, p. 10597.

Raheem, D., Carrascosa, C., Oluwole, O. B., Nieuwland, M., Saraiva, A., Millán, R. and Raposo, A. (2019). Traditional consumption of and rearing edible insects in Africa, Asia and Europe. *Critical Reviews in Food Science and Nutrition*, 59, pp. 2169–2188.

Rawski, M., Mazurkiewicz, J., Kierończyk, B. and Józefiak, D. (2020). Black soldier fly full-fat larvae meal as an alternative to fish meal and fish oil in siberian sturgeon nutrition: The effects on physical properties of the feed, animal growth performance, and feed acceptance and utilization. *Animals*, 10, pp. 1–19.

Ritchie, H., Rosado, P. and Roser, M. (2017). Meat and dairy production. https://ourworldindata.org/meat-production

Roser, M. and Rodés-Guirao, L. (2013). Future population growth. https://ourworldindata.org/future-population-growth

Röthig, T., Barth, A., Tschirner, M., Schubert, P., Wenning, M., Billion, A., Wilke, T. and Vilcinskas, A. (2022). Insect feed in sustainable crustacean aquaculture. *Journal of Insects as Food and Feed*, 9(9), pp. 1115–1138.

Rumbos, C. I., Mente, E., Karapanagiotidis, I. T., Vlontzos, G. and Athanassiou, C. G. (2021). Insect-based feed ingredients for aquaculture: a case study for their acceptance in Greece. *Insects*, 12, p. 586.

Singapore Food Agency (SFA). (2022). Consultation on regulation of insect and insect productions (omports and locally farmed/processed). https://www.reach.gov.sg/Participate/Public-Consultation/Singapore-Food-Agency/consultation-on-regulation-of-insect-and-insect-products

Shumo, M., Osuga, I. M., Khamis, F. M., Tanga, C. M., Fiaboe, K. K. M., Subramanian, S., Ekesi, S., van Huis, A. and Borgemeister, C. (2019). The nutritive value of black soldier fly larvae reared on common organic waste streams in Kenya. *Scientific Reports*, 9, pp. 1–13.

Soetemans, L., Uyttebroek, M. and Bastiaens, L. (2020). Characteristics of chitin extracted from black soldier fly in different life stages.

International Journal of Biological Macromolecules, 165, pp. 3206–3214.

Sogari, G., Menozzi, D. and Mora, C. (2019). The food neophobia scale and young adults' intention to eat insect products. *International Journal of Consumer Studies*, 43, pp. 68–76.

Szendro, K., Nagy, M. Z. and Tóth, K. (2020). Consumer acceptance of meat from animals reared. *Animals,* 10, pp. 1–10.

Tomberlin, J. K., Sheppard, D. C. and Joyce, J. A. (2002). Selected life-history traits of black soldier flies (Diptera: Stratiomyidae) reared on three artificial diets. *Annals of the Entomological Society of America*, 95, pp. 379–386.

van Huis, A. (2022). Edible insects: Challenges and prospects. *Entomological Research*, 52, pp. 161–177.

van Huis, A., Rumpold, B. A., van der Fels-Klerx, H. J. and Tomberlin, J. K. (2021). Advancing edible insects as food and feed in a circular economy. *Journal of Insects as Food and Feed,* 7, pp. 935–948.

Vilcinskas, A. (Ed.) (2013). *Yellow Biotechnology II: Insect Biotechnology in Plant Protection and Industry*. Springer.

Wilson, A. C. C. and Duncan, R. P. (2015). Signatures of host/symbiont genome coevolution in insect nutritional endosymbioses. *Proceedings of the National Academy of Sciences*, 112(33), pp. 10255–10261.

WWF-UK. (2019). Driven to waste: the global impact of food loss a waste on farms. https://wwf.panda.org/discover/our_focus/food_practice/food_loss_and_waste/driven_to_waste_global_food_loss_on_farms

Yen, A. L. (2015). Insects as food and feed in the Asia Pacific region: Current perspectives and future directions. *Journal of Insects as Food and Feed*, 1, pp. 33–55.

Externalities in Food Security

https://doi.org/10.1142/9789811278297_0024

Chapter 24

Food and Nutrition Insecurity Caused by the Interplay of Conflict, Pandemic and Disasters: A West Timor Story

Jonatan Lassa[1] and John P. Talan[2,3]

[1]*The Northern Institute, Charles Darwin University, Australia*
[2]*Institute of Resource Governance and Social Change, Kupang, Indonesia*
[3]*Resilience Development Initiative (RDI), Bandung, Indonesia*

24.1 Introduction

In many developing countries of Asia and the Pacific, food and nutrition security may be affected by acute crises and chronic threats that occur simultaneously. Existing vulnerability and long-term conflict legacies may interact with the current impacts of natural hazards and pandemics to form cascading crises that compound the ability of poor people already suffering from insufficient nutrition and food insecurity.

While most literature tends to address single threats and their effects on food security, in reality, many low- and middle-income countries suffer multiple crises. In this chapter, we illustrate the impact of cascading and compounding crises by presenting a detailed study of West Timor, a region that Western scholars once called "Africa in Asia" [Booth, 2007], that shares its boundary with Timor Leste and Northern Australia, and is semi-arid and prone to droughts, cyclones and other biosecurity threats.

In the last 80 years, research suggests that West Timor is vulnerable to ecological crises, including ongoing water problems, food production, biodiversity crisis, and human security issues. The ecological crisis in the early 20th century was characterised by the increase in human and animal populations combined with Dutch colonisation, which triggered agricultural practices that demanded more agricultural land, resulting in deforestation and increased soil erosion, later referred to as The Timor Problem [Ormeling, 1955]. 60 years after the Dutch left Indonesia, food and water insecurity problems continued as the most problematic development issues in West Timor. Consequently, West Timor continued to be the target of international and national food assistance and social protection until the first decade of the 21st century [Lassa, 2009]. International humanitarian non-governmental organisations and the central government remain key advocates that often nudged local governments to allocate more resources to increase food security and agricultural production.

Today, climate change and recurrent El Nino and La Nina events, combined with a lack of institutional capacity and good governance, have exacerbated the current biosecurity and climate crisis. Population change, rapid urban development and the East Timorese crisis in the last 20 years are among the pressures that shape the environmental crisis in West Timor. The beginning of the 21st century was a trying time for West Timor ecology. The impact of El Nino on livelihoods, such as livestock, was severe with the potential extinction of some of the large animals, for example buffalo [Lassa and Banunaek, 2018], and other strategic crops like Timor apples [Suek, 2020] and Timorese citrus [Mudita, 2013], among others.

This chapter elaborates on the lives of vulnerable groups in West Timor, especially the East Timorese, who were involuntarily uprooted and mitigated to West Timor in 1999. It originated from a referendum in 1999 when East Timor reclaimed its independence after more than 20 years of being annexed as the youngest province in Indonesia. Thousands of East Timorese fled from their ancestors' land because of armed conflict between pro-independence versus pro-Indonesia integration groups.

After Timor Leste was recognised as a sovereign country in 2002, most refugees gradually returned to East Timor. In some pockets of West Timor, there have been "new citizens" (a.k.a. "warga baru") who remained or decided to stay in West Timor for various reasons. One of the main reasons is that they were part of the pro-Indonesia militia [Damaledo, 2018; Sakti, 2023], and the other is that their local patrons were the leaders of the pro-Indonesian group. As a form of loyalty to the leaders, they decided to stay. They became Indonesian citizens despite the consequences of living in poverty and limited access to basic rights and livelihood assets. It explains why most residents in the former East Timor refugee settlements tend to group themselves based on the same village or areas of origin in East Timor.

Those who stayed often lived in marginal conditions in the first decade of the 21st century, when the economic situation of West Timor was still full of rampant chronic poverty and malnutrition. They had to adapt to complex conditions in their temporary shelters. Most families often moved from camps and settlements inside of

West Timor. They lived in uncertainty for years, especially when the Indonesian government stopped refugee assistance around 2003–2004.

The main problems faced by former East Timorese refugees who were still in the transitional shelters (often called 'refugee camps' by the locals) include the lack of available land for settlements and cultivation, and the problem of integration with local residents. They are often socially excluded and seen as a group with split loyalties, and are subject to social bullying and stigma [Damaledo, 2018].

For years, the new citizens had to adopt various ways to meet their food needs, such as getting permits or renting from the local landlord to do land clearing and opening up new cultivation on a profit-sharing arrangement. They enjoyed a more stable life and livelihood in their current locations. In the last 10+ years, the community also survived on diversified food and income streams such as cash crops, which they call ' fast money', used for the family's daily needs or their children's educational needs. When COVID-19 occurred, local markets were disrupted as the government restricted mobility and activities that affected marketing of their cash crops. The pandemic also limited their access to the other jobs they usually do in their effort to meet family food needs. It created imbalances in their daily life struggles.

This part of our research aims to understand how the most vulnerable groups and individual families cope with COVID-19.

We primarily adopted a *life history approach* to this ethnographic research. The life story interviews were exploratory research. Our key objective is to spell the stories out and see the world from the survivors' perspectives. We are mindful of our subjectivity and biases in framing and structuring the stories.

Because of COVID-19, most of the fieldwork had been completed by John Talan using pandemic safety procedures. Verbal agreements were used instead of paper-based agreements. In this chapter, only one story is selected based on its richness, as the respondents were happy to share their stories with the world.

24.2 Insights from the Life History of MS

In the ethnographic research approach that we share in this chapter, we have selected a respondent, MS, whose life and life history offer a generic representation of many East Timorese living in transitional housing. We also argue that the narrative through the lens of a person named "MS" represents the experience of some of the most vulnerable groups in rural West Timor, Indonesia.

The story shares views from a middle-aged former East Timorese refugee woman, MS, who is not adequately educated. Previous research had discussed the important connection between ageing and forced migration of former East Timorese older women refugees who have experienced displacement several times in East Timor's history [Sakti, 2023]. Sakti argues that the older former East Timorese refugee women told stories about their experiences of displacement and hardships during the war at different times. The former East Timor refugee middle-aged woman in this story, MS, has experienced at least once being displaced by the daily life difficulties she faces, especially in her household's domestic affairs such as providing food for family members.

We also find that the older the former East Timorese refugee women are, the more displacement events they experienced, and they then narrated these stories to the younger refugees. Just as the older generation carries out their daily activities centred on the home and family environment [Sakti, 2023], MS's story represents the younger generation who share similar everyday experiences. MS married her husband in 1996 when still a teenager at 16. A year later, she had a miscarriage but was soon pregnant and gave birth again to a boy, and after only two months, the baby died under 'strange circumstances', according to her narrative. A year later, she got pregnant again and gave birth to a third child. The child survived, but it was not a good time. The political momentum then led to a referendum that separated Timor Leste from Indonesia in 1999. MS and her husband were among the 500,000 refugees who involuntary migrated to West Timor, Indonesia, in 1999. As of 2023, she has been living for 24 years in various places in West Timor.

She is now aged 41. She gave birth to her 4th to 7th children in refugee camps. She gave birth to her latest (13th) child, a baby boy, in mid-2020 during the COVID-19 crisis. She was very sick and almost died during the pregnancy.

Consequently, the baby was premature. MS received demands from her husband's extended family to have many children, which later became a big challenge when her family faced the COVID-19 outbreak. She narrated, "We have to have many children because my husband's siblings do not have any offspring. But after the 13th child, I decided to take out my uterus because I was very sick and almost died during the last pregnancy."

The baby was born prematurely. He is now two years old and stunted. She blamed the stunting on premature birth. According to MS, when she gave birth amid her illness, the doctor who assisted in the delivery process thought that her baby would not last long. Since the baby was born prematurely during the pandemic, MS left the baby to be treated in the hospital for ten days when she had to return home to continue her recovery process which in turn resulted in an unknown illness. MS also added that COVID-19 made it worse as her family had difficulty providing proper food for the baby.

Before COVID-19, 12 members (including ten children) in her family lived under one roof. After COVID-19, the oldest daughter, 24 years old, who is already married, returned to stay with her, bringing together the son-in-law and two grandchildren living with her. In addition to her husband, only one child contributed to the household income by working odd jobs. During COVID-19, with a total of 16 people, the family would immediately experience food shortages.

Marriage customs in their culture is one factor that added to their burden of surviving. MS and her eldest daughter, who was married and had two children, cannot live in the original village of their husband's family because they had not fulfilled their customary obligations (e.g., dowry), so their family must live with the wife's family.

The COVID-19 outbreak has had a typical impact on the families of former East Timorese refugees by disrupting the balance that began to form after moving from the refugee camp to the new resettlement that is their current "*kampung*" (village). The pandemic has hit the ability of this community's families to ensure their food security due to restrictions on markets where buying and selling of their cash crops occurs and also disruption of access to cash through the cessation of non-agricultural work.

The following sections (24.2.1–24.2.6) will illustrate how an affected family accessed food during multiple crises and uncertainties from 1999 to 2022.

24.2.1 *Uprooted and Multiple Displacements*

MS and her family were forced to flee to Camp Tuapukan in Kupang Regency in 1999. Staying for a month in her 2 × 2 m^2 room in

Tuapukan camp was one of the darkest times in MS's life, so she reflected:

> *"In 1999, we came to live in Tuapukan for a month. Our camp was very crowded. People throng around. People were sick, and some just died. Hospitals were also overcrowded with people. People throw away waste anywhere."*

She recalled that poor sanitation facilities and lack of water caused the refugees to contract various diseases; unfortunately, some died.

Sponsored by the government, the Indonesian National Army moved MS and her family to a camp in the Sulamu sub-district, a remote location in the interior of the Kupang district. They were no longer crowded together since they had more freedom to build makeshift buildings for their homes; however, sanitation and clean water facilities were minimal. Each refugee family had to build an emergency latrine for itself to defecate a bit more appropriately, even though the building was considered an emergency building.

In 2002, when Timor Leste began to enjoy political stability as a young independent country, her extended family, including her mother and brothers and sisters, who were also refugees, decided to return to their hometown in the Viqueque district. She could not return as her husband is an Indonesian citizen.

Her family started to feel isolated as they lived alone in Sulamu after the departure of the extended family back to Timor Leste. Her uncle, who worked as a civil servant and lived in Tuapukan camp (around 40 km from Sulamu, but back in 2002, it could take more than three hours to reach the camp by public transport), asked her family to move to Tuapukan to be close to each other. Her husband followed this arrangement because, based on their marriage tradition, in a new family where a husband has not completed the customary marriage obligations in the form of a dowry, the husband must move and live in the wife's family surroundings. In brief, MS and the family moved to Tuapukan in 2002, when she was pregnant and about to give birth to another child. It was more comfortable for her to be looked after by known relatives when giving birth.

The family struggled to survive without access to jobs and gardens. In the first four years from 1999–2003, while in the refugee camp, the family received social protection assistance from the government, including 50 kg of rice and Rp. 700,000 (AUD 70) per month. After 2003, the assistance was stopped, and they were no longer considered refugees.

Fortunately, living in a new location provided some new opportunities for families such as MS; they have a house with clear land status which also means they now share a sense of place — have neighbours, have a more permanent address and can find a regular job — something they longed for after the crisis in 1999.

However, getting a house and what they longed for does not automatically lead to a good quality of life. Water scarcity haunted and coloured their days in the new location. It often took hours to be able to get water as they had to walk 3–4 km to get water from the river, especially in the dry season.

24.2.2 *Combining Access to Land and Job Security to Ensure Food Security*

In 2006, after four years of resettling back in the Tuapukan camp, the MS family had the opportunity to settle down in a resettlement location initiated by CIS-Timor (*Circle of Imagination Society* — a non-governmental organisation headquartered in Kupang focusing on empowering displaced communities), in collaboration with the Kupang Regency government seeking resettlement locations for former East Timorese refugees. Together with 49 other families, MS and her family received a new shelter 6 × 6 m^2 in Raknamo Village. The shelter sits on a 20 × 20 m^2 piece of land. The 50 houses built at that location were called location 50/Lorosae I. Lorosae is synonymous with 'land of the rising sun' in the East (of Timor).

Since then, the family has relied on gardening. Having a garden of their own brings a more comfortable feeling to the MS family. MS viewed gardening as the backbone of the family's food supply. When the harvest is not disrupted due to climatic conditions or pests, they can have food supplies to be consumed for a year, with additional income generated from her husband's other work as he often works off the farm as a labourer in a construction project (when there is an opportunity) and as a motorcycle taxi (Ojek) driver. He sometimes teamed up with other daily labourers to seek employment (also when there is an opportunity).

> *"Here we can ask local landlords to share with us based on a verbal arrangement. We often want to make a big plot but don't have the labour to do so. So we land clear and create a new garden to grow crops."*

Her family owns a garden with an area of approximately 50 acres (about 20 hectares). They usually plant corn, cassava and legumes such as green beans, peanuts and rice beans in the garden. Even though they produce quite a lot of corn, the harvest from their garden is not sufficient for the consumption of 13 members of their family in a year. Only when her husband gets 'construction project' labour jobs which is interspersed with motorcycle taxi driving can they ensure their family's food needs. With this additional work, they can get cash so the stored corn supply can last longer.

MS revealed the opportunity for her family to clear shrubs to make arable land plots from the local forest nearby to produce their food needs as a garden. Sometimes, this did not end well. As she narrated, the scheme is prone to moral hazards as a local landlord might decide to take a certain proportion of the share unilaterally. They resolved cases like this at the police station with a request to show proof of land access rights. Without a legal document, these local resident families refuse to share the produce. According to her, they initially worked on forest land or shrubs, which they cleared to become arable gardens.

During the gardening season, she and her husband routinely go to the garden in the morning from 0700. Work in the garden starts from preparing the land, planting, caring for the plants, clearing weeds, to harvesting. They prepare or clear the land of grass so that their crops grow optimally. A successful garden crop means the MS family's life in a year will be much easier to cope with. They have lunch in the garden delivered by their children. The MS family has breakfast in the morning with coffee if they have it or with water and boiled cassava if that is available in the garden. Plain water is enough for them if they do not have coffee or cassava from the garden. After dozens of years of living in that location, those are the habits that they adapted to their living conditions. The cash can usually be obtained from other jobs MS's husband does. She often uses the income from her husband to buy food and children's school needs. 'Project work' can be obtained by soliciting friends or neighbours with information and links to project work. The type of wages received by her husband varied, and may be daily, weekly or piecemeal. If the husband gets a lot of project work that year, they will eat rice more often and occasionally interspersed with side dishes, such as fish, at least 1–2 times a week.

24.2.3 *COVID-19 Pushed Rural Families to Readopt Food Subsistence Temporarily*

When the pandemic hit Indonesia in March 2020, the MS family was again in one of their most difficult situations.

> *"Recently in 2020, this has not been working. People say you can't get out. When we go out, we have to check our body temperature. We immediately isolate. So we are all afraid of work."*

The mobility restriction policy implemented by the government to control the spread of COVID-19 impacted the MS family. The family's access to food is hampered, and their only food source for two years is their garden and the arable land. Widespread rumours and unverified information often created confusion, causing fear and uncertainty, as expressed by MS. As a result, the husband had to stop his work as a labourer on various construction projects or as a motorcycle taxi driver.

24.2.4 *African Swine Fever and Cyclone Seroja Add More Weight to the COVID-19 Crisis*

West Timor has been impacted by the widespread transmission of African Swine Fever (ASF) since early 2020 till now as we write this chapter (April 2023). Some figures suggested more than half a million pigs died from ASF causing losses of at least IDR 2.3t (USD 163 million) in West Timor alone [Antara, 2023]. Unfortunately, the ASF virus attack in 2020 also caused two of MS's pet pigs to die and these had to be thrown away. According to her, currently, the cage is empty and cannot be filled again after the ASF virus attack.

At the end of 2021, when the interview took place, although MS's husband had returned to work on several construction projects, their family condition had not fully recovered. The reason was their garden was affected by the Seroja cyclone. Therefore, part of the corn they were about to harvest rotted due to excessive rain. At least half of their crops were spoiled and unharvestable.

24.2.5 *Reduction in Food Intake and Frequency*

During that time, their family's diet changed. In the days before COVID-19, the MS family ate more than two meals a day, usually corn at noon and rice at night. But as they consumed corn more often, their food reserves soon ran out because there were 16 members in their family. During COVID-19, food intake and frequency reduction was the knee-jerk response of the MS family. Since MS was in charge of household food management, she must take measures so that there was adequate food the next day.

While MS blamed her two-year-old's stunting on premature birth, we have reasons to believe that food shortage is another reason for the stunting.

In non-pandemic conditions, their daily food (carbohydrate) composition is 3 kg of ground corn mixed with 3 cups of rice for one-time cooking and for the whole family to eat at night. During the day, they cook corn by boiling it. Suppose they consume ground corn day and night; then the corn they produce can last six months. Sometimes, they even consume the corn intended as seeds for planting. If this happens, they must buy or ask for the seeds from neighbours when planting season arrives. During the pandemic, they had to drastically reduce the amount of food they ate due to food shortages.

24.2.6 *Returning to Food Subsistence is not an Easy Journey*

To increase the amount of food, she asked her children to pick as many *marrunga* (moringa) leaves as possible to mix with the food they were cooking, given lots of water to make it like porridge and enough for them as a family. She told this story while crying. While sobbing MS recounted her conversation with her children about the day:

> *"These kids said, how come this is the year we eat like this? I said what do you want to eat? What is it we eat? Until I said, get Marungga! Kids said we didn't know eating the stuff! I said I don't know what to eat when we don't have it. Eat it! I have a big boy [recently dropped out of high school]. He said he didn't want to eat. I was angry. I took a small stick and hit him. I said, "If you don't want to eat, what will you eat?" He said, "We usually have good food. Why are we eating this now?" I said to eat well if you must work on a project so we can eat well. But now, when you have no job, you could not even go out?"*

She said they experienced a difficult situation for a year, from the middle of 2020 to the first half of 2021. Farm products such as cassava leaves, which they usually sell to the market for additional cash, also cannot be sold because the market is closed.

The situation during the pandemic brought changes to the MS family. If, before the pandemic, the food they ate was ground corn mixed with rice, they could also buy vegetables such as mustard greens, kale, and fish. In mid-2020, after the pandemic started attacking Indonesia, MS said her husband could no longer work freely. Because of this issue, most of the men in their village were afraid to travel. One issue that worries them is that those who come out will be arrested and isolated and cannot be visited by their wives and children.

One of their family's regular expenses is transportation for the children who go to school. Together with her husband, MS hopes that her children will be able to study until they graduate from high school so that they could have the opportunity to get better jobs. Consequently, she maintained the consumption of corn in his family to save money to transport one of his sons to high school, which takes 30 minutes from home. MS has to pay for daily transport costs for Rp. 20,000 if the husband cannot drive him to school. During the pandemic mobility restrictions, the high school boy stayed at home. But the allocated transportation costs must be used to buy internet quota to attend online schooling from home.

During COVID-19, there were increased tensions between their children's school needs and the provision of food. As a housewife, MS said, "I had to think hard to ensure that these two daily needs are fulfilled — I had to control and limit the family's daily food consumption."

24.2.7 *Access to Cash Assistance and Food Loans*

The shortage of food at the household level left a burden for MS as a woman. In the context of the lack of food at home, she had to deal with the condition of her starving children. As a housewife, MS must be good at managing the use of food in her family.

> *"Because every day I weigh my food! I want to take rice, we have to give out money. Sometimes he (the husband) is a part-time motorcycle taxi driver, and sometimes he gets Rp. 10,000 or Rp. 20,000. He buys 1–2 kg of rice."*

During the pandemic, the husband's only job was driving motorcycle taxis. It was based on order — when neighbours needed transportation services for certain purposes and called their husbands at their houses. She would feel a little relieved because her husband could bring 2 kg of rice home from the motorcycle taxi. "I sometimes cried when we didn't have enough food all day — we then could not eat as a family." She added: "We'll talk or take them for a walk to distract them from thinking about food."

Under such circumstances, she will try to borrow from neighbours but only if the neighbours have sufficient reserves. Commonly they will share their food even though they often do not have enough themselves.

MS borrowed 1–2 kg of rice from the nearby kiosks. She could get rice at a slightly higher price from the seller based on the promise that she would pay back when she received the cash assistance (using the Family Hope Program card or PKH — a form of cash transfer for low-income families with school children). Her family has received PKH assistance since 2019 because their children are still in school, and four are registered as recipients of PKH assistance. She received the PKH once every three months in the amount of Rp. 2.200,000 (USD 150). The assistance received every three months makes it difficult for her to make anticipatory arrangements for three months, not only for food needs but also for the children's school needs, monthly and daily, such as transportation costs. The last PKH assistance was received in November 2021 (one month before this interview); according to MS, she immediately paid her debts. When she gets the money, MS usually divides it into school needs for her children and the rest is used to pay off debts and buy food.

Once, because of the difficulties she was experiencing, she borrowed from a loan shark. However, sometimes when the debt collector visited to collect the pay, she had to hide or escape to sell cassava leaves at the nearby local market. After paying off the loan, she decided to stop borrowing from daily loans.

Living away from the extended family is challenging for MS. Sometimes, she feels homesick about not meeting her parents and siblings in Timor Leste. Still, she does not dare to dream because she realises it costs a lot to visit her hometown. She hopes the pandemic will end soon so they can freely farm and sell garden produce and her husband can return to project work so their family will no longer suffer from hunger as she did during the pandemic.

24.3 Effect of COVID-19 on Food and Nutrition Security

One of the significant impacts of COVID-19 on vulnerable communities is the reduced ability to provide food at the household level due to the lack of jobs and access to markets to sell their agricultural produce.

MS's story in Section 24.2 above represents one dramatic scenario of how low-income families from marginalised backgrounds struggle to sustain their food security. Under normal conditions, the lives of former East Timorese refugees in West Timor were predominantly shaped by a combination of farming food crops and cash crops in the rainy season, commercial crops to generate cash during the harvest season, and other off-farm activities such as selling labour in construction projects during the dry season or by becoming migrant workers to other islands in Indonesia (Kalimantan, Sulawesi, Papua, etc.) or also to foreign countries such as Malaysia.

Losing access to markets and labour jobs means their families have less (consumption of) rice. Access to such work is a favourite for the respondent's family, especially for children who prefer rice consumption compared to the type of food they produce on the farm they process. When the husband was involved in a construction job as a labourer, the family consumed corn twice a week (MB, 32 years old). Food subsistence is generally insufficient to meet family needs for a year.

In addition to the obstacles to food supply due to the closed access to jobs and markets from COVID-19, the costs that must be incurred to buy credit/internet quota for the needs of children who are required to undergo online education during the pandemic have contributed to worsening efforts to provide the family food: "School children also because school at home, (online) online. Before COVID-19, they went to face-to-face schooling, which was good. During COVID-19, the teacher only gave questions. Where do we get the money to top up our bandwidth? Where do we get the money to top up credit? Because there are so many questions. We filled 100,000 also in less than one week. Only 3–4 days were gone because the children went to high school, junior high, and elementary school" (EC, 36 years old). This situation creates a dilemma between spending for school needs or buying food amid a lack of income due to COVID-19.

24.3.1 *COVID-19 Affects Access to Markets and Cash*

In the West Timor region, the impact of COVID-19 on the families of ex-East Timor refugees comes in the form of obstacles to selling agricultural produce to the local market. Access to local markets to sell agricultural products is a balance point in their livelihood where apart from producing their food for their families by farming, the agricultural products that are sold can help them provide options for types of food that they do not grow, such as rice so that their families can have other options besides the corn and cassava they grow, especially for children who have difficulty with these types of food. On the other hand, types of work outside of agriculture are difficult to reach due to restrictions on activities during COVID-19, so these families struggle to provide food for their families, especially children. Most only eat corn from the garden. If they are able to sell cassava or sweet potato leaves, they can buy 1 or 2 kg of rice. "We try for small children because half don't want to eat corn" (AC, 30 years old).

24.3.2 *Activity Limitations and Job Loss During COVID-19*

COVID-19 has also cut off another livelihood mechanism that developed among the former East Timor refugee community, namely the network for work as building construction workers, especially for adult men in the summer. With this mechanism, the limitations for summer agricultural production are overcome to generate cash so they can support their families. When the pandemic occurred, this mechanism stopped and disrupted the food system of ex-refugees as described by MS: "...(during) 2020 unable to work. People say you can't get out. When we go out, we have to check our body temperature. We immediately isolate. So we are all afraid of work." As a result, her family depends on the corn harvest from their farm. With 11 children, their food reserves did not last long, and they faced a family food crisis. She was forced to borrow food from neighbours at a purchase price several times the average price. However, MS was not always able to get the loan in the midst of a community of residents who were also struggling through the pressure of the situation due to COVID-19. In the most challenging circumstances, she and her family managed not to eat for a day, and the way she used to keep her children alive was to give them warm water so they would not get sick.

24.3.3 *COVID-19 Worsens Impacts of Disasters and Potentially Increases Vulnerability to Stunting*

For the families of ex-refugees in West Timor, the conditions of the agricultural land that they have access to only allowed them to produce certain types of food crops such as corn, cassava, bananas and beans; access to markets plays an important role for the food security system and provision of nutrition for children. Losing access to markets and cash deprives them of their ability to provide food for their families and adequate nutrition for growing children amid the harsh conditions they experienced even before COVID-19.

The pandemic has worsened the living conditions of former East Timorese refugees who are also dealing with a water crisis in resettlement areas. Under normal conditions, during the dry season, ex-refugees must spend a budget of at least US$1 for 75 litres of water to provide drinking water for a week. In the conditions of the pandemic, the absence of jobs and access to cash has made efforts to provide drinking water even more challenging to fulfil, forcing them to access water of poor quality from available sources.

By only having simple house assets and a minimal yard area, COVID-19 returned their living conditions to the difficulties experienced in the early 2000s, two decades ago. At that time they were still living in refugee camps, no longer getting food and cash assistance from the government, and did not have access to jobs and so they experienced food difficulties. Raknamo Village, which is one of the resettlement destination villages where around 50% of the villagers are former East Timorese refugees, has the status of a village with the highest stunting rate in Kupang Regency with a total of 64 stunted children in 2020 (statement of the village head based on data collection by 'Posyandu' cadres together with 'Puskesmas' (health centre) officers); these have the potential to be increasingly vulnerable due to the challenges of food shortages faced by these families.

24.4 Concluding Remarks

In addition to COVID-19, Cyclone Seroja in 2021 and ASF outbreaks during 2020–2023 further compromised the livelihoods and food insecurity of the uprooted ex-East Timorese communities in West Timor. In generic disasters where emergencies are often brief, the communities can rely on their social capital, such as extended family support and local churches. Our field research suggests that the local church had also run out of resources as incomes and offerings drastically reduced since religious services were disrupted.

COVID-19 is an extended emergency that pushed the most vulnerable groups, represented in MS's stories, to develop multi-tiered options, including optimising their produce from their garden and lands for subsistence farming, quantity and eating frequency adjustment, erratic service jobs, access to food loans and government cash assistance. Reducing the total daily food consumption in the family has helped them get through the tough times due to the pandemic. Cash assistance from the government can be used as collateral to apply for loans to the nearest kiosk, especially in the most precarious situations.

MS's story represents the layered pressures former East Timorese refugee women faced during the COVID-19 crisis. In general, the communities were silent about their savings. Nevertheless, COVID-19 substantially eroded savings based on data from Indonesia [Masagus *et al.*, 2023].

This research found that the most vulnerable groups already on the list of existing cash transfers aimed at school children and education development can access their cash assistance. However, there is no top-up cash assistance to meet their extra demand when their regular income was reduced due to COVID-19.

The education cash transfer that MS received was mainly for educational purposes, but they shifted it substantially to food. Our findings suggest that families like MS can utilise cash programs to help complement food and livelihoods. However, the complexity of the situation, as shared by MS, suggests that marginal and low-income families with many children barely escape from the risk of malnutrition, especially stunting.

Historically, West Timor is a fragile place often associated with famine and hunger, at least in 20th-century Indonesia. Despite gaps in nutrition security as indicated above, we argue that food insecurity in West Timor during COVID-19 did not result in widespread famine and hunger. Some of the reasons are partly due to the increasing government fiscal capability and its commitment to continue and expand its existing cash assistance for low-income families. We argue that the 21st-century pandemic crisis in West Timor offers a different outlook than the 20th century, where the region had been challenged by recurrent droughts resulting in hunger and famine [Lassa, 2009].

We argue that there is a need to fix existing social protection policies in Indonesia. For example, a more adaptive social protection policy needs to be more flexible to top up existing cash assistance to anticipate potential acute malnutrition due to income shocks experienced by low-income families, as their income might be only sufficient to access food and other nutritional intakes at a certain level during large crises.

Acknowledgements

We are grateful for the willingness of 25 'warga baru' in Kupang and Atambua, who generously allocated their time for the interviews by John Talan [Lassa, 2023]. Talan (second author), contracted by the first author, and funded by JICA, conducted ethnographic interviews using a reflective approach between November 2021–March 2022. Special thanks to MS, who was willing to share her story with the world to know her experience facing uncertainties over the last 20+ years.

Publisher's Note

Written informed consent for publication of the interviews was obtained from all participating adult subjects and from parents or legal guardians for minors or incapacitated adults. There was no compensation in any form for the participants. The Author of this chapter understands that publication of the interviews could lead to identification of the participants and their relatives, and agrees to indemnify and keep indemnified the Publisher against any suit, demand, claim or recovery, finally sustained, by reason of any loss of identity privacy.

References

Antara. (2023). 500,000 pigs in NTT died from the ASF virus. https://kupang.antaranews.com/berita/106302/500000-ekor-ternak-babi-di-ntt-mati-akibat-virus-asf

Booth, A. (2007). Africa in Asia? The development challenges facing Eastern Indonesia and East Timor. *Oxford Development Studies,* 32(1), pp. 19–35.

Damaledo, A. (2018). *Divided Loyalties: Displacement, Belonging and Citizenship among East Timorese in West Timor*. ANU Press.

Lassa, J. (2009). Understanding food and nutritional policy in NTT Province 1958–2008. *Journal of NTT Studies*, 1(1), pp. 28–45.

Lassa, J. (2023). COVID-19 Impact on the Most Vulnerable Communities in Indonesia. In M. Caballero-Anthony, Y. Mine and S. Ishikawa (Eds.), *Human Security and Empowerment in Asia: Beyond the Pandemic*. Routledge.

Lassa, J. and Banuanek, R. (2018). Long term trend of cattle and buffalo in Timor Tengah Selatan 1970–2016. *RGSC Brief #15*. http://irgsc.org/index.php/2018/01/31/irgsc-brief-long-term-trend-of-livestocks-tts/

Lassa, J., Talan, J., Klaas, H. and Yuliana, S. (2022). *Sail Through the Storms with Cash Transfer: Survivor's Stories of Cash and Vouchers Assistance in Indonesia During Disasters and Covid-19*. Xlibris.

Mudita, I. W. (2013). *Community Biosecurity In West Timor, Indonesia: The Role of Local Communities and Governments In Managing Huanglongbing and Other Diseases and Pests of Citrus*. PhD Thesis, Charles Darwin University, Australia.

Ormeling, F. J. (1955). *The Timor Problem: A Geographical Interpretation of an Underdeveloped Island*. J. B. Walters.

Ridhwan, M. M., Rezki, J. F., Suryahadi, A., Ramayandi, A. and Ismail, A. (2023). The impact of COVID-19 lockdowns on household income, consumption, and expectations: evidence from high-frequency data in Indonesia. *Bulletin of Indonesian Economic Studies*, DOI: 10.1080/00074918.2023.2167930.

Suek, R. E. (2020). Miracle in Timor Island. In J. Lovett, S. Widinugraheni and A. Milligan (Eds.), *Plant Biosecurity and Biodiversity in Dryland Areas in a Time of Climate Change*, pp. 65–67. Australian Plant Biosecurity Science Foundation.

Victoria, K. and Sakti, V. K. (2023). Ageing at the margins: gendered and southern narratives of displacement among the East Timorese in Indonesia. *Journal of Ethnic and Migration Studies*, 49(4), pp. 1065–1081.

https://doi.org/10.1142/9789811278297_0025

Chapter 25

Creating an Environment for Agri-Food Innovation

Andrew D. Powell

CEO, Asia BioBusiness Pte. Ltd., Singapore

25.1 Introduction

Many inventions destined to become true innovations with deep societal impact have initially met pushback from stakeholders. The printing press, the telephone, the steam engine, the automobile, the mobile phone and the internet are just a few examples that disrupted existing social structures and raised concerns about safety, privacy, and social impact.

While innovations in agricultural and food technologies have the potential to enhance food production, improve food safety, and address today's pressing global challenges such as climate change and food security, they are also not immune to pushback. It could be argued that new foods or drinks, ingredients, additives, or technologies used in food production are more likely to encounter resistance because of the deep emotional and cultural connection people have with food, when compared with other innovations. Any change in the *status quo* can bring disquiet, concern, and sometimes controversy.

Most recently resistance has been seen towards genetically modified (GM) food, but significant resistance was met when coffee was introduced to Europe in the 17th century; canning was first used in the 19th century; microwave technology, additives (E numbers) and novel ingredients (aspartame, sucralose, acesulfame potassium) in the 20th century. We are also now seeing resistance in some consumers to the so-called "future foods" (plant-based protein products, cultivated meats, and precision fermentation-derived products) who see them as over-processed, unnatural, or poor in nutritional content.

25.2 An Environment for Innovation

The possibility of resistance to new technological innovation is often ignored by technologists who focus on the technology itself and the addressable market for their potential innovation. While companies may address many risks along the pathway to commercialisation such as those associated with technology development, finance, intellectual property, and regulatory environment, market acceptance and social license to operate are often not acknowledged. It is important, however, to ensure that there is a market for their products long before the product is ready to be taken to the consumer. If controversy around a technology develops before the products get to the market, then all the time and investors' money risk being wasted. Proactively managing this market risk through effective communication is vital to ensure that there is an environment in which the product can be marketed.

Companies and technologists are not solely responsible for creating a conducive environment for marketing of a novel product, however. Regulators play a crucial role in creating an environment for marketing novel food products by establishing standards and guidelines that ensure the safety and efficacy of these products, conducting risk assessments, reviewing and approving new products, and monitoring compliance. The regulatory framework provides a clear path for food manufacturers to follow so they can bring their products to market, while protecting the health and well-being of consumers.

But new regulations, standards and operating protocols for a new food product do not appear overnight and take foresight and preparation by the agencies charged with ensuring new products are safe for public consumption. Regulators often face the "pacing problem" first highlighted by Downes in his book *The Laws of Disruption* where technological innovation outpaces their ability to develop laws and regulations [Downes, 2009]. The situation, as described by Downes, where "technology changes exponentially, but social, economic, and legal systems change incrementally" is currently very evident in the development of artificial intelligence and machine learning applications.

GM crops and food where policies were developed slowly and with inconsistent approaches around the world is an example of the pacing problem in the agrifood area. The GM crop case has been well studied with respect to the link between technology advocacy, consumer acceptance and regulations [Arujanan and Teng, 2018]. In principle, biotechnology, as an innovative technology, was believed by most mainstream scientists to confer large potential benefits to increase agricultural productivity. Multinational companies that invested millions to develop crop varieties with traits to benefit farmers, such as pest resistance, did not anticipate the arousal of consumer concern about the technology by groups opposed to the technology, and its dominance by companies, and the resulting paralysis in regulatory approval in many developing countries prevented them from benefiting from biotechnology [ISAAA, 2019]. Only belatedly did the industry respond by conducting communication initiatives based on 'risk communication', an approach discussed in later sections of this chapter.

There is potential for a similar situation to develop in the cultivated meat space. Singapore, however, showed considerable foresight in initiating policy development in cultivated meat some years ago before any product was close to market. This has allowed Singapore to be a leader in this area with the approval of a commercial product for sale (albeit in limited quantities) in 2020 [Phua, 2020] and the approval of meat produced using serum-free media in 2023 [Shu, 2023].

A regulatory vacuum without sound, science-based regulations can create an environment where misinformation holds sway and leads to misperceptions being propagated. This misinformation can, in turn, influence the development of policies and regulations and, when policies are finally developed, lead to a patchwork of inconsistent regulations in different countries which can not only impact the deployment of the technology at a global level but the very innovation process itself.

The regulatory environment in many countries in Asia is inconsistent with stated government policies that promote innovation in agriculture and food to solve the impending crisis of food insecurity. While the willingness to drive the agrifood sector forward through technology is often stated at the highest levels in government, the utilisation of solutions offered by both government and industry-supported research are often hampered by misguided regulatory policy, and the pace of the regulatory process. This is a major disincentive for investors in the agrifood space as it increases the risk that their investments face.

Another example where regulatory policy is retarding the potential impact of a technological solution is the "line-of-sight" requirement for the use of drones in agriculture. While cameras and virtual reality headsets can be used in recreational use of drones in racing competitions and in the military, their use in agricultural applications, e.g., for targeted fertiliser and pesticide applications and disease monitoring, is hampered by the users being required to have sight of the drone at all times.

25.3 The Communication of Innovation

When an invention has the potential to evolve into being a true innovation, technologists naturally want to talk about it. Public relations tools can be used to raise awareness and excite the public about the technology and its value, and science communication tools can be used to inform, educate, and enthuse. When performed well these tools have considerable power, but these tools have limited value when there is resistance to a technology/innovation. In fact, their use in such situations can increase the levels of concern. A third set of tools and techniques should be employed called 'risk communication'. This set of tools, however, is rarely utilised or the need recognised by technologists.

25.4 Communication in Controversy: Risk Communication

Risk communication is a social science-informed approach for communicating effectively in high concern, low trust, sensitive, or controversial situations. An appreciation of the need for such techniques was first noted in the medical world, where doctors often must communicate difficult news to patients who are under stress.

Over the past three decades, risk communication has become recognised as a necessary component in effective risk management and decision making. Risk communication helps to enhance knowledge and understanding, build trust and credibility, encourage dialogue and, finally, influence attitudes, decisions and behaviours. All these are critical when parties in a controversy need to come together and establish common ground.

Risk communication techniques can be applied to a wide range of situations and have been applied to situations where people have developed a concern about technology or techniques, e.g., stem cells [Giles, 2010], cloning [Rudenko and Matheson 2007], nanotechnology [Malakar *et al.*, 2022], GM crops [Teng, 2008] and GM food [Frewer, 2004].

A fundamental concept of risk communication is that people experiencing stress typically (1) have difficulty understanding and remembering information and (2) want to know that you care before they care what you know. A central theorem of risk communication is that people's perceptions of risk are influenced by factors other than numerical data. Research has shown that there is a low correlation between the technical seriousness of a risk and peoples' perception of that risk [Renn, 2004]. This often results in two problems: (1) risks that are likely to harm people do not upset them so they fail to take appropriate precautions and (2) risks that are not likely to harm people do nonetheless upset them and so they take unnecessary precautions.

Appropriate communication is essential for all stakeholders in high-concern situations whether they are thought leaders, policymakers, managers or researchers. Whilst many stakeholders in food and agriculture, e.g., researchers/academic lecturers have communication skills appropriate to their own specialist areas, communicating effectively in high-concern or high-stress situations presents very different challenges, and a different set of communication skills is essential in such situations.

Risk communication has broad application in business and is a vital component in ensuring freedom to operate in its broadest sense — providing the right information to create a business-conducive environment [Wiedemann *et al.*, 2021].

Risk communication is crucial in the communication around food innovation because it enables consumers to make informed decisions about the safety and benefits of new food products. When introducing new food products, companies must provide information about the potential risks associated with their consumption, including possible allergic reactions or other adverse effects.

In addition, risk communication can help build trust between consumers and food innovators. By being transparent about the potential risks and uncertainties associated with new food products, innovators can demonstrate their commitment to safety and responsible innovation.

Effective risk communication can also help prevent misinformation and fearmongering about new food products. By providing accurate and clear information, consumers are less likely to rely on rumours or hearsay, which can lead to unwarranted concerns or even panic.

25.5 Risk Communication Theories, Tools, and Techniques

Four risk communication theories have been defined by Covello [2021]. Two of these theories address the people who are receiving the messages while the remaining theories address how the message is delivered.

25.5.1 *Trust Determination*

Trust determination theory is the basis for techniques on how to gain another person's trust in order to accept one's view and is captured by the expression "People need to know that you care before they care about what you know."

Trust determination theory states that when people are upset they are often distrustful and if people think they may lose something, their acceptance of a message is based on trust and credibility. Therefore, this theory emphasises that there are critical factors which determine if someone will trust a person who is trying to convey a message when people have high concern about the issue. There are four critical trust and credibility factors: 1) Empathy and Caring; 2) Dedication and Commitment; 3) Competence; and 4) Honesty and Openness.

What these factors imply is that, commonly, in situations where people are not sure about an issue, they will have questions such as:

- Do they care about what I care about?
- Are they listening to my concerns?
- Are they dedicated and committed professionals?
- Are they competent and knowledgeable about the areas in my concerns?
- Are they honest, open, forthright, truthful and candid?

If a speaker is able to show empathy and caring right from the start when speaking to a group who are uncertain or doubtful about biotechnology, there is an increased likelihood that their position may be considered and accepted. This can be achieved by using various strategies. Non-verbal, visible cues are important as part of the oral communication. Up to 75% of the message in high-risk/

low-trust situations have nothing to do with the content and is completely non-verbal. Factors like eye contact, pointing, an open posture, sitting slightly forward vs. slouching or sitting too close, and tone of voice are all noticed by an audience which is searching for signs of empathy and caring.

Active listening where the listener listens, processes, and then responds without interrupting the speaker also helps display empathy and caring and to achieve a position of trust.

In addition to being perceived as having the attributes of a trustworthy and credible person or organisation, being perceived as having the support of third parties having the attributes of trustworthiness and credibility also contributes to your perception with respect to trust.

It is therefore important to determine, for the country or domain of interest, what the "credibility ladder" on an issue is. A credibility ladder is a list, in decreasing credibility, of the organisations or persons trusted by the public on any particular issue. For food issues, doctors, university professors and teachers are likely to be high on the credibility ladder in most countries, while companies, non-governmental organisations and consultants are commonly found to be low on the credibility ladder. Trust determination theory also tells us that credibility can be transferred from a higher source to a lower source: A lower credibility source takes on the credibility of the highest credible source that agrees with its position on an issue.

25.5.2 *Risk Perception Theory*

Risk perception theory teaches how to minimise the perception of risk as a factor that reduces trust and acceptance by another person.

Many factors affect the perception of risk, and it is important to appreciate that people who are upset have perceptions of risk that are very different from scientific experts.

The theory emphasises that people's perception of risk is strongly influenced by as many as 40 risk perception factors that vary depending on the subject of concern, but the 4 key factors are:

- Trust
- Benefit
- Fairness
- Control

Perceived trust is the most important. Then people need to feel they are in control and that there are benefits to them from accepting a technological innovation. In the case of GM food, the public was (perhaps still is) still largely uninformed about most of the benefits of GM food, such as the positive effects of reducing pesticide use in GM crop production, the higher yields which have allowed food prices to remain low, etc.

An understanding of risk perception helps explain why simply delivering factual messages via public relations or science communication strategies does not work.

Typically, the response to situations where there is resistance from consumers is the launching of education programs. This so-called "deficit model" approach, where a knowledge deficit in someone's minds is filled with information, is flawed, however, and unlikely to achieve the desired outcome, and may even make the situation worse. It fails to appreciate the different ways experts and lay persons perceive risk [Hansen *et al.*, 2003].

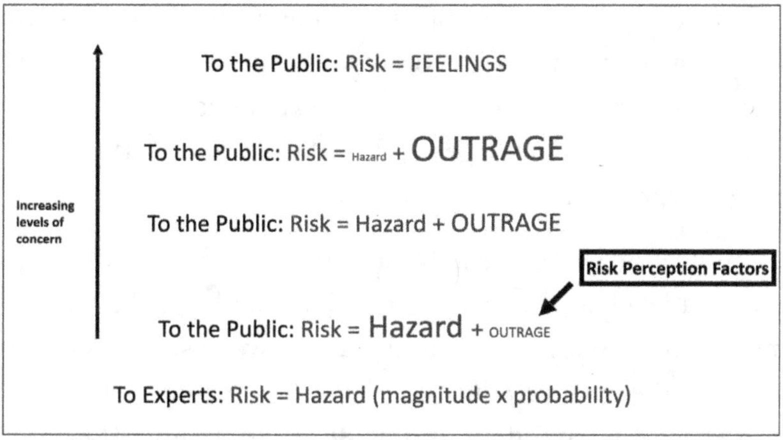

Figure 25.1 The impact of outrage on the importance of hazard.

While the experts look at the introduction of a new technology through an analytical lens (Risk = Hazard), consumers/lay people are more emotional in their assessment of the technology and are impacted by a concept called "Outrage" (Figure 25.1). Outrage is dependent on the risk perception (or outrage factors) noted above. If they are ignored in any communication then outrage builds until it totally outweighs the hazard [Covello and Milligan, 2010; Sandman, 2012; Slovic, 2000].

As many of the risk perception factors have little basis in fact, educating a person in the facts of a new product or technology, particularly when there are high levels of outrage, will not reduce their concerns, and may in fact only further increase the levels of outrage. This, for a technologist, is counterintuitive and contrasts with the facts or, at least, the statistical significance required by science.

25.5.3 *Mental Noise Theory*

Mental noise theory teaches how to craft messages in simple ways that people under stress can readily accept. When people are under stress or concerned, their ability to take on board information is hindered by mental noise or cognitive static and this can cause the loss of up to 80% of incoming messages. Language must be simple, and the number of messages should be limited to three and the messages repeated to combat this static.

Communication should be kept clear and concise by using language that is at a level significantly lower than the language used at the average education level of the audience (Covello suggests four years lower than the average education level of the audience). Technical jargon should be avoided, and answers kept short (two-minute answers), presentations should be short (15 minutes maximum), and when dealing with the media, answers should be very brief, 10 seconds or less. These messages should be decided upon in advance and message maps prepared (see later). Simplicity in language may be checked using a checklist consisting of vocabulary, number of syllables, length of sentence, length of paragraph, passive or active construction, and position of verb in sentence. This is particularly important in written communication on risk issues, especially in food.

25.5.4 *Negative Dominance*

Negativity is problematic in communication on risk issues because when people are upset or stressed, they tend to think negatively and put more weight on negative information.

The rule of thumb which this theory provides is that it takes three positive messages to equate to one negative message. Therefore, to overcome one negative media article will require four positive articles (3+1). Negativity words should also be avoided, e.g., "no", "not" (or "can't", "don't", "won't"), "never", "nothing", and "none". This is because when people are stressed or in high-concern situations, they will tend to hear the negative more than the positive. Negative terms like these also drown out the positive, appear defensive, create an absolute, are difficult to defend, indicate an unwillingness to respond, and sometimes closes options for more dialogue.

25.6 Putting Risk Communication into Practice for Companies and Regulators

Development of a risk communication strategy is a proactive process and not a trivial undertaking. The process requires anticipation, preparation, and practice for the effective delivery of messages to address the situation of concern [Covello and Milligan, 2010].

Anticipation and preparation will include identifying and prioritising stakeholders; identifying scenarios; identifying issues, concerns, questions; identifying risk perceptions and outrage; creating message maps of key issues; developing credibility ladders; identifying partners (e.g., journalists); and identifying and training (the right) spokespeople.

One of the most important tools for preparing clear and effective risk communication messages is the "message map". Message maps contain detailed, hierarchically organised information in blocks designed to respond to anticipated questions or concerns. A message map is a visual aid that provides, at a glance, the messages to be delivered. Message maps allow risk communicators to develop messages in advance and can be tested through focus groups and other empirical studies. All the messages should be vetted for scientific accuracy and consistency by stakeholders in academia, government, and industry.

The development and use of message maps ensure that key messages are consistently delivered by all those within a company, business organisation, public institutions (e.g., regulatory), private, or non-governmental organisation.

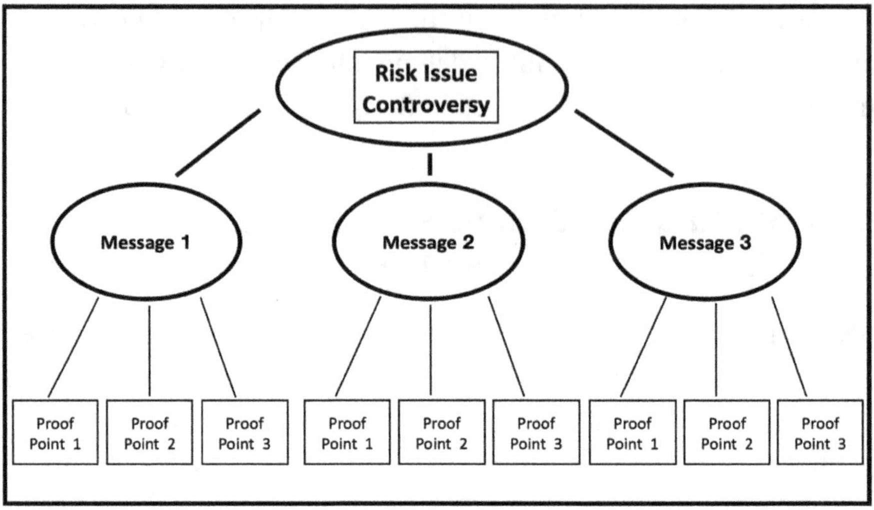

Figure 25.2 Message map example.

Message maps can be constructed in table form, in an Excel format, or in a figure similar to Figure 25.2.

The message map is a cornerstone of communication and allows consistent messaging through an organisation, regulatory or commercial. Any staff member who is likely to interact with external stakeholders should be familiar with the content of the organisation's message maps and have practiced delivering the messages to ensure that they are effective voices of the organisation, i.e., speak clearly, display empathy and care, and not have any behavioural quirks that deflect from the reception of the message.

In addition, entities engaging with the public must also continually monitor traditional and social media for the development of issues that may need to be addressed. Message maps and risk communication have found wide application in changing public and regulatory mindsets towards GM crops derived from biotechnology [Navarro and Hautea, 2011; Teng, 2008].

25.7 Conclusion: Trust and the Environment for Agri-Food Technological Innovation

The creation of an environment for agri-food innovation requires a comprehensive approach that addresses the potential resistance and concerns associated with new technologies and products. While innovations in agriculture and food have the potential to bring significant benefits, they can also face pushback due to the deep emotional and cultural connections people have with food.

Both regulators and companies have the responsibility to create an environment that allows agrifood innovation to flourish. This environment depends on these players being seen as worthy of trust. Risk communication is an essential tool for the creation of this environment. Without this trust, investment in technology will be wasted and food security put at risk.

In Asia, a region which holds the majority of humanity, and which is subject to a plethora of problems that constrain agriculture and food production, technology-based innovations are essential to overcome many of these problems, such as those arising from climate change and natural resource degradation. Innovations which originate from either the public sector (e.g., Golden Rice) or private industry (e.g., novel food) need to be given the appropriate environment to prove their utility. Appropriate communication such as Risk Communication holds much promise to do so.

References

Arujanan, M. and Teng, P. (2018). Legal, Regulatory and Labeling Status of Biotech Crops. In M. Kuntz (Ed.), *Transgenic Plants and Beyond*, pp. 45–89. Elsevier.

Covello, V. T. (2021). *Communicating in Risk, Crisis, and High Stress Situations: Evidence-Based Strategies and Practice*. John Wiley & Sons.

Covello, V. T. and Milligan, P. A. (2010). *Risk Communication: Principles, Tools, & Techniques*. United States Nuclear Regulatory Commission. https://www.nrc.gov/docs/ML1015/ML101590283.pdf

Downes, L. (2009). *The Laws of Disruption: Harnessing the New Forces That Govern Life and Business in the Digital Age*. Basic Books.

Frewer, L. (2004). The public and effective risk communication. *Toxicology Letters*, 149(1–3), pp. 391–397.

Giles, T. D. (2010). Communicating the risk of scientific research. *Journal of Technical Writing and Communication*, 40(3), pp. 265–281.

Hansen, J., Holm, L., Frewer, L., Robinson, P. and Sandøe, P. (2003). Beyond the knowledge deficit: recent research into lay and expert attitudes to food risks. *Appetite*, 41(2), pp. 111–121.

International Service for Acquisition of Agribiotechnology Applications (ISAAA). (2019). *Global Status of Commercialized Biotech/GM Crops: 2019*. https://www.isaaa.org/resources/publications/briefs/55/

Lorenko, L. and Mattheson J. C. (2007). The US FDA and animal cloning: Risk and regulatory approach. *Theriogenology*, 67(1), pp. 198–206.

Malakar, Y., Lacey, J. and Bertsch, P. M. (2022). Towards responsible science and technology: How nanotechnology research and development is shaping risk governance practices in Australia. *Humanities and Social Sciences Communications,* 9, pp. 17–31.

Navarro, M. J. and Hautea, R. A. (Eds). (2011). *Communication Challenges and Convergence in Crop Biotechnology*. International Service for the Acquisition of Agri-biotech Applications (ISAAA).

Phua, R. (2020). Lab-grown chicken to be sold in Singapore after 'world's first' approval for cultured meat. *CNA*. https://www.channelnewsasia.com/singapore/eat-just-lab-grown-chicken-cultured-meat-first-approval-sfa-450071

Renn, O. (2004). Perception of risks. *Toxicology Letters*, 149(1–3), pp. 405–413.

Rudenko, L. and Matheson, J. C. (2007). The US FDA and animal cloning: risk and regulatory approach. *Theriogenology*, 67(1), pp. 198–206.

Shu, C. (2023). Good Meat approved to sell serum-free cultivated meat in Singapore. *TechCrunch*. https://techcrunch.com/2023/01/18/good-meat-regulatory-approval/

Sandman, P. M. (2012). *Responding to Community Outrage: Strategies for Effective Risk Communication*. American Industrial Hygiene Association. http://psandman.com/media/RespondingtoCommunityOutrage.pdf .

Slovic, P. (2000). *The Perception of Risk*. Earthscan Publications.

Teng, P. S. (2008). Risk communication: communicating on GMO topics under challenging conditions. *Biosafety Journal, Korea*, 9(2), pp. 44–63.

Wiedemann, P. M., Clauberg, M. and Börner, F. (2021). *Risk Communication for Companies*. S. Fischer Verlag. https://preparecenter.org/wp-content/uploads/2021/04/Risk-communication-for-companies.pdf

https://doi.org/10.1142/9789811278297_0026

Chapter 26

Think, Feel, Eat: Socio-Psychological Factors Shaping Public Acceptance of Novel Foods

Tong Jee Goh, Mengxia Huang and Shirley S. Ho

Wee Kim Wee School of Communication and Information, Nanyang Technological University, Singapore

26.1 Introduction

Attaining food security is a mounting challenge as the world grapples with a growing population. Food security refers to having consistent physical and economic access to safe food, and the ability to meet the nutritional needs for an active and healthy lifestyle [Food and Agriculture Organization (FAO), 2006]. This definition covers four pillars, namely, availability, access, utilisation, and stability. Utilisation refers to absorption of nutrients; stability occurs when the first three pillars are sustained over time [World Resources Institute (WRI), 2019]. It is estimated that a 56% increase in food production is required to sustain the growing population. World issues, such as climate change, are pressuring food systems [WRI, 2019]. World crises not only signal the urgent need to produce larger quantities of quality food with the available natural resources but also underscore the importance for countries to attain food security at the local level.

Advancements in food technologies hold some answers to strengthening food security. In introducing a series of "Transformative Twelve" technologies for advancing food systems, the World Economic Forum [WEF, 2018] included scientific means for producing novel foods. Although regulatory authorities have not established a universal definition of novel foods, they are known as non-traditional foods that have yet to be formally introduced into a country's food system [European Commission, 2022]. What beholds is the scaling of innovations alongside growing public acceptance to fulfil the potential of food technologies.

Public acceptance is fundamental in determining which novel food technologies will achieve long-term implementation. In this chapter, we provide an overview of several novel foods and key factors that shape public acceptance. Following, we establish the implications of consumers' decision-making processes on food security. Next, we review some of the informational interventions, and those that attempt to shift affective and attitudinal responses. We conclude with recommendations for further research into consumers' acceptance.

26.2 Novel Food Technologies and Food Security

26.2.1 *Nano-Engineered Food*

The nutritional aspect of food is inextricably linked to the safety aspect. Food safety sets the standard for making nutritional food that is critical for preventing diseases and promoting growth available and accessible [World Health Organization (WHO), 2022].

Delivering safe food is therefore key to the attainment of food security. Applications of nanotechnology have enabled food producers to contribute to food security. Nanotechnology reduces materials to sizes as small as one-billionth of a metre (1×10^{-9} m) [Chaudhry *et al.*, 2017]. Nano-engineered food can be produced through applications of nanotechnology. For instance, nano-fertilisers, nano-pesticides, and plant growth regulators can be introduced during cultivation to improve crop quality [Lugani *et al.*, 2021]. The technology can also be applied in parts of the post-harvest value chain, from food processing to preservation and packaging, to raise food safety. Key examples are nano-sensors that detect pathogens on crop surfaces and edible antibacterial nano-coatings that keep food fresh [Lugani *et al.*, 2021]. The WEF [2018] estimated that malnutrition would reduce by 5% with improved access to quality food. Safe applications of nanotechnology would enable consumers to enjoy fresh and nutritious food.

26.2.2 *Alternative Proteins*

Concerns over the resource-intensive nature of food production have prompted the establishment of sustainability as the fifth pillar of food security. Sustainability refers to maintaining sufficient natural resources to support food production [WRI, 2019]. Concerns over using large amounts of resources to produce meat have prompted research and development (R&D) of alternative proteins, which refer to proteins that can substitute conventional animal-based proteins. They include plant-based meat, cultivated meat, insects, and algae [WEF, 2019]. Plant-based meat is manufactured by extracting and processing proteins from plants and adding other ingredients and additives to attain the sensory profile of meat [The Good Food Institute, 2021]. Cultivated meat is created by extracting stem cells from live animals and cultivating the cells in nutrient-rich environments. The muscle and fat cells formed are then processed into the final product [Whiting, 2020]. R&D has unveiled the environmental prospects of cultivated meat. Producing meat in laboratory settings helps reduce greenhouse gas emissions and land usage. Additionally, the environmental benefits of entomophagy, which include utilising minimal water and space [Rumpold and Schlüter, 2013b], promise the viability of insect rearing. The high protein content makes insects good dietary replacements [FAO, 2021]. If the uptake of alternative proteins goes up by another 10%, greenhouse gas emissions can be reduced by up to 8%, while usage of natural resources can drop by at least 12% [WEF, 2018]. These projections emphasise the critical role that dietary changes can play in attaining food security.

26.2.3 *Food From High-Tech Farming*

The agricultural sector is propelled by the prospect of achieving food security through the deployment of advanced technologies. High-tech farming creates the possibility of producing crops and livestock through controlled environment agriculture [Al-Kodmany, 2018]. It involves employing technologies such as the Internet of Things, artificial intelligence, and data analytics to create optimal agricultural conditions. For instance, systems that are designed to cultivate crops can be digitally controlled to achieve the appropriate balance of sunlight, humidity, and temperature [Onag, 2021]. The use of technological devices such as remotely operated vehicles, robotic cages, drones, and smart sensors to monitor conditions of breeding grounds helps ensure the quality of seafood [Musenga, 2021]. With the assistance of technology, the expansion of farming practices into once untapped spaces reduces land use, while raising the accessibility of food.

26.3 Cultural, Social, and Psychological Factors that Shape Acceptance of Novel Foods

From an economic perspective, the novelty of food technologies lies in the recency of introductions into the consumer market, and not necessarily to the "cutting-edge" characteristics of the science and technology involved [European Commission, 2022; Siegrist and Hartman, 2020]. Notwithstanding the prospects of novel food technologies for food security, public acceptance depends on consumers' awareness of the potential pros and cons in terms of health and environment. Other considerations lie in public perception of safety regulations. When consumers make decisions, they would draw upon their cultures, knowledge, mental shortcuts, and the media. In this section, we review the cultural, social, and psychological factors that affect consumers' attitude and acceptance of novel food technologies.

26.3.1 *Culture of Food Consumption*

The impact of cultural groups' established way of eating is best exemplified through entomophagy. Tropical regions in Asia, Africa, and Latin America carry long traditions of entomophagy due to the abundance of insect species [Raheem *et al.*, 2019]. For instance, Thai communities with traditions of entomophagy would consider further consumptions [Tan *et al.*, 2015]. Comparatively, Western societies are less accepting of insect-based products [Toti *et al.*, 2020]. Key reasons are cultural associations of insects with threats, disgust, and savagery [Looy *et al.*, 2014]. Cultural ideations of what are presumably edible in relation to morality, food origins, and civilisation perpetuate reticence [Rozin and Fallon, 1987]. Possibly supported by the cultural acceptance of entomophagy, food manufacturers in Thailand have applied novel technologies to produce insect-based products [Durst and Hanboonsong, 2015]. The entrenchment of cultural values regarding what are acceptable is a strong factor in determining what people are willing to incorporate into their diets.

26.3.2 *Media Framing and Media Use*

Media frames are useful tools for drawing attention to science issues; they also help public interpret the content. Media outlets set frames by defining narrative scopes of various issues. Consequently, some aspects get more spotlight than others [Nisbet and Newman, 2015]. For instance, news framings of health and environmental threats of food technologies [Rickard and Feldpausch-Parker, 2016] can inadvertently sideline the potential benefits. Risk and benefit frames shape consumers' risk and benefit perceptions. Media outlets can also draw public attention to a science issue through policy frames. One such example is framing GM food around the inadequacy of governance [e.g., McCluskey *et al.*, 2016]. The pressure that media outlets exert on policymakers through framing can ignite more debates involving policy and help alter public acceptance of food technologies.

26.3.3 *Heuristic Cues*

Consumers also rely on heuristic cues to form perceptions of novel foods. Relying on heuristic cues involves using mental shortcuts. One reason is a lack of knowledge on food technologies [Gupta *et al.*, 2015]. Esoteric science makes it reasonably difficult for consumers to be well versed in the potential of food technologies in resolving food crises. Consumers' ability to form perceptions despite possessing little knowledge highlights the strong influence of external cues and the propensity to react to related cues [Cobb, 2005].

The cognitive miser model [Fiske and Taylor, 1991] explains people's tendency to devote minimal mental effort to make decisions. Consequently, in a low-information scenario, people rely on mental shortcuts, and this even constitutes a rational process.

26.3.3.1 *Trust in Authorities*

Trust in authorities is a heuristic that shapes risk and benefit perceptions. Trust in governments' policies for technological development and an understanding of authorities' approach for addressing concerns about potential risks can influence public perceptions [Bennett and Radford, 2017]. When limited experience and low familiarity hinder consumers' in-depth understanding of food technologies, belief in authorities' concern for consumers' welfare would boost confidence in the little-known technologies. Importantly, the key role that trust plays in boosting the efficiency of public engagement about technology [Duncan, 2011] suggests that people's belief in authorities could shape their perception more than their knowledge. Trust in authorities is therefore a crucial heuristic in that it is based less on the inherent qualities of novel foods than on the perceptions of the reliability of regulations and robustness of science in finding acceptable trade-offs between risks and benefits.

26.3.3.2 *Perceived Naturalness*

As limited knowledge may hinder consumers' ability to analyse food safety, another reasonable heuristic is the lay perception of naturalness: the non-artificiality of production. When confronted with the notion of altering "natural" compositions, the mental conflicts that consumers encounter would conjure images of "tampering with nature" [Shaw, 2002]. The association of ingesting "foreign" bodies embedded in "unnatural" products with risks provides a logical explanation [Harrison *et al.*, 2013]. This is the case for nano-engineered food. Studies in Europe and Asia showed that a preference for naturalness was associated with stronger risk perception of nano-engineered food as well as support for labelling and banning them [Chuah *et al.*, 2018; Siegrist *et al.*, 2008]. However, nanomedicine was reportedly more accepted [Porcari, 2019], potentially due to the healing effects of medical technology. Although the contrast appears to contest the naturalness heuristic, it emphasises "unnaturalness" as a perception that people hold towards novel foods and which can be quickly dispelled in the presence of another seemingly more compelling heuristic tool. Essentially, the naturalness heuristic shows that even without deep scientific understanding, a reliance on related cues to evaluate food technologies carries strong implications for the future of novel foods.

26.3.3.3 *Spillovers from Past Perception*

Evaluating food technologies based on perceptions of past technologies is another cognitive shortcut. Technological spillover occurs when the reality of a technology influences the prospects of future technologies [Cuppen *et al.*, 2020]. Given the lay public's awareness of the alterations involved in producing genetically modified (GM) food, there is little wonder that they would associate nano-engineered food with GM food on the basis of "manipulation of nature" [Gupta *et al.*, 2017]. Speculations about nano-engineered food can also arise from drawing analogies with asbestos, dioxin, Agent Orange, and nuclear power [Macoubrie, 2005]. There is ground for spillover effects from these materials because animal and cell culture studies revealed that there was some degree of resemblance between engineered nanomaterials and asbestos [Lam *et al.*, 2004; Muller *et al.*, 2005; Oberdorster *et al.*, 2005]. Herein also lies a potential contextual spillover effect since perceived similarity of technologies can lead to rejection. The precedence that the highly televised GM debate sets for nano-engineered food also spells the reality of a historical spillover since lingering concerns over food safety can invoke strong reactions towards nano-engineered food. Currently, there is no known empirical evidence of spillover effects manifesting in cases involving alternative proteins. However, this does not rule out the possibility that the different degrees of cell modifications involved in the productions of plant-based meat and cultivated meat can induce similar technological spillover effects between these two types of alternative proteins, as in the cases of GM and nano-engineered food [Chriki and Hocquette, 2020]. Altogether, the relative novelty of engineered food products implies that spillover effects can impinge on its future, potentially beyond what existing regulations can prevent.

Growing empirical evidence of how perception of GM food can spill over to nano-engineered food puts the challenges of its development into perspective. Among the public in Singapore, people with negative pre-existing attitude towards GM food displayed weaker intention to consume nano-engineered food compared to those with positive pre-existing attitude [Ho *et al.*, 2020]. Risk perception of GM food among French and Germans was associated with an unwillingness to pay for nano-engineered food [Bieberstein *et al.*, 2013]. Likewise, risk perception of GM organisms among Americans significantly correlated with support for the labelling of nanotechnology products [Akin *et al.*, 2019]. Based on the common association between GM-related entities and nano-engineered food across various regions, the case that we have made about spillovers is tenable. In this regard, the challenge for developing nano-engineered food lies not so much in communicating its inherent qualities alone, but in disentangling the novel food technology from a multitude of the preceding technologies.

26.3.4 *Knowledge*

The role of knowledge in influencing acceptance of novel foods is debatable. Proponents of the science literacy model [Miller, 1983] argue that knowledge deficit is a major barrier to acceptance. From this perspective, knowledge of promises of novel food technologies for humankind is key for raising public acceptance. Studies show evidence for the influence of information on acceptance of insect-based food, organic food, and cultivated meat [Barsics, 2017; Lombardi *et al.*, 2019; Woolf *et al.*, 2019; Wang *et al.*, 2019]. However, Piha *et al.* [2018] found contrasting associations between objective knowledge, which is commonly measured through true-false questions, and the attitude towards insect-based food: the association was significant among Northern Europeans, but was non-significant among Central Europeans. However, subjective knowledge, which measures self-reported knowledge, was significantly associated with the outcome. On the other hand, Ho and Goh (forthcoming) found that general science literacy was negatively associated with Singaporeans' support for the development of urban farms, while objective domain-specific knowledge was positively associated with the outcome.

These results highlight several important considerations about the inconsistent influence of knowledge. Drawing the link to Connor and Siegrist's [2010] argument that factors other than knowledge could be influencing acceptance, we raise the possibility that cross-cultural difference could have contributed to such inconsistencies. The authors also acknowledged that dimensions of knowledge that questions capture could be another contributing factor. Hence, while prevailing results have lent some support to the science literacy model, it is crucial for scholars to recognise that knowledge of novel foods can be defined by their nuances, in terms of their economic, environmental, health, technological, and social risks and benefits. Hence, detailed analyses of the influence of various dimensions would be useful for providing insights on the role of knowledge in the context of novel foods.

26.3.5 *Food Neophobia and Food Technology Neophobia*

Another group of factors that can hinder consumers' acceptance of novel foods pertains to food neophobia. Conceptually, food neophobia is a personality trait that causes people to avoid new and unfamiliar food; ethnic food is one example [Pliner and Hobden, 1992]. Taking account of people's tendency to reject novel foods based on technologies employed in manufacturing, food technology neophobia captures an aversion to eating foods produced by novel technologies due to fear [Cox and Evans, 2008]. The key factors resulting in the aversion to food technologies include risk perception, media influence, and health and environmental concerns [Giordano *et al.*, 2018]. Studies in various countries such as Canada, Chile, Italy, and South Korea showed that consumers with food technology neophobia held negative attitudes towards nano-engineered food and GM food, which affected their purchase willingness [e.g., Matin *et al.*, 2012; Kim *et al.*, 2014; Sodano *et al.*, 2016]. Specifically, food technology neophobia towards nano-engineered food could have arisen from people's understanding of the health impact of the toxicity profiles of nano-engineered ingredients and the translocation of what they believe to be harmful nano-materials used in the post-harvest process onto food products [Nile *et al.*, 2020]. In summary, food neophobia is a fear response towards unfamiliar food.

26.4 Implications of the Factors that Shape Public Acceptance of Novel Food

26.4.1 *The Influence of Science Knowledge on Food Acceptance*

Promises of food technologies are substantiated by scientifically espoused knowledge on the health and environmental benefits. The scientific knowledge that consumers think they possess can encourage acceptance of novel foods. An international study reported that over 30% of the consumers surveyed considered the ability to help reverse climate change a key reason for switching to alternative proteins and 75% indicated that the prospect of healthier diets is a major motivator for doing so [Witte *et al.*, 2021]. Consumption intentions that are informed by outcomes suggest that consumers link their perceived knowledge of the science underlying food innovations with the results that technologies can deliver. If the above figures for alternative proteins had reflected rejection, the huge figures across all novel food technologies would speak of massive knowledge inadequacy that could stifle the attainment of food security.

Given evidence on relative roles that knowledge and heuristic cues play, the influence of scientific knowledge on decision making suggests that knowledge adequacy can override the tendency to rely on heuristic cues. Factors for acceptance vary across food technologies. Hence, knowledge adequacy implies that it is necessary to build domain-specific knowledge, which can include knowledge of how the science underlying specific food innovations relates to risks and benefits. Accordingly, there is also room for building knowledge on the implications of the acceptance of specific food technologies on equitable food security. The possibilities for knowledge building signal the potential to foster knowledge-driven decisions.

Importantly, raising the dominance of knowledge means overcoming potential constraints posed by heuristic cues and preventing biased decisions.

26.4.2 *The Influence of Heuristic Cues on Food Acceptance*

Granted, non-expert consumers tend to rely on heuristic cues, which in most cases mean basing decision making on incomplete pictures of R&D advancements. The efforts that notable organisations undertook in addressing inaccurate perceptions of food technologies illustrate the potential impact of heuristic cues on food security. Addressing the oft-cited claim that GM foods are unsafe, The Royal Society [2016] stated categorically that no substantial evidence points towards the health detriments of consumption and that doing so does not alter a person's genes. Amid escalating concerns over consuming carcinogenic by-products of food irradiation, a tripartite study concluded that there are no risks associated with applying ionising radiation to preserve food; even high doses can eliminate foodborne diseases and raise the availability of safe food [Joint FAO/IAEA/WHO Study Group on High-Dose Irradiation, 1999]. In other words, if authorities (e.g., scientific organisations and public agencies) lapsed in their attempts at overriding heuristic cues with substantial knowledge on safety standards, persistent reliance on heuristic cues among target populations of novel foods can cost opportunities to benefit from transformative food technologies.

Notwithstanding situations in which heuristic cues can result in biased decisions, mental shortcuts can facilitate decision making. Organisational trust guides non-expert consumers to accept novel foods. In this regard, Siegrist *et al.* [2003] argued that assessments of organisations' trustworthiness are dependent on how much organisations' efforts align with consumers' values. Hence, consistent efforts in conducting R&D and providing updates on food safety standards would raise the visibility of organisations' commitment to safeguarding public welfare, which in turn would raise public acceptance of novel foods and the attainment of food security. To raise awareness of entomophagy, the FAO has been supporting local insect-rearing initiatives and engaging in public education. Underscoring the importance of building trust through robust regulations, the WHO [2019] called for harmonisation of country- or region-based food safety regulations with international standards. Evidently, the WHO recognises the paramount importance of consumers' trust in strong regulatory systems in bolstering food innovations. Hence, as far as consumer engagement is concerned, organisations need to be strategic in reducing consumers' reliance on heuristic cues that hinder acceptance and leverage the trust heuristic to boost confidence, promote innovations, and strengthen food security.

26.5 Socio-psychological Interventions to Promote Consumer Acceptance of Novel Foods

26.5.1 *Cognitive Interventions Through Information Exposure*

Experimental interventions have displayed the effects of information exposure on consumers' reactions. Lombardi *et al.* [2019] found that compared to the instance when participants were exposed to general information on the difference between conventional food products and those that contained mealworms, the exposure to specific information on individual benefit (i.e., health) and collective benefit (i.e., food security and environmental benefits) of the latter product resulted in stronger willingness to pay for insect-based products. Russo *et al.*'s [2020] neurophysiological study found that claims on the tastiness and healthfulness of crackers that contained earthworm flour caused food tasters to move towards the product; the healthfulness claims induced stronger reactions. Additionally, a video that presented information on the product's nutritional value and contribution to environmental sustainability reduced the tasters' aversion to the product. This result corroborates the earlier result on individual and collective benefits.

Regarding GM food, Raza *et al.* [2021] also found that the knowledge gain that resulted from exposure to information on its health and environmental benefits was significantly associated with perceived risk reduction. Based on the concept of on-pack communication, Biondi and Camanzi [2020] found that participants who were exposed to claims on the nutritional, environmental, hedonic (i.e., gustatory pleasure) and innovative (i.e., of the food processing) aspects of a novel vegetable oil held strong perceptions of the product accordingly. Particularly, assessments on the nutritional aspect enhanced participants' assessments on all the other three aspects, introducing what is known as a halo effect. Together, these studies suggest that in addition to making health claims, additional information on the sensory, sustainability, and scientific aspects of novel foods has the potential to alter consumers' responses.

26.5.2 *Affective Outcomes of Exposure to Aspects of Novel Foods*

Exposure to novel foods also altered emotional reactions towards, and in turn impacted, consumption intention. Krings *et al.* [2022] found that consumers rated meat dishes that were introduced as "regular meat" (i.e., meat from farmed animals) more favourably compared to those introduced as "clean meat". Food technology neophobia moderated this result: consumers who rated high on this factor (vs. low) were more favourable of the regular-meat dishes. Similarly, burgers said to contain patties made with novel ingredients, including mealworms (i.e., novel burgers; vs. burgers with regular beef patties) received lower ratings on sensory liking; the willingness to eat novel burgers was also significantly lower [Tan *et al.*, 2016]. Also concerning alternative proteins, another study that considered the extent of processing insects found that consumers displayed the least level of liking and willingness to consume tortilla chips that were mixed with whole crickets. Relatedly, the chips containing insects (i.e., either in the bit or whole forms) evoked stronger negative emotions such as "sickened" and "grossed out". Conversely, reduced visibility of crickets elicited positive responses [Gmuer *et al.*, 2016]. In summary, how alternative proteins are presented to consumers can evoke different emotions.

Additional findings illustrate how affective evaluation depends on social contexts of consumption. For instance, Motoki *et al.* [2022] found that anticipating eating novel foods with friends and at festivals increased expected positive arousal and calmness. The more positive the emotional responses were, the stronger the willingness to try novel foods. In relation to the earlier point on presentation of alternative proteins, this result suggests that while some characteristics of novel foods induce negative affective responses, introducing other interventions can help overcome the constraints to acceptance.

26.5.3 *Attitudinal Outcomes of Exposure to Aspects of Novel Foods*

Research also presents substantial evidence on the impact of psychological interventions. Based on the notion of social representation, Bryant and Barnett [2019] found that nomenclatures of cultivated meat connotated different ideas. Particularly, "lab-grown meat" received the poorest attitudinal response compared to "animal-free meat", "clean meat" and "cultured meat". Additionally, "clean meat" was deemed to be vastly different from "lab-grown meat". Overall, non-technical nomenclatures impacted the positivity of evaluations, which in turn raised consumption intention. Similarly, Siegrist *et al.* [2018] found that consumers who were exposed to descriptions of organic meat (vs. technical descriptions: made using biotechnology) perceived stronger naturalness of organic meat. In one instance, the participants assigned to the cultured-meat and organic-meat conditions perceived traditional meat to be more natural than each respective type of meat, despite the absence of descriptions of traditional meat. It is plausible that with respect to traditional meat, perceptions of the larger difference with cultured meat than with organic meat could have steered consumers to pick a "safer option". Overall, exposure to cultured meat reduced the willingness to buy cultured meat. Between the two cultured-meat conditions, the non-technical condition (vs. technical condition) evoked a stronger willingness to buy cultured meat. While it appears to be difficult to eliminate consumers' negative evaluations, interventions that highlight the non-technical aspects and reduce anchoring to traditional meat could pave the way towards raising positive evaluations and driving acceptance.

26.6 Prospects for Research on Factors Influencing Consumer Acceptance

The evidence that supports the effectiveness of (a) information that stress personal and collective benefits and (b) on-pack communication suggests the prospects of using strategic platforms for positioning novel foods vis-à-vis food security. Foremost, regarding front-of-packing messaging, future research can examine the relative effectiveness of personal and collective benefits across a wider range of novel foods, and also study the effectiveness of including scientific vs. non-scientific explanations of manufacturing and the respective products' contributions to food security. Additionally, testing the effectiveness of endorsements by authorities and product spokespersons on food packaging is another viable direction. Further research can investigate how message modality (e.g., images, text, audio) and platform choice (e.g., social media vs. traditional media) can affect advertising outcomes across different consumer groups.

Another insightful finding is that of the halo effect [Thorndike, 1920], in the sense that consumers rely heuristically on a positive attribute of a novel food to make conclusions of other attributes, or even the product as a whole. Prevailing evidence points to the halo effect of health information on the sensory aspects of novel foods. Particularly, the halo effect on consumers' evaluations of environmental benefits and product innovativeness is useful for informing research that aims to examine how consumers' evaluations of specific attributes can impact their perception of how consuming novel foods contributes to food security. Further, research can also examine how the halo effect can lead to biased expectations of novel foods and what types of interventions can be introduced to achieve a more balanced understanding of the prospects of novel foods for food security.

Regarding the effect of visual stimulus on consumers' reactions, research has shown that the visibility of insect parts evoked negative emotions. On the same note, future research can examine the effect of colour of insect-based food. Besides, food tasting experiments can expand the scope of sensory stimuli by examining the impact of gustatory and olfactory interventions on affect and acceptance.

Essentially, these directions revolve around direct experiences. Yet, Rousset *et al.*'s [2008] examination of how other eaters' facial expressions influenced target consumers' consumption desire point us in more research directions: examine the impact of displaying (a) others' reactions towards and (b) consumers' ratings of sensory qualities on packaging and different advertising platforms.

With respect to introductions of novel foods, research has shown that names and descriptions can connotate various ideas, which in turn evoke different reactions. On this note, we propose that future research examine differences in reactions due to variations in the language used to introduce novel foods in promotional efforts and front-of-pack messaging. Related to the use of technical language (vs. non-technical), one example is testing the effects of product descriptors that incorporate scientific terms (e.g., "This product contains the *Histidine* protein from the *Acheta domesticus* cricket species."; Rumpold and Schlüter, 2013a) and one that does not (e.g., "This product contains parts of crickets."). The same approach can be taken in the context of nanotechnology and high-tech farming.

26.7 Conclusion

Public acceptance of novel foods bears major implications for food security. Consumers' direct experiences and encounters that are mediated by media and communication can affect the prospects of novel foods in attaining food security. The factors that predict acceptance provide some leverage for prompting consumers to incorporate novel foods into their diets. Meanwhile, stakeholders need to be cognizant of the hurdles and explore cognitive, affective, and attitudinal interventions that can raise acceptance.

Acknowledgment

This research is supported by the Ministry of Education, Singapore, under its Academic Research Fund Tier 1 (Grant Number: RT16/20).

References

Akin, H., Yeo, S. K., Wirz, C. D., Scheufele, D. A., Brossard, D., Xenos, M. A. and Corley, E. A. (2019). Are attitudes toward labeling nano products linked to attitudes toward GMO? Exploring a potential "spillover" effect for attitude toward controversial technologies. *Journal of Responsible Innovation,* 6(1), pp. 50–74.

Al-Kodmany, K. (2018). The vertical farm: a review of developments and implications for the vertical city. *Buildings,* 8(2), p. 24.

Barsics, F., Megido, R. C., Brostaux, Y., Barsics, C., Blecker, C., Haubruge, E. and Francis, F. (2017). Could new information influence attitudes to foods supplemented with edible insects? *British Food Journal,* 119(9), pp. 2027–2039.

Bennett, D. and Radford, T. (2017). Public Perceptions of Nanotechnologies: Lessons from Genetically Modified Foods. In Q. Chaudhry, L. Castle, and R. Watkins (Eds.), *Nanotechnologies in Food*, pp. 60–80. Royal Society of Chemistry.

Bieberstein, A., Roosen, J., Marette, S., Blanchemanche, S. and Vandermoere, F. (2013). Consumer choices for nano-food and nano-packaging in France and Germany. *European Review of Agriculture Economics,* 40(1), pp. 73–94.

Biondi, B. and Camanzi, L. (2020). Nutrition, hedonic or environmental? The effect of front-of-pack messages on consumers' perception and purchase intention of a novel food product with multiple attributes. *Food Research International,* 130, p. 108962.

Bryant, C. J. and Barnett, J. C. (2019). What's in a name? Consumer perceptions of in vitro meat under different names. *Appetite,* 137, pp. 104–113.

Chaudhry, Q., Watkins, R. and Castle, L. (2017). Nanotechnologies in Food: What, Why and How?. In Q. Chaudhry, L. Castle, and R. Watkins (Eds.), *Nanotechnologies in Food*, pp. 1–18. Royal Society of Chemistry.

Chriki, S. and Hocquette, J.-F. (2020). The myth of cultured meat: A review. *Frontiers in Nutrition*, 7(7), p. 7.

Chuah, A. S. F., Leong, A. D., Cummings, C. L. and Ho, S. S. (2018). Label it or ban it? Public perceptions of nano-food labels and propositions for banning nano-food applications. *Journal of Nanoparticle Research*, 20, p. 36.

Cobb, M. D. (2005). Framing effects on public opinion about nanotechnology. *Science Communication*, 27(2), pp. 221–239.

Connor, M. and Siegrist, M. (2010). Factors influencing people's acceptance of gene technology: The role of knowledge, health expectations, naturalness, and social trust. *Science Communication*, 32(4), pp. 514–538.

Cox, D. N. and Evans, G. (2008). Construction and validation of a psychometric scale to measure consumers' fears of novel food technologies: The food technology neophobia scale. *Food Quality and Preference*, 19(8), pp. 704–710.

Cuppen, E., Ejderyan, O., Pesch, U., Spruit, S., van de Grift, E., Correljé, A. and Taebi, B. (2020). When controversies cascade: Analysing the dynamics of public engagement and conflict in the Netherlands and Switzerland through "controversy spillover". *Energy Research & Social Science*, 68(7), p. 101593.

Duncan, T. V. (2011). The communication challenges presented by nanofoods. *Nature Nanotechnology*, 6, pp. 683–688.

Durst, P. B. and Hanboonsong, Y. (2015). Small-scale production of edible insects for enhanced food security and rural livelihoods: Experience from Thailand and Lao People's Democratic Republic. *Journal of Insects as Food and Feed*, 1(1), pp. 25–31.

European Commission. (2022). Novel food. https://food.ec.europa.eu/safety/novel-food_en#:~:text=What%20is%20Novel%20Food%3F,novel%20food%20came%20into%20force.

Fiske, S. T. and Taylor, S. E. (1991). *Social Cognition*. McGraw-Hill.

Food and Agriculture Organization. (2006). Food security: Policy brief. https://www.fao.org/fileadmin/templates/faoitaly/documents/pdf/pdf_Food_Security_Cocept_Note.pdf

Food and Agriculture Organization. (2021). *Looking at Edible Insects from a Food Safety Perspective*. https://www.fao.org/3/cb4094en/cb4094en.pdf

Giordano, S., Clodoveo, M. L., De Gennaro, B. and Corbo, F. (2018). Factors determining neophobia and neophilia with regard to new technologies applied to the food sector: A systematic review. *International Journal of Gastronomy and Food Science*, 11, pp. 1–19.

Gmuer, A., Guth, J. N., Hartmann, C. and Siegrist, M. (2016). Effects of the degree of processing of insect ingredients in snacks on expected emotional experiences and willingness to eat. *Food Quality and Preference,* 54, pp. 117–127.

Gupta, N., Fischer, A. R. H. and Frewer, L. J. (2015). Ethics, risk and benefits associated with different applications of nanotechnology: A comparison of expert and consumer perceptions of drivers of social acceptance. *Nanoethics,* 9, pp. 93–108.

Gupta, N., Frewer, L. and Fischer, A. (2017). Acceptance of Agri-Food Nanotechnology: Insights from the Evolution of Food Technology, Novel Foods and the Psychology of Novel Food Acceptance and Evidence from Present Study. In Q. Chaudhry, L. Castle, and R. Watkins (Eds.), *Nanotechnologies in Food*, pp. 39–59. Royal Society of Chemistry.

Harrison, K. L., Geller, G., Marshall, P., Tilburt, J., Mercer, M., Brinich, M. A., Highland, J., Farrell, R. M. and Sharp, R. R. (2013). Ethical discourse about the modification of food for therapeutic purposes: How patients with gastrointestinal diseases view the good, the bad, and the healthy. *AJOB Primary Research,* 3(3), pp. 12–20.

Ho, S. S., Goh, T. J., Chuah, A. S. F., Leung, Y. W., Bekalu, M. A. and Viswanath, K. (2020). Past debates, fresh impact on nano-enabled food: A multigroup comparison of presumed media influence model based on spillover effects of attitude toward genetically modified food. *Journal of Communication,* 70(4), pp. 598–621.

Ho, S. S. and Goh, T. J. (forthcoming). Making space for food: The socio-psychological and communication factors shaping support for urban farms in Singapore.

Joint FAO/IAEA/WHO Study Group on High-Dose Irradiation. (1999). *High Dose Irradiation: Wholesomeness of Food Irradiated with Doses Above 10kGy.* https://apps.who.int/iris/handle/10665/42203

Kim, Y. G., Jang, S. Y. and Kim, A. K. (2014). Application of the theory of planned behavior to genetically modified foods: Moderating effects of food technology neophobia. *Food Research International*, 62, pp. 947–954.

Krings, V. C., Dhont, K. and Hodson, G. (2022). Food neophobia as a psychological barrier to clean meat acceptance. *Food Quality and Preference,* 96, p. 104409.

Lam, C. W., James, J. T., McClusky, R. and Hunter, R. K. (2004). Pulmonary toxicity of single-wall carbon nanotubes in mice 7 and 90 days after intratracheal instillation. *Toxicological Sciences,* 77(1), pp. 126–134.

Lombardi, A., Vecchio, R., Borrello, M., Caracciolo, F. and Cembalo, L. (2019). Willingness to pay for insect-based food: The role of information and carrier. *Food Quality and Preference,* 72, pp. 177–187.

Looy, H., Dunkel, F. V. and Wood, J. R. (2014). How then shall we eat? Insect-eating attitudes and sustainable foodways. *Agriculture and Human* Values, 31, pp. 131–141.

Lugani, Y., Oberoi, S. and Rattu, G. (2021). Nanotechnology in Food Industry-Applications and Future Perspectives. In V. K. Maurya, K. M. Gothandam, S. Ranjan, N. Dasgupta, and E. Lichtfouse (Eds.), *Sustainable Agriculture Reviews 55*, pp. 71–92. Springer.

Macoubrie, J. (2005). *Informed Public Perceptions of Nanotechnology and Trust in Government.* Woodrow Wilson International Center for Scholars. https://search.issuelab.org/resource/informed-public-perceptions-of-nanotechnology-and-trust-in-government.html

Matin, A. H., Goddard, E., Vandermoere, F., Blanchemanche, S., Bieberstein, A., Marette, S. and Roosen, J. (2012). Do environmental attitudes and food technology neophobia affect perceptions of the benefits of nanotechnology?. *International Journal of Consumer Studies*, 36(2), pp. 149–157.

McCluskey, J. J., Kalaitzandonakes, N. and Swinnen, J. (2016). Media coverage, public perceptions, and consumer behavior. *Annual Review of Resource Economics*, 8, pp. 467–486.

Miller, J. D. (1983). Scientific literacy: A conceptual and empirical review. *Daedalus*, 112(2), pp. 29–48.

Motoki, K., Park, J., Spence, C. and Velasco, C. (2022). Contextual acceptance of novel and unfamiliar foods: Insects, cultured meat, plant-based alternatives, and 3D printed food. *Food Quality and Preference*, 96(1), pp. 104368.

Muller, J., Huaux, F., Moreau, N., Misson, P., Heilier, J. F., Delos, M., Arras, M., Fonseca, A., Nagy, J. B. and Lison, D. (2005). Respiratory toxicity of multi-wall carbon nanotubes. *Toxicology and Applied Pharmacology*, 207(3), pp. 221–231.

Musenga, G. (2021, April 7). Advanced technology and aquaculture: Drones and artificial intelligence to make a difference. *Agrilinks*. https://www.agrilinks.org/post/advanced-technology-and-aquaculture-drones-and-artificial-intelligence-make-difference

Nile, S. H., Baskar, V., Selvaraj, D., Nile, A., Xiao, J., and Kai, G. (2020). Nanotechnologies in food science: Applications, recent trends, and future perspectives. *Nano-Micro Letters*, 12(1), 45.

Nisbet, M. C. and Newman, T. P. (2015). Framing, the Media, and Environmental Communication. In A. Hansen and R. Cox (Eds.), *The Routledge Handbook of Environment and Communication*, pp. 325–383. Routledge.

Oberdorster, G., Oberdorster, E. and Oberdorster, J. (2005). Nanotoxicology: An emerging discipline evolving from studies of ultrafine particles. *Environment Health Perspectives*, 113(7), pp. 823–839.

Onag, G. (2021). IoT sensors enable urban farming in Singapore. *FutureiOT*. https://futureiot.tech/iot-sensors-enable-urban-farming-in-singapore/

Piha, S., Pohjanheimo, T., Lähteenmäki-Uutela, A., Křečková, Z. and Otterbring, T. (2018). The effects of consumer knowledge on the willingness to buy insect food: An exploratory cross-regional study in Northern and Central Europe. *Food Quality and Preference*, 70, pp. 1–10.

Pliner, P. and Hobden, K. (1992). Development of a scale to measure the trait of food neophobia in humans. *Appetite,* 19(2), pp. 105–120.

Porcari, A., Borsella, E., Benighaus, C., Grieger, K., Isigonis, P., Chakravarty, S., Kines, P. and Jensen, K. A. (2019). From risk perception to risk governance in nanotechnology: A multi-stakeholder study. *Journal of Nanoparticle Research,* 21, p. 245.

Raheem, D., Carrascosa, C., Oluwole, O. B., Nieuwland, M., Saraiva, A., Millán, R. and Raposo, A. (2019). Traditional consumption of and rearing edible insects in Africa, Asia and Europe. *Critical Reviews in Food Science and Nutrition,* 59(14), pp. 2169–2188.

Raza, S. H., Zaman, U., Ferreira, P. and Farías, P. (2021). An experimental evidence on public acceptance of genetically modified food through advertisement framing on health and environmental benefits, objective knowledge, and risk education. *International Journal of Environmental Research and Public Health,* 18(10), pp. 5264.

Rickard, L. N. and Feldpausch-Parker, A. M. (2016). Of sea lice and superfood: A comparison of regional and national news media coverage of aquaculture. *Frontiers in Communication,* 1, p. 14.

Rousset, S., Schlich, P., Chatonnier, A., Barthomeuf, L. and Droit-Volet, S. (2008). Is the desire to eat familiar and unfamiliar meat products influenced by the emotions expressed on eaters' faces? *Appetite,* 50(1), pp. 110–119.

Rozin, P. and Fallon, A. E. (1987). A perspective on disgust. *Psychological Review,* 94(1), pp. 23–41.

Rumpold, B. A. and Schlüter, O. K. (2013a). Nutritional composition and safety aspects of edible insects. *Molecular Nutrition and Food Research,* 57(3), pp. 802–823.

Rumpold, B. A. and Schlüter, O. K. (2013b). Potential and challenges of insects as an innovative source for food and feed production. *Innovative Food Science & Emerging Technologies*, 17, pp. 1–11.

Russo, V., Songa, G., Marin, L. E. M., Balzaretti, C. M. and Tedesco, D. F. A. (2020). Novel food-based product communication: A neurophysiological study. *Nutrients,* 12(7), pp. 2092.

Shaw, A. (2002). "It just goes against the grain": Public understandings of genetically modified (GM) food in the UK. *Public Understanding of Science,* 11(3), pp. 273–91.

Siegrist, M., Earle, T. C. and Gutscher, H. (2003). Test of a trust and confidence model in the applied context of electromagnetic field (EMF) risks. *Risk Analysis,* 23(4), pp. 705–716.

Siegrist, M. and Hartmann, C. (2020). Perceived naturalness, disgust, trust and food neophobia as predictors of cultured meat acceptance in ten countries. *Appetite,* 155, p. 104814.

Siegrist, M., Stampfli, N., Kastenholz, H. and Keller, C. (2008). Perceived risks and perceived benefits of different nanotechnology foods and nanotechnology food packaging. *Appetite,* 51(2), pp. 283–290.

Siegrist, M., Sutterlin, B. and Hartmann, C. (2018). Perceived naturalness and evoked disgust influence acceptance of cultured meat. *Meat Science,* 139, pp. 213–219.

Sodano, V., Gorgitano, M. T., Verneau, F. and Vitale, C. D. (2016). Consumer acceptance of food nanotechnology in Italy. *British Food Journal,* 118(3), pp. 714–733.

Tan, H. S. G., Fischer, A. R. H., Tinchan, P., Stieger, M., Steenbekkers, L. P. A. and van Trijp, H. C. M. (2015). Insects as food: Exploring cultural exposure and individual experience as determinants of acceptance. *Food Quality and Preference,* 42, pp. 78–89.

Tan, H. S. G., Fischer, A. R. H., van Trijp, H. C. M. and Stieger, M. (2016). Tasty but nasty? Exploring the role of sensory-liking and food appropriateness in the willingness to eat unusual novel foods like insects. *Food Quality and Preference,* 48, pp. 293–302.

The Good Food Institute. (2021). The science of plant-based meat. https://gfi.org/science/the-science-of-plant-based-meat/

The Royal Society. (2016). GM plants: Questions and answers. https://royalsociety.org/-/media/policy/projects/gm-plants/gm-plant-q-and-a.pdf

Thorndike, E. L. (1920). A constant error in psychological ratings. *Journal of Applied Psychology,* 4(1), pp. 25–29.

Toti, W., Massaro, L., Kais, A., Aiello, P., Palmery, M. and Peluso, I. (2020). Entomophagy: A narrative review on nutritional value, safety, cultural acceptance and a focus on the role of food neophobia in Italy. *European Journal of Investigation in Health, Psychology and Education,* 10(2), pp. 628–643.

Wang, X., Pacho, F., Liu, J. and Kajungiro, R. (2019). Factors influencing organic food purchase intention in developing countries and the moderating role of knowledge. *Sustainability,* 11(1), p. 209.

Whiting, K. (2020). How soon will we be eating lab-grown meat? *World Economic Forum.* https://www.weforum.org/agenda/2020/10/will-we-eat-lab-grown-meat-world-food-day/

Witte, B., Obloj, P., Koktenturk, S., Morach, B., Brigl, M., Rogg, J., Schulze, U., Walker, D., von Koeller, E., Dehnert, N. and Grosse-Holz, F. (2021). Food for thought: the protein transformation. *Boston Consulting Group and Blue Horizon.* https://web-assets.bcg.com/a0/28/4295860343c6a2a5b9f4e3436114/bcg-food-for-thought-the-protein-transformation-mar-2021.pdf

Woolf, E., Zhu, Y., Emory, K., Zhao, J. and Liu, C. (2019). Willingness to consume insect-containing foods: A survey in the United States. *LWT — Food Science and Technology,* 102(2), pp. 100–106.

World Economic Forum. (2018). *Innovation with a Purpose: The Role of Technology Innovation in Accelerating Food Systems Transformation.*

https://www3.weforum.org/docs/WEF_Innovation_with_a_Purpose_VF-reduced.pdf

World Economic Forum. (2019). *Meat: The Future Series; Alternative Proteins.* https://www3.weforum.org/docs/WEF_White_Paper_Alternative_Proteins.pdf

World Health Organization. (2019). *Promoting Harmonized Food Safety Regulation in a Time of Change, Innovation and Globalized Trade.* https://www.who.int/docs/default-source/resources/promoting-harmonized-food-safety-regulation-en.pdf

World Health Organization. (2022). Food safety. https://www.who.int/health-topics/food-safety

World Resources Institute. (2019). *Creating a Sustainable Food Future: A Menu of Solutions to Feed Nearly 10 Billion People by 2050.* https://files.wri.org/d8/s3fs-public/wrr-food-full-report.pdf

https://doi.org/10.1142/9789811278297_0027

Chapter 27

Future-Gazing into the Trends Affecting Asian Food Security

Luke Tay

Cornucopia FutureScapes, Singapore

27.1 Introduction

The 2000s have been called "The Asian Century", marking the expected shift in the preponderance in world affairs away from the West and towards Asia. Whether or not Asia ends up holding such sway, by its mass of population, economy, cultural vibrancy and diversity, or geopolitical heft, its prospects and performance — good, bad, or weirdly surprising — will be key to shaping world futures at large. The development path of Asian food systems and food security outcomes across the region will play an enabling and perhaps even a decisive role in these wider developments.

Reviewing the preceding chapters of the book, one is struck by the congruence between its scope and perspectives raised in a survey of food system stakeholders conducted in 2022 [Tay, 2022] of their mid- to longer-term outlook on issues for the food system, summarised in Table 27.1.[1]

Table 27.1 Summary of key issues from 2022 stakeholder survey.

Cornucopia FutureScapes Food Foresight Opinion Leaders' Survey (Early 2022)
• **Notable concerns** raised included the climate emergency, OneHealth, the food-health nexus and personalised nutrition, food system synergies with energy and water systems, circularity and combatting food loss and waste, rivalry between legacy and emerging food categories, avoiding an over-concentration on a narrow range of species for food, flexing agricultural heritage systems, scaling up regenerative agriculture, the future of work in agrifood, and a just transition for smallholders.
• **Urban food systems** were seen as a focal point for applied technological innovation and policy redesign, including to elevate self-sufficiency and resiliency in the face of disruption. This should be planned together with reconceptualising and transforming periurban and rural areas, and national and cross-border infrastructure, as a system.
• **Resiliency** of food systems was a key concern, across production, the supply chain, the agrifood workforce, consumer access and affordability, and in terms of anticipation of perturbations.
• A range of **technologies and innovations** of interest were cited, including controlled environment agriculture, functional foods, digitalisation of the food system, food system applications for the "omic" sciences, nature-based solutions including bioremediation, fermentation, food production from the air, and mechanisms for emissions trading.
• "**Food citizenship**" and shifting food values and expectations were flagged as themes of interest, and how communities may partner with stakeholders to lift themselves out of food insecurity; the key role of food-related knowledge, information, and resilience against misinformation were noted.
• A greater focus on **food system governance** was considered key, including joined up with adjacent policy areas, and with greater intervention and subvention under the rubric of securitising the food system. Universal basic nutrition, as an aspect of "Universal Basic Income", was one noted concept.
• In **international trade and industrial policy**, momentum towards nearshoring, reshoring, and friendshoring was noted, as were opportunities for "**green growth**" for the food system.

[1] Cornucopia FutureScapes Food Foresight Opinion Leaders' Survey (early 2022).

But how will such a wide range of factors shaping the future of food systems interact, and to what end? Moreover, the food system is perhaps one of those most exposed to the shaping push and pull of developments in the broader world system: even as "inside-out", food systems performance has effects on wider human and planetary wellbeing, and there is also a decisive "outside-in" effect from environmental, geopolitical, economic, social, and broader technological trends, with these extrinsic factors also significantly shaping the possibilities, opportunities, imperatives, and constraints faced by actors in the food system.

Futurists assess the salient factors and issues that shape emerging outcomes for a given system, and frame and analyse them as "driving forces". Besides gauging the level of impact they have, a key consideration is how uncertain their trajectories and outcomes may be [Centre for Strategic Futures, 2012]. Such "critical uncertainties" among the driving forces multiply the range of possible future states for the system by the range of possible permutations of their interactions — all the more so across longer timescales — so much so that it is absurd to hold to one single "forecast" or "official version" of the future of food.

Futures thinking, or put in more utilitarian and actionable terms, "strategic foresight" is one means to make sense of this palpable complexity and uncertainty, for informed pro-action. In particular, the scenario method helps flesh out how a range of plausible futures could take shape based on how critical uncertainties and their interactions play out differently, the holistic contemplation of which enables "future-ready" "re-visioning", "re-missioning", and forward planning by food system stakeholders, individually and collectively, to position for various futures beyond their control, and to "lean in", exercising their considerable individual and collective agency, to shape actual outcomes in preferred directions.

This chapter uses a scenario frame to characterise the "critical uncertainties" which will shape Asian food systems' development and performance, posit scenario outcomes from various permutations of their direction and interaction, discuss implications, and conclude with broader reflections on the unfolding Asian food century.

27.2 Critical Uncertainties Shaping the Asian Food System

Looking ahead towards the mid-21st century, we may start by posing a framing focal question looking out a decade hence to the century's one-third mark: ***What will the Asian food system look like in 2033?***

Apropos to the question, some major forces shaping outcomes would include: climate effects on regional agrifood production and value chains; emerging global and regional geopolitical and geoeconomic contours; advances in technology and innovation (whether originating in food-centric domains, or beyond), social and demographic change and its effect on the food "demand-scape" and civil society's actions in the food domain; and dominant agrifood policy approaches among Asian states.

27.2.1 *Whither the Climate?*

Climate may be considered a "critical uncertainty". The reality of the "climate emergency" is settled science, and its ravages are an increasing challenge for food systems today. Realisation of the importance of food systems to addressing climate change was reflected in how the 2022 United Nations Climate Change Conference (COP27) was the first to emphasise food-climate linkages as a key theme. Looking towards mid-century, the coherence and robustness of global climate mitigation efforts can be seen as highly uncertain. Moreover, the salutary effects of even concerted decarbonisation (or ill effects of unhindered emissions growth) on the food system may be more palpable only further into the 21st century.

Key uncertainties for Asia, given its geographic expanse and diversity, would be how acute and varied extreme weather effects would be on food production and value chains across the region, through known mechanisms such as sea level rise, of particular concern to littoral and maritime Asia, and volatile weather and glacial melt at the Tibetan plateau affecting river-irrigated agricultural systems across the East, Southeast, and South Asian continental massif.

In weighing climate impacts, we must of course look beyond the food system we have today, to how and how successfully it may adapt at local, national, regional and wider scales, through techniques such as "climate-smart agriculture", controlled environment agriculture, adjustment to crops and growing areas, measures to address climate factors influencing food loss and waste, and so on.

Global heating is but one of a range of environmental and biodiversity-related pressures facing the food system, in which the food system is likewise complicit. To what extent may the Asian food system both mitigate its overall ecological footprint to conform to planetary limits, and adapt to overcome challenges that arise, including contamination and threats to food safety, and plant, animal, and zoonotic diseases? What may be the impact of known concerns such as African Swine Fever, zoonotic Avian Influenza, and fall armyworm and locust infestations — along with novel threats — moving forward, influenced by rising temperatures and changing wind and weather patterns?

27.2.2 *Geopolitics and Geoeconomics*

With the unwinding of the (first!) Cold War in the 1990s, "The End of History" was proclaimed by Francis Fukuyama [1989]. The West and its allies had prevailed. Liberal democracy and free market capitalism had been vindicated as the world's default operating system. Globalisation would extend connectivity and trickle-down prosperity across the former Second and Third Worlds, including through an increasingly global food industry, eager to surmount barriers to cross-border trade and investment, contesting and at times collaborating with indigenous players and interests.

Today, history is back. The world has seen the rollback of free trade amid rising protectionism and spiking geopolitical threat concerns, upheavals in leading liberal democracies, the rise of China on its own terms, the mistrust and ill-will stoked by COVID-19, and the Russia-Ukraine war and inter-state tensions in the "Indo-Pacific", centred on a brewing US-China rivalry, joined by other players in and beyond the region. In this febrile environment, zero-sum strategic calculus and geopolitical risk management trump profit maximisation and comparative advantage for governments, and global industry alike. Macroeconomic upheaval and potential monetary transition (de-dollarisation and the rise of a potential digital Yuan zone, for instance) could change the food business and reorient food production and flows.

Avoiding simple extrapolation of the current trajectory of superpower confrontation into the future is key to sense the possible outcomes. Global divides may indeed worsen and calcify into a "Cold War 2". However, if the U.S. and China achieve a *détente* and better manage their differences, emphasising and actualising areas of win-win cooperation, including on climate and food systems, a "G2" [Bush, 2011] world where the U.S. and China partner amicably to steer the world system could arise with new momentum for global exchange and cooperation. Table 27.2 is an illustration of both possible trajectories' implications for the food sphere.

Table 27.2 Illustration of two possible trajectories for future food situations.

"Walled Belt" — *Cold War 2 erupts between the U.S. and China*	"Abundance Road" — *Win-win U.S.-China "coopetition" and coordination*
• A "Sinosphere" covers much of "Belt & Road" Asia and Africa, with privileged food trading relationships locked in by treaty, contractual, financial and physical infrastructure to China; the West and China jostle to dominate Latin American source markets. • Substantial autarky in essentials including food and energy at national and bloc levels to reduce import/export dependency on potentially hostile/vulnerable markets. • Increasing state command and control of strategic resource sectors, with national food companies co-opted as arms of food security policy at home and abroad. • Global fisheries and their regulatory bodies are arenas of conflict. • Weaponisation of food trade/aid/investment as a tool to compete and coerce; largely confined within the blocs, and as strategic overtures to non-aligned markets. • Agritech securitised and regulated. Deliberately incompatible standards lock-in bifurcation and trade/investment rigidities. • Geoengineering to advance own production, with (deliberate) indifference to wider consequences.	• A flat world hyperconnected by multi-directional flows of food trade, investment, and knowledge/data, with the U.S. and China as key players, "system administrators" and beneficiaries. • The global food system more integrated than ever yet with much reduced average food miles and emissions footprint; "global circle of food neighbourhoods." • Market principles and a multitude of multinational food e-businesses dominate, regulated and supported by robust internationally harmonised rules and standards, with greater emphasis on environment, social and governance. • Great power "coopetition" in ag-eco-tech for sustainable food systems, and food aid/investment for least developed countries. Collaboration on geoengineering and energy-water tech "moonshots" that help the global commons. • Regulatory compatibility/convergence spurs faster and broader Agritech progress and adoption. • Good intellectual property protection mitigates guardedness against commercial espionage.

Table 27.2 (*Continued*)

"Walled Belt" — *Cold War 2 erupts between the U.S. and China*	"Abundance Road" — *Win-win U.S.-China "coopetition" and coordination*
• Rigid and brittle food markets; food insecurity especially for the non-aligned. • Eco-nationalist indoctrination to patriotic food habits. Taboo to eat exports and cuisines of the adversary. • Food sector an arena for "grey zone" conflict: misinformation, sabotage, etc. • Globally uncoordinated climate response; emphasis on national and bloc-level food system adaptation and resiliency, emergency planning, stockpiling, rationing and punishment of food waste.	• New generations revere planetary-human wellness link; profound reducetarian, locavore/grow-it-yourself, and wellness/nutrition-oriented shifts in consumption. • Cosmopolitan world food culture takes root, with celebration of local variety and heritage food systems. • Antifragile global food system, networked and with high data transparency anticipates issues (droughts, OneHealth eruptions, etc.), enacting proactive measures to avert/mitigate crises.

Certainly, beyond these starkly mirror-imaged outcomes, there are many other possible future trajectories. A new cold war could turn hot, with potentially existential implications for world civilisation, hence the increasing focus on conceptualising approaches for the post-nuclear holocaust restart of human systems, such as in the work of The Centre for the Study of Existential Risk at the University of Cambridge, and the Alliance to Feed the Earth in Disasters.

Alternatively, a multipolar world (dis)order may arise, for instance if key powers like the European Union, India, or Brazil assert their own geostrategic autonomy. A world of somewhat unfriendly blocs would likely have heavy-handed industrial policies to ensure geographic and policy control over critical value chains including food production, and to shape and regulate consumption.

In Asia, some or most of the nations could converge in greater economic and indeed political regionalism, emulating the European Union model, and perhaps growing around an "ASEAN+" nucleus. This could be a building block for renewed globalisation in a more liberal scenario, or of a more autarchic "world of regions" in one with less globalisation, with food flows adapting to different realities. If a new Cold War develops, such a grouping could position itself as non-aligned, and insistent on preserving its autonomy to deal with both antagonists — hence playing a useful if precarious role as a connector, including for food trade.

In essence, the food sector, like others which became substantially globalised and liberalised since the 1990s despite several lingering areas of protectionism, will need to anticipate and adapt to alternate geopolitical imaginaries.

This applies particularly to Asia, given China's presence, rivalry with the U.S. and uneasy relations with India and numerous other regional powers, and contested territorial claims in the region astride major international trade routes.

A geopolitically charged future would affect the range of considerations — from crop mixes to agrifood finance investment and partnership flows, regulatory realignments, input and export market preference and access, and non-tariff barriers.

If food insecurity surges and threatens countries' strategic position or domestic political stability, we can contemplate futures where states step forward to command and control their domestic food systems and cross-border food trade.

27.2.3 *AgriFood Tech Transformation*

Looking ahead, new technology and innovation, both in areas currently focused on food use cases and beyond, will shape possibilities for the food sector, and pathways to deliver on food security.

What future agrifoodtech paradigms and possibilities may there be? Earlier chapters have covered various emergent technologies in depth. Distilling from these, the following can be considered as overlapping frontiers for further tech advancement towards new capabilities, options, and enhanced performance for the food system:

- **Novel foods and new/enhanced production methods** that advance core metrics like yield, labour and land productivity and feed conversion ratio, seen through a new frame such as the carbon performance, overall ecological efficiency, and positive or negative externalities of different food production systems [Quintieri *et al.*, 2023];
- **Synergies across the food-energy-water nexus**: how may food production be not only more frugal in energy and water consumption, but perhaps even generative of one or both in the process;
- **Circularity, and reducing loss and waste**, including through enhanced biosecurity;
- **Resiliency and consistency of production**, including through controlled environment agriculture, and for renewal of food production in the wake of catastrophes;
- **Pre-farm to post-fork**: enhancements and synergies across the extended value chain, from agri-inputs, seen in a holistic sense, to outcomes beyond satiation and nutrition for the end-users; this includes artificial intelligence (AI) [Mavani *et al.*, 2022],

automation, and Internet of Things technology for situational awareness, decision support, and optimisation across the food system for all stakeholders — producers, logisticians, retailers, consumers, regulators;

- Emerging food solutions may also impactfully serve as part of mitigative or adaptive "**climate tech**" [Cornelli *et al.*, 2023], for instance where carbon is sequestered as part of the production process, or where production setups help protect against coastal tidal surges, preserve and enhance the arability of land, soil, and area climates, or enable the expansion of cultivation to previously barren areas;
- Techniques that **harness traditional knowledge and nature-based solutions** for "regenerative" and "**agroforestry**" approaches;
- Enabling substantial **food production by urban households** and communities for their own consumption;
- Enabling food production in or from **novel/underutilised spaces** like the atmosphere, underground, and the sea; and
- Enhancements to the **risk assessment, approval and regulation** of the food system, particularly novel foods.

Overall, technological advancements have the potential to empower the food sector with more options and tools to create and capture value, deliver enhanced production and resource efficiency and sustainability, and better meet human needs and wants.

Key uncertainties include the scalability, pace and extent of growth and diffusion, and take-up of novel foods and agrifoodtech. This will depend not only on their intrinsic qualities and advantages in production or for the end-user. Their competitiveness against legacy foods and their interests, and "social licence" and market appeal, will be key.

Furthermore, implicit assumptions about which types of actors create, possess, and use these technologies may also need re-examining. Will key technologies be cornered by particular national or corporate interests? Will they lend themselves to a flatter market structure where more players can compete (a 3D food printer in every kitchen?), or to yet greater market concentration at national, regional, and global scales?

Contrasting future trajectories can be imagined where new agrifoodtech sparks a paradigm shift in how food is made, moved, and consumed. Will novel proteins, for instance, dominate Asia in the future, or face significant headwinds and failures, remaining a niche? A synthesis where heritage food systems, currently prevailing industrialised agriculture and food methods, and new-age technologies blend creatively and productively is conceivable — for instance if organic or agroforestry modes embrace bioengineered varietals and precision farming techniques. A technologically bifurcated food system can be imagined, both between developed and emerging markets across Asia, and within developed markets, for example based on socio-economic stratification, or contrasting food values and preferences.

27.2.4 *Social Engagement*

People are of course the "end-users" of the food system, but are increasingly playing more varied and active roles across it. Asia itself is home to an estimated 450 million smallholder farmers [Rigg *et al.*, 2016], who are themselves consumers and influential socio-political actors.

Globalisation, urbanisation and growth have made many less aware of how and where their food is made, but rising disruptions, not least COVID-19, economic stressors, environmental concerns, and controversies over nutrition and safety have turned more people into conscious consumers (such as through the rise of community-supported agriculture), activists and advocates for food system transformation, home and community farmers and circular/sharing economy participants.

Across a region known for its vibrant and variegated agricultural heritage and cuisine, how will the food culture evolve? How may food values, preferences and beliefs change, including affected by socio-economic status, gender, ethnicity, religion, ideology, education, and (mis)information? How will generational and demographic change shape developments? Moving forward, how will "food citizens" across Asia relate to the food sector? What will they expect of it, and of governments? And broadly, what will the outcome of these uncertainties mean to Asians' disposition towards an evolving food sector? Will the predominant sentiment be one of engagement, indifference, hostility, or disengagement, across food citizens' varied roles?

27.2.5 *Dominant Food Policy Paradigms*

Considering the range of demands, stressors and new technological possibilities shaping sector developments and food security outcomes, Asia's governments will be tackling extraordinary complexities and multifaceted challenges moving forward, matched by the wide range of policy models, levers, and innovations that they may jointly or individually pursue.

Asian states' awareness, capacity, capabilities, ideologies, focus and attention — and decision makers' shifting priorities and interests amid the flux of bureaucratic, national and international politics — will together shape the intentionality, level of attention and focus, policy programme and approach, effectiveness and outcomes of food system governance.

Certainly, the great diversity of national agronomic and geostrategic situations (for instance, between food-surplus and -deficit countries, and in the level of wealth and development) defies oversimplification, but one can consider whether Asia's governments may tend towards *laissez-faire*, benign neglect, or different flavours of hands-on interventionism. Whether and how seamlessly states see and flex synergies between food policy and other adjacent areas of governance like health, workforce and the economy, education, etc., will also shape food governance futures.

27.3 Future Food Scenario Frameworks

Across the critical uncertainties discussed above, we may contemplate future scenarios such as:

- Whether climate change-related effects on food systems across Asia are generally severe, uneven, or (surprisingly) moderate and surmountable
- In terms of geo-political-economic space for the food system, would there be an easing of tensions and differences and incipient "re-globalisation," or a world comprised of chunks of states, where much of Asia forms a bloc, or a fragmented Asia where strategic cooperation and economic flows have been largely degraded?
- Across Asia, are the food sector and food security policy domains generally neglected, or do states take a commanding role, or do they generally follow market mechanisms, and pursue synergies in a holistic policy programme with other domains?
- Do emerging agrifood technologies dominate the ecosystem, or mostly fail to gain traction, with today's prevailing foods,

methods and technologies remaining dominant and evolving incrementally, or does the agrifood sector become distinctly segmented between high-tech, currently mainstream, and agroforestry and whole/natural foods categories, or would there be a blending and synthesis across modes?
- Are Asian food citizens actively engaged with an evolving food sector, alienated and indifferent to it, or zestfully carving out alternatives to the mainstream?

Table 27.3 summarises how these Critical Uncertainties may each branch out differently. The red, green and lilac shaded cells represent different combinations of permutations of outcomes of the critical uncertainties, which develop into three distinct scenarios of ***what the Asian food system will look like in 2033***, elaborated further below. (In grey are potential branches of certain critical uncertainties not explored in the scenarios considered here).[2]

27.4 Food System Asia 2033 Scenarios

Based on these (Table 27.3), three plausible scenarios emerge of possible futures for the regional food system:

---

[2] This author has been researching on emerging issues and trends across the food system, particularly in Asia. At a food systems and foresight workshop conducted for food officials from various Asian countries, the author took on board additional perspectives, and developed a set of scenarios which have been further revised and updated.

Broadly, this approach follows the "inductive" scenario methodology, where various critical uncertainties are considered and their potential branching outcomes listed, with scenarios developed based on logically consistent permutations of branches. A narrative is developed to explain how each particular scenario developed out of the combination and interaction of factors.

Table 27.3 Asian food system 2033 scenario framework.

Critical uncertainty	Some possible outcomes of each critical uncertainty			
Climate Effects	Severe	Uneven	Moderate	—
Geo-Pol-Econ Impetus	Re-globalisation	Asian bloc	Divided world, divided Asia	Fragmented Asia
Food Governance	Laissez-faire / neglect	Command	Holistic	—
AgriFood Tech Paradigm	New dominant	Synthesis	Conventional dominant	Segmented
Social Engagement	Alienated	Engaged	Community food sovereignty	—

27.4.1 *Scenario 1 — Carbon Sync*

It is 2033. After narrowly avoiding starting World War III, the world's great powers do humankind and the earth a favour and reach a tentative understanding that leads with time into a renewal of collaboration, at first episodic and transactional, then increasingly deep, synchronised, and geared at greening the food system as the foundation of its enduring resilience. Multilateralism is revived under a reinvigorated United Nations system, facilitating cooperation, knowledge exchange, and agrifood trade flows.

This geopolitical reset enables a green reset also. Advancing food, energy, water, and circularity technologies are spurred by the peace dividend's spurt of economic growth, unhindered by restrictions on technology dissemination.

Climate change effects have been uneven but significant around the world. At different times, different breadbaskets across Asia and the world have experienced climate-related crop failures and production diseases. But Asia and the world have learned the lesson from the bad old days of the 2020s when restricted food flows in times of disruption led to waves of food insecurity and ill will. Instead, major producers such as India, Indonesia, and Vietnam led the way in strengthening the norm of preserving international food flows amid shocks, and collaborating towards more sustainable, and thus resilient, food systems in such areas as anticipation of supply disruptions, and development of shared stockpiles of key inputs and food supplies. "What goes around, comes around" now played out in a positive, pragmatic, and virtuous circle.

Renewed international exchange and cosmopolitanism, reflected in diets, furthered the convergence and fungibility of transcontinental food flows and preferences. Wheat and rice flows between Asia and the rest of the world grow, buttressing food security at global levels.

Various "ancient grains" — sorghum, millet, quinoa, farro and amaranth among them — are now being grown where terrain, soil and changing climate allow. Such diverse grains cultivation is now typically done as a polyculture on agroforestry lines, mixed with fruit, forest vegetables and oilseeds.

Vast swathes of such agroforestry plantations — run by indigenous cooperatives, settler smallholders escaping Asia's overcrowded cities, or large Asian multinational corporations alike — have sprouted across the region. Their expansion helps to bioremediate and rewild degraded lands, and serves as a cordon between settled areas and Asia's unspoilt natural vestiges.

The signature of the age is the eclectic synthesis between traditional crops and practices, cutting edge technology, and business and social enterprise model innovation: much of these plantations' varietals have been gene edited to buttress their resilience to drought, flood, heat, and pestilence, and to enhance their nutritive and nutraceutical value. Deep in the plantations, farmers and technicians labour alongside a menagerie of autonomous cobots, in a man-machine-AI interface that optimises yields.

Transcending the earlier focus on economic growth as a means to advance military power, governments in this more pacific era can focus on enhancing human welfare, in synergy with nature, harnessing policy innovations and market-based mechanisms for sustainability.

Unlike the meagre, overblown and often fraudulent gestures of the past, close adherence to rigorous Environment, Social and Governance standards is *de rigueur* among Asia's leading agrifood businesses — a reputational hygiene factor and point of pride among the regions' Family Offices.

Amid guilt and outrage at the imminent disappearance of several Pacific islands beneath rising waves, the COP 33 of 2028 agreed on a "green sprint" to bring the world back onto the Paris Agreement's 1.5°C track. Critical to that was the Treaty of Singapore of 2029. After a marathon negotiating session, the host state managed to gain countries' unanimous agreement to a robust, binding, standardised universal carbon offset regime, backed by the new Greenback-Yuan global digital currency. Designed by a caucus of global corporates, green groups, universities, and fintech wizards, the regime achieved an accurate, optimal, and verifiable mechanism for measuring effective carbon sequestration, underpinned by advances in climate and data science.

As part of the deal, global oil and mining majors were strong-armed into agreeing to a binding transition plan to taper hydrocarbon extraction and roll their reserves, infrastructure and expertise into the Green Sprint — principally by radically scaling up solar, wind, and green hydrogen power generation, and the eco-extraction of rare earths enabling the new green economy — sustaining a lifeline of revenues and paying back in cash and kind the eco-reparations imposed on them by the international community, granting a just transition and an economic lifeline to their stakeholders.

Food-energy system synergies reached a new peak as agrivoltaic plantations sprouted in deserts and arid borderlands — doubling up as climate engineering keeping creeping desertification at bay across tracts of North and Central Asia. Meanwhile, off Asia's lengthy coastlines, and gradually deeper out to sea, belts of wind/tide and multi-trophic mariculture farms proliferated with an ecological setups with a variety of fish, shellfish, crustaceans, and micro- and macro-algae, alongside a proliferation of seasteads, particularly across the formerly fortified shoals and islands of the South China Sea Multinational Eco-Investment Zone.

The "green sprint" would have been an uphill crawl without the active engagement and support of Asian and global publics. Sensitised to the ravages and ripple effects of previous generations' climate failures, Asia's new and demographically leaner generation of consumers with a green conscience and a post-hedonistic wellness focus tapered their consumption of land animal meat, embracing increasingly tasty and affordable plant-based, cell-cultured, and fermented analogues.

Green leadership and policymaking — a new wave of more progressive and systemic earth systems thinking among Asia's rising mandarins — lay at the core of the Asian and world food system's brewing transformation. With the fiscal and cognitive burden of superpower confrontation having eased, the world's governments could pivot to a joined-up human and eco-wellness and development agenda.

The dominant paradigm across both liberal and illiberal jurisdictions around Asia is to link agrifood, health, climate, innovation, and rural-urban-international development policies. The citizens of Asia are further coaxed towards healthy and sustainable living by robust taxation on less healthy and ecological consumption and lifestyles. More "nanny states" impose social credit schemes that name and shame steak eaters, food wasters, and unhygienic food establishments.

At ASEAN+++ and APEC meetings, leaders and countries' "face" and soft power standing are measured by their eco-performance, reported on with stark accuracy by an international bureaucracy armed with an arsenal of AI, big data, and Internet of Things eco-surveillance capabilities.

New generations of Asians born at the 1/3 mark of the century can look forward to a world that is gradually turning the corner on the climate emergency; a world without hunger that weaves the best of traditional knowledge and advanced technology to produce and consume what it needs, and revivify the earth.

27.4.2 *Scenario 2 — Fortress Food Factory*

This 2033 Asian food future is rather more tense, grim, and unequal. A stark red-blue line runs jaggedly across Asia. Food, trade, logistics, tech, data, people, and idea flows rarely breach it.

Brewing superpower rivalries, triggered by territorial disputes, East and West, have ripened into a full-fledged Cold War 2, dividing the world into rival armed camps — one embracing most of the Eurasian land mass, South Asia, Africa and the Middle East; the other, most of maritime Australasia, the Pacific, the Americas, and Europe. One with more pretensions towards freedom and democracy, the other emphasising the welfare of the collective. A small residue of non-aligned "basket case" states without agricultural nor mineral potential twist in the wind, not worth the effort to co-opt or subdue.

With national economies mobilised and geared towards a multi-domain arms race, scant resource and policy attention are paid to issues and domains not upholding the hard power, social order and cohesion of each bloc.

The near-total breakdown of the multilateral system has meant that the already faltering United Nations-mediated climate process has sputtered into irrelevance. The legacy, dirty but cheap carbon-based industrial and energy sectors, which had been tapering, found a second wind in the energy crisis and remilitarisation which marked the limited conflicts across Eastern European and Asian flashpoints in the 2020s. These further ravaged the climate and decisively tipped its trajectory such that the Paris glide to 1.5°C moved plainly out of reach.

The "Great Sweat" of 2029 saw hundreds of millions of people perish in record global heatwaves and droughts. The drastically accelerated melting of the polar ice shelfs and most of the remaining icepack of the Tibetan Plateau saw sudden, epic flooding, killing tens of millions more, submerging much of archipelagic and coastal Asia's cities and agricultural deltas.

With cities like Shanghai, Sydney, Jakarta and Dhaka succumbing to the waves, both halves of divided Asia had to deal with multitudes of climate refugees, food crises, and infrastructure and economic damage in the hundreds of billions. A breakdown in human and animal health systems, and the desperate logging and clearance of jungle areas for shelter and firewood sparked outbreaks of animal and zoonotic disease, causing further devastation to human life and food systems. Whereas in the early 2020s the world had been angsting about the future of animal agriculture, for the foreseeable future the sector would be a scant remnant of its former scale, dominated by criminal gangs and extractive state monopolies. Grimly, Asia and the world are now involuntarily "reducetarian".

With these disasters affecting both sides of the Cold War 2 and causing an inward focus, with the coming of the 2030s tensions have somewhat eased. But wariness remains as to whether one side or the other would move to seize less damaged arable borderlands in the other's sphere.

Amid global crises, each bloc's governments took greater control of essential sectors, including food and agriculture, to restore production and ensure adequacy and continuity of food supply.

A silver lining was that much of the technology developed for military purposes — among them satellite surveillance, robots and drones, nuclear power, biological warfare and defence, AI, logistics and engineering capabilities — could be cross-deployed as part of an urgent push to jump-start the largely plant, mycelium, microorganism, and aquaculture-based food sources that could be revived.

With much of Asia's previous staple growing areas heat- and water-stressed and salinified, staple cultivation moved upland and northward. Gene editing and smart farming solutions featured greatly as means to coax more product out of unwilling soil, as did greenhouse, indoor, and underground farming at scale, with controlled environmental agriculture — often powered by dedicated microreactors — boosting production. Inundated coastal cities were turned into surreal food factories, with indoor farms, insulated from the elements, occupying abandoned skyscrapers, and streets — now canals — adapted for automated aquaculture.

High-tech, state-directed, centrally planned agrifood programmes took hold in both halves of divided Asia. The leading powers of each bloc, controlling some of the last remaining nutritive surpluses, exerted power over lesser bloc members to whom they gave or withheld assistance.

Across overcrowded inland cities and sprawling displaced persons camps, nutrition and taste took a backseat with a focus on meeting basic calorific needs. AI-informed "smart rationing" took hold, with the algorithm issuing nutrient allowances frugally based on omic readings, occupation, political reliability, and usefulness to the state.

Gradually, to eke out every possible efficiency, AI and machine learning was extended to encompass the entire planned agrifood economy. Central nutrition metabolic algorithms planned inputs, coordinated production and logistical operations, and overwatched the system to limit loss, waste, contamination, and criminality.

The bloc governments also controlled and revived a limited barter trade across the divide with their adversaries — one side trading what surplus starches it had in exchange for proteins.

In this future, alienated and oppressed subjects of both empires struggled to eat to live, resentful of their smart rations, and eking out a high-tech subsistence.

27.4.3 *Scenario 3 — Distant Plates*

The final scenario envisioned is one where, over the next decade, climate change effects continue to manifest, but at an intensity seemingly moderate and manageable.

Geopolitically, the growing rivalry between superpowers of the early 2020s did not lead to a two-sided cold or hot war. Each faced economic setbacks and some sociopolitical instability, limiting their strength and appeal. With time, this led to a peeling away of support of most other powers, who chose non-alignment, and pursuit of their own interests, typically as regional blocs.

Across Asia, China, Russia and India have each carved out spheres of influence deep into the Eurasian land mass. The rest of East Asia, Southeast Asia, and the Southwest Pacific have formed a loose SEAPAC confederation — a free trade area, strengthened by high external tariff walls, a common digital currency, and convergent food safety, quality, and nutrition standards.

SEAPAC typifies the world of 2033 — not by and large a hostile one, but an unsociable one of insular regions, each going it alone with generally limited flows and exchanges between them. The lesson of COVID-19, and subsequent geopolitical conflicts, trade embargoes, and so on in the mid-2020s was that globe-spanning value chains are serially prone to disruption and manipulation. The risk from frequent extreme weather affecting food production and logistics also multiplied with distance. Instead, reshoring, nearshoring, and friendshoring of key value chains is now the norm, and years of realignment in this direction have led to fairly stable, highly regionalised and autarkic markets.

The global food industry has adapted also. Transcontinental food majors have now adjusted to be contiguous in their operations to their anchor regional blocs. Within their regional redoubts, they have largely captured and coopted the agrifood policymaking establishment, and reached accommodations with existing structures of middlemen and smallholders.

Agrifood policy is one of benign neglect. Cosy oligopolies mean that food prices are fairly high, good margins are enjoyed, and there is limited incentive for agrifoodtech innovation that rocks the boat on established capital, product lines, and interests. The "GAP"[3] and "HACCP"[4] best practice of the legacy food industry of the 2020s has become the dominant practice of the regionalised food sector of the 2030s — no more, no less. The sclerosis of the regional food sector is also a form of "resilience" — nothing new ventured, nothing lost. And if a localised weather disaster decimated the harvest in one part of SEAPAC, another could pick up the slack across the sprawling region.

After brief flashes of interest in regional nodes like Singapore, the cultured meat fad fizzled and has been dismissed as a vanity project of foreign interests. Instead, building on indigenous culinary heritage like *tempeh*, and the rich climate-resilient range of heritage grains and pulses across the region, "low-tech" "highly processed" plant-based meat, in regional flavours and formats with regional ingredients, is a vibrant category, fitting seamlessly into 101 regional dishes and local cuisines. Fermentation and mycoculture also feature more significantly.

Meanwhile, the region's consumers don't expect and perhaps don't know any better. Prices are higher than they could be under globalisation. There's undernutrition, but not much starvation. And for town and rural dwellers, there's lots of room to carve out one's own food space — community farms, kitchens, and agroforestry plantations that supplement diets and incomes.

---

[3] Good Agriculture Practice.

[4] Hazard Analysis and Critical Control Points.

27.5 Asia's Food Future: Where Will You Be?

These sketch scenarios are but some of the possible trajectories that Asian food systems and the lived experience of food (in)security in the region may take, based on the twists, turns and interactions of factors such as climate effects, politics, economics, technological advancement, food policy frameworks, and peoples' engagement with the food system beyond consumption.

Contemplation of scenarios prompts questions and reflections, rather than ready answers. Which future conforms and which diverges the most from one's expectations and planning parameters? As a food citizen, and in other professional and institutional roles in the food system, in which future would you rather inhabit, and bequeath to subsequent generations? What factors extrinsic to the food sector should it seek to shape and influence? How? For the food sector itself, how may different stakeholders — policy, enterprise, civil society, academia — nationally, regionally and beyond enhance dialogue and collaboration around shaping the future of the ecosystem?

The Asian food system has, so to speak, a lot on its plate, and a key role in shaping future outcomes for the region, and the world. Thinking deliberately and imaginatively beyond present conditions to inform forward planning will be the bedrock of its future readiness, agency, and resilience.

References

Bush, R. C. (2011). The United States and China: a G-2 in the making?. *Brookings*. https://www.brookings.edu/articles/the-united-states-and-china-a-g-2-in-the-making/

Centre For Strategic Futures, Singapore. (n.d.). *Foresight: A Glossary.* https://www.csf.gov.sg/media-centre/publications/foresight-glossary/

Cornelli, G., Frost, J., Gambacorta, L. and Merrouche, O. (2023). Climate tech 2.0: social efficiency versus private returns. *BIS Working Papers No 1072.*

Fukuyama, F. (1989). The End of History?. *The National Interest*, 16, pp. 3–18.

Mavani, N. R., Ali, J. M., Othman, S., *et al.* (2022). Application of artificial intelligence in food industry — a guideline. *Food Engineering Reviews*, 14, pp. 134–175.

Quintieri, L., Nitride, C., De Angelis, E., Lamonaca, A., Pilolli, R., Russo, F. and Monaci, L. (2023). Alternative protein sources and novel foods: benefits, food applications and safety issues. *Nutrients*, *15*(6), p. 1509.

Rigg, J., Salmanca, A. and Thompson, E. C. (2016). The puzzle of East and Southeast Asia's persistent smallholder. *Journal of Rural Studies,* 43, pp. 118–133.

Tay, L. (2022). Food opinion leaders' survey. https://www.linkedin.com/feed/update/urn:li:activity:6930568215529963520/

https://doi.org/10.1142/9789811278297_bmatter

Index

www.ingramcontent.com/pod-product-compliance
Lightning Source LLC
LaVergne TN
LVHW010537300926
849162LV00002B/161